# PALESTINE
# AND
# TRANSJORDAN

The great interest of this volume is that it predates the establishment of the state of Israel. It is devoted to what was then called Palestine, and to 'Transjordan', the lands east of the river Jordan that now comprise the Kingdom of Jordan. The geographical rather than political approach to the region presented in this handbook is instructive.

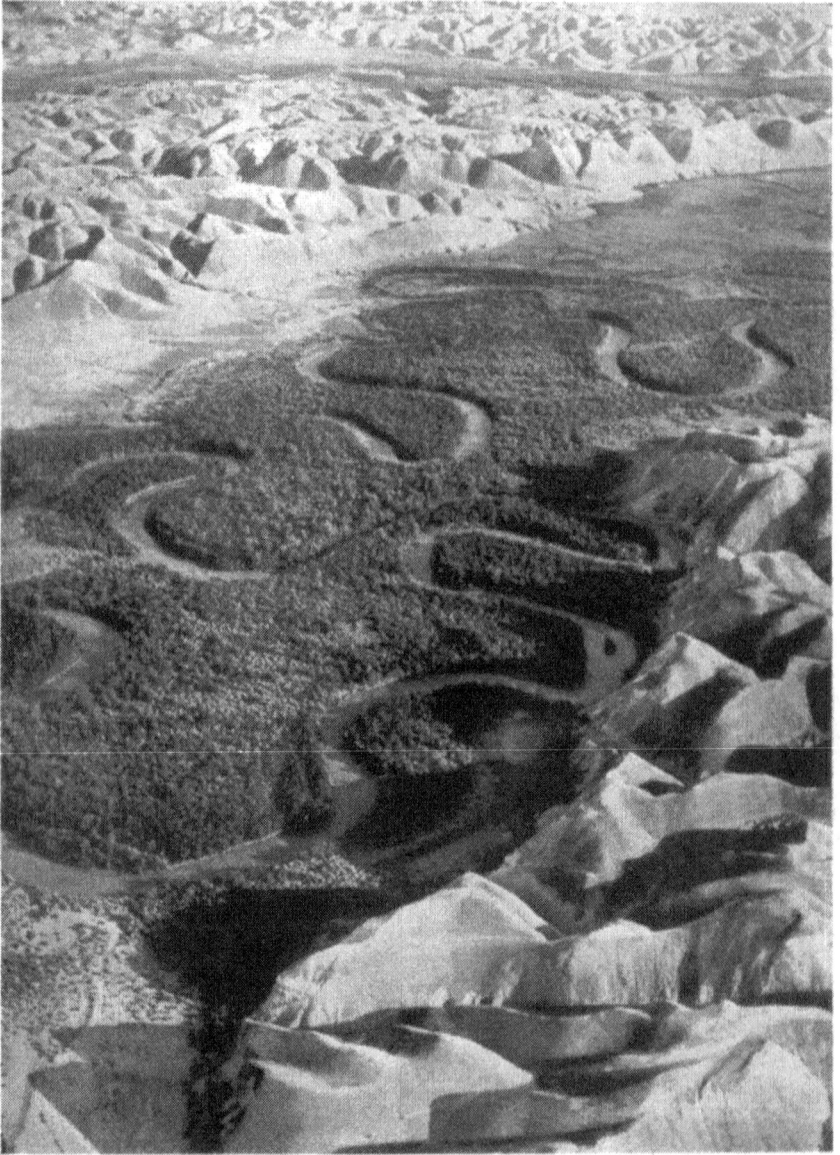

1. *The meanders and 'gallery' vegetation of the Jordan. View south at latitude 32° 08' near the Ghor Faria. The Jordan here flows at 1,150 feet below sea-level. The valley of the Zerka (Jabbok) of Transjordan is seen in the distance*

# PALESTINE
# AND
# TRANSJORDAN

## NAVAL INTELLIGENCE DIVISION

**Routledge**
Taylor & Francis Group

LONDON AND NEW YORK

First published in 2006 by Kegan Paul.

This edition first published in 2009 by
Routledge
2 Park Square, Milton Park, Abingdon, Oxfordshire OX14 4RN

Simultaneously published in the USA and Canada
by Routledge
711 Third Avenue, New York, NY 10017

First issued in paperback 2016

*Routledge is an imprint of the Taylor & Francis Group, an informa business*

*British Library Cataloguing in Publication Data*
A catalogue record for this book is available from the British Library

ISBN 13: 978-1-138-97786-0 (pbk)
ISBN 13: 978-0-7103-1028-6 (hbk)

**Publisher's Note**
The publisher has gone to great lengths to ensure the quality of this reprint
but points out that some imperfections in the original copies may be
apparent. The publisher has made every effort to contact original copyright
holders and would welcome correspondence from those they have been
unable to trace.

# PREFACE

IN 1915 a Geographical Section was formed in the Naval Intelligence Division of the Admiralty to write Geographical Handbooks on various parts of the world. The purpose of these handbooks was to supply, by scientific research and skilled arrangement, material for the discussion of naval, military, and political problems, as distinct from the examination of the problems themselves. Many distinguished collaborators assisted in their production, and by the end of 1918 upwards of fifty volumes had been produced in Handbook and Manual form, as well as numerous short-term geographical reports. The demand for these books increased rapidly with each new issue, and they acquired a high reputation for accuracy and impartiality. They are now to be found in Service Establishments and Embassies throughout the world, and in the early years after the last war were much used by the League of Nations.

The old Handbooks have been extensively used in the present war, and experience has disclosed both their value and their limitations. On the one hand they have proved, beyond all question, how greatly the work of the fighting services and of Government Departments is facilitated if countries of strategic or political importance are covered by handbooks which deal, in a convenient and easily digested form, with their geography, ethnology, administration, and resources. On the other hand it has become apparent that something more is required to meet present-day requirements. The old series does not cover many of the countries closely affected by the present war (e.g. Germany, France, Poland, Spain, Portugal, to name only a few); its books are somewhat uneven in quality, and they are inadequately equipped with maps, diagrams, and photographic illustrations.

The present series of Handbooks, while owing its inspiration largely to the former series, is in no sense an attempt to revise or re-edit that series. It is an entirely new set of books, produced in the Naval Intelligence Division by trained geographers drawn largely from the Universities, and working at sub-centres established at Oxford and Cambridge, and is printed by the Oxford and Cambridge University Presses. The books follow, in general, a uniform scheme, though minor modifications will be found in particular cases; and they are illustrated by numerous maps and photographs.

The purpose of the books is primarily naval. They are designed first to provide, for the use of Commanding Officers, information in a comprehensive and convenient form about countries which they may be called upon to visit, not only in war but in peace-time; secondly, to maintain the high standard of education in the Navy and, by supplying officers with material for lectures to naval personnel ashore and afloat, to ensure for all ranks that visits to a new country shall be both interesting and profitable.

Their contents are, however, by no means confined to matters of purely naval interest. For many purposes (e.g. history, administration, resources, communications, &c.) countries must necessarily be treated as a whole, and no attempt is made to limit their treatment exclusively to coastal zones. It is hoped, therefore, that the Army, the Royal Air Force, and other Government Departments (many of whom have given great assistance in the production of the series) will find these handbooks even more valuable than their predecessors proved to be both during and after the last war.

J. H. GODFREY

*Director of Naval Intelligence*

1942

The foregoing preface has appeared from the beginning of this series of Geographical Handbooks. It describes so effectively their origin and purpose that I have decided to retain it in its original form. I would like to add that in dealing with a country such as Palestine it is impossible to avoid matters of political controversy. The Admiralty does not necessarily agree with the particular presentation of such matters in this volume.

This volume has been prepared by the Oxford sub-centre of the Naval Intelligence Division under the direction of Lieut.-Colonel K. Mason, M.C., M.A., R.E., Professor of Geography in the University of Oxford, and is the work of a number of contributors, whose names are given in Appendix I, page 581.

E. G. N. RUSHBROOKE

*Director of Naval Intelligence*

NOVEMBER 1943

# CONTENTS

## PART I. PALESTINE

PAGE

I. INTRODUCTION . . . . . . . . 1
Boundaries and Area (1)—Geographical and Administrative
Divisions (3)—History and People (4)—Place-names (6)—
Topographical Glossary (7).

II. PHYSICAL GEOGRAPHY . . . . . . 8
GEOLOGY (8)—REGIONAL TOPOGRAPHY (12): The Plains (12)
—The Mountain Region (15)—Galilee (15)—Samaria (16)—
Judaea (18)—The Shephelah (20)—The Jordan Trench (21)
—The Negeb (23)—RIVERS AND LAKES (25): Rivers of the Medi-
terranean Seaboard (25)—The Jordan (28)—The Lakes (30).

III. THE COAST . . . . . . . . . 33
Ras en Nakurah to Haifa (33)—Haifa to Tel Aviv and Jaffa (37)
—Jaffa to Rafa (43).

IV. CLIMATE, VEGETATION, AND FAUNA . . . 47
CLIMATE (47): Pressure (48)—Winds (49)—Temperature (51)—
Humidity (53)—Evaporation, Visibility (54)—Cloud (55)
—Rainfall (56)— Dew, Snow, Thunder and Hail, Miscellan-
eous (60).

VEGETATION (61): Biological types (64)—Botanical Divisions
(65)—Plant Life of the Divisions (66): Mediterranean Region,
The Coastal Plain (66)—The Main Mountain Block (72)—
—Steppe Region (75)—Desert Region (76).

FAUNA (78).

V. HISTORY . . . . . . . . . . 81
EARLY TIMES TO THE ROMAN SETTLEMENT (81):
Earliest Culture (81)—The Biblical Period (83)—From Nebu-
chadnezzar to Antiochus IV (87)—The Maccabaean Revolt (89).

THE ROMAN PERIOD (90):
Roman Palestine (90)—Herod the Great (91)—Revolt against
Rome (94)—The Jews of the Dispersion (95)—Jews and
Christians (96).

ARAB AND LATIN RULE (99):
The Arab Conquest (99)—Arab Rule in Palestine (100)—
The Crusades (103)—The Latin Kingdom (106).

THE OTTOMAN EMPIRE (109):
The Ottoman Empire (109)—Napoleon's Invasion (110)—
Mehemet Ali (112)—Ottoman Rule in the Nineteenth Century
(114)—The European Powers (114) Jewish Immigration
(116)—The Young Turk Revolution (117)—The War in
Palestine, 1914-1918 (117)—Jewish Immigration during the
Ottoman Period (120)—Zionism (121).

THE MANDATE (123):
After the War (123)—Arab Reactions (124)—Arab Outbreaks
(125)—A New Solution (130).

PAGE

VI. THE PEOPLE . . . . . . . . . . 133
    RACE AND NATIONALITY (133): The Arabs (133)—The Palestin-
    ian Christians (138)—The Jews (138)—LANGUAGE (139)—
    RELIGION (143): Moslems (143)—Jews (144)—Christians (148)
    —CULTURE (155): Music (156)—Drama, Art, and Architecture
    (157)—Town Planning, Literature (158)—Periodicals, Libraries
    (159)—Museums, Popular Culture, Costume (160)—The Arab
    Village (163)—Domestic Arts (165)—Mats and Basketry
    (167)—Domestic Animals (168).

VII. DISTRIBUTION OF THE POPULATION . . . 171
    CENSUS FIGURES (171): Estimates, The Census of 1931 (171)—
    Place of Birth (172)—Nationality, Citizenship (173)—POPU-
    LATION INCREASE (174): Causes, Natural Increase (174)—IMMI-
    GRATION AND EMIGRATION (177): Categories of Immigration
    (177)—Incentives to Immigration (178)—Illegal Immigration,
    Origin of Immigrants (180)—Social Effects of Immigration
    (181)—Emigration (182)—DISTRIBUTION (183): Present Distri-
    bution (183)—Urban Immigration (184)—Casual Labour (186)
    —The Towns (187)—Municipal Areas (190).

VIII. ADMINISTRATION . . . . . . . . 191
    CENTRAL GOVERNMENT (191): The League of Nations (193)—
    The Departments (194)—LOCAL GOVERNMENT (197): The
    Municipalities (197)—Town Planning (200)—COMMUNAL
    AUTONOMY (200): The Jewish Community (200)—The
    Moslem Community (202)—JUSTICE AND CRIME (204): Adminis-
    tration of Justice (204)—Law (206)—Police and Prisons
    (207)—LANGUAGE AND RELIGION (208)—LAND OWNERSHIP
    (208)—EDUCATION (213): Arab Schools (215)—Jewish Schools
    (216)—Technical and Scientific Education (218)—Other Non-
    Government Schools (218)—The Hebrew University (219).

IX. PUBLIC HEALTH . . . . . . . . 220
    Vital statistics (220)—Causes of Death (222)—Infectious
    Diseases (222)—Malaria (224)—Kala-azar, Tuberculosis (230)
    —Venereal Diseases (231)—Ankylostomiasis (232)—Schistoso-
    miasis (233)—Ophthalmic Diseases (233)—Rabies (234)—
    MEDICAL SERVICES (235): School Medical Service, Medical and
    Ancillary Professions, Hospitals and Dispensaries (235)—
    Laboratory Services, Infant Welfare (236)—Quarantine
    Services (237)—Lunacy (238).

X. AGRICULTURE AND INDUSTRIES . . . . 239
    AGRICULTURE AND FORESTRY (239): Soils (239)—Crops (243)
    —Irrigation (247)—Research Stations (250)—Pests (251)—
    Fungous Pests (252)—Forestry (253)—Afforestation (255)—
    MINERAL INDUSTRIES (256)—OTHER INDUSTRIES (260)—
    Electricity (262)—Oil and Soap (263)—Wine (264)—Tobacco
    (265)—Building (266)—Textiles (269)—Oil-refining (269)—
    Minor Industries, Fisheries (270)—Tourists (271)—Trends of
    Industry (272)—Labour (273)—Histadrut (275)—Labour
    Legislation (277).

PAGE

XI. BANKING, FINANCE, AND COMMERCE . . . 279

BANKING (279): Currency (280)—PUBLIC FINANCE (281):
Revenue (282)—Expenditure (283)—COMMERCE (284): Balance
of Trade (285)—System of Foreign Trade (288)—Imports
(289)—Exports, Tariff Policy (290)—Internal Trade (292).

XII. PORTS AND INLAND TOWNS . . . . . 295

PORTS (295): Acre (295)—Haifa (300)—Jaffa (307)—Tel Aviv
(311)—Gaza (315)—INLAND TOWNS (318): Beersheba (318)—
Beisan (319)—Bethlehem (320)—Hebron (321)—Jenin, Jericho
(322)—Jerusalem (323)—Khan Yunis (330)—Lydda (331)—
Nablus (332)—Nazareth (333)—Petah Tikva (334)—Ramallah,
Ramleh (335)—Safad (336)—Tiberias (338)—Tulkarm (339).

XIII. COMMUNICATIONS . . . . . . . 340

History of Railways (341)—Development of Roads (344)—
RAILWAYS (345): Index to Railways (346)—Administration
(346)—Traffic (347)—Junctions, Workshops, Fuel (348)—
Water-supply (349)—Construction Details (349)—Descrip-
tion of Railways (350–372)—Abbreviations (351)—ROADS (372):
The Coastal Road (373)—The Central Road (379)—The
Transverse Roads (384)—Jordan valley road (390)—SHIPPING
SERVICES (391)—CIVIL AVIATION (392)—SIGNAL COMMUNI-
CATIONS (395).

PART II. TRANSJORDAN

XIV. PHYSICAL GEOGRAPHY . . . . . . 399

Introduction (399)—TOPOGRAPHY (403): Western Highlands
(406)—Ajlun Highland (407)—Northern Belka (410)—Southern
Belka (411)—Highland of Maan (417)—The Desert (419)—
CLIMATE (421): Pressure, Winds (421)—Temperature, Humidity
(422)—Visibility, Cloud (423)—Rainfall (424)—Snow, Thunder
(425)—VEGETATION (425): Soils, Botanical Divisions (426)—
Mediterranean Zone (426)—Steppe Zone (429)—Desert Zone
(432)—FAUNA (433).

XV. HISTORY OF TRANSJORDAN . . . . . 434

EARLIEST TIMES TO ALEXANDER (434): The Israelite Occupation
(435)—The Assyrian and Persian Empires (437)—FROM
NABATAEANS TO GHASSANIDS: The Hellenistic Period (438)—
Roman Rule (441)—Administration and Culture (443)—Roman
Arabia (444)—The Ghassanids (446)—ARAB AND TURKISH
RULE: The Rise of Islam (448)—Moslem Rule to 1914 (450)—
Exploration in the Nineteenth Century (453)—THE WAR OF
1914–1918 (455)—AFTER THE WAR 1919–1939 (460).

PAGE

XVI. THE PEOPLE AND THEIR GOVERNMENT . . 465

THE PEOPLE (465): Beduin tribes (466)—Non-Arab Communities (468)—Births and Deaths (469)—Religion (470)—Education (471)—Culture (472)—GOVERNMENT: Central Government (472)—Divisional Government, Municipal Government (473)—ADMINISTRATION: Justice (474)—Lands, Public Security (475)—PUBLIC HEALTH: Medical Organization, Diseases (476)—Pests (481).

XVII. ECONOMIC GEOGRAPHY . . . . . . 482

Minerals (482)—Industries (484)—Agriculture (487)—Soils (489)—Irrigation (491)—Crops (493)—Livestock (494)—Forestry (495)—State Forests (496)—Commerce (497)—Finance (500)—Currency, Banking, Department of Development (502)—Public Works (503)—RAILWAYS (503): History (503)—Samakh-Deraa (505)—Deraa-Maan-Nakb Shtar (508)—ROADS (513): Allenby Bridge-Amman (514)—Desert trunk road (515)—Others (517)—Air Routes (520)—THE PORT OF AKABA AND THE ADJACENT COASTS (521).

APPENDIXES: A.   Table of Strata and Igneous Rocks . . . 525
            B.   Chronological Table . . . . . 527
            C.   The Holy Places . . . . . 530
            D.   Some Historical Sites in Transjordan . . 540
            E.   The Royal Navy in Palestine, 1936–1938 . 547
            F.   Time, Calendars, Festivals, Weights and Measures . . . . . . 550
            G.   Meteorological Tables . . . . . 555
            H.   Conversion Tables . . . . . 566
            I.   Authorship, Bibliography, and Maps . . 581

INDEX . . . . . . . . . . 590

# TEXT-FIGURES AND MAPS

GENERAL AND PHYSICAL

1. Palestine, Transjordan, and surrounding countries    *facing p.* 1
2. Regions and main place-names . . . . *facing p.* 3
3. Geological map of Palestine and Transjordan . *facing p.* 9
4. Geological section across Judaea . . . . *p.* 11
5. Generalized relief map . . . . . . *p.* 14
6. Topographical sections across Palestine . . *facing p.* 15
7. Rivers and Lakes . . . . . . *facing p.* 28
8. The Dead Sea . . . . . . *facing p.* 29

THE COAST

9. Haifa and the Bay of Acre . . . . . *p.* 34
10. The Coast from Atlit to Nathanya . . . *p.* 38
11. The Coast north and south of Jaffa . . . *p.* 40
12. The Dunes north of Ascalon . . . . *p.* 42
13. The Coast from Gaza to Rafa . . . . *p.* 44

CLIMATE AND VEGETATION

14. Rainfall Distribution . . . . . *p.* 57
15. Rainfall, Rain Days, and Monthly Averages . . *p.* 58
16. Annual Rainfall Section, Jaffa to Amman . . *p.* 59
17. Vegetation Regions of Palestine and Transjordan . *p.* 67

HISTORY

18. The Kingdoms of Israel and Judah . . . *p.* 84
19. Palestine at the time of Christ . . . *p.* 92
20. Roman Palestine, A.D. 400 . . . . *p.* 98
21. Palestine of the Crusades . . . . . *p.* 104

POPULATION, ADMINISTRATION, AND PUBLIC HEALTH

22. Jewish Immigration into Palestine . . . *p.* 179
23. Estimated density of Population, 1940 . . *p.* 185
24. Administrative divisions and centres . . . *p.* 198
25. Jewish-owned land, April 1942 . . . *p.* 212
26. Malarious Areas and Malarial Control . . . *p.* 229

AGRICULTURE, INDUSTRIES, FINANCE, AND COMMERCE

27. The Soils of Palestine . . . . . *p.* 240
28. Springs, Wells, and Irrigation . . . . *p.* 248
29. Consumption of Electricity . . . . *p.* 262
30. Export of Soap . . . . . . *p.* 264
31. Export of Wine . . . . . . *p.* 265
32. Investment in private building, 1924–1940 . . *p.* 267

(ix)

33. Building Licences in the four Chief Towns, 1932–41    .    *p.* 267
34. Production, Consumption, and Imports of Cement    .    *p.* 268
35. Revenue from Customs Receipts and Land Fees   .    .    *p.* 284
36. Capital brought into Palestine by Immigrants    .    .    *p.* 287

PORTS AND INLAND TOWNS

37. Plan of Acre at the time of the Crusades    .    .    .    *p.* 296
38. Plan of Acre   .   .   .   .   .   .   .   *p.* 296
39. Plan of Haifa and Mount Carmel    .    .    .    .    *p.* 302
40. The communications of Haifa    .    .    .    .    .    *p.* 302
41. The port of Haifa   .   .   .   .   .   .   *facing p.* 306
42. Old Jaffa sea-front, south of the harbour    .    .    .    *p.* 308
43. Jaffa Harbour   .   .   .   .   .   .   *p.* 311
44. Jaffa and Tel Aviv   .   .   .   .   .   .   *p.* 313
45. Gaza   .   .   .   .   .   .   .   .   *p.* 316
46. Plan of Jerusalem   .   .   .   .   .   .   *p.* 324

COMMUNICATIONS*

47. Ramleh road-centre   .   .   .   .   .   .   *p.* 376
48. Jerusalem road-centre   .   .   .   .   .   *p.* 381
49. Telegraphs, Telephones, and Wireless Stations    .    .    *p.* 394

TRANSJORDAN

50, 51. The Highlands of Ajlun and the northern Belka   .   *pp.* 404, 405
52, 53. The Southern Belka   .   .   .   .   *pp.* 412, 413
54. The Highland of Maan   .   .   .   .   .   *p.* 416
55. Roman Sites and Roads   .   .   .   .   .   *p.* 445
56. The Cultivated Zone of Transjordan   .   .   .   .   *p.* 486
57. Water-supply of Transjordan   .   .   .   .   *p.* 490
58. Communications   .   .   .   .   .   .   *p.* 504
59. The Pipe-line and desert motor-road   .   .   .   *p.* 516

HISTORICAL SITES

60. The Church of the Holy Sepulchre   .   .   .   *pp.* 532–3
61. Plan of Jerash   .   .   .   .   .   .   *p.* 542

*62. The Communications of Palestine   .   .   .   *in pocket at end.*

# ILLUSTRATIONS

1. The Meanders and Gallery Vegetation of the Jordan . (*frontispiece*)

GENERAL AND REGIONAL

2. Relief model of Palestine . . . . . . *facing p.* 14
3. Plain of Esdraelon from Carmel . . . . . 16
4. Plain of Esdraelon from the Mount of Precipitation . . 16
5. The Horns of Hattin, Galilee . . . . . . 17
6. Cactus at Kefr Kenna ('Cana of Galilee') . . . . 17
7. The Hill of Samaria (*mod.* Sebustya) . . . . . 18
8. The Wilderness of Judaea from the air, between Jerusalem and Jericho . . . . . . . . . 19
9. Monastery of St. George, Wadi Kelt . . . . . 20
10. The Brook Kidron, south-east of Jerusalem . . . 20
11. Modern Jericho and the Jordan trough, near the north end of the Dead Sea . . . . . . . . . 21
12. Nebi Musa near Jericho, and the Nahr Mukallik . . . 21
13. Plain of Gennesaret and the Sea of Galilee . . . 30
14. Waterfall near Metulla . . . . . . . 30
15. Lake Tiberias with Mount Hermon in the distance . . 31
16. The Dead Sea and the Transjordan escarpment . . . 31

THE COAST

17. The Coast of northern Palestine near Ras en Nakurah . . 36
18. The sea-wall of Acre . . . . . . . 36
19. The Bay of Acre from the citadel of Acre . . . 37
20. Haifa and the Bay of Acre . . . . . . . 37

VEGETATION

21. Rocky soil steppe, lower slopes of Palestine escarpment . . 70
22. Oakwood with heavy undergrowth of *Styrax officinalis* at Sheikh Abreik, near Nazareth . . . . . . . 70
23. Huleh swamp and lake . . . . . . . 71
24. Sand-dunes south of Jaffa . . . . . . . 74
25. Maquis near Zichron Jacob, Samarian hills . . . 74
26. Garigue in mountains behind Zichron Jacob . . . 74
27. The banks of the Jordan . . . . . . . 75
28. Gallery forest of the Jordan meanders . . . . 75

HISTORY

29. Egyptians under Rameses II assaulting the fortress of Dapur in Galilee (*from Karnak*) . . . . . . 82
30. Semitic captives taken by the Egyptians (*NW. wall of Abydos*) . 83
31. Tell ed Duweir, the mound of ancient Lachish . . . 86

32. Tell es Sultan, the mound of ancient Jericho    .    *facing p.* 86
33. The Jebusite Wall, Mount Ophel, Jerusalem    .    .    .    87
34. The Israelite Wall and part of the Hellenistic Round Tower at
    Samaria    .    .    .    .    .    .    .    .    .    87
35. The ruins of Herod's Palace, Samaria    .    .    .    .    94
36. Samaria, modern Sebustya    .    .    .    .    .    94
37. Nineteenth-century Jewish village of Zichron Jacob    .    .    122
38. Rehovot, the Jewish centre of the orange industry, south of Jaffa    122
39. Nahalal, in the plain of Esdraelon    .    .    .    .    123
40. The Wailing Wall at Jerusalem    .    .    .    .    .    123


THE PEOPLE

41. Semitic types from the palace of Rameses III at Medinet Habu,
    Egypt .    .    .    .    .    .    .    .    .    134
42. Palestinians of the second millennium B.C.    .    .    .    135
43. Mixed types of Arab fellahin to-day    .    .    .    .    136
44. Beduin and their tents    .    .    .    .    .    .    137
45. Jewish types    .    .    .    .    .    .    .    .    138
46. A beduin encampment    .    .    .    .    .    .    139
47. A hill-side village in Samaria    .    .    .    .    .    139
48. Moslems at prayer    .    .    .    .    .    .    .    144
49. Samaritans at prayer .    .    .    .    .    .    .    144
50. The Orthodox ceremony of 'the Washing of the Feet' at the
    Church of the Holy Sepulchre, Jerusalem    .    .    .    145
51. The Palestine Archaeological Museum    .    .    .    .    160
52. The Hebrew University    .    .    .    .    .    .    160
53. Costumes of Arab women    .    .    .    .    .    .    161
54. Ashdod, an Arab village of southern Palestine    .    .    .    162
55. An Arab village of the coastal plain    .    .    .    .    162
56. Mud-brick dwellings of an Arab village    .    .    .    163
57. Bethany on the Jericho road. A stone-built village of the
    Judaean hills    .    .    .    .    .    .    .    163
58. Gleaning near Bethlehem    .    .    .    .    .    164
59. Grinding corn .    .    .    .    .    .    .    .    164
60. Ain Miriam, the Virgin's Spring, Nazareth .    .    .    164
61. Mat-making from papyrus .    .    .    .    .    .    165
62. Reed huts on the shore of Lake Huleh    .    .    .    .    165


AGRICULTURE AND INDUSTRIES

63. Ploughing in Palestine    .    .    .    .    .    .    244
64. An orange-grove in the coastal plain    .    .    .    .    244
65. Irrigation pumps on the Auja    .    .    .    .    .    245
66. Ben Shemen, a Jewish agricultural school    .    .    .    245
67. Afforestation near Nazareth. The Balfour forest in 1929    .    252
68. The Balfour forest in 1935    .    .    .    .    .    .    252

69. Papyrus growing at Lake Huleh . . . *facing p.* 253
70. Arab women carrying papyrus for mat-making . . . .253
71. Palestine Potash Company's salt-pans at the northern end of the Dead Sea . . . . . . . . . 258
72. Artificial reservoir and hydro-electric power station of the Palestine Electric Corporation at the junction of the Yarmuk and the Jordan . . . . . . . . 258
73. Ain es Siyah Pumping-station for Mount Carmel water-supply 270
74. Oil storage tanks and workers' settlement on the Bay of Acre east of Haifa . . . . . . . . 270
75. Arab fishermen . . . . . . . . 271
76. Fellah watering sheep and goats . . . . . 271

PORTS AND TOWNS

77. Marino Sanudo's plan of Acre at the time of the Crusades . 296
78. Aqueduct from Kabri to Acre . . . . . . 297
79. Acre. Jazzar's Mosque from the east . . . . 297
80. Haifa. The main wharf and transit sheds . . . 304
81. Haifa and the lower slopes of Carmel . . . . 304
82. Haifa port, breakwater, and oil dock from the south . . 305
83. Haifa from the north-east . . . . . . 305
84. Jaffa Harbour from the air, looking north-east . . 308
85. Jaffa Harbour from the air, looking south . . . 308
86. Tel Aviv. The lighter basin . . . . . 309
87. Tel Aviv. View south from the stadium . . . 309
88. Beisan . . . . . . . . . 320
89. Beersheba . . . . . . . . 320
90. Bethlehem. The Church of the Nativity . . . 321
91. Bethlehem. General view . . . . . . 321
92. 'David's Pool' at Hebron . . . . . . 322
93. Hebron. General view . . . . . . 322
94. Jenin and the plain of Esdraelon . . . . 323
95. Modern Jericho . . . . . . . 323
96. Jerusalem. The Haram esh Sherif across the Kidron from the Garden of Gethsemane . . . . . . 324
97. Jerusalem. View north up the valley of the Kidron from near the Pool of Siloam . . . . . . 324
98. Jerusalem. The old city, the Haram esh Sherif, and the Mount of Olives, seen from the air to the south . . . 325
99, 100. Jerusalem. Streets in the old city . . . 326
101. Jerusalem. The Jaffa Gate . . . . . 327
102. Jerusalem. The Damascus Gate . . . . 327
103. Jerusalem. The Ecce Homo Arch . . . . 330
104. Jerusalem. The Church of the Holy Sepulchre . . 330
105. Jerusalem. The old city . . . . . 331
106. Jerusalem. The Jewish Agency in the new city . . 331

107. Nablus, the Biblical Shechem . . . . *facing p.* 334
108. Nazareth in Galilee . . . . . . . . 334
109. Safad . . . . . . . . . . 335
110. Tiberias from the north . . . . . . . 335

COMMUNICATIONS

111. Railway bridge over the Wadi Ghazza, south of Gaza . . 358
112. Battir station, Lydda–Jerusalem railway . . . . 358
113. Masonry bridge over the Kishon, km. 13·1, Haifa–Samakh railway . . . . . . . . . . 359
114. Railway bridge over the Yarmuk near Naharayim . . . 359
115. The coast road into Syria at Ras en Nakurah, 12 miles north of Acre . . . . . . . . . 380
116. On the road from Jerusalem to Jericho . . . . 380
117. Old Jisr Banat Yakub from the Syrian side . . . . 381
118. Lydda airport. View eastwards from the air . . . 381

TRANSJORDAN

119. The Yarmuk valley between Samakh and El Hammeh . . 406
120. The Yarmuk valley between the railway stations of Wadi Khaled and Esh Shajara . . . . . . . . 406
121. Es Salt . . . . . . . . . 407
122. Amman . . . . . . . . . 407
123. Bab el Mojib. Junction of the Wadi Mojib (Arnon) with the Dead Sea . . . . . . . . . 418
124. View westwards down the Wadi Kerak . . . 419
125. The Seil Kerak in flood . . . . . . 419
126. Lake deposits of salt and clay of the Lisan peninsula, Dead Sea 430
127. View eastwards from the Deir plateau near Petra . . . 430
128. Oleanders in full bloom in the Sik gorge at Petra . . 431
129. Vegetation at Amman . . . . . . 431
130. Dolmen between Dana and Shobek . . . . 434
131. Gilgal (stone circle) near Petra . . . . . 434
132. Amman, from south-east of the theatre . . . 435
133. Kerak. East face of the castle battlements . . . 435
134. View south down the depression from Azrak . . 446
135. The keep at Kasr Azrak . . . . . . 446
136. Camels grazing at Kasr Azrak . . . . . 447
137. Camel caravan in southern Transjordan . . . 447
138. Tunnel on the railway south of Amman (km. 105·1) . . 512
139. Railway bridge over dry wadi near Maan (km. 331·6) . . 512
140. The desert near pumping-station H4 in wet weather . . 513
141. Auto-patrol laying the surface mat over a desert culvert . 513
142. Motor-mechanical angle-dozer clearing a track in the lava belt 513
143. Akaba from the sea . . . . . . . 522

144. Akaba. View up the Araba depression    .    .    *facing p.* 522
145. Akaba wireless post    .    .    .    .    .    .    . 523
146. Akaba Customs House and Fort from the west    .    .    . 523

HOLY PLACES AND HISTORICAL SITES

147. The Church of the Holy Sepulchre, Jerusalem    .    .    . 530
148. Interior of the Church of the Nativity, Bethlehem    .    . 530
149. The Mosque El Aksa, Jerusalem    .    .    .    .    . 531
150. Kubbet es Sakhra, the Dome of the Rock, Jerusalem    .    . 531
151. The Roman theatre at Amman    .    .    .    .    .    . 542
152. Jerash. Monumental gate leading to the Temple of Artemis    . 542
153. Meshatta from the air    .    .    .    .    .    .    . 543
154. Petra. The Khazna Firaun, Pharaoh's Treasury    .    .    . 543

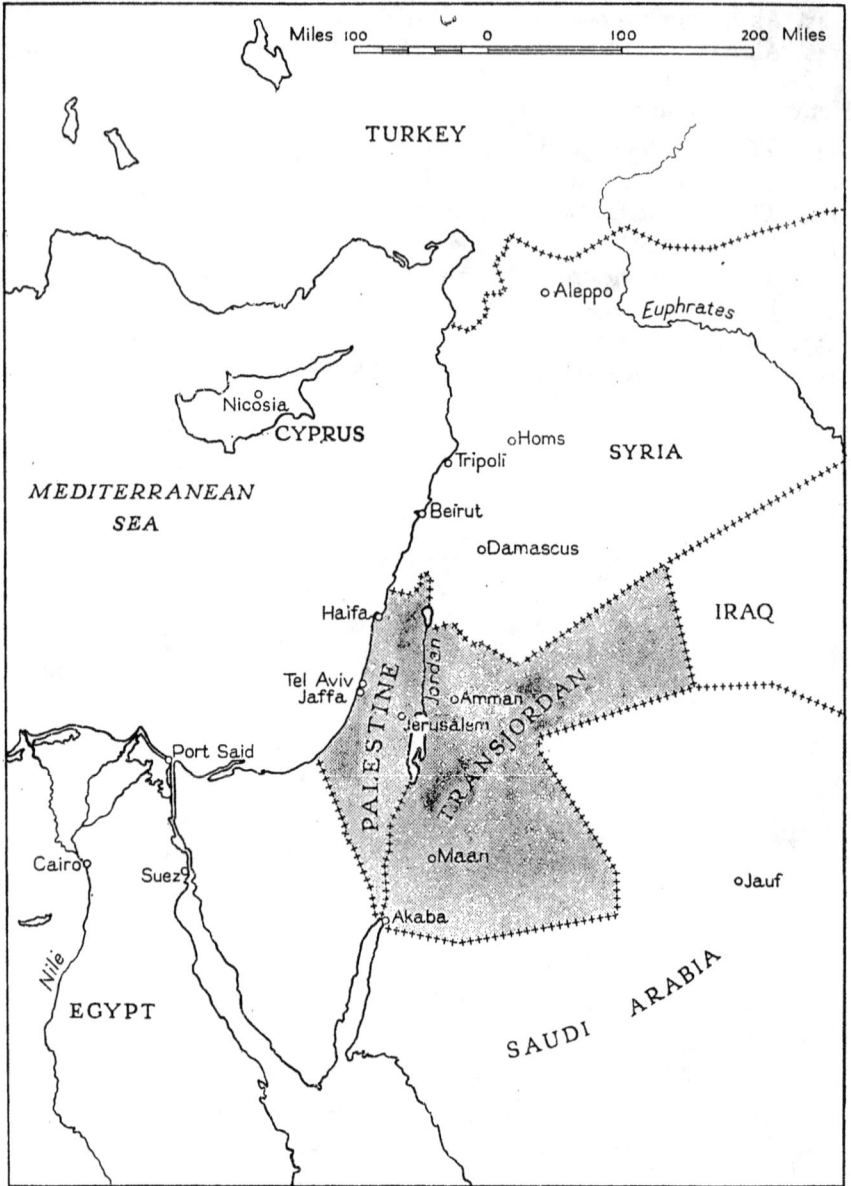

FIG. 1. *Palestine, Transjordan, and surrounding countries*

# PART I. PALESTINE

## CHAPTER I

## INTRODUCTION

*Boundaries and Area*

PALESTINE has been called 'the least of all lands', and within the limits set by the Mediterranean on the west, the deep rift of the Jordan valley on the east, the mountains of Lebanon on the north, and the Sinai desert on the south, it is geographically well defined. It lies on the western edge of the continent of Asia, between latitudes 29° 30′ and 33° 17′ N. and longitudes 34° 13′ and 35° 42′ E., and its political boundaries are with Syria and Lebanon on the north, with Syria and Transjordan on the east, and with the Sinai province of Egypt on the south-west. The greatest distance from north to south is about 270 miles, and from east to west a little under 70 miles. The area is about 10,000 square miles, including 261 of water: Lake Huleh, Lake Tiberias or the Sea of Galilee, and the Dead Sea.

More exactly the land boundary runs as follows: From Ras en Nakurah on the Mediterranean (lat. 33° 06′ N., long. 35° 06′ E.) to a point west of Kadas, north to Metulla, and east to a point a short distance west of Banyas (lat. 33° 15′ N., long. 35° 41′ E.). Thence south, running east of Lake Huleh to Jisr Banat Yakub, south of the lake, then a few yards east of the river Jordan and Lake Tiberias to El Hammeh, 5 miles east of the southern end (lat. 32° 41′ N., long. 35° 40′ E.). From El Hammeh along the middle of the river Yarmuk to the Jordan confluence; thence along the Jordan, the Dead Sea, and the Wadi Araba as far as the sea 2 miles west of the village of Akaba (lat. 29° 33′ N., long. 34° 58′ E.). From Akaba along the gulf to Bir Taba and then north-westwards to the Mediterranean immediately north-west of Rafa (lat. 31° 19′ N., long. 34° 13′ E.).

These boundaries are not coterminous with those of biblical Palestine, which varied considerably from time to time. They enclose a larger area than the combined kingdoms of Israel and Judah, and include both the proverbial limits of the Holy Land: Dan—Banyas, the generally accepted site of the town of Dan, is just outside—and Beersheba. They comprise the former Ottoman sanjaks of Jerusalem, Belka, and Acre, and much of the southern sanjak of the vilayet of

Beirut. To these four districts has been added a strip of almost un-inhabited land south and south-west of the Dead Sea, formerly a part of the sanjak of Maan.

The northern and north-eastern frontiers were laid down in the Anglo-French Convention of 23 December 1920 (Cmd. 1195), and after delimitation on the ground were confirmed in 1923 (Cmd. 1910; Treaty Series No. 13—1923). The frontier with Transjordan was fixed by the High Commissioner for Palestine and Transjordan on 1 September 1922 in an order authorized by Article 86 of the Palestine Order in Council. In the south and south-west the frontier follows the former boundary between Egypt and the Ottoman Empire. The sanjaks of Belka, Acre, and Beirut were in the Ottoman period parts of the vilayet of Beirut. Jerusalem was an independent sanjak under the direct control of the Porte. The strip of territory between the Dead Sea and the gulf of Akaba was a part of the vilayet of Damascus. Palestine was then generally known in the East as 'Southern Syria'.

On the east and the west the boundaries are the obvious physical ones. On the south, history made the old frontier between the Otto-man Empire and Egyptian Sinai, as drawn in 1906, inevitable. Only on the north and north-east were alternatives practicable. There the boundary might have been drawn along the northern limit of the old sanjak of Beirut; or a natural line would have been from the mouth of the river Litani until it turns at right angles towards the north, then slightly south-east skirting the mountains of Lebanon and Mount Hermon to Banyas and turning again to join the present boundary at Lake Huleh.

Thus Palestine, between the desert and the sea, is part of the borderland where East meets West, and is also on the only line of land communication between Asia and Africa. Within its narrow limits two of the great faiths of the world, Judaism and Christianity, saw their beginnings, and from them has come the inspiration to which Western civilization owes much of its being. Later a third great faith, Islam, found also a centre in Palestine—the Land of Three Faiths.

In these circumstances Palestine, known to millions as 'the Holy Land', has always far exceeded in significance its size and its resources. In material wealth it has never been of importance; in spiritual wealth it has for twenty centuries exceeded all other lands. To-day it is still a small and poor land, but the name Palestine means to millions an inspiration and a hope, a past and a future.

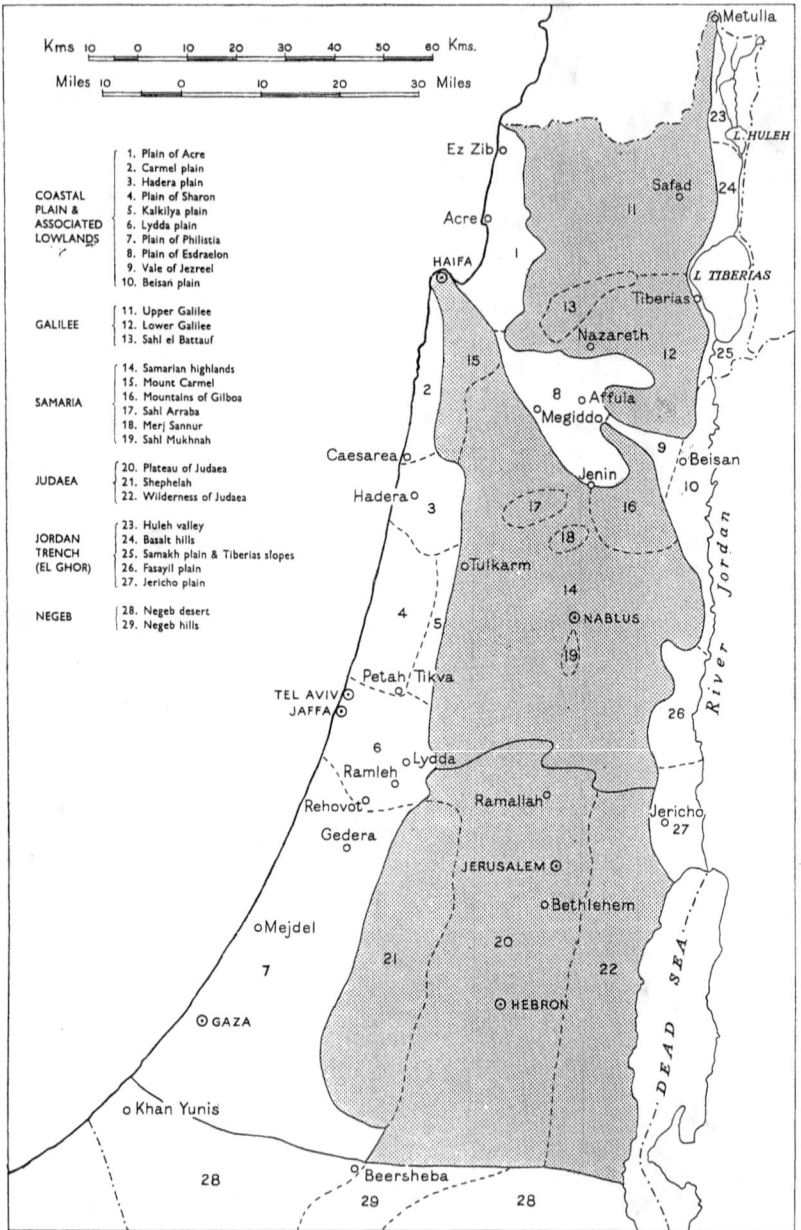

Kms 10   0   10   20   30   40   50   60 Kms.

Miles 10   0   10   20   30 Miles

COASTAL
PLAIN &
ASSOCIATED
LOWLANDS

1. Plain of Acre
2. Carmel plain
3. Hadera plain
4. Plain of Sharon
5. Kalkilya plain
6. Lydda plain
7. Plain of Philistia
8. Plain of Esdraelon
9. Vale of Jezreel
10. Beisan plain

GALILEE

11. Upper Galilee
12. Lower Galilee
13. Sahl el Battauf

SAMARIA

14. Samarian highlands
15. Mount Carmel
16. Mountains of Gilboa
17. Sahl Arraba
18. Merj Sannur
19. Sahl Mukhnah

JUDAEA

20. Plateau of Judaea
21. Shephelah
22. Wilderness of Judaea

JORDAN
TRENCH
(EL GHOR)

23. Huleh valley
24. Basalt hills
25. Samakh plain & Tiberias slopes
26. Fasayil plain
27. Jericho plain

NEGEB

28. Negeb desert
29. Negeb hills

Metulla

L. HULEH

Ez Zib

Safad

Acre

HAIFA

L. TIBERIAS

Tiberias

Nazareth

Affula

Megiddo

Beisan

Caesarea

Jenin

Hadera

Tulkarm

NABLUS

Petah Tikva

TEL AVIV
JAFFA

Ramleh   Lydda

Rehovot

Ramallah

Jericho

Gedera

JERUSALEM

Bethlehem

Mejdel

HEBRON

GAZA

Khan Yunis

Beersheba

DEAD SEA

River Jordan

FIG. 2. Regions and main place-names

Although it is a small country, communications not only within it but also with other lands have been well developed. From Haifa to Alexandria the distance in a direct line is 320 miles, to Cyprus 170 miles, to the Piraeus 750, and to Brindisi, 1,120 miles.

*Geographical and Administrative Divisions*

Palestine is a land of great topographical variety. Three parallel north–south strips form the chief relief features, and each of these can be further subdivided on a basis of local topography. On the west a coastal plain of varying width borders the Mediterranean. Inland, a dissected highland zone, widening from about 25 miles in the north to 40 in the south, contains the mountains of Galilee, Samaria, and Judaea, and falls abruptly on the east to the great trench of the Jordan valley and its southward continuation, the Wadi Araba. In the Negeb desert of the south, climate, imposing its own uniformity, constitutes a fourth region which overrides the topographical continuation of the three former zones.

There is a remarkable diversity of climate. In the Jordan valley conditions are tropical, intolerable to Europeans in summer, but warm, sunny, and ideal in the depth of winter. In the mountainous region the winters are as cold as those in England. Heavy snowfalls are not infrequent, and central or other means of heating the houses is essential to comfort. Rain is frequent during the four or five months of winter. It is very heavy while it lasts, but interspersed between periods of sunshine and blue skies, which, though cold, make a pleasant winter. In the plain it is never cold. Only on an occasional wet winter day is a fire needed in Haifa or Tel Aviv. The weather on the coast has been compared, not inappropriately, with that of the Riviera. Even in summer, if care is taken to dress suitably, there is no discomfort from the heat. The principal discomfort arises from the dust which permeates everything, especially when raised by the wind in late summer. The asphalting of roads during the past twenty years both in the towns and in many parts of the country has greatly reduced this discomfort.

But in spite of this diversity, there are only two seasons throughout Palestine, summer and winter, the transition from one to the other being almost abrupt. The wet and dry seasons are everywhere clearly differentiated.

This variety of topography and climate produces variations in the fertility of the country. The Jordan valley is largely sterile, because much of the soil is alkaline, but in the north the loams of old lake basins make cultivation possible, and tropical fruits grow in oases such as Jericho. The mountain region is also sterile, but for other reasons—scarcity of water and soil. Here, however, there are also oases, larger than those of the valley, in particular around Hebron, Ramallah, and Nablus, and in the north around Safaḍ. The only agriculturally satisfactory parts of Palestine are the coastal plain and the plain of Esdraelon. In the south, even before Gaza is reached, the coastal plain passes gradually into the desert of the Negeb, a desert comprising almost half the country but with less than 5 per cent. of the population, where the cause of sterility is the lack of water, not of soil. The Government of Palestine has been searching for underground water here over a long period, but the salinity of the water that has been found makes it useless for cultivation. It seems that the relatively large area of the Negeb is doomed to remain only a wandering place for beduin and their half-starved flocks.

In a small country such as Palestine the administration is necessarily to a large extent centralized. There is, however, a certain amount of decentralization, the country being divided into six districts under district commissioners who have representatives in the sub-districts into which the districts are divided (fig. 24).

## History and People

From the beginning of history until the Ottoman period Palestine seems always to have been the battleground on which neighbouring Powers fought one another for mastery. It is for this reason that the Israelites and their descendants, the Judaeans, kept for the most part to the mountains, away from the road between Africa and Asia on which the rival armies met. Another consequence of this endless rivalry between neighbouring empires, bringing with it the unenviable position as a partial buffer between them, is that only for brief and infrequent periods has Palestine or any part of it enjoyed any sort of political independence. When not incorporated in a neighbouring empire Palestine was often dependent on the whim of some foreign tyrant who could dictate to its nominal rulers as he wished.

The many conquests of the country and the occupation of it by foreign armies have made of its population a mixture of peoples for which there are few parallels elsewhere. Some of these peoples have amalgamated in course of time, and the backbone of the present population, the fellahin of the villages, though largely from Arabia and replenished from Arabia, is the result of that amalgamation. But many alien elements have not been assimilated, and modern Palestine has been described as 'a Babel of Tongues' and 'a Museum of Nationalities'; hence the difficulties which beset the administrator, bent on the welfare of all sections of the population. Very few inhabitants consider themselves Palestinians. They are in their own eyes Arabs, Jews, Armenians, Circassians. The most that they can be persuaded to admit is that they are Southern Syrians.

It is not the purpose of this book to suggest a solution to the outstanding political problems, but to relate the facts which may help towards it. In the section on Transjordan (p. 465) it is shown how throughout the centuries there has been impact between the desert and the sown. In Palestine and Syria, and still more in Transjordan, the peasantry throughout the ages has received an increment of Arab blood, and in recent years there has been mass immigration of Jews from near and far. Under Ottoman rule Palestine and Syria were one, and this problem, not yet serious, was an Ottoman affair. Towards the end of that rule Arab nationalism grew throughout the states bordering Arabia, and the hopes of Jews for a return to Palestine increased throughout the world. The atmosphere of war from 1914 to 1918 was not the best in which to plan a settlement of such conflicting fundamental desires, and in the stress of war none of the parties to the pacts then made—Allies, Arabs, or Jews—could foresee the post-war conditions under which adjustment would be possible. Even afterwards, at Versailles and Geneva, there were so many major problems to be solved that it was difficult to find a final solution to this one of western Asia, and it was still outstanding when war broke out again in 1939.

The political problems are intensified by another which is fundamentally geographical. In twenty years the population has doubled. Much of this increase is due to two factors: Jewish immigration and the Arab birth-rate; for the Arabs have been increasing at a rate of 2·5 per cent. each year for over fifteen years, and are consequently finding it difficult to supply their needs in traditional manner in a land of limited resources. It is also true that most of the Jewish landholdings are in the plains; nevertheless a large proportion of these areas still belongs to the Arabs. Thus the Arab problem can only be solved either by increased intensity of cultivation, or by a check to the increase in numbers, or by the development of industry, none of which will be easy to accomplish. The Jewish problem, on the other hand, is essentially urban, and for the ultimate stability of the Jewish population its solution is more important than that of land settlement. It does not appear impossible, therefore, that the development of industries by the Jews, if it would give additional employment to the Arabs, might lead the two peoples to live side by side in mutual benefit, and so settle the outstanding political problems of both. Unfortunately the Arabs object to industrialization, and the Jews tend to restrict to their own people the labour required for such enterprises.

These problems are not only of concern to Palestine, but are to a large extent international, since they affect three separate peoples, the British, the Arabs, and the Jews, each with world-wide connexions. Britain, as the mandatory Power, pledged to serve the interests of Jew and Arab alike, is legally answerable to the League of Nations and morally to world opinion. Her own imperial interests are also involved, and since Palestine is so favourably situated to become a focus of routes by land, sea, and air, it is obviously to the benefit of Britain in particular and of the world as a whole that Palestine should be friendly and peaceful. The conflict between two conceptions of life which is now troubling Palestine is part of a wider struggle in many parts of the world. Against this background it is possible to study in the geography of this small country the prospects of solution. The proximity of Palestine to unsaturated markets outside the temperate zone is an incentive to further effort.

### Place-names

The spelling of place-names has not yet been crystallized in Palestine. The Palestine Government in co-operation with the Permanent Committee on Geographical Names for British Official Use adopted a standard spelling for many names; this spelling appears to be still provisional and liable to change. Official maps on different scales, and adjacent maps on the same scale, are inconsistent. There appear to have been three major changes in twelve years. Moreover, the historical and modern names for a place often differ widely, and the earlier name is often more familiar to the English reader, while the official name is unknown locally. Jewish development has also brought with it a number of Hebrew place-names, sometimes for newly settled sites, sometimes for settlements that have taken the place of Arab villages or have grown up beside them. Sometimes both Hebrew and Arabic names survive in addition to the biblical or historical name. In the following pages no one system of nomenclature has been adopted. As a rule the most familiar name has been taken, but the alternative has generally been added on the first reference. In the spelling of transliterated Arabic and Hebrew names the customary usage has been followed, subject to the following general rules. All diacritical signs have been omitted, since to the ordinary reader they are meaningless; the letter *k*, except in 'Iraq', has been preferred to *q*; the terminal *h* has been appended after *e* (e.g. Huleh, not Hule or Hula); the article *el, ez, ed*, &c., has as a rule been omitted from before the name of a river, and in names when an alternative is possible *e* has been preferred to *a*, e.g. 'Tell' has been preferred to 'Tall'. With these exceptions, names have been written as far as possible to agree with those on official large-scale maps of Palestine, which are inconsistent with small-scale maps, rather than with those in official reports, which often agree with neither.

The following Arabic words are in common use in place-names; followed by a personal or descriptive name.

## *Topographical Glossary*

| | | | |
|---|---|---|---|
| Ain | spring | Khan | caravanserai |
| Ard | earth | Khirbet, khurbeh | ruin |
| Bab | gate | | |
| Bahr | lake | Mar | saint |
| Banat | daughters | Merj | meadow |
| Beled | village | Mina | harbour |
| Ben, beni | son, sons | Mughara | cavern |
| Bet, beit | house | Nahr | river |
| Bilad | district | Nebi | prophet |
| Bir | well | Nekb | pass |
| Birkeh, birket | pool, cistern | Ras | promontory, peak, head |
| Burj | tower | | |
| Dahr | mountain ridge | Sabkha | saline depression |
| Deir | monastery | Sahl | plain |
| Derb | way | Sanjak | province |
| Ghadir | swamp | Seil | torrent |
| Ghor | low ground, valley | Sheikh | lord |
| Husn | fortress | Sidi | saint, holy man |
| Jebel | mountain | Suk | market, bazaar |
| Jezireh | island | Tarik | road |
| Jisr | bridge | Tell | artificial mound, generally covering a ruined city |
| Kabr | tomb | | |
| Kala, kalat | castle | | |
| Karya | village | Umm | mother |
| Kasr | castle | Vilayet | province |
| Kefr (*Heb.* Kefar) | village | Wadi | watercourse, often dry |
| | | Wata | plain |
| Khabra | rain-water pool | Weli | tomb of saint |

## CHAPTER II

# PHYSICAL GEOGRAPHY

PHYSICALLY Palestine and Transjordan fall into five distinct regions: (i) the coastal plain, together with the plain of Esdraelon; (ii) the mountain districts of Galilee, Samaria, and Judaea; (iii) the Jordan trench and its structural continuation, the Wadi Araba; (iv) the southern deserts, known generally as the Negeb; and (v) the plateau east of Jordan, forming the State of Transjordan (p. 399). The two states offer the varieties of soil, climate, and vegetation of a continent: mountain and plain, barren hills and pleasant valleys, lake and sea-board, deserts and broad stretches of deep, fruitful soil. With the exception of the volcanic rocks of Galilee and similar masses east of Jordan, the country is built mainly of a light-coloured limestone, extremely porous, but interspersed with beds of marl. The hills of Palestine are therefore ill watered in spite of a fair winter rainfall, and are poor in cultivable land; on the other hand, an active circulation of underground water-supplies causes abundant springs, especially in the north. Running water, when present, carves deep gorges isolating blocks of highland like natural fortresses, with the valley-sides hollowed out by caves. Palestine is indeed the land of grottoes and caverns.

## GEOLOGY

THE whole region lies along the broken edge of the old land-mass which to-day makes up Arabia and north-east Africa. It is covered by a veneer of wind-borne sediments in the desert region of the south, which thins out northwards and westwards where it is covered by beds of gradually thickening marine deposits (fig. 3).

The old mass forming the basement is now exposed only south of the Dead Sea in the walls of the Wadi Araba, where it appears on both sides and extends far to the south-east beyond the frontier. It comprises crystalline schists cut by bosses of grey granite which are themselves in turn pierced by basic dikes (originally molten matter) following north-north-west lines. This old basement was levelled in very early geological times, and on it were deposited sandstones of many ages from late pre-Cambrian times to Lower Cretaceous. A sea lay to the north and west during most of this long period, occasionally encroaching eastwards, flooding the edge of the desert

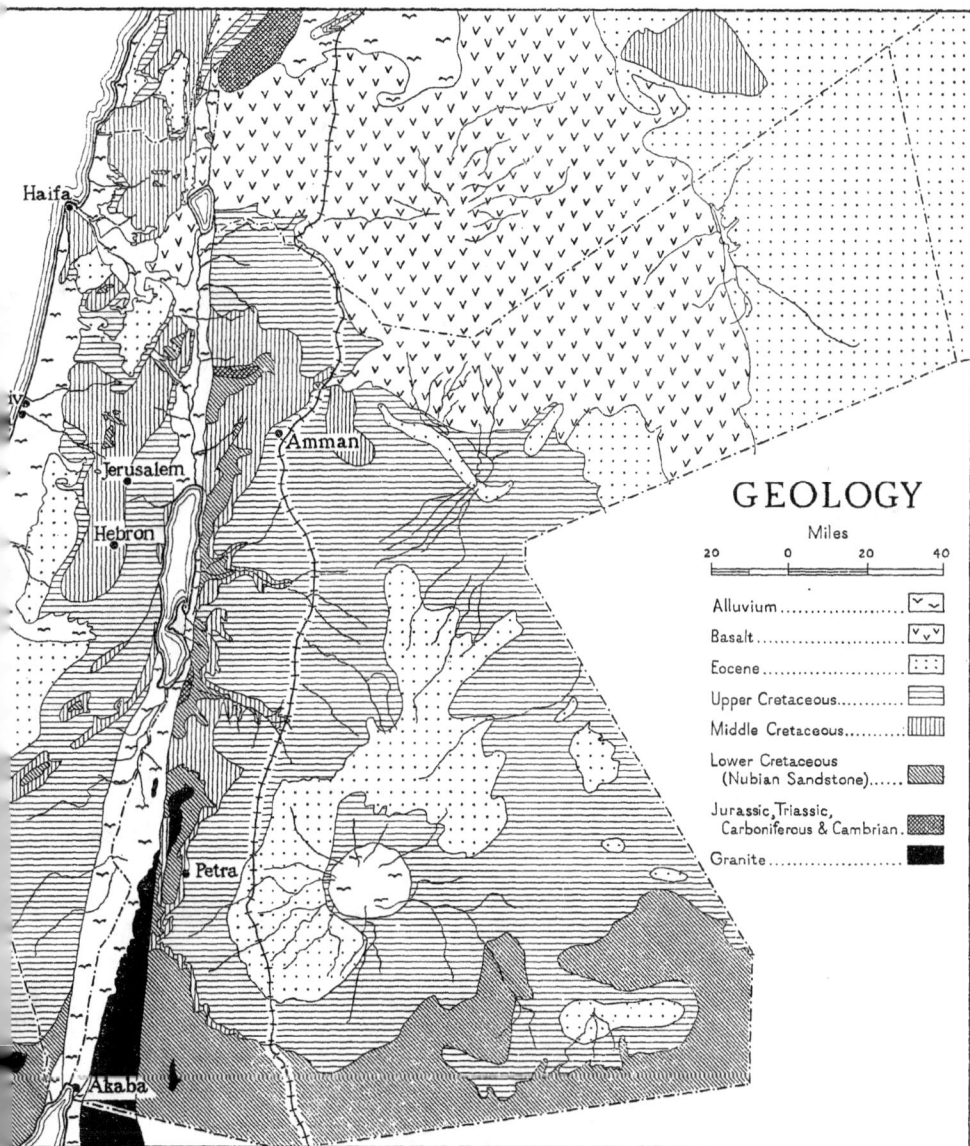

GEOLOGY

Miles

20    0    20    40

Alluvium..................... ⟨⌄⌄⟩

Basalt.......................... ⟨ᵛᵥᵛ⟩

Eocene....................... ⟨∷∷⟩

Upper Cretaceous........... ⟨▤⟩

Middle Cretaceous........... ⟨▥⟩

Lower Cretaceous
(Nubian Sandstone)...... ⟨▨⟩

Jurassic, Triassic,
Carboniferous & Cambrian. ⟨▦⟩

Granite..................... ⟨■⟩

FIG. 3. *Geological map of Palestine and Transjordan*

and then retreating, perhaps leaving behind lagoons which later evaporated to form beds of gypsum. Such beds are found between strata of normal marine origin, the fossils of which, entombed in the sandstones and sandy limestones, serve to date the strata. These marine sediments thickened greatly towards the north-west during the Middle Mesozoic, forming eventually a wedge-shaped block with the thick end in Syria and the thin edge in Transjordan, where it fades out.

The whole region was submerged at the end of the Lower Cretaceous age, and in the Middle and Upper Cretaceous a thick sheet of limestone was deposited. This was composed of several varieties of rock, some dolomitic and some shaly, and in beds both thin and massive. The uppermost deposits are more chalky and mixed with many layers and nodules of flint, part of the formation near the top being a series of thin-bedded cherts. Marine deposition continued into the Lower Eocene age, when apparently the sea receded for a while and some slight erosion took place in the west before another submergence occurred during which the thick beds of Middle Eocene limestone were laid down. About the end of this time the whole series of beds began to fold, and elevation occurred, particularly in the east. The sea persisted along the west coast, however, after a very short interruption, into the Miocene age, except in the north, where land emerged finally about the Middle Miocene.

The folding alluded to above resulted in a gentle arching of the sediments along a north-north-east axis in northern Palestine, akin to, but much feebler than, that found in the ranges of Lebanon and Anti-Lebanon in Syria. In southern Palestine, however, the sedimentary mantle is rucked up into a group of curving folds running north-east near the Dead Sea and almost west at the Sinai frontier. They have no counterpart in Transjordan, but resemble the structures lying north of Damascus. They suggest a southward movement of a Palestine block relative to a Transjordan block, and a crowding of pliable sediments on the western basement against a south-eastern obstacle in a manner which did not occur over the eastern block, where the rigid unyielding basement of the old African Arabian continent under the shallow sediments permitted only a slight warping.

The folding was not strong and was succeeded by considerable fracturing during the Miocene. Strong vertical movements of blocks occurred, resulting in the Jordan trough being formed. At first two basins were formed, with a land barrier between them. The southern was partly filled in the late Miocene or Pliocene age by sediments grading from sands and silts below to gypseous limestones and dolomites and bedded gypsum above. The former represent the coarse detritus of the weathering escarpment edges of the newly formed plateau margins of the trough; the latter are the deposits of a highly saline sea, a more extensive ancestor of the Dead Sea, with its surface at least 500 feet above the present level. The northern basin contained a freshwater lake until the Upper Pliocene age, when it seems to have been embraced by the southern 'Bitter Sea'. Before the junction took place a second spasm of strong vertical movement of the land-blocks occurred, and the floor of the Dead Sea trough dropped to its present relative level 5,000 feet below the edge of the escarpment of the eastern plateau and 2,600 feet below sea-level. The Dead Sea is certainly the remains of a sheet of sea-water much more extensive than the sea of to-day.

In the next phase, violent fracturing took the place of folding in late geological times, during which individual blocks of land moved vertically up or down relatively to each other along the fractures or 'fault-planes'. The Jordan valley, the Dead Sea, the Wadi Araba, and the gulf of Akaba form a single depressed unit along a series of faults parallel to and in prolongation of each other. The plain of Esdraelon north of the Carmel ridge is a sunken block fractured from the hills of Samaria; and it is probable that another fault follows closely the shore of the eastern Mediterranean and is responsible for its harbourless coastline. Less conspicuous fractures trending north-north-east can be traced among the Judaean hills and occasionally in Transjordan. All this fracturing was accompanied by volcanic activity, which lasted a long time and resulted in the formation of large tracts of lava in the north of the area.

Open sea conditions obtained on the western coastlands from the Oligocene age onwards and are shown by the succession of foraminiferal marls, shaly limestones, and salt-water sandstones and conglomerates. The last of the series is a false-bedded calcareous sandstone deposited before the uplift of the coast above sea-level in the Pliocene age. The latest phase is one in which debris eroded from the Judaean hills has been deposited over the gently tilted marine sediments and subsequently fringed with coastal sand-dunes. Unlike the late strata of the Dead Sea neighbourhood there is no covering of lava along the coast.

The brief outline of geological history given above is not controversial, but there has been considerable argument and speculation about the mechanics of the formation of the Jordan valley and Akaba trough. It is often called a 'rift valley', which implies that the early sedimentary plateau was arched, and that the central segment or 'keystone' dropped and so produced the rift. If this occurred the trough was caused by tension or a release of pressure on either side. Others call it a 'ramp valley', holding that the region was under compression, and that in order to release the strain the central block was broken and forced down, the escarpments on either side overriding the narrow wedge in the centre. Neither theory can yet be

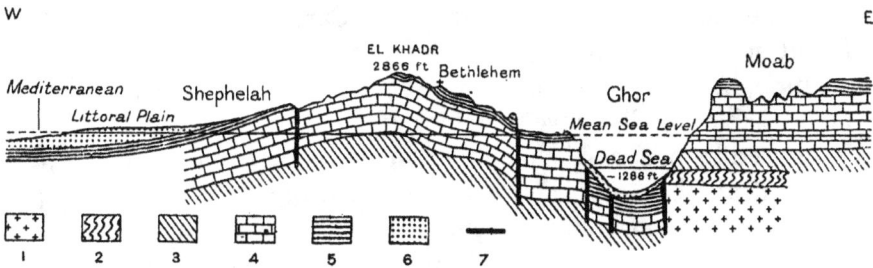

FIG. 4. *Geological Section across Judaea*

1. Crystalline;   2. Primary;   3. Cenomanian Sandstone;   4. Cenomanian Limestone;   5. Senonian calcareous marl;   6. Pliocene and later;   7. Fault.

proved, though it is indisputable that the basement of the Jordan trough has sunk relatively to the Judaean hills and the Transjordan plateau. This deeply entrenched valley, much of it far below sea-level, is the most striking feature of Palestine; it is, however, only one local incident of the breaking down of south-east Europe, western Asia, and north-east Africa. The Black Sea, the Aegean, the eastern Mediterranean, a host of fertile depressions in Turkey, the 'rift valley' system of the Red Sea, the gulf of Aden, Abyssinia, and east Africa as far south as Lake Nyasa, all result from the same fracturing of the earth's crust. In all these regions the vertical movements of crustal blocks were accompanied or followed by volcanicity.

A simplified geological section across the country from west to east about the latitude of Bethlehem is given in fig. 4. The vertical displacement of the beds is easily seen, as are the gentle warping of the marine sediments west of the Ghor or Jordan trough and the almost horizontal beds of similar deposits spread out on the ancient crystalline basement east of the trough.

Much detailed work has been carried out to ascertain the lie of the beds in Palestine for the practical purpose of utilizing the valuable underground supplies of water. These supplies are of the first importance in a land where the rainfall is seasonal, and insufficient owing to irregularity from year to year. The porosity of the rocks of the Judaean hills relegates these uplands almost entirely to pasture. Agriculture in the valleys and lowlands depends mainly on the underground water issuing as springs.

Apart from water-supplies, the rocks of Palestine and Transjordan have yielded little of value. Some beds of the Upper Cretaceous are known to be rich in phosphates. Manganese is found associated with dolomites and sandstones regarded as Carboniferous. Gypsum is found in certain localities, and the Dead Sea contains useful salts in solution, including potash. In spite of some indications of petroleum, no workable supplies have been located. The grottoes and caves have been used by man as his habitation in transition from the tent of the desert to the house of the town, for which the rocks provide ample quantities of good building stone, and some useful road metal.

## REGIONAL TOPOGRAPHY

### (i) *The Plains*

The plains comprise the coastal lowland, which runs the whole length of the land, from the Negeb in the south to Ras en Nakurah or 'the Ladder of Tyre', and the plain of Esdraelon in the north, which stretches for nearly 40 miles from the coast at the bay of Acre inland to the Jordan south of Lake Tiberias. Between the southern part of the coastal plain and the Judaean hills is a range of low hills, known as the Shephelah, with a small elevated plain between it and the main slopes of Judaea. These will be described with the mountain region, with which they have more in common (p. 20).

In the north the plain of Acre extends for 20 miles in a semicircle round the bay of Acre, with a breadth of from 5 to 9 miles. Between the town of Acre and Ras en Nakurah the coastal plain becomes more and more constricted, until there is only just enough room for a road. The great spur of Mount Carmel, projecting north-west towards Haifa, reduces the coastal plain to a bare 200 yards, by which the coast road and railway pass along the edge of the sea. South of Cape Carmel the plain remains comparatively narrow until near Caesarea (Kisarya) it begins to widen out to form the plain of Sharon which extends southwards as far as Tel Aviv and Jaffa. This great fertile plain, the width of which at Tulkarm is 10 miles, and throughout its length little less, lies behind an almost straight coastline protected by sand-dunes and has suffered in the past by being badly drained. The recent deposits brought down from the hills, and produced also by the erosion of sandstone hills in the plains, are already carved into scattered sandstone ridges, on which stand the village settlements. Drainage and irrigation by wells are the principal features of the agricultural economy of this region, the chief centre of the citrus cultivation.

Near Jaffa a spur of low hills approaches the coast, with the perennial river Auja reaching the sea north of Tel Aviv and the intermittent stream of the Wadi Kebir following the southern edge of the spur and turning north inland of Jaffa. Then the plain widens again behind a broad belt of sand-dunes and includes the towns of Lydda and Ramleh. Here is the ancient 'plain of Philistia', which extends south for 60 miles to the frontier and beyond, being about 20 miles wide at Gaza.

A fertile soil, suitable warmth, sufficient water-supplies, all tend to make this coastal plain a rich agricultural land in comparison with the inland plateaux of Samaria and Judaea. Orange-trees surround the settlements with a belt of dark colour; palms, cactus, and Barbary fig-trees border the irrigated gardens. Farther inland, where it is drier, cereals take the place of citrus, then almonds and olives, and then the vine.

The plain of Esdraelon, or Megiddo, was formed by the dislocation of a belt of country along a line of faults, which traverse the northern end of the hills of Samaria and leave the Carmel ridge as an upstanding fragment. It is bounded on the north by the hills of lower Galilee, from which the southern outlier Mount Tabor (Jebel et Tur) stands up as a landmark from the plain; and on the south by the ridge of Carmel and the mountains of Gilboa (Jebel Fakkua). These two project from the hills of Samaria north-west and north-east enclosing a re-entrant of low ground north of Jenin, between which town and Nazareth the plain is widest, 16 miles from north to south. Esdraelon may be divided into three parts: (1) on the west, the plain of Acre, part of the coastal plain, is separated from Esdraelon proper by spurs of the mountains of Galilee which reach out southwards almost to the Carmel ridge; (2) in the centre, Esdraelon proper, or the valley of Megiddo; and (3) in the east, the Emek or Vale of Jezreel which is more undulating and is gashed on the south by the Nahr Jalud which drains past Beisan, 400 feet below sea-level, to the

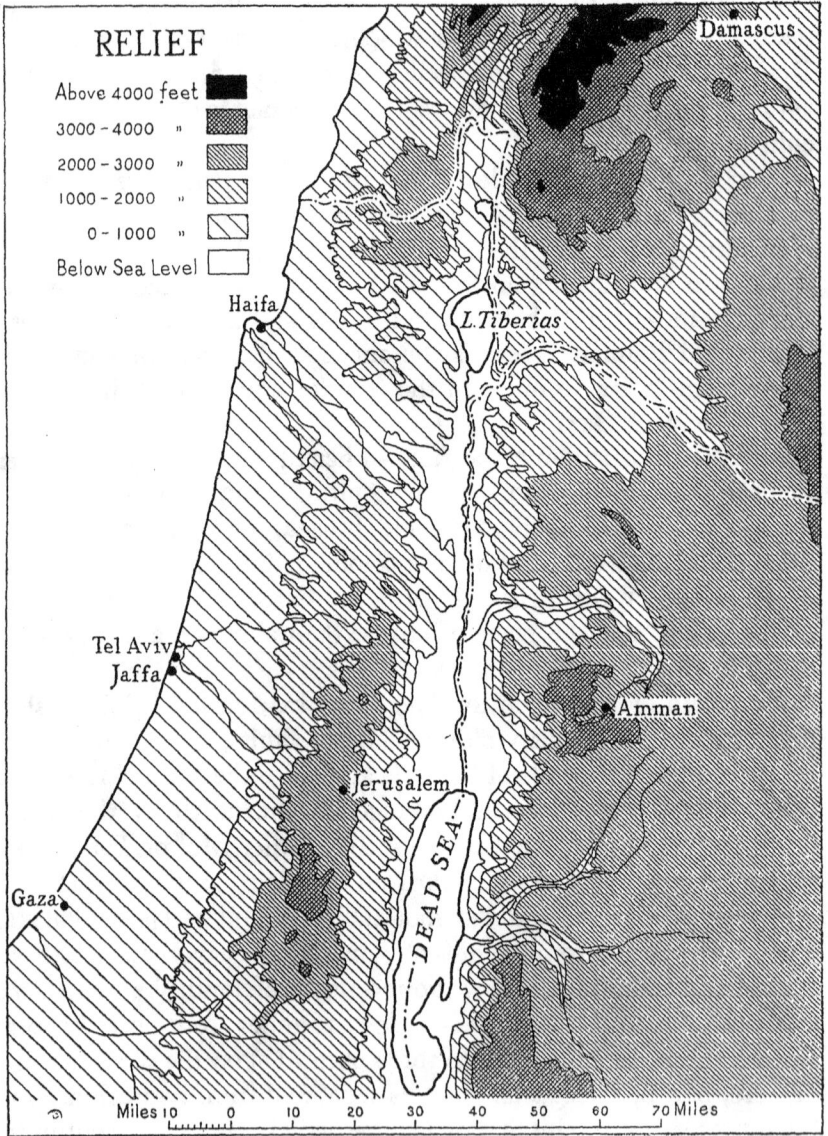

FIG. 5. *Generalized Relief Map*

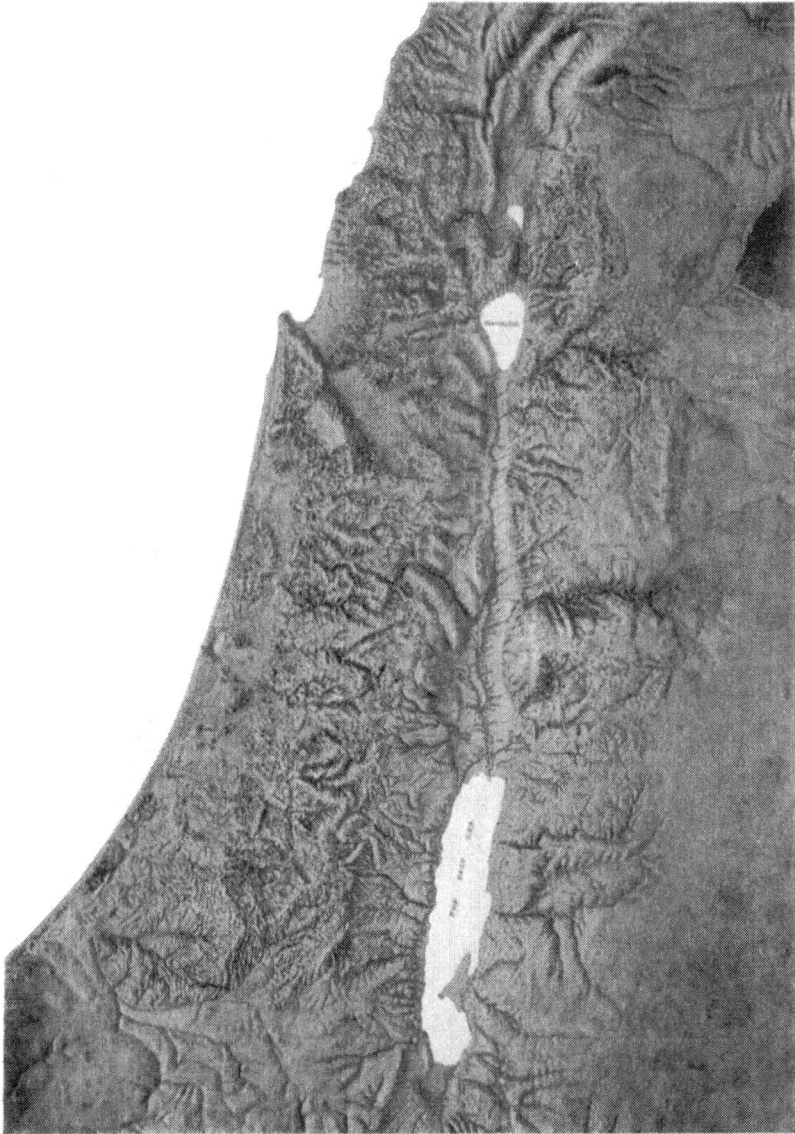

2. *Relief model of Palestine*

SECTION ON LINE ATLIT-TIBERIAS

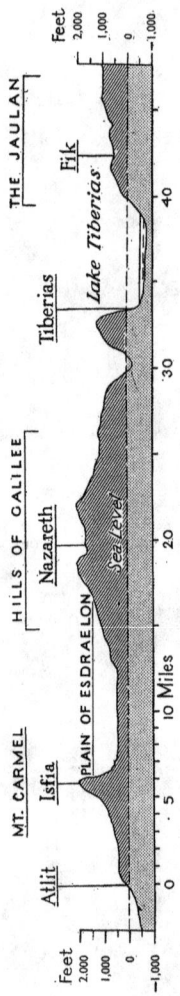

MT. CARMEL    HILLS OF GALILEE    THE JAULAN

Atlit    Isfia    Nazareth    Tiberias    Fik

PLAIN OF ESDRAELON    Lake Tiberias

Sea Level

Feet
2,000
1,000
0
-1,000

Feet
2,000
1,000
0
-1,000

0    5    10 Miles    20    30    40

SECTION ON LINE TIRA-BEISAN

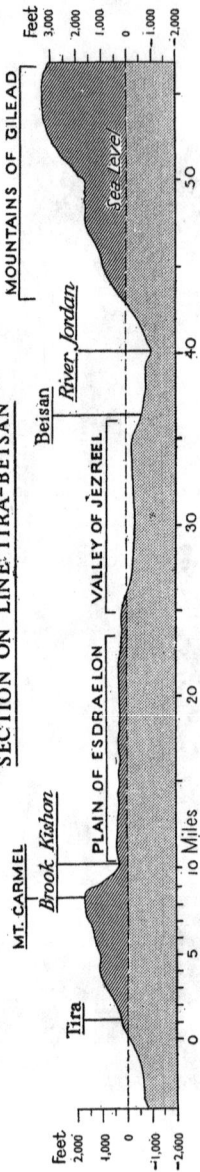

MT. CARMEL    MOUNTAINS OF GILEAD

Tira    Brook Kishon    Beisan

PLAIN OF ESDRAELON    VALLEY OF JEZREEL    River Jordan

Sea Level

Feet
2,000
1,000
0
-1,000
-2,000

Feet
3,000
2,000
1,000
0
-1,000
-2,000

0    5    10 Miles    20    30    40    50

SECTION ON LINE JAFFA-JERUSALEM

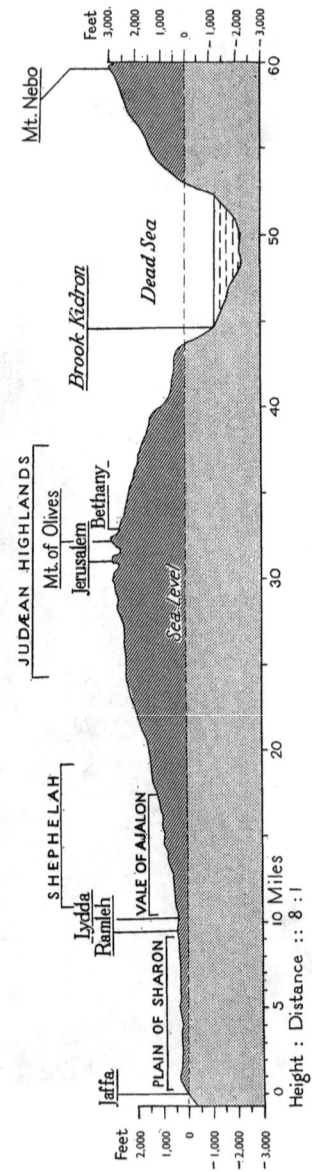

SHEPHELAH    JUDÆAN HIGHLANDS

Jaffa    Lydda    Ramleh    Jerusalem    Mt. of Olives    Bethany    Brook Kidron    Mt. Nebo

PLAIN OF SHARON    VALE OF AJALON    Dead Sea

Sea Level

Feet
2,000
1,000
0
-1,000
-2,000
-3,000

Feet
3,000
2,000
1,000
0
-1,000
-2,000
-3,000

0    5    10 Miles    20    30    40    50    60

Height : Distance :: 8 : 1

Fig. 6. Topographical Sections across Palestine

bed of the Jordan, 400 feet lower. The plain of Esdraelon, with its rich deep black earth, formed by the decomposition of the basalts of Galilee—themselves the result of the volcanic activity which accompanied the foundering of the plain—has been for centuries under-cultivated, in parts derelict and disease-infected, mainly on account of the neglect and insecurity that accompanied the rule of the Ottoman Sultans. In recent years most of it has been acquired by the Jewish Agency for Palestine and settled with Jewish immigrant cultivators (fig. 25, p. 212). In consequence, the early prosperity has begun to return to what should ultimately be the granary of Palestine.

## (ii) *The Mountain Region*

The mountain region is divided historically into Galilee, upper and lower, Samaria, and Judaea. Galilee is north of the plain of Esdraelon between lakes Huleh and Tiberias and the sea. Samaria and Judaea together form the limestone backbone of Palestine.

*Galilee.* Upper Galilee is a mountainous limestone plateau, structurally an offshoot of the loftier mountains of Lebanon, and showing more of the effects of folding than the hills of Samaria and Judaea. It is approximately 16 miles from north to south and 25 from west to east. It is dominated on the north-east by Hermon; in fact this mountain, standing up to 9,232 feet beyond the frontier, dominates the view as far as the coast at Haifa, 70 miles away, and even farther south in Judaea. The watershed of upper Galilee lies towards the east. The long tongue of Palestinian country bordering the western edge of the Jordan trough north of Lake Huleh rises to a maximum height of nearly 2,900 feet and falls almost sheer to the trough, which is here about 300 feet above sea-level; but the highest points are a few miles west of Safad: Jebel Jarmak (3,963 ft.), Jebel Heidar (3,435 ft.), and Jebel Arus (3,514 ft.). A first-class road climbs up to Safad and skirts this limestone group to find its way by a gap and dry valley westward to the coast at Acre. South of the gap the hills are lower and more broken, and the limestone becomes covered more and more with basaltic lavas.

Upper and lower Galilee are separated from each other by the plain of Asochis (Sahl el Battauf), a plain about 9 miles long from east to west, 2 miles broad, and at about 500 feet above sea-level. Its eastern end is less than 7 miles from the plateau edge, which falls steeply to the western shore of Lake Tiberias. The highest point of the escarpment immediately behind the town of Tiberias is 817 feet; the surface of the lake less than 2 miles away is 686 feet below sea-level.

Lower Galilee is lower in altitude than upper Galilee. Broadly speaking, it comprises several parallel ridges, running from east to west with open valleys between them, but the features are much less regular than farther north. From Haritiya ('Harosheth of the Gentiles'), at the southernmost tip of the plain of Acre, to the southern end of Lake Tiberias is 28 miles; from north to south lower Galilee is rarely 7 miles across. Nowhere do the hills reach 2,000 feet. The 'Horns of Hattin', west of the town of Tiberias, are only 1,070 feet; Mount Tabor (Jebel et Tur) stands up at the south-east end to 1,850 feet. Jebel Turan, immediately south of the Sahl el Battauf, and Jebel es Sikh, north-east of Nazareth, reach 1,800 and 1,880 feet respectively; between them winds the road from Tiberias through Nazareth to Haifa, picking its way wherever accidents of topography lessen the gradient. The city of Nazareth on the southern border of this upland stands at 1,600 feet and near the highest point of the road. In the plain of Esdraelon is the outlying hill of Jebel ed Dahi, or 'Little Hermon', 1,690 feet above sea-level.

Throughout Galilee rain is more abundant than in Judaea and springs more numerous. There are more streams of running water, more trees and woods of dwarf oak, terebinth, and Aleppo pine; indeed 13 per cent. of the country here is still wooded, a high proportion for Palestine. In the depressions where the products of the decomposition of limestone and basaltic rocks have combined to form a fertile soil, fields of corn are common, Compared with Judaea, Galilee is a garden; compared with Lebanon it is semi-desert.

*Samaria*, roughly covering the same region as the ancient kingdom of Israel, lies between the plain of Esdraelon and the plateau of Judaea, with which it is continuous. Its northern boundary runs south-eastwards along the Carmel ridge to the edge of the Jordan trough, but includes the projection northwards known as the mountains of Gilboa (Jebel Fakkua); its southern is an indeterminate line roughly from west to east, passing immediately north of Ramallah; its western includes the slopes of Carmel and the hills behind Tulkarm; its eastern is the Jordan escarpment. These boundaries enclose a territory of about 1,600 square miles, about 50 miles long from Mount Carmel, behind Haifa, to Ramallah, and rather under 30 miles from Tulkarm eastwards to the Jordan escarpment. In climate and vegetation Samaria is transitional between Galilee and Judaea, less green and well-watered than Galilee, less dusty and brown than Judaea. Mountainous throughout, its heights never

3. *The Plain of Esdraelon from Carmel*

4. *The Plain of Esdraelon from the 'Mount of Precipitation'*

5. *The Horns of Hattin, Galilee*

6. *Cactus at Kefr Kenna ('Cana of Galilee')*

reach those of upper Galilee, and it is lower than Judaea between Jerusalem and Hebron.

Mount Carmel, 1,800 feet, in the extreme north-west, is famous in biblical history, as are also mounts Ebal (Jebel Eslamiya), 3,084 feet, and Gerizim (Jebel et Tur), 2,890 feet, the twin heights which enclose the valley where lies Nablus—successor to Shechem, and principal town of Samaria—and guard its approaches from the south. These and Tell Asur, 3,290 feet, are the highest summits in Samaria.

The approaches by several wadis from the plain on the west are easier than in northern Galilee. On the east the descent to the Jordan is less sheer and difficult than farther south; and the desert conditions of the descent from Judaea to the Dead Sea are not found on the paths that lead from Samaria to the Jordan, where a number of streams, several of which are perennial, course the slopes. Of these the most important is the Wadi Faria (Farah), which in its lowest course is known as the Wadi Jauzala (Jozeleh). This short stream, rising at about 2,240 feet, enters the Jordan at 1,160 feet below sea-level. The shorter, steeper Wadi Malih, farther north, is saline, as its name denotes (*malih* = salt).

Samaria, though mountainous, is interspersed with a number of small plains and open valleys. The rounded slopes contrast with the deep gorges and rugged plateaux of Judaea. Two such plains are located near the junction of the Carmel ridge and the projection ending in the mountains of Gilboa (Fakkua), immediately south of Jenin: the Sahl Arraba (the 'plain of Dothan') at about 800 feet, and the Merj el Ghuruk (or Merj Sannur) 1,150 feet. The latter is lake or marsh for half the year. The Sahl Mukhnah is south of Nablus, and along it runs the first-class plateau road from that town to Ramallah and Jerusalem. The western portion of Samaria, known as Mount Ephraim—at one time the name of the entire group with the exception of Carmel—is at a lower level.

Though there are numerous paths and tracks, only one first-class road climbs up from the coastal plain. This goes from Tulkarm to Nablus by the Wadi Zeimar which is also taken by the narrow-gauge railway. Six miles before reaching Nablus it joins the central ridgeway road, which makes use of Sahl Arraba to reach Jenin, whence it connects with the roads which serve the plain of Esdraelon.

Though in some respects the least interesting part of Palestine to-day, Samaria was historic ground during the early military history of the Jews. While it was still a northern district of a united state, the defence of its northern front led to Barak's victory of the Kishon and to Saul's defeat on Mount Gilboa. After the secession from Judah, Israel had to defend itself, and its citadel Samaria, fortified by Omri and defended by Ahab, gave its name to this 'northern kingdom'. Assyrian conquest from the north overwhelmed it earlier than Judaea, which seldom supported it and was exposed by its collapse.

*Judaea.* There is no defined boundary between Samaria and Judaea, and it has been taken above as a line roughly from west to east passing immediately north of Ramallah, 10 miles north of Jerusalem. But there is a marked difference between the topography of the two regions, Samaria being more eroded into mountain and valley than Judaea, which remains a high plateau, less dissected because of its drier climate. As one goes south the landscape becomes harsher and more rugged. Bare rocks, washed clear of soil, with stretches of loose broken stones, seemingly endless, are the chief surface features, with here and there pockets of earth protected from the rush of ephemeral torrents of winter rain and eagerly cultivated by the poor *fellahin*. Only around Ramallah and Bira, about 10 miles north of Jerusalem, and Hebron, a city some 19 miles south of it, is there any serious cultivation. Jerusalem itself stands on a hill-top amid rocks and fields of stones: here, as elsewhere, opportunities for cultivation are very limited.

The Judaean tableland is about 48 miles from north to south; the distance from Ramallah to Beersheba is 51 miles. From east to west it widens gradually from 15 miles in the north to 25 in the south. It slopes gradually to the plains on the west and very steeply to the Jordan valley, a fall of 4,000 feet in 25 miles between Jerusalem and the north end of the Dead Sea. On the west the descent is in two steps: to the Shephelah plateau, and thence to the coastal plain.

The highest point is 3,336 feet, near Halhul, 3½ miles north of Hebron. Other heights are Nebi Samwil, 2,904 feet, 5 miles north of Jerusalem, and Jebel et Tur ('the Mount of Olives'), 2,680 feet, overlooking Jerusalem from the east. South of Hebron the land falls away rapidly, reaching the plain after 20 miles.

Sir George Adam Smith has described the general character of the Judaean plateau in a vivid passage.

'The greater part of the Judaean plateau consists of stony moorland, upon which rough scrub and thorns, reinforced by a few dwarf oaks, contend with multitudes of boulders, and the limestone, as if impatient of the thin pretence of soil, breaks out in bare scalps and prominences. There are some patches of cultivation, but though the grain springs bravely from

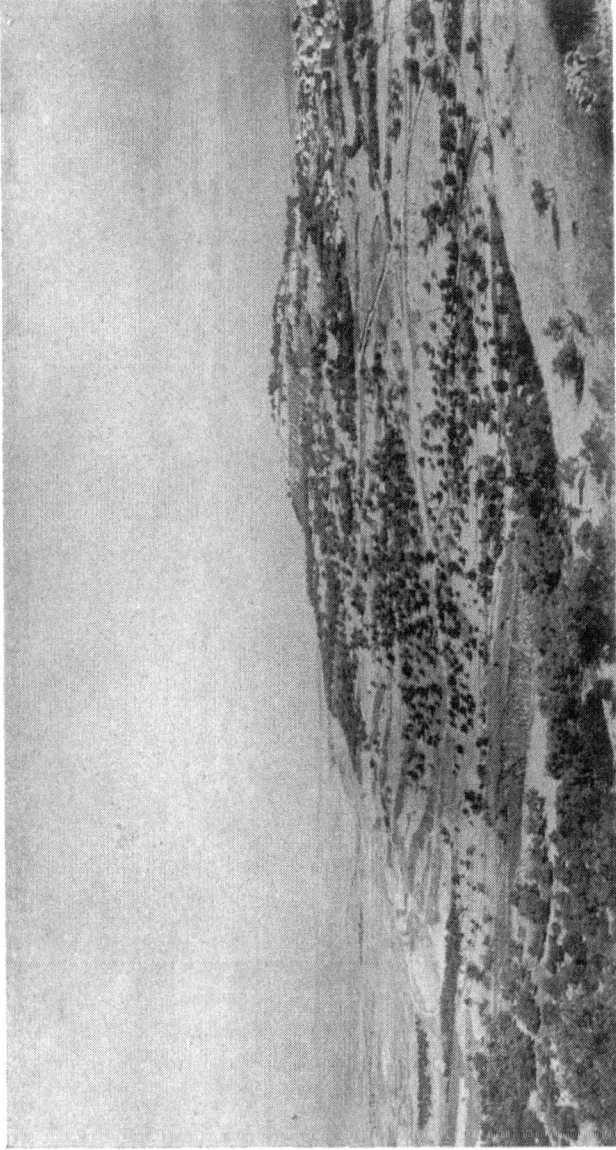

7. *The Hill of Samaria* (mod. *Sebustya*)

8. *The Wilderness of Judaea, from the air, between Jerusalem and Jericho*

them, they seem more beds of shingle than of soil. The only other signs of life, besides the wild bee and a few birds, are flocks of sheep and goats, or a few cattle, cropping far apart in melancholy proof of the scantiness of the herbage. Where the plateau rolls, the shadeless slopes are for the most part divided between brown scrub and grey rock; the hollows are stony fields traversed by dry torrent-beds of dirty boulders and gashed clay. Where the plateau breaks, low ridge and shallow glen are formed, and the ridge is often crowned by a village, of which the grey stone walls and mud roofs look from the distance like a mere outcrop of the rock; yet round them, or below in the glen, there will be olive-groves, figs, and perhaps a few terraces of vines. . . .

'The prevailing impression of Judaea is of stone—the torrent-beds, the paths that are no better, the heaps and heaps of stones gathered from the fields, the fields as stony still, the moors strewn with boulders, the obtrusive scalps and ribs of the hills. In the more desolate parts, which had otherwise been covered with scrub, this impression is increased by the ruins of ancient cultivation—cairns, terrace-walls, and vineyard towers.'

On the west, the approaches to the plateau from the plain, in order from north to south, are:

(a) the Wadi Dilb, which rises near Ramallah;

(b) the Wadi Malaka with the two Beth Horons, where Judas Maccabaeus defeated the Syrians in the second century B.C.;

(c) the Wadi Salman, the main route in ancient times, which drains north through Lydda, collects the winter waters of the first two, and reaches the sea by Jaffa;

(d) the Wadi Ali, along part of which runs the modern road to Jerusalem;

(e) the Wadi Sarar, in part the Wadi Ismain, now followed closely by the railway from Jaffa to Jerusalem;

(f) the Wadi Samt (Vale of Elah), up which the Philistines, the Syrians, and Richard Cœur de Lion advanced to Jerusalem;

(g) the Wadi Afranj ('valley of Zephathah'), west of Hebron.

The road southward from Hebron leaves the plateau by the Wadi Khelil to Beersheba, where the Wadi Bir es Saba, of which it is a tributary, flows west and north-west as the Wadi Ghazza to the sea near Tell Ujal.

On the east the descent is precipitous from an average height of 2,500 feet above sea-level to 1,300 feet below, in the sunken trench of the Ghor. Rain on this side is most exceptional, and in consequence the land is a veritable desert, 'the wilderness of Judaea'. The only natural lines of communication are the Wadi Kelt and the Wadi Mukallik. The present first-class road from Jerusalem to Jericho takes the headwaters of the Mukallik but makes a long detour round the Wadi Kelt in order to find an easier gradient. Elsewhere the plateau ends in a succession of precipitous terraces, the easternmost often 1,000 feet above the bottom of the Ghor. These walls of rock are, however, carved up by a number of deep gorges which render passage from north to south almost impossible, though all except the Wadi Kelt in the north and the Feshshet ed Derwish or Wadi Umm Beghak, running into the south-west of the Dead Sea, are dry save for part of the winter.

The wilderness of Judaea, and that of Tekoa which begins 5 miles south of Jerusalem, fully deserve their names; they are real deserts, rough and rocky, with parched and barren wastes, and with no trace of tree or field, excepting the occasional oases in the beds of a few streams and around one or two springs. Population there is none apart from the anchorites of the monasteries, of which the principal are those of St. George in the Wadi Kelt, and of Mar Saba, 10 miles to the south. Nomad beduin are only temporary visitors.

The *Shephelah*, midway in more than one respect between the plateau of Judaea and the coastal plain, is different in structure and landscape (fig. 4). It stretches almost from the confines of Samaria to a point east of Gaza and covers an area 30 miles long and from 5 to 8 miles wide, curving gently and concave to the sea. Its western boundary runs approximately from a point 3 miles west of Tell Jazar (Gezer) and 14 from the coast to a point 15 miles east of Gaza. North of this district the characteristic features of the Shephelah are not found, and the low hills which extend from Samaria to the plain are spurs of the mountain backbone.

The height of the Shephelah averages from 500 to 800 feet above the sea, but in one or two places reaches 1,500 feet. Mainly composed of soft chalky limestone with an undulating surface sloping westward and intersected by wadis, the land, especially in the valleys, is fertile. The higher parts are separated from the Judaean plateau by the line of a depression forming broad shallow valleys—the Wadi Najil, the Wadi Sur, and the Wadi Samt (Vale of Elah)—a well-watered fertile region growing cereals and olives, with evidence of having once supported a far larger population than now. Cut off from the plateau by an abrupt escarpment, it was the contested frontier between the Israelites of the plateau and the Philistines of the coastal plain, the scene of their ceaseless warfare and of the legendary feats of Samson.

10. *The Brook Kidron, south-east of Jerusalem*

9. *Monastery of St. George, Wadi Kelt*

11. *Modern Jericho and the Jordan Trough near the north end of the Dead Sea.
Escarpment of the Belka highland across the plain*

12. *Nebi Musa, near Jericho, and the Nahr Mukallik at the foot of the Jordan
escarpment.  View southwards*

Later it formed the similar battleground of the Maccabees and the Syrians (p. 89), and of Saracens and Crusaders (p. 103).

### (iii) *The Jordan Trench (El Ghor)*

The Jordan trench begins at the northern frontier of Palestine, where the headwaters of the Jordan, collected by a few larger streams, flow through marshland to form Lake Huleh, 230 feet above sea-level. At Lake Tiberias ('the Sea of Galilee'), 10 miles to the south, it is already nearly 700 feet below sea-level, while at the north end of the Dead Sea the floor of the trench has dropped a further 580 feet. South of the Dead Sea it begins to rise again and its name, 'El Ghor'— properly only given to the trench between Lake Tiberias and the Dead Sea, but more often applied to the whole feature—changes to the Wadi Araba. Under this name it is known until it reaches the sea at the head of the gulf of Akaba, its base having risen above sea-level west of Petra. The gulf is merely the flooded extension of the trench, the sea having broken into it east of Mount Sinai and submerged it as far as the small Transjordan port of Akaba, close to the southernmost point of Palestine. From the southern base of Mount Hermon to the foot of the Scorpion cliffs (Akrabbim), 8 miles south of the Dead Sea, the distance is 168 miles; from Hermon to Akaba about 100 miles more.

The width of the trench ranges from less than 3 miles to more than 14. The river Jordan, the boundary of Palestine throughout most of its length, flows through its centre, so that the eastern half is generally in Transjordan territory. Except for the break caused by the Emek Jezreel, the Ghor is flanked on the Palestine side by continuous hills and mountains interrupted only by a few watercourses, occasionally with perennial streams. The chief stream-beds from north to south are:

(*a*) the Wadi Hindaj, opposite Lake Huleh, known in its uppermost reaches as Wadi Fara;

(*b*) the Amud, Rubadiya (or Tuffa), and Hamam, flowing into Lake Tiberias, and the Wadi Bira (or Sherrar) joining the Jordan south of it;

(*c*) the Nahr Jalud, draining the Emek Jezreel past Beisan into the Jordan;

(*d*) the Shubash, Malih, Faria (or the Wadi Jauzala), Ahmar, and Auja, rivers of Samaria;

(*e*) the Kelt and the Mukallik, of northern Judaea, the last entering the Dead Sea direct.

Farther south the great eastern walls of the Judaean plateau, 3,500 feet high, are cut by impassable ravines and gorges, the names of which are unimportant.

The Huleh valley, including Lake Huleh, is about 15 miles long and nearly 5 miles wide. For the first 6 miles the floor is a fertile alluvial plain; the remainder is mainly marshland and lake, the most considerable margin of dry land being slightly higher ground to the west of the lake, where rich wheat lands come close to the shore. Towards the southern end the lake tapers to a width of a few hundred yards and is eventually almost enclosed by low volcanic hills. On the south-west there are plantations of eucalyptus trees.

South of Lake Huleh the Ghor is narrowed by basaltic hills through which the Jordan has cut a deep gorge in order to reach the lower level of Lake Tiberias. Here the trench widens to nearly 8 miles, the whole being filled by lake, which leaves only just enough space for a road on either side. A small strip of Palestinian territory passes up the eastern side of the lake, but there is a 7-mile gap along the north-eastern shore which belongs to Syria. Tiberias on the western shore and Samakh on the southern are the only important settlements, the latter being on the railway between Haifa and Deraa, the junction for Damascus and Amman.

The breadth of the Ghor for the first 12 miles south of Lake Tiberias is from 3 to 4 miles. Then it expands westwards, merging in the plain of Beisan, which, if included in the Ghor, doubles the width. South of the Wadi Malih, at the southern end of this plain, the hills once more close in and the valley is at its narrowest; but it soon widens again to an average of 3 miles. East of Ras Umm el Kharruba (692 ft.), which encloses the Ghor el Faria, the faulted trough of the lower Wadi Faria, the Jordan trench is 6 miles wide and 900 feet below sea-level. There is now a general widening, especially westwards to the plains of Fasayil and Jericho, and a width of 10 miles is maintained to the latitude of the latter, when it increases to 14 miles, conformable with a receding bay in the Transjordan scarp. It is about 9 miles wide at the northern end of the Dead Sea.

Throughout most of its length the Ghor is very fertile, but little cultivated, the extreme heat at the bottom of the trench and the radiation from the rock walls making heavy work by a non-tropical people such as the Jews, or even by the Arabs, very difficult. Moreover, in the south, where the valley widens, water-supply is inadequate without costly irrigation, and much of the soil is rank. The valley is therefore almost uninhabited, the large village of Jericho

(Eriha), a short distance north-west of the Dead Sea, being in fact an oasis in the desert, as are the other insignificant settlements.

Jericho was once an important outpost town covering the Jordan crossings immediately north of the Dead Sea. Engeddi, at the mouth of the Wadi Ghar, about half-way down the western coast of the Dead Sea, was once a town supported by the fertile land surrounding it. King David fortified it; under the Romans it was the centre of a toparchy; in the time of Josephus its palms and balsam were famous; as late as the Crusades, its vineyards were celebrated throughout Syria. To-day a few ruins mark its site and only a dozen poverty-stricken Arabs scratch a bare existence from the soil. From Engeddi leads one of the very few tracks from the Dead Sea up into Judaea, though its lower climb is by a staircase rather than along a road. It passes through the Wadi Ghar to Hebron and Jerusalem.

The Palestine shore of the Dead Sea and for some miles westward is indeed a true desert, and, except at Engeddi, incapable under present conditions of supporting life. The Palestine Potash Company houses its workers at the northern and southern ends of the Dead Sea, and at the northern end there is a hotel and bathing-place. But to a large extent the Ghor has been abandoned to nature and is now the resort of the fauna of Palestine rather than of man.

For a more detailed description of the Jordan, of lakes Huleh and Tiberias, and of the Dead Sea, see below, pp. 28–32.

## (iv) *The Negeb*

Southern Palestine or the Negeb is the fourth principal natural division of Palestine—an indefinite desert region within artificial political boundaries, and separated on the north by the line between the habited and the uninhabited which shifts from season to season and from year to year. Its population is almost entirely nomadic, especially in the centre and south, and the sites of occupation are continually changing.

The area is approximately 4,520 square miles (12,577,000 *dunams*), and is nearly as large as the rest of Palestine.[1] Excluding the portion near the coast which has some features in common with the coastal plain farther north, the Negeb falls into two parts: the long slope upwards to the south-east, which is very sparsely inhabited, and the mountain and desert of the east and south. Judging by the remains of Byzantine and later towns, the first of the two parts once had

[1] The figure is from the Royal Commission Report, p. 234. The remainder of Palestine is given as 13,742,000 *dunams*. One *dunam* equals 0·23 of an acre.

a population, not large but of some consequence.  The Negeb is entirely dependent on its rainfall, always scanty and uncertain, for its water-supply.  There is no evidence that this was ever sufficient to support the population that the ruins suggest, and it is possible that these were chiefly military posts with the miscellaneous collection of services necessary for their maintenance, and were not entirely dependent on the land for their supplies.

Beersheba, 30 miles south of Hebron and the southern limit of the Holy Land, is on the edge of the Negeb.  It is now a village, which, previously abandoned, was reoccupied only in 1899 or 1900.  Forty-five miles along the desert road to Egypt is the frontier police-post of El Auja el Hafir.  These are the only regularly inhabited places in the Negeb.

The north-western part of the Negeb is a plain, sloping gently upwards from the coast behind a belt of sand-dunes which widens beyond the Egyptian boundary west of El Arish.  For some 15 or 20 miles south-eastwards from the coast there is some scattered cultivation and grass in spring.  A large expanse of sandy desert, about 15 miles wide, extends northwards of the Wadi Abyad, the depression that drains the mountains along the Egyptian border farther south, and leads westwards towards the Wadi El Arish, and east of this expanse broken hills reach north-eastwards towards Beersheba, which is at about 900 feet above sea-level.  These are outliers of the Judaean hills and are drained by various watercourses, dry except after rain, which is eventually collected by the Wadi Ghazza.  A higher ridge of rocky desert extends south-westwards from the southern end of the Dead Sea to beyond the Egyptian frontier, and forms the watershed—if such a term is permissible in a country which is almost entirely devoid of water—between the catchments of the Arish and the Ghazza on the north-west and the Fukra and Araba on the south-east.

This ridge is rough and broken ground, mostly between 1,500 feet and 2,000 feet, but rising south-westward towards the frontier to heights above 3,000 feet.  The boundary crosses the ridge south-east of Kuseimeh, an Egyptian police-post on the desert road from Suez to Beersheba.  Hereabouts are the highest points: Jebel Kharuf (3,262 ft.), Jebel Lussan (3,140 ft.), Jebel Maghara (3,040 ft.), Jebel Samaweh (3,300 ft.), and others unnamed.  They are roughly half-way between the Mediterranean and the head of the gulf of Akaba.

The desert road from El Auja to Beersheba keeps generally to the stony ground along the northern foot of the ridge, thereby avoiding the more difficult sand-desert to the north and the broken country to the south. Most of the ruins referred to above are hidden away in the upper ravines of the ridge, not far from the head of the Wadi Roman, which lies in a deep depression parallel to the ridge and on the south-east side of it. North of the ridge there is still a little cultivation; to the south and east of it there is none, and here the country becomes more rugged, stony, and broken. The ridge falls in broad steps to the edge of the Araba escarpment, but these steps are much broken and cliffs of 500 feet are common; the escarpment itself is generally precipitous, especially in the north where it ranges from 1,200 feet below sea-level to 1,800 feet above.

### RIVERS AND LAKES

The rivers and lakes of Palestine are few. The former are of little economic consequence, except to the slight extent in which they supply water for irrigation. None is navigable except for very small boats. The largest, the Jordan, is entirely an inland river, ending in the Dead Sea. Those which reach the sea are, from north to south, the Naamin (*class.* Belus) immediately south of Acre; the Kishon or Mukatta directly east of Haifa; the Zerka or Crocodile river between Tantura (Dor) and Kisarya (Caesarea); the Hadera or Mifjir, and the Iskanderuna, both south of this latter site; the Auja or Yarkon, which enters the sea through the northern suburbs of Tel Aviv; the Rubin, seven miles south of Jaffa; and the Ghazza beyond Gaza. These are all perennial streams in their lower courses, though when the dry season is a month or two old, they carry little water, and are then fed by springs, often low down in their course.

### *Rivers of the Mediterranean Seaboard*

The Naamin and the Kishon drain lower Galilee, the latter being by far the most important. The *Naamin* rises east of Haifa among the Galilean foothills and flows sluggishly northwards through the plain of Acre, forming marshland behind the coastal dunes, until it enters the Mediterranean beyond the southern outskirts of Acre. A tributary, the Halazun, which joins it in the marshes, is of more consequence and has two principal sources: the Khashab, rising in the mountains near Rama, and the other in the edge of the Sahl el Battauf (the 'plain of Asochis'). The Naamin basin is at most 10 miles from north to south and 19 from source to coast.

The *Kishon* carries a much greater volume of water and is deemed one of the principal rivers of Palestine, second only to the Jordan. It has two main tributaries: the shorter, which under the name of Rummana rises almost within sight of Mount Hattin, less than 10 miles west of Tiberias, flows westwards along the southern edge of the Sahl el Battauf as the Khaliadiya, and enters the main river as the Malik; and the main Kishon, which rises in Mount Gilboa east of Jenin, and flows through the plain of Esdraelon and along the northern foot of Carmel until it reaches the sea in the eastern suburbs of Haifa. It drains the whole of the sunken plain of Esdraelon and part of lower Galilee, being also fed by springs low down in the Carmel ridge and in the hills to the north. The length of the Malik is about 25 miles; that of the Kishon, known also in its upper reaches as the Sitt, rather more than 35 miles. The plain near the mouth of the Kishon was formerly marshy and enclosed by dunes, and the course of the river was constantly shifting. Agricultural and industrial development, partly Jewish, partly sponsored by the Government, has now controlled the water. The sand-dunes have been levelled and the marshes to a large extent drained.

The *Zerka* or Crocodile river—it derives the latter name from the belief that crocodiles were to be found in it as late as the nineteenth century—drains the south-west side of the Carmel ridge and part of the plain of Sharon. It has several short tributaries. After passing the spur of Zichron Jacob, it forms two branches which reach the sea 3 miles apart. The extensive marshes behind the coastal dunes were a source of disease until they were drained, between 1920 and 1930, by the Palestine Jewish Colonization Association, under a concession from the Government.

The *Hadera* or Khudaira, known also as the Mifjir, the 'Dead river' of the Crusades, enters the sea 2½ miles south of Caesarea. It is formed by several tributaries: the Ara, which is fed by springs in Carmel; the Abu Nar, which rises east of the Sahl Arraba ('plain of Dothan') and is perennial for most of its course; and the Massin, which rises north of Nablus. These wadis undergo several changes of name throughout their courses. The marshes of the lower Hadera were infested by malarial mosquitoes until drained by Jewish settlers.

The next river is the *Iskanderuna*, the 'Salt river' of the Crusades. Draining the western side of the Samarian watershed as the Hawwatat, its main sources are the Tin and the Zeimar which rise near Nablus. Other tributaries are fed by springs in the western foothills of Samaria. The Iskanderuna enters the sea 7 miles south of Caesarea. In its lowest reaches this river is sometimes known as the Wadi

Hawarith, a name taken from the local Arabs, sometimes as the Wadi Kalansawa, and its plain as the Emek Hefer.

The *Auja* or Yarkon is fed by four principal tributaries: (i) the Kalkilya, which, after reaching the plain near the village of that name, is used for irrigation, and only a small surplus reaches the main stream; (ii) the Ishkar, known in its middle course as the Kana, and in its headwaters as the Jarra; (iii) the Sarida or Ballut, the upper tributaries of which are the Ishar, the Kub, and the Nimr; and (iv) the Kebir or Musrareh, which, rising as the Dilb near Ramallah in northern Judaea, changes its name several times before it joins the Auja 2 miles from its mouth. The Auja is the southernmost stream in Palestine that can fairly be termed a river, and one of the very few on which boating is possible, even near the sea. Up its tributary valleys run the principal routes, both ancient and modern, to northern Judaea and Samaria. Its three northern tributaries drain almost the whole of southern Samaria nearly as far north as Nablus; the Kebir, the rest of southern Samaria and northernmost Judaea. It traverses that portion of the plain where stand the towns of Ramleh, Lydda, and Petah Tikva, and enters the sea by Jaffa and Tel Aviv. Much of its water is derived from a strong spring in the plain at Ras el Ain (*class.* Antipatris), where the Ishkar and Ballut unite, but there are many other springs along its course. The waters are used for irrigating the neighbouring citrus plantations, and for some years past there has been a project for utilizing the water more widely.

The only three remaining rivers of any importance flowing into the Mediterranean are the Rubin, the Sukreir, and the Ghazza. The *Rubin*, rising near Bira, north of Jerusalem, cuts a deep valley—the Sarar or the 'vale of Sorek', now followed by the railway—and reaches the sea about 7 miles south of Jaffa. It is only perennial in its lowest reaches. The *Sukreir*, of less importance, finds a way through the sand-dunes 9 miles farther south; it is joined by several small streams in the plain of Philistia, but all are dry in summer. The *Ghazza*, which enters the sea 6 miles south-west of Gaza, originates in the Khelil or Abrek near Hebron and in the Wadi Milh many miles to the south. These two streams unite 3 miles east of Beersheba and as the Wadi Bir es Saba cross the northern Negeb, collecting some water in winter from several wadis. Eight miles from the coast the Ghazza (locally the Shellala) is joined on the right bank by the Sharia, which is fed from the southern Shephelah. The Ghazza is never a continuous stream and is made up of a series of pools in winter, fed by occasional springs and a scanty rainfall; but its course and those of its tributaries are witness to underground supplies of water which are reached by wells.

## The Jordan

The Jordan, historically and geographically, is the principal river of Palestine. It has several headwaters. The streams from Anti-Lebanon are the longest, the Wadi et Teim, later the Hasbani, rising north of Hermon, and several other streams from Syria joining to form the main channel. The Liddan, which also has several sources in Syria, receives its strongest volume from Tell el Kadi,[1] just within Palestine territory, and from Banyas (*class.* Paneas, the biblical Dan), a little to the east, where, at the very foot of Hermon, a fountain bursts out in the cave of the ancient god Pan, now destroyed by recent earthquakes. All these sources unite about 6 miles north of Lake Huleh, but the stream soon branches again at Es Salihiya and the waters, with those of other streamlets from the enclosing escarpments, form marshland across the whole width of the trough for a distance of 5 miles north of the lake.

Lake Huleh is briefly described below (p. 30). A few streams which rise in upper Galilee, but are mostly fed by springs low down on the Jordan side of the watershed, add water to the lake or the Jordan immediately to the south of it. Such are the Hindaj, Wakkas or Shababik, Musheirifa, and Shahyan. There are a number of small hamlets with olive-groves dependent on these springs, tucked away in their valleys. From Lake Huleh to Lake Tiberias is another 10 miles. The total fall between the two lakes is 916 feet. The river here forms a series of cascades in a narrow gorge and receives no reinforcement. Before entering the gorge it is crossed by the Jisr Banat Yakub ('the bridge of Jacob's daughters'), on the 'Way of the Sea' (*Via Maris*), the ancient road from Egypt to Syria and central Asia. Where the Jordan enters Lake Tiberias it is 60 feet wide and passes peacefully through a small delta.

The lake and its tributaries are described below (p. 30). The Jordan valley, or the Ghor, is 65 miles long from Lake Tiberias to the Dead Sea, with the escarpments so close on either side as to leave a plain sometimes not more than 2 or 3 miles wide, in which the river almost doubles its length by meanders. In this section the Jordan falls from 686 feet below sea-level at Lake Tiberias to 1,290 feet

---

[1] Even at Tell el Kadi there are two sources: one where the stream is already 12 feet wide and 3 feet deep as it gushes from the ground, the other a short distance above, quieter and shallower.

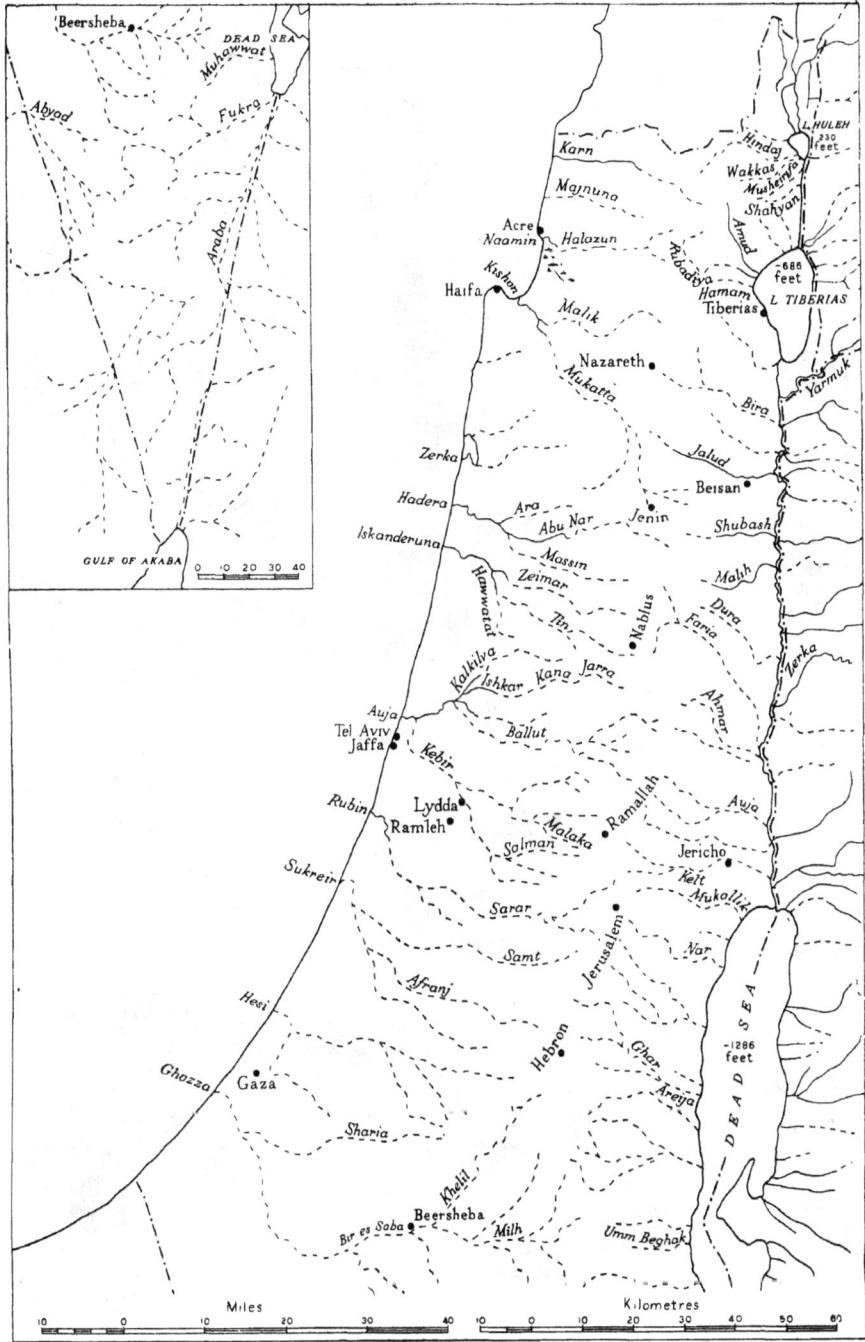

FIG. 7. *Rivers and Lakes*

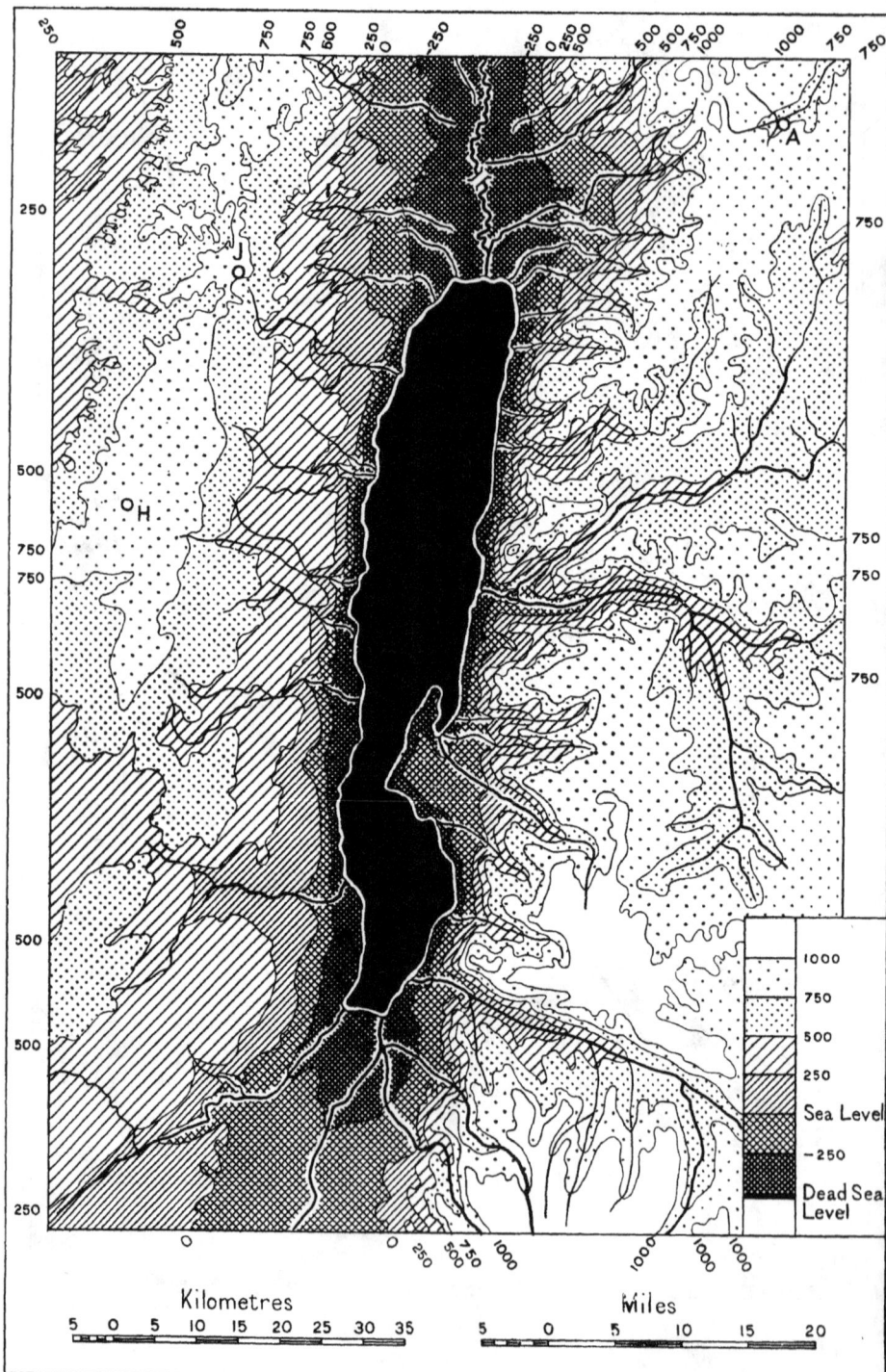

FIG. 8. *The Dead Sea*
(*Heights in metres; J. Jerusalem; H. Hebron; A. Amman*)

at the Dead Sea. Deeply sunken as is the valley bottom, it is covered with Pliocene and more recent sediments through which the river has cut its bed still lower, sometimes as much as 150 feet. Springs abound, and there are many tributaries on both banks. Those in Palestine have been mentioned on page 21. The most important feeder on the left bank is the Yarmuk, which enters about 5 miles south of the Sea of Galilee, part of its course serving as a boundary between Syria and Transjordan, and as a natural route for the railway to Deraa. This and other left-bank tributaries are described in Chapter XIV.

Vegetation is luxuriant, but rank (*frontispiece*). Six miles south of Beisan, where the valley closes in, there is very little cultivation and almost no permanent population. The streams that feed the Jordan are often impregnated with salts, useful for other purposes, but harmful to agriculture. Every year during the rainy season the valley bottom is flooded, and a residue of mud and gravel, drift-wood and derelict tree-trunks, rotting vegetation and refuse is left behind. Near the river are ugly mudbanks, sometimes 25 feet high, with occasional beds of shingle, foul with ooze and slime, which make approach to the river difficult. Farther south, movement becomes easier. The jungle disappears, but only because the soil is so poisoned that it is incapable of supporting any vegetation. As the Dead Sea is approached, the plain is dotted with barren dust-coloured hillocks and ridges of yellow marl, deposited and carved into strange shapes by the annual floods. Not inaptly they have been likened to refuse heaps of a chemical factory. Swamp abounds and there is much malaria. Near Jericho the valley widens and its character changes: it becomes desert rather than wilderness, in which Jericho and such small valleys as Ain Duk form oases because of their springs of sweet water.

In the summer, the river is about 30 yards wide in its lower reaches, a rapid muddy stream with an uncertain current that is sometimes dangerous to the bather. Its depth varies from 3 feet at the fords to 10 or 12 elsewhere.

The Yarmuk, just above its confluence with the Jordan at the village of Naharayim, has been dammed to supply hydro-electric power for the Palestine Electric Corporation. A mile lower down the Jordan is the old Saracen bridge of Jisr el Majami, which carries the road from Beisan to Tiberias and Syria; near it is the railway bridge on the route from Haifa to Damascus and Amman. Three miles to the south the pipe-line from the Iraq oilfields to Haifa passes under the

Jordan. Below the confluence of the Nahr Jalud, the principal right-bank tributary, which drains the plain of Beisan, is the Jisr esh Sheikh Hussein. Close to the junction of the Zerka (*anc.* Jabbok) tributary from Transjordan and the Faria from the west is the Jisr Damiya, the bridge which once took the main road from central and perhaps southern Palestine to Gilead and Bashan. It was in ruins until 1941, when it was rebuilt.

A number of minor tributaries join the Jordan south of the Faria, the best known being the Kelt, which rises a few miles north of Jerusalem, and after passing Jericho reaches the Jordan about 4 miles before the latter enters the Dead Sea. East of Jericho is the modern Allenby bridge, the principal one over the Jordan, which carries the road from Jerusalem and the coast to Amman, the main line of communication to Transjordan from the west.

### The Lakes

During its course through the trench the Jordan expands into three considerable sheets of water, Lake Huleh, Lake Tiberias, and the Dead Sea, locally known as the Bahr Lut.

*Lake Huleh.* The Huleh basin covers about 44 square miles or 28,160 acres. Of this, Lake Huleh may be said to extend over 8,825 acres, of which 4,934 are swamp and marsh. It is a shallow expanse of water with an indeterminate shoreline, about 4 miles from north to south and at its widest 3 miles from east to west. A few unimportant streams flow into it from both east and west. The swamp extends for another 5 or 6 miles to the north and the whole is gradually contracting on account of the deposition of silt. The marsh is overgrown with papyrus from 13 to 17 feet high (p. 71)—one of the densest masses of papyrus in the world—and is a principal source of malaria in Palestine, the Arabs of the neighbourhood being riddled with it (fig. 26, p. 229). For this reason draining of the swamp has long been desirable. Moreover, the reclamation of land would provide especially fertile land for cultivation, a fact already recognized by the Ottoman Government in 1914, when they granted the first concession to two merchants of Beirut. Little was done, however, for many years, and it is only recently that any progress has been made with a new project.

*Lake Tiberias* is 13 miles long and 8 miles at its widest. It is 686 feet below the level of the Mediterranean, and its depth ranges to about 700 feet, varying 3 or 4 feet between summer and winter. Its shores are mainly of pebbles and sand, and brooks lined with oleanders run

13. *View southwards from the road to Tabgha across the Plain of Gennesaret and Sea of Galilee towards Tiberias*

14. *Waterfall near Metulla, one of the sources of the Jordan*

15. *Lake Tiberias with Mount Hermon in the distance*

16. *The Dead Sea and the Transjordan escarpment from the Judaean foothills*

into it. The lake is hemmed in on east and west by mountains, often rising steeply from the water's edge and in places barely leaving room for the road. On the west there are two small plains: that of Ghuweir—formed by the riverain deposits of three streams which rise in Galilee, the Amud, the Rubadiya (or Tuffa), and the Hamam —lines the lake for about 4 miles and is more than a mile wide; that of Tiberias, farther south and more restricted, is occupied almost wholly by the town of that name. On the east there is no affluent of any consequence, except the Semak, which forms a useful route to Kuneitra in Syria.

The surroundings of the lake are among the most beautiful and fertile in Palestine. Black basalt rock backs the shores and plains. There are several hot springs on the west of the lake, especially near Tiberias. Fish are plentiful. The western shore in particular occupied a prominent position in biblical times, when at least nine towns were sited around the lake. All but Tiberias have gone or are only represented now by villages, for in the absence of irrigation, the region cannot support a large population.

*The Dead Sea.* The third of the Jordan lakes is the largest and by far the most remarkable. It is 47 miles long from north to south and 10 miles at its widest; it has an area of 340 square miles. The Transjordan boundary bisects it. Its eastern shore is described on p. 411. Its surface is 1,290 feet below the level of the Mediterranean, and its waters are 1,308 feet deep towards the north-east, so that rock-bottom here is sunk about 2,600 feet below mean sea-level. Towards the southern end it shallows, before merging into salt swamps and marsh. A few streams, none of them of much significance except the Jordan, enter the Dead Sea, but none issues from it. It has been estimated that about 6½ million tons of water enter daily at certain seasons. The level is mostly controlled by the high rate of evaporation, caused by the great heat during most of the year, and evidenced by the impenetrable mist that often covers the sea.

The shores of the Dead Sea consist mainly of a low beach of gravel, varied by marl or salt-marsh. Two-thirds of the way south a broad, low promontory projects from the eastern side; it is known as El Lisan, or 'the tongue', and on it there is now a small aircraft landing-ground, 1,082 feet below mean sea-level, the lowest on earth.

On the Palestine side of the sea the mountains, never far from the shore, come down to the water's edge at three places: Ras Fashkha, Ras Mersed, and Jebel Usdum. The last named, at the extreme south-west end, is a ridge of rock-salt, 300 feet high and 5 miles long.

Of the streams that enter from the west, very few are perennial. The Ain Fashkha originates in the escarpment near Ras Fashkha, from several hot brackish springs (temp. 70° to 80° F.); the Ain el Ghuweir (temp. 90° F.) is very similar, and there are others farther south. Of longer streams the Wadi Nar, carrying water only in winter, rises near Jerusalem as the Kidron; the Ain Jeddi, a short stream which enters the sea near Engeddi, whose fertility was once renowned (p. 23), has now lost all its importance; the Kelb or Areija, rising as the Wadi Arrub a little north of Hebron, enters the sea south of Engeddi.

The affluents are mostly saline; some sulphurous springs flow into the sea; other chemicals impregnate the water from springs below the surface. There is bitumen in the surrounding rocks, and at times, especially after earthquakes, lumps of bitumen are seen floating in the sea, a phenomenon known to the ancients who gave to the sea the name of Asphaltites.

# CHAPTER III

# THE COAST

THE coast of Palestine trends in a general south-south-westerly direction for about 140 miles, from the Syrian frontier at Ras en Nakurah to the Egyptian border at Rafa. South of Acre the shore is sandy with dunes spreading inland, almost the only break being immediately south of the bay of Acre, where the seaward end of Carmel forms a rocky promontory. At Nakurah, on the frontier, there are cliffs. Occasionally in the north the beach is fringed with rocks and cut up by small creeks, while here and there in the south there are low cliffs not more than 80 feet high. The bay of Acre, which lies between the small promontory on which Acre stands and the headland of Mount Carmel, is the only marked indentation in the coastline. Its importance is increased by the fact that it lies at the seaward end of the plain of Esdraelon, the natural route inland from the coast to Damascus. Despite the swell, it has the best anchorage on the coast. In northern Palestine the main lines of communication lie close to the shore, as in Syria, but south of Caesarea where the Carmel range recedes inland and the lowland broadens, the main road and railway also diverge from the coast. Communications to the east follow the principal wadis that drain the central highlands. The low-lying plains behind the coastal dunes—Acre, Sharon, and Philistia—are cultivated, especially the plain of Sharon, where oranges, cucumbers, melons, and other vegetables are grown. For more detailed description the coast will be divided into three sections: (i) Ras en Nakurah to Haifa, (ii) Haifa to Tel Aviv and Jaffa, (iii) Jaffa to Rafa. Each section is subdivided into the coastline, the coastal plain, and the communications.

The short strip of Palestinian coast at the head of the gulf of Akaba is described with the coast of Transjordan, on p. 521.

## Ras en Nakurah to Haifa (fig. 9)

Between Ras en Nakurah and the port of Haifa, a distance of 20 miles, the coast trends in a general south-south-westerly direction. In this stretch there are low sandy beaches, and a few rocky points and fringing rocks north of Acre. The coastal plain is from 2 to 4 miles broad, widening into the plain of Acre in the south, and backed inland by the mountains of Galilee (p. 15).

The promontory of Ras en Nakurah, or the Ladder of Tyre, which

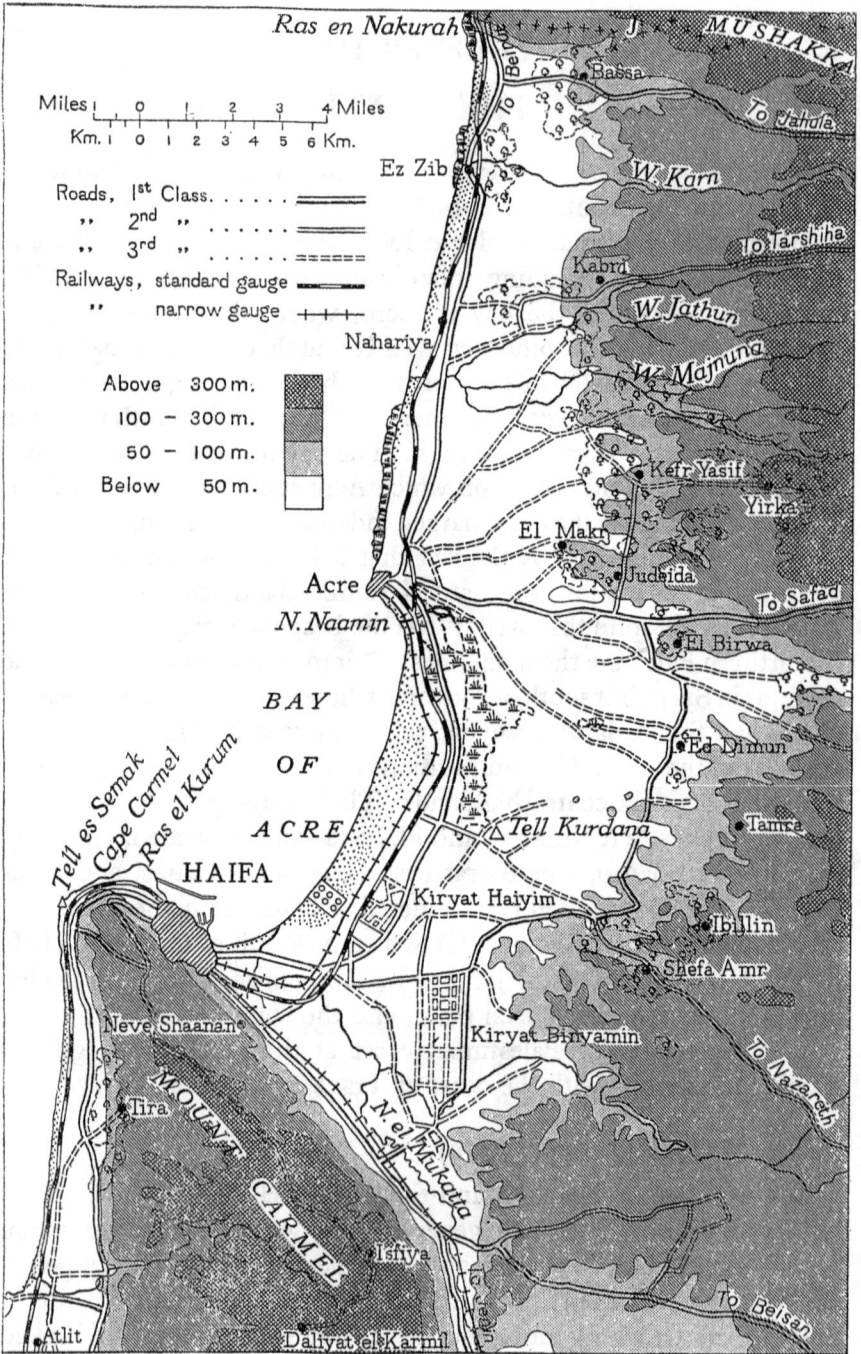

Fig. 9. *Haifa and the Bay of Acre*

marks the boundary, rises gradually from a height of about 350 feet close to the sea to 1,174 feet 2 miles inland. It is the end of a spur from Jebel Mushakka, and falls on the south side abruptly to the coastal plain; its northern slopes in Syria are more gradual. The coast is rocky for about a mile south of the promontory, then there is a sandy beach more than 7 miles long, with sand-dunes stretching 300–700 yards inland, but broken at Ez Zib by low cliffs; this continues as far as 2 miles south of the fair-sized village of Nahariya. From here to Acre, for just over 4 miles, the shore is rocky.

Acre stands on a triangular promontory projecting about 700 yards seawards south-west from the plain; it is a town of 9,800 inhabitants (1941), mostly Moslems. There are outer and inner anchorages and a small harbour for coasting vessels and local boats, with a lighthouse on the point (p. 295).

Between Acre and Ras el Kurum, the promontory immediately west of Haifa, the open bay of Acre, 7½ miles wide, faces north-west and the shoreline recedes 2½ miles inland. The shore is sandy and is backed throughout by sand-dunes, which have a breadth of more than a mile at one place; they average about 50 feet in height, but vary between 20 and 180 feet. A mile south-east of Acre is the mouth of the Nahr Naamin (*anc.* Belus), which has its source in the Tell Kurdana (141 ft.), 6 miles to the south-east, and is bordered by marshes up to a mile wide or more all along its course. For a mile south of the Nahr Naamin the sand-dunes are backed by a plantation of palm-trees, with the Naamin marshes behind. Two miles east of Haifa is the mouth of the Nahr Mukatta or Kishon, whose tributaries, rising in Mount Tabor and Mount Gilboa, unite in the plain of Esdraelon (*mod.* Merj ibn Amir), 15 miles from Haifa. The belt of sand-dunes is very narrow here, and the river flows parallel to the shore for nearly a mile. It is shallow at its mouth, and heavy surf usually breaks across the bar. It is crossed by two road bridges and a railway bridge, all within 2 miles of the sea. Beyond the mouth of the Nahr Mukatta the sand-dunes narrow to a breadth of 200 yards, factories and palm-trees taking their place on the outskirts of Haifa.

Haifa, the first port of Palestine, lies at the southern end of the bay of Acre, at the foot of Mount Carmel, which rises steeply behind the town to a height of nearly 1,000 feet. It has an estimated population of 114,400 (1941), though only 50,400 according to the 1931 census. The number is divided almost equally between Arabs and Jews. The port and town are described in detail in Chapter XII (pp. 300–7).

The coastal plain north of Acre is well watered throughout by

streams which descend at right angles to the coast, the chief being
the Wadi Karn, which reaches the sea by the village of Ez Zib,
and the Wadi Majnuna, 5 miles to the south. Between these two is
the Wadi Jathun, whose waters are led southwards across the plain by
aqueduct to Acre (photo.78). The plain is studded with many villages,
and other settlements nestle among the olive-groves and orchards
which cover the lower slopes of the mountains. The road and railway, close to the shore at Ras en Nakurah, continue northwards into
Syria through Beirut, Tripoli, and Latakia; southwards to Acre they
are never more than 2 miles from the shore. One and a half miles
south of Ras en Nakurah a road climbs eastwards, roughly parallel
to the boundary, and joins the road from Tiberias to Metulla near
Jahula. An indifferent second-class road leads inland from Nahariya
to Tarshiha (10 miles), taking the slopes north of the Wadi Jathun.
The best road, graded as first-class, strikes inland from Acre to Safad,
and so leads northwards to Metulla and into Syria, north-eastwards
by Jisr Banat Yakub to Damascus, and south along the Jordan
valley to Tiberias and Beisan.

South of Acre, where the plain is broader, much of the land behind
the dunes is taken up by the marshes of the Nahr Naamin, though
these are gradually being reclaimed. In this section a narrow-gauge
(1·05 m.) railway from Haifa to Acre runs close to the shore behind
the dunes. As yet it has not been removed, though it is now to some
extent superseded by the new standard-gauge line from Haifa to
Beirut, which follows the same alinement to Acre, passing between
the marshes of the Naamin and the dunes, and through the palm-belt
immediately south-east of Acre. The new standard-gauge line continues northwards along the shore past Ras en Nakurah to Tripoli.
The railway workshops are about 3 miles east of Haifa, midway
between its eastern outskirts and Kiryat Hayim (Haiyim, Haim).

A new well-made but winding first-class road along the inland
edge of the plain links the Acre–Safad road with Haifa, and from
it a similar road branches over the hills through Shefa Amr to
Nazareth. But the most important road inland is that from Haifa
through the gap south-eastwards to the fertile plain of Esdraelon.
The main road leads to Beisan and the Jordan; first-class branches
from it lead south-south-east to Jenin and so to Nablus, and north-
east through Nazareth to Tiberias. Haifa is also the terminus of the
narrow-gauge railway which takes the same gap down to the Jordan
valley, and from Samakh climbs the Yarmuk valley to Deraa in Syria,
to connect with Damascus and Amman. Through this gap also comes

17. *The Coast of Northern Palestine near Ras en Nakurah*

18. *The sea wall at Acre*

19. *The Bay of Acre from the Citadel of Acre*

the pipe-line from the Kirkuk oilfields of Iraq. It keeps to the north of the Nahr Mukatta to the refinery south of Kiryat Hayim, and from it pipes lead to the Iraq Petroleum Company storage tanks on the coast 3 miles east of Haifa. The Haifa airport is close to the railway workshops and oil refinery.

Thus, within a circle of 3 miles radius, at this southern end of the plain of Acre are located the best port and harbour in Palestine, the air-port, oil refinery, and storage tanks, and the point of convergence for road and railway routes.

## Haifa to Tel Aviv and Jaffa (figs. 9, 10, 11)

In this section the long spur of Mount Carmel rises steeply near the coast, and limits the coastal plain in the north to a few hundred yards, but the plain widens southwards to 2 miles between Atlit and Tantura, and at Caesarea broadens rapidly to form the plain of Sharon. From Caesarea the coast trends south-south-west for 30 miles to Tel Aviv; it consists of sandy beaches with occasional low red cliffs all the way to within 2 miles of Tel Aviv, where there are undulating sandhills 50–80 feet high.

From the town of Haifa the shore of the bay trends north-west for a mile to Ras el Kurum, at the northern end of a flat plain a mile wide extending from the base of Mount Carmel. Between Ras el Kurum and Tell es Semak, a low peak 2 miles west-south-west, rises Cape Carmel, a bold headland at the north-western end of Mount Carmel. It rises 500 feet almost sheer from the sea, and the ridge then extends for 12 miles south-east, reaching its maximum height of 1,861 feet 8 miles inland. At the base of the headland the coastal plain is never more than 200 yards wide. There is a lighthouse near the point.

From Tell es Semak the coast trends southwards for 8¾ miles to Atlit, where there is a sandy rock-strewn beach with ledges of rock parallel to the shore and about a mile away. The coastal plain gradually increases in width from about 400 yards in the north to a little over 2 miles behind Atlit. Ancient Atlit (Castellum Peregrinorum, or Petra Incisa) stands on a rocky promontory extending 700 yards westwards, with a small bay on the southern side about half a mile wide. The high square tower, among the ruins of the great Crusaders' castle, is conspicuous from the sea. There are salt-pans immediately inland and to the south, with the small modern hamlet and railway station of Atlit a mile inland.

Between Atlit and Tantura, a distance of 6 miles, the coastline

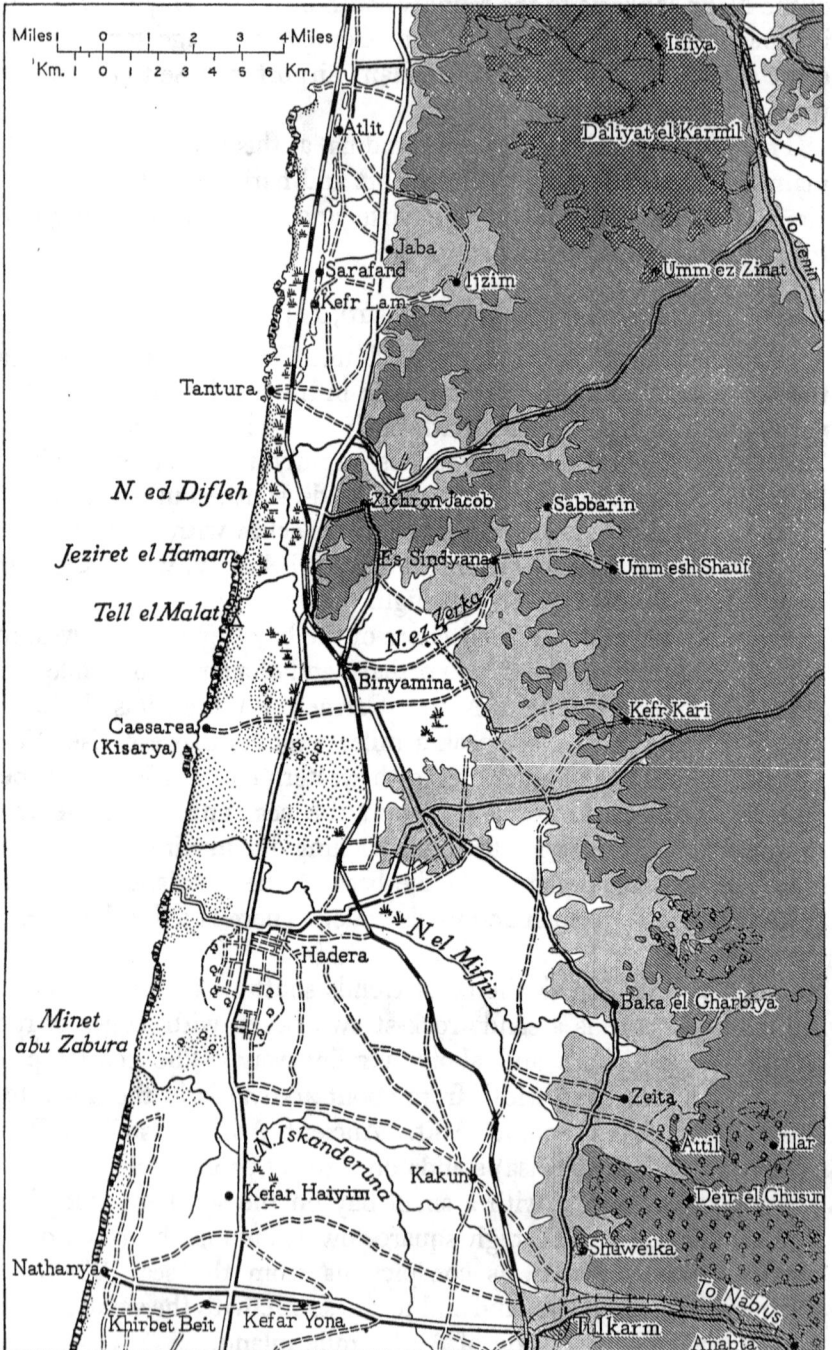

FIG. 10. *The coast from Atlit to Nathanya (Key on fig. 9)*

is rocky in the north and south with small sandy coves, and a 3-mile strip of sand in the middle. Half a mile behind the coast is a low ridge, 85 feet high, parallel to the shore, with two small villages, Sarafand and Kefr Lam, on it. The railway follows the seaward edge of the ridge, while the road keeps to the foot of Mount Carmel, 2 miles farther inland. Tantura (*anc.* Dor) is a village of 750 inhabitants with a landing-place on the sandy beach inshore of some black, rocky islets and sheltered from the north by a small promontory. The ancient port, where boats still shelter, was on the south side of the village, inside the islets. Two miles to the south is the marsh-bordered mouth of the Nahr ed Difleh, or Oleander river, which, in Roman times, formed the southern limit of Phoenicia.

The coast from Tantura continues directly south-south-west for nearly 8 miles to Caesarea (*mod.* Kisarya). For the first 4 miles there is unencumbered sandy beach extending for about 400 yards inland and formerly backed by marshes, now drained for another 400 yards. Opposite the small, black, rocky islet, known as Jeziret el Hamam, which is close inshore, the beach is bordered by rocks. Two and a half miles north of Caesarea is the mouth of the Nahr Zerka (or Crocodile river) with a hill, Tell el Malat, on its southern bank. Inland the precipitous face of a flat-topped spur from the Carmel ridge, 458 feet high, stands up from the coastal plain, with the large Jewish village of Zichron Jacob on its summit, 3½ miles south-east of Tantura. It is reached by a good first-class road. Another large village, Binyamina, lies amid fertile surroundings at the southern foot of the spur, 4 miles from Caesarea. Southwards the foothills of Mount Carmel rapidly recede inland and the plain of Sharon opens out. Caesarea was once the principal port of Palestine, and the centre of Roman administration; in Roman times it received its water-supply by aqueduct from the Crocodile river; the ruins of the ancient mole which extend seawards for 300 yards mark its site from the sea. The number of ruins indicates its past importance, but the modern village, dependent on wells, has a population of only 350. It has a summer anchorage for small boats, half a mile off shore. Sand-dunes extend inland from Caesarea to within a mile of Binyamina, which can only be reached by rough tracks from the coast.

For a mile south of Caesarea the coast has off-shore rocks, then for 3 miles there is a sandy beach backed by dunes through which the Nahr Mifjir finds an outlet. Between this and the mouth of the Nahr Iskanderuna rocky stretches alternate with small sandy patches, with two small lakes inland, the remains of marshland reclaimed by

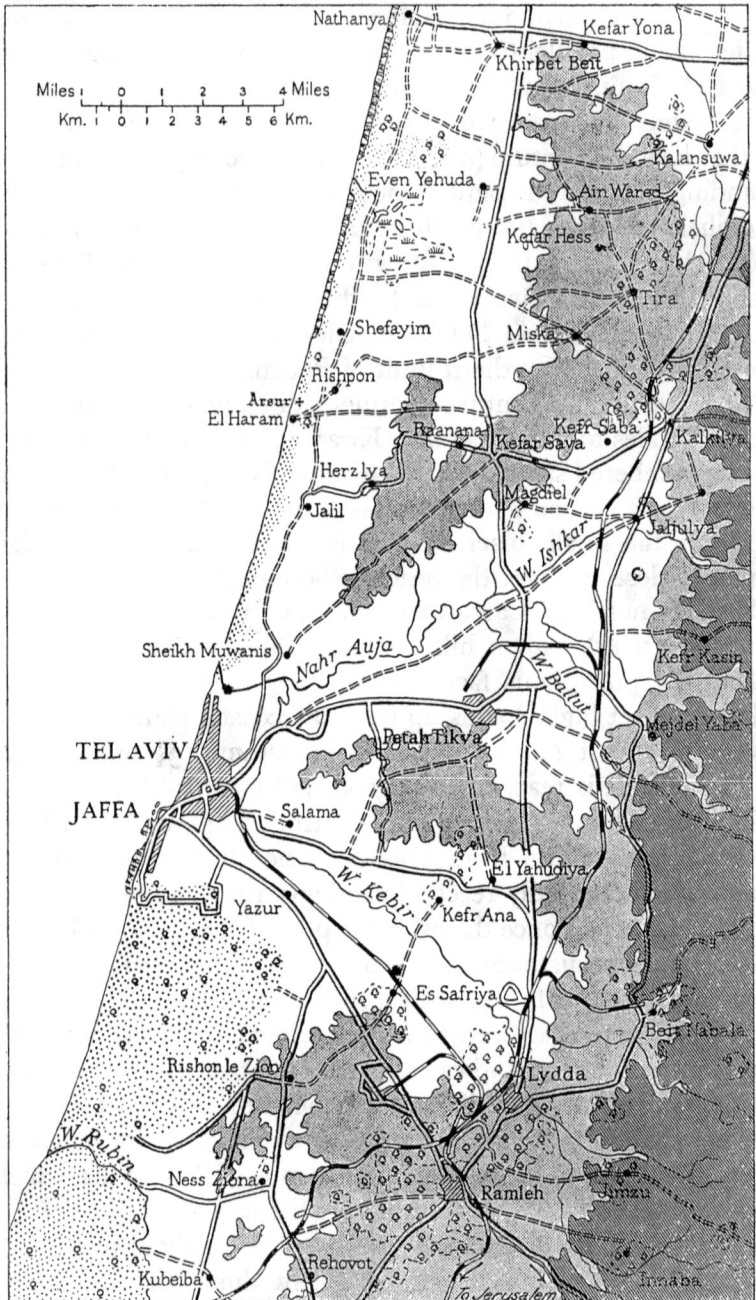

FIG. 11. *The Coast north and south of Jaffa (Key on fig. 9)*

the prosperous village of Hadera. The lowest reaches of the Nahr Iskanderuna are enclosed on either bank by sand-dunes rising to 60 feet. North of the river the dunes reach the coastal road 2 miles inland near the southern edge of the Hadera cultivation.

A similar alternation of low cliffs and occasional sandy patches continues southwards for 12 miles from the Iskanderuna mouth. Then for a distance of 10 miles there is one long uninterrupted beach of sand to the mouth of the Nahr Auja, immediately north of Tel Aviv. South of the Nahr Iskanderuna the sand-dunes are rarely more than 400 yards wide, but there is one patch south of Nathanya which extends inland for over 2 miles. Ten miles south of Nathanya is El Haram, a loading-place for small craft; the village stands on the top of a hill and is conspicuous from the sea. Half a mile to the north of El Haram was the Crusaders' port of Arsur (*class.* Apollonia), on a conical hill, marked now by a minaret. Sandhills continue to the mouth of the Auja where the northern outskirts of Tel Aviv begin; these with Jaffa and the southernmost suburb of Bayit Vegan, occupy 6 miles of sea-frontage.

Jaffa is the second most important port on the coast, but vessels have to anchor some distance off shore. Lighters and small boats convey passengers and cargo to landing-stages in Jaffa and Tel Aviv. Both towns are described in detail in Chapter XII (pp. 307–14).

Behind the coast the plain broadens to 10 or 12 miles and forms one of the most fertile tracts of land in the whole of Palestine. Wells abound and there are numerous villages, many of them new Jewish settlements, both in the plain of Sharon itself and on the mountain slopes which rise gently to the east. The plain is the centre of citrus-fruit cultivation, and olive-groves cover the hill-sides.

Between Haifa and Jaffa four main streams enter the sea and form the outlets of the intricate wadi systems of the western slope of the Samarian highlands. From north to south they are the Zerka or Crocodile river, which has its mouth $2\frac{1}{2}$ miles north of Caesarea, and the Mifjir, or 'Dead river' of the Crusades, which enters the sea $2\frac{1}{2}$ miles south of the town. The Iskanderuna, or 'Salt river' of the Crusades, reaches the sea near Minet abu Zabura, 8 miles south of Caesarea; the Auja, north of Tel Aviv, is the most important of all coastal streams south of the Litani, and the outlet of one of the greatest and most complicated wadi systems in the central uplands. Among its numerous tributaries there are three principal arms—the Wadi Ishkar, along which a second-class road runs to Nablus; the Wadi Deir Ballut or Sarida; and the Wadi Kebir, which takes

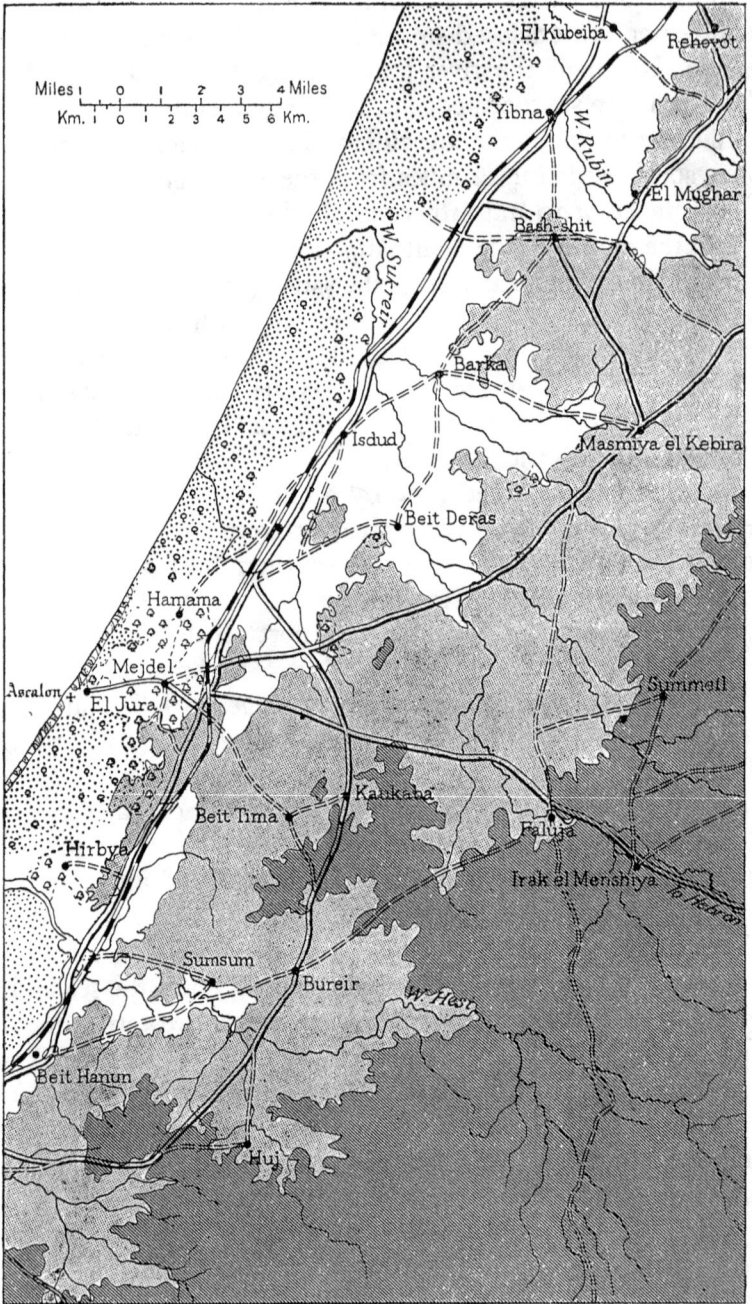

FIG. 12. *The dunes north of Ascalon (Key on fig. 9)*

the Jaffa–Jerusalem road. The plain between these rivers is richly cultivated, and there are numerous settlements and villages.

In the north the standard-gauge railway from Haifa to Jaffa which, together with the main road, rounds Cape Carmel close to the sea, follows the shore southwards, often less than 300 yards inland, though the road keeps to the foothills of Carmel, which rise abruptly from the plain, as far south as Tantura, where the railway moves inland to join the road, and both pass through Binyamina. From here onwards the road passes through the chief agricultural settlements of the plain, while the railway increases its distance from the coast to 10 miles at Tulkarm, rail and road junction 23 miles north-east of Tel Aviv and 10 miles by direct first-class road inland from Nathanya. Tulkarm stands at the entrance of the deeply cut valley of the Wadi Zeimar, a tributary of the Nahr Iskanderuna, along which run a narrow-gauge railway and the main road to Nablus; the railway joins a line from Affula at Sebustya station; the road is continued south through Ramallah to Jerusalem, joining the road from Haifa and Jenin at Deir Sharaf. The coastal road keeps much nearer to the sea than the railway after crossing the Nahr Mifjir near Hadera.

Jaffa and Tel Aviv, though important road centres, are not directly served by the coastal railway, but the standard-gauge line from Jaffa to Jerusalem meets this railway 11 miles south-east of Jaffa at Lydda. Besides the local roads that radiate to the large villages and small towns in the neighbourhood, there are first-class roads south-east to Jerusalem and south to Gaza.

## Jaffa to Rafa (figs. 11, 12, 13)

The shoreline from Jaffa to the Egyptian boundary at Rafa is remarkable for its straightness. Except at very occasional wadi-mouths, there is no break in the monotonous regularity of the coast, and the low sandy foreshore is only interrupted by stretches of low cliff at a few places.

From Jaffa the coastline trends south-south-west for 29 miles to Ascalon, and is bordered by sand-dunes, occasionally edged by rocky outcrops, the whole way. Inland of Jaffa and Tel Aviv the plain of Sharon is interrupted by a low ridge, an offshoot of the Judaean hills, from 150 to 250 feet high. South of this ridge is the plain of Philistia, from 18 to 25 miles wide, well cultivated in the north, but diminishing in fertility as it approaches Gaza in the south, where the Tertiary sediments become increasingly covered by sand. The plain is generally level, but occasional sandstone ridges stand up to altitudes of about 250 feet.

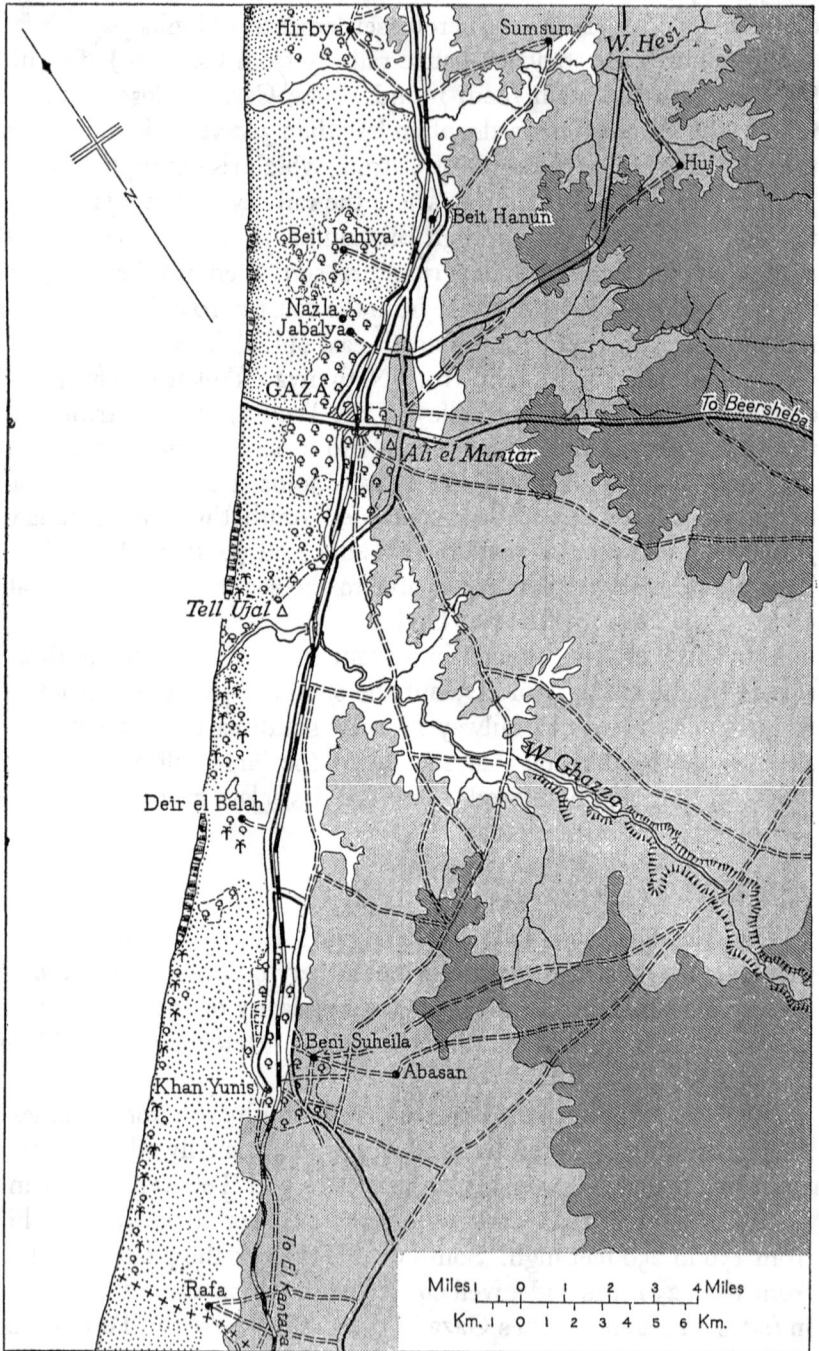

FIG. 13. *The coast from Gaza to Rafa (Key on fig. 9)*

Immediately south of the southern suburbs of Jaffa the sand-dune belt stretches for 4 miles inland and continues uninterruptedly for 8 miles southwards, until broken by the course of the Wadi Rubin. The dunes have an average height of 140 feet, but occasionally reach over 200 feet. A similar belt lines the coast beyond the Rubin, past the mouth of the Wadi Sukreir, but from here the breadth narrows to 2 miles, and, tapering southwards, disappears for a short distance 3 miles north of the site of Ascalon, about 26 miles from Jaffa. Here, round the cluster of villages of Hamama, Mejdel, and El Jura, lying back from the coast, orchards have survived the encroachment of the dunes, and for 6 miles the shoreline is bordered by low cliff.

The ancient city of Ascalon was built on ground abutting on bold cliffs about 60 feet high. Little remains of it. The modern village of El Jura is less than a mile to the north-east, surrounded by orchards and mulberry-trees, but with sand-dunes threatening three sides of it. There is a summer anchorage off shore, but it is quite unprotected, and only a track leads up from the shore either to Hamama or to Mejdel, and thence to the coastal road and railway, 3 miles inland from the shore at this point.

Near Ascalon the coast begins to curve gradually more towards the south-west. It is backed by sand-dunes almost the whole distance to the Egyptian border, but there are occasional stretches of low cliff. About half-way between Ascalon and Gaza there is a break, occupied by the village and fruit-trees of Hirbya. Gaza is about 2 miles from the coast, and its gardens, orchards, and olive-groves put up a ceaseless struggle against the encroaching dunes. Its suburbs to the north, Jabalya, Nazla, and Beit Lahiya, are almost completely surrounded by sand. Gaza, which is on the coastal road and railway, is protected on the south by the ridge of Ali el Muntar, and by olive-groves hedged by cactus, which proved effective obstacles to the British advance in March 1917; but it has a good road leading to the shore. Ships can anchor about a mile and a half off shore and discharge their cargoes by large boats, but the anchorage is very exposed and vessels are seldom seen.

Six miles south of Gaza is the mouth of the Wadi Ghazza, which marks the southern end of the attenuated plain of Philistia. Tell Ujal (122 ft.) is a conspicuous hillock on the flat sandy right bank of the wadi. The sand-belt is only about a mile wide at this point, and 3 miles farther on the coast rises to low cliffs for another 3 miles near Deir el Belah. The rest of the coast to Rafa, rather more than 7 miles away, is sandy, with a regular belt of dunes, from 120 to 200 feet high, averaging $2\frac{1}{2}$ miles in width, with palms on the seaward face, and the village of Khan Yunis in the lee of the landward edge.

The northern part of the plain of Philistia, round Lydda, Ramleh, and Rehovot, is the most thickly populated district of Palestine; water from wells is ample and cultivation is intense; orchards and olive-groves spread up into the Shephelah and the lower slopes of the Judaean hills. But the wadis have only short perennial courses, if any, and very little water reaches the sea by them. The only wadis that break across the plain and through the dune-belt are the Rubin, about 7 miles south of Jaffa; the Sukreir, about half-way between Jaffa and Ascalon; and the Ghazza, about 6 miles south-west of Gaza. The Wadi Sarar, the chief tributary of the Rubin, is important, for its upper valley forms the natural route of the railway from Lydda to Jerusalem; the road to Hebron follows the valley of the Wadi Afranj, which drains into the Sukreir.

Except at Jaffa and Gaza there are no good roads fit for wheels from the shore across the dune-belt to the coastal road and railway, though there is an indifferent one at El Jura through Mejdel. Except in the extreme north near Lydda, Ramleh, and Rehovot, the railway to Egypt keeps close to the inland edge of the dune-belt, and from Yibna, near Rehovot, is never more than 4 miles from the sea, and rarely more than three. The main road also, though farther inland between Rehovot and Mejdel, follows the railway closely from this latter village to Gaza. South of Gaza the new coastal main road skirts Khan Yunis and Rafa, and it is now first class.

It is interesting to recall that the British advance in 1916 from the Suez Canal to El Arish on the Egyptian side of the frontier, and subsequently to Gaza, was made possible only by the laying of the railway and a water pipe-line which kept pace with it, and that the sand was made passable for motors by constructing a 'road' of wire-netting held in place by pegs.

The southern end of the plain of Philistia is narrower and more desolate than the north, and more broken by sandstone hills. Wells become less numerous, and south of Gaza water is a main anxiety. A number of tracks cross this country, but the last road of any importance is that which leads from Gaza to Beersheba.

## CHAPTER IV

# CLIMATE, VEGETATION, AND FAUNA

## CLIMATE

PALESTINE, though a small country, has a variety of climates ranging from sub-Alpine through temperate and Mediterranean to tropical. The mountains of northern Galilee have climatic features similar to those of parts of Switzerland, the deserts of the Negeb to those of parts of the Sahara; in the plain of Sharon and on the slopes of the Shephelah one might be in the Italian Riviera; the climate of the Judaean hills has been likened to that of central Germany; in the Jordan trench the summer heat is as unbearable as that of any place on earth, though mid-winter is as pleasant as an English summer.

These variations are caused both by the position of the country and by its relief. Palestine lies in the transitional region between the comparatively well-watered lands of the Mediterranean and the deserts of Asia and Africa. Its highland backbone emphasizes the parting between the two. Westerly winds bring rain from the Mediterranean to the western slopes; but in the south where such winds pass over the deserts of Africa and Sinai they have little moisture to spare for the Negeb. On the climate of this small country has depended much of its history and must depend many of its prospects.

Meteorological readings have been taken since the middle of the nineteenth century at several places in Palestine, but only since the war of 1914–1918 have official stations been set up. Other non-official observations have been made in many parts, but often deal only with rainfall. The official and non-official stations used in the following description are given below. They are divided into three climatic belts—the coast, the inland belt, and the Jordan depression—and are given from north to south in their respective regions. Unofficial stations are in italics. For the Tables see Appendix G, pp. 555 ff.

| Station | Altitude (feet) | Number of years of records |
|---|---|---|
| 1. *Coast* | | |
| Acre . | 61 | 5–10 |
| Haifa . | 52 | 9–18 |
| Tel Aviv | 105 | 5–10 |
| *Jaffa (Sarona)* | 66 | 10 |
| Gaza . | 158 | 18 |

| Station | Altitude (feet) | Number of years of records |
|---|---|---|
| *2. Inland* | | |
| Nazareth . . . . . | 1,608 | 15 |
| Jenin . . . . . . | 525 | 18 |
| El Latrun . . . . . | 656 | 6–12 |
| Jerusalem . . . . . | 2,485 | 20–40 |
| Beit Jemal . . . . . | 1,148 | 5–10 |
| Bethlehem . . . . . | 2,342 | 3 |
| Hebron . . . . . | 2,900 | 18 |
| Beersheba . . . . . | 938 | 18 |
| *3. Jordan Depression* | | |
| Tiberias . . . . . | −653 | 9–15 |
| Beisan . . . . . | −387 | 5–8 |
| Tabgha . . . . . | −682 | 3–4 |
| Jericho . . . . . | −820 | 18 |
| Dead Sea (north end) . . . | −1,260 | 4–5 |
| „ (south end) . . . | −1,210 | 4–5 |

## Pressure

In winter the eastern Mediterranean is a region of relatively low pressure, across which a succession of depressions passes from west to east over Palestine. It is flanked on the north by the high-pressure system of Eurasia, which extends to the Balkans and Turkey, and on the south by a high-pressure system over north Africa. As summer approaches, the Mediterranean centre of low pressure gradually moves eastwards to the Persian Gulf, which then becomes a region of intensely low pressure. In the Mediterranean, pressure is highest at the western end, but the gradient from west to east is slight. Summer pressure conditions are very stable and the passage of depressions at this season very rare.

A remarkable feature in the distribution of pressure is caused by the Jordan valley, where actual pressure is abnormally high both in winter and in summer. The means at Tiberias (−653 ft.), for instance, are 30·8 inches in January and 30·4 inches in July, compared with 30·1 and 29·7 at Haifa. The absolute maximum recorded at Tiberias in 1911 was 31·22. Farther south, isolated readings at Jericho (−820 ft.) indicate pressures between 30·3 and 31·5 inches; and on the Dead Sea shores less accurate observations by aneroid barometer give a mean of about 31·5 inches. These high figures are, of course, the direct result of the depth of the trough below sea-level. They are not strictly comparable with those of the pressure systems described above, and the general circulation of the winds is therefore not affected.

WINDS

(a) *Surface Winds* (Table I, pp. 555 ff.)

The depressions which move eastwards from the western Mediterranean between late autumn and mid-spring, and from then till June from north Africa, produce variable winds, mainly from the S., SW., and SE. On the coast the easterly, and in the inland belt the westerly component is more marked. In the Jordan depression the topographical influence is strong, N. and NW. winds prevailing round the Dead Sea. Farther north, E. winds are most numerous at Tiberias, but calm conditions are prevalent.

In summer, depressions are very rare and the west–east pressure gradient controls the winds, which are lighter, less variable, and have a larger westerly and northerly component. On the coast, however, SW. or S. winds still prevail, though they are often masked by the marked alternation of land and sea breezes. Inland, W., SW., and even NW. winds are most common. In the Jordan depression there is great local variety—the prevalent wind at Tiberias being W., at Jericho N. or NE., and near the Dead Sea N. and S. The Dead Sea produces its own winds, a daily rhythm of outflowing breezes by day and inflowing ones by night. At the northern end there is (1) a dry N. wind from the Jordan valley at night, (2) a moist S. wind from the Dead Sea landwards during the day until 16.00 hours, followed by (3) a hot, dry W. wind until the first hours of the night. At the southern end the winds are generally hotter and their directions more complicated. There is a light S. or SE. wind at night, and a weaker but moister N. wind by day.

In neither winter nor summer are the winds normally strong, and the number of calm days at most stations is high (Gaza 49%); but strong winds occur at times with the passage of winter depressions, and occasionally they reach gale force (force 8). Such gales occur on the average twice a year, mostly in January or February. The most frequent directions are from between S. and W., though in the N. occasionally from between NW. and E. All anchorages are exposed to the NW., and before the port of Haifa was constructed ships were often unable, as at Jaffa to-day, to communicate with the shore for days. On Lake Tiberias and the Dead Sea, tempests caused by winds from the N. break out at times almost without warning, but do not last long.

(b) *Local Winds*

(i) Land and sea breezes are a very marked feature on the coast in summer, the sea breeze being particularly welcome for its moderating effect on the temperature.

These breezes follow the normal course, the sea breeze usually setting in about 10.00 hours, increasing until noon or early afternoon—the maximum varying with the locality and local weather conditions—and dying down to calm at sunset. The land breeze ordinarily rises about 20.00 hours or later, and lasts until sunrise. In the middle of summer, therefore, the sea breeze reinforces the prevailing wind in the afternoon, so that it is always fresh and frequently strong. The land breeze is, however, much weaker than the sea breeze, and if opposed by the prevailing wind, may merely result in night calms. Minor variations occur by reason of local topography, especially in the neighbourhood of Haifa.

These breezes are strongest in July and August, when the midday heat is considerably tempered by the cooling sea breeze. They are noticeable in May and may be prominent until the end of September; they may be perceptible even in the cool season if not obscured by stronger influences. In calm weather they rarely penetrate more than 20 miles inland or the same distance out to sea. The effects of the sea breeze may be felt up to 3,000 feet over the land, that of the land breeze up to 1,500 feet over the sea. An important effect of the sea breeze is to raise the daytime humidity along the coast.

(ii) *The Scirocco*, sometimes also known as the *Khamsin* or *Simoom*, is an oppressive, hot, dry, dust-laden SE. or E. wind originating in the Arabian desert. It occurs mainly from April to May or early June, and from September to November inclusive; and especially in May and October. The highest temperature may occur in spring or autumn because of the scirocco—on one occasion the temperature reached or exceeded 104° F. on four successive days from this cause. The effect on the new-comer to the country is to lower his activity, physical and mental. The scirocco is dreaded by all for the discomfort it brings.

The wind blows in front of depressions as they pass eastwards. The first indications are a fall in atmospheric pressure, a rapid decrease in humidity at night as the dry air approaches, and the appearance of high cirrus cloud. The air, cool at first, later becomes oppressively hot, and as the wind strengthens—occasionally reaching gale force—violent dust-storms may occur, sometimes reducing visibility to less than 50 yards. The wind then veers abruptly to the NW.; there is a rapid fall in temperature and rise in relative humidity; the dust clears, although the wind may remain strong; the high cloud (cirrus) decreases, and is replaced by broken cumulus; the atmosphere freshens.

Occasionally a strong, dry, and dusty E. wind occurs during winter. This wind is, however, bitterly cold, especially when its direction is a few degrees north of east. It is known as the 'cold scirocco'.

(iii) *Dust-devils* occur in coastal regions, usually but not necessarily originating over shallow depressions or near low ridges. In many places there is a preliminary whirl of dust near the ground from which the columnar 'devil' rises; on the other hand, near Beersheba the columns rise straight from the surface without any preparatory phase. Dust-devils reach a fairly uniform height of 600 to 700 feet, drift with the prevailing light wind, and rotate in either direction. They come to an end by lifting upward from the surface or by dissipation. A wind exceeding 11 or 12 knots is usually too strong for rotating dust-devils, and *dust-clouds* are then more common. *Sandstorms* or *dust-storms* are not frequent in Palestine. Any strong wind in the hot season may raise clouds of driven dust, but as the dust remains close to the ground they are dust-clouds and not true dust-storms.

## TEMPERATURE (Table II, pp. 557 ff.)

Differences of altitude, topography, and wind all lead also to extreme variation in temperature and ranges of temperature. Temperatures fall as height increases, temperature ranges increase with distance and shelter from the sea, and, while sea winds are usually mild, land winds from the east may be either hot and dry in summer or bitingly cold in winter. On the whole, however, the temperature both in summer and winter is pleasant and healthy. Moreover, as distances are so short, it is always possible to move to an ideal climate a short distance away; when it is cold at Hebron or Jerusalem one can reach the warmth of Jericho or the coast in about an hour.

Winters are moderately cool on the coast, with mean daily maximum temperatures[1] in January and February of roughly 65° at all

---

[1] Explanation of terms used in describing temperature:

*Monthly mean*—the average temperature throughout the whole month (day and night together).

*Mean monthly maximum*—the average of all the highest temperatures recorded during the month in question in all the years of observation; i.e. the highest point to which one may expect the temperature to rise during that month. This must be distinguished from the *mean daily maximum* during any month, which is the average of all the daily maxima during that month averaged over all the stations, and minima of about 47°. Inland it is colder, with a January mean temperature of about 50°, mean daily minima down to 40° and occasional frosts, especially in Hebron and Jerusalem and farther north (absolute minimum, Hebron 19°; El Latrun 27°). The Jordan depression has a most enjoyable and healthy winter, similar in many ways to a perfect English summer; temperatures are higher than on the coast (Jan. mean daily maximum, Tiberias 65°; Jericho 68°).

In summer, temperatures vary greatly from place to place, but the means usually lie between about 73° and 83°, except on the higher parts and in the Jordan depression (80–90°). On the coast the range of temperature is comparatively small, and maxima rarely exceed 95°. In the upland region the range of temperature is greater than on the coast, but while in Galilee and Samaria mean summer temperatures tend to be a degree or two lower than on the coast, in southern Judaea and the Negeb the heat is greater (Beersheba, Aug. mean daily maximum, 94°). In the Jordan valley the summer heat becomes stifling; at Jericho mean daily maxima remain above 100° from June to September and temperatures between 110° and 120° have been recorded at all stations.

Spring and autumn often have their normal temperature increase or decrease interrupted by hot spells due to scirocco winds blowing between May and October, and any place may have its highest temperature of the year in any one of these months (e.g. El Latrun 106° in May). The highest temperatures of the year in fact rarely occur in midsummer, owing to the strength of the sea breezes, which are most prevalent at that time. Autumn is always warm, September being as hot as and often hotter than June. October is very variable owing to incipient winter conditions and there is a sharp fall from then to December.

## Diurnal Range of Temperature

This is usually greater in summer than in winter, and inland than on the coast. The summer increase of diurnal range is interrupted where the sea breeze effect is marked. Towards the interior the daily range increases rapidly to as much as 25° within a few miles of

years of observation, i.e. the point to which one may expect the temperature to rise at some time on every day of the month.

*Absolute maximum*—the highest temperature ever observed.

Provided that the figures are all derived from the same period of years, the mean daily maximum (M.D. max.) is always higher than the monthly mean, the mean monthly maximum (M.M. max.) always higher than the mean daily maximum, and the absolute maximum highest of all.

the coast, and reaches its greatest heights in the Jordan valley, where the mean range is nearly 30°. In the Dead Sea region there is a considerable difference between the two ends of the sea. The (night) minima are much lower at the southern end, so that the daily ranges are greater there, sometimes in the ratio of $1\frac{1}{2}:1$.

On the coast and in some places in the hills in summer the daily temperature regime is dependent on the sea breeze. Temperatures increase rapidly till 10.00 hours, then remain fairly uniform until 17.00 or 18.00 hours, after which they fall again. If the sea breeze is delayed the temperature continues to rise, only to fall as much as 10–20° when it does eventually set in.

Certain extraordinary fluctuations in temperature have been recorded. At Beit Jibrin in the Shephelah the temperature has been known to rise from 42° at sunrise to 85° at noon late in April. At Tell el Kadi, in the north, a storm of wind and rain brought the temperature down within a quarter of an hour from 88° to 72°. Variations as great as from freezing-point to 80° in the course of twenty-four hours have been known. In addition 'we must not forget that temperature in the shade quite inadequately expresses the intense fervour of the direct rays of the sun, when no cloud intervenes to mitigate the heat. On the sea-coast the sun temperature often reaches 145°, sometimes over 150°, and in the Jordan valley and in the narrow gorges which debouch into the basin of the Dead Sea, the heat is blistering. One of these wadis is appropriately termed Wadi en Nar, the Valley of Fire' (G. E. Post).

## HUMIDITY (Table III, p. 560)

Generally speaking, the air in Palestine is dry, and in summer away from the coast, very dry (Jericho, May 43%). In winter and along the coast humidity is higher (65–80%). Normally there is a fairly steady transition from a maximum in mid-winter to a minimum in early summer, but along the coast the prevalence of sea breezes increases the humidity during the season of their greatest intensity, so that the air is driest in spring and autumn (Haifa, October minimum). At all coastal stations the mean summer humidity is near 70 per cent. The annual range of humidity increases rapidly with distance from the sea, and the summer values drop to low levels as the desert is approached, reaching their lowest in the Jordan valley.

There is also a large diurnal variation of relative humidity, partly due to temperature changes and partly to land and sea breezes. The daily range, from a maximum in the early morning about 07.00 hours to a minimum shortly after noon, may amount to as much as 10 per cent. in winter and 20 per cent. in summer.

In all regions, especially near the coast, humidity depends largely upon wind direction. Scirocco winds are always dry, and may bring the relative humidity down to as little as 9 per cent (Jerusalem). Sea breezes in summer are relatively damp, and bring heavy dews at night in the coastal region. In winter SW. and W. winds are humid, but in summer, coming fresh from the cooler water of the open sea, they are comparatively dry.

## EVAPORATION (Table IV, p. 560)

In a country without rain for six months of the year, evaporation is very important. In the south and the Jordan valley it exceeds precipitation; open cisterns or pools without sources to feed them quickly dry up in summer, and the problem of water conservation is of immense importance. Even in Jerusalem the annual evaporation (old method)[1] is calculated at 41·6 inches as compared with a rainfall of about 21 inches. Near the Dead Sea evaporation is about 5 to 10 times as great as on the coast, and in especially dry weather it is said to amount to as much as 0·9 inch a day. As a rule evaporation is greatest during periods of highest temperature and lowest humidity.

## VISIBILITY

### Fog and Mist

In general, fog (Table V, p. 561) and mist are uncommon in Palestine. At sea they occur most often in summer and least in winter, fogs exclusively, and mists most frequently, in the morning.

*Frequency of Mist and Fog at Sea in the Eastern Mediterranean*
*(per cent. of observations)*

| Jan. | Feb. | Mar. | Apr. | May | June | July | Aug. | Sept. | Oct. | Nov. | Dec. |
|------|------|------|------|------|------|-------|-------|-------|------|------|------|
| 3 | 4–6 | 5–7 | 8–13 | 15–20 | 20 | 10–15 | 10–15 | 5–12 | 3–4 | 3–5 | 3–6 |

The coastlands have annually about 12 days with fog. Occasionally this lasts well into the day, and once in spring at Gaza, a thick fog lasted for 7 hours. Inland, fogs are slightly more frequent (about 16 days). Ground fogs are not uncommon at night, but are soon dis-

---

[1] Methods of calculating evaporation have changed, so that records are not always comparable. The figures in Table IV are based on more modern methods.

sipated when the sun rises. The Jordan valley has most fog. Here as many as 10 days with fog have been recorded in a month near Lake Tiberias, and near the Dead Sea intense evaporation causes thick fogs which may last until midday. The season of occurrence varies with local conditions.

In addition to this, visibility may be considerably limited locally by the scirocco or dust-storms, especially in the Negeb.

## Mirage

Mirage is liable to be encountered whenever there are large horizontal or vertical differences of temperature. Elevation of the horizon or superior mirage, giving the impression of exceptional visibility as objects below the normal horizon are seen, occurs often on the coast, when hot, light winds blow off shore, since the surface layer of air over the sea is cool and the air above is abnormally warm. The converse, depression of the horizon, or inferior mirage, giving exceptional clarity to objects above the normal horizon, occurs when the decrease of air density with height is abnormally small near the surface. This is liable to happen in the desert or over shallow coastal waters and flat coasts, when the air in immediate contact with the surface may be heated to much higher temperatures than that above.

## CLOUD (Tables VI, VII, pp. 561-2)

The eastern Mediterranean is a region of sun and light compared with western Europe, and even the western Mediterranean; in summer there are periods of weeks when not a cloud is to be seen in the sky.

Throughout the country most cloud occurs in winter (about 5 tenths), brought by the depressions passing over the country. In summer the amount is everywhere very small (0-2 tenths). There is in general rather more cloud on the coast, among the mountains, and locally in the Jordan valley (Tiberias) than elsewhere. The south and the interior, especially the lower Jordan valley, are almost cloudless (Table VII) in summer. When the sea breeze persists at night, clouds form over high ground, especially along the coast, and deposit heavy dew. They become very thick for a few hours in the early morning as the dew evaporates.

Records of the number of overcast skies exist for Haifa, where they occur mainly in winter, associated with S. and SW. winds. There are none at all in summer.

RAINFALL (Figs. 14, 15, 16; Tables VIII, XI, pp. 562-4)

The ruling feature of the climate is the division of the year into a rainy and a dry season. The rainy season opens in November, sometimes in October, and ends in April. Outside of this there are only occasional and exceptional showers of rain associated with thunderstorms.

It is possible to distinguish three phases of the rainy season: the Former, main, and Latter rains. The first rains, the Early or Former rains of the Bible, occur in October and November (1-5 in.), and are heaviest in the coastal region. Until they come, the land is too dry and hard for ploughing, but after the first few showers the soil is softened and ploughing commences. If rain does not come by the middle of November disaster threatens the farmer. The Mishna, compiled in the second century A.D., says 'men shall begin the form of praise appropriate to the manifestation of Almighty power in the giving of rain, from the first day of the Feast of Tabernacles (which may fall on any day between 20th September and 19th October). On the third day of Marcheshwan (8th October to 7th November) shall they begin to pray urgently for rain. If the 17th day of Marcheshwan come without rain having fallen, then shall they begin to celebrate three days of fasting.' The rainfall is not exceptionally heavy until about the middle of January, but in the next six weeks, as a rule, the greater part of the year's rainfall occurs (December-February, 10-20 in. on the coast and mountains; 2-6 in. in the south and the Dead Sea region). After the middle of March the heaviness and frequency of the main rains slacken. The Latter rains (March-April, 1-5 in.) then begin and continue for about a month. They are heavier than the Former rains in the inland region, although not on the coast.

These are the normal conditions, but exceptions are not infrequent (maxima and minima, Table VIII). There have been years in which the Former rains have failed completely, others in which the rains have amounted to but a fraction of the normal. In one recent year there was no rain at all during February, usually one of the wettest months. In wet years, on the other hand, the total may be more than twice that which falls in years of scanty rainfall. For agriculture the Former rains, immediately preceding ploughing and sowing, and the Latter rains, shortly before the harvest, are the most important. The main rains serve to fill the wells and cisterns, to feed the springs, and to supply the wadis with water.

Even during the main rains in January and February, the rainfall

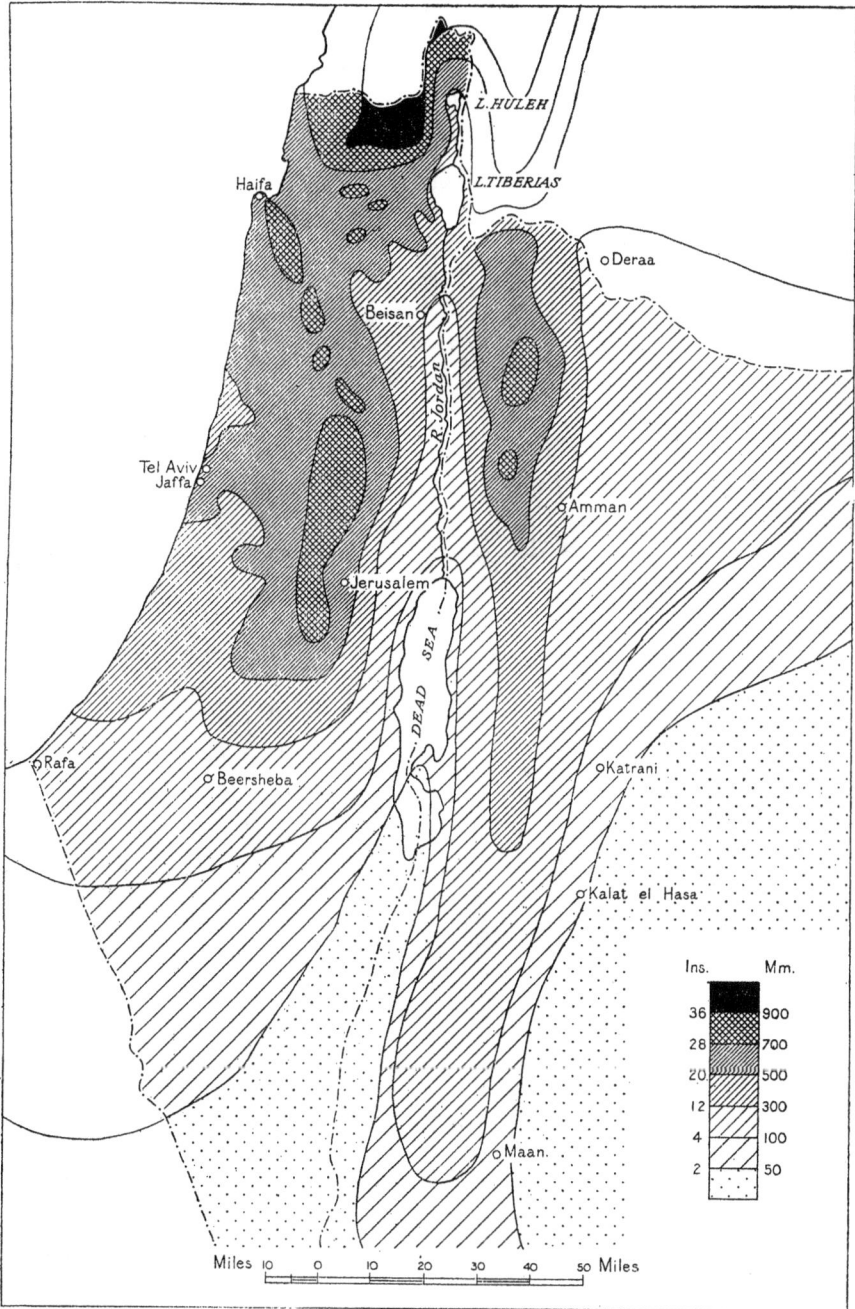

FIG. 14. *Distribution of Rainfall (average annual, 1901–30)*

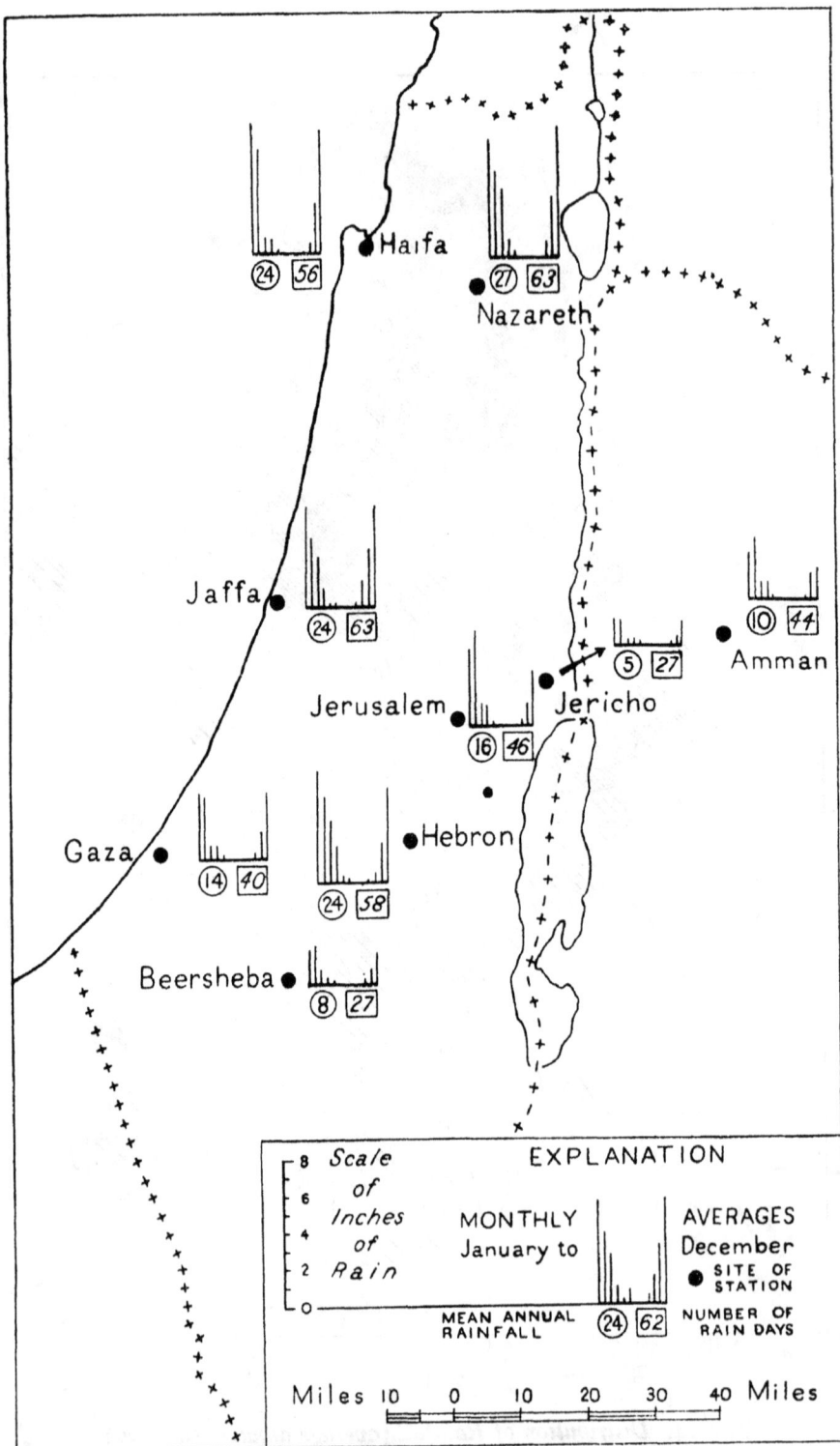

FIG. 15. *Rainfall, Rain Days, and Monthly averages*

is not continuous. The storms endure perhaps for three days, and then there follows a week of sunny spring-like weather, succeeded in its turn by another continuous downpour. The intensity of the rain also varies greatly from gentle showers to violent storms and cloud-bursts. There are few winters without such heavy downfalls, which wash away roads and railways and flood the lower portions of the towns. In the course of these, 3 or 4 inches of rain, and sometimes more, may fall within twenty-four hours, e.g. at Haifa, nearly 11 inches on 9 December 1921 (maximum in 24 hours, Table VIII).

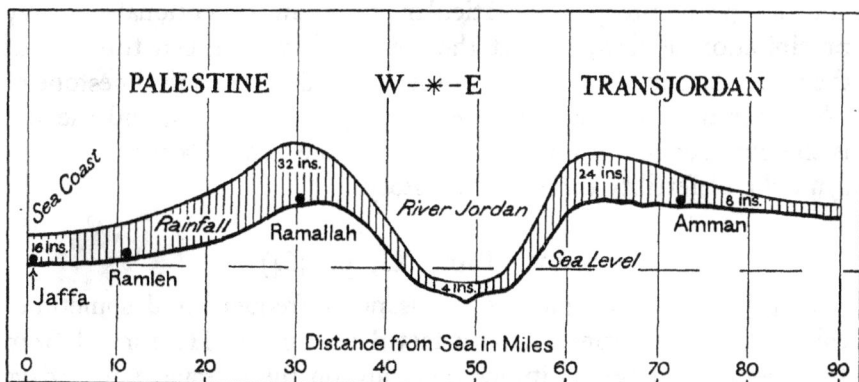

FIG. 16. *Annual Rainfall Section from Jaffa to Amman (almost all October to April)*

The amount of rainfall varies in different parts of the country. Generally speaking, the amount is more plentiful in the north than in the south, on the high ground than the plains, and on the coast than inland. The coastlands have from 25 inches in the north to 16 inches in the south; the plateau from 16 to 30 inches according to locality and altitude; Galilee is the best watered region of the country (28–30 in.). In the southern Negeb and the lower Jordan valley rain is rare (1–5 in.), and in the Beersheba district the amount is very small (about 8 in.). In the coastal region the Former rains tend to be heavier than the Latter rains (Haifa, October-November 3·2 in.; March-April 1·6 in.). Inland the converse is true (Jerusalem, 1·4 in. and 2·1 in.). The rain always comes with W. and SW. winds, and is generally preceded by a strong wind of at least twenty-four hours' duration.

The rainfall of Palestine would be adequate if it were more evenly distributed. The average rainfall at Jaffa, for instance, is about the same as that of London, and more than that of Berlin. In

Europe, however, the fall is distributed fairly evenly throughout the year: in Palestine the whole of it falls in a few winter months when it is of relatively little use for cultivation. For six months in the summer there is no rain, and the land is parched, dependent on irrigation, and on dews.

## DEW (Table X, p. 564)

Dews are both frequent and copious, especially in the north, and enable crops such as cucumbers, melons, and tomatoes to be cultivated during the dry season without irrigation. Mount Carmel and its promontory, in particular, have an exceptionally heavy precipitation of dew, so that the country here is green throughout the year. Also in consequence of this heavy dew, the soft limestone of which the mountain is composed rapidly disintegrates, and the soil is thereby frequently replenished. Thus the name Carmel has been symbolic of fertility throughout history.

## SNOW (Table XI, p. 564)

In the mountain regions snow is not infrequent and sometimes collects in drifts from 10 to 12 feet deep, cutting Hebron off from Jerusalem. At lower altitudes there are on the average 1 to 3 days with snowfall annually. More frequent snowfall, however, is not exceptional, and there are, on the other hand, many winters with no snow at all. In February 1920, snow lying on the ground prevented communication between one part of Jerusalem and another for many days, and some of the old houses in the city collapsed under the weight.

## THUNDER AND HAIL (Tables XII, XIII, p. 565)

Thunder-storms occur chiefly in the cold season. The greatest number is usually recorded in November or December. Their incidence varies greatly from year to year and from place to place. They are most common in the Jordan valley.

Hail not infrequently accompanies thunder during the winter rains. It may occur at any time between November and May (2–6 days per year), but mainly between December and March. There is none during the summer months.

## MISCELLANEOUS

### (i) *Length of Day*

The earliest time of sunrise is 04.58 early in June, and the latest

06.57 early in January (local time). Sunset ranges from 17.00 at the beginning of December to 19.05 early in July. Thus the longest day is about 14 hours and the shortest less than 10. There is very little twilight, full daylight following quickly after dawn, and darkness after sunset.

### (ii) *Changes in Climate*

There have been many discussions about the question of climatic change in Palestine since biblical times, and especially a decrease in rainfall. It has been argued that biblical Palestine, and even Palestine in the first centuries of the present era, must have supported a population appreciably larger than the present one, or than any that has lived in the country during the past fifteen centuries. This is suggested by the remains of towns in parts of the country where a population of the size indicated could not possibly find sustenance at the present day, and even in regions which are now entirely desolate. The existence of a larger population, which, in the absence of minerals, must have depended primarily on agriculture, argues a greater productiveness of the land and hence a larger rainfall than at present. Evidence of this type is presented by Mr. Ellsworth Huntington as a basis for the conclusion that there has been some, although no very great, decrease in rainfall. Nevertheless opinion is divided. 'One of the reasons', says Sir George Adam Smith, 'for the conclusion that the climate has suffered a change for the worse, through the diminution of the rainfall, is the alleged decrease of the woodlands of the country. In all probability these were never much greater in ancient Palestine than they are today. The references to climate and weather in the Bible and the Mishna are fully consistent with the present conditions.' C. R. Conder concludes that 'the change in productiveness which has really occurred in Palestine is due to decay of cultivation, to decrease of population, and to bad government'.

## VEGETATION

IN spite of its small size, Palestine has a comparatively rich flora. That is to say, the number of different kinds of plants found within its borders is high. The astonishing number of species (about 3,000 vascular plants) is all the more remarkable when one considers the climatic extremes to which the vegetation is subjected. It has been truly said that water-supply is primarily the factor limiting plant growth in Palestine. The exiguous rainfall, however, is supplemented to some extent by dew (p. 60). In many parts of Palestine, at the height of the dry season, this may be very heavy, and certain plants are adapted to make use of these nightly precipitations. Certain sand-dune grasses (*Aristida Forsskalii, A. scoparia, Danthonia Forsskalii*, &c.) possess enormous root systems, covered with absorbent hairs, spreading horizontally just below the surface. There seems no doubt that these roots are capable of absorbing dew.

An adverse factor during the dry season is the effect of the intense insolation on the organic matter in the soil. Soil temperatures of 130–144° F. have been recorded during the height of summer; these tend to destroy the organic matter present and prevent the production of beneficial organic substances which are normally produced as the result of bacterial decay.

The following factors probably contribute to the wealth of the natural flora: (*a*) a large percentage of the plants develop and flower during the rainy season; (*b*) many of the plant communities are 'open' ones with bare soil between the individual plants which allows the development of large numbers of small annual and perennial species between the larger plants; (*c*) a relatively short period is required by the majority of the species to complete their annual life-cycle. Close observation of any particular area in the spring shows how quickly the different species succeed one another, flowers and seed being produced and the plants dying down in a remarkably short time. In the plain of Sharon near Jaffa and Tel Aviv, however, one gets the impression that a single red-flowered species predominates for two or three months. This is an illusion, since at least four species possessing red flowers follow one another in quick succession. These include an anemone (*Anemone coronaria*), a buttercup (*Ranunculus asiaticus*), a tulip (*Tulipa montana*), and a poppy (*Papaver* sp.). Climatic factors are generally considered to be of major importance in affecting the composition of plant communities. There are, however, two others which exercise an influence. Edaphic or soil factors play an important role in the synthesis of plant societies. Biotic factors, or the influence exerted by other living creatures, are of particular significance in Palestine. The wholesale cutting down, during the 1914–1918 war, of what still existed of the timber of Palestine was a major disaster, since no reafforestation could be carried out at the time and the ubiquitous goat effectively prevented natural regeneration.

At the present time violent changes are taking place in the vegetation of Palestine, due in the main to improved methods of agriculture carried out by Jewish immigrants. The hitherto rich marsh flora of the coastal plain is being ousted as a direct result of drainage operations. Marshy ground, when drained, is very fertile and, as it is easily acquired, many of the marshes are being transformed into areas of cultivation. Most of the marshes in the plain of Sharon have already disappeared, and the draining of the great Huleh marsh is projected. The direct result of this transformation is to exterminate many interesting marsh plants such as water-lilies and sedges.

The wild flora of cultivated fields has undergone great changes with the advent of the Jewish immigrant. The primitive Arab plough removes and kills shallow-rooted annuals but leaves behind many perennials with deeper rooting systems. With the coming of the European plough and tractor, however, very few such perennials remain in the ground after a few years. Sixty years ago, in the plain of Esdraelon, Barkey reported the presence of enormous tufts of thistles (probably *Cynara syriaca*) scattered about in great profusion. The peasants of the time drove their ploughs between the tufts, whereas modern methods have almost eliminated the plant from Jewish settlements. Many other species have succumbed to the same treatment. In the fertile plains of Gennesaret and Beisan large numbers of bushes of the lotus (*Zizyphus Lotus*) and the Christ-thorn (*Z. Spina-Christi*), which are characteristic plants of these districts, have disappeared from the areas of intensive Jewish cultivation. Such plots as are still in Arab hands are covered with these bushes and only the spaces between the plants are tilled.

The introduction of alien plants has also changed the face of the countryside in many districts. An Australian eucalyptus (*Eucalyptus rostrata*) is widespread in Palestine, especially in the Hadera and Jaffa districts. The prickly pear (*Opuntia Ficus-indica*) or cactus also, as in other Mediterranean countries, is widespread as a common constituent of hedges (photo. 6). Weeds of cultivation inevitably accompany introduced crops, and many have established themselves on arable land.

The mountain flora has suffered much from the activities of Arab charcoal and lime burners. The increased settlement creates a demand for lime and charcoal, and large areas of shrubby vegetation have been denuded for this purpose. Only systematic reafforestation can counteract this wholesale destruction.

Along the sea coast many of the mobile dunes have been fixed by planting special sand-binding species such as marram grass (*Ammophila arenaria* var. *australis*), tamarisk (*Tamarix* sp.), and sand wormwood (*Artemisia monosperma*), in order to produce a more stable surface. Plants which normally inhabit such localities quickly disappear from the stabilized dunes, and at Tel Aviv, which is largely built on sandhills, much of the original dune vegetation has entirely died out.

*Biological Types.* It has been pointed out that a large proportion of Palestine plants complete their life-cycle within the limits of the rainy season. Such species avoid the extreme conditions of the summer months and are frequently mesophytic, that is, they are moist-soil plants, ill equipped to withstand extreme climatic conditions. To this class belong most of the annuals, which suffer greatly from winter droughts when they occur. Some of these annuals, peculiar to the rainy season, develop and ripen their fruit within a few weeks. Such are the 'ephemerals', and they often inhabit places where the rainfall is scanty, such as the Jordan valley or in rocky habitats. Examples are pearlwort (*Sagina apetala*), twin speedwell (*Veronica didyma*), annual daisy (*Bellis annua*), the curious Rose of Jericho (*Anastatica hierochuntica*), and many others. There are, however, some annual species which continue into the dry season, such as certain larkspurs (*Delphinium rigidum* and *D. peregrinum*), mountain knotgrass (*Paronychia argentea*), wart grass (*Coronopus squamatus*), and several members of the daisy family. A few annuals are capable of developing during the dry season, such as trailing heliotrope (*Heliotropum supinum*), a spurge (*Euphorbia lanata*), and crotons (*Crozophora* spp.).

It is noticeable that those annual species that complete their life-cycle entirely within the limits of the rainy season are mesophytic, whereas the species which linger on into the dry season are more or less xerophytic, that is, specially equipped to withstand conditions of drought. These will be referred to later.

Those plants which persist from year to year, the perennials, have been divided into two classes. First, there are those which are dormant during the dry season. These disappear from the landscape during the summer heat, remaining below ground in the form of bulbs, tubers, or 'rootstocks'. They are admirably adapted to withstand intense drought. Entire families are included in this class such as the Lily, Iris, Orchid, and Amaryllis families, and many other examples could be cited. The second class of perennials embraces all those which exist more or less actively during the dry season. They consist of herbs and the majority of the dwarf shrubs, whose aerial parts disappear during the dry season. Regeneration is brought about by buds which develop on old aerial branches. Most plants of this class are xerophytic and include Grasses and members of the Pea, Sage, and Convolvulus families.

The methods by which these plants reduce their 'water-loss' to a minimum are as follows:

1. By the development of a thick outer wall (cuticle) to the cells of the leaves, as in most evergreens. Examples are the evergreen oak (*Quercus calliprinos*), buckthorn (*Rhamnus Alaternus*), laurel (*Laurus nobilis*), St. John's Bread (*Ceratonia Siliqua*), and the oriental strawberry tree (*Arbutus Andrachne*).

2. By a reduction of leaf-surface in addition to (1). Included here are the lentisk (*Pistacia Lentiscus*), the olive (*Olea europaea* var. *Oleaster*), and the lotus.

3. By a reduction of leaves to scales or spines, as in species of tamarisk and *Thymelaea hirsuta*.

4. By reducing leaves to rudiments or dropping them at the beginning of the dry season. Stems are usually green and perform the functions of leaves. They are generally known as 'switchplants'. Examples are joint-pine (*Ephedra campylopoda*), thorny asparagus (*Asparagus stipularis*), Spanish broom (*Spartium junceum*), white broom (*Retama Raetam*), and a genista (*Genista fasselata*).

5. By a rich investiture of hairs in such plants as hyssop (*Origanum Maru*), Palestine woundwort (*Stachys palaestina*), thymeleaved savory (*Micromeria serpyllifolia*), and the common varthemia (*Varthemia iphionoides*).

A few xerophytes shed their leaves at the beginning of the rainy season and remain green during the dry season. Examples are the terebinth (*Pistacia Terebinthus* var. *palaestina*), one of the oaks (*Quercus infectoria*), a hawthorn (*Crataegus Azarolus*), and lotus.

## Botanical Divisions

That Palestine possesses a Mediterranean flora is only true in part, since the climate does not conform, over a large part of the country, to Mediterranean standards.

The botanical exploration of the country has been carried out fairly thoroughly by various workers in the past and particularly in recent years by Alexander Eig and his colleagues. Only the desert territories of the Negeb are little known. The whole country can be divided into three main botanical regions, as follows (fig. 17):

1. *Mediterranean Region.* The limits are the Syrian border in the north, the sea coast in the west, the eastern slopes of the main mountain block in the east, and a southern boundary which roughly follows a line drawn from Gaza to Hebron.

2. *Steppe Region.* There are two principal areas included in this region. First, a narrow strip stretching from Lake Tiberias along the eastern slopes of the Samarian and Judaean mountains down to the near Negeb. Secondly, the near or upper Negeb itself. Certain elements of the flora of the Negeb invade the contiguous coastal belt of the Mediterranean region with which, edaphically, it has much in common.

3. *Desert Region.* The intense insolation is responsible for the high salt-content of the soils of this region, which in some instances is so extreme as to inhibit altogether the growth of plants. Plants that live under such conditions are either ephemerals that complete their life-cycle in the short space of the rainy season or are plants displaying outstanding xerophytic adaptations. The areas of this region include the lower Jordan valley with the adjacent lower slopes of the mountains; the Wadi Araba and the far or lower Negeb.

### Plant Life of the Divisions

#### 1. Mediterranean Region

This region may be divided roughly into the coastal plain and the main mountain block.

(a) *The Coastal Plain.* The coastal part of the plain by reason of the light character of its soils is known as the 'light soils belt' and is of special interest. Narrow in the north, it widens southwards where it passes gradually into the semi-light soils of loess in the Negeb. Light soils readily absorb water, they warm up quickly and are well aerated, so that in general, plants of the rainy season develop on them much earlier than they do on heavier soils.

Of the 300 species found in the area, half are found nowhere else in Palestine. A feature of the soils of the belt is the high percentage of sand and the low, sometimes very low, proportion of calcium carbonate. Many of the plants growing in the belt are probably of species which dislike the presence of calcium. In fact, such species in Palestine find here their only refuge.

The belt may be divided into four main types of plant habitats,

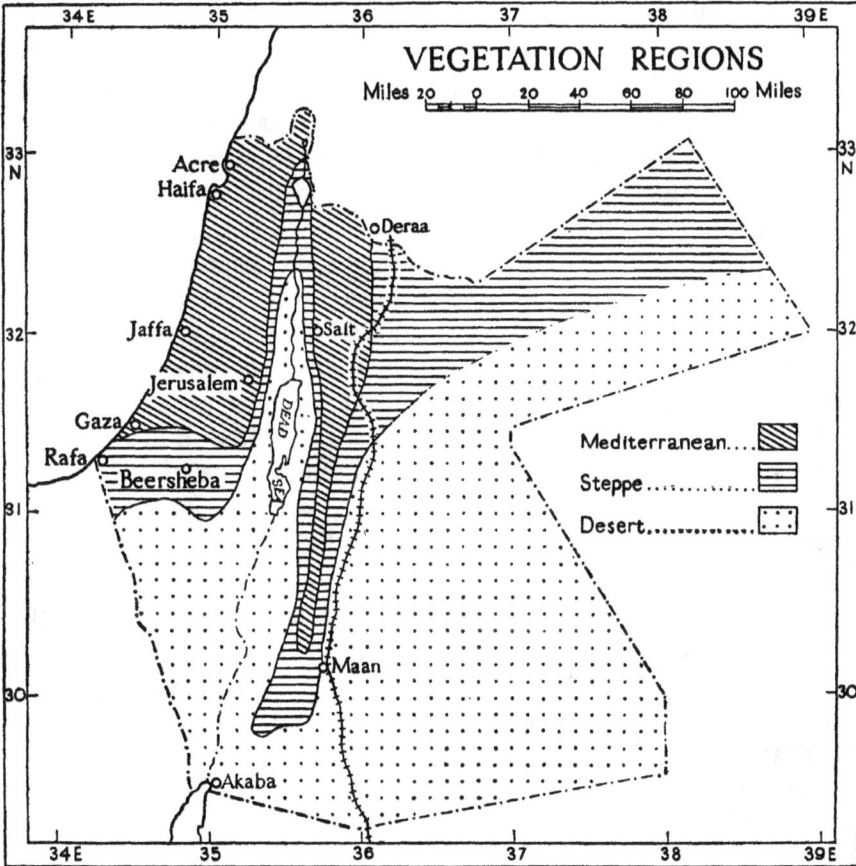

FIG. 17. *Vegetation regions of Palestine and Transjordan*

namely sea-shore, dunes, kurkar hills, and sandy clay plains.

(i) *Sea-shore*. The shore may be high with no large dunes in the immediate hinterland, as between Hadera and Tel Aviv, or low with dunes in close proximity, as along the coast from Jaffa to the Egyptian border. The plants of this region, few in number, are subjected to the action of waves during storms or at least to salt-water spray. They are usually fleshy plants and include seakale (*Cakile maritima*), prickly saltwort (*Salsola Kali*), sea spurge

(*Euphorbia Paralias*), and others. On the high sea-coast, on steep rocks, and on ancient walls adjoining the sea-shore may be found samphire (*Crithmum maritimum*), golden samphire (*Inula crithmoides*), and sea lavender (*Limonium virgatum*). The attractive Morning Glory (*Ipomoea littoralis*) is found in the neighbourhood of wadi outlets.

(ii) *Dunes*. The desert sands of the Negeb are continuous with the sand-dunes of the southernmost portion of the coastal belt. Dunes of the wind-blown mobile type are very numerous in the south, and at Rafa, for example, are from $1\frac{3}{4}$ to 3 miles wide and may attain a height of 150 feet. Here, one may travel long distances without meeting any vegetation at all. Lacking any traces of humus, these drifting dunes are too dry to support any but the most specialized types of plants. In places one may find scattered tufts of marram grass, a species much prized for its sand-binding properties, one or two other grasses (*Danthonia* and *Aristida* spp.), a convolvulus (*Convolvulus secundus*), and perhaps isolated shrubs of a milk vetch (*Astragalus tomentosus*). Passing northwards the dunes tend to become lower and narrower, and with the increase of atmospheric precipitation more plants make their appearance. This increase in vegetation tends to stabilize the dunes and at the same time produces a small amount of humus. The scattered grass tufts are then augmented by a number of sedges and various perennials like white broom, sand wormwood (*Artemisia monosperma*), and an evening primrose (*Oenothera Drummondii*). All these plants are still rather widely spaced with short-lived annuals making their transitory appearances between them (photo. 24).

In the moister valleys between the dunes, where there are distinct traces of humus, the flora becomes richer. This is still more pronounced where the dunes cover a stratum of heavy soil which is impervious to rain. In such circumstances certain perennial marsh plants may be found side by side with the more typical sand-dune species. Such a condition formerly existed in the plain of Acre near Kiryat Hayim where the dune summits were occupied by dune plants exclusively, while in the rather wide valleys between, marsh-loving species of sedges and rushes together with other hydrophytic plants were found. In the north of the dune-belt, where the sand has become more or less fixed, certain areas are dominated by the lentisk, the 'mastic' of commerce. Such areas occur around Hadera and between Binyamina and Caesarea (fig. 10). In other localities the white broom is a conspicuous feature.

An interesting feature of the dune flora is the occurrence of two distinct blossoming periods. The warm airy soil encourages the early development of the annuals, which wither and die in a relatively short time. On the other hand, the perennial species begin to flower only towards the end of the rainy season and continue in flower during the greater part of the dry season. The cause lies in the nature of the root systems, which in annuals are only superficial, but in perennials are deep enough to tap the water resources of the lowest levels.

Where sandy fields border on fields of heavy soil the number of species increases greatly. Here are seen ragweed (*Ambrosia maritima*), a procumbent star thistle (*Centaurea procurrens*), a camomile (*Ormenis mixta*), and love-in-a-mist (*Nigella arvensis*).

(iii) *Kurkar Hills*. This term is used for the old dunes which have become hardened by incrustations of lime. They are not homogeneous in structure but contain calcareous sand concretions intermixed with layers of pure sand. They extend along the coastal plain parallel to the sea coast in several ranges. Their stability and better water-holding power produce a fairly rich vegetation of low annuals, bulbous perennials, and semi-shrubby plants. Characteristic species include a heliotrope (*Heliotropium rotundifolium*), a figwort (*Scrophularia xanthoglossa*), a scabious with white or bluish flowers (*Scabiosa argentea*), a dark purple iris (*Iris atropurpurea*), and a number of grasses.

(iv) *Sandy Clay Plains*. These occupy the largest area of the light soils belt and consist of undulating plains and valleys of red sandy clay soils which vary somewhat in their content of clay. The soils are always very poor in lime. Economically, it is the most important area, since such soils are admirably suited to citrus cultivation. The largest continuous block of sandy clay soils stretches north of the Auja river to Binyamina and the marsh reclaimed near Zichron Jacob. A second large area extends south of the Auja and north of the Rubin. Although these soils contain a high proportion of sand (up to 95%), their moisture-retaining properties are greatly increased by the small amount of colloidal clay present. Thus, a rich and varied flora grows on these soils, the exact composition varying with the clay content. The vegetation consists of low-growing annual and perennial herbs or semi-shrubs. Many of the smaller plants are members of the pea and bean family such as lupins, clovers, and medicks, although they prefer more lime in the soil. The French lavender (*Lavendula Stoechas*) and Christ-thorn occur here, also a crimson tulip (*Tulipa sharonensis*), the procumbent star thistle, and a number of grasses. One of these, *Desmostachya bipinnata*, in northern Sharon, is a conspicuous constituent of a type of grass steppe which is a characteristic feature of the northern limits of the light soils belt. This grass is a tall tough species with a strong vertical rootstock and is an indicator of soils suitable for fruit-tree plantations. Historical accounts show that in the latter part of the last century much of the light-soil part of Sharon was occupied by 'park-like' forests of oak (*Quercus ithaburensis*), and it is assumed that *Desmostachya bipinnata* was a dominant constituent of the forest undergrowth. To-day, only traces of these forests exist in the grass steppe in the form of solitary trees or scattered stumps. In the plain of Sharon, a member of the daisy family, *Ormenis mixta*, with white flowers in the spring, dominates the scene over large areas.

Here and there in this region are areas where the clay content of the soil is high and where a little below the surface is a hard impermeable pan layer locally known as 'Nazzaz'. The top soil is therefore not easily dried out, and although the 'Nazzaz' layer is not penetrable by the roots of plants, a large number of low-growing shallow-rooted annuals and perennials find their home in the top soil.

It has been mentioned that the eastern, somewhat ill-defined boundary of the light soils belt passes into a zone of heavier soils. This zone, which comprises the remainder of the coastal plain, extends to the lower slopes of the main mountain block and from north to south comprises a fairly flat, narrow strip, widening southwards to the loess soils of the near Negeb. This area has been the centre of cultivation for centuries and therefore little of the original wild flora remains. The soil is red to brown in colour, loamy in texture, and is rich in mineral salts, although, as usual with Palestinian soils, it is deficient in humus. Unlike the light soils, it contains an adequate content of lime brought down from the hills by the scouring action of rain. The flora of this region is limited to such areas as are not actually under cultivation. Many of the species of the sandy-clay soils are found here as well as certain shrubby elements which invade from the hills to the east. The rainy season, as usual, brings its spate of annuals which come and go with their usual rapidity.

*Hydrophytic Plants.* As mentioned above, the marshes that once dotted the Sharon and Philistine plains are fast disappearing as a result of drainage operations. The natural flora of these regions is thus being exterminated, and it is only a matter of time before these water-loving plants will be found only in close proximity to permanent

21. *Rocky soil steppe, lower mountain slopes of Palestine escarpment*

22. *Oak-wood with heavy undergrowth of Styrax officinalis, at Sheikh Abreik near Nazareth*

23. *Huleh Swamp and Lake*

watercourses. A feature of these 'hydrophytes' is that the annual species, as well as most of the perennial herbs, dwarf-shrubs, and semi-shrubs, develop after the rainy season is over. Only after the rains have ceased and the hot summer sun has heated the soil do these plants awake from their winter rest. The hydrophytes of Palestine may be divided into (a) those which are submerged in or float on the surface of water, e.g. duckweeds (*Lemna minor* and *L. gibba*), water lilies (*Nuphar luteum* and *Nymphaea alba*), water buttercup (*Ranunculus aquatilis*), and the like; (b) plants known as 'reeds' which may grow actually in the water, or on the banks of streams or in marshes, e.g. tall grasses (*Phragmites communis* and *Arundo Donax*, &c.), sedges (*Cyperus* spp., *Cladium Mariscus*), rushes (*Juncus* spp.), irises, and so on; (c) trees and shrubs which are usually seen near flowing water, e.g. tamarisk, willows (*Salix* spp.), the oriental plane (*Platanus orientalis*), though this is rare; a poplar (*Populus euphratica*), oleander (*Nerium Oleander*), willowherb (*Epilobium hirsutum*), and others; (d) annual and perennial herbs which are not submerged, e.g. horsetail (*Equisetum ramosissimum*), mints (*Mentha* spp.), watercress (*Nasturtium officinale*), various grasses, sedges, and rushes.

On occasions one finds in the marshes near the sea such halophytes as sea lavender (*Limonium vulgare*), golden samphire, and sea plantain (*Plantago crassifolia*).

*The Huleh Swamp.* This large swamp north of Lake Huleh consists of a dense jungle of vegetation with comparatively few areas of open water (photo. 23). The main body of the swamp is composed of a mass of papyrus (*Cyperus Papyrus*), 13–17 feet high, intermixed with a few species which root in the matted rhizomes of the papyrus. These include water horehound (*Lycopus europaeus*), the purple-flowered loosestrife (*Lythrum Salicaria* var. *tomentosum*), knotweeds (*Polygonum* spp.), though the most characteristic plant is a fern, *Dryopteris Thelypteris*. The periphery of the swamp is occupied by a community of 'reeds' which includes the grass *Phragmites communis*, various sedges, mints, rushes, and other denizens of a typical reed community. As the swampy ground extends outwards, a broad zone of the low-creeping dog's-tooth grass (*Cynodon Dactylon*) makes an appearance. There is evidence to show that the swamp is gradually encroaching on the lake so that in time it is possible that the entire lake may become another gigantic papyrus swamp. If the project for the draining of this area eventuates, the complete destruction of the natural aquatic flora is inevitable (p. 30).

(b) *The Main Mountain Block.* This range, mainly composed of limestone, presents in the main a desolate aspect; the forests that once covered it have long since been destroyed, and the somewhat steep faces are scoured by torrential winter rains or subjected to the intense summer sun. In the latter half of the nineteenth century there were still many forests in various parts of western Palestine, but only a few poor remnants can now be found. The last great wave of destruction took place in the war of 1914–1918, when the Turkish authorities cut down many of the trees, including cultivated species, since no other fuel for trains was available. Natural regeneration of these wooded areas was prevented by the grazing of goats.

Fortunately there are, scattered about the country, various fine old oaks or terebinth trees, either solitary or in groups, preserved as 'sacred' trees. These are said to shade the tombs of saints or else, perhaps, to be haunted by spirits. Such trees are frequently all that is left of extensive forests in localities which are now completely deforested.

Traces of oak forests (*Quercus ithaburensis*) are still to be found in the northern parts of the coastal plain. Although this species appears to flourish best in plains, it seems to thrive fairly well as high as 2,000 feet, provided there is a sufficiently deep and good soil. It is the predominant tree in the hills and lower mountains of Samaria and lower Galilee, though it is rare, or even disappears completely, in the higher ranges of the Samarian mountains, in upper Galilee, and in the Judaean mountains. Probably the most complete remnant of what was once an extensive oak forest is to be found in the western Nazareth hills. The commonest under-shrub of these oak communities is the storax (*Styrax officinalis*), while other fairly common ones are the thorny broom (*Calycotome villosa*), a buckthorn (*Rhamnus palaestina*), and a hawthorn (*Crataegus Azarolus*).

The Aleppo pine (*Pinus halepensis*) which once clothed the summits of the highest peaks is now represented here and there, as on Mount Carmel, by a few scattered specimens. The evergreen oak, which in earlier days produced a forest zone lying between the high forests of the Aleppo pine and the lower zone of the deciduous oak, now constitutes a predominant element in the 'maquis'. Maquis is a secondary community of shrubs, mostly evergreen and drought-resisting, which follows the destruction of the trees. In a well-developed maquis the principal elements may grow taller than a man, while the spaces between are occupied by semi- and dwarf-shrubs. The annual and perennial ground flora is always rather poor. In western Palestine this zone extends from the northern boundary of the mountains of upper Galilee to the south of the Judaean mountains. It is specially concentrated on the western slopes facing the sea and reaches an altitude of 4,000 feet. Its abundance on slopes and inclines of wadis is probably due to the fact that in such situations it escapes the attention of the Arab farmer.

As stated above, the most important species of Palestine maquis is the evergreen oak, though sometimes the community is mixed and contains no predominant element. The maquis is often very dense, with abundant climbers, making penetration into the thickets very difficult, while the lack of adequate light in the lower strata is the reason for the paucity of annual and perennial herbs (photo. 25).

Among the principal shrubs of the maquis, in addition to the evergreen oak, are the following: hawthorn (*Crataegus Azarolus*), laurel (*Laurus nobilis*), wild pear (*Pyrus syriaca*), storax, terebinth (*Pistacia Terebinthus* var. *palaestina*), lentisk, buckthorns (*Rhamnus Alaternus* and *R. palaestina*), strawberry tree (*Arbutus Andrachne*), Spanish broom (*Spartium junceum*).

Maquis reaches its most complete development in the northern limits of the mountain block where the rainfall is comparatively high. As one passes down towards the near Negeb climatic conditions become less favourable and a deterioration sets in. As with the ancient forests, the maquis has suffered much from the hand of man. The Arab peasant continues to use the plants for fuel or for the preparation of charcoal, while in places, on Mount Tabor for example, large areas were devastated in the 1914–1918 war.

Where conditions for growth become less favourable, either as a result of continued destruction by man or worsened soil conditions, the 'garigue' type of vegetation makes its appearance. The shrub elements become smaller and less common; the semi- and dwarf-shrubs, 'the under-scrub', increase in quantity, and a more scattered community arises, with rocky soil and stones and bare tracts appearing between the plants. The species are always much below man's height, the shrubs poorly developed, but because of the increased light at ground-level, a rich annual and perennial flora develops in the rainy season (photo. 26).

Of all the shrub elements of maquis, the evergreen oak is the last to succumb to the destructive work of man owing to its astonishing regenerative powers after cutting or burning. Thus we find it a constant component of garigue together with stunted specimens of hawthorn, storax, buckthorn, terebinth, and others. In fact, in garigue communities known to be formed from devastated maquis, one meets most of the shrubby elements of the latter. Less common in Palestine is a type of garigue which is not constituted of the remnants of a broken down maquis. As an example may be quoted a chain of low hills between Kefr Kenna near Nazareth and Sejera, lying between Mount Tabor and Tiberias. This area is covered with low shrubs of the yellow-flowered thorny broom which is the dominant species here, although the shrubby burnet (*Poterium spinosum*), another spiny plant, is an important partner. Semi-shrubs found in the garigue include two hairy rock roses (*Cistus villosus* and *C. salvifolius*), a tree mallow (*Lavatera tomentosa*), and woody spurge (*Euphorbia thamnoides*). In addition to the shrubby burnet many dwarf shrubs belonging to the sage family are found, while a number of perennial grasses are also present.

A further stage of deterioration in the vegetation of the hills and mountains is brought about by still worse soil and moisture conditions or even both together. The shrubs become very scanty, even the semi-shrubs become rarer, and the ground becomes dotted with dwarf shrubs and perennial herbs. The name 'batha', a Hebrew term, has been applied to this community, which is the commonest to be observed in the mountains. Many miles of mountain slopes are covered with this dreary vegetation, particularly monotonous in the dry season, but brightening somewhat during the rains, when a rich annual and perennial herb flora temporarily flourishes. The principal component of the batha is the shrubby burnet, probably the most widely spread dwarf shrub in Palestine. It is a low, much branched spiny shrub, often present in such large numbers as to cover entirely the surface of the soil. At other times it is more open in its distribution with a sprinkling of other dwarf shrubs and perennial herbs; here and there also, perhaps, a solitary remnant of maquis or garigue. The burnet is much used by the Arabs as fuel, both for domestic purposes and for the burning of lime.

The wild flora of much of the uncultivated parts of the light soils belt of the coastal plain has been described as a type of batha. It is a degenerate plant community which has followed the destruction of the oak forests, but its composition is often very different from that of the more typical batha of the mountains. The shrubby burnet is seldom dominant and quite often absent, while the grass-steppe found in some parts of the plain of Sharon has no equivalent in the open batha of the hills.

24. *Sand dunes south of Jaffa*

25. *Maquis near Zichron Jacob, Samarian hills (dominant element, Quercus coccifera)*

26. *Garigue in the mountains behind Zichron Jacob (dominant elements, Pistacia Lentiscus, Salvia Cistus villosus, Quercus coccifera)*

27. *The banks of the Jordan*

28. *Gallery forest of the Jordan meanders*

## 2. Steppe Region

(a) *The Eastern Slopes of the Samarian and Judaean Mountains.*
Climatic conditions along this narrow strip differ in several respects
from those of the western slopes. The rainfall is lower and the effect
of the arid regions to the east is more manifest. The mountain slopes
are steeper than those of the western side and in consequence soil and
moisture conditions are very poor. Large expanses of rocky soil and
stones are much in evidence and the vegetation is much scattered,
conforming to a type known as 'rocky soil steppe' (photo. 21). Passing
eastwards from the Mediterranean batha, the shrubs become scarcer,
the dwarf shrubs decrease in number and size, and fresh species make
their appearance. The shrubby burnet disappears from the scene as
the slopes descend to the Jordan depression below. Such shrubby
elements as are present include the woolly wormwood (*Artemisia
Herba-alba*), the carob, buckthorn (*Rhamnus palaestina*), white broom,
thorny saltwort (*Noaea mucronata*), and others. In the neighbourhood of Lake Tiberias the mountain slopes are dotted here and there
in small groups with shrubs of Christ-thorn and lotus, while in the
adjoining fields the groups approach one another and form an almost
impenetrable thicket resembling some forms of maquis or garigue.
As one passes southwards along the mountain slopes, and conditions
become more arid, the vegetative covering becomes more scanty and
the general colour of the landscape is governed by rocks and stones
rather than by plants.

(b) *The Near Negeb.* This area, as will be seen on the vegetation
map (fig. 17), is a transverse strip with Beersheba as its centre. It has
a low rainfall, rarely exceeding 12 inches, and a large part of it is given
over to the intensive cultivation of barley. It is an intermediate
region dividing the Mediterranean communities of the coastal plain
and western slopes of the mountains from the desert flora of the
greater part of the Negeb. The flora of the uncultivated parts is a type
of steppe with scattered tufts of xerophytic grasses and, in the rainy
season, many species of gaily coloured annuals. On the semi-desert
soils in the east an annual leguminous plant, *Trigonella arabica*,
sometimes makes a fine show in the rainy season with its attractive
white or yellow flowers covering large areas of uncultivated fields.
To the west, where the soil is light loess, a plant forming fairly
dense communities is an asphodel with white and reddish flowers,
*Asphodelus aestivus*. This plant, however, is more strictly a Mediterranean species. In the dry season the uncultivated tracts present

an arid desolate aspect with, here and there, only occasional masses of prickly pear to break the dull monotony of the sandy ground.

### 3. Desert Region

(a) *Lower Jordan Valley.* The climatic conditions in this low-lying valley are tropical. Rainfall is very low, under 8 inches, while insolation is intense. It is convenient to divide the region into three main areas: (1) the Jordan valley in the narrow sense, restricted to the river-banks; (2) the hills and ravines of the broken ground along the river-banks; (3) the wide plain extending to the mountains.

(1) A dense and fairly wide gallery forest of trees and shrubs lines both banks of the river. Here are found a poplar (*Populus euphratica*), various willows, tamarisk, oleander, the chaste-tree (*Vitex agnus-castus*), and a shrubby fleabane (*Conyza Dioscoridis*) (photos. 27, 28).

(2) The broken ground, the 'badlands', found immediately outside the forest belt is in strong contrast to the green riparian gallery forest. The soils of these much eroded hills are almost barren and the intense insolation coupled with low precipitation produces a varying degree of salinity. In consequence, only scattered grey plants which can withstand saline conditions are to be found, belonging mostly to the goosefoot family (*Chenopodiaceae*). The principal elements are species of sea blite (*Suaeda*), saltwort (*Salsola*), and orache (*Atriplex*), while during the short rainy season a richer ephemeral flora makes a fleeting appearance (*frontispiece*).

(3) The plain extending to the mountains varies in width and is mostly composed of grass steppe, of which the dominant plant is a species of spear grass (*Stipa tortilis*). This generally grows somewhat densely, occasionally covering the surface of the ground. Where the ground is wetter and more saline, a sea lavender (*Limonium Thouini*) accompanies the grass, while in places it may even become dominant. Associated also with spear grass is an interesting annual member of the daisy family, *Aaronsohnia Factorovskyi*, the only species of a genus which is restricted to the desert regions of eastern Palestine. Other companion plants are a yellow hawkbit (*Leontodon hispidulus*) and a couple of sand spurreys (*Spergularia diandra* and *S. media*). The *Stipa* steppe extends to the mountains on the west and even covers the lower slopes of the mountains themselves. The eastern boundary of the steppe is occupied frequently by a mixed xerophytic-halophytic flora which gradually merges into the more typical halophyte vegetation of the 'badlands'. Sometimes the grass invades the hill-tops of this broken ground also. Although the plain

is green enough during the rains, it presents a desolate aspect during the months of the dry season.

The closed-in nature of the Dead Sea, coupled with a high degree of evaporation, produces a steamy tropical atmosphere. Most of the plants of this area are concentrated at the oases, in wadi ravines, or in rock-clefts. The oases are frequently composed of dense hydrophilous 'reed' communities containing a number of plants of mixed origin which can only be described as weeds. Such communities are not typical of tropical conditions. The more representative tropical plants consist mainly of grey and often woolly xerophytic shrubs. Here occurs the Sodom Apple or 'Dead Sea fruit' (*Calotropis procera*: loc. *ushr*), a large strange-looking bush with apple-like fruits full of threads and air. Also the velvety Indian mallow (*Abutilon denticulatum*), senna (*Cassia obovata*), and spiny species of acacia. Many of these shrubs flower during the hottest months, August to October, their blossoms standing out conspicuously in the otherwise desolate landscape. On the cliffs may sometimes be seen solitary date palms in inaccessible spots. A scanty vegetation of saltwort, orache, sea blite, &c., is found in the neighbourhood of salt-springs or on the sea-beaches.

(*b*) *The Wadi Araba.* Botanically, this southern extension of the Jordan rift has not been studied intensively, but we know something of its vegetation from the accounts of Hart and Tristram. The north end of the valley, the Ghor, is a sunken plain traversed by watercourses arising from the highlands in the east. That part which directly borders on the southern end of the Dead Sea is a marshy area characterized by a heavy concentration of salt. It is known as the 'Sabkha' and is quite barren. Extending southwards, salt marshes of a milder type occur, and in these are found a number of fleshy halophytes seen elsewhere only in the vicinity of the sea. Such plants include the sea sow-thistle (*Sonchus maritimus*), golden samphire, sea blite, saltwort, and orache. Farther on, the marshy areas become less frequent and fresher, and in them are found jungles of large decorative grasses such as silver spike (*Imperata cylindrica*), reed grass (*Phragmites communis*), and plume grass (*Erianthus Ravennae*). Tamarisks and various shrubby halophytes are also to be seen. The vegetation changes gradually as one passes towards the drier and less acutely saline soils of the south. Communities of tropical trees and shrubs make their appearance, while the halophytes decrease in frequency. The Sodom Apple, a poplar (*Populus euphratica*), and castor-oil tree (*Ricinus communis*) may be seen, together with shrubs of *Acacia laeta*, salvadora (*Salvadora persica*), Christ-thorn, and balsam (*Balanites aegyptiaca*). In the south these communities of trees and shrubs may become very dense, but towards the north they are more scattered, owing probably to the destructive activities of a fluctuating population, who from time to time have carried out a primitive agriculture there. From the fertile Ghor one climbs to the more arid continuation of the Araba, passing through broken and difficult limestone country, across open gravel plains, stony slopes, and areas of shifting sand, down to Akaba on the sea. The vegetation is largely xerophytic, and tropical and halophytic elements are common. Occasional springs produce miniature oases with specimens of poplar, the prickly unsightly shrub, *Prosopis Stephaniana*, and various halophytes. In places bulbous plants, species of *Allium* and *Pancratium*, are common. A parasitic relative of the mistletoe, *Loranthus Acaciae*, produces a handsome display of crimson flowers on plants of acacia, buckthorn, or Christ-thorn. A fairly common shrub is *Calligonum comosum*, which often grows in shifting sand and has whitish tortuous branches. In places rolling sand-dunes are marked by bushes of tamarisk and *Anabasis*, the latter a curious plant with jointed stems and much-reduced leaves. Most of the species found in the Araba are found in Sinai also, and many have their centre of distribution in tropical Africa.

(*c*) *The Lower Negeb.* Of the vegetation of this area little is known, but it is possible to arrive at some estimate of its composition by analogy with better known areas with similar edaphic and climatic conditions. The flora has much in common with that of Sinai, of which it is really a part; it is essentially tropical, though containing some Mediterranean and steppe infiltrations towards its northern limits. Many of the species found in the Dead Sea area and the Araba occur here. In places, grey halophytic bushes are a conspicuous feature of the landscape. The majority of the plants are xerophytic herbs and shrubs, although many brightly coloured annuals enliven the scene in the short-lived rainy season, particularly in the neighbourhood of the wadis.

## FAUNA

PALESTINE, as a consequence of its remarkable varieties of climate, elevation, and topography, is the home of a great variety of fauna. European, Asiatic, and African, tropical, sub-tropical, and temperate types, are all to be found there. Eight thousand species of fauna are said to be known in Palestine to-day and this large number is also said to be only one-third, or even one-fifth, of the number that exists. The number of species within general knowledge is, however, very much less.

According to the Bible, the principal animals of Palestine were the lion, the leopard, the hyaena, the jackal, the fox, the bear, the wild ass, and several species of antelope, among the wild animals; the sheep, the goat, the ox, the pig, the horse, the dog, and the dromedary among the domesticated ones.

Of these, few if any have become extinct; those that have disappeared seem to have been known until recently. Among the fauna of to-day are the roe deer, the fallow deer, the bubale and the addax (both varieties of antelope), the wild sheep, the Syrian bear, the leopard, the jungle cat and the cheetah, although in some instances specimens are met very occasionally. Wild swine are found in the Jordan valley. The gazelle and Sinaitic ibex are by no means extinct, but they are seen far less often than formerly. More prevalent are the wild cat, the striped hyaena, the mongoose, the spotted weasel, the wolf, the jackal, and the fox. Of the smaller animals there are several species of hare, two of porcupine, spiny mice, the dwarf hamster, gerbils, jerboas, voles, dormice, shrews, bats, and both the European and the desert hedgehog. The European house-mouse and several varieties of black rat have been imported.

Three hundred and seven different species of birds have been noted. Most of these are migrants, coming to Palestine only in the summer or the winter.

Venomous snakes are of rare occurrence and the number of their species is small. These, however, include two kinds of viper. Fifty-seven varieties of reptiles have been counted, distributed among the three orders Ophidia, Lacertidae, and Chelonia. The crocodile survived until, at the earliest, the last quarter of the nineteenth century. Sixty-eight different species of fish native to the waters of Palestine, fresh and marine, have been identified, but it is known that the list is far from exhaustive. Some of these migrated from the Red Sea through the Suez canal. There are said to be 4,700 species of insects in Palestine, of which 2,000 are beetles and 1,000 butterflies. This large number is believed to be at the most a third of those that should ultimately be identified.

*Pests* (p. 251). The most destructive are the field-mouse, scale insects, ticks, woodboring insects, and fruit flies. So far as human beings are concerned the several varieties of mosquito and sand-fly are perhaps the most objectionable. Locusts are not indigenous, but they invade or threaten to invade Palestine periodically, and if they succeed, do great damage. They come from the Nejd, and less often from the Sudan. The most recent occasion of the threat of a locust invasion was in 1929, but by tireless and widespread measures taken in Transjordan and the Sinai peninsula the locusts were kept out of the country. Co-operation between the neighbouring governments has now been organized to deal with any future threat. The scale insect, known in Palestine as Black Scale, has long been prevalent in the north and has done much harm to citrus fruit. Hitherto, it has been kept from the valuable orange-groves of the Jaffa district, but much vigilance has been necessary to this end. The spread of this, and other pests, is dealt with tirelessly by the Government Department of Agriculture.

## CHAPTER V

# HISTORY

## 1. EARLY TIMES TO THE ROMAN SETTLEMENT

### Earliest Culture

UNTIL the last twenty years little was known of the ancient culture of Palestine, but its main outlines have now been determined by archaeological excavation. Like most other countries, Palestine passed through the usual 'ages' when first stone, then copper and bronze, and finally iron were the materials of the chief implements and weapons. But even the assignment of the earliest Bronze Age in Palestine to about 3000 B.C. is tentative, and depends on comparisons with better dated cultures in Egypt and Mesopotamia. Moreover, principal stages overlap, and all regions do not develop at the same rate.

At no period has there been a characteristically Palestinian architecture or art, or even a general culture. To material civilization the inhabitants of Palestine do not appear to have made any contribution whatever. While they were producing religious and poetical masterpieces, and giving to mankind the most lofty conception of deity, they were content to adapt to their social and material needs the manners and crafts of their neighbours.

The inhabitants of Palestine in the earliest Palaeolithic periods are unknown, but Neanderthal man with his *Mousterian* culture appeared early—perhaps before he arrived in Europe—occupying caves in Mount Carmel, on the maritime plain, in the valleys near Samaria, on the Judaean highlands, and in Moab. These Palestinian men were larger and more developed physically than their counterparts in Europe; they preyed on mammoth, rhinoceros, and other powerful animals, and they buried flint implements with their dead.

An *Aurignacian* culture, like that of central France, followed and long coexisted with the Mousterian, but survived it, with more skilful flint technique, vigorous sculpture, the use of fire, of clothes sewn with bone needles, of magical ceremonies, and sculptured cult-figures connected therewith—though not cave-paintings as in France and Spain. Between the old and the new Stone Age the curious *Microlithic* culture was widespread, characterized by tools of very minute stone flakes inserted in wooden hafts, some of which are worn as if by reaping. But there is no other evidence for the practice of agriculture yet, though wheat and barley are known to have been growing wild in Palestine at this period.

Very rude constructions of stone blocks announce the first builders, and probably also the first places of worship. With the domestication of plants and animals, and the new art of grinding stone tools instead of chipping them, the *Neolithic* way of life begins, and a new type of man appears in caves at Jebel Sunin and Gaza, akin to hill-folk in south Persia and Arabia. Caves are so common in the limestone hills that much of the evidence still comes from cave dwellings and cave burials. But there are also traces of dolmens and other structures of rude stone in Sinai and Galilee and east of Jordan—known as *gilgals* in antiquity and *jiljiliyeh* to-day. The worship of Earth-Mother and Corn-Goddess becomes apparent, in sacred 'high places', at 'pillars', and in 'groves'. With the use of stone hoes in cereal agriculture and of rock-cut press-beds for wine and oil, and with the making of pottery, the record of early culture becomes fuller and more varied.

Some time before 3000 B.C. a tall, aggressive people entered from the north-east, bringing copper implements and fortifying their 'fenced cities' with stone-faced earthworks; examples remain at Hazor and Jericho, and sometimes on earlier sites, with water-tunnels for times of siege, as at Gezer and Jerusalem, and crowded palaces for the chieftains. Terraced agriculture became general, and a rude plough came in probably from Egypt, but wheeled transport did not yet compete with the laden ass. The saddle-quern, spindle-whorl and loom, the potters' wheel, and other mechanical devices came into use. Traffic with Egypt is indicated by carnelian beads of Sixth Dynasty style (*c.* 3000 B.C.) and must have begun soon after the invasion of Canaan by Sa-hu-re of the Fifth Dynasty.

Bronze superseded copper about 2500 B.C. also from north Syria; and iron about 1200 B.C., probably from Asia Minor. Gold was already known to the first metal-workers, but in a country so often overrun it remained rare till the rise of the great kings of Jerusalem, David and Solomon.

The worship of 'high places' and 'pillars' and a serpent-cult became more elaborate, with ritual dances and the sacrifice of children. Egyptian representatives of deities appear alongside the ruder native figures, probably during the Twelfth Dynasty occupation of Palestine about 1800 B.C., when Egyptian paintings show rich tribute brought thence by Asiatic vassals.

This Egyptian dominion was ended by the Hyksos invaders from the north-east, with their new weapon of war, the horse-drawn

29. *Egyptians under Rameses II (XIX Dyn.) taking the fortress of Dapur in Galilee (mod. Tabor?) by assault [from Karnak]*

chariot, and a fresh type of fortress, rectangular with deep fosse and glacis and towers of brick, as at Gaza. They buried their dead in pit-tombs, but their general culture was not high.

## The Biblical Period

By the tireless investigations of archaeologists the story of man in Palestine is gradually being pushed back farther and farther. Occasional references to the country and its inhabitants have been found in the early Babylonian and Egyptian records and have often been confirmed by discoveries in the land itself.

Continuous history begins about 1600 B.C. when Egypt threw off Hyksos domination; soon after 1500 Thothmes III, of the Eighteenth Dynasty, was reconquering Palestine and Syria as far as the Euphrates. His decisive battle at Taanach near Megiddo (1479), on the edge of the plain of Esdraelon, was the first of those struggles to which 'Armageddon' owes its name. Egyptian protectorate stimulated traffic with Syria, and even with Babylonia. At Beth-shan (Beisan) Egyptian temples were built and rebuilt over the 'high place' of the local god Merkal. Fine houses, bazaars, and skilled craftsmen in the cities, and widespread agriculture, testify to prosperity, further illustrated by Egyptian records of tribute. After 1400 B.C. Hittite aggressors out of Asia Minor penetrated as far south as Judaea, detaching small Palestinian states from an enfeebled Egypt, and wrecking those that resisted. Among these was Jerusalem, first mentioned in the Tell el Amarna correspondence.

The invasion of Palestine by the Israelites under Joshua, from beyond Jordan, is dated by some as early as 1450, by others as late as 1200, when a collapse of the city wall at Jericho and desertion of the town occurred; but desert people bring little material culture. Similar disasters have been traced at Taanach, Lachish, Ain Shems, Gerar, and other places, but the Jebusite fortress of Zion held out till its capture by David after 1000 B.C., when the countryside had been long settled and its Canaanite peoples enslaved.

About 1200, also, the ruinous attacks of 'land-raiders' from Asia Minor who had wrecked the Hittite Empire, and of 'sea-raiders' out of the Mediterranean, completed the collapse of old Canaanite culture and cut off the traffic with Egypt, while they opened new connexions with Cyprus, Crete, and the Greek islands. In the pottery and other arts of the coast towns this western influence is evident. The Philistines, who came from oversea, gave the country their name (*Pulisata*

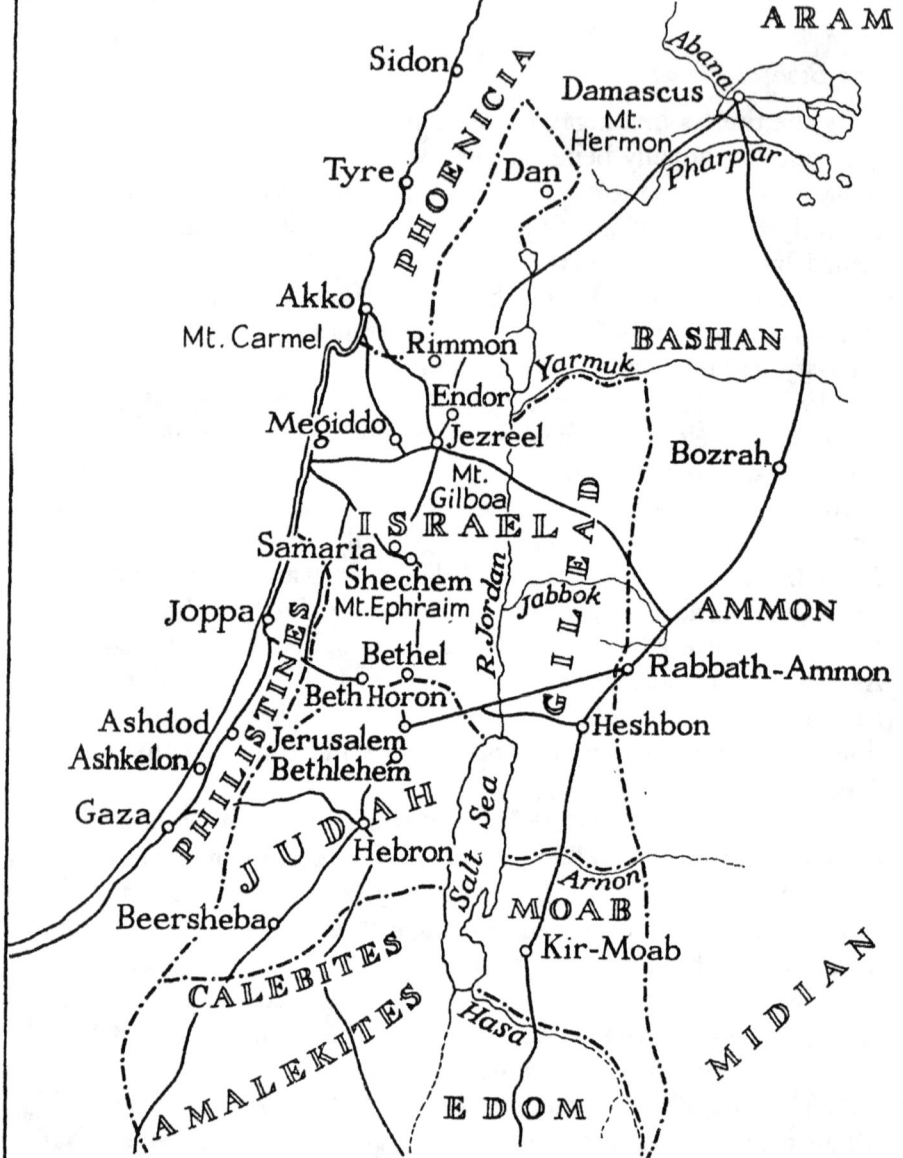

FIG. 18. *The Kingdoms of Israel and Judah*

in Egyptian, *Palestina* in Greek) and long struggled with the Israelite tribes in the hill country, disarming them for a while in spite of heroic counter-attacks under the 'Judges', local leaders, political and military. Northward, Israelite conquest at its farthest extended to the foot of Mount Hermon and the sources of the Jordan, southward to the Dead Sea a little below the latitude of Hebron; the lowland plain of Jezreel, however, remained in the hands of the Canaanites. The far south, beyond Hebron and the lands of the tribe of Judah, was the territory of Simeon, but its position and identity were always somewhat indefinite. Simeon seems to have dwelt among the Amalekites in the Negeb and to have been soon merged with them. On the other side of the Jordan, opposite Samaria, Israelite land extended to the desert and to a less extent farther south, where the Jordan gorge and the Dead Sea impose natural barriers towards Ammon and Moab.

The Bible describes the invasion and partial conquest of the land by Joshua and his successors; the period of disintegration and continual contests with Canaanites, Philistines, Amalekites, and other peoples; the consolidation of the Israelite territories under Saul, David, and Solomon, the only period in which there was a fully independent Israelite state; the separation of this state into the rival kingdoms of Israel and Judah; and the political deterioration that led to the destruction of the kingdom of Israel by Sargon of Assyria in 722–721 B.C., and then of Judah by Nebuchadnezzar of Babylon in 587–586.

During these centuries the limits of Hebrew or Israelite Palestine varied. It reached its greatest extent under Solomon, in fact, 'from Dan to Beersheba'; beyond the latter lay the indefinite territory originally assigned to Simeon, which, however, passed out of Solomon's control, except the route to his port on the Gulf of Akaba. On the west not only had the Canaanite outpost at Jerusalem passed into Israelite possession and become the capital, but Solomon's rule reached the Mediterranean coast, from Mount Carmel and the river Kishon to a point more than half-way to Joppa (Jaffa) and about opposite to Shechem (Nablus). Farther south towards the sea only a narrow strip of plain was left to the Philistines. On the east, Israelite territory came down to the river Arnon, half-way along the shore of the Dead Sea, absorbing at the same time the kingdom of Ammon. With the separation of the two kingdoms of Israel and Judah about 935 B.C. there was not much change in their total extent, but by 722 B.C., when that of Israel disappeared, Judah had been reduced to a parallelogram stretching from Bethel in the north to the desert beyond

Beersheba in the south, and from the eastern edge of the coast plain to the Dead Sea (fig. 18).

Of the splendours of Solomon's temple and palace, the biblical descriptions emphasize the Phoenician craftsmanship, and enough has survived of this style of work, in silver bowls and ivory carving, to give precision to the record; at Samaria the 'ivory house' of Ahab is represented by many fragments of its inlaid decoration. The lavish use of ivory in this period is characteristic, and well attested at Megiddo, Lachish, and Beth-Pelet. For long the dominant influence in design was Egyptian, but with successive Assyrian conquests, Mesopotamian traffic and craftsmanship spread, while Ahaz copied for the Temple an altar seen at Damascus.

By the time of Hezekiah, *c.* 700 B.C., the inscription in the Siloam tunnel at Jerusalem (p. 326) reveals that alphabetic writing was in general use; personal names occur on seals and seal-impressions as early as Ahab's time (*c.* 850 B.C.); at Lachish dispatches were written with a reed-pen on potsherds (*c.* 585 B.C.); and there is a written calendar from Gezer. At Lachish also similar writing occurs on a vase of about 1200 B.C.; and the inscribed sarcophagus of Ahiram at Byblos, in Phoenicia, may be earlier still. Into Palestine the alphabet was clearly introduced ready-made during a period when many peoples and cultures intermingled there and required a simpler mode of writing for the Aramaic dialect, now generally spoken, than either Babylonian cuneiform or Egyptian hieroglyphic characters.

Though the quarrel between the Northern and Southern Kingdoms dissolved the wide dominion achieved by David and Solomon, both remained prosperous. The protests of Hebrew prophets against luxury and oppression of the poor by the rich are confirmed by fragmentary evidence of opulence in Ahab's palace at Samaria, and by the record of Assyrian and Babylonian plunder when the two kingdoms fell. On the other hand, the clumsy and inartistic pottery and other offerings at local 'high places', where old Canaanite worship persisted in spite of priest and prophet, show that outside the palaces and the national sanctuaries the general level of culture was low.

From the death of Solomon until the destruction of the kingdom of Judah, a period of some four hundred years, the history of Palestine was one of almost continuous strife between Israel and Judah and, for the greater part of the time also, of defensive warfare against foreign invaders from the north or the south. Assyria, Babylonia, Syria, and Egypt in turn coveted both the land of Israel and those parts of Palestine, for example Philistia, over which the people of Israel or of

31. *Tell ed Duweir, the mound of ancient Lachish*

32. *Tell es Sultan, the mound of ancient Jericho*

33. *The Jebusite Wall, Mount Ophel, Jerusalem*

34. *The Israelite Wall and part of the Hellenistic Round Tower at Samaria (Sebustya)*

Judah had no permanent control, and made frequent invasions with a view to annexing them. These greater powers made Palestine the battlefield in wars which had little direct connexion with its peoples. Opposing armies generally met along the coastal plain. Those coming from the north crossed the Jordan either through Banyas at the source, or across the Jisr Banat Yakub, the 'Bridge of the Daughters of Jacob', a couple of miles south of Lake Huleh, or still farther south, below Lake Tiberias and opposite Beisan. All these three routes lead into the plain of Esdraelon, near the western end of which is the historic site of Megiddo, at the foot of the Carmel range, where the road from Egypt and the coast crosses the ridge and reaches the central plain.

### From Nebuchadnezzar to Antiochus IV

With the fall of the kingdom of Judah the country became a part of the Babylonian Empire. Many of its leading men were exiled, as had been the leaders of the people when the kingdom of Israel fell before Assyria (722). Never again did it gain full independence, for in the time of the Hasmoneans and their successors, the house of Herod, it had only a limited local autonomy. Palestine continued henceforth, as it had been for the greater part of past history, a dependency of a greater power.

Assyrian and Babylonian deportations were compensated by settling aliens from elsewhere, who brought relics of their own culture into the local chaos, which was little affected by provincial governors or garrisons. Those Hebrews who escaped to Egypt with Jeremiah became acclimatized there; only 'by the waters of Babylon' Ezekiel and others conserved priestly traditions and the national ideal. In 537 B.C., when Cyrus included the country in the Persian dominion, a small number of Jewish exiles returned, and were encouraged to set up again an autonomous community, religious and civil. In Palestine, however, they met with difficulties from their neighbours, the Samaritans, descendants of Assyrian colonists, who had mingled with the Israelites remaining in the land, had adopted their religion, and now desired to share with the returning exiles in the rebuilding of the Temple. Their offer, however, was rejected, as they were not pure Israelites. The returning exiles complained also of the local representatives of the suzerain who, as a consequence either of personal hostility, of inadequate instructions, or perhaps of supineness, hindered the work of rebuilding. However, Darius, a successor of Cyrus, intervened, and the rebuilding of the Temple was at length completed. The city was refortified on the old foundations (p. 326), and a Judaean self-governing community was reorganized by Ezra and Nehemiah. In 444 B.C., ninety years after the return under Zerubbabel, the rule of the Jewish Law was fully re-established in Jerusalem. But the priesthood cared little for culture or craftsmanship, and the restored exiles, like their kinsmen of the Dispersion (p. 95), devoted themselves to religion, agriculture, and commerce, not to the arts.

For the next eighty years the history of Palestine, as of the Persian Empire of which it formed part, was almost blank. Provincial modes of life and local forms of worship were undisturbed. But as the Persian monarchy weakened, subject states such as Egypt, Phoenicia, and Cyprus revolted, and in the reign of Artaxerxes III Ochus there were similar disturbances in Palestine, followed by ruthless suppression. Some historians even suspect a new exile about 340 B.C. This was the period of Holofernes and the *Book of Judith*.

Alexander of Macedon invaded Asia in 334, and in the following year his victory at Issus brought about the downfall of the Persian Empire. A new and more virile power had arisen. The West competed with the East for the dominion of the world. So far as Palestine was concerned, the victory of Issus and the destruction of Tyre led directly to the occupation by Alexander of the coastal plain, the highway of all the armies that had struggled for the mastery of Asia and of Africa. The only resistance was at Gaza, which held out till the siege-train could be brought forward from Tyre. Whether Alexander ever visited Jerusalem is doubtful, though there is a legend of his encounter with the High Priest.[1] It was not Judaea but Persian Egypt, now in his rear, that he could not ignore. In his treatment of vassal states he observed the Persian tolerance of local customs; this little upland state under its High Priest, less interested in secular dominion than in liberty to pursue its religious ideals, interfered with no one, and for a brief period Judaea was indeed a theocracy.

Alexander died in 323, and the division of his conquests among rival 'successors' in Egypt, Syria, and elsewhere made Palestine once more the cockpit of Asia. For the first hundred years, indeed, under

---

[1] The story runs that, before he set out for the conquest of Asia, Alexander was visited in a dream by a handsome and dignified old man who promised him success in his undertaking. On his entry into Palestine he summoned Jerusalem to surrender. A deputation with the High Priest at its head waited on him outside the walls. Alexander recognized the visitor of his dreams. Henceforth the Judaeans were high in the conqueror's favour, and Jews to this day name their boys Alexander in honour of their protector.

the Ptolemaic dynasty of Egypt, Judaea remained in great measure autonomous, while on the coast of Syria Greek culture spread rapidly (p. 438). The Ptolemies tolerated, and perhaps encouraged, this separatism; it was with the aggression of the Seleucid kings of Syria that trouble began.

Antiochus III of Syria (223), though defeated, after initial successes, at Raphia (Rafa) in 219 B.C., routed the Ptolemies at Paneas (Banyas) on the north frontier in 198. Once again only Gaza held out in the far south.

During the first years of the Syrian period Palestine was happy in being without history, for Antiochus III and his immediate successor, Seleucus Philopator, continued the policy of the Ptolemies. Nevertheless, without compulsion, hellenization spread with the planting of Greek colonies, and its subtle influence made new conquests among the indigenous population. The attractions of the new civilization could not be withstood in spite of the opposition of the Jewish national state, in the strong hands of the Temple priesthood, which not only resisted the spread of Greek culture in Palestine, but encouraged the Dispersed elsewhere to hold aloof from it wherever they were numerous enough to establish what the Greeks called a *synagogue* ('congregation') and to maintain their own tradition and belief.

## The Maccabaean Revolt

A change came with the accession of Antiochus IV Epiphanes in 175 B.C. If Antiochus had been satisfied that hellenization should succeed by its own attractions, Palestine might have become part of the Greek world, like his other provinces and dependencies. But this process was too slow for him. The main barrier was Judaism, the Jewish religion, in many respects the antithesis of Hellenism. To this a great part of the Jews had a fanatical devotion, though even among them there was a Hellenistic party. To suppress Judaism, therefore, Antiochus set himself to destroy the Jews. His attempt led to the Maccabaean revolt (168), in the course of which the Syrian armies were repeatedly defeated, and in the event the country gained complete independence from Syria. The heroes of the revolt were the Hasmonean family, Mattathias and his five sons, of whom Judas Maccabaeus ('the Hammer') is the most famous post-biblical hero of the Jewish people. Guerrilla warfare was the prelude to more regular operations, in which the Syrians were repeatedly and signally defeated. In the hills the Graeco-Syrian troops could not withstand the attacks of the Judaeans hiding behind the rocks and in the gullies;

and when converging forces attempted to force him into the plain, Judas was too quick and too agile for his enemies. He was now no longer a rebel and guerrilla chief, but a national leader.

Jerusalem was, however, still in the hands of the enemy, and until the capital was recovered the victory could not be complete. By now Antiochus was realizing that the Judaean outbreak was not merely a police matter but a serious war. But the very size of the Syrian army seems to have been a disadvantage in so restricted an area, while the Judaeans again had the advantage of irregular formations, the broken country, and a great leader. The victory of Judas at Bethzur, a few miles to the south, laid Jerusalem open. Judas entered it, cleansed it of Hellenistic idolatries, and set up his capital there. After his later defeat and death in the battle of Elasa (161 B.C.) his brother Jonathan became High Priest and leader of the people; he made good the losses of Judas, and extended his territories. Simon, the last of the brothers, succeeded him (143), extended his rule still farther, and was the only son of Mattathias to leave a successor in the direct line. Simon was not only High Priest; he was also recognized as *Ethnarch* or independent political ruler by Syria and later by Rome.

The revolt of Mattathias and his sons began as a war for religious liberty and to preserve the way of life that made this liberty possible. These aims were secured, but the desire for political independence followed; and when this was precariously achieved, there followed an imperialist desire, not merely to control neighbouring lands, but to annex them. But the pinchbeck Hasmonean Empire collapsed, and with it political independence. The Hasmonean family fell generation by generation from the ideals of its founder, until there was little to choose between it and other little oriental despots; it was finally extinguished by murder. Fanatical nationalism, meanwhile, precluded compromise with foreign ideas and cultures. Even in craftsmanship, Greek models were replaced, in pottery for example, by clumsy imitations of old Canaanite forms. Only two centuries later even the Jewish religion, for whose sake Mattathias and his sons had drawn sword, faded away from the land where it was born, and survived only among the Jews of the Dispersion.

## 2. THE ROMAN PERIOD

*Roman Palestine*

Meanwhile, Rome had been obliged or induced to intervene between Syria and Egypt, the latter an ancient ally, the former a bad

neighbour to Roman Cilicia. Roman influence over the Hasmonean
house had been considerable, even before the invasion of Syria by
Pompey in 64 B.C. His intervention in Palestine was provoked by
dissension between rival princes. The dominion of Alexander
Jannaeus (103–76) had extended from the southern shore of Lake
Huleh to the borders of the Nabataean country in the south, and
from the coast and the Kishon, on the west, to Rabbath Ammon
(Philadelphia, now Amman) and beyond, on the east. The whole of
this territory was Jewish, with the exception of the free city of Ascalon
on the coast and a small portion of the ancient kingdom of Ammon
beyond the Jordan (p. 442).

Pompey broke this unity into five fragments. The whole of the
coast-plain, Samaria, Idumaea in the south, and Gilead across the
Jordan, were annexed to the new Roman province of Syria. All cities
were declared 'free' and self-governing. Those in Gilead across the
Jordan, Greek in population, united as the *Decapolis* for defence
against their nomad neighbours.[1] Most of the Moabite country went
to the Nabataeans of Petra. The district east of Lake Tiberias and the
upper Jordan became a part of the Ituraean confederacy. Hyrcanus,
the Jewish High Priest and Ethnarch, retained only Judaea proper,
Peraea on the other side of the Jordan, and Galilee which was separated
from Judaea by the vale of Jezreel and Samaria. But even this was
temporary. Six years later the Proconsul Gabinius deprived Hyrcanus
of his civil powers, and divided his territory into five independent
cantons—*synedria* or *synodoi*. Hyrcanus remained High Priest, and
Antipater, an Idumaean, was made Fiscal Superintendent of the five
*synedria*. In 47 B.C., however, Caesar restored the title of Ethnarch to
Hyrcanus, but made Antipater governor of Judaea, which now included three of the *synedria* together with his native Idumaea which
was detached from Syria.

## Herod the Great

Further changes came after the death of Julius Caesar when Mark
Antony governed the eastern provinces, in concert with Cleopatra of
Egypt. Antipater had two sons, Phasael and Herod, and they were
given influential positions under him. His fortunes and those of his
family were obviously rising, and those of the former ruling house
were in decline. At one period Antigonus, a nephew of Hyrcanus,

[1] Originally ten, as the name denotes; eight were afterwards added. Of the
original cities, nine were on the eastern side of the Jordan; the tenth was Scythopolis, the modern Beisan (p. 441).

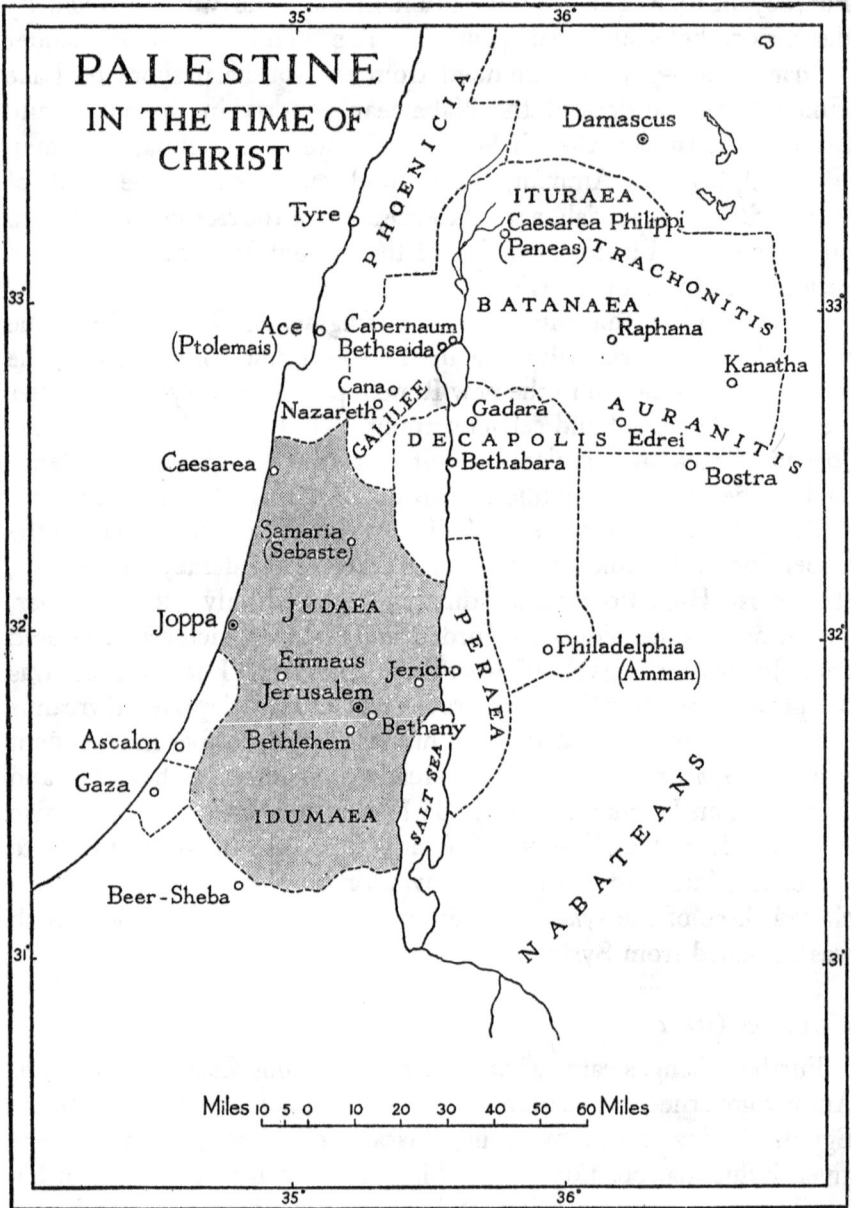

FIG. 19. *Palestine at the time of Christ, showing boundaries of principalities.*
*Roman province of Judaea stippled*

rebelled and, with the help of the Parthians from Mesopotamia, took Hyrcanus prisoner and caused Herod to flee to Rome. Phasael, the elder brother, had poisoned himself. Antigonus was hailed king by the people, but his reign was brief (39–37 B.C.). In Rome Herod was created 'King of the Jews' and with a Roman army soon secured his kingdom. Antigonus, the last of the Hasmonean princes, was taken prisoner and beheaded.

Throughout the Hasmonean period the head of the State had been the High Priest, sometimes enjoying that dignity only, at others joining it to that of civil head (Ethnarch). Herod returned to the older precedent, by which the civil and religious offices were kept entirely separate. He was the first ruler of Judaea who was not fully a Jew in blood. His mother was a Hasmonean princess, but his father was an Idumaean.

Herod, known in history as Herod the Great, ruled over a kingdom that (as delimited by Augustus) extended from Dan almost to Beer-sheba and from the coast to the other side of the Jebel Druse, far beyond the Jordan. Only the lands of the Decapolis on both sides of the Jordan were outside his sway. On the coast the boundary was a few miles north of Caesarea (fig. 19).

With the conquest of Syria and Palestine, Hellenistic zeal for material and intellectual culture had been smothered by Roman indifference and political support of the Temple priesthood. But the nationalist ideal also had lost the stimulus of persecution, the attempt to re-establish genuine Hebrew culture had failed, and 'Pharisee' exclusiveness found a rival in 'Sadducee' compromise with Hellenistic and liberal ideas: and with the 'Sadducees', in the Gospels, stand the 'Herodians'.

Herod was a great builder of cities, palaces, and fortresses, and many remains of his buildings survive, free but unintelligent copies of classical architecture, such as his 'Beautiful Gate' of the Temple area. In the 'Tomb of Absalom', beyond the Kidron, Ionic pillars support a Doric entablature, with an Egyptian cornice and a pyramid above. Among other monuments was a larger and more elegant Temple in Jerusalem, to take the place of the modest shrine of the exiles who returned with Ezra and Nehemiah. Adjoining the Temple was his principal palace, but he had others at Samaria and elsewhere (photo 94). More Roman than Jewish in sympathy, and in blood half an Idumaean, he never had the full-hearted allegiance or acceptance of his subjects, who looked on him as imposed on them by force, the alien representative of Roman conquerors rather than their freely chosen ruler.

Thus under Roman control, but through a local prince, the customs, art, and language of the Greek world at last imposed themselves on Palestine. At Beth-shan the Canaanite temples of Merkal and Astarte were converted into Greek fashion, and dedicated to Dionysius and Atargatis. A measure of western influence is the enormous number of wine-jars, with trade-marks of Rhodes, found all over Palestine; and the new taste for architecture and painting in the traditional cave-tombs, such as that of Apollophanes at Marissa, with frescoes of processions and animals with their names. After Herod's dynasty ended, Roman governors followed his example, and the general prosperity of the country, like that of the cities beyond Jordan—Ammon, Gerasa, and Gadara—were reflected in great Jewish synagogues and secular buildings alike (p. 442). In Palestine the people of the old hill-villages came down into open country, and founded new settlements under the old names, which remained prosperous and ostentatious as long as Roman defences kept at bay the Parthian and the Saracen.

## Revolt against Rome

Herod the Great died in 4 B.C., and his kingdom was divided between his three sons; but none of them inherited his statesmanship or diplomacy, and they soon sank to be Roman office-holders. After them, the government was formally in the hands of a Roman *procurator*, within the province of Syria. As the birth of Jesus was contemporary with the death of Herod, Palestine during His life and ministry was, in effect, under Roman rule (fig. 19).

Popular resentment was covertly fomented by the priesthood and the Pharisees against direct Roman administration, until a rebellion broke out in A.D. 66, which lasted four years, in spite of unceasing dissension among the rebels; one party always considering the other insufficiently thorough, but all united in hostility to the more moderate men, who would have liked an accommodation with Rome. The revolt ended with the capture and sack of Jerusalem by Titus in August A.D. 70.

Only in one centre did the Jewish resistance survive the fall of Jerusalem for a moment. Masada, the fortress on the Dead Sea, hitherto impregnable, still had a Jewish garrison, which fought as if final victory were in their grasp. The Romans had superior might and military proficiency. When at length it was obvious to the most fanatical of the defenders that their cause was hopeless, they killed themselves, men, women, and children, rather than surrender. Only a couple of women with their children, who had hidden themselves,

35. *The Ruins of Herod's Palace, Samaria*

36. *Samaria, modern Sebustya*

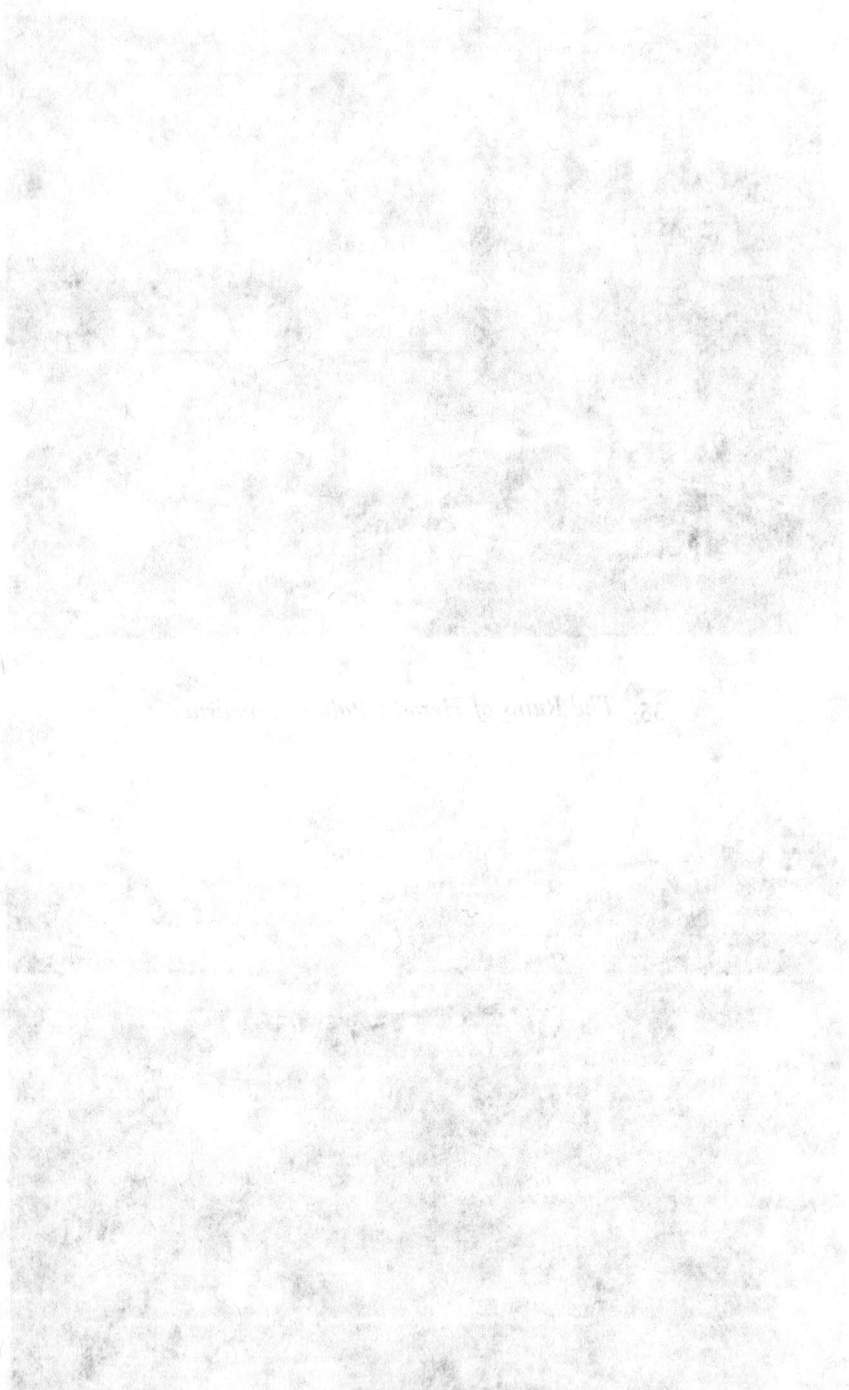

survived. This is accepted in Jewish history as the final extinction of the Jewish State, which had already long been a shadow.

But despite Roman massacres and expulsions, there was still a Jewish population in the country, degraded and impoverished, politically powerless, but spiritually renewing its strength, and with sufficient hope, or despair, to revolt again in 132 under Simon Bar Cochba, 'the Son of a Star', who had convinced himself and many followers that he was the Messiah. This revolt caused the Romans considerable difficulty for three years, and was suppressed ruthlessly. The last stand was at Bether, now Battir, still known as Khirbet el Yehud ('the Ruin of the Jews'), whose hill stands out prominently at the last station on the railway to Jerusalem.

*The Jews of the Dispersion*

Much more significant were the fortunes of Jewish communities outside Palestine. The forced migrations after the Assyrian conquest of Samaria (722 B.C. and later) to Mesopotamia and Media led to no permanent settlement. The 'exiles' to Babylonia, after Nebuchadnezzar's conquest of Jerusalem (597, 586, 582) were allowed by Cyrus to return in 537, but only some did so and more (some 5,000 persons) returned with Ezra, probably under Artaxerxes I (*c.* 457).[1] Others remained in Babylonia and were reinforced by later exiles under Artaxerxes III (358–338), when others were sent to Hyrcania. From these eastern centres many Jews spread through Persia, Media, Armenia, and parts of Asia Minor and elsewhere.

Refugees from Nebuchadnezzar's invasion joined an earlier settlement at Tahpanhes (Daphne) in the eastern delta of the Nile, and there was a community at Elephantine in upper Egypt under Persian rule. But the principal Jewish colony in Egypt was afterwards in Alexandria, where it occupied a large distinct quarter: later refugees under the high priest Onias settled at Heliopolis about 170 and built a temple. There were also many Jews in Cyrenaica under the Ptolemies.

From the Palestinian home, Jews spread also widely in Syria, after the death of their persecutor Antiochus IV Epiphanes (p. 89), and in Cilicia and many parts of Asia Minor under Roman rule. There were Jews in Greece before 150 B.C., a settlement of deported Jews in Rome after Pompey's reorganization of the East (63 B.C.), and another at Puteoli in Campania in 4 B.C. The Sephardim claimed to be descended from Jews who settled in Spain before the beginning of the

[1] Some historians assign this event to the reign of Artaxerxes II (*c.* 387 B.C.).

present era. St. Paul proposed to visit them on one of his missionary tours.[1]

Wherever there were ten Jewish settlers they formed an organized congregation for worship (*synagogue*) and for affairs, under an *ethnarch* ('national-leader'). Through the local communities funds were contributed to maintain the temple-worship at Jerusalem. From Julius Caesar and Augustus the Jews acquired distinct legal status, exemption from military service, and other privileges; but after the revolt and destruction of Jerusalem, these were strictly limited to religious matters. Some Jews, such as the family of Paul the Apostle, had full Roman citizenship. That many Jews became hellenized is clear from the translation of the Law and other sacred books into Greek at Alexandria about 250 B.C. And while some Jews may have lapsed altogether, there were certainly many converts to Judaism who made pilgrimage to Jerusalem in large numbers; and Jewish monotheism as expounded by Philo of Alexandria, an older contemporary of Jesus, influenced Greek and Roman thought and belief. There were, however, periodical persecutions under Tiberius (A.D. 19) and Caligula (A.D. 38).

## *Jews and Christians*

Bar Cochba's revolt marked the final breach between the Jews and the Christians. Hitherto the latter had been a part of the Jewish people, albeit heretics in religion. It was apparently St. Peter who realized that a man could be a follower of Jesus without being a Jew (*Acts* x); that the Christianity that was developing was something more than a reformed Judaism; and that it was no longer necessary to accept fully the Law, which was the kernel of Judaism. Thus there came to be two classes of Christians—Jewish Christians on whom the Jewish Law was binding, and other Christians on whom lay a lighter yoke. This development was probably not realized at the time. The leaders of the new movement were all Jews. There had long been a class of 'god-fearing' Gentiles, 'Proselytes of the Gate', men and women who accepted most of the teachings and many of the laws of Judaism, without formally entering the Jewish community. The earliest Gentile converts of the Christians were, if not solely, almost

---

[1] Lord Beaconsfield used to argue that, even if the Jews of to-day could be held responsible for the Crucifixion, his branch of Jewry, the Sephardim, were exempt, since they were living in Spain centuries before that event. Some of the Jewish communities of Germany, now destroyed, had histories that went back to the beginning of the present era when the Rhineland was on the frontier of the Empire and beyond it was only barbarism.

entirely among these. To Jews in general, these had never been true Jews, so there was no appreciable change.

Gradually, however, the new sect and the parent body became more widely separated; and as Christianity grew, Judaism became more hostile, foreseeing a struggle in which it might not, after all, be victor, and, if it were victor, could only be so after great anxiety and at a considerable price. Contempt for an insignificant group of heretics changed to fear of a religious rival. There was also, on the part of the Jews, the horror of law-breakers, though by no means all the Christians broke the Jewish Law; very many observed it even in details, and the first generation of Christians not only believed themselves to be Jews, but were accepted as such. A definite move towards separation was made by the Jews about the end of the first century when a passage was introduced into the Jewish daily ritual, so worded that no conscientious Christian could recite it. It is to this date, A.D. 80 or 90, that separation should be assigned. Thus doctrinal differences grew more acute. But while to the Jews the Christians were heretics, to the outside world they were Jews.

The refusal, however, of the Jewish Christians to join with their fellow Jews in the revolt of Bar Cochba put them irrevocably outside the pale. A national barrier was henceforth erected above the religious one between the two halves of Jewry. Hadrian, however, oppressed both equally, defiling and destroying alike the Holy Places of the Christians, the Jews, and the Samaritans. But the polytheistic Romans did not as a rule persecute religions, which were far too numerous in their empire to make anything but toleration practicable. Once extinguished politically, Jews were allowed to follow their religious lives without interference. After the death of Hadrian, Jewish scholars reopened their schools of learning in Galilee, which became, for centuries, a centre of Jewish scholarship. Here were composed the Palestinian *Talmud*, the inspiration of many generations of Jewry, and the *Zohar*, the Bible of Jewish mysticism.

The adoption of Christianity by Constantine (324) as the official religion of the Empire caused further change; for the Jews were considered enemies of Christendom, and for some centuries the lot of the Jews both in Palestine and in the Dispersion was unenviable. Under Julian (361–3) there was momentary relief and even official encouragement for rebuilding the Temple at Jerusalem, but his reign was brief, and darkness again descended on the Jewish people.

When the Empire was divided in 395, Palestine became a part of the Eastern or Byzantine system. There was occasional rebellion, but for

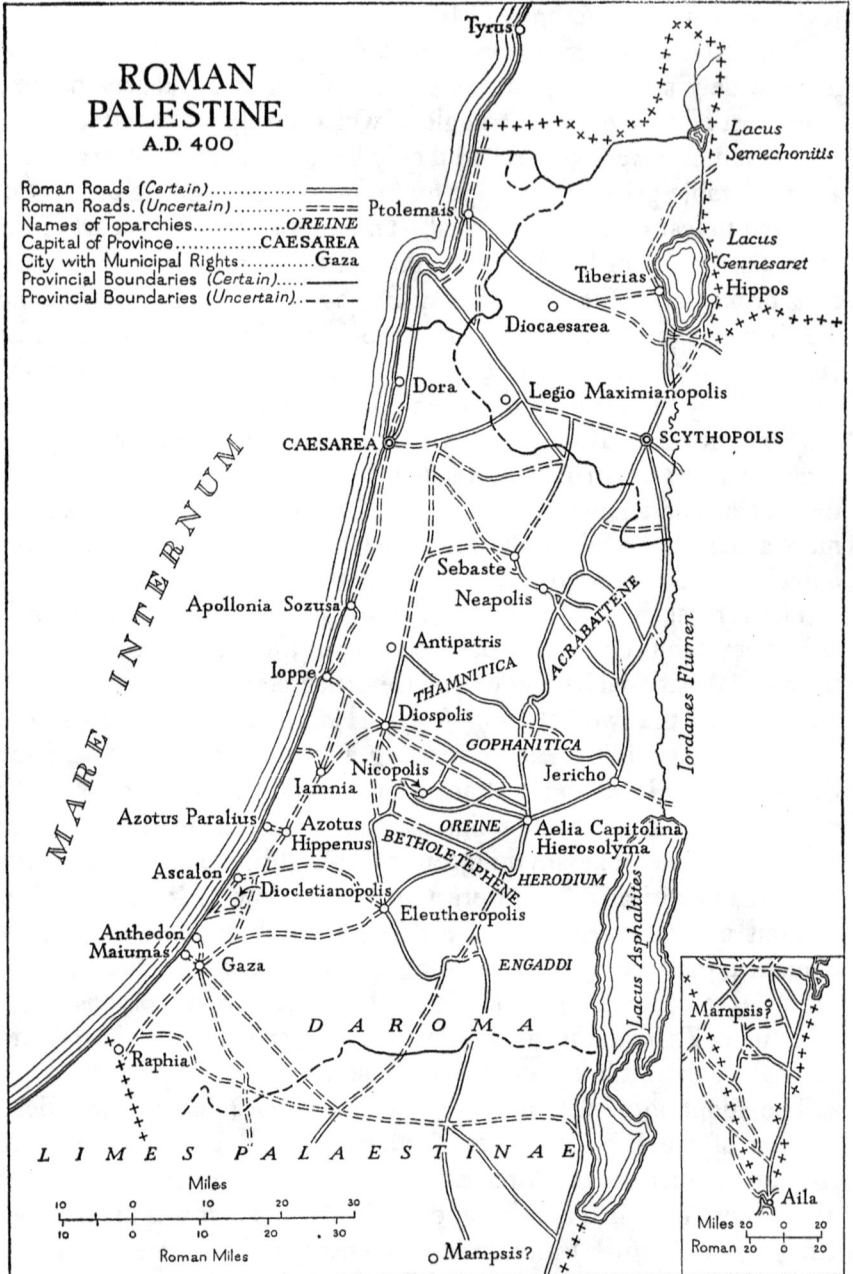

## ROMAN PALESTINE
### A.D. 400

Roman Roads (Certain)............... ═══
Roman Roads. (Uncertain)........... ════
Names of Toparchies...............*OREINE*
Capital of Province.............**CAESAREA**
City with Municipal Rights............Gaza
Provincial Boundaries (Certain).....═══
Provincial Boundaries (Uncertain)..─ ─ ─

Tyrus

*Lacus Semechonitis*

Ptolemais

*Lacus Gennesaret*

Tiberias
Hippos

Diocaesarea

Dora

Legio Maximianopolis

**CAESAREA**

SCYTHOPOLIS

*MARE INTERNUM*

Sebaste

Neapolis

*ACRABATTENE*

Apollonia Sozusa

Antipatris

*Iordanes Flumen*

Ioppe

*THAMNITICA*

Diospolis

*GOPHANITICA*

Nicopolis

Jericho

Iamnia

Azotus Paralius

Azotus
Hippenus

*BETHOLETEPHENE*

*OREINE*

Aelia Capitolina
Hierosolyma

Ascalon

*HERODIUM*

Diocletianopolis

Eleuteropolis

Anthedon
Maiumas

Gaza

*ENGADDI*

*Lacus Asphaltites*

D   A   R   O   M   A

Mampsis?

Raphia

Aila

*L   I   M   E   S      P   A   L   A   E   S   T   I   N   A   E*

Miles
10        0        10        20        30
10        0        10        20        . 30
Roman Miles

Miles 20    0    20
Roman 20   0    20

Mampsis?

FIG. 20.  *Roman Palestine*, A.D. 400

the most part the land had rest (fig. 20). It was a period of religious devotion, of the cult of the Holy Places, of road construction, of the great buildings of Justinian. Suddenly in 611 the Roman defences collapsed with the invasion of the Persians under Chosroes II. The Jews of Galilee joined the invaders, and for fourteen years the Christians suffered severely. Jerusalem was sacked in 614, the Church of the Holy Sepulchre was burned, and the Holy Cross carried to Persia. But the Jews also suffered, and the peace which restored Syria and Palestine to Byzantium in 628 was at first welcomed by both. The hatred, however, of the Christian monks for the Jews was insatiable and after only a year or two the Jews of Palestine were exterminated, except those who fled to the desert or into exile.

### 3. ARAB AND LATIN RULE

*The Arab Conquest*

The end of the Byzantine period was now at hand. Roman frontier guards were familiar already with the Saracens, one of many tribes of nomad raiders, who gave their name to the general Arab force which arose suddenly within the desert. There had long been a large caravan traffic, both between Mesopotamian and Syrian centres, and from Yemen by the west coast of Arabia to Egypt and through Palestine northwards, as well as east of the Dead Sea from Petra, by Gerasa (Jerash) to Damascus (p. 442). To protect these important trade-routes the Romans had supported the Hasmonean and the Herodian dynasties. Later, the Ghassanids, vassals of Rome, and the Lakhmids, subsidized by Parthia, controlled the wide desert region between Parthia and Roman Syria: both were Christian, and had intimate relations with the Arab tribes to the south, among whom both Christianity and Judaism had spread. But by the seventh century these frontier states had decayed, and the sheikhs of more or less Christianized Arabs provided levies for frontier defence against Saracen and other marauders.

What changed the whole situation was the creation of a new trading-centre at Mecca, on the western road, by an exceptionally gifted tribe, the Koreish. This depended, like the older trading-centres, on the security of the caravan-routes, by which Meccan caravans reached Gaza or Damascus. In a local quarrel with the richer Koreish, Mohammad and his first adherents made their famous 'flight' to Medina in 622, whence they intercepted the north-bound traffic and became rich and numerous. A raid on Mutah, east of the Dead Sea, in 629 was defeated, and Mohammad died in 632 (p. 448).

Mohammad's teaching, as was to be expected in the circumstances of his life, owed something both to Judaism and to Christianity, but far more to its repudiation of the more controversial doctrines of both creeds, which divided men rather than united them, and to its insistence on the five essentials—surrender (*islam*) to the will of God revealed through the Prophet, prayer, fasting, charity, and pilgrimage—the last a concession to the vested interest of Mecca in its pre-Islamic sanctuary. On the common ground of surrender to God, every Moslem found brotherhood and freedom from man's oppression; and it was not till after 900, and after much experience of controversy among sects of its own, that Islam was given philosophic basis by Ashari. This system, definite and immutable, and embodied in the Prophet's writings (the *Koran*), was administered after the founder's death by a popularly elected 'successor' (*khalifa* or *caliph*), who in fact nominated the next, and chose his own 'helper' (*wazir*) and other officers. Universal military service, habitual among desert folk, and brought to high efficiency for the defence (and attack) of a caravan, supplied the needs of the fighting force by organized raiding, and recruited this warrior caste by voluntary enlistment of conquered peoples; for the choice offered them was between conversion, which presumed co-operation in the 'holy war' (*jehad*); submission, which meant tributary autonomy; and suppression. By wise management, the second of these was made preferable to the third, and the first to the second; with the result that the warrior class, which paid no tribute, tended to outgrow revenue, and depended for subsistence on further conquest, while association in conquest rallied tribes and peoples, hitherto self-governed, behind the military colonies, such as Basra and Kufa, which defended the early frontiers, and inevitably acquired political as well as strategical significance. In each conquered territory the 'canon law' of Islam, sacred and immutable, did not displace, but was supplemented by, a 'civil law' based in each region on local usage (*adat*) and the ordinances of rulers (*gervanin*).

### Arab Rule in Palestine

Abu Bekr, the successor of Mohammad, attacked south Palestine with larger forces in 634, while Khalid ibn Walid raided the Persian outpost at Hira farther east, and then, crossing the desert westwards, threatened Damascus. The Byzantine army in Palestine was defeated between Jerusalem and Gaza. Abu Bekr died soon after, but under the new caliph Omar, Khalid in 635 received the surrender of

Damascus from the civil population, which welcomed the Arabs as deliverers from Byzantine misrule. Though compelled to withdraw, his victory over the emperor's new levies on the Yarmuk river in 636 was decisive (p. 450). Mesopotamia was overrun in 637, Egypt conquered in 640, Persia defeated in 641, and the Byzantine fleet destroyed in 655.

The Arab victory was of supreme importance for the future of Islam and therefore for the history of the world. Two of its causes were the weakness of the Byzantine Empire and the preference of the Syrian population for Arab rule. The military efficiency of the invaders is not so easily determined. Individually they were brave and practised combatants with sword and bow. Their leaders were experienced in minor warfare, and evidently were skilful enough to adapt the tactics and strategy of the desert to greater tasks. On the other hand, the invaders were severely tested only during the battle of the Yarmuk, and it may be that defects in the opposing army and the accident of a sand-storm turned the scale in their favour. Other alleged causes—that they were an army of horsemen, or that they owed their success to enormous numbers—do not bear critical examination. Most of the Arabs fought on foot, and became great horsemen only after conquering the horse-ranches of Syria and Persia. At the Yarmuk a maximum estimate is 24,000 men, and 10,000 more likely; and the invasion of Egypt in 639 was begun with 4,000 men. The part played by the new faith, also, has probably been overstated, and perhaps misconceived. The popular view, supported by Moslem tradition, that the Arabs set out to conquer the world for their faith, can hardly be maintained. The influence of Islam consisted rather in this, that in virtue of a common faith, the Arab tribes for the first time acted together, and that a common direction and purpose were secured by the authority of the caliphs, the 'successors' of Mohammad.

Henceforth, for almost 1,300 years, with the exception of the brief Crusade period (1099–1291) Palestine was a Moslem province, under Arab rule and later under Turkish. Christians and Jews alike had only the religious liberty, and the limited civil status, of subject nationalities (*millets*) under their religious chiefs, and were liable to tribute. For the full political and civil rights of Islam are entrusted only to Moslems.

Even before the Arab conquest there had been immigration into Palestine from Arabia; and the conquest inevitably increased this. Moreover, the native population, a conglomerate, only superficially

hellenized and christianized, of many races and peoples that had
successively settled 'this side of Jordan' since the dawn of history,
soon for the most part accepted Islam, and spoke Arabic instead of the
kindred Aramaic or Syriac. Most important of all, Omar's conquest
brought peace. Palestine was no longer a frontier province towards
Parthia, nor a battle-field between Egypt and western Asia; and under
the genial administration of Moawiya, from 656 till he was proclaimed caliph at Jerusalem in 660, its people were able to live their
own lives, undisturbed either by war or by persecution. For it is
clear from the continued use and repair of churches and synagogues
alike, at Gerasa in Transjordan and elsewhere, that the deep an-
tagonism between new faith and old arose later. Arabic did not even
become the official language till 694, and the first Moslem coinage is
of about the same date. The transference of the capital of the caliphate from Mecca to Damascus in 661 brought Palestine nearer to the
centre of affairs. Moreover, to the Moslems, as to Jews and Christians,
Jerusalem was a holy city, and in 684–691 Abd el Malik further
weakened the prestige of Mecca by beautifying Jerusalem and com-
pleting the 'Dome of the Rock'. The replacement of the Omayyad
dynasty by the Abbasid (749) ended the original supremacy of the
Arabs. The transference of the caliphate from Damascus to Baghdad
in 750 shifted the Moslem centre eastward, and, in view of the extension of Islam over what had been Parthian and Persian dominions,
diminished the prestige and prosperity of Palestine. The new mixed
armies of foreign mercenaries included more and more Turki and
Mongol adventurers; and the authority of the caliphs in Baghdad was
challenged by heretical as well as dynastic opponents. The Car-
mathian revolt in Africa (895–919) and pillage of Mecca (929) drove
many Moslems to Jerusalem; and when the Fatimite caliphs, claiming
descent from the Prophet's daughter, invaded Egypt from the west
(969) and declared themselves independent, Palestine suffered once
more, as under the successors of Alexander (p. 89), from the quarrels
of powerful neighbours, and became intermittently a frontier province
of Egypt. Whereas Harun ar Rashid had granted to Charlemagne
access and facilities for Christian pilgrims to the 'Holy Places', and
the Church of the Holy Sepulchre had been rebuilt in 831, a new
fanaticism is illustrated under the Tulunids and other military adventurers, Arab, Turk, and Mongol, in the destruction of the Church of
the Holy Sepulchre by the mad Fatimid, Hakim Bi-amrillah (996),
and by the rise of the Druses and other heretical sects in Syria. There
were fierce revolts in Palestine in 1011–1013 and 1024–1029. In 1072

Baghdad employed Seljuk Turks[1] to invade Syria and Palestine. Damascus and Jerusalem were captured, and there was much devastation, but the projected invasion of Egypt was repelled, and Palestine was recovered by the Fatimids.

### The Crusades: A.D. 1097–1291

It was the sufferings of the Palestinian Christians, and the devastation of their 'Holy Places' by Seljuks and Fatimids alike, that roused the indignation of Peter the Hermit, a soldier from Picardy, who made pilgrimage in 1093, and through his preaching inspired the Crusades, the first invasion of the East by the West since Alexander and the Romans. The opponents of the West were two: Byzantium and Islam. The Eastern Empire had long been in decay, although it endured until the fifteenth century. Though it tolerated the first Crusaders, it became their prey in 1204 for two generations. Islam was far tougher, and when the Crusaders finally retired from Palestine in 1291, Islam was stronger there than ever. There were many Crusades, but the First (1097–1099), which led to the conquest of Palestine, and the Third (1189–1192), sent in vain to recover Jerusalem after the defeat of Guy de Lusignan at Hattin (1187), are the most important.

The First Crusade falls into two parts. The earlier was a Peoples' Crusade, excited by wandering preachers, of whom Peter the Hermit is the best known. It was in five divisions, three of which were destroyed before they reached Constantinople; the other two in Asia Minor by the Seljuk Turks. The other part, the Crusade of the Princes, was more successful. Of its many contingents, the most important were those of Lorraine under Godfrey de Bouillon and his brother Baldwin, who reached Constantinople on 23 December 1096;

[1] The Seljuk 'Sultans of Rum' in Anatolia, A.D. 1067–1300 (for whom see the Handbook, *Turkey*, vol. i, pp. 282–284), took little part in affairs south of Taurus, but their relations with the Seljuks of Baghdad should be noted. In 1040 the Oghuz Turks of western Asia, recently conquered by the Arabs and converted to Islam, overthrew their conquerors and occupied Merv. Hence, under the leadership of the Seljuk clan, they spread westward to found four main principalities, Iran, Kerman (S. Persia), Syria, and eventually Rum (i.e. 'Roman' Anatolia): Togrul Beg joined the service of the last Abbasid caliph about 1050, and occupied Baghdad in 1055. He was by no means the first Turkish mercenary in the service of the Abbasids. Though originally not very numerous, and wandering herdsmen rather than warriors, the Seljuks easily imposed their rule over the settled populations, without destroying or displacing them, while they adopted Arab and Persian cultures, and combined them with Greek craftsmanship, as their fine buildings show. They left no literature, but their Ottoman successors owed much to their administrative experience.

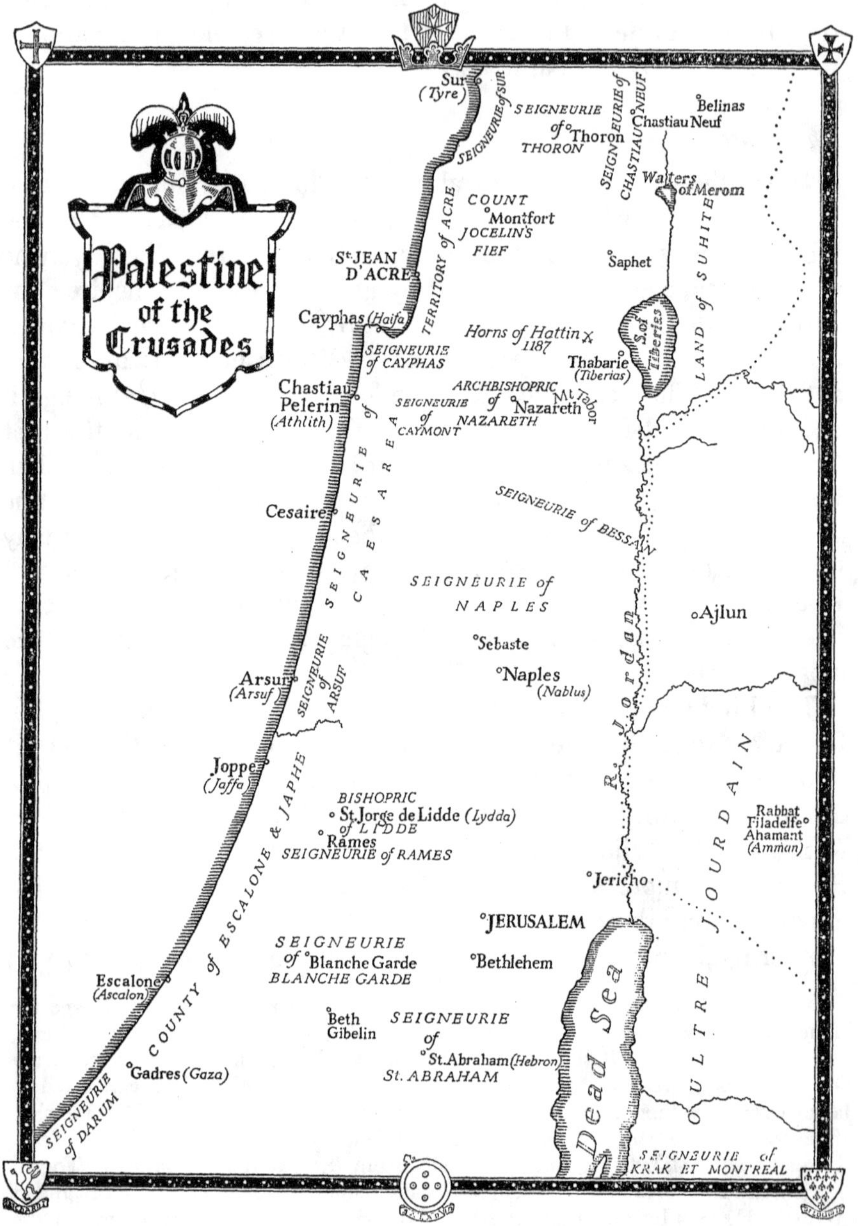

Palestine
of the
Crusades

Sur
(Tyre)

SEIGNEURIE of SUR

SEIGNEURIE
of Thoron
THORON

SEIGNEURIE of
CHASTIAU NEUF

Belinas
Chastiau Neuf

Walters
of Merom

COUNT
Montfort
JOCELIN'S
FIEF

Saphet

St JEAN
D'ACRE

TERRITORY of ACRE

LAND of SUHITE

Cayphas (Haifa)

SEIGNEURIE
of CAYPHAS

Horns of Hattin X
1187

Thabarie
(Tiberias)

S. of
Tiberias

Chastiau
Pelerin
(Athlith)

SEIGNEURIE
of
CAYMONT

ARCHBISHOPRIC
of Nazareth
NAZARETH

Mt Tabor

SEIGNEURIE of CAESAREA

SEIGNEURIE of BESSAN

Cesaire

SEIGNEURIE of
NAPLES

Ajlun

R. Jordan

Sebaste

Arsur
(Arsuf)

SEIGNEURIE
of
ARSUF

Naples
(Nablus)

Joppe
(Jaffa)

COUNTY of ESCALONE & JAPHE

BISHOPRIC
St Jorge de Lidde (Lydda)
of LIDDE
Rames
SEIGNEURIE of RAMES

OULTRE JOURDAIN

Rabbat
Filadelfe
Ahamant
(Amman)

Jericho

JERUSALEM

SEIGNEURIE
of Blanche Garde
BLANCHE GARDE

Bethlehem

Escalone
(Ascalon)

Beth
Gibelin

SEIGNEURIE
of
St.Abraham (Hebron)
St. ABRAHAM

Dead Sea

SEIGNEURIE
of DARUM

Gadres (Gaza)

SEIGNEURIE of
KRAK ET MONTREAL

FIG. 21. *Palestine of the Crusades*

the Provençals under Raymund of Toulouse and the Papal Commissary, Bishop Adhemar, who joined them in the following April; and the Normans, mainly from south Italy, who assembled at Durazzo under Bohemund of Otranto and his nephew Tancred, and arrived in Palestine about the same time. Others, under Hugh of Vermandois, a brother of the King of France, Robert of Normandy, Stephen of Blois, and Count Robert of Flanders, had joined them in Constantinople. The size of these armies has been variously estimated, from 150,000 to 600,000, but only about 40,000 reached Palestine. Dissensions and jealousies broke out among the princes and nobles, almost as soon as they met. Some were sincerely inspired by religious motives; others thought more of the things of this world, and looked forward to be ruling princes rather than penitents and pilgrims. Thus, Bohemund carved out for himself a principality of Antioch, Baldwin the county of Edessa, and Raymund that of Tripoli, all before entering the Holy Land.

The route of the invaders was overland from Constantinople, through Asia Minor and Syria, then in the recent occupation, not everywhere effective, of the Seljuk Turks. The Byzantine Emperor was not reconciled to their loss; and in eastern Asia Minor survived Armenian principalities, the sympathies of whose rulers and peoples were likewise with the Christian invaders. Moreover, the inhabitants as a whole were hostile to the Seljuks. Among the Seljuks themselves there was dissension; the last of their great emperors, Kaikhosru II, had recently died, and his empire had fallen to pieces. There was also hostility between the Shia caliph of Cairo and the Sunni princes of Syria. All these circumstances helped the Crusaders.

In May 1097 the Crusaders crossed the Bosporus, and with the help of the Emperor Alexius besieged and took Nicaea (*mod.* Iznik). A fortnight later the Seljuks were defeated in battle at Dorylaeum (*mod.* Eskişehir) and the Crusaders marched south-east towards Heraclea (*mod.* Erc̣gli). Here Tancred and Baldwin turned southward into Cilicia and began to carve out the principality of Antioch. The main army, however, turned north-east to make touch with the Armenians, and then south towards Antioch, in besieging which from 21 October 1097 to 3 June 1098 some assistance was received from Genoese ships in St. Simeon, the port of Antioch.

After renewed disputes the army moved south-east and was kept three months by the fruitless siege of Arka near Tripoli. At this point Godfrey de Bouillon took control of affairs. Bohemund remained in Antioch; the others pressed forward along the coast, following the route of so many earlier conquerors, and then, turning inland, besieged Jerusalem, which submitted after a month's siege on 15 July 1099. In the march from Antioch along or near the coast further assistance was rendered by Italian ships which supplied not only provisions and munitions but men and material for the sieges of Antioch and Jerusalem. The capture of Jerusalem was celebrated by a massacre of all the Moslems and Jews in the city. Palestine became the kingdom of Jerusalem, and in Syria the principality of Antioch and the counties of Tripoli and Edessa were only little inferior in status (fig. 21).

It is usual to speak of a series of separate Crusades, but the whole period of the Latin kingdom comprised one continuous Crusade, recruits coming to the kings of Jerusalem in an almost uninterrupted stream. By this means alone was the kingdom kept in existence. The Second Crusade in 1146, preached by St. Bernard, was led by Louis VII of France and Conrad III of Germany. The Crusaders from northern Germany, however, were permitted to fulfil their vows by attacking their heathen neighbours, the Wends, and did not turn towards the Holy Land at all. Those of Scandinavia, the Low Countries, and England went by sea, and on the way drove the Moors from Lisbon and founded the kingdom of Portugal. When at length these detachments reached the East, they were practically the only forces that Conrad had at his disposal. The armies of Conrad and Louis kept apart until they joined King Baldwin, by which time they had for the most part wasted away. The combined forces attacked Damascus and failed.

## The Latin Kingdom

From 1099 until the rise of Saladin (1173–1193) the Latin kingdom enjoyed relative peace and prosperity. The government was of feudal type with a king and powerful nobles almost independent of him. Its weakness was the great gulf between the small governing class of western adventurers and the native population. To remedy this weakness, or to lessen it, the fighting force had to be continually replenished from the west. This made the Latin kingdom in effect a dependency of Europe, in some respects of the Papacy. The Latin Church was established in Palestine, and its Patriarch, though elected by the clergy, was confirmed by the Pope. The Latin Patriarch was independent of the king, and at times rivalled him in power. There were also the Christian Orders of Knighthood, the Hospitallers of St. John, the Templars, and the Teutonic Knights, powerful and wealthy, owing spiritual allegiance to the Pope, but in temporal matters independent of him, as well as of the king. Godfrey de Bouillon, the leader of the First Crusade and the conqueror of Jerusalem, refused the title of king. He would not wear a crown where his Master had suffered, but took the title of 'Protector of the Holy Sepulchre'. His successors, however, had no such qualms. They were kings of Jerusalem in name as well as in fact, and for centuries after the expulsion of the last of them, European rulers continued to enjoy this empty title, as their heirs and nominal successors. The kings of Jerusalem being in origin Franks or French—in the wide medieval sense—the French Government later put forward the claim, accepted by the Ottoman Sultan in 1535, to protect the Christian, or later the Catholic, population of the Levant: it was also, on the termination of the war with Turkey in 1918, the historical basis for the grant of a French Mandate to protect Syria and the Lebanon; the original claim covered Palestine also.

The separation between the governing class and the people did not persist; gradually the two began to merge. Inevitably, the more numerous gained the upper hand, and in the resulting amalgam the East was more apparent than the West. As has happened often in Levantine history, western Asia consumed its European guests or masters: the Crusaders' memorials are vast ruined castles and churches, a few place-names, and periodical outbursts of fanaticism among their Moslem subjects.

The Third Crusade, which touches English history most closely, began in 1189. Like the First, it was a war for the recovery of the Holy Sepulchre, for Jerusalem had fallen to the Saracens at Hattin and Tiberias two years earlier. It was led by the three great kings of Europe; Philip Augustus of France, the Emperor Frederick I of Germany, and Richard Cœur de Lion of England. The rivalries between these monarchs precluded success. The one place in Palestine that remained in Christian hands was the foothold of the army that for two years had been besieging Acre (fig. 21). This army was the focus of the new Crusade. The Moslem enemy was Saladin, the Kurdish general of Nureddin, Seljuk ruler of north Syria since 1146: he had conquered Egypt in 1173, and taken Jerusalem from Guy de Lusignan in 1187. The German contingents left Regensburg in May 1189, crossed Hungary, entered the dominions of the Eastern Empire, and passed into Asia Minor, marching west of the route of the First Crusaders. On the river Salef (the Gök Su in Cilicia), the Emperor Frederick died after an accident. His troops marched on, but of the army that left Europe only a thousand men survived to reach Acre.

The English and French contingents travelled together by sea. A winter in Sicily led to quarrels between Philip Augustus and Richard, and in the spring they separated. Philip sailed straight for Acre. Richard captured Cyprus on the way. He reached Acre on 8 June, and within less than five weeks Acre was captured. But the quarrels of Richard and Philip here broke out again and were embittered by those between Guy de Lusignan and Conrad of Montferrat, rival claimants to the kingdom that no longer existed. Philip Augustus returned to France, and Richard was left as outstanding leader. He had some successes, took Arsuf, Joppa (Jaffa), and Ascalon on the coast, and arranged a truce for three years by which the coast from Tyre to Jaffa was left in the hands of the Crusaders. But the Crusade had failed; the Holy Sepulchre had not been recovered; Jerusalem remained in infidel hands. Richard never entered the Holy City. He marched far enough inland for it to be seen—to the height now known as Nebi Samwil—according to Moslem traditions, the burial-place of the prophet Samuel. But Richard averted his gaze. If he was not worthy to recover for Christendom the Holy City, he said, he was not worthy to look upon it.

Later Crusades effected little. The long-deferred Sixth took place in 1227 under the Emperor Frederick II, but under Papal ban, on account of secular disputes. In February 1229 he secured by treaty ten years possession of Jerusalem and the other Christian Holy Cities, with a corridor to Acre, which was still in Frank possession, and crowned himself King of Jerusalem on 18 March. But he could not celebrate the services of the Church there, since every city in which he set foot was placed under Papal interdict. Jerusalem, Nazareth, and Bethlehem remained under Christian rule for fifteen years; but the hold of the Crusaders became precarious and reinforcements were excommunicated. Even to hold the Holy City no assistance was to be given to the enemies of the Pope. One of these expeditions, in 1240–1241, was led by Richard of Cornwall, brother of Henry III of England. In the end the Franks allied themselves with the ruler of Damascus against the Sultan of Egypt. Deserted by their allies at the battle of Gaza, they were defeated by the Egyptians under Beibars, afterwards Sultan, and Jerusalem passed out of Christian control in 1244. Ascalon fell three years later and Acre itself in 1291.

Meanwhile Saladin's dominion had been broken by Mongol invaders, some uninvited, others summoned by Damascus or by Egypt, where the *Mamluks* (military slaves) of the Fatimid dynasty long maintained themselves. Another invasion of central Asian tribes, under

Hulagu Khan, who had taken Baghdad in 1258, was repulsed near Jezreel by the Mamluks in 1260, and Palestine remained for 200 years a dependency of Egypt. The raids of Genghiz Khan (1225–1227) and Tamerlane (1401) damaged Syria more than Palestine, and expended their violence in Anatolia. In the intervals between invasions, Palestine shared in the prosperity which Syria enjoyed through its caravan trade. It was only when the discovery of the Cape route to the Indies by the Portuguese (1498) diverted much of this trade at its sources that these western depots were paralysed (p. 453).

## 4. The Ottoman Empire

### The Ottoman Empire

Like the Seljuks, the Ottoman Turks had been driven out of central Asia by Mongol tribes. In 1227 they were reluctantly given land near Ankara by the Seljuk Sultan of Konya. There Othman (Osman I, 1288–1326) made himself powerful and independent, and his followers became known by his name. His son Orkhan captured Brusa (1326), Nicomedia, and Nicaea, struck back at other Moslem principalities of Anatolia, and secured foothold in Europe (1335) at Gallipoli, Bulair, and Rodosto. Under Murad, Adrianople became the Ottoman capital (1367); his son Bayazid (1396) was recognized by the caliph in Egypt as 'Sultan of the Land of Rum'. In 1453 Mohammad II captured Constantinople and reorganized the Ottoman Empire, which now included the troublesome Karamanian principalities of south-eastern Anatolia and most of the Greek islands. The Knights of St. John, however, held out in Rhodes till 1523, the Genoese in Cyprus till 1571, and the Venetians in Crete nearly a century longer.

Selim I conquered the Mamluk rulers of Egypt in 1517, occupied Syria and the Hejaz, and obtained from the last Abbasid Caliph, Mutawakkil, the title of Caliph and the custody of the sacred banner of the Prophet. Of more practical significance was the reunion of all the resources of Islam, from the Tigris and the Nile to the Danube, under the Ottoman Sultans, only qualified by the rivalry between Sunni Turks and Shia Persians—accentuated by the expulsion of Shias from the dominions of Selim I—and by internal contrasts between the provinces north of the Taurus, which retained much of their Byzantine heritage of culture, and those to the south and east, which had accepted Islam to be rid of Constantinople—Emperor and Patriarch alike—and which had adopted not only the creed and the language but also the culture of the Arabs, matured under the convergent influences of Egypt, Persia, and Syria itself.

Ottoman rule in Palestine lasted just 400 years, from Selim's conquest in 1517 to the capture of Jerusalem by British forces in 1917. At first Ottoman rule, in Palestine as elsewhere, was efficient. Jerusalem was heavily fortified, on the old lines, in 1537 (p. 327) and much new building was undertaken, in the best period of Turkish architecture which followed Seljuk models. But, in spite of occasional revivals, its deterioration is marked by local revolts of Daher el Omar and Ahmed el Jazzar at Acre: the latter in 1791 expelled French traders who had been there for more than a century.

## Napoleon's Invasion

Napoleon, occupying Egypt in 1799, was threatened by Turkish forces organized in Syria by Ahmed el Jazzar. At the same time a British fleet was off the coast. Having pacified Egypt temporarily, Napoleon determined to strike before he was attacked. He sent four divisions, about 13,000 men in all, across the desert of Sinai with instructions to join forces at El Arish. For his heavy artillery the desert seemed too difficult, and despite the British blockade he decided to send it by sea, to take advantage of the shallow coastal waters, where the British frigates could not close the land. El Arish was easily taken and the combined army entered Palestine. At Gaza, forward enemy troops were dispersed, and the town submitted without opposition. Napoleon, in his dispatch to the Directory, boasted that he had beaten the enemy on the very spot on which Samson had carried off the Gates of Gaza.

Jaffa was more vigorously defended, but at a cost of a thousand men it was stormed after a forty-eight hours' siege, the defenders fighting from street to street. It illustrates the heterogeneous collection of peoples in Palestine that the garrison consisted of men in various costumes and of all colours, *Magharbeh* from north Africa, Albanians, Kurds, Anatolians, Karamanians, Damascenes, natives of Aleppo, and black men from Tekrour. Five thousand troops surrendered when Jaffa fell and were granted their lives; but Napoleon overruled such leniency. He had those prisoners who belonged to the towns on his prospective march set aside. The remainder, 3,800, were butchered in cold blood, to the horror even of his own officers. Jaffa was made the base of the invaders, and from there Napoleon issued a proclamation to the people of Palestine to the effect that he had come to deliver them from the Mamluk of Egypt and from Jazzar.

The problem before Napoleon was now the same as that which has confronted all invaders from the south, before and since. To reach Damascus and northern Syria it was necessary to strike inland over Carmel and the hills of Samaria and to secure the Jordan crossings. The communications to these pass through the plain of Esdraelon, which is open to the west at the bay of Acre, and they are secure only if the invader has command of the sea. Napoleon had not that command and was therefore forced to divert part of his strength required for the conquest of Syria in order to seize Haifa and the key fortress of Acre.

The double task in a hostile country proved impossible. Kléber's division occupied Haifa without opposition, but a British naval division under Sir Sidney Smith blockaded the port and on 16 March captured the artillery which was being sent by sea for the storming of Acre. The result of this setback was that, after ten days of preparation, the assaults were beaten back with heavy losses and Napoleon had to settle down to siege warfare.

Meanwhile other French columns under Murat and Junot, engaged in clearing the way to the Jordan crossings, were continuously harassed by Jazzar's troops and irregulars. Junot was surprised at Nazareth and driven out; Kléber was in difficulties in the same neighbourhood; the French in Safad were suffering a minor siege; Murat alone was successful at Jisr Banat Yakub, the Jordan crossing south of Lake Huleh. To resolve these difficulties Napoleon had to intervene with troops required for the capture of Acre, and thus gave time for reinforcements to be brought up by sea for its defence.

Napoleon's policy of striking terror into the population by burning their villages and massacring the inhabitants cowed the survivors for a time and enabled him to renew the siege of Acre. But it was too late. British marines and the captured guns were now taking part in the defence. Assault after assault was driven back with heavy loss, and when after two months of siege a breach was made and for a short time the French flag flew on a part of the ramparts, the French were routed by British seamen, supported by gunfire from the ships, and pursued by fresh Turkish reinforcements which had arrived by sea at the critical hour. The tide had turned. A last desperate assault led by Napoleon was decisively beaten.

The defeat before Acre was the ruin of Napoleon's hopes. The whole country rose against the invaders, and Napoleon had to face the truth that without command of the sea he could neither conquer the country nor hold it. Disease broke out in his army, and there was

incipient mutiny. There was no alternative but retreat. The siege
was raised on 20 May. The wounded and such guns as could be
removed were embarked at Jaffa, but were captured by the British.

The line of retreat to Gaza was strewn with dead and abandoned
material. The column was harassed by Arabs and by British who
landed in small boats from the sea. Everything on the line of march,
including the town of Jaffa, was destroyed by the French, and as far
as Khan Yunis near the Egyptian frontier the plain looked like a sea
of fire from the burning crops. Gaza had conducted itself peaceably
and was spared, though its fortifications were razed to the ground
and a fine of £1,000,000 was imposed on its inhabitants. The
wretched peasantry of the surrounding country were left destitute.
This ended Napoleon's attempt on Palestine and Syria. Years later,
contemplating the past in his exile on St. Helena, he dated the beginning of his decline and fall, not from Moscow but from Acre, the
scene of his first defeat.

### Mehemet Ali

In the confused years which followed, Mehemet Ali, an Albanian
in the Turkish service, massacred his Mamluk masters (1811),
became ruler of Egypt, and made himself indispensable to the Sultan
during the Greek War of Independence. When the Sultan suspected
and attacked him in 1831, he invaded Palestine and Syria, stormed
Acre in 1832, and defeated the Turkish army at Nisib (Nizip) in
1839.

His intrigues with the Powers nearly involved them in a general
war, but he was compelled to withdraw from Syria, which had revolted, and he was compensated by recognition as hereditary pasha of
Egypt. Mehemet's representative in Syria and Palestine was his son
Ibrahim, who also commanded his armies. Ibrahim's rule was just
but heavy, and was interrupted by revolts. The eventual withdrawal
of the Egyptians was forced by the Powers supporting Turkey, among
which Britain took the lead. A European fleet, mainly British, attacked
the Syrian coast towns. The peoples of Syria and Palestine, at first
not hostile to the Egyptians, found them hard taskmasters. Their
attitude consequently changed, and by the last months of the
Egyptian occupation the people as a whole were on the side of their
former Turkish masters and their allies. In the course of their retreat,
the armies of Mehemet suffered much at the hands of Arab irregulars.

The share of the allied fleet in the reconquest of Syria in 1840 was
important. The camp at Juneh bay, where the invading force landed,

was secured by its guns. The rapid blows at widely separated points
on the coast were made possible by the transport and gunfire which it
provided. The cutting of Ibrahim's sea-communications with Egypt
was a deadly blow when the Syrians turned against him. These easy
triumphs of the allies over the coast towns were much beyond what
may normally be expected from such operations. Only Acre was
strongly fortified. The capture of Sidon in a single day and the surrender of Acre after a few hours' bombardment were obviously due to
the cowardice and demoralization of the Egyptian garrisons. Beirut
was held for more than a month against a combined attack by sea and
land, and the principal achievement of the fleet at this point was the
landing of the allied forces. The garrison of Tripoli was withdrawn
by Ibrahim, although it was not attacked. Jubeil, Haifa, and Jaffa
could not be, and were not, seriously defended.

On 26 October the Turkish admiral summoned the town of Acre to
surrender, but the demand was rejected. On 3 November the allied
squadron, under Admiral Sir Robert Stafford, began the attack on the
fortress which was believed to be almost impregnable. About midday
*Phoenix* opened fire and soon the action became general. The squadron
was stationed in two divisions, as the town and fortress of Acre presented two points to the sea. Commodore Napier in *Powerful* led the
way to the northward, closely followed by four other ships of war,
while five other British frigates, with the Turkish and Austrian vessels,
stood to the south. The frigate *Castor* took up her position about 700
yards from the batteries, which poured forth a tremendous and in-
cessant fire. By half-past five the defending guns had been silenced,
and a small boat having reported in the middle of the night that the
Egyptian troops were leaving the town, 300 Turks and a party of
Austrian marines landed at daybreak and took possession without
opposition. The havoc made by the guns of the squadron in the walls
and town was great, but, notwithstanding the long-continued fire
from the batteries, the ships escaped with little damage. The allied
losses were only 14 British and 4 Turks killed and 42 wounded. This
attack on Acre was, it would seem, the first occasion on which the
advantages of steam were employed in battle. Four steamships were
engaged in the action, and their guns did great execution; for the new
motive force enabled them, with rapidity, to take up the most ad-
vantageous positions. No previous bombardment of a coast town had
been so quickly successful. It took the allied fleet only a few hours
in 1840 to capture the town. Eight years earlier, in 1831–1832,
Ibrahim had, with the support of the surrounding population, spent

six months to secure it. The victors in 1840 lost 18 killed and 42 wounded; in 1832 about 4,000 killed and wounded with 2,000 deaths from disease.

### Ottoman Rule in the Nineteenth Century

During the early years of the nineteenth century the rule of the Sultan in Palestine was not very effective. He appointed governors and they duly took up office, but, as a rule, local chieftains practically ignored them, and ruled in their own right. Prominent among these was Ahmed el Jazzar (p. 110), Pasha of Acre, who had annexed also the district of Gaza. His nominee and successor, Suleiman Pasha, whom the Porte felt it best in the circumstances to accept, annexed Damascus and Tripoli, and for twenty years a large part of Syria acknowledged him as its ruler, and Acre as its capital city. Tribute and a shadowy acknowledgement were paid to the Sultan, and these seemed to satisfy him. Apart from the Gaza district, about this period, Transjordan, the Nablus district, the Jordan valley, and the Hebron district were more or less independent of Constantinople. The relations of the people to their rulers were approximately feudal, the nobles or chieftains being the descendants of men who either by character or by valour had earned their selection as heads of their communities. Ibrahim, during the Egyptian occupation, suppressed most of these small independent or semi-independent rulers, and when he had to withdraw from the country, the Sultan inherited the improvement. Another service, which continued after the Egyptian occupation, was the introduction of Palestine and Syria to Europe. After medieval pilgrimages ceased, the Levant had become almost unknown country to Europeans, but in the time of Ibrahim began a new trail, not of pilgrims, but of travellers, who often published their impressions. Among English travellers and writers were politicians and missionaries.

### The European Powers

One result of Mehemet Ali's revolt and expulsion from Palestine was a revival of interest in Palestine among the European Powers. There had been rivalry between the English and the French almost since the opening of modern history. Syria, lying on the road to India and the Far East, had been a subject of interest to both peoples or their governments since the end of the sixteenth century. France had been accepted as Protector of the Latin Church in the Ottoman Empire in 1535; England had a consul at Aleppo, with jurisdiction as far south as Jerusalem, in 1583. Until the nineteenth century, however, the interest of these Powers had been intermittent, and France had permitted her rights, or those of the Latin Church, in the Holy Sepulchre, to be encroached upon by the Orthodox Church and consequently by Russia. So far as French interest was active, it showed itself in northern Syria rather than in Palestine, or even in the Lebanon. In fact, in the earlier years of the nineteenth century British prestige, strengthened by the support given to the resistance to Napoleon, and later by the expulsion of Mehemet Ali from Syria and Palestine, despite French opposition, had unquestionably risen above that of France. There was also a quickening of interest in the population of the country on the part of missionary, educational, and charitable organizations. To this the protection given by British consuls to the Jewish residents in Palestine, and the establishment of the protestant bishopric (p. 153) in 1841, accompanied and followed by medical missionaries, undoubtedly contributed. In 1838 Britain appointed a consul to Jerusalem[1] and the British example was soon followed by other European Powers and by the United States. After the expulsion of Ibrahim and the Egyptians, rivalry shifted to the Lebanon, where the Maronite Christians were under French protection, and their enemies, the half-Moslem Druses, looked to Britain for support. Here the conclusion was in favour of the French, for in the inevitable clash (1860) the Maronites, with French support, overcame their enemies, and many of the Druses withdrew to the Hauran. Even to this day, however, the British are looked upon by the Druses as friends.

Later, the tide of pilgrims recommenced, this time from Russia. These pilgrims were read as a hidden threat, an army in disguise, their hospices and other institutions as possible hiding-places from which a hostile army might sally forth one day. France, anti-clerical at home, was clerical abroad. Her mission was to introduce and foster French culture in the Near East. The newly created Germany and Italy also developed a political interest in Palestine, cloaked in religious, educational, or archaeological wrappings. British interest in Palestine had died away. British institutions were few; their buildings, compared with those of the other European peoples, insignificant. Yet, perhaps because of this modesty, British influence among the people of Palestine was not less than that of its rivals.

---

[1] A selection from the archives of this consulate, edited by A. M. Hyamson, has been published by the Jewish Historical Society of England, *The British Consulate in Jerusalem in relation to the Jews of Palestine 1838–1914* (Pt. I, 1939; Pt. II, 1941).

Others might give and promise more, but Britain was trusted. Many foresaw the end of Ottoman rule in Palestine; there were few who did not hope that Britain would take the place of the Turk. But apart from a few Jews, the bishop, and some missionaries, there were no British subjects except the consul and his family. The main function of the bishopric was to spread Anglican Christianity among the Jews and the Arab population in turn. But British public men, notably the Earl of Shaftesbury, began to revive an interest in the settlement of the Jews in Palestine, which had been going on for nearly three centuries, and had been stimulated by Napoleon's brief encouragement of the idea of a Jewish state under the protection of France. Following Shaftesbury's suggestion in 1839, British protection granted to the foreign Jews in Palestine—almost without exception Russians who were refused protection by their own Government—became effective a few months later. At the same time, France was renewing the historic claim to protect all oriental Christians; and this claim was contested by Russia as protector of the Orthodox Church. Later, Italy also disputed the right of France to protect Italian subjects, and consequently a large proportion of the Latin ecclesiastics. One of the innumerable quarrels between Christian communities—on this occasion around trivial rights in the Church of the Nativity at Bethlehem—was a direct cause of the Crimean War, France championing her Latin protégés and Russia the Orthodox Church.

### Jewish Immigration

From about 1880 the Jews also became a political factor in Palestine. The flow of Jewish immigrants into Palestine began to grow under pressure of persecutions in Russia and Romania. The story of the Zionist movement is told in brief on p. 121. The Sultan did not object to Jewish settlers, but was afraid of the troubles they might bring with them. Russia, while oppressing Jews at home, was anxious to keep control of Russian subjects who found their way to Palestine, for use in high diplomacy. Britain already claimed an interest in the well-being of the Jews in Palestine. Here were opportunities for further foreign interference. Above all, Zionism, in so far as it was a political as opposed to a cultural movement, a nationalism like the other new nationalisms, threatened to establish a new state—at the best, a second Lebanon—at the expense of the Ottoman Empire. The Sultan did not want another Lebanon, and stipulated that immigrants should abandon their previous citizenship, and become Ottoman subjects; also, that if they settled anywhere in Ottoman territory, it should not be in Palestine.

*The Young Turk Revolution* of 1908 raised hopes in Palestine as elsewhere, and the 'Young Arabs' joined the 'Young Turks'. Palestine, like all other parts of the empire, sent representatives to the newly constituted parliament in Constantinople, and Palestinian Arabs were given high and responsible office in the new administration. But the revolution belied its promise. In its working, the new constitution showed itself little different from the old. The principal change was in personnel. Its basis was not freedom and encouragement for the many nationalities among the people of the Ottoman Empire, but Ottomanization more rigid than before. But the era of nationality and of nationalism, that had opened a generation before, had touched the Arab population of Syria and Palestine. The Arabs had begun to realize that they, also, formed a nationality, and they looked forward to the reawakening of an Arab culture, and also of Arab autonomy. Disappointed in their hopes in the Young Turk movement, they persisted, but necessarily in secret. Damascus and Beirut were the centres of the new movement, but it spread also into Palestine. Thus was aroused a longing, a hope, that was to cause much trouble later to the British. And the new Arab nationalism, which at first was mainly cultural, gradually became nationalist in the European political sense.

## The War in Palestine: 1914–1918

When war with Turkey broke out in November 1914, the Suez canal was, in effect, Egypt's military frontier on the east. Egyptian territory stretched for another hundred miles, but this territory, except for an oasis here and there, was almost waterless desert. The British were prepared to remain passive, but not so the Turks. There are three routes from Palestine across the desert of Sinai. The Turks chose for their main effort the central route through Beersheba and El Auja el Hafir, but they also sent subsidiary forces along the other two. By the beginning of February 1915 these had crossed the desert, and were within striking distance of the Suez canal. The British forces, on the African side, had some support from warships in the canal. The Turks attacked on the night of 2 February, and managed to put three pontoons across the canal, but the men who crossed were killed or taken prisoner. A further attempt on the following day met with similar failure, and the Turks withdrew.

There was no new move on either side for almost a year. Then
the British crossed the canal and advanced a few miles into the desert.
From this line the British Army, under Sir Archibald Murray,
advanced eastwards, fought three successful engagements, and by
9 January 1917 reached the Palestine frontier at Rafa. The original
intention was not to invade Palestine, but to secure the Egyptian
frontier. But with the successes gained, this decision was abandoned
and Murray was ordered for political reasons to advance to the conquest of Palestine. He did not, however, receive the additional forces
he required: indeed, one of his four divisions was withdrawn.

Following on the track of every previous invader of Palestine from
Egypt—along the coast road—Murray's army took Rafa and advanced
to the outskirts of Gaza, accompanied step by step by the railway and
a sweet-water canal. In the latter, an old popular expectation seemed
about to be realized, that when the Nile flowed into Palestine,
Turkish rule there would cease. The road was blocked at Gaza by
Turkish forces. Murray's plan was to cut off Gaza from reinforcements from the north and east and then to take it by storm. The
attack was made on 26 March but failed, although success was very
near; and after another unsuccessful attack on the following day, the
British force withdrew 5 miles to the Wadi Ghazza. Murray's next
intention was to consolidate his previous gains, and not to attempt to
advance again until the end of the hot weather. But he received
instructions to advance without delay. In the meanwhile the Turks
had strengthened their position, not only at Gaza, but eastwards as
far as Beersheba on the central road. The British advanced again
on 17 April, using some tanks for the first time on an eastern battle-
field. Mechanical difficulties and the excellent Turkish gunnery
quickly put them out of action. After this heavy defeat for the British,
operations relapsed into trench warfare.

In July 1917 Murray was replaced by Sir Edmund (afterwards
Viscount) Allenby, the immediate purpose being to relieve the threat
to Baghdad by a further attack on Palestine. The obvious British
line of advance was through Gaza, where were the advantages of
adequate water-supply and of naval support from the sea. But Gaza
was strongly held, and its capture would be both lengthy and costly.
The more practicable and less difficult course was to turn the Turkish
left at Beersheba. The autumn was spent in preparations, which
in themselves served a purpose, for the knowledge of them kept the
German and Turkish armies in northern Syria from marching,
as they had intended, on Baghdad. Each side intended to forestall

the other, but the British struck first. On 31 October they attacked Beersheba and took the village. On the following day they advanced on Gaza. The Turks, under German direction, counter-attacked at Beersheba, but were defeated. By 16 November not only Gaza but Jaffa had been occupied, and the remains of the Turkish army cut in half, part being north of Jaffa and the remainder preparing to defend Jerusalem.

Allenby did not allow the Turks to recover. His main forces turned east towards Jerusalem by roads that the Philistines and Antiochus had trodden many centuries before. Anxious to avoid fighting in the immediate vicinity of the city, he planned to envelop it. Jerusalem surrendered on 9 December, and two days later Allenby entered the city on foot. This success gave great encouragement to the Arab army of the Emir Feisal based on Akaba, and to his supporters east of the Wadi Araba and the Dead Sea (p. 458).

The Turks made an ineffectual attempt to recover Jerusalem before the end of the year, and after its defeat Allenby advanced the whole of his front—which had been extended from Jaffa to Jericho—by a few miles. For some months there was discussion in London and Paris between the advocates of concentration on the western front and of the exploitation of 'side-shows'. In the end the advocates of an advance in Palestine won, and the preparations were being pushed forward when the great German attack in France in March 1918 necessitated the withdrawal of every man who could be spared, and further advance was consequently delayed.

The beginning of the end came in September 1918. On the morning of the 19th Allenby's forces a few miles north of Jaffa attacked the Turks. Within three hours the enemy's lines had been pierced. The cavalry swept on beyond Carmel to the historic plain of Megiddo. Within twenty-four hours Nazareth, the headquarters of the German Commander-in-Chief, was taken. By the capture of Affula and Beisan the line of retreat of the forces north of Jerusalem was cut. All the German and Turkish troops in Palestine were being driven towards Nablus, from which the only road still open led down the mountainside into the Jordan valley, still known as the Valley of Death. The Army was supported by the Royal Air Force. With command of the sea, there was nothing to fear from the west. On the other side, in Transjordan, the Arab forces of Feisal and Lawrence were waiting. Few Turks escaped. Haifa was occupied on 23 September. Two days later there was a fierce battle at Samakh on the southern shore of Lake Tiberias. At its close there was no longer any organized hostile force in Palestine, and a few days later the same could be said of Syria. After four centuries Ottoman rule had come to an end.

## Jewish Immigration during the Ottoman Period

The new Jewish immigration into Palestine which began in 1882 was caused by the Russian and Romanian persecutions (p. 116), the flood from which turned towards North and South America, to England, and to south Africa; but a trickle flowed towards Palestine. There had been Jewish immigration to Palestine even before 1880, and even a few small attempts at agricultural settlement on the part of Palestinian Jews. But the immigration that opened in 1882 differed in essentials from its predecessor. The earlier immigration was religious—a movement of men who wanted a retreat in which to devote themselves to their religious pursuits, to study and to pray. In the Holy Land they were vicarious residents, the representatives of Jewry outside, whose sympathies were with them, and who would have liked, or thought they would have liked, to settle in Palestine also, but were unable to do so. The new immigration continued to include these elements, but to an ever-increasing extent it consisted of young men and women of a different character, on whom their religion rested relatively lightly—in some cases not at all—who came to Palestine not as fugitives but as pioneers, with a mission to rebuild there a Jewish community dependent on its own exertions, perhaps to lay the foundations of the restored Jewish state of which Jews had dreamed for two thousand years. The old immigrants had come to Palestine to pray and to die: the new came to work and to live.

The new movement was not altogether new. It had to some extent existed for centuries, and there had been several recent attempts, in which in the nineteenth century Englishmen were especially interested, to create in Palestine self-supporting Jewish communities, recruited from without and healthy in body and mind, as the beginning of a Jewish renaissance. One such attempt began with the establishment by French Jews of an agricultural school near Jaffa, at Mikveh Israel, in 1870. At this stage the movement was evidently looked on with favour by the Ottoman Government, which presented the land on which the school was established. No hint of politics appeared, or existed. Mikveh Israel may be considered the mother of Jewish agricultural settlement in Palestine, though it was primarily a school for native Jews of Palestine, with a sprinkling of Jewish boys from abroad.

The earliest real agricultural settlement, founded in Petah Tikva in

1878, failed at first but was revived in 1883. This also was originally intended to be a settlement of Palestinian Jews from Jerusalem, but when the colony was re-established it was by Jews from Russia (p. 137). Petah Tikva has grown continuously from 1883 and is now a small town with a municipality and a population of about 17,000 as estimated by the Jewish Agency. The revival of Petah Tikva was, however, preceded by the establishment of other Jewish settlements by Jews from Russia and Romania—Rishon le Zion, Zichron Jacob, and Rosh Pinna, all of which have grown. To-day there are over 250 Jewish agricultural settlements, large and small, in Palestine. Some, Rishon le Zion, Rehovot, Nathanya, Hadera, are small towns rather than villages. Some are industrial, but all depend to a greater or less extent on agriculture (photos. 37, 38).

The effects of the anti-Jewish outbreak of 1881 in Russia and in Romania turned what had hitherto been an academic movement on a very small scale into one with practical possibilities. The *Choveve Zion* Society ('Lovers of Zion') was formed for agricultural colonization but was in no sense a political movement. Its participants wanted only the opportunity for Jews to settle in Palestine, to cultivate the land there, and to found and bring up healthy, self-respecting families, that would benefit and bring credit to the country as a whole, and at the same time revivify the sorely stricken spirit of the Jewish people. They were also, like their predecessors, to be the vicarious representatives of European Jewry. The enthusiasm of the new society far outran its means and experience, and these attempts would probably have proved as unsuccessful as their predecessors, had not a warm-hearted and far-seeing French Jew, Baron Edmond de Rothschild, come to their assistance and devoted a fortune to place them on stable foundations. It was an Englishman then resident at Haifa—Laurence Oliphant—who first introduced Rothschild to these new-comers and their plans. The *Choveve Zion* movement continued on modest lines for some seventeen years, until it was absorbed by the new political Zionism under Herzl, with whom leaders of the *Choveve Zion* were not always in complete sympathy. Rothschild, however, continued on his course, being dependent on no one, and his organization directed and helped existing settlements, and established new ones.

## Zionism

Theodor Herzl was a Viennese newspaper correspondent in Paris, practically isolated from the stream of Jewish life, when in 1896 the

Dreyfus affair turned his attention to the Jewish question, and to a possible solution by a Jewish state in which Jews could build up a Jewish nation and be 'as other peoples'. He very soon localized his projected state in Palestine. In 1904 he died at the age of 44, worn out by his efforts, which, so far as Palestine was concerned, were a complete failure. His only success had no connexion with Palestine —the British Government's offer of territory in east Africa, now Kenya, for an autonomous Jewish settlement under a Jewish governor to be appointed by Britain. To Herzl's irreconcilable followers, however, there was no alternative to Zion.

After the death of Herzl, the importance of the Zionist organization, both in Jewry and outside, fell to a very low level. The accepted leaders of Jewish communities in Europe and America were never captivated by it. They were all full citizens, in sympathy, in duty, as well as in benefit, of their respective countries. They were sympathetic towards the success of the new settlements in Palestine, towards the welfare of the Jewish population. But that was as far as their interest went.

The fortunes of Zionism remained at a low ebb until the outbreak of war between Turkey and the Allies. Jews and non-Jews realized at once that the non-Turkish parts of the Ottoman Empire would go into the melting-pot when the time came for a settlement. Zionism might then become practical politics. Contact was made between Zionists and representatives of the British Government, always sympathetic. The movement was then in the hands of the 'practical' or 'cultural' Zionists, more concerned with the spirit of Jewish colonization and Jewish culture than with a Jewish state. There were also discussions on the part of the Government with the leaders of English Jewry. The formula adopted in the Balfour Declaration (1917) was a compromise between the two opposed Jewish opinions.

'His Majesty's Government view with favour the establishment in Palestine of a national home for the Jewish people, and will use their best endeavours to facilitate the achievement of this object, it being clearly understood that nothing shall be done which may prejudice the civil and religious rights of existing non-Jewish communities in Palestine, or the rights and political status enjoyed by Jews in any other country.'

There was no mention of a Jewish state or other political entity in this declaration. The term used, 'a national home for the Jewish people', was vague, and open to several interpretations. The reiterated claim on the part of the Zionists, among whom the political nationalists began again to raise their heads, to secure a far stronger

37. *Nineteenth-century Jewish village of Zichron Jacob*

38. *Rehovot, the Jewish centre of the orange industry, south of Jaffa*

39. *Nahalal in the plain of Esdraelon.  A* moshav, *or modern Jewish small-holder agricultural settlement, with public buildings in the middle, farm-houses forming a circle, and the holdings extending outwards*

40. *The Wailing Wall at Jerusalem*

phrase—'the reconstitution in Palestine of the National Home of the Jewish people'—was definitely rejected. A Jewish state was not ruled out by the declaration, but an offer of very much less would have still been in accordance with its terms. Moreover, the British Government did not promise to create anything. That was the task of the Zionists and the Jewish people. The British promise was only to 'use their best endeavours' to facilitate the achievement of this object.

The promise, modest and indefinite as it was, caused a certain amount of excitement and suspicion in the Arab world as soon as it became known. The Arab Revolt against Turkey was in progress in alliance with Britain. For a moment it seemed that the promise to the Zionists, which had probably been much exaggerated by the time it reached Feisal's camp at Akaba, would bring the revolt to a premature end. But the British Government acted promptly. It sent D. G. Hogarth with assurances to the Sherif of Mecca, at that time the head of the Arabs who were in alliance with Britain. The promise of a Jewish national home would be fulfilled only 'in so far as is compatible with the freedom of the existing population, both economic and political' (Cmd. 5964: 1939). The Arabs were satisfied, and the revolt continued until it was crowned with success.

## 5. THE MANDATE

*After the War*

Palestine having been occupied and the war brought to a successful end, the disposal of the conquered lands came forward for decision. Feisal, provided the Arabs were given the self-government they had been promised in the Arab lands, was quite willing to agree to a special status for Palestine, at any rate so far as it was Jewish. The Jews of Palestine and of the Dispersion, so far as they were able to express their views, were anxious for a British protectorate, with the Balfour Declaration as a charter, in a Palestine separated from the neighbouring lands, in which they would be free to develop along their own lines. The Arabs of Syria and Palestine were at one in their objection to any separation. They also wanted a British protectorate, or an American one which everyone recognized was unattainable. The only exceptions were perhaps some of the Lebanese, who wanted a separate State of the Lebanon under French protection. No one elsewhere desired any sort of French control, or, apart from some Jews, any sort of Jewish national state. The settlement was not made formally until July 1922, when the Mandate for

Palestine, which it had previously been decided by the Allied and Associated Powers should be entrusted to Britain, was approved by the League of Nations. The Mandate incorporated the terms of the Balfour Declaration. It recognized the historical connexion of the Jewish people with Palestine, and placed on the Mandatory Power the responsibility for introducing such political, administrative, and economic conditions as would encourage the establishment of the Jewish 'national home', the development of self-governing institutions, and the safeguarding of the civil and religious rights of all its inhabitants. In furtherance of the first of these objects, a Jewish Agency was to be constituted in order to advise and co-operate with the Administration of Palestine in matters concerning the Jewish national home, and, subject to the control of the Administration, to share in the development of the country. The Administration of Palestine should facilitate Jewish immigration under suitable conditions and encourage close settlement of Jews on the land, 'while ensuring that the rights and position of other sections of the population are not prejudiced'. Hebrew was to be one of the official languages of Palestine. The British Government was, however, careful to explain in a document (Cmd. 1700: 1922) issued at the same time as the Mandate, and similarly accepted by the Council of the League of Nations, that it had no intention of constituting Palestine as a Jewish State. The most that could be read into the Balfour Declaration, it said, was that a Jewish national home 'should be founded *in Palestine*'. The declaration, and the Government that made it, never contemplated 'that Palestine as a whole should be converted into a Jewish National Home', nor 'the disappearance or the subordination of the Arabic population, language, or culture in Palestine'.

*Arab Reactions*

In the meanwhile there had been two outbreaks in Palestine on the part of the Arabs, directed against the Jewish immigrants. In spite of all assurances, the Arabs had become very suspicious of Jewish intentions, and the support which the British Government proposed to give them. There was also a growing Arab nationalism that demanded self-government, under British supervision and protection, for the people of Palestine, and, in some quarters, for union with Syria.

The earlier of these outbreaks occurred while the Military Administration was still in control. One of its consequences was the substitution of a civil administration, with Sir Herbert (afterwards Viscount) Samuel as High Commissioner. Sir Herbert, an ex-Cabinet Minister and member of the Jewish community, of moderate Zionist sympathies, threw himself into the work of administering the country in the interests of all classes of its population, on the lines of the policy laid down by His Majesty's Government. Jewish immigration was facilitated within reasonable limits; government and military works gave opportunities for employment for new settlers as well as for the indigenous population; the beginnings of industry were laid, and the existing small agricultural settlement extended and developed. However, neither the Jewish nor the Arab element in the population was satisfied. The one wanted more, the other less. Sir Herbert Samuel retired after five years in office, and was succeeded by Viscount Plumer, one of the heroes of the war and a very successful Governor of Malta. His three years of office coincided with a period of economic depression, during which the Zionists realized that it was essential that they should moderate their pace. The moderation reacted on the Arabs, and in consequence, during Lord Plumer's administration, there was peace in the land. After Lord Plumer came Sir John Chancellor, an experienced and successful colonial administrator. Under him the economic situation began to improve, and the Zionist hopes and expectations to expand; and, with the Zionist expansion, came a renewal of the suspicions and fears of the Arabs. These were still further encouraged by the agreement between the Zionists and other Jews, the so-called 'non-Zionists', to co-operate for the Jewish settlement and development in Palestine; the subject of a Jewish state or any sort of political Judaism, to which the 'non-Zionists' strongly objected, was by mutual consent left in suspense. The suspicions and fears of the Arabs culminated in another outbreak (1929), fiercer than either of its predecessors, in which the Jewish population suffered severely.

### Arab Outbreaks

Although this outbreak can be traced to the feeling of uneasiness on the part of the Arabs, which would sooner or later, if not relieved, have made a clash inevitable, the immediate cause was to be found in the rival claims that met around the 'Wailing Wall' (photo. 40). The rights of Jews and Arabs with regard to this wall, which is on the one face a Jewish Holy Place and on the other a Moslem one, are very carefully defined under the *status quo* (Appendix C). Neither side had in reality accepted that definition, and when in the years before 1929 the Jews seemed to be gradually extending their rights and claims, the Moslems became at the same time more suspicious and more uneasy.

The Moslem Arab motives were to some extent political as well as religious, for the ancient wall which was supposed to be sacred to both parties had become a battleground in the political war between them. The action of some headstrong young Zionists who, in August 1929, seized the opportunity of a Jewish fast-day to march to the wall with flags, despite the prohibition of the Government and against the wishes of responsible Jewish leaders, and to make a demonstration there which made no pretence to any religious complexion, brought matters to a head. The Moslems had their demonstration the following day. Both peoples were boiling. In these circumstances, incidents arose almost spontaneously, and within a few days serious clashes, mainly instigated by the Arabs, occurred in Jerusalem, Hebron, Safad, Jaffa, and elsewhere.

Under Lord Plumer, Palestine had been practically denuded of troops, and the combined strength of the Army and Palestinian Police Force was quite inadequate to control events. Some of the Royal Air Force was brought into Palestine from Transjordan (which itself was infected by the prevailing unrest, and needed careful watching) and the combined British forces, including the Police, were put under the officer commanding the Royal Air Force. Reinforcements were sent from Egypt, and by their assistance the outbreak was suppressed after seven days, in the course of which 133 Jews were killed and 339 wounded. Of the Arabs, 116 were recorded as killed and 232 as wounded, many of them by rifle fire of the police or military forces; but as the Director of Health said in his report, 'it is known that a considerable number of unrecorded casualties from rifle fire occurred among the Arabs'.

The Government appointed a commission of Members of Parliament, drawn from the three parties, under the chairmanship of Sir Walter Shaw, a retired Colonial Chief Justice, to inquire into the immediate causes of the outbreak, and to make recommendations for avoiding a recurrence. This commission recommended that the Government should define its policy clearly, and should reiterate, in particular, that the rights and position of the non-Jewish communities would be fully safeguarded. The machinery for the control of immigration should be reformed, and steps taken to avoid excessive influx, as in 1925 and 1926 (p. 181). Steps should be taken to find means for increasing the fertility of the land; in the meanwhile the eviction of peasant cultivators should cease and the cultivators should be provided with much needed credit. The limitations of the powers of the Zionist Organization should be clearly defined. The commission made no formal recommendation for constitutional development, but expressed the opinion that 'the absence of any measure of self-government is greatly aggravating the difficulties of the local Administration'; it also recommended the early appointment of a commission to inquire into rights and claims regarding the Wailing Wall (p. 538). The Government accepted these conclusions and appointed Sir John Hope-Simpson to go further into the questions of immigration and land. His report carried the recommendations of the commission somewhat further. When this also was in effect adopted, the Arabs showed moderate satisfaction, the Zionists intense hostility. In the end nothing much was done, and events followed their course until a new outbreak occurred in 1933.

Sir John Chancellor had in the meantime retired, and had been succeeded by General Sir Arthur Wauchope. During his term of office there were two Arab outbreaks, both anti-British. The second, also anti-Jewish, which began in April 1936 and continued with one or two short intervals until the declaration of war in 1939—when all differences in Palestine were sunk in the universal Jewish and Arab support of the British cause—was in effect a rebellion whose objects were (a) to prohibit Jewish immigration; (b) to prohibit the transfer of Arab lands to Jews; (c) to establish a national government responsible to a representative council (Colonial No. 129 (1937), p. 23). The Arabs were encouraged in their action by the successful rebellions of the neighbouring Egyptians and Iraqis, and more recently by the apparent success of the Syrians, who by these means had gained the limited independence they had demanded.

The suppression of the outbreak was difficult. It not only had the support of practically the entire Arab population of Palestine, but also—at any rate in its aims—the sympathy of the neighbouring Arab governments and peoples, and also of Moslems farther afield.

The trouble began with a relatively trivial incident; the murder of two Jews by Arab bandits on 15 April 1936. It was immediately followed by the murder of two Arabs in the same neighbourhood; by angry Jewish demonstrations in Tel Aviv at the funeral; by the circulation of rumours in Jaffa that Arabs were being murdered in Tel Aviv; and by murderous attacks on Jews in Jaffa. 'Arab National Committees' sprang into existence in all the Arab centres of Palestine. The first of them, at Nablus, proclaimed a general strike, which was at once taken up by the others. The five Arab political parties, as a rule opposed on personal grounds to one another, united to form the 'Arab Higher Committee', whose membership included a Greek Orthodox

Arab and a Roman Catholic Arab, as well as Moslems. Attempts by the High Commissioner to pacify the Arabs were met by an intensification of the strike. The announcement of another large Labour Immigration schedule on 18 May made the Arabs only the more determined. There was still, however, little bloodshed, the weapons employed being, for the most part, the strike, non-cooperation with the Government, and damage to Jewish property, in particular to plantations and crops.

The position was, however, continually growing worse. Before the end of May, attacks on isolated Jews, firing at Jewish villages, and attempts to derail trains and otherwise interfere with communications, became almost of everyday occurrence. Very soon armed Arab bands, recruited not only in Palestine but also in Syria and Iraq, appeared in the hills, and the country was soon in the midst of a rebellion in the course of which hundreds of lives, British as well as Arab and Jewish, were sacrificed. The outbreak, originally anti-Jewish, became also anti-British. As time passed, the extremists among the Arabs got more and more control and many Arabs also were murdered, presumably for being lukewarm to the cause. The attacks were no longer sporadic but organized. From the second week in May, military reinforcements were arriving from Egypt and Malta. They were mainly used for the defence of key-points, patrolling the roads, escorting convoys, and protecting the railway lines. No serious attacks were made on the bands in the hills, but a large number of Arabs, including some prominent men, were arrested and confined in camps. These measures had no appreciable effect on the outbreak. The extent of the sympathy it enjoyed was shown by a memorandum to the High Commissioner, signed by practically every Arab judge, official, and clerk—but not the police officers—who showed their sympathy if not with the methods, certainly with the aims, of the insurgents.

Meanwhile, the Arab bands became more powerful and active. At their head was Fawzi ed Din el Kauwakji, a Syrian soldier of fortune or patriot, perhaps both, who had served with distinction in the Turkish army during the war, and after the French occupation of Syria had obtained the *légion d'honneur* for his work as an intelligence officer. On the outbreak of the Druse rising in 1925 he had joined the insurgents and been sentenced to death by the French, but on its suppression he had escaped to the Hejaz, where he became military adviser to King Ibn Saud. Finally he had received a commission in the Iraqi army, which he had resigned to take command of the rebels in Palestine. Under him the outbreak became a war, with drilled and disciplined forces on both sides. The damage done by the rebels against government, Jewish, and Moderate Arab lives and property increased at a still greater rate. Pitched battles were fought, and aeroplanes were brought into action on the government side. Further reinforcements arrived in September, and by the end of that month there were about 20,000 British troops in Palestine. Further, an Order in Council authorized the application of martial law.

Under this combined pressure, the outbreak was formally brought to an end by the Arab Higher Committee on 12 October 1936, in response to an appeal by the Arab kings and emirs. The Royal Commission, which had been in being for some months, thereupon sailed for Palestine. But the rebellion had been long out of the hands of the Arab Higher Committee. The men in arms were in control, and without their agreement the appeal could be little more than a pious hope. The murder of two senior government officials, one a British Christian in September 1937, the other a Palestinian Jew, in October, brought matters to a head. The Arab Higher Committee was dissolved and steps taken to arrest and exile its members. Haj Amin el Husseini, Mufti of Jerusalem and head of the Arab Movement, fled from Palestine. At the same time a modified form of martial law was introduced.

At the end of 1938 the outbreak began to die down. There were two causes. One was the continued pressure of the British forces, still further strengthened; the other the apparent tendency on the part of the Government to modify its policy. In the meanwhile, however, the outbreak had gone so far that a large part of Palestine, including towns such as Jaffa and Hebron, and even the old city of Jerusalem, had passed completely out of the hands of the Government and had to be reconquered. Troubles continued until the declaration of war in September 1939, but by the latter part of 1938 they had been reduced to isolated outrages, committed in some instances for political reasons, but as frequently, if not more so, acts of revenge or even of brigandage.

The Royal Navy played a valuable part, and showed its versatility in a number of unusual roles, when co-operating with the military and civil authorities to bring the disorders to an end in the period 1936–1938. A summary of the special activities undertaken by His Majesty's ships and their personnel during this period is contained in Appendix E to this volume.

To illustrate the scale of the disturbances, some figures may be of interest. During the year 1938 were recorded 5,708 separate cases of terrorist activity. In the course of these, 216 British, 390 Jews, and 598 Arabs were wounded, and 77, 255, and 503 respectively killed; in addition it was estimated that more than a thousand members of armed bands were killed, and about the same number wounded, in encounters with the British forces.

## A New Solution

The Royal Commission, under Lord Peel, found that the problem was insoluble so long as the Mandate remained unamended; for the Mandate required the Administration to carry out two policies that were irreconcilable; to facilitate and encourage Jewish expansion and development, and at the same time to safeguard the existing rights and interests of the indigenous Arab population. The commission recommended that the present Mandate be brought to an end, that Palestine be divided into three parts, the one in which there was a Jewish majority to be formed into a Jewish sovereign independent State, the second, in which the Arabs predominated, into a similar Arab State, and the third containing the Christian Holy Places to be placed under a permanent British Mandate. With this solution no one was satisfied. The Arabs declined any mutilation of Palestine. The Jews for the most part shared their objections, perhaps for different reasons. A minority of the Zionists, anxious for a Jewish State at almost any price, was willing to accept partition, but provided only that the provisional boundaries suggested for their territory by the Royal Commission were extended. Parliament and the League of Nations showed themselves anything but enthusiastic for the Royal Commission's solution. Only the Government, tired of the endless attempts to solve the apparently insoluble, and believing that the Jews at any rate would accept partition, approved the Royal Commission's recommendations.

The Royal Commission's boundaries were admittedly provisional; and there were other details to be settled, for instance, the economic and financial relations between the proposed states and with the Mandatory Power. To examine these, a new Partition and Technical Commission was appointed. Among its instructions was one to draw the boundaries so as to 'necessitate the inclusion of the fewest possible Arabs and Arab enterprises in the Jewish area and vice versa'. The provisional boundaries had left only a few hundred Jews on the Arab side; on the other hand, almost half the population of the proposed Jewish State would have been Arab, and in the district of

Galilee, which was to have been included, 85 per cent. of the population was Arab. Yet even the advocates of partition among the
Zionists would only accept that solution if the borders of the proposed Jewish State were considerably extended.

In these circumstances the conclusions of the Partition Commission
were inevitable. They were that the partition of Palestine was
impracticable and unworkable—not only on the question of boundaries; and that if the Government was determined to pursue its
announced policy, and if the instructions given to the Partition
Commission were to be observed, the frontiers of the new Jewish
State provisionally suggested by the Royal Commission would have
to be so drastically contracted that it would be no larger than a
moderately sized English county. This report put an end to 'partition'.

The British Government had consequently to start anew. At first
it attempted to bring the Jews and Arabs together, to a round-table
conference under British chairmanship, for agreement on a constitutional settlement. In this it failed. Large delegations came to
London, of Jews, Zionist and non-Zionist, Palestinian, British, and
foreign, and of Arabs, not only from all parties in Palestine, but also
from the neighbouring Arab governments. The Jews met the representatives of the Arab States, and discussed the problem with them.
There were many discussions between the Government representatives and the Jews and the Arabs separately. But the Palestinian
Arabs resolutely refused to meet the representatives of the Jewish
Agency for Palestine, whose existence, constituted under the terms
of the Mandate, they refused to recognize. The British Government,
having failed to get any agreement between the Jews and the Arabs,
put forward tentatively its own solution. This was at once rejected
by the Jewish delegation, who at the same time withdrew from the
conference. The Arabs also did not accept the proposals, but showed
themselves more amenable. Further discussions between the British
and the Arabs ensued, and in the end the British Government
published a new Statement of Policy (Cmd. 6019: 1939). There was
to be established within ten years an independent Palestine State,
in which Jews and Arabs would share in the government and the
essential interests of each community would be safeguarded. During
this time steps would be taken to educate Palestinians in administration by giving them an ever-increasing share in its work and
responsibilities. At the end of five years British and Palestinians
would co-operate in drawing up a constitution for the country. Under

this constitution the Holy Places, the religious bodies, the different communities, the special position of the Jewish National Home, the strategic needs of the country, and the interests of certain foreign countries would all be safeguarded. In the meanwhile Jewish immigration would be limited to 75,000 in the period of five years. This would raise the Jewish population of Palestine to about a third of the whole. Further Jewish immigration would then be permitted only with the agreement of the Arab section of the population. With regard to land, the country was to be divided into three zones. In the one, in which the population was largely Jewish, acquisition of land by Jews was to be unrestricted. In the second, such acquisition would be permitted exceptionally. In the third, the districts entirely Arab, it would be prohibited. The new immigration procedure was put into force at once. War then broke out. Some months later the new land legislation was enacted, but further action under the new Statement of Policy was suspended.

## CHAPTER VI

# THE PEOPLE

## RACE AND NATIONALITY

A RACE has been defined as a group of people who possess the majority of their physical characteristics in common and transmit them to their offspring. In this sense there is no pure race in Palestine, though religious communities which habitually intermarry tend to exhibit hereditary and racial uniformities, and their community of culture tends to unite them in a nationality—a term sometimes confused with race, though distinct from it.

In the population of Palestine as a whole, in modern as in all earlier times, two strongly contrasted racial types predominate over all others:

(a) the *Anatolian*, sometimes called 'Armenoid', and in Europe 'Alpine', derived from the Mountain Zone to the north, with characteristic high, short skull, with steep flat back and retreating forehead; dark hair and eyes, dense skin, strongly curved nose, thick lips, large ears; thick-set with broad hands and feet, and much body hair; best represented among Armenians and inhabitants of Asia Minor, and common among Nestorian Christians;

(b) the *Mediterranean* or 'Brown Race', a long-headed type with prominent occiput, oval face, dark hair and eyes, olive complexion but clear skin, slight build, and slender limbs; represented by the better-bred beduin of the desert, and Palestinian Arabs of desert origin.

Both types have inhabited Palestine from early times, and are represented in Egyptian paintings of Asiatic captives and vassals, about 1500 B.C., and on Assyrian and Egyptian carvings (photos. 41, 42). Both have also been reinforced by kindred invaders, from the north and from the east respectively; and in periods of peaceful intercourse they have interbred and originated intermediate types.

## The Arabs

In comparison with Syria, Palestine owes more of its historical and modern population to the Arab immigrants, who have entered in small parties, more or less continuously between the greater invasions, and have been absorbed among the sedentary 'people of the land', commonly called *fellahin* as in Egypt. All those peoples, who had been well mixed before the advent of the Arab conquerors in the seventh century A.D., accepted both the Arabic language of the new-comers, which was closely akin to the Aramaic already spoken generally in the country, and also, with few exceptions, their Moslem faith. Thus 'Arab' in Palestine came to mean Arab-speaking, and as a rule Moslem. Many of these earlier peoples were Semites, like the invaders from Arabia, and amalgamation with them was therefore not very difficult, but the non-Semite folk, or Semitic elements less close to the new-comers, were also very largely absorbed, in so far as they had not already become assimilated. Thus the Arab people of Palestine which now comprises over two-thirds of the population—and until twenty years ago nine-tenths—is to a relatively small extent Arab in blood, although Arabic-speaking and Moslem in tradition and in culture (photos. 43).

The meaning of the new term 'Arab Nationality', which, as commonly used, denotes the greater part of the population of Palestine, whether Moslem or Christian, is discussed by Eric Mills in his report on the *Census of Palestine 1931*, vol. i, p. 73. This Arab nationality, he points out, has no legal existence, since there is no Arab community in any formal sense: 'its basis is perhaps best described as an awareness, on the part of members of some of the non-Jewish religious communities, of the possibility of common factors in the aims of the several communities'. The Arab nationality in Palestine is in fact a political creation, a reaction from the creation or existence of a Jewish nationality. Arab nationality having been accepted as a description in the 1931 census, out of 772,904 individuals so described (of whom 766,222 were Palestinian citizens) 690,420 were Moslems, 73,281 were Christians, and 87 were Jews by religion. Of the 9,116 'others', who described themselves as 'Arabs', most were presumably Druses and Bahai (p. 144). In addition there were some 66,300 described as Nomads or *Beduin*, who should unquestionably be included in the 'Arab' total.

The *Beduin* or Nomads may be accepted as pure Arabs by blood. With only slight qualification, this is true also of the principal families of the aristocracy of Palestine—the Husseini, Khaldi, Abdul Hadi, Nashashibi, and others. In origin they are Arab, but like other principal families in the Ottoman Empire, they often took their wives from other communities, and as a consequence the ancestry of these

41. *Semitic types from the Palace of Rameses III at Medinet Habu*

*Galilean (Merom)*

*Philistine (XX Dyn.)*

*Syrian*

*Amorite*

*Judaean (XXII Dyn.)*

*Arab*

42. *Palestinians of the 2nd Millennium B.C.*

families is now somewhat mixed. These purer Arabs fall into two divisions, the *Kais* of the north and the *Yaman* of the south; but this distinction is now generally forgotten.

The Beduin, like their near kinsmen in Arabia, dwell in portable tents of black goats'-hair ('the tents of Kedar') (photos. 44). Tents of different tribes vary in form: some, such as those of the Taamireh, are as a rule rectangular, others are circular, others oval. Small in numbers, the tribes generally avoid open places for their camps, not only for shelter but in order not to be conspicuous; for similar reasons they pitch their tents at some distance from their watering-places. Natural caves in the wadis are preferred by some families, as they afford better shelter and protection. There is little or no cohesion between the various tribes. Their watering-places are springs, standing pools of rain-water, and cisterns roughly cut in the rock in the valley bottoms. On the border between 'the desert and the sown', the people tend to change their mode of life; the nomads become partly or wholly sedentary, the sedentary become semi-nomadic. Thus the people on the western edge of the Judaean desert, as, for example, the Taamireh, who were originally *fellahin*, take their cattle out into the desert and live a nomadic life; on the other hand, genuine beduin in the desert regions, such as the Rashayideh of Ain Jedi, remain so long in certain places as to become almost sedentary.

The beduin of Palestine are to be found with few exceptions on or near the southern and eastern boundaries. They belong to both sides of the frontier, dwelling mostly in Sinai or Transjordan, and passing farther into Palestine as the summer advances and pasture becomes scarce. In years of drought they will wander as far north as Syria. At the time of the harvest many beduin help the agriculturists of Palestine. As a body they have a justifiable reputation for raiding, but as a rule they confine their attentions to one another. Only under pressure of urgent necessity do they now risk a raid on the settled population, and in Palestine they are very little inclined to engage in raiding anyone.

The *fellahin*, or peasants and agriculturists, are different. They are descendants of all the peoples who have conquered the land or settled in it from before the beginning of history. The Canaanites, Hivites, Horites, and other 'peoples of the land' in the Bible, are all represented among them. So are also the Israelites, the Edomites from the south, and presumably also the Philistines from oversea. Later comers from Babylonia, Syria, Greece, and Rome have all left descendants among them. So have the Europeans of the Crusades, as is evident from the physical appearance of the Christian natives of Bethlehem and the neighbouring Beit Jala, whose women still wear medieval European costume.[1]

Here and there other small secluded groups have survived; the small group of Jewish Arabs in Pekiin, south of the Acre–Safad road, is perhaps the last remnant of the original Galilean Jews. The handful of Samaritans at Nablus trace their origins back to the Assyrian conquest. Some distance east of Tulkarm, in a remote, barely accessible valley, is an Arab village, the physical appearance of whose inhabitants is altogether different from that of any other Arab community in Palestine or elsewhere. On the coast of Sinai, outside Palestine, along the marsh or salt lake of Sabkhet el Bardawil—the suggested alternative to the Red Sea as the locality of the destruction of Pharaoh's forces—live the Bardawil fishermen. In the neighbourhood is the site of an outpost of the Latin kingdom. Its inhabitants are undoubtedly descendants of the Crusading soldiers and local women. The tradition of the villagers is that they are of European descent, and the name of Baldwin, the King of Jerusalem, who sent them there, is preserved in their name Bardawil. Lastly, in Jericho and its neighbourhood the prevailing type has an obvious negroid admixture, attributed to slaves or servants brought from Africa in Roman or later times. The men of Jericho and those of Bethlehem are very far apart physically, but both claim Arab nationality like all the other Arabic-speaking inhabitants of Palestine.

The Arab-speaking *town population*, apart from the leading families already mentioned (p. 134), is as mixed in origin as are the *fellahin* peasantry, but the mixture in many cases is far more recent, and is still continuing. This population, popularly described as Levantine, has a large *fellah* element: it has also pure Arab elements, but they are in a minority; a certain number of Jews, oriental and

---

[1] This mixture of races is well illustrated by a passage in C. S. Jarvis's *Yesterday and To-day in Sinai*. He is writing of El Arish in Sinai which, although not politically, is geographically a part of Palestine, and whose inhabitants are very closely akin to those of southern Palestine. 'For the next 3,000 years' after the foundation of the town, he says, 'it saw the passage of innumerable invading and retreating armies—Syrians, Hittites, Assyrians, Persians, Romans, Greeks, Jews, and French. Stragglers from every passing army dropped out and stayed at El Arish, marrying into Arishy families and plying their trades. Napoleon in 1799 occupied the town for over a year, the French leaving their mark on the next generation, whilst the Turks from the days of Mohammed Ali until the British occupation maintained a battalion of Bosnians or Albanians there, many of whom, on completion of their service, appear to have intermarried and settled down, with the result that the Arishia of to-day are of every type.'

43. *Mixed types of Arab fellahin to-day*

44. *Beduin and their tents*

European, have been absorbed, mainly Jewish women by marriage; but it also has elements that have arrived in Palestine more recently: in fact, in the towns, everyone who has not actively kept himself connected with his own community has been thus assimilated and speaks Arabic as his native tongue. The Greek-speaking element is still relatively large. Of the Christians in Palestine in 1931, 1,684 men and women gave Greek as their normal language; 508 were born in Greece or the Greek islands, and 170 in Cyprus; 632 described themselves as Greek nationals and 29 as Cypriots. These do not, however, by any means comprise all of Greek blood in Palestine.

Almost all the Moslems and the oriental Christians are Arabs. There are exceptions, the Egyptians, Circassians, the Magharbeh of north Africa, and the Bosnians among the Moslems. The Turkish-speaking community (1,268 in 1931), about the same size as the Greek, is the remnant of the Turkish military and administrative class, of which the greater part left the country in 1918, with the Turkish Army. The remainder, and other elements, such as refugees from Armenia, of Turkish origin and speech, have been rapidly assimilated into the Arabic-speaking population, for 6,303 persons claimed in 1931 to have been born in Turkey. The number of Kurds and Turkoman nomads is small. The Egyptians are a very recent element in the population. They came first with Allenby's army towards the end of the war of 1914–1918. Some remained, and others have since joined them. Unskilled labourers almost without exception, they belong to one of the lowest strata in the population. In 1931 there were 1,383 Egyptian Moslems in Palestine, and 2,316 Palestinian Moslems had been born in Egypt.

The Russian conquest of the Caucasus in about 1860–1870 caused many Moslem tribesmen of the Caucasus and adjacent provinces, unwilling to live under Christian rule, to seek refuge in a Moslem land. The Treaty of Berlin in 1878 gave impetus to this movement, and Abdul Hamid made use of it to plant colonies of these virile and truculent fighting-men on the marches and desert fringes of his empire; more especially Circassians, on the eastern border of Syria and Palestine, and in what is now Transjordan. There are at present about 900 Circassians in Palestine. Similarly, on the occupation of Bosnia and Herzegovina by Austria in 1878, many Bosnian Moslems (who are Islamized Serbs) emigrated into Turkish territory. Some of these were established within the ruined city of Caesarea.

There was also an influx of Moslems from north Africa into Syria and Palestine early in the eighteenth century, from the mercenary infantry of the Pashas. Some had, indeed, settled in Jerusalem from religious motives even earlier; and others followed in the nineteenth century in consequence of the French conquest of Algeria. An ancient group of these 'western' Magharbeh in the old city of Jerusalem, between the Wailing Wall and the Dung Gate (also called the 'Gate of the Magharbeh'), was established there by the charity of the Abu Madian *waqf*, or charitable foundation. Few have come from these western lands recently, and in 1931 there were left in Palestine only 485 Moslems born in north Africa, apart from Egypt.

## The Palestinian Christians

Under Ottoman rule, in Palestine as elsewhere, religious community coincided with nationality (*millet*: see *Turkey*, vol. i, p. 336) among the subject peoples. Christians formed such *millets* under their respective patriarchs; and in the early days of the Anglican Bishop, his Palestinian converts often claimed British citizenship, though without success. The members of the two Armenian Churches, with the few Armenian Protestants, mainly in Jerusalem, still describe themselves as of Armenian descent and nationality, being usually recent refugees from massacre and plunder in Turkey. Most of the Armenians in Palestine speak colloquial Armenian among themselves, but the majority know some Arabic, and some know Turkish. Christians of European and American origin have their respective civil nationalities. With these exceptions, however, the indigenous adherents of Christian communities in Palestine describe themselves as Arabs, and speak Arabic.

## The Jews

The Jewish communities of the Ottoman Empire likewise formed a *millet*, represented by the Chief Rabbi at Constantinople, and under his jurisdiction in confessional matters. In Palestine there are now many Jewish sects (pp. 144 *sqq.*), the members of which differ racially, even more than culturally; for instance, the Yemenite Jews are Arab, and the Daghistani Jews are Caucasian highlanders. Many had never been Ottoman subjects, and moreover there has not been for many centuries any Jewish state of which they could claim to be nationals (photos. 45).

The Jew is to a great extent a product of his environment, and tends to be assimilated to it. But in addition to common descent and common religion, all Jews have a common tradition and history, and form

Old Jew from Safad

Immigrant Zionist Jew

An Ashkenazi Jew

Bokharan Jewess

Yemenite Jew

45. *Jewish Types*

46. *A beduin encampment*

47. *A hill-side village in Samaria*

a homogeneous community. And most of the Jews of the world disclaim anything else.

In Palestine, however various their origins—and very many are Ashkenazim (p. 146) from central and northern Europe—the Jews tend to segregate themselves, in all-Jewish districts, in villages and in town-quarters alike; and culturally and intellectually they have come to form a self-contained community, and are creating a Jewish nationality like that which has come into being in the 'ghetto-countries'. But a Jewish nationality is still very different from a Jewish nation; and as many of the persecuted Jews from Spain in the fifteenth century, and from Germany in the twentieth, had (owing to long intermarriage) only a small proportion of Jewish blood, the Jewish population of Palestine is physically of very mixed descent, and far from constituting a Jewish race.

## Language

Arabic is, and has been for very many centuries, the language of the majority of the inhabitants of Palestine. After the Arab conquest it displaced both Aramaic and Greek. English is the language of the Mandatory Government. Among the Jews, however, the language most generally spoken is Hebrew. All three are official languages. Legislation is promulgated in all of them, although when the versions differ in meaning, that of the English version prevails. All three are used in the courts and government offices, and on coins and postage stamps. Telegrams are accepted in any of the three.

Hebrew has been since biblical times the language of prayer, of scholarship, and of literature for the Jews, and also to some among the Jews of the East the language of social and commercial intercourse. In a wider field it has to some extent been the *lingua franca*, the means of intercourse between Jews of different parts of the world separated otherwise by linguistic barriers. In this last respect, however, it has had a serious and, until recent years, always growing competitor in Yiddish or Judaeo-German, the language of the Jewish ghetto communities of central and eastern Europe and the chief means of communication between Jewish settlers in Palestine and their kinsmen elsewhere.

The renaissance of Hebrew which has restored it to the position of a living language, for everyday use in Palestine, had its beginning in the cultural reformation led by Moses Mendelssohn towards the end of the eighteenth century. Although the main purpose of his movement was to lead European Jewry into European life and thought, a subsidiary aim was the revival of the Hebrew language. This movement, at first entirely literary and confined to a small circle, gradually passed beyond pure scholarship and literature into popular poetry and fiction. It remained, however, artificial and self-conscious until it became a part of the nationalist Zionist movement for return to Palestine and for return to Hebrew (p. 121). The new settlement in Palestine, which was expected to draw its members from all the lands of the Dispersion, would be a Babel unless it had a common language. To adopt Arabic, the language of Palestine, would frustrate the aims of the settlers, for it would be the first step towards a new assimilation there. Yiddish was the language of the *Ashkenazim* and *galuth*, or 'exile', only; and as it was hoped to incorporate both the Sephardim who spoke Ladino or Español and also the oriental Jews of western Asia, the decision that Hebrew should be the language of the Jews in Palestine carried general acquiescence, except among the extreme Orthodox sect which considered the secularization of the sacred tongue to be sacrilege. Outside Palestine, however, Hebrew as a living language was almost entirely ignored or discouraged, probably not on religious grounds, but lest it should create a new barrier between the Jews who spoke Hebrew and the remainder of the world.

For like the rest of the Near East, Palestine at the beginning of the twentieth century was a region in which all the Great Powers of Europe were competing for influence, and in this competition the Jewish citizens of the different states took their part. The *Alliance Israélite* had its network of schools throughout the region, which took their place in the army of the intellect and of the spirit that was to bring French culture and civilization to the East; and its language of instruction was French. The Germans, rather later, brought the German language and *kultur* through the *Hilfsverein der Deutschen Juden*, an organization like the *Alliance Israélite* for the assistance and education of Jews in the backward lands. The Anglo-Jewish Association spread English culture, with English as the language of education. The Russians and the Italians made no direct efforts to influence the Jews, and worked mainly among other sections of the population.

In 1913 this political propaganda clashed with the new Hebrew movement. The *Hilfsverein* attempted to introduce German as the language of instruction in the newly founded Technical Institute at Haifa. Palestine Jewry boycotted the new institute, withdrew its children from all schools of the *Hilfsverein*, and opened schools of its own on a Hebrew basis. This was the beginning of the present Hebrew public school system of Palestine, which in 1940 educated 56,900 children, 68 per cent. of the Jewish school population. In 1931, 165,488 Jews returned Hebrew as the language used in ordinary life. This figure, however, cannot be taken as accurate. 'At the census taken in 1922 Jews were encouraged to return Hebrew as their usual language. In 1931 propaganda was conducted by one section of the Jewish community to the end that all Jews should return Hebrew as their language, while a section of the orthodox sub-communities sought to encourage Jews to return Yiddish or Español' (*Census of Palestine 1931*, vol. i, p. 221). The figures of the partial census of 1917, over which the British military authorities had no control, were still more exaggerated, as a part of a nationalist campaign. Even the Jewish Agency itself, in the report of a census of the Jews of Jerusalem, which it conducted in 1939, stated that literacy and language were omitted from the questionnaire 'as the possible replies were expected to be of a rather subjective character'.

Tabulated returns of these three censuses follow:

*Number of Jews using Hebrew, Yiddish, or Español in 1931 and 1922*

| | Persons | | Hebrew | | Yiddish | | Español | |
|---|---|---|---|---|---|---|---|---|
| | *1931* | *1922* | *1931* | *1922* | *1931* | *1922* | *1931* | *1922* |
| Palestine | 174,610 | 83,794 | 165,488 | 80,396 | 4,694 | 1,946 | 865 | 357 |
| Jaffa | 7,209 | 5,087 | 5,787 | 19,498 | 296 | 356 | 136 | 49 |
| Tel Aviv | 45,568 | 15,065 | 43,906 | | 1,054 | | 113 | |
| Jerusalem | 51,222 | 33,971 | 47,950 | 32,341 | 1,429 | 999 | 481 | 174 |
| Haifa | 15,293 | 6,230 | 14,687 | 5,683 | 457 | 332 | 40 | 39 |

*Number of Jews per 1,000 using Hebrew, Yiddish, Español in 1931 and 1922*

| | Hebrew | | Yiddish | | Español | |
|---|---|---|---|---|---|---|
| | *1931* | *1922* | *1931* | *1922* | *1931* | *1922* |
| Palestine | 948 | 959 | 27 | 23 | 5 | 4 |
| Jaffa | 803 | 968 | 41 | 18 | 19 | 2 |
| Tel Aviv | 942 964 | | 26 23 | | 5 2 | |
| Jerusalem | 936 | 952 | 28 | 29 | 9 | 5 |
| Haifa | 922 | 912 | 29 | 53 | 3 | 6 |

The absolute and the proportional statistics for other languages are not shown.

*Results of an Internal Census of the Jewish Community in Palestine during the War and taken as at 1916–1917*

| Locality | | Usual language spoken by the Jews in different localities | | | | | | | |
|---|---|---|---|---|---|---|---|---|---|
| | *Persons* | *Hebrew* | *Yiddish* | *Español* | *Arabic* | *French* | *Other languages* | *Not recorded, and children less than one year of age* |
| Total persons  . | 32,485 | 14,144 | 10,025 | 1,180 | 4,393 | 132 | 430 | 2,181 |
| Jaffa   .    . | 4,117 | 962 | 1,133 | 378 | 904 | 49 | 30 | 661 |
| Tel Aviv   . | 2,192 | 1,011 | 630 | 32 | 62 | 17 | 111 | 329 |
| Haifa   .    . | 1,406 | 177 | 353 | 22 | 813 | 6 | 11 | 24 |
| Tiberias   . | 3,066 | 1,822 | 1,065 | 4 | 125 | 8 | 5 | 37 |
| Safad  .    . | 2,688 | 135 | 1,783 | 5 | 628 | 2 | 18 | 117 |
| Hebron    . | 757 | .. | 218 | 424 | 42 | .. | .. | 73 |
| Colonies   . | 15,100 | 8,224 | 4,593 | 301 | 965 | 50 | 238 | 729 |
| Workers' groups | 1,799 | 1,100 | 250 | 12 | 363 | .. | 17 | 57 |
| Yemenites   in colonies   . | 1,360 | 713 | .. | 2 | 491 | .. | .. | 154 |
| Per 1,000   . | 1,000 | 436 | 309 | 36 | 135 | 4 | 13 | 67 |

In 1931 the census gave sixty languages spoken normally and in everyday use. Arabic and Hebrew were the principal ones: 779,081 individuals, of whom 2,216 were Jews, returned Arabic as their native or adopted tongue. 165,488 gave Hebrew as their normal language. Yiddish was spoken by only 4,694 (4,610 Jews, 84 'others'). *Español* or *Ladino*, the other Jewish tongue, had only 865 normal speakers, all Jews. There must have been very few Jews who did not speak at least one other language; even among the native Jews, French, German, and to a less extent English, were common, the result of the activities of the foreign Jewish educational organizations and the English missionary institutions. Among many of the Jews, however, the speaking of Hebrew, and a pretence of ignorance of all other languages, are considered patriotic. In the older Jewish villages Arabic is widespread among those born in the country, while among Arabs whose work or business brings them in contact with Jews, Hebrew is spreading. Arabic is taught in some of the Hebrew schools; Hebrew in none of the Arab schools. In 1931 French was very prevalent among the Arabs of the towns; latterly English has taken first place among all residents in the larger towns, except perhaps in Tel Aviv.

## RELIGION

In Palestine the broad religious classifications—Moslem, Christian, and Jew—are not sufficient. The differences between the several sects within each great religious division, if not wide, are often deep, and in any conspectus of the texture of the population these have to be taken into consideration.

### The Moslems

Setting aside such semi-Moslem communities as the Bahais, the Druses, and others as heresies, Islam is represented in Palestine by the Sunnis and the Shias, of whom the former are in an overwhelming majority; only 4,100 Shias were recorded in the census of 1931. With the exception of the brief period of Fatimite domination, Palestine has been overwhelmingly Sunnite since its conquest by the Arabs in 636. The Sunnis, or observers of the *sunnas* (precedents or traditions), fall into five great schools. Of these four—Shafi, Hanbali, Hanafi, and Maliki—are represented in Palestine, the Shafi school comprising 70 per cent. of the Sunnis of Palestine and the Hanbali 19 per cent.

The *Shias* were the 'party' of Ali, first cousin of the Prophet, and arose when Persian and other non-Arab converts to Islam brought with them ideas derived from their former religions, especially that of the revelation of divinity in a series of *imams* ('prophets') descended from Ali, and of the eventual return of one of these imams as *Mahdi* ('guided of God') to open the Messianic Age. They do not accept the Ommayad caliphate or its successors. The Shias broke up early into sects. In Palestine they are for the most part *Mitwali* (*Matawila*) from the Lebanon, and are settled close to the Lebanese frontier. They expect the second coming of the Twelfth Imam, a boy who disappeared down a well in Baghdad about A.D. 874. Their spiritual centre is at Kerbela in Iraq, but in the Lebanon they are an organized community with religious courts which apply their own law.

The Circassian refugees in Palestine (p. 137) are also Shias, and the Bahais (*below*) are derived from Shias.

*The Druses.* In northern Palestine, especially in the Haifa and Acre sub-districts, are a few villages of Druse settlers from the Hauran. They had 7,028 inhabitants in 1922 and 9,198 in 1931.

The Druses, a nationality based on a mystical religion, appeared in the Lebanon soon after A.D. 1000 as the followers of Ismail el Daruzi who proclaimed that Hakim, Fatimite caliph of Egypt, was divine. Other doctrines were preached by Hamza, the Persian vizir of Hakim;

but only the initiated (*uqal*, *akil*) know the principles of their faith, which appear to combine beliefs from Islam, Judaism, and Christianity with primitive pagan practices. The uninitiated (*jahel*, *juhal*) 'observe but do not inquire', and all alike conform outwardly to the dominant faith wherever they may be. From the Lebanon the Druses spread to the Hauran between 1700 and 1750, and in both districts have defended their independence against all aggressors. In 1861 the Lebanon became a privileged province under Christian auspices; but there are many Druses outside and especially south of it; and those who migrated to the Hauran are now the most numerous and have overflowed into northern Palestine, where they are peaceable, monogamous, with high morality, good education, and strong sense of justice. They are almost all engaged in agriculture.

*The Bahais.* Around Haifa and Acre are a few Bahais—265 in 1922, 350 in 1931—adherents of a modern Shiite sect founded in 1844 at Tabriz by a Persian, Mirza Ali Mohammad, who announced himself as the *bab* ('gate') by which believers have access to the 'hidden' Twelfth Imam. Later he declared himself the Imam, and was put to death at Tabriz in 1850. The moral teaching of his son Mirza Yahya became very popular and was much persecuted in Persia: there were at one time many Babi converts in North America. After a schism in 1863 the dissentient Baha-ullah declared himself Imam and gave his own name to his sect, which alone persists. Bahais accept Mohammad and the Koran, but hold that revelation is progressive. Baha-ullah died at Acre in 1892: his son and successor Abbas Effendi Abdul Baha settled at Haifa, received the honour of knighthood in 1919, and was buried there in 1921. His tomb is a place of pilgrimage.

### The Jews

The two principal classes into which the Jews fall are the *Sephardim* and the *Ashkenazim*. These do not, however, represent differences in ritual, except on minor points. They are geographical in origin.

The *Sephardim* are the descendants of those Jews who settled in the Iberian peninsula before the opening of the Christian era and were expelled from Spain in 1492 and from Portugal in 1497. Many *Sephardi* communities in the East still speak Español or Ladino, a Spanish dialect (p. 140). Until recent years the Sephardim composed not only the largest section of the Jews of Palestine, but considered themselves, and were accepted there, as the *élite* of Jewry. They derive their name from Sepharad (*Obadiah*, xx), which was the

48. *Moslems at prayer*

49. *Samaritans at prayer*

50. *The Orthodox Church Ceremony of the Washing of the Feet at the Church of the Holy Sepulchre, Jerusalem*

traditional name applied to Spain by Jews in the Middle Ages. Steeped in the culture of Spain in its greatest period, the Sephardim, while in their former homes and for some centuries later, were, intellectually as well as materially, far in advance of the Ashkenazim of northern and central Europe, who were for the most part confined in ghettos, intellectual and physical. In Europe and America they retained this high level, and ultimately, to a large extent, merged in the surrounding population. In Palestine they retained their exclusiveness and deteriorated. The term *Sephardim* is now often used to denote any community of Jews which is not definitely Ashkenazim (whether or not it follows the Sephardi rite of prayer) and which follows the usage of the Sephardim in the pronunciation of Hebrew.

The Sephardim proper began to reach Palestine after the expulsion from Spain in 1492. For the most part they settled at Safad, which they made the centre of Jewish mysticism, and in Jerusalem, which had by this time again obtained a Jewish population and relaid its foundations as a centre of Jewish learning.

Other small groups of oriental Jews in Palestine are all loosely included among the Sephardim. These are all recent arrivals, their communities having been founded by immigrants during the nineteenth century. The only one that can be said to be prosperous is the Bokharan community, men of substance (as a rule) who came from the Khanates of Bokhara and Khiva, and from Samarkand in Russian Turkistan; they claim descent from the exiles who were taken to Babylon by Nebuchadnezzar in 587 B.C. They are not numerous, and all live in Jerusalem, as their ancestors lived, and speak the language, Judaeo-Persian, that their ancestors spoke in central Asia. They began to settle as recently as 1893.

The Yemenite Jews are the best known of these oriental communities. They came from the Yemen in south Arabia, where the political and social conditions still resemble those of Arabia in the early years of Islam, under which the Jews were burdened with disabilities, and from Aden and the Protectorate (photo. 45). Descendants of those Jewish tribes of Arabia who refused to accept Islam, they are physically more like Arabs than Jews, being perhaps related in origin with those who departed with the Queen of Sheba after her visit to King Solomon, or more likely with those engaged in the caravan trade between south Arabia and Petra (p. 447). The immigration of Yemenite Jews into Palestine began between 1880 and 1890, and has continued practically without cessation, although not in large numbers. Their native tongue is Arabic, they have their own strict ritual, and they are almost without exception artisans or craftsmen, though a few are hawkers. Among their women are found the best Jewish domestic servants of Palestine. Only within very recent years have one or two gained entry into the professions. They have settled in all parts of Palestine, forming villages of their own on the outskirts of Tel Aviv, Haifa, and Jerusalem, and of the larger Jewish villages. Including those not born in the Yemen but of Yemenite origin, they are said to number about 20,000; but this is an exaggeration.

Other small oriental Jewish communities are those of the Persian Jews (some of whom come from Iraq), the Moroccan Jews, and those from Urfa in Asia Minor. Their numbers are not large and their position is low: most of them have settled in Jerusalem, where they are professional beggars. The Jews of Georgia also live mainly in Jerusalem and form a small separate community, but they are of higher standing than the others. There are even a few Falashas, black Jews from Ethiopia, very recent arrivals in Palestine, who are hardly distinguishable in appearance, custom, or language from their neighbours in Ethiopia. They too are connected in legend, if not in history, with the visit of the Queen of Sheba. Their religion is certainly Judaism, but rather debased, and their traditions support a Palestinian origin.

The *Ashkenazim* are the Jews of northern and central Europe, and originally of German lands. In the *Talmud* the biblical Ashkenaz is son of Gomer, whose name was thought by some to resemble that of Germany. But though in the early Middle Ages they lived mainly in Germany and northern France, in physical build they approximate more than other Jews to central European types, and most modern Ashkenazim are of Polish or other east European origin. In ritual, their main difference from the Sephardim is in their pronunciation of Hebrew. Throughout the world it is computed that about 90 per cent. of the Jews are Ashkenazim.

In Palestine, where they now form the overwhelming majority of the Jewish population, they are for the most part very recent. For instance, until 1837 when earthquakes in Safad and Tiberias destroyed the Jewish quarters and the survivors had to leave, it is said that there were not a dozen Ashkenazim in Jerusalem. About that time, however, the Ashkenazim began to leave Russian territories for Palestine. Being men of religion, who devoted themselves to study and prayer, they were practically without means, and depended for subsistence on the *chalukkah*, a system by which funds have been

collected throughout the Jewish Dispersion since its beginning
for the maintenance of Jewish worship and its ministers in the Holy
Land. The Ashkenazi *chalukkah* contribution from Russia, however,
began only in 1777, and to meet the new demands of these Russian
immigrants, the collection had to be considerably increased.

Included among the Ashkenazim are the *Chassidim* or Pietists, who
arose in eastern Europe in the eighteenth century as a consequence
of the Cossack persecution of the Jews in Poland. Chassidism is a
mystical movement, and its leaders are as a rule miracle-workers, or
believed to be so by their followers. The Chassidim are opposed to
the more rational-minded Talmud Jews, and in Europe there have
been long-standing contests between them. They are not very influential in Palestine and are to be found mostly in Jerusalem, where
their synagogue is the second most noteworthy in the city. Steeped in
their beliefs and their mysticism, they take no part in the life of the
people, or in politics.

At the other extreme are the recent arrivals from Germany, who
have established in Palestine a few Jewish congregations, where a
Liberal Judaism of very assimilative character is preached. The
Liberal Jews—found mostly in Germany and North America, with
a smaller number in England and the British dominions—are
on the very edge of Judaism, and fade imperceptibly into Unitarianism and Deism, their Jewish origin being almost their only distinguishing feature.

On the edge of Jewry also, but not within it, are two other communities, both consequences of schisms of many centuries ago and
now represented by very few members in Palestine.

The *Samaritans* are the lineal descendants of the new settlers
placed in Samaria by the Assyrians on the destruction of the kingdom
of Israel in the eighth century B.C. (p. 87). These amalgamated with
those Israelites who were not exiled. Their offer to share in the rebuilding of the Temple of Jerusalem was rejected on the ground that
they were not pure Israelites, and the feud has persisted almost until
the present day. The Samaritans strictly observe biblical Judaism,
accepting the Pentateuch, but rejecting the Prophets and the rabbinical writings. They practise animal sacrifice, and celebrate the
Passover on Mount Gerizim, which they believe to be the site of
Solomon's Temple (photo. 49).

Their numbers were once fairly large, but the outlying settlements
have disappeared, and for many years the remnant has been concentrated in Nablus. The 1931 census gave 182 Samaritans in

Palestine, of whom 160 were in Nablus. Their language is Arabic, but their ritual language Aramaic: their educational and material standard is low.

The *Karaites* are the remnant of a reforming anti-rabbinical movement in Mesopotamia in the eighth century. They are said to number about 12,000 in all. The Karaite community of Palestine was never large; before 1914 it is said to have numbered from 80 to 100, but most of these are believed to have emigrated to Cairo, which has long been the main centre of Karaism.

## The Christians

It is only to be expected that many Christian sects, like the thirteen Jewish, should be enumerated in the census of Palestine; but only a few are either numerous or important. It is necessary to distinguish between communions which either originated in Palestine or have long historical position there, and the Palestinian establishments—some of them ephemeral—of sects centred elsewhere, for whom the 'Holy Land' has a sentimental attraction. The best known are the Orthodox Churches, Greek and Russian; the Latin or Roman Catholic Church, known in Palestine as the Latin Church, and the eastern (*Uniate*) churches in union with it; the Armenian, Coptic, Abyssinian, and Jacobite churches; and the Protestant churches—Anglican (with the Episcopal Church of Scotland), Presbyterian, Lutheran, and numerous 'free' or non-conformist communions of European or American origin.

*The Orthodox Church.* Of all the Christian communities the Orthodox, known also as the Greek Orthodox or Greek Church—and popularly as *Roumi* (i.e. Byzantine)—is the largest and usually the most important. It is under the direction of the Patriarch of Jerusalem, who traces his succession back to the Bishops of Jerusalem, of whom St. James, the 'brother of the Lord', was the first. On the destruction of Jerusalem in A.D. 70 the seat of the Church was removed to Caesarea, and its head was entitled 'Metropolitan'. At the Council of Chalcedon in 451 the see became a patriarchate. Under the Latin kingdom the patriarchate was exiled to Constantinople, where it remained till it returned to Jerusalem in 1867.

When the British civil administration was formed in 1921 the patriarchate was found to be in considerable difficulty—financial, on account of the cessation of its revenue from Russia and Romania, on which it had long depended, and constitutional, on account of protracted contest between the Patriarch Damianos and his synod. The financial difficulties were relatively easy to solve. The patriarchate owned large estates in Palestine. A financial commission was appointed by the Government, and after some years the estates were made to yield a sufficient revenue to meet the expenses.

The constitutional difficulties have not yet been solved. They derive from two controversies (a) between the clergy and the laity as to their shares in the government of the Church; (b) between Greek and Arab, for ecclesiastical offices and privileges. As the laity is mainly Arabic-speaking, and the higher clergy mainly of Greek descent, these questions are interconnected: and in 1923 the appointment of a Bishop of Nazareth, who could not speak Arabic, brought the dispute to a crisis. The Patriarch is also officially president of the Confraternity of the Holy Sepulchre, and guardian of the Sacred Shrines on behalf of those Christian communities which do not claim ownership of any of them; but he has never had funds for their maintenance and has had to appeal for assistance from without. Moreover, as expenditure on repairs by any one of the Churches might result in a claim to ownership, the Government, Ottoman or Palestinian, has sometimes had to effect urgent repairs at its own expense. The jurisdiction of the Patriarch is practically coextensive with Palestine and Transjordan. He is assisted by a number of titular bishops who bear the title 'Metropolitan' or 'Archbishop'. They have no real diocesan jurisdiction, their functions being either to represent the Patriarch in the districts, or to assist in the ecclesiastical ceremonies in Jerusalem.

Members of the Orthodox Church in Palestine in 1931 numbered 39,727, or over 40 per cent. of the total Christian population. Most of them are in the Jerusalem, Bethlehem, and Jaffa sub-districts. The liturgical language is not always Greek, which is, however, spoken by the higher clergy; but the lay members and the lower clergy are almost entirely Arabic-speaking, and the services are often sung in Arabic. During the last two generations there has been a movement for union between the Orthodox and Anglican Churches.

*The Latin Church.* The second largest Christian community in Palestine is the Roman Catholic or 'Latin' Church. Its members numbered 14,245 in 1922 and 18,895 in 1931. Many members of this church in Palestine belong to one or other of the religious orders: Franciscans, Dominicans, Carmelites, Benedictines, Salesians, and others, or the corresponding foundations for women. Of the large number of foreigners among them (17%), 615 are British, 591 Italian, and 513 French.

The Roman Catholic Church in Palestine is under the jurisdiction of the Latin Patriarch of Jerusalem. It was established in Jerusalem by the Crusaders in 1099, but for centuries there had been Latin pilgrims and monasteries in the Holy Land. For two centuries the history of the patriarchate and of the kingdom was practically identical. On the capture of Jerusalem by Saladin (1187) the patriarchate removed to Acre, and after the fall of that city in 1291, there was no resident patriarch, though the title was conferred on a prelate of the Roman Curia. In 1847 the see was revived and occupied by a patriarch residing in Jerusalem. While the patriarchate was in abeyance, the Latin Holy Places were in the charge of the Franciscan Order under the 'Father Custodian of the Holy Land', a title which still survives. Its holder is appointed by the General of the Franciscan Order, and is invariably an Italian. He is assisted by a French Vicar, a Spanish Procurator, and a council of five of whom one is always British, one French, one Italian, and one Spanish. There is also an Apostolic Delegate for Palestine.

*The Uniate Churches.* In Palestine there are six independent Catholic communions which have acknowledged the supremacy of the Pope, but preserve their own liturgies and customs—the Melkites, the Maronites, the Armenian Uniates or Catholics, the Syrian Catholics (Uniates who have separated from the Jacobites, p. 152), the Assyrian Catholics or Chaldaeans, and the Abyssinian Uniates. But of these only the Melkites and the Maronites are numerous.

The Melkites, who originated in the sixth century, are the largest of the Uniate communities of Palestine. Their rite is Byzantine (Orthodox), but their liturgical language is Arabic. The Patriarch as a rule lives in Syria at Damascus or in the Lebanon, but there is a Melkite Archbishop of Galilee at Haifa, and a seminary for priests in Jerusalem. There were 11,191 Melkites in Palestine in 1922: 12,645 in 1931, of whom all but a thousand were in the northern district, for the most part in Haifa, Acre, Nazareth, and their neighbourhoods.

The Maronites are to be found for the most part in Syria, in the Lebanon. They are certainly the oldest of the Uniate Churches, and are said to represent most closely the ancient Church of the country before the Arab conquest. In 1931 there were 3,431 (in 1922, 2,382) in Palestine, mostly in the Haifa sub-district, some in Safad and its neighbourhood. Their rite is Syrian, and their liturgical language Syriac. This Church is governed by a patriarch who resides in the Lebanon, but there is a Maronite Bishop of Tyre and Palestine, who resides at Tyre.

The Armenian Uniates of Palestine are mostly in Jerusalem, where they own a handsome cathedral. They derive from the Armenians of Cilicia who allied themselves with the Crusaders, ecclesiastically as well as militarily. The Armenian Catholic Patriarch of Cilicia, at Azzem near Beirut, is now represented in Jerusalem by a Vicar-General. The Armenian Uniates have retained the Armenian liturgy and rites, modified to suit Vatican standards. They numbered 271 in 1922 and 330 in 1931.

The Syrian Catholics of Palestine are also for the most part in Jerusalem, with a theological seminary at Bethany. They are governed by a titular Patriarch of Antioch, who resides in Beirut. In Palestine there were 323 in 1922 and 171 in 1931, but the Assyrian Catholics may have been counted among them in the earlier year.

Of the Assyrian Catholics in Palestine, 106 in 1931, 40 were living in Jerusalem and 52 in the Haifa–Acre neighbourhood.

A few Abyssinian Uniates have retained an oriental ritual, but are in communion with Rome.

On one occasion in the year, the 'Carnival of the Rites', nine days before the general carnival, representatives of all the Latin and Uniate Communities of Jerusalem meet each on successive days, before the Convent of the Réparatrices, to pray on behalf of those who might be tempted by the attractions of the carnival. The Mass is recited on different days, according to six different rites, and sermons are preached in as many languages. Nowhere else, not even in Rome, is there a similar occasion.

*The Armenian Church.* After the Orthodox and Latin Churches the Armenian (Gregorian) Church has the largest number of followers in Palestine: 2,939 in 1921; 3,167 in 1931. Two-thirds of these live in Jerusalem and most of the remainder in Haifa and Jaffa. The history of this national church, founded by St. Gregory the Illuminator, goes back at least to A.D. 250. In early days it paid much respect to the Church of Jerusalem, whence it derived its lectionary and its arrangement of the Christian year, but it has been for many centuries quite distinct from the Orthodox, and also from the Roman Catholic Church. In the fifth century there were Armenian convents on the Mount of Olives, and in the seventh century there were seventy in Palestine. From early times there has been a Bishop of the Armenian Church in Jerusalem, and there was already an Armenian Patriarch in 1006. His jurisdiction formerly extended to the Armenians of Cyprus and Syria; now it is limited to the Gregorian Church of Palestine. In September 1921, a new Armenian Patriarch was enthroned after formal approval of his election by King George V, the first occasion on which a British sovereign has supervised the election of the head of an Eastern Church. Their Cathedral of St. James the Great and St. James the Less, together with a vast patriarchate, schools, chapels, and gardens, occupies most of the south-west quarter of the city within the walls, and possibly encloses part of the gardens of Herod's Palace.

*The Coptic Church.* Though there are said to have been more than 2,000 Copts in Palestine in 1900, there were only 297 in 1922 and 219 in 1931, resident in Jerusalem, Jaffa, and Ramleh. The Copts are members of the ancient Church of Egypt, said to have been founded by St. Luke, but differentiated by the Monophysite doctrine—that Christ had one composite nature—of which Egypt was the centre. Their name is synonymous with Egyptian and their language is derived from the ancient language of Egypt. Their ritual is still very primitive, not having developed since their separation from other Christians in 639; its language, originally Greek, has long been Coptic. The Coptic Patriarch of Alexandria still includes 'Jerusalem, the Holy City' in his title, but the head of the Coptic Church in Palestine is a Metropolitan bishop who lives at Jaffa, where there is a large Coptic convent for the care of pilgrims from Egypt, who are numerous at Easter.

*The Abyssinian Church.* Membership of the Abyssinian Church in Palestine has risen from 85 in 1922 to 282 in 1931, almost all employed in the service of the Church, which is ancient, monophysite, and in communion with the Copts. There are several Abyssinian convents in Jerusalem, a church outside the walls, and a monastery on the bank of the Jordan. Pilgrimage to Jerusalem is a religious duty and covers many sins. The Abyssinian Church has always been bitterly opposed to missionaries of other churches. Among the Abyssinians, as among the other oriental communities, church and state are almost synonymous, and a change of religion, even from one sort of Christianity to another, is treasonable.

*The Jacobites.* The Syrian Orthodox Church, founded by the monophysite Jacob Bardaeus in the sixth century, had 813 members in 1922 and 1,042 in 1931, mainly in Jerusalem and Bethlehem; most of its congregations have long been farther east. These Syrian Christians are in communion with the Coptic Church; their liturgy, attributed to St. James, is in Syriac, and preserves the ancient ritual of Antioch. The Jacobite convent in Jerusalem is built round the traditional house of St. Mark.

*The Anglican Church.* Among the numerous foreign churches with an establishment in Palestine, the Anglican Church has a special interest, being the church of the Mandatory Power. Members of the Anglican confession in Palestine numbered 4,553 in 1922 and 4,799 in 1931; of the latter, 38 per cent. were Palestinian citizens.

The history of the Anglican Church in Palestine begins in 1825 when the London Society for Promoting Christianity among the Jews began its activities on a modest scale at Jerusalem, Safad, and Tiberias, and also in Syria. English interest in Palestine and the Jews was then very active and the new movement immediately secured support. In 1839, when Mehemet Ali was in control of Palestine, permission was given to erect a church in Jerusalem, but in the following year Mehemet was driven out of the country and another ten years passed before Christ Church near the Jaffa Gate was completed. By the following year a hospital, schools, and other institutions had been opened. Meanwhile, an Anglo-Prussian bishopric of Jerusalem had been established, at the instance of King Frederick William IV of Prussia, who proposed the nomination of a bishop by the British and Prussian sovereigns alternately. The proposal was welcomed by Queen Victoria and her government, but there was much opposition on the part of High Churchmen, who objected to the connexion with a non-episcopal communion, and who felt that the proposed bishop would be a rival to the Orthodox Patriarch. However, in 1841, Parliament approved the arrangement, and Queen Victoria appointed Michael Solomon Alexander, a convert from Judaism, to be the first 'Bishop in Jerusalem'.[1] The Jerusalem bishopric is the oldest of the twenty-one dioceses which do not come within any ecclesiastical province but are directly under the metropolitical jurisdiction of the Archbishop of Canterbury.

Bishop Alexander, whose activities were largely missionary, provoked strong protests on the part of the Jews not only of Palestine but also of England.[2] He died while on a journey in 1845, and was succeeded, on the nomination of the King of Prussia, by Samuel Gobat, a Swiss pastor, who was more interested in the Arabs than in

---

[1] The statute constituting the bishopric is said to have convinced Newman of the heretical character of the Church of England, and thereby turned him towards Rome.

[2] 'The Statement of Proceedings relating to the Establishment of the Bishopric' relates that 'his chief missionary care will be directed to the conversion of the Jews, to their protection, and to their useful employment'. For details of many of these disputes, see *The British Consulate in Jerusalem 1838–1914*, edited by A. M. Hyamson, Part I, 1939; Part II, 1941.

the Jews. He held the see for thirty-three years, during which he had fair success among Arabic-speaking members of the Orthodox Church, despite his instructions to 'establish and maintain relations of Christian charity with other Churches represented at Jerusalem, and in particular with the Orthodox Greek Church; taking special care to convince them that the Church of England does not wish to disturb, or divide, or interfere with them'. Before he died he had formed groups of Arab-speaking Anglican Protestants in all parts of Palestine and Transjordan in which Christians were to be found. Bishop Gobat was succeeded by Joseph Barclay, who died after two years. Prussia then withdrew from the arrangement, and there was an interregnum for six years; but in 1887 the Archbishop of Canterbury, at the express wish of the Orthodox Patriarch, appointed an Anglican bishop in the person of George Francis Blyth. Successors were in due course appointed, and the relations between them and the Orthodox patriarchate have always been excellent. Under Blyth the Cathedral Church of St. George, with schools and other subsidiary buildings, was erected, and a fund, supported by friends in all English-speaking lands, was established. The American Episcopalian Church supports an American chaplain who is one of the canons of St. George's, and shares in its work, and the name of the President of the United States is coupled with that of the King in the State prayers. The Anglican Church in Palestine cares for the spiritual welfare of most of the British Government officials and also, in war-time, of officers and men of the Imperial Forces from all parts of the Empire. For a time the jurisdiction of the bishop extended over Anglicans in Egypt, the Sudan, Cyprus, and Syria, but it is now limited to Cyprus, Syria, and Iraq, in addition to Palestine and Transjordan. Its institutions include secondary schools for boys and girls in Jerusalem and Haifa, which are attended by Moslems and Jews as well as by Christians.

The Church of Scotland has a beautiful church dedicated to St. Andrew, close to the Jerusalem railway station. A number of other Reformed Churches (English, American, Swedish, &c.) also work in Palestine. Before the present war the German Lutherans carried on an extensive evangelistic and philanthropic work; this is now under the care of the Anglican Bishop.

*The German Templists.* Among the settlements of millenarian believers in Palestine, the 'German Templists' are of special interest. This sect, which has its name from *Ephesians* ii. 21, arose in Württemberg in the middle of the nineteenth century. Of its members 250, led by Christopher Hoffmann, came to Palestine in 1869 to establish the ideal Christian community in the Holy Land, and thence to regenerate the religious and social life of Europe. While holding themselves Christians, they reject many of the dogmas of Christianity, and base their teaching mainly on Old Testament prophecies. Their first settlement was at Haifa: others followed at Jaffa, Jerusalem, Sarona and Wilhelma near Jaffa, and a new Bethlehem (Beit Lahm) near Nazareth. In 1931 they numbered 1,113, almost half living in Jaffa and its neighbourhood. They engage for the most part in agriculture and are to a less extent shopkeepers and artisans. Industrious, law-abiding, and friendly disposed towards their neighbours, these Württemberg peasants and small shopkeepers are in normal times among the most valuable and steady elements in the population of Palestine.

*The American Colony* is also a millenarian sect. The present one came into existence in 1881, but it had a predecessor, similar in teaching, some forty years earlier. This arose out of one of the American 'revivalist' movements, led by a Father Miller who prophesied that the world would come to an end in 1843 and collected some 50,000 followers in the United States. Their expectation was disappointed, but Mrs. Minor of Philadelphia, a wealthy disciple, led a colony to Palestine to prepare for the new era, which devoted itself to agriculture at Urtas near Bethlehem. When Mrs. Minor died in 1855, few were left. Eleven years later a new 'American Colony' arrived and were known as 'Adamites', from their leader, G. J. Adams. After continuous misfortunes the settlement was soon dispersed, and their houses, in the 'German Colony' of Jaffa, were acquired by the German Templists.

The present 'American Colony' was founded in 1881 by Mrs. Spafford, an American millenarian and philanthropist. Some of her American followers were of Swedish origin, others came direct from Sweden, others from the Jewish population of Palestine. At first it devoted its energies, and the founder's fortune, to benefit the poorer Arabs of Jerusalem. Later, as funds diminished, commerce and tourist traffic were undertaken, and after Mrs. Spafford's death in 1923 there were further changes, and a schism; but the 'colony' remains a sect, differing in many respects from other Christian bodies.

## CULTURE

The sphere of culture is somewhat indefinite. It can be taken to cover a variety of activities, some only slightly related. The field is that of thought and feeling rather than of action. Things of beauty belong to culture: practical use is not the principal consideration. In this loose sense there is more than one culture in Palestine. But in this matter the division is not between Arab and Jew, but between European and oriental. In the European community, Jewish and non-Jewish, including also the few Arabs with European education or long residence in Europe, there are gradations of culture as in Europe and America. But within these gradations Jew and non-Jew are alike. Similarly, among the orientals, Jewish and non-Jewish, in many of the divisions of culture Palestinian Jew, Christian, and Moslem, and Yemenite or Bokharan Jew are nearer to one another than is European Jew to Yemenite or Bokharan.

## Music

Nowhere is this more evident than in music. The Jews, to a large extent highly cultured European people, have brought with them the music of Europe, much of which they themselves had created, and in Palestine almost from the days of their arrival they have imported, adapted, or created for themselves means of expressing themselves in the medium which is, relatively, so large a part of their life. There is in Palestine no group of European Jews, small or large, in which a violin or piano is not found and in use. From no group of Jewish men and women, no matter how poverty-stricken, or whatever their occupation, is a sense of music entirely absent. Visitors to communal settlements, where the necessities of life are obviously very scarce, have been astonished when in reply to the question: 'What would you like to make your life more comfortable?' the request is for a piano. The natural consequence is the active encouragement of music in all classes of Jewry. Nowhere is interest in music, and understanding of it, more widespread. A symphony orchestra of the first rank and international reputation is maintained, partly with outside assistance, and its concerts are among the events of Palestinian life, in the country as well as in the town. Individual recitals are frequent. There has been more than one attempt to maintain a Hebrew opera company, by which the favourite operas of European music-lovers and also less familiar ones were given. Palestine Jewry maintains schools of music in all principal towns.

Among the oriental section of the population, not only is the music of an entirely different character, alien to the European, but its pursuit is almost primitive. In this respect no comparison between the two sections is possible. Few city Arabs or oriental Jews are musical executants: but in the country, the gramophone has not yet silenced the shepherd's pipe or the primitive stringed instrument of the *fellahin*.

## Drama

After music comes the drama, with related forms of public entertainment. Here also there is a sharp division between Western and Eastern. For the latter there are occasional theatrical performances by companies from Egypt or Syria, but neither the plays nor their presentation rank very high. Public entertainment among the Arabs is for the most part in the form of café performances; among the oriental Jews there is practically none. With the Western Jews the case is very different. The Habimah Dramatic Company, formerly of Moscow, retains its international reputation and in normal times is frequently on tour in Egypt, Europe, and America; though the medium is Hebrew, the drama is, however, really Russian. The *Matate*, which has now given performances with fair continuity for twelve or fifteen years, specializes in satire, and gives sketches rather than plays. Its inspiration it draws from within Palestine, and it is in truth a product of Palestinian Jewry. A third dramatic company, the *Ohel*, is different again, half-way between the two. It was formed in Palestine and is of Palestine; originally, perhaps still mainly, amateur, its members are drawn from working men and women who devote their leisure to this form of self-expression.

## Art and Architecture

Art exhibitions are frequent, at any rate in Jerusalem and Tel Aviv, and artists are even more numerous. But Palestine Jewry has not produced any special school of painters or sculptors, nor any artists of distinction. Art in Palestine is merely an overflow of that of the Continent, to a large extent not very praiseworthy imitation of the decadents of Europe. Sculpture, which is on a very much smaller scale, seems to give greater promise. Yet the striving after art is evident, and a promise of better things to come. Among the orientals, art in the conventional sense is practically unknown.

Architecture can hardly be said to exist as an art in Palestine. There are many modern buildings, but few of architectural merit. In Palestine, especially in Tel Aviv and the new suburbs of Haifa and Jerusalem, each builder or house-owner is as a rule his own architect, with the inevitable results. Tel Aviv, a city twenty-five years old, is a heterogeneous collection of erections (photo. 87). Of the principal new buildings of Jerusalem, Government House, the Archaeological

Museum, and the General Post Office were entrusted to an English architect of genius. The War Cemetery, also the work of an English artist, is worthy of its purpose, its site, and its setting. But the group of university buildings suffered from plurality of architects and styles.

On the types of houses in Palestine Mr. Mills has a short paragraph in his *Report on the 1931 Census* (*see also* photos. 54 to 57):

'In the towns all types of house, from the dignified stone constructions built scores of years ago, to the dignified and undignified detached residences and tenements, built of stone or reinforced concrete, and copied from European countries, and purporting to satisfy European requirements, are found. Houses in the villages are constructed of the material found most easily. In the hill country, stone is employed; in the villages of the southern part of the maritime plain, mud bricks are commonly the material of construction.'

But many families, Arab and Jewish, live in far less susbtantial structures—in huts, in tents, in large packing-cases (known as 'lifts') in which refugees from Germany had brought their property, in constructions of mud and stones and petroleum-tins.

### Town Planning

A Central Town Planning Commission, with local commissions subsidiary to it, was included in the Civil Administration from the first, to control building and to preserve and increase amenities in the best-known centres of Palestine. Progress has been impeded by political disturbances and the indifference of local authorities; but recently the planning regulations have been enforced, and some unauthorized buildings have been pulled down. A large part of Jerusalem, and the reclaimed area which formed part of the harbour scheme at Haifa, were better treated. Jerusalem, for the first fifteen years of the new regime, had an active, devoted, and cultured mayor, an Arab who had lived many years in Constantinople and knew western Europe well, and by him were laid the lines of development of a beautiful city. In Haifa the Government kept control over the new area, which is growing up worthy of the city (photo. 80).

### Literature

The Arabs of Palestine produce very little literature: eighty-three books of original literature in the eight years preceding 1931. The Jews, on the other hand, are essentially a people of the book, in a wider sense than Moslems. In the past, after the period of the Bible, some Hebrew classics were produced in Palestine. In recent days, with the revival of Hebrew, there has been a remarkable output of books, for the size of the Hebrew-speaking population. Many, but not all of these, are translations, an appreciable number from European classics. Little original work has been produced[1] although there is an almost continuous inflow of men of letters. But masters of Hebrew literature, fairly prolific in Europe, such as Bialik the poet, and Ahad Ha'am the philosopher and essayist, became dumb when they settled in Palestine. Almost the only literary work of any consequence produced by the Jewish settlement in Palestine has been the adaptation of Hebrew, until our own day almost a dead language, to everyday use.

## Periodicals

The newspaper press, both Jewish and Arabic, is prolific. It is difficult to find any community in which there are so many periodicals: one in Hebrew for every 498 Hebrew-speaking Jews. In every Arab village there is at least one man who can read, who may be seen daily seated with a newspaper with all the male inhabitants around him. There are also a number of periodicals in English and other languages. With one or two exceptions, however, the newspaper press is not of a high level, being far more concerned with politics and propaganda than with news, of which there is generally but a meagre supply.

There are many printing-presses, mostly Hebrew, and a few publishing firms, all Jewish.

## Libraries

Libraries are few, but that of the Hebrew University at Jerusalem with about 400,000 volumes is the greatest library in the Middle East. The other principal libraries are the Khalidi, with about 7,000 Arabic manuscripts, besides Arabic and European books, the Armenian Patriarchate library (26,000 volumes), the library of the French School of Archaeology, all three in Jerusalem, and the Municipal Library of Tel Aviv. There is also a central library for the scattered Jewish communal settlements. The various Schools of Archaeology and Oriental Research make their own libraries available to recommended students. Of these there are always some at work in Palestine, and several permanent establishments. They are all foreign institutions, with the exception of the Palestine Jewish Exploration Society and the archaeological faculty of the Hebrew University, but they draw some

[1] Eleazar Ben Yehuda's *Dictionary of Modern Hebrew* and Joseph Klausner's *Life of Jesus* and *History of Modern Hebrew Literature* may be mentioned.

of their staff from the local population, and in other ways influence the thought and culture of Palestine. Lectures on historical and literary subjects are given in all parts of the country, many by European and American residents or visitors, but the very great majority in Hebrew by Jewish residents.

## Museums

Though a small and poor country, Palestine is exceptionally rich in museums. Pre-eminent among them is the magnificent Archaeological Museum in Jerusalem, the gift of an American benefactor, John D. Rockefeller Jr. Within its walls the varied and detailed past of Palestine is being reconstructed. The museum has the first claim on objects of archaeological interest discovered in the country, and, such discoveries being of almost daily occurrence, it has plenty of material for detailed reconstruction. The Palestine Folk Museum, in the Citadel at Jerusalem, has been formed and directed by British residents to collect and preserve articles pertaining to Palestinian and Transjordanian life and history: it has no endowment and is dependent on donations and the zeal of its supporters, who are gradually forming a collection that will illustrate the life and customs of the indigenous peoples.

The Hebrew University has an archaeological museum, the gift of a South African benefactor. At Tel Aviv the late mayor, Meir Dizengoff, a few years before his death, presented to the municipality his house with the nucleus of an art collection, which is still being supplemented, specializing in the works of Jewish artists.

## Popular Culture

With the oriental population the cinematograph and the broadcasting service are more popular than music or literature. Films are always assured of a full house, whether in a Jewish or an Arab centre. The displays are of varying quality, but sooner or later English favourites reach Palestine. The broadcasting service provides, as elsewhere, both information and amusement. In Arab villages it has to some extent supplanted the newspaper.

## Costume

In Palestine this is almost as varied as the population. Here is a scene within the walls of Jerusalem:

'A narrow street . . . with funny little open shops on each side, and sometimes arches across the street with houses built on them and some-

51. *The Palestine Archaeological Museum*

52. *The Hebrew University*

*Christian Arab woman*
*from Ramallah*

*Married Christian Arab woman*
*of Bethlehem*

*Beduin woman*

*Fellah woman*

53. *Costumes of Arab women*

times gardens up in the air and sometimes goats feeding on the tops of the houses. There are all sorts of people in the streets, black, white, brown, yellow, and chocolate-coloured. There are Bedouins out of the desert in their burnouses, Arabs of the town in tarbushes, Greek popes in high hats, policemen in hats that look like black fezzes, white friars in sun-helmets and white clothes, and black friars in black clothes, without boots or hats, Galician Jews in long purple or scarlet velvet robes, fur caps, and side-curls, Jewish boys in funny felt hats and side-curls, and Yemenite Jews who look like Arabs but have side-curls, and there are many other funny-looking people besides. Then there are camels and lots and lots of donkeys and horses and motor-cars and mules and goats and sheep, black, white, and black and white' (*Palestine Old and New*, pp. 118–119).

In Jerusalem there are twenty communities, each with its special costume, and further, within each community perhaps twenty varieties. Every Arab town and village or group of villages has its special costume, differing sufficiently from those of its neighbours for its inhabitants to be distinguished at a glance, yet similar to them. In Bethlehem the married women wear the tall head-dress made familiar by pictures of Europe in the Middle Ages. *Fellah* women wear on their heads circlets of silver coins. Some wear very long skirts that, if allowed, would trail yards behind them, but are tucked into their girdles. Their infants they strap on their backs or, when they are a little older, place them on their shoulder, where they sit unsupported as if riding horses (photo. 43 ). The top of their head-dress is as a rule flat, for they carry water-jars and other burdens on it—too often the ubiquitous petroleum tin. To this is attributed their noticeably graceful carriage. The man of the village wears on his head a flowing *keffiya*, bound with a rope of camel-hair, and a loose garment (*abba*) from his shoulders, but when at work he tucks it into his waist. Seeing an Arab of the lower class at work, one realizes the meaning of the phrase, 'to gird up one's loins'. The middle and upper class townsman (*effendi*) as a rule wears a *tarbush* or *fez*, a reminiscence of Turkish days. During the disturbances they wore the *aggal* and *keffiya* as a sign of national solidarity, except the *ulema* (Moslem clergy) who wear the tarbush with a handkerchief twisted around it. During the same period the Palestinian Jews also abandoned it. On the outbreak of the war the Arabs for the most part reverted to the tarbush. Those of all classes who have made the pilgrimage to Mecca wear green in their head-gear. The Arab gentleman's outdoor dress is the *jibir*, a long coat, hanging perfectly plain from neck to heel, with a low collar like that of an Anglican priest. It is often made of very fine cloth and gives an appearance of dignity. But many of the younger members of these families have abandoned the ancestral costume. They retain the tarbush, but otherwise their clothes are European.

In the villages, and to some extent among the lower classes in the towns, the Moslem women go unveiled. Among the better classes, however, veiling is general, although exceptions are becoming commoner. In the matter of veiling, which is a long-standing custom, not a religious duty, Palestine is behind Egypt and even Syria. Beneath their veils the women wear clothes of western fashion. In Egypt, among the upper classes, absence of the veil is the rule rather than the exception. In Syria it is frequent although still exceptional. In Palestine it is still very rare. Palestinian Arabs who brought brides from Beirut used sometimes—before relations between Jews and Arabs had become seriously strained—to settle in Tel Aviv, so that their wives might continue to live (as they had been accustomed) as Europeans. On the other hand, there are Arab Moslem girls who, educated at an English school or university and having lived there in the same manner as the other girls, on their return to their homes in Palestine have been secluded in the women's quarters and not permitted to go abroad unveiled. Prominent Palestinian Arabs, except those who hold religious office, invariably adopt European dress immediately they leave Palestine, and dress their wives as European women.

Differences in dress between Christian and Moslem villagers are only in detail. In the towns Christians, both men and women, dress for the most part as Europeans.

Among the Jews there are several varieties of dress, for a Jew wears the costume of the country from which he or his father has come. The overwhelming majority of the Ashkenazim wear the ordinary European costume, varied only in details. Those younger men who come from Russia wear the Russian shirt, generally black, which has become the uniform of the *Chalutz* or Zionist pioneer. The older generation, the *Chassidim* or 'pious ones', wear the dress that was customary in Poland in the fifteenth and sixteenth centuries, a long ungirdled coat (*kaftan*, in silk for festivals), a small cap, and over it a pointed velvet one with a sable brim (*streimel*; the rabbis wearing it with thirteen sable points), half shoes, and black or white stockings. The men, in this class all strictly observant Jews, keep their heads always covered, as do their married women. The *Chalutzim* never wear hats or caps. The women of the Polish and Lithuanian com-

54. *Ashdod, an Arab village of Southern Palestine*

55. *An Arab village of the coastal plain*

56. *Mud-brick dwellings of an Arab village*

57. *Bethany, on the Jericho road. A stone-built village of the Judaean hills*

munities wear bodices embroidered with silver and gold. Their daughters and nieces, the *Chaluzoth*, have not only discarded the parental costume, but even that of Europe, and often go about in shorts, imitating their male companions, to the scandal of the Arabs.

The oriental Jews as a rule wear the traditional Jewish costume of the land from which they or their parents or more remote ancestors have come. The Bokharan Jews dress as Bokharans: those from the Yemen as Arabs. Sephardi Jews of Palestinian origin often wear white underskirts and coloured over-coats, but they are rapidly adopting the more or less European dress of the Palestinian Christians. Most of them wear the tarbush, though they also discontinued the practice, at least temporarily, during the disturbances.

## The Arab Village

The village usually climbs a hill-side or crowns a hill-top—situations good for defence—and looks like a miniature walled city because the houses are joined by high walls with few windows outside. The streets are narrow and irregular, sometimes mere passages, with open spaces near the mosque, the church, or the well.

Palestinians excel in traditional masons' craft. Naturally the towns have the finer houses, but good examples are to be seen in the villages. The flat-roofed houses, of mud brick or of stone, with roof-beams sometimes supported on arches, go back at least to classical times; the vaulted types are common from the early Middle Ages, when timber became scarce. Their roofs also are sometimes flat, but sometimes the vaults appear, dome-like, above the roofs, and similar cupolas are shown in Assyrian representations of enemy towns. Quite recently this folk architecture has been employed in the Rockefeller Museum.

The building of a new house, especially of cross-vault type, is a great event in a village, a crowd of helpers singing and working at high speed: 'No joy like the joy of vaulting' is the proverb. The placing of the keystone is followed by sacrifice of sheep, feasting, congratulations, and presentation of gifts.

The house of the *fellah* has only one room, divided into a larger raised portion for the family and a lower for their livestock; on a hill-side the stable may be underneath. With security and prosperity, more villagers build separate cowsheds. There is no sanitation, except a primitive privy in houses of leading sheikhs, mostly north of Jerusalem. The thick walls, low door, and small windows are suited to the climate. The house is cool in summer and warm in winter, but dark, and serves mostly for sleeping and shelter in intemperate weather; indeed, often it is in part a cave in the hill-side. Much work is done in the yard or on the roof. Nowadays rooms are added to the old houses, windows are glazed, and new houses are being built with upper stories and larger, lighter rooms.

*Furniture.* There are usually no chairs, tables, or bedsteads. The floor is plastered and sometimes pebble-polished; rugs and reed-mats are laid over it, with piled bedding, cushions, and quilts; the walls are sometimes plastered, with or without pebble-polish or whitewash. Cupboards are contrived in the walls, with shallow clay shelves to hold oil-lamps and other objects, and a clay rack for spoons; the edges are often ornamented in clay or patterned in blue. Tall corn-bins in sun-dried clay hold the year's supply. Ornamented chests contain festal dresses and personal effects; on the walls hang coloured baskets and leather bags for coffee, rice, and other dried goods; cherished saddle-bags or saddles may be kept in this room, but usually in the stable or yard with agricultural implements.

Some houses have a fire-place; but usually smoke finds its way out through a hole in the wall or roof, closed in rainy weather; guest-rooms have an open hearth in the middle. A proverb says: 'Marble outside and soot within.' Cooking is mostly done in the yard or in a little cookhouse, with often a bread-oven. Portable clay braziers are used, for warmth and for cooking: corn is still often ground in a hand-mill, and coffee roasted on a pan and pounded in a mortar. Wooden bowls, baskets, and straw platters supplement ubiquitous earthen-ware, but in almost any house now there will be modern additions, glass, cutlery, a primus stove, and paraffin lamp. Housework is simple; the bedding is rolled up, and the floor swept with a home-made hand-broom.

*Food.* The staple food of the *fellah* consists of bread, olive-oil, and vegetables, supplemented by milk (usually soured), clarified butter, and eggs; for sweetening, honey and grape-treacle; meat is rare except on festivals, its absence compensated by excellent home-baked bread. Among a large choice of favourite vegetables are onions, tomatoes, beans, egg-plant, and wild mallow; the young leaves of many wild plants are eaten raw as salad. Fruits vary with the district; oranges, bananas, melons, and pears are very local; apricots, almonds, peaches, grapes, figs, mulberries, pomegranates, and prickly pear are common; all are eaten raw. Chief condiments are pepper, red pepper, and dried *zatar* (*Origanum syriacum*, the white marjoram, believed to be the true hyssop) mixed with *simmak* (*Rhus coriaria*). Pepper is the

58. *Gleaning near Bethlehem*

59. *Grinding corn*

60. *Ain Miriam, The Virgin's Spring, Nazareth*

61. *Mat-making from Papyrus*

62. *Reed huts on the shore of Lake Huleh*

first mention of something not home-grown; but rice, coffee, tea, and sugar are bought when funds permit.

This diet is admirable, but there is rarely enough of it to feed the family well. Real dearth is occasionally caused by crop failure; more often the bad financial position of the *fellah* compels him to sell the more nourishing foods—chickens, eggs, and milk especially—which should feed his children. Little is done to store or preserve food, except to dry fruits. The hungriest time is just before harvest when 'a mouse would go away disconsolate'.

*Cooking and Meals.* Baking is by far the most important method of cooking. On the housewife depends the quality of the bread, for she has to clean the corn by handpicking it, also often to grind it, and to sift the meal before mixing the dough. She usually knows how to make both girdle- and oven-bread; both are leavened with sour dough, but the girdle-bread, when needed in a hurry, as for visitors, may be made without leaven; it is like a thin pancake, delicious when fresh. The round cakes of oven-bread are often of high quality, and keep well. Fancy bread, popular in towns, is occasionally made in the country by adding scraps of meat or aromatic seeds; special cakes are also made for funeral feasts.

The chief meal, at evening, generally consists of a stew made with vegetables or lentils. Meat may be stewed, baked, or grilled; eggs are usually scrambled with oil; rice is boiled, seasoned with oil, and coloured yellow with bastard saffron (*Carthamus tinctoria*). *Knafe*, a favourite dish at festivals, is a home-made vermicelli.

In some villages a primitive steamer is made by putting a pottery sieve on top of the cooking-pot and joining the two with dough; a stew cooks in the pot below, and above, in the sieve, are pellets of dough. This exactly resembles the outfit for making *kouskous* in the Aures, Algeria, and may be an introduction from north Africa.

Meals used to be served in a large wooden bowl, round which all sat; but these outsize bowls are hard to come by nowadays, and a low table is laid, with platters and bowls.

## Domestic Arts

*Pottery.* The making of pottery is still a live craft with interesting and primitive processes and products. Some ware is only baked by the sun's rays; some is made by hand and baked in an open fire; some wheel-made and kiln-fired.

The sun-dried vessels, made in summer and used by the village housewife for her oven, braziers, cornbins, and chicken coops, are made of the marl used in plastering walls, mixed with the finest chopped straw. The vessels are built up by hand from the ground in stages, and not moved till dry.

*Hand-made and open-fired pottery* is a woman's craft, also in summer when water-jars and other household wares are needed in the village; occasionally it might be termed a by-craft, when the wares are sold in the district outside, as with the cooking-pots of El Jib (near Ramallah) and Kefr el Labad (near Tulkarm). The pots are usually piled mouth to wind; the fuel fired in a pile of brushwood or dung; when the potter judges that the pots are baked, she fishes them out with a long stick. The products are: large and small water-jars, jar lids and dipper jugs (commonly sold in a set of three pieces), large washing-bowls, small food-bowls, cooking-pots, egg pans, braziers, foot-baths, and sieves. At Ramallah, Sinjil, and other places pots are ornamented with designs painted in red.

Potter's wheel and kiln are used by men. The black smoked-ware of Gaza, and the fine reddish ware from Hebron, usually to be seen at the Jaffa Gate of Jerusalem, are sold all over the country. Village centres with one or two kilns are many, each supplying a small district round them, as, for example, Jaba near Sebustya and Irtah near Tulkarm. The chief products are: water-jars, jugs plain and spouted, milk pots, drinking-bottles, and bowls. Plain ware is sometimes ribbed on the wheel; at Hebron water-jars are ornamented with a fine wooden comb. Pots are sometimes ornamented after baking with patterns in oil paints of violent colours.

*Spinning and weaving* are still carried on, but many towns and villages, known to have been weaving centres, now have few or no looms working. As with the pottery, there are interesting survivals of primitive practice. Hand-spinning is still practised by men and by women in many places; both sheep's wool and goats' hair are used. Three types of loom are still in use:

(1) *The horizontal ground-loom*, identical with the beduin loom, pegged out on the ground, is used only by women, in the villages, for sacks, rugs, saddle-bags, and hammock-cradles made from handspun wool, occasionally dyed at home with madder and other vegetable dyes (e.g. Hebron district), but more usually by a dyer in the nearest town. The manner of weaving and the class of weave all resemble the technique of the desert tent-weaver, but the products are not so good, either in quality or in pattern.

(2) *The vertical loom*, like a large tapestry loom, is used only by men. The yarn is made from goats' hair spun on a hand spinning-

machine. It is woven into a material resembling tent-cloth, in warp-face weave, but no pattern is attempted except simple stripes and checks in the natural colours, grey, black, and white; it is pleasant to look at, very strong, and could be used for rugs, but is usually made into sacks. This craft has been noted in Hebron, Nablus, Safad, and a few other places.

(3) *The treadle loom* is chiefly used by men, and rarely by women in some institution under European influence. The old looms, in village or town, are of the Mediterranean type, usually small with compact frame, but there are a few great looms like those of Damascus at the *Alliance Israélite* school in Jerusalem. Only one of the old weaving-centres is still alive and busy, Mejdel, near Gaza, where cotton goods are made from imported yarn, and woollen material from both hand-spun and machine-spun yarns. This is the only place in Palestine where the traditional woman's dress is still made of local material, a cotton striped in various colours. Yet even here the craft has declined, for Mejdel had 500 looms in 1909 and a few years later only 200.

Weavers in the villages and small towns (e.g. Ramallah) chiefly make *abayas* in black and white from hand-spun and machine-spun wool. A few of the towns, e.g. Nablus, produce shepherds' coats in gay colours. At Bethlehem a speciality is the red-striped women's coat worn in that district, which keeps three or four weavers employed.

There is no doubt that, of all the crafts, weaving has suffered the most from importation of factory-made goods. A primitive agri-cultural system which has lost its crafts cannot but be in a parlous condition; here the loss of the weaving craft accounts in part for the poverty of the villagers.

*Mats and Basketry*

*Mats* for flooring and fencing are woven by men on a horizontal loom identical with the mat-loom of modern Egypt. The materials are various reeds used plain for the weft and twisted into a rope-like yarn by hand for the warp. At Abu Dis near Jerusalem the reeds are *Juncus maritimus*, from the Jordan valley. Round Lake Huleh, mats are woven by women on vertical looms from the papyrus rush; here also the weft is plain, the warp hand-twisted. The mats, thick and soft, are used for flooring. Another kind, made there on a frame, is used to cover the local huts. These mat-crafts are seasonal (photos. 61, 62).

*Basketry.* Coiled, plaited, and wicker-work are all known; but only the coiled basketry is made and used all over the country; the other two are local. Coiled basketry is made of corn straw, chosen by the girls at harvest time. Platters and baskets are made by women; the stitch is open, worked with the awl; the straw is sometimes used plain or dyed, and there is much pattern-work.

*Plaited basketry* of reeds from the coastal marshes and also of halfa grass—e.g. the two-handled baskets used for carrying earth in excavation—is made in the villages of the foothills by men and women during the winter months, a most useful by-craft.

*Wicker baskets*, large, round, and flattish for carrying goods to market, are made in Hebron district from branches of lentisk and pomegranate (photo. 53).

## Domestic Animals

Among the domestic animals of Palestine cattle come first, and of these the small, bristly Arab cow is most numerous. It has, in the course of generations, adapted itself to the local conditions, which are not very favourable to imported cattle. Its supply of milk is small; it is more useful as the main working animal of the *fellah*. The Beirut cow, higher in the scale, according to European standards, may be only a better-fed variety of the Arab cow. Although little larger than the Arab cow it gives four times the amount of milk, but it is more difficult and expensive to feed, as are the other varieties of cattle. Still better as a milk-producer—its principal purpose—is the Damascus cow, but this is more liable than the two previously mentioned varieties to suffer from climatic changes and disease. A good cross is between the Beirut and Damascus cattle. The Gaulan cow, which gives good beef, can be used as a draught animal, and also gives almost twice as much milk as the Arab cattle. It is often crossed with the European breeds which have been introduced into the country by European settlers. The value of the results has varied. The number of domestic buffaloes diminishes with the draining of the marshes, and they are now in effect limited to the Huleh district. Their economic value is not great.

The Palestine sheep belong to the fat-tailed variety. They have been native to Palestine for at least 3,000 years. But by far the most important animal for milk is the goat, of which there are two varieties, the black mamber goat (*Capra mambrica*) and the red or red-white Damascus goat. Both sheep and goats are mountain animals. They roam the hills for pasture, the goat a menace to afforestation, but the

Government is very chary of interfering with the 'poor man's cow'.

Among the beduin the one-humped camel, or dromedary, is the most important domestic animal. It is the beast of burden and the riding animal of the desert. By the fellah it is used for ploughing. Its wool and its milk are used by its owners. Even its meat is eaten occasionally, particularly on long desert journeys when food would be difficult to carry, although very few owners can afford to kill a camel for such a purpose. The centres of breeding are in the deserts of southern Palestine, of Transjordan, and of Syria.

The horse in Palestine goes back almost to the beginning of history, and there are many references to it in the Bible. It is somewhat small and delicately formed. It is not the proverbial purebred Arabian horse, the *Assileh*, although this is still to be found in Transjordan. The donkey, of a larger type than is generally met with in Europe, is, like all other domestic asses, a descendant of the wild Nubian species. It is in many respects the most valuable of all the domestic animals of Palestine. Mules are also bred, but are by no means as common as either horses or asses.

Most of the dogs of Palestine are pariahs. Formerly they were the scavengers of Palestine, but the British administration has deprived them largely of this function. Their numbers have been and continue to be reduced, partly as a precaution against rabies, which is almost endemic in Palestine (p. 234). Some of these pariah dogs have been domesticated and are kept by private owners, especially by shepherds for guarding their flocks. In the rural districts they live and hunt in packs, and become especially active in the evening. The *saluki* is a beduin dog, of greyhound type, bred in the desert.

There are domestic cats everywhere, but they do not attach themselves to one household. They are more in the nature of predatory animals. Rabbit-breeding has become an industry in very recent years. The first specimens were imported. There is some fear that in the end it may prove a plague instead of a source of wealth.

Poultry-keeping is very widespread. There is no Arab village in the country not overrun with chickens. In the Jewish villages poultry farming and egg production are managed on more scientific lines. Nevertheless, the needs of the country far outstrip the local egg production and most of the eggs consumed come from abroad. In 1939 Palestine imported 68 million eggs; according to the statement of the Jewish Agency 58,816,000 were produced on Jewish farms during the same period. The import of eggs, although still very much larger than in 1934 and previous years, has been falling since 1937, the year of the highest figures (92,909,000). In 1941 the number was only 38,760,969. The number of other poultry bred in Palestine is very small. Domestic pigeons are more plentiful.

The most recent government enumeration of livestock is that of 1937. This showed 20,053 horses, 8,989 mules, 92,205 donkeys, 28,085 camels, 169,145 cattle, 6,064 buffaloes, 209,422 sheep, 361,424 goats, and 2,660,092 poultry. Camels, buffaloes, and especially sheep and goats all show reductions on earlier figures.

## CHAPTER VII

# DISTRIBUTION OF THE POPULATION

## CENSUS FIGURES

### Estimates

THERE have been many estimates both of the population of Palestine from biblical times until our own day and of the Jewish population from time to time, but none has been more than a guess. Some of these Jewish estimates are given below:

| | | | | | | | | |
|---|---|---|---|---|---|---|---|---|
| A.D. 1170 | . | . | . | 1,440 | 1914 | . | . | . | 84,660 |
| 1523 | . | . | . | 3,700 | 1918 | . | . | . | 56,000 to 60,000 |
| 1839 | . | . | . | 12,000 | 1920 | . | . | . | 66,574 |
| 1880 | . | . | . | 35,000 | 1922 (Census) . | . | 83,794 |
| 1895 | . | . | . | 47,000 | 1931 (Census) . | . | 174,610 |
| 1900 | . | . | . | 70,000 | 1941 (Govt. Est.) | . | 474,102 |

The figures of the total population in biblical and early historical times are even less reliable. Account must be taken of popular prejudice against any 'numbering of the people', which goes back to King David's time (2 *Samuel* xxiv), and of the suspicion that a census is preparatory to taxation or conscription. Even in 1931, if the beduin had known that they would be counted, they would have struck tents and flitted overnight. The average standard of living in early days was probably lower than it is in wide districts of the country to-day, but unless the character and fertility of the country have changed radically (as there is no reason to believe), it can never have supported a population much larger than at present. It is probable that during the last century of Ottoman rule the population of Palestine remained fairly constant. A Turkish estimate of 1914 was 689,300, but the territory did not coincide with the present administrative Palestine. With the return of the refugees after the war it was approximately 673,200 in 1920. But in the following twenty years it doubled. The sources of this almost unprecedented increase in population will now be considered in some detail.

### The Census of 1931

The first census of the population of Palestine was taken on 23 October 1922; the second on 18 November 1931. The latter was far more detailed, scientific, and reliable, and, despite the difficulties of numbering a Moslem people, it can be accepted as giving a fairly accurate account of the population in 1931. Unfortunately this is the latest count. The internal disturbances in 1936 and the war in 1941 prevented the intended census in these years, but the Administration has published estimated totals for every year since 1931. The figures of the two counts and the subsequent estimates are as follows:

|  | Total | Moslems | Jews | Christians | Druses |
|---|---|---|---|---|---|
| 1922 Census . | 752,048 | 589,177 | 83,794 | 71,464 | 7,928 |
| 1931 ,, . | 1,035,821 | 759,712 | 174,610 | 91,398 | 9,148 |
| 1932 30 June . | 1,052,872 | 771,174 | 180,793 | 90,624 | .. |
| 1933 ,, . | 1,104,884 | 789,980 | 209,207 | 95,165 | .. |
| 1934 ,, . | 1,171,158 | 807,180 | 253,700 | 99,532 | .. |
| 1935 ,, . | 1,261,082 | 826,457 | 320,358 | 103,371 | .. |
| 1936 ,, . | 1,336,518 | 848,342 | 370,483 | 106,474 | .. |
| 1937 ,, . | 1,383,307 | 875,951 | 386,074 | 109,762 | .. |
| 1938 ,, . | 1,418,619 | 895,159 | 399,808 | 111,796 | .. |
| 1939 ,, . | 1,469,974 | 915,486 | 427,812 | 114,623 | .. |
| 1940 ,, . | 1,529,559 | 941,362 | 456,743 | 119,007 | .. |
| 1941 31 Dec. . | 1,585,500 | 973,104 | 474,102 | 125,413 | .. |

It will be seen that whereas the total population has increased by 53 per cent. in the ten years ending on 31 December 1941, Moslems have increased by 28 per cent., Jews by 171 per cent., and Christians by 37 per cent., during the same period.

Moreover, 85,647 beduin were estimated in 1922 and 66,337 and 216 gipsies were enumerated in 1931. The figures for 1931 are probably near the normal; but the total varies from season to season and from year to year; for as summer advances there is always an influx from Sinai and Transjordan in search of pasture, with a corresponding reflux as soon as the rains begin (p. 466).

Although, in the census of 1931, religion was considered the most important basis of classification, race or nationality was also recognized. The report of this census also supplies figures for country of birth, place of permanent residence, and 'nationality' within citizenship, but the totals are not always consistent. In a population in which immigration plays so large a part, the first of these is very important; the second is less so, inasmuch as it affects only temporary residents; the third has already been discussed (p. 134).

### Place of Birth[1]

Of 693,159 Moslems (less nomads and gipsies) recorded in the 1931 census, 680,653 (98·2%) had been born in Palestine, 8,725 in neigh-

[1] The census of 1922 did not record the place of birth. The information regarding immigrants furnished annually until and including the year 1934 also does not give this information, but instead the country of previous residence, which is by no means identical.

bouring Arab lands, 2,316 in Egypt, 485 in the other north African lands, 88 in Europe, and 92 in America.

Of the 174,610 Jews only 73,195 (42%) were Palestinian by birth. Of the others, 80,347 came from Europe (35,776 from Poland, 27,354 from Russia, 1,181 from Germany, 612 from Austria, 493 from Czechoslovakia); 652 from British possessions (80 from India); and 831 from America (672 from U.S.A.). The number born in eastern and south-eastern Europe as a whole was 76,474 (43·7%); in oriental countries other than Palestine, 19,642 (11·2%); but only 4,941 (2·8%) in western and central Europe (exclusive of Poland) and the New World.

Of the 91,398 Christians in Palestine in 1931, 73,564 (80·5%) were born there. Of the others, 4,565 came from the British Empire (176 from India), 852 from Germany, 668 from Russia, 553 from Italy, and 321 from U.S.A., most of those from Russia and Italy being men and women of religion. From the British Empire came government officials, members of His Majesty's forces, police, and other temporary residents. Excluding these special classes, Christian immigrants into Palestine were mainly from Asiatic countries.

## Nationality

Exclusive of the 66,337 nomads, all of whom were Arabs, and of 216 gipsies who were neither Arab nor Jew, 772,904 persons returned themselves as Arab by nationality, 174,809 as Jewish, and 21,555 as Europeans, Armenians, &c. Of the Moslems, 99·6 per cent. described themselves as Arabs. The remainder were principally Egyptians and Turks. Of the Christians, 80·2 per cent. were Arabs, the remainder for the most part Europeans and Armenians. More individuals described themselves as Jews by nationality than by religion (174,809 : 174,610), the difference being made up of 21 Moslems, 25 Christians, and presumably 153 others, of no classified religion. On the other hand, 87 professed Jews were of Arab 'race' and 145 of 'other races'. Of 10,101 'others' by religion, 9,116, principally Druses, described themselves as Arabs.

## Citizenship

The total number of Palestinian citizens in the country in November 1931 was 874,905, of whom about 27,500 were estimated to have acquired citizenship by naturalization.

Of the 693,159 Moslems (less nomads and gipsies), 686,560 (99%) were Palestinian citizens and 61 others had applied for naturalization.

Next in number came the citizens of Transjordan (2,179), of Syria (1,597), and of Egypt (1,383).

Of the 174,610 Jews, 100,704 (57·6%) were Palestinian citizens, and 7,902 had applied for naturalization. Of those who had not, 23,107 were Polish citizens, 8,771 citizens of the Union of Soviet Republics, 3,986 French citizens, 2,629 Romanians, 2,370 Persians, 2,222 United States citizens, 2,128 Lithuanians, and 2,062 citizens of the United Kingdom, exclusive of the administrative and military personnel. The rest of the British Empire provided 126 citizens, Germany 1,010, Austria 689, and Czechoslovakia 1,090. The Imam Yahia of the Yemen had 1,771 Jewish subjects in Palestine.

Of the 91,398 Christians, 78,291 (85·6%) were Palestinian citizens and 133 had applied for naturalization; 4,748, mostly officers of the Government, members of the armed forces, police, and their dependants, were citizens of the United Kingdom, and 50 were citizens of other parts of the empire. Of the 1,934 German nationals, most were members of the Templist sect (p. 154); the 1,267 Syrian citizens were French-protected subjects.

Comparison of these figures with those for countries of birth shows that a great majority of the Jews born in the territories of the Union of Soviet Republics, and a smaller proportion of the Polish-born Jews and of Egyptian Moslems, had acquired Palestinian citizenship. On the other hand, most of the Jewish citizens from British soil and from the United States and a smaller proportion of the United States Christians, previously naturalized in these countries, had acquired Palestinian citizenship by naturalization; while of 3,986 French-Jewish citizens in Palestine, only 254 Jews then in Palestine had been born in France.

## POPULATION INCREASE

### Causes of Increased Population

For the remarkable recent increase in the population of Palestine there are two major causes and one minor; for the northern frontier was rectified in 1923, and about 10,000 persons (9,700 Arabs and 300 Jews) were thereby annexed. The major causes were (a) natural increase by excess of births over deaths, and (b) excess of immigration over emigration. These two causes operate in different ways, and have very different consequences, now and in the near future.

### Natural Increase

The population of Palestine had probably remained fairly constant over a long period. The birth-rate was always high, but three important factors tended to neutralize this. The death-rate, mainly due to disease, was also high: military conscription year by year took a heavy toll of the young men: and, with most of the world open to emigrants, there was a constant flow of emigration from Palestine, especially to North and South America. The high birth-rate kept the population from falling; the other factors kept it from rising. In the twenty years during which the British have been responsible for administering the country, these three factors have disappeared. Conscription has been abolished; since 1930 all countries have been closed to Palestinian immigrants; British sanitary administration has brought the death-rate down to a fraction of what it was in the Ottoman period.

In recent years, also, the Jews, especially those of the United States of America, have devoted much work and wealth to both preventive and curative medicine, mainly, though not entirely, among the Jewish section of the population. Much of the preventive work—draining the marshes for instance—distributes its benefits without consideration for race, religion, citizenship, or nationality. Other organizations, such as the Venerable Order of the Hospital of St. John of Jerusalem (p. 235), have also devoted skill, energy, and money to healing the people of Palestine, thereby contributing to reduce the death-rate. Consequently, the population, 689,300 in 1914 and 673,200 at the end of the war and after the return of refugees in 1920, increased to 752,048 in 1922, to 1,035,821 in 1931, and to an estimated one of 1,585,500 at the end of 1941.

In considering birth-rate, death-rate, and infant mortality it must be remembered that a large proportion of the Christian population consists of religious celibates and of temporary residents—middle-aged government officials, consular staffs, &c.; and that in the Jewish population there is an abnormal proportion of men and women between the ages of 20 and 40 who are European immigrants. Births and deaths are not all registered, especially among the beduin, but, apart from them, the number of failures to register is not likely to be considerable, relatively or absolutely.

The birth-rate has remained high, especially among the Moslems; for the whole country 38·58 per 1,000 in 1941 (50·06 in 1928), for the Moslems 49·2 (55·5 in 1926, the highest that has ever been recorded). The death-rate, after rising from 18·8 in 1922 to 26·9 in 1928, fell to 13·9 in 1939, but rose again to 18·5 in 1940 and 16·3 in 1941: the average for the years 1922 to 1940 inclusive being 21·55. The Moslem death-rate (excluding beduin) has throughout been much the highest (20·9 in 1922, 21·4 in 1941), including as it does all ages and most of the poorer classes; the Jewish is always the lowest, with a fall in 1930 from 11·6 to 9·5 (7·9 in 1941); the Christian varies with the total rates, but is considerably below them; 13·5 in 1922, 11·1 in 1941.

The high birth-rate of Jews in Palestine is not due to high fertility, but to the high proportion of persons within the reproductive age. The decline in the Jewish birth-rate from 38·16 in 1924 to 20·67 in 1941 results from the increased number of unmarried or as yet child-less immigrants, and is reflected in the reduction of the birth-rate for the whole country.

On the other hand, the Jewish death-rate (9·3 for 1931–1935, 8·2 for 1936–1938, 7·9 for 1939–1941) is much lower than that of eastern and even than that of western Europe (Romania 20·6, Poland 14·6, Italy 14·1, U.K. 12·2) and compares with Canada 9·7, Australia 9·0, New Zealand 8·2, being favourably affected by the age-distribution resulting from immigration of young, able-bodied adults, a temporary factor. The Jewish rate of natural increase in 1931 was 10·9 per 1,000.

A further factor is the reduction of the infant mortality from 156·6 in 1922 to 116·3 in 1941, most marked among Jews (from 128·9 to 55·6) and least, as would be expected, among Moslems (from 162·8 to 131·7), though still much higher than in some European countries (U.K. 58; Switzerland 47; Sweden 46), and reinforced by high mortality in the early years of childhood.

The conclusion to be drawn from the figures is as follows: The average annual increase of the population of Palestine is the highest recorded anywhere to-day. From 1922 to the end of 1938, the settled population increased on an average by 4·8 per cent. per annum. In Europe the annual rate from 1900 to 1930 was 0·8 per cent.; in Egypt (1917–27) 1·1 per cent.; in India (1921–31) 1·0 per cent. About half of the population increase in Palestine since 1922 has been due to immigration, but even excluding this, the rate of increase is very high. Principal causes are a high net reproduction among Moslems, and a favourable age-composition of the Jewish population. Among Moslems fertility is extremely high. The result is a rapid rate of Moslem population increase: 21·4 per 1,000 in 1931.

If the 1931 rates of fertility and mortality persist, and immigration ceases, the much more rapid rate of increase among the Moslems must result in the marked fall of the Jewish percentage of the population; it has indeed been calculated that to maintain the present percentage an annual immigration of about 32 per 1,000 Jews now in Palestine would be necessary.

## IMMIGRATION AND EMIGRATION

### Categories of Immigration

Under Article 6 of the Mandate for Palestine the Mandatory Power is under an obligation to 'facilitate Jewish immigration under suitable conditions . . . while ensuring that the rights and position of other sections of the population are not prejudiced'. The Mandatory Power has not, however, interpreted this instruction as giving Jews an absolute monopoly of immigration into Palestine. The regulations divide immigrants into two categories. In the one there is no differentiation between Jew and non-Jew so long as certain conditions are fulfilled. So long as neither the Police nor the Health Authorities object, any prospective immigrant who is in free possession of a minimum amount of capital can obtain an immigration certificate and permission to settle in Palestine. He may be accompanied by his wife and children (being minors) and in certain circumstances by other dependent relatives. Similarly any authorized resident of Palestine may send for his wife, minor children, and dependent relatives. Approved educational institutions, irrespective of the community they serve, may bring students and pupils from abroad, so long as their maintenance in Palestine for a reasonable period is assured. Similarly monks, nuns, priests, rabbis, and other such persons are free to settle in Palestine, so long as some approved organization takes responsibility for their maintenance. These rules apply to Jews, Christians, Moslems, and persons of no religion. The test is solely financial or economic.

It is in the second and larger class of immigrant—the so-called 'Labour Schedule' immigrants—that there is an advantage to the Jews. A bona-fide employer in Palestine, who needs a certain class of labour and cannot obtain it in the country, may obtain immigration certificates without difficulty, especially if he has qualified individuals in mind. But these nominated individuals form only a very small proportion of the labour immigration. The great majority are authorized in bulk and anonymously, when the Palestine Government, after consulting the Jewish Agency for Palestine, has estimated the prospective need for additional labour during the next six months. Government decides the total number and classifies them by sex, by

N

trade, and by age; most are unskilled or of no particular trade. It then places all, except a small reserve of which it retains control, at the disposal of the Jewish Agency. For many years the men among these 'Labour Schedule' immigrants were permitted to bring their wives and minor children with them. This concession, however, was abused by fictitious 'wives' and was withdrawn, and only a limited number of immigration certificates are now issued under the Labour Schedule to authorize the entry of couples instead of individuals.

*Incentives to Immigration*

Immigration into Palestine has come in waves (fig. 22). There has been more than one incentive. Among a certain class, especially noticeable in times of economic depression, idealism and enthusiam have been the great incentives. These have been the true Zionists, men and women willing and eager to sacrifice the comforts and prospects of life, in order to live and work in Palestine, and help to rebuild it as a Jewish centre. Side by side with them is a parallel class, who may be termed messianic Zionists, to whom Palestine is the 'Holy Land', and Judaism a religion, not a nationalism as among the class first named; men who wish to settle in Palestine, there to practise their faith unhindered, and to await the millennium. These go to Palestine to pray and die rather than to work and live.

But there are other immigrants, less idealistic, and especially noticeable in periods of prosperity, who, half-deliberately, half in consequence of Zionist propaganda, look upon Palestine as an *el Dorado*, a country to which one goes not so much to do good as to do well. At first this element was to a large extent ephemeral. It came to Palestine in times of abundance, but withdrew at the first hint of depression, as shown by the emigration figures. These people were, however, caught by the last and greatest 'boom', for when the reaction came they found the whole world closed to most of them, and they had to remain in Palestine.

Contemporary with the last 'boom', and to a large extent a cause of it, was another type of immigrant, the refugee from central Europe, of Jewish faith and Western culture, and European-born for many generations. Some were men of high intellect and international renown, and they brought a culture, of which there had been too little among the immigrants hitherto. Although they brought only a fraction of their property, large sums of money in the aggregate were contributed by sympathizers in Britain and America to restore them as self-respecting members of society. These new-comers were not for the most part Zionists (though many have since become Zionists), for before their expulsion from their homes they had no thought of emigration. It is impossible to say how many of such refugees have entered Palestine, but since Hitler's rise to power in 1933 their number probably amounts to some scores of thousands: citizens of Germany, Austria, Czechoslovakia, and Danzig; and of other countries

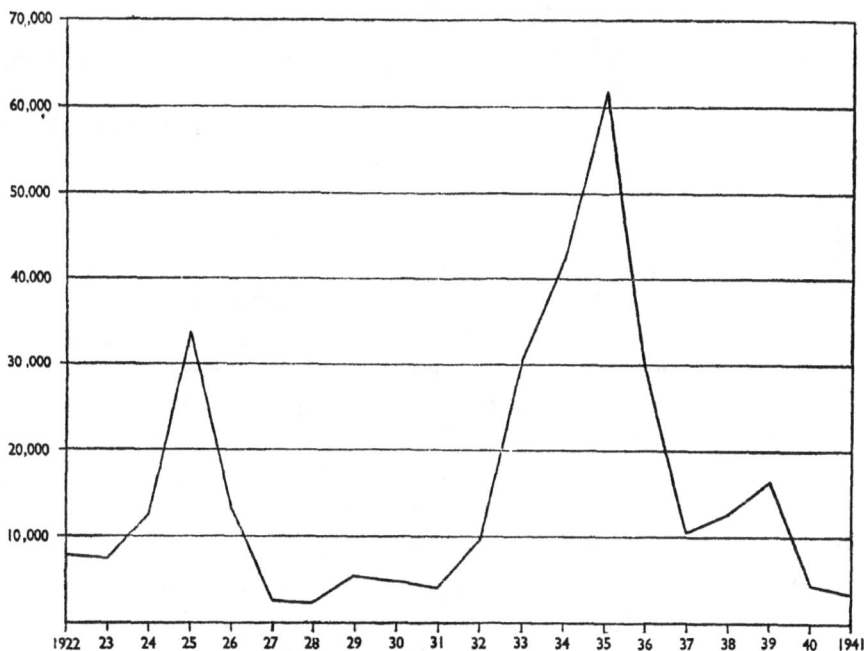

FIG. 22. *Jewish Immigration into Palestine*

under National-Socialist influence—Italy, Hungary, Romania, and Bulgaria.

The regulations define an immigrant as anyone who intends to remain in Palestine longer than one year; and most immigrants have the intention of settling in Palestine permanently. But this is not always the avowed or real intention. Students coming to places of education in Palestine are supposed to return to their homes at the conclusion of their studies; but few do so. Among European non-Jewish immigrants, the British officials, consular officers and police, and their families and servants, and the European and American archaeologists and other advanced students, almost all leave the country permanently after a longer or shorter stay.

## Illegal Immigration

All immigration totals are rendered incomplete by the omission of the 'illegal immigrants', who manage to settle in the country by evading the regulations. Evasion takes two forms. In the earlier period, especially from 1925 to 1933 or 1934, large numbers of prospective immigrants came in the guise of temporary visitors and failed to leave the country when their permits expired, and, with the connivance of many residents, were able to conceal themselves. This practice was eventually brought to an end by imposing stringent conditions on all 'travellers' or temporary visitors.

The second form of evasion has so far proved more difficult to control. There was always some infiltration across the land frontiers, and occasional landing of small boatloads of persons who had not qualified, and could not qualify, for admission through the legal channels. Until a few years ago this was not serious: then politics entered into the game. Resentment at the refusal of the Government to entrust to the Zionist Organization the regulation and control of immigration, led to the entry of parties without passports or papers of identity, in unseaworthy vessels, who landed secretly at night or openly approached the coast, secure in the knowledge that their vessel could proceed no farther, and that the humanity of the Palestine Government and its officers would permit them to land. The National-Socialist Government of Germany, and (it is believed) the Fascist Government of Italy, adopted a similar practice, placing Jewish subjects, seized indiscriminately, on overcrowded, insanitary, unseaworthy vessels, whose captains were instructed to take them to Palestine, or at any rate not to return with them. This practice was countered by including those persons who were known to have entered Palestine illegally and could not be returned to their countries of origin, against the next Immigration Schedule and (more recently) by transferring shiploads of illegal immigrants to Mauritius until the end of the war.

Figures of registered immigration since the civil administration began in 1920 are given opposite, and are shown on fig. 22.

## Origin of Immigrants

Immigrants to Palestine are drawn from almost all countries and from all the five continents. In accordance with the policy laid down in the Mandate, most of them are Jewish. Of them the great majority come from Europe, and a very large proportion from eastern Europe.

## Number of Registered Immigrants into Palestine, 1920–1941

| Year | Jews | Non-Jews | Total |
|---|---|---|---|
| 1920–1 . . . | c. 14,784 | c. 138 | 14,922 |
| 1922 . . . . | 7,844 | 284 | 8,128 |
| 1923 . . . . | 7,421 | 570 | 7,991 |
| 1924 . . . . | 12,856 | 697 | 13,553 |
| 1925 . . . . | 33,801 | 840 | 34,641 |
| 1926 . . . . | 13,081 | 829 | 13,910 |
| 1927 . . . . | 2,713 | 882 | 3,595 |
| 1928 . . . . | 2,178 | 908 | 3,086 |
| 1929 . . . . | 5,249 | 1,317 | 6,566 |
| 1930 . . . . | 4,944 | 1,489 | 6,433 |
| 1931 . . . . | 4,075 | 1,458 | 5,533 |
| 1932 . . . . | 9,553 | 1,736 | 11,289 |
| 1933 . . . . | 30,327 | 1,650 | 31,977 |
| 1934 . . . . | 42,359 | 1,784 | 44,143 |
| 1935 . . . . | 61,854 | 2,293 | 64,147 |
| 1936 . . . . | 29,727 | 1,944 | 31,671 |
| 1937 . . . . | 10,536 | 1,939 | 12,475 |
| 1938 . . . . | 12,868 | 2,395 | 15,263 |
| 1939 . . . . | 16,405 | 2,028 | 18,433 |
| 1940 . . . . | 4,547 | 1,064 | 5,611 |
| 1941 . . . . | 3,630 | 555 | 4,185 |

Many immigrants from western Europe and America were born in eastern Europe and have continued to live with their children in an east European atmosphere. The Jewish immigration into Palestine, until the organized ill-treatment of the Jews of Germany, was overwhelmingly east European, and even after the great increase of immigration from Germany and Austria, Germany came only second among the countries from which came the immigrants, especially among those nominated by the Jewish Agency.

Immigrants came also from Great Britain, the British Empire, and the United States of America. These came under no pressure, nor was their incentive as a rule religious, but nationalist—to refound a Jewish people in Palestine.

A third class of Jewish immigrants is drawn from eastern and especially from Moslem lands. The culture and way of life of the Jews of Bokhara, Georgia, Kurdistan, and Iraq is altogether different from that of the Jews of Europe and America. They are far closer akin to the Arab-speaking population, and particularly to the native Jews of Palestine.

### Social Effects of Immigration

The influence of Jewish immigrants since about 1880 has entirely changed the character of the Jewish population of Palestine. Previously it was overwhelmingly parasitic, consisting of old men and women and of younger persons who devoted their lives to study and prayer, and produced nothing. The change came, even before 1880. The new pioneers still more looked forward to a Jewish restoration in Palestine, but of a very different character (pp. 116, 120).

## Emigration

Some emigrants, mainly Arab, left as a direct consequence of Ottoman misrule, and to escape from poverty and lack of security. The emigration fever is said to have first attacked the population of Syria, of which Palestine was then a part, about 1860. The country people flocked to the towns and the townsmen to Egypt. America is said to have been 'discovered' at the centennial exhibition in 1876, and the flow to the New World began.

In America they would start as pedlars, some to become shopkeepers; the exceptions merchants. Not a few of these merchants prospered and retired to their original homes with which they always kept up connexion. Many young men went out to join elder relatives and returned to Palestine to seek brides. Much of the prosperity of Bethlehem and Ramallah, small Christian towns, is based on South American commerce; most of the little palaces that surround Bethlehem were built with South American money. Less important destinations for Arab emigrants are Cairo for those from Hebron, and Amman for those from Nablus; from both, the emigrants are of the small shopkeeping class.

Minor streams of emigration followed from Syria, and to a less extent from Palestine, to South America, the British Dominions and also, to a small extent in the person of merchants, to Great Britain, where for the most part they settled in the Manchester district. The British occupation of Egypt and later of the Sudan encouraged emigration in those directions. It should be remembered, however, that of all these emigrants relatively few came from Palestine, and of these few most went to South America. In 1912, 400 young men left Safad and its vicinity for South America, and in 1913 there were about 3,000 emigrants from the *sanjak* of Jerusalem, which included Bethlehem and Ramallah, the principal Palestinian centres of emigration. These 3,000 were about equally divided between Moslems, Christians, and Jews. The Moslem emigrants always remained on a lower economic level and seldom made sufficient money to justify their return to Palestine. Still scattered through South America are little colonies of Christians from Bethlehem or Ramallah. The Palestinian Jews kept less to themselves, being absorbed into the Jewish communities of the lands in which they settled, and, unlike the Christians, they did not show any great desire to resettle in Palestine before the era of intensive Zionist propaganda.

Since 1930 South America and all other countries have been closed to emigrants from Palestine, and the human traffic between Palestine and America, north and south, is now one-way only, eastward but not westward.

Records of emigration have been kept for most of the mandatory period, but are inadequate, since it is in many cases impossible for a man to say whether or not he would return to Palestine.

*Number of Recorded Emigrants from Palestine, 1922–1941*

| Year | Jews | Non-Jews | Total |
|---|---|---|---|
| 1922 . . . . | 1,451 | 1,348 | 2,799 |
| 1923 . . . . | 3,466 | 1,481 | 4,947 |
| 1924 . . . . | 507[1] | 604[1] | 1,111 |
| 1925 . . . . | 2,151 | 1,949 | 4,100 |
| 1926 . . . . | 7,365 | 2,064 | 9,429 |
| 1927 . . . . | 5,071 | 1,907 | 6,978 |
| 1928 . . . . | 2,168 | 954 | 3,122 |
| 1929 . . . . | 1,746 | 1,089 | 2,835 |
| 1930 . . . . | 1,679 | 1,324 | 3,003 |
| 1931 . . . . | 666 | 680 | 1,346 |
| 1932 . . . . | .. | .. | .. |
| 1933 . . . . | .. | .. | .. |
| 1934 . . . . | .. | .. | .. |
| 1935 . . . . | 396 | 387 | 783 |
| 1936 . . . . | 773 | 405 | 1,178 |
| 1937 . . . . | 889 | 639 | 1,528 |
| 1938 . . . . | 1,095 | 716 | 1,811 |
| 1939 . . . . | 1,019 | 977 | 1,996 |
| 1940 . . . . | 693 | 492 | 1,185 |
| 1941 . . . . | 426 | 790 | 1,216 |

[1] July–December only.

## DISTRIBUTION OF POPULATION

*Present Distribution*

In a country made up of desert and cultivated land, and of mountain and marsh, the distribution of population is inevitably uneven. Since nearly half of Palestine consists of the almost empty Negeb, figures given for the country as a whole do not convey the true picture.

The total area of Palestine is 10,000 square miles, of which 261 are water, 89 are swamps and dunes, 4,452 are the Negeb desert. In Palestine, north of the Negeb, there are both inhabited and un-inhabited districts, but there is no considerable empty district. The total population in 1931 was 1,035,821 (107 per square mile); of the Negeb, or Beersheba sub-district, 51,082 (11 per sq. m.); and of the remainder of Palestine 984,739 (193 per sq. m.). In the census of 1931 the Jaffa sub-district, in which were Jaffa, Tel Aviv, and some of the principal Jewish villages, was the most thickly populated part of the country. Here the density of population was over 1,157 to the square mile. Next came the Jerusalem sub-district (853) and the Haifa sub-district (448). Elsewhere the highest was the Ramleh sub-district (232), another Jewish agricultural area. In the Beersheba sub-district bordering on the Negeb it was 14 (fig. 23).

The considerable increase of population since 1931 (p. 172) has not been spread equally over the country. The empty spaces remain empty, and in the Arab districts the growth has not been very great. The new population has for the most part gone to the four towns, Jerusalem, Jaffa, Tel Aviv, and Haifa, and to the Jewish villages along the coast from north of Haifa to south of Jaffa, and in the plain of Esdraelon. By this means the density of population in the Haifa, Tulkarm, Jaffa, Ramleh, and Nazareth sub-districts has been increased. Nowhere else has there been appreciable change. Jewish settlers have reclaimed areas of marsh and sand-dunes in the plains of Esdraelon, of Acre, and of Sharon, but this was before 1931, by which year settlement in those regions was already well advanced. Excluding the urban populations of Jerusalem, Jaffa, Tel Aviv, and Haifa, the density in 1931 was 208 per square mile in the coastal plain, 153 in Galilee, 136 per square mile in the mountain districts of Samaria and Judaea, and 194 in the plain of Esdraelon.

*Urban Immigration*

This agricultural revival and expansion, although the most notice-able part, is by no means the most important numerically of the Jewish revival in Palestine. In 1914 it was estimated that of a total Jewish population of 84,660, 11,660 or about 14 per cent. lived in the villages. The census of 1931 gave a total Jewish population of 174,610, of which 46,143 or 26 per cent. lived in the villages but only 26,939 (15%) were mainly occupied in agriculture. Many of the villages were even then becoming urbanized or industrialized. There are no reliable later figures, and the Jewish population has

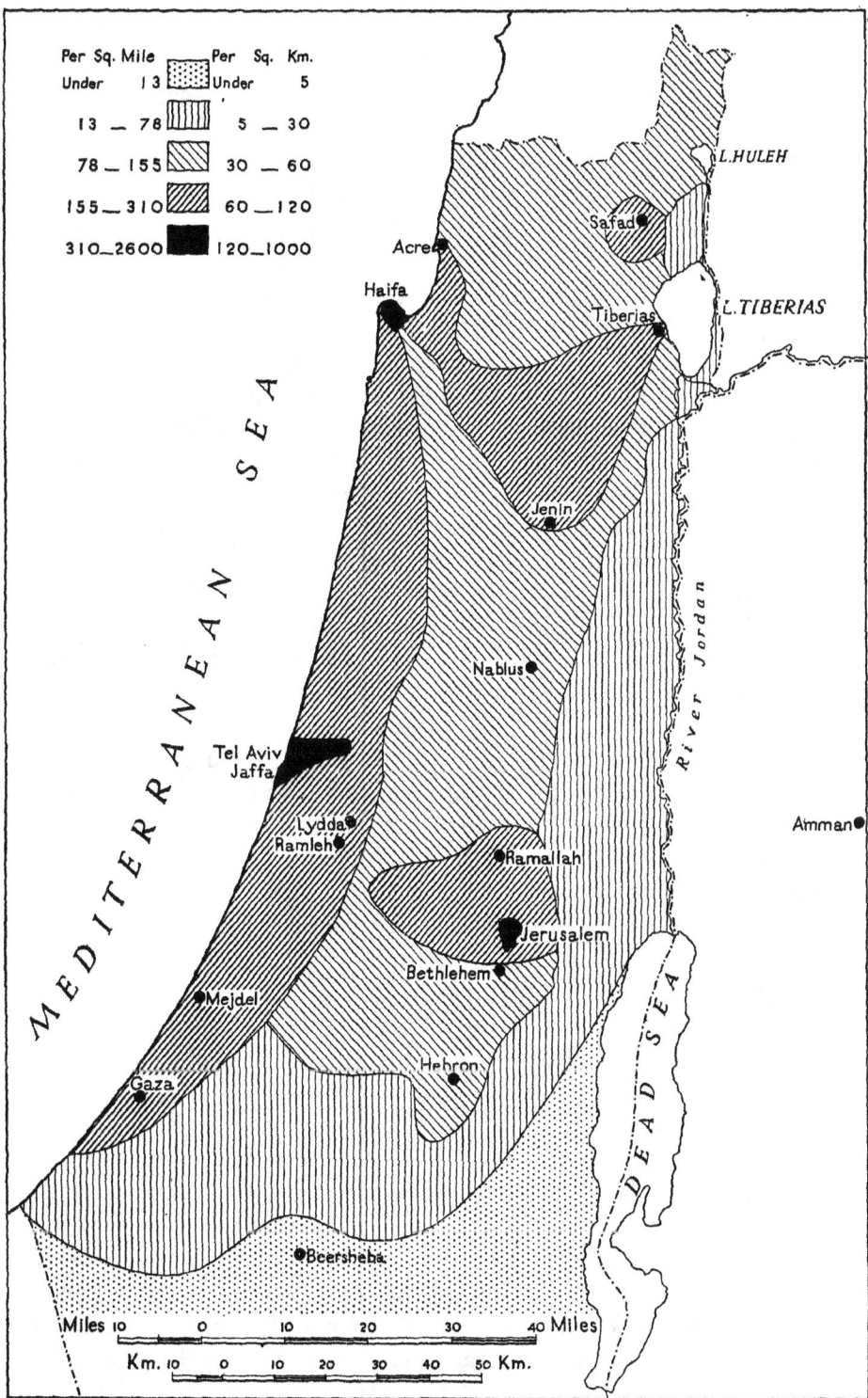

**Per Sq. Mile**  **Per Sq. Km.**

Under 13  Under 5

13 — 78  5 — 30

78 — 155  30 — 60

155 — 310  60 — 120

310 — 2600  120 — 1000

MEDITERRANEAN SEA

L. HULEH

Safad

Acre

Haifa

Tiberias

L. TIBERIAS

Jenin

River Jordan

Nablus

Tel Aviv
Jaffa

Amman

Lydda
Ramleh

Ramallah

Jerusalem

Bethlehem

Mejdel

Hebron

DEAD SEA

Gaza

Beersheba

Miles 10  0  10  20  30  40 Miles

Km. 10  0  10  20  30  40  50 Km.

FIG. 23. *Estimated Density of Population, 1940*

in the meanwhile more than doubled, but there is no reason to believe that a larger proportion of the Jewish population is engaged in agriculture to-day than ten years ago. Of 222,251 Jewish immigrants in the years 1931–1940, the great majority have passed into the towns —Tel Aviv, Haifa, and Jerusalem. The first-named, in 1920 merely a suburb of Jaffa with a population of a few hundreds, is now a municipality with a population, all Jewish, estimated at 141,000. After Tel Aviv the most important Jewish centre is Haifa, which has grown, from 24,634 inhabitants with 6,230 Jews in 1922, to 114,400 with 57,100 Jews in 1941. The opening of the harbour at Haifa in 1933, and later of the oil refinery by the Consolidated Refineries Limited, accelerated development. Tel Aviv is the principal commercial centre of Palestine; Haifa the industrial one. Jerusalem is secondary in both respects; but it is the administrative capital and the headquarters of the principal Jewish and other institutions. As it is not a centre of industry, or even of agriculture, it has less attraction for new-comers who have to earn their living. But with Tel Aviv it is the largest town in Palestine, and until the rise of Tel Aviv it was the largest Jewish centre in the country. The population of Jerusalem in 1941 was about 141,000, of whom 85,700 or 60·8 per cent. were Jews.

In the other towns of Palestine the Jewish population is small, except in Jaffa, which in 1941 had 23,800 Jews (28%), who are all concentrated on the Tel Aviv border, and in all respects, except municipally, belong to Tel Aviv. Tiberias had 5,381 (63%) in 1931; Safad (1931), 2,547 (27%); Acre, 200–300. There are no Jews in Nablus, Gaza, Nazareth, Bethlehem, Ramleh, Lydda, or Mejdel. Thus, despite the establishment of 257 'colonies' or agricultural settlements, the Jewish population of Palestine is predominantly urban and industrial. Commerce, large and small industry, and the professions, take almost six Jews for one who devotes himself to agriculture.

*Casual Labour*

Into these figures, however, enters one element of doubt. A large proportion of the Jewish immigrants in the past twenty years have entered under the Labour Schedule (p. 177), on the nomination of the Jewish Agency. These young men and women have not come to any definite employment, nor are the majority fully trained in any trade. Many have had some training in agriculture, but little practical experience. In Palestine they join the ranks of casual labour, in which they may remain for years. Probably almost without exception these *chalutzim* or agricultural pioneers are anxious to settle on the land; but there is no land for them. As many as possible—and perhaps more than is wise—are crowded into the Zionist communal settlements, but far more are left outside. For these there is not even enough agricultural employment for wages; moreover, this employment is largely seasonal. As a consequence, among these *chalutzim* there is always a large floating element taking and seeking work wherever it can be found, one day in the fields, another in building, a third as navvy or dock-labourer or porter, but never settled anywhere. For this reason statistics of population in Tel Aviv or Haifa or the rural settlements are not altogether satisfactory. Lack of employment will lead to an abnormal influx into Tel Aviv, the capital of Palestinian Jewry, and this again will probably be followed, especially if a new Labour Schedule is under consideration, by the removal of large batches of unemployed to the communal settlements, where their presence is less obvious, and where—the principle of an equal share of everything having been adopted—there will always be food and shelter. The population of Tel Aviv in 1941 was estimated at 141,000, but no one can say what proportion consisted of this floating population.

Of the non-Jewish arrivals (p. 181) a large proportion are not in the true sense immigrants. They are temporary residents—civil servants, British police, consular officers, members of the staffs of banks and other European institutions, even missionaries and religious persons—who stay in Palestine with their families for a longer or shorter period, but never transfer their domicile. The only non-Jewish immigrants—apart from a few hundred Armenian refugees who ceased coming two decades ago, and the Moslem Circassians and Bosnians transferred to Palestine by the Ottoman Government during the nineteenth century (p. 137 )—are Arabs, most of whom are of Palestinian origin and are returning home, many from Spanish America where they or their parents had gone as emigrants at the end of the nineteenth century or beginning of the twentieth. They are mainly Christians, but there are Moslem *fellahin* among them.

## The Towns

In comparing the size of the urban and rural populations of Palestine, the question at once arises—what is a town? The Ottoman system seems to have been to grant the attributes of a municipality to any close grouping of population of 5,000 and upwards, and thereby designate it as a town: of those, some are now far smaller. These towns or municipal areas were taken over by the new Government, which in course of time added two or three. Other villages whose population passed the 5,000 limit during the past twenty years were, however, not raised to the dignity of towns. The result is that there are to-day in Palestine twenty-four centres with municipal councils. Their populations range from 3,000 in Jenin (1938) to 141,000 in both Tel Aviv and Jerusalem (1941). With four exceptions, however, these are not towns in the English sense, despite their designations and municipal councils. Most of them are villages; some not very large. With the exception of Nablus, Petah Tikva, Acre, and Mejdel they are entirely dependent on agriculture. The four Palestinian towns that are towns in the English sense are Jerusalem, Tel Aviv, Haifa, and Jaffa. Their population consists solely of townsmen: 238,873 in 1931; that of the remainder of the country, 730,395, is almost entirely rural, apart from 66,553 nomads and gipsies. Thus 23 per cent. of the sedentary population was urban and the rest rural. Immigration since 1931 having been mainly of an urban character, these proportions have not since been altered in favour of the rural population.

The distribution of the three main religious communities between the four towns and the rural districts is worthy of notice. Of the 973,104 Moslems in 1941, 109,900 (11%) lived in these towns; of 474,102 Jews, 307,600 (65%); of 125,413 Christians, 64,200 (51%). In considering the proportion of Christians it should be remembered that these include a relatively very large number of Europeans, and also most of the civil servants, of whom a very large proportion is Christian.

Of the population of Jerusalem in 1931, 35 per cent. was foreign born, of Tel Aviv 71 per cent., of Haifa 31 per cent., and of Jaffa 14 per cent. These differences are explained by the fact that Tel Aviv is entirely Jewish, while Jaffa consists of Arabs and oriental Jews, many of whom were born in Palestine. Jerusalem and Haifa have large European populations, Jewish and Christian.

'In general, towns in Palestine are only in the very early stages of development: towns depend upon an economic background, and the background for the four main towns does not yet emerge in sharp outline. Jaffa and Tel Aviv both have a sense of security in the development of agriculture, particularly that part of it concerned with the cultivation of oranges and grape-fruit, but Tel Aviv does not bear in its age, sex, and conjugal constitutions the marks of a progressive commercial or industrial development like that of Haifa or Jaffa. The development of Haifa and its port works may have a considerable effect on both Jaffa and Tel Aviv; and the age and sex constitutions of its population imply a strong sense of confidence in the future, a confidence not based on present prosperity so much as on anticipated development. Jerusalem has no very well defined features assisting towards an estimate of its future. In the material sense, it will probably remain a residential centre for the professional classes, and through them will provide a general but limited market for the natural produce of the country. That the town was ever established where it stands is something of a mystery, since it lacks natural resources and has few, if any, strategical values. Yet its influences in the world have been incalculably greater than those of any other historical city; and even if, at times, the response to these influences was material, the influences themselves were of the spiritual order. Its origin and its history are alike supranatural; and, doubtless, this quality of mystery has given it a dominance in the world of an order totally different from that of the great cities upon which the world now depends for its material existence.' (Mills, *Census of Palestine 1931 Report*, vol. i, p. 31.)

This was written in 1931. One may add that the citrus industry, on which Jaffa and Tel Aviv were then largely dependent, has since been sorely stricken, and although it will recover to some extent, it may never rise again to the level of prosperity of the mid-thirties; that the opening of the harbour at Haifa in 1933 affected unfavourably the prosperity of Jaffa, which was still further reduced by the attempt to direct to Tel Aviv much of the remaining passenger and goods traffic—an attempt which damaged Jaffa without bringing much benefit to Tel Aviv; and that Haifa, with the opening of the harbour and the pipe-line from Iraq, the erection of petroleum refining plant, and the laying of a road across Palestine and the desert to Iraq, shows signs of permanent advance to prosperity.

Tel Aviv, one of the two largest towns, has grown very rapidly during recent years and, as the Jewish metropolis, may continue to grow. Equal in size of population is Jerusalem, once the largest urban centre in the country; Haifa, now the principal port, is third. Both of these have increased in population during the past twenty years, but neither at the rate of Tel Aviv. After these three come Jaffa, formerly the principal port, and then Gaza, Nablus, Hebron, Petah Tikva, Lydda, Ramleh, Nazareth, Safad, Tiberias, Acre, Bethlehem, and other smaller municipalities. But except Gaza, Nablus, and Hebron, they are little more than overgrown villages dependent on agriculture; at the best, market towns and nothing more.

Many of the towns of Palestine go back to a very early period of history. Jerusalem, Hebron, Nablus (Shechem), and Gaza are mentioned in the Bible. Samaria and Jezreel, successive capitals of the kingdom of Israel, are now represented by Arab villages, Sebustya and Zirin respectively. Nazareth, Jaffa (Joppa), and Bethlehem are prominent in New Testament history, and Bethlehem's story goes back earlier. Tiberias dates from the beginning of the present era. Acre and Ramleh came into prominence only with the Crusades, although Acre appeared in the conquest-list of Thothmes III of Egypt, about 1500 B.C. Safad and Haifa are of later appearance, the latter little more than a century old. Tel Aviv and the small Jewish towns are of yesterday. The principal towns are described in Chapter XII.

### Municipal Areas including Suburbs and Larger Villages of Palestine and their Population, 1913–1938

(Towns with less than 5,000 inhabitants have been omitted)

| | Consular estimate 1913 | 1922 Census | 1931 Census | 1941 Estimate |
|---|---|---|---|---|
| Jerusalem | 95,000 | 62,578 | 90,503 | 141,100 |
| Jaffa | 55,000 | 32,524 | 51,866 | 85,300 |
| Haifa | 30,000 | 24,634 | 50,403 | 114,400 |
| Gaza | 30,000 | 17,480 | 17,046 | 27,400 |
| Hebron | .. | 16,577 | 17,531 | 21,000 |
| Nablus | 25,000 | 15,947 | 17,189 | 21,900 |
| Tel Aviv | .. | 15,185 | 46,101 | 141,000 |
| Safad | 15,000 | 8,761 | 9,441 | 11,000 |
| Lydda | .. | 8,103 | 11,250 | 15,700 |
| Nazareth | .. | 7,424 | 8,756 | 11,300 |
| Ramleh | .. | 7,312 | 10,421 | 13,600 |
| Tiberias | .. | 6,950 | 8,601 | 11,000 |
| Bethlehem | .. | 6,658 | 6,815 | 8,200 |
| Acre | .. | 6,420 | 7,897 | 9,800 |
| Dura | .. | 5,834 | 7,255 | .. |
| Mejdel | .. | 5,097 | 6,226 | .. |
| Petah Tikva | .. | 3,032 | 6,880 | 17,400 |

## CHAPTER VIII

# ADMINISTRATION

### Central Government

THE Civil Administration of Palestine was initiated on 1 July 1920 with Sir Herbert Samuel as High Commissioner. Previously the country had been administered by the military authorities who, in accordance with international law, preserved as far as was practicable the *status quo ante*. The Mandate for Palestine was not approved by the Council of the League of Nations until 24 July 1922, but in the special circumstances the continuance of the military administration was not considered desirable, and the Mandate, even before its terms had been formally approved, was entrusted to Great Britain. The Mandate for Palestine is an 'A' Mandate, that is to say that, as laid down in Article 22 of the Covenant of the League, Palestine is considered one of the 'communities (that) had reached a stage of development where their existence as independent nations can be provisionally recognized, subject to the rendering of administrative advice and assistance by a Mandatory, until such time as they are able to stand alone'. However, of the three 'A' Mandatory territories, Palestine was considered an exception.

The other two 'A' Mandates, those for Iraq, and for Syria and the Lebanon, are relatively straightforward. Into that for Palestine was introduced the complication of a promise to facilitate 'the establishment in Palestine of a national home for the Jewish people'. As a consequence it was found that the project of a national government with very restricted powers supervised by British advisers was not practicable, but that the administration of the country had to be from the beginning in the hands of British officials, representative of the Mandatory Power. The High Commissioner, although he held that title, had powers and functions very similar to those of a Governor of a Crown Colony. In the last resort the decision in matters of administration rested with the Secretary of State for the Colonies in London.

One of Sir Herbert Samuel's first acts after his assumption of office as the first High Commissioner was to appoint an Advisory Council consisting of four Moslem Arabs, three Christian Arabs, three Palestinian Jews, and ten British officials, with himself as Chairman. This council was to scrutinize all proposed legislation and to advise the High Commissioner on all matters of public policy. But it had no legislative powers; these rested with the High Commissioner. This council remained in existence for about a year, at the end of which period it was to have been replaced by a Legislative Council with larger, but still limited, powers. The Arabs, however, refused to participate in a council with such limitations, nor would they co-operate, when it was proposed to revive the former Advisory Council. As a consequence, an Advisory Council, consisting solely of British officials, was appointed. The Executive Council, consisting of the three or four senior British officials under the chairmanship of the High Commissioner, which was constituted at the same time as the original Advisory Council, has remained without change in constitution throughout the whole period of the Civil Administration. The present system of government is that ordinances are considered first by the High Commissioner in Executive Council, and after they have received the provisional approval of the Secretary of State in London, are submitted to the Advisory Council. They are then published in the *Official Gazette*, a period of at least a month (except in cases of urgency) being allowed for comment or criticism by unofficial interests likely to be affected, and then—often after amendment—they are enacted. When a proposed ordinance is likely to affect communal Jewish interests, the 'Jewish Agency' (p. 194) is consulted at the first stage before submission to the Executive Council, in accordance with Article 4 of the Mandate.

The Constitution of Palestine is formally enshrined in the Palestine Order in Council, 1922, made by His Majesty King George V on 10 August of that year. The High Commissioner derives his authority from this instrument, which has been amended as occasion required. If the members of the Executive Council are unanimous in an opinion that the High Commissioner does not accept, he must submit to the Secretary of State a statement of his reasons for differing from them.

The principal executive officer, after the High Commissioner, is the Chief Secretary. He is the normal means of communication with the High Commissioner, to whom heads of departments, however, also have direct access whenever they so desire. The Chief Secretary, in the words of Sir Anton Bertram, an authority on colonial administration,

'is responsible for the general supervision of all departments, co-ordinating their work, recommending to Government the acceptance or rejection of their proposals, and defending their approved policy in Council. He is like a minister in charge of all departments. In this respect his position may be compared with that of Mussolini in Italy; but he is responsible, of course, to the High Commissioner for all that he does.' (*Colonial Administration.*)

Heads of departments invariably report to the Chief Secretary, who must also be in close touch with the District Administration, the branch that is closest to the population. Through this contact, in the absence of any kind of representative body, he can advise the High Commissioner regarding public opinion. In the words of another high authority on colonial government, Lord Lugard, the Chief Secretary's task

'is to foster that sympathy, mutual understanding, and co-operation between the government and the people without which no government is really stable and efficient.' (*The Dual Mandate in Tropical Africa.*)

The Chief Secretary should also be the sole channel of communication between the High Commissioner and members of the public and public bodies; for it is one of his functions to enable the High Commissioner, by affording him the relative information, to take a decision on every case that is submitted to him. In practice, however, many matters of minor importance are decided by the Chief Secretary without reference to the High Commissioner. Attached to the Secretariat is a Press Bureau whose head is responsible for the scrutiny of, and liaison with, the local press.

The Economic Adviser is the principal adviser to the High Commissioner on all economic questions involving decisions by, or the intervention of, Government. He presides over the standing Committee for Commerce and Industry, the advisory body, including Arab and Jewish representatives, to which tariffs and similar proposals are referred before action is taken by Government.

The Financial Adviser is responsible for the formulation of the Government's financial policy, for the preparation of the annual budget, and for general control of finances.

## The League of Nations

Palestine, although under British administration, and governed, in effect, as a Crown Colony, is not a part of the British Empire; the national status of its inhabitants is that of Palestinian citizens under British protection, not British subjects. On British territory, therefore, Palestinians are alien. The Mandate under which the country is administered requires an annual report by the Mandatory Power to the Council of the League of Nations. In the past the Mandates

Commission of the League has once a year examined the Report on Palestine, and a representative of the British Government, sometimes the Secretary of State, and generally one also of the Palestine Government, often the High Commissioner, used to appear before it to answer questions and to give explanations. The Mandates Commission then reported to the Council of the League, which had power to express opinions, but could not interfere in the administration of the country, which remained the sole responsibility of the Mandatory Power. The terms of the Mandate, however, could not be altered except by the Council of the League.

The religious communities and other considerable sections of the population have also the right to approach the Mandates Commission, through the High Commissioner. They have made full use of this power, and every year the Mandates Commission has been deluged with memoranda and petitions, most of them dealing with trivial matters, but some occasionally even questioning the legality of the Mandate. The Jewish Agency for Palestine, although more representative of Jewry outside the country than within, without fail submits memoranda and petitions. At first it claimed the right of direct access to the Mandates Commission. This was rejected, and it now sends its memoranda, in the same manner as the other petitioning bodies, through the High Commissioner.

There is one further international check upon the Government of Palestine. All the Mandates provide that, if any dispute should arise between the Mandatory and any member of the League of Nations, relating to the interpretation or the application of the provisions of the Mandate, it shall be submitted to the Permanent Court of International Justice, if it cannot be settled by negotiation. It is not only the International Court, however, which may pronounce upon the legality of the acts of the Government of Palestine. The Palestine courts also exercise that authority. They may decide whether legislation or executive action is in accordance with the provisions of the Mandate as laid down in the Order in Council. They have exercised that power on many occasions.

## The Departments

The task of the departments is to maintain the government in a state of efficiency and to afford direct assistance in material development.

The senior department is the legal one, that of the Attorney-General. In the first year of the Civil Administration there was a

Legal Secretary who, together with a Financial Secretary, shared to some extent with the Chief Secretary the supervision of the departments and of the communications between them and the High Commissioner. This followed the system of government in the Sudan, which also is not a Crown Colony and, like Palestine in its first years, is under the control of the Foreign Office. When, however, the Colonial Office assumed responsibility for Palestine, the usual administrative system of the Colonial Empire was introduced. The Attorney-General is not only the principal law officer of the Government, but also the legal adviser of the High Commissioner and of all the departments of government, and the legal draughtsman.

The other principal departments, whose titles sufficiently describe their functions, are Health, Education, the Treasury, Police and Prisons, Public Works, Customs Excise and Trade, Railways, Agriculture, Migration. Minor ones are Antiquities, Lands, Land Settlement, Surveys, Posts and Telegraphs, and Labour.

The head of the Department of Health is the Director of Medical Services.[1] The Treasurer was previously also Financial and Economic Adviser; he is now only the Chief Accounting Officer. There is also a Government Auditor, an official of the Colonial Audit Department in London.

The Department of Migration is concerned with the issue of Palestinian passports and the grant of visas for Palestine, Great Britain, and other parts of the empire. A part of its work is the organization or control of immigration and the collection of the material on which the High Commissioner bases his decisions in regard to immigration policy. In this part of his duty the Commissioner of Migration works in consultation with representatives of the Jewish Agency for Palestine, which is especially interested in all questions of immigration. Until a few years ago the Department also controlled the entry and departure of all individuals, but this function has now been transferred to the Police. Immigration into Palestine falls into several categories, of which the principal[2] are: (a) persons of independent means, that is, possessing a minimum capital of £1,000; (b) persons with a definite prospect of employment in Palestine, and (c) dependants of permanent residents or immigrants. Authorized immigrants were permitted to be accompanied

---

[1] See pages 235–8.
[2] This classification has been adopted as a matter of convenience. It is not official: compare Chapter VII, p. 177.

by their wives and minor children, but glaring abuses of this privilege in recent years necessitated its partial curtailment in so far as category (b) is concerned. For the same reason, the definition of 'dependant' in category (c) has had to be restricted. At the same time the Palestine Citizenship Order in Council was amended so that a woman marrying a Palestinian citizen no longer automatically acquires Palestinian citizenship.

Until a few years ago the number of immigrants admitted under all categories except (b) was unlimited, anyone able to fulfil the conditions being admitted, unless there were valid medical or police objections. The High Commissioner now lays down the maximum number of immigrants to be admitted during a given period, and apportions this maximum among the several categories. The size of category (b), that of labour immigrants, is calculated on estimates of the expected new employment and cessation of employment during the coming period of six months, existing unemployment being taken into consideration. In making this estimate the views of the Jewish Agency are always given consideration, but as a rule there is a great gap between the Zionist expectations and the more sober, and also better informed, anticipations of the Commissioner of Migration. Once a Labour Schedule is approved, after a small deduction has been made for non-Jewish immigrants, the remainder of the immigration certificates available are placed at the disposal of the Jewish Agency.

Another function of the Commissioner of Migration is the naturalization of aliens, and the decision in all complicated cases of citizenship where British and Palestinian citizens are concerned. Under the Palestine Citizenship Order in Council of 1925, all Ottoman citizens habitually resident in Palestine on 1 August of that ye automatically became Palestinian citizens, unless they opted to retain Ottoman citizenship, in which case they were expected to leave Palestine. For persons born subsequent to that date the *jus sanguinis* applies. The children of Palestinian citizens, whether born in Palestine or not, are Palestinian from birth. Further, children born in Palestine of parents who are stateless become Palestinian citizens. With regard to aliens settled in Palestine the conditions of naturalization are very light. They are (a) residence in Palestine for not less than two years during the three immediately preceding the date of application; (b) good character; (c) a knowledge of one of the three official languages; and (d) statement of intention to reside permanently in Palestine. The fee payable for naturalization is 10s. in two instalments. This compares with £10, the fee payable for a similar service in Britain.

The Commissioner of Migration acts in certain respects (issue of passports, visas, &c.) as Consul for Great Britain. He formerly performed similar functions on behalf of the Governments of Egypt and Iraq. He is also the nominal head of the Office of Statistics. The Director of Lands is concerned mainly with the leasing of government lands, but he also supervises the registration of all transfers of land.

## LOCAL GOVERNMENT

Side by side with the Central Administration is the local administration under the direction of District Commissioners, originally designated Governors. The number of districts has varied from time to time. There are at present six. Under the Military Administration before 1921 there had been twelve. At one period, between 1927 and the disturbances in 1936, there were only three, and for a still briefer period, two (fig. 24).

The apex of the system of the local government is the District Commissioner, who has been described as the eye of the Government. He and his assistants are the visible representatives of the Government throughout the length and breadth of the land. They are the authorities to whom the countryside turns in all cases of difficulty. The districts are divided into sub-districts, each in the charge of an Assistant District Commissioner, below whom are District Officers, who are Palestinians. Under the District Officers are the headmen of villages (*Mukhtars*). The principal man of the village is as a rule chosen for this office. His chief functions are: (a) to keep the peace within the village; (b) to send to the nearest police station information of any serious offence or accident occurring in the village; (c) to assist government officers in the collection of revenue; (d) to publish in the village any public notices or proclamations sent by the District Commissioners; (e) to keep a register of all births and deaths within the village, and to send a copy to the Senior Medical Officer once a quarter.

Similarly, there are Mukhtars of the older quarters of the towns, but their functions are more limited.

### The Municipalities

In the towns there are municipal councils under mayors appointed by the High Commissioner from among the elected members, and

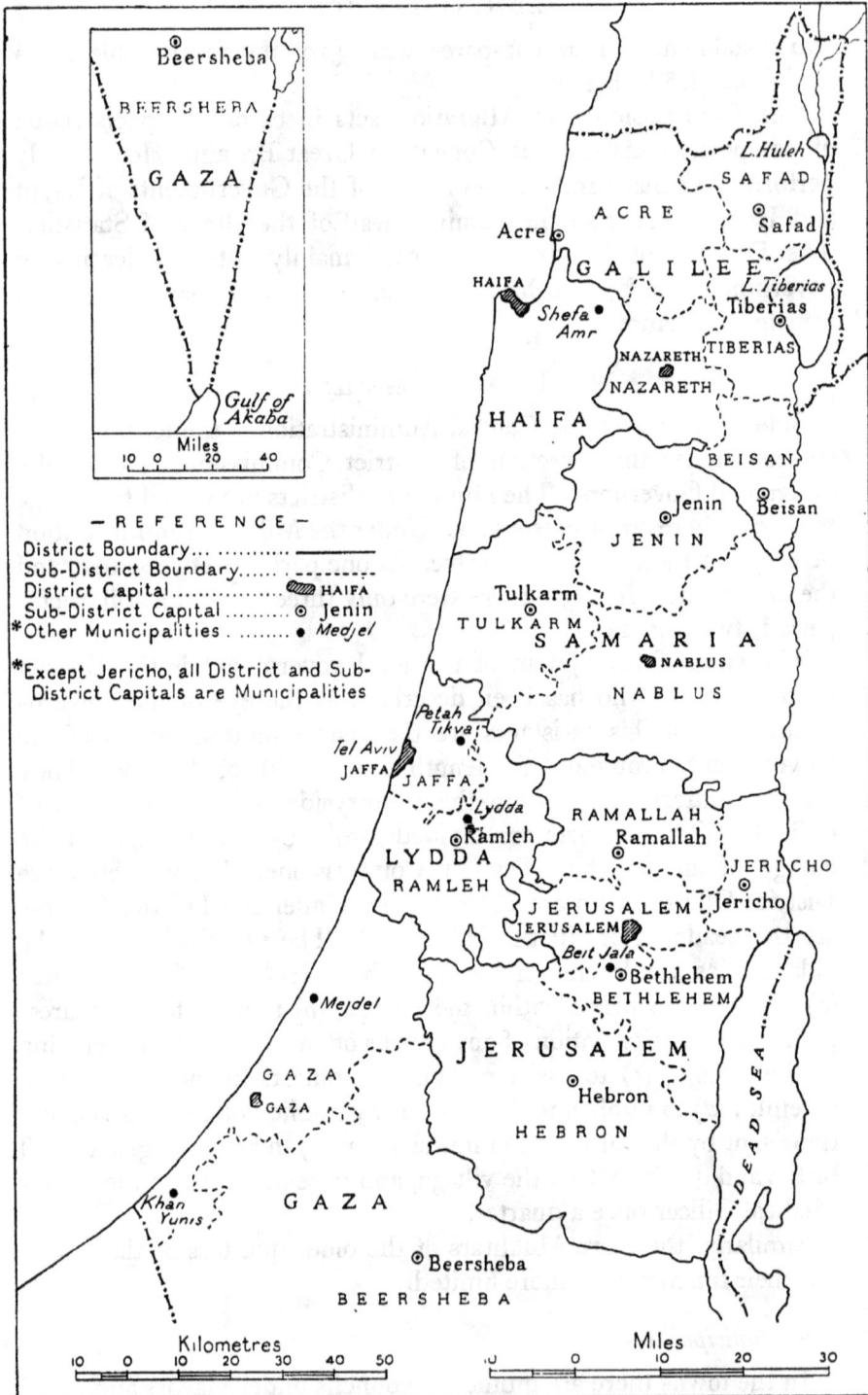

FIG. 24. *Administrative divisions and centres of Palestine.*

in two or three instances also deputy mayors. The High Commissioner has also the power to nominate two additional members of the Jerusalem and Haifa councils to provide for the representation of elements of the population, such as foreign communities, which might not otherwise be adequately represented; but this right has not been exercised. The system of municipal government was reorganized in 1934, and the first elections under the new system were held in that year.

The electorate of the municipal councils consists of male Palestinian citizens of 25 years and upwards, who have during the preceding twelve months paid either an urban property tax of ten shillings as owner, or municipal rates amounting to one pound. Since urban property tax is not payable by owners of property within the walled city of Jerusalem, those owners of property who would in other circumstances have been liable to pay ten shillings per annum are enfranchized there. Qualified electors of the age of 30 years and upwards may be elected members of the councils, provided they are resident in the borough. In Tel Aviv and Petah Tikva (p. 202) the franchise is wider; women as well as men are entitled to vote there and to be elected, and the wives of electors are equally qualified with their husbands: the minimum age for an elector is 21 years, and for a municipal councillor 25 years. Municipal areas are divided into wards for electoral purposes. Community rolls—that is, the separate representation of communities—have been abolished, except at Tel Aviv and Petah Tikva. Within municipal areas, urban districts, under urban committees, may be created, if the inhabitants as a whole so desire. These committees may provide additional conveniences and amenities. In no instance, however, has advantage been taken of this provision.

The revenues of the municipalities are derived from (a) a property rate, payable by owners, not exceeding 10 per cent. of the rateable value of buildings, &c., or 6 per cent. of the capital value of unoccupied land; (b) a general rate, payable by occupiers, not exceeding 15 per cent. of the rateable value of property; (c) an education rate, not exceeding $7\frac{1}{2}$ per cent., payable by occupiers; (d) a sewage rate payable by occupiers; and (e) miscellaneous fees payable for licences, &c. In some cases there are also grants to municipalities by the Central Government. The budgets of the municipalities are subject to approval by the Central Government.

For populated areas smaller in size than municipalities, and also for town quarters with special characteristics, local councils are provided. These possess more limited powers than the municipal councils. There is no general definition of these powers. They are laid down in each individual case, and include the power to levy rates. Apart from these constituted authorities, the heads of the principal families in the villages, and the sheikhs among the beduin tribes, exercise probably equal authority, if not greater, in the absence of all legal sanction. In the Jewish villages a similar position is occupied by councils, elected by all the adult inhabitants, which are in effect recognized by the Government, although they have no legal status.

## TOWN PLANNING

In one field of activity, that of town planning, the Central Government exercises an appreciable amount of control. There are local commissions in all of the towns, but above them all is the Central Town Planning Commission, whose membership now consists solely of government officials. In many parts of Palestine, town planning, which may include the preservation and care of sites of archaeological, historical, or even aesthetic value, is obviously a matter that concerns a far wider public than the local one. It is, in some cases, the concern of the peoples of half the world. For this reason a centralization that could otherwise perhaps hardly be defended is, in Palestine, a necessity. In matters of town planning, the local commission, on which the Government is also strongly represented, is to a large extent the agent of the central commission.

## COMMUNAL AUTONOMY

### The Jewish Community

The religious communities in the Ottoman period were organized in *millets*—national units with considerable autonomy in their internal government. Likewise, in 1926 the Government of Palestine enacted a Religious Communities Ordinance. This was merely an enabling ordinance, empowering a community to apply for autonomous organization, whose limits would be defined in regulations to be approved by the High Commissioner. The Jewish community was the only one to apply for such an organization, and the regulations governing it came into force in 1928. However, all the religious communities, including the Jewish, have complete autonomy in matters of personal status—marriage, divorce, inheritance, &c.—so far as Palestinian citizens and subjects of foreign Powers, excepting those of Europe, America, and Japan, are concerned. In these matters, the relative ecclesiastical law prevails. The regulations constituting and governing the Jewish community, however, go much further. They provide for both religious and lay authorities. The principal religious authority is the Rabbinical Council, consisting of the two chief rabbis and six other rabbis, the *Ashkenazi* and *Sephardi* branches of Jewry having equal representation. The Rabbinical Courts are vested with jurisdiction in matters of personal status of Jews, and of religious endowments for the benefit of Jews, but they exercise jurisdiction only over those Jews who are registered as members of the community. Any individual who desires not to be included in the community may have his name removed from the register, and cannot then be subjected to either the religious or lay authorities of the community. The *Agudat Israel*, the extreme Orthodox section which has a strong element of messianism in its Zionism, and moreover is doubtful of the orthodoxy of its fellow-Jews, has opted out of the community in a body.

The lay organs of the community which are established by the regulation are: (*a*) an elected Assembly (*Assefat Hanivcharim*); (*b*) a General Council (*Vaad Leumi*); (*c*) Committees of Local Communities (*Vaad ha-Kehillah*). The Assembly is supposed to be elected for a period of three years according to regulations drawn up by the General Council and approved by the High Commissioner. The Assembly is to elect the General Council each year, and consider a budget presented by the Council. It may authorize the imposition upon members of the community, through local communities, of rates for educational and philanthropic purposes, and the maintenance of the religious offices; and the charging of fees on account of the ritual killing of animals, of licences for the baking of unleavened bread, and for burial. The amount of these rates and fees must be approved by the Government each year; and the whole budget must likewise be submitted to the Government for approval. The General Council has the function of administering the affairs of the community in accordance with the resolutions of the Assembly, and acts as the representative of the community in its relations with the Government.

Although the Assembly should be elected every three years, elections have in practice been far less frequent. The Assembly does not even meet regularly every year. Its income is also somewhat irregular, considerable difficulty being encountered in its attempts to collect the taxes due.

*A Local Community* is constituted in any place where not less than thirty adult Jews, who are registered as members of the community, have their residence. Only one local community can exist in each town or village; but any congregation or section comprising not less than thirty adults may claim the satisfaction of its special religious or cultural needs according to its own principles, and is entitled therefore to a proportionate share of the revenue of the community. The Committee of the Local Community is the recognized representative of the community before the District Administration.

In the election of the General Council of the Jews of Palestine, men and women equally may exercise the franchise. This right was quoted by the *Agudat Israel* as one of the reasons for which they were unable to have any share in the Jewish community, as organized. They objected to it 'as giving women active and passive right of election, which is not practised in any existing Jewish Community' and as being 'against Jewish morals and religion' (*Permanent Mandates Commission*, Minutes of 7th Session, p. 182).

The health and education systems of the Jewish community are to a large extent the responsibility of the communal organization, but for these purposes it receives considerable assistance from the Government and from foreign Jewish organizations. In Tel Aviv and Petah Tikva, whose populations are practically entirely Jewish, the Municipal Council and the local communal council have been combined.

Outside the official communal organization there are a number of arbitration committees before which many Jewish litigants bring their cases.

## The Moslem Community

Under Ottoman rule the Moslems were above the *millet* systems. They constituted both the ruling class and the whole state. The law of the land was theirs. The other communities were subject races to whom the general law did not in some respects apply; for them special provision had to be made. British rule, however, made all the communities equal. The Moslem community, if it had wished, could also have come under the Religious Communities Ordinance, and regulations for its government would have been framed. It did not ask to do so, but nevertheless retained its own jurisdiction in matters of personal status. In common with the other communities it was also guaranteed absolute religious liberty. The *Sharia* courts and Moslem religious endowments (*waqf*) were also left under it. Some sort of organization was, however, necessary, and by an Ordinance of December 1921 a Supreme Moslem *Sharia* Council was instituted. The Council consists of a President, known as the *Rais el-Ulema*, and four members, of whom two represent the district of Jerusalem, one Nablus, and one Acre. The members are chosen by an electoral college for a period of four years, but the method of election of the President has not yet been decided. Embodied in the High Commissioner's Order are the regulations, drawn up by a Moslem Committee, laying down the functions and powers of the Council. The members of the Council receive salaries from the Government. The revision of the constitution of the Supreme Moslem Council has been under consideration for some time.

The *Sharia* or Moslem religious courts have exclusive jurisdiction in matters of personal status of Moslems and Moslem religious endowments (*waqf*). There are Sharia courts in fourteen towns in Palestine, each presided over by a *kadi*. In each town there is also a Moslem jurist (*mufti*), whose duty it is to give canonical rulings on points of Moslem religious law. The appointment of kadis and muftis is subject to the approval of the Government which, however, has not the power to remove a mufti once his election has been approved. There is an appeal from the Sharia courts to the Moslem religious court of appeal, which sits in Jerusalem and consists of a president and two members.

The *Waqfs* are religious endowments, not necessarily Moslem, although in effect generally so. These endowments consist of property appropriated or dedicated (by a document called a *waqfiah*) to charitable uses and the service of God. They are divided as regards their administration into two categories, those formerly administered or supervised by the Ottoman Ministry of Waqf, and those which are independent of government control. Of the endowments formerly under the control of the Ministry, there are two classes: (1) *Mazbuta waqfs*, or waqfs administered and controlled directly by officials of the Ministry of Waqf; (ii) *Mulhaqa waqfs*, or waqfs which were under the general supervision of the Ministry, but were not under their direct administration. This latter class of foundation is a family settlement corresponding in general with an English trust.

By the High Commissioner's Order of the 20 December 1921 all Waqfs are placed under the control of the Supreme Moslem Sharia Council. The total Waqf revenue is estimated to amount to about £50,000 per annum, of which £30,000 is derived from a fixed payment by the Government in lieu of the tithe payable on lands dedicated by former rulers for charitable purposes, which tithe was commuted in 1927. The accounts of the Supreme Moslem Council are subject to audit. The social activities of the Waqf administration include the maintenance and assistance of schools, soup kitchens, a hospital, an orphanage, &c.

The disturbances culminating in the murder by Arab terrorists of an Acting District Commissioner and his police escort in September 1937 led to the dismissal of Haj Amin el Husseini, the Mufti of Jerusalem, from his membership of the General Waqf Committee, of which he was chairman. The Committee was at the same time temporarily dissolved. The Government thereupon appointed a commission under the chairmanship of a British judge to administer the Waqf revenue and to exercise the financial control previously exercised by the Supreme Moslem Council and the General Waqf Committee. This commission, which includes a Moslem member, is of a temporary character.

## JUSTICE AND CRIME

### Administration of Justice

The judiciary is regulated by the Palestine Order in Council. By this, three divisions have been established. At the base are the *magistrates' courts*, which exercise both civil and criminal jurisdiction. They try civil cases up to the value of £100, or concerning the re-covery of land; and criminal charges for which broadly the maximum penalty is one year's imprisonment. Most of the magistrates are Palestinians (Arabs or Jews); but British barristers have been appointed as stipendiaries in the larger towns. Further, a number of British officials hold magisterial warrants, by which they may dispose of the simpler criminal cases.

Next above the magistrates' courts are the *district courts*, of which there are five, centred at Jerusalem, Jaffa, Nablus, Tel Aviv, and Haifa. They are composed of a British president and two Palestinian judges, and they have jurisdiction in all civil matters outside the competence of the magistrates' courts, and in all criminal matters except capital cases. Further, they hear appeals from the magistrates' courts in their area, and also act as land courts to decide cases of disputed ownership.

The highest division is the *Supreme Court*, composed of a British Chief Justice, one or more British puisne judges, and four Palestinian judges. The Supreme Court has two branches of jurisdiction. As a Court of Appeal it hears appeals from district courts and from those courts which try suits for ownership of land; as a High Court it exercises jurisdiction, new to Palestine and borrowed from English constitutional tradition, for testing the legality of government action by petitions in the nature of writs of *Habeas Corpus*, injunction, and mandamus.

Capital cases are tried by a special court of criminal assize, in which the Chief Justice, or another British judge of the Supreme Court, sits with the full district court. A further appeal lies in civil cases of a certain value from the Supreme Court to the highest tribunal of British administration, the Judicial Committee of the Privy Council in London. That is an application of His Majesty's prerogative in all countries in which he exercises jurisdiction.

*Cases entered (other than religious courts)*

| | | 1930 | 1940 |
|---|---|---|---|
| Supreme Court: | Civil . . . . | 210 | 279 |
| | Criminal . . . | 217 | 147 |
| | Total . . . . | 427 | 426 |
| High Court: | Civil . . . . | 101 | 114 |
| Court of Criminal Assize: | Criminal . . . | 59 | 62 |
| Special Tribunal: | Civil . . . . | 3 | .. |
| District Courts: | Civil . . . . | 2,501 | 1,937 |
| | Criminal . . . | 2,282 | 1,962 |
| | Total . . . . | 4,783 | 3,899 |
| Land Courts: | Civil . . . . | 515 | 88 |
| Magistrates' Courts: | Civil . . . . | 64,025 | 40,746 |
| | Criminal . . . | 23,481 | 88,408 |
| | Total . . . . | 87,506 | 129,154 |
| Municipal Courts: | Criminal . . . | 10,770 | 7,012 |
| Special Magistrates' Courts: | Criminal . . . | 14,825 | 4,021 |
| TOTAL | Civil . . . . | 67,355 | 43,164 |
| | Criminal . . . | 51,634 | 101,612 |
| | | 118,989 | 144,776 |

*Municipal Courts* sit in Jerusalem and Jaffa, where a stipendiary presides, and in Tel Aviv, Gaza, Acre, Petah Tikva, and Rehovot, where the courts consist of honorary magistrates. Offences for which the punishment is a fine of not more than £5, or imprisonment for not more than fifteen days, are tried in these courts.

Among the beduin of southern Palestine minor cases are decided, in accordance with tribal custom, by the sheikhs. There is, however, an appeal to a higher tribal court, consisting of the local district officer and two sheikhs. The more serious criminal charges are dealt with by the Jerusalem District Court which visits Beersheba periodically. Minor charges involving a punishment of not more than a year's imprisonment may be dealt with by District Commissioners and other officers of the Government, to whom magisterial powers have been granted. Foreign citizens charged with any but trivial offences are entitled to be tried by a British magistrate or a court containing a majority of British judges.

The religious courts are a part of the system of communal autonomy and are dealt with on pages 200–4.

There are no juries in Palestine. Local conditions render their employment impossible. On the other hand, the population of Palestine is extraordinarily litigious. The table on p. 205 shows that there is an average of over 12,000 cases a month in all the courts of Palestine in a population of about a million and a half.

*Law*

At the beginning of the British period the system of law administered was the Ottoman code, which then prevailed throughout the Ottoman Empire, an inheritance from the Napoleonic period. This was modified from time to time by ordinances issued by the High Commissioner, and occasionally by Orders in Council. Under the Order in Council which enshrines the Constitution of Palestine, the courts were directed in the first place to apply Ottoman legislation as modified by any legislation of the Palestine Government. If this legislation was inadequate, the principles of English Common Law and Equity should be applied. Thus the Ottoman code of civil law was taken into use with little amendment. In this connexion it should be mentioned that in Palestine, as under Ottoman law, most matters of family rights are governed by religious law and are under the jurisdiction of the respective ecclesiastical courts. The Ottoman criminal law, however, proved hardly workable, even after drastic amendment, by a modern European government. Consequently, in 1938, it was entirely replaced by a new criminal code, on English lines. The Ottoman code of criminal procedure, also Napoleonic, was at the same time replaced by English procedure. The Ottoman commercial code, which also had a French origin, was similarly abolished. In all departments of law, excepting that relating to land transactions, there has been a tendency to model the law of Palestine on that of England.

*Police and Prisons*

The Department of Police and Prisons, under an Inspector-General, is the most costly of the departments of government. Its average annual ordinary expenditure during the five years ended 31 March 1939 was £814,544 (£1,351,947 in 1938–9). As its name implies, it is a combination of two departments, the Police, the more important one, being responsible for internal security. More recently, one of the functions of the Department of Migration, the control of frontiers for persons entering and leaving the country, has been transferred to the Police. Of the Police the British Section is the largest. The Palestinian Section includes both Arabs and Jews. The British and Palestinian personnel both carry out normal police duties, but the maintenance of the mechanical transport of the whole force rests with the British Police.

There are two central prisons, one in Jerusalem, formerly a hospice for Russian pilgrims, and the other at Acre in the Citadel, once the centre of the resistance to Napoleon. Most male prisoners sentenced to less than five years' imprisonment are employed in jail labour-companies in road-making, quarrying, and similar occupations. So far as beduin and, to a large extent, fellah prisoners are concerned, out-door employment is essential in order to avoid serious deterioration in the health of those who have been accustomed to spend the greater part of their lives in the open air. One of the difficulties in the way of the correction of criminals in Palestine is the ineffectiveness of prison in these circumstances. The standard of living of the fellahin and beduin is very low, even lower than that of the prison. As a consequence the prisoner is better fed and better housed than in his own home. His work in a labour-company is, if he is a fellah, not very different from his normal employment. Since imprisonment for debt still holds in Palestine, and many debtors prefer to go (or cannot avoid going) to prison rather than pay their debts, the prison population of Palestine is always relatively large. For young offenders there are reformatories.

## LANGUAGE AND RELIGION

In the courts, in communications with the Government, in municipal affairs, and in similar matters, any one of the three official languages—English, Arabic, and Hebrew—may be used. This equality of the three languages is in accordance with Article 22 of the Mandate. In practice, however, Arabic only is used in the all-Arab districts, and Hebrew in the all-Jewish. Ordinances and government notices are promulgated in all three languages, but in case of a difference the English version prevails. Inscriptions on coins, currency notes, and postage stamps are in the three languages, and telegrams are accepted in any one of the three. The regular days of rest of the various creeds are official days of rest for members of the respective communities. In practice it is not possible—for instance in the Post Office, where most of the telephonists are Jewish—for this rule to be rigidly observed, but every effort is made. The principal religious holidays are also official days of rest for the members of the several communities, and there is much balancing and weighing of the relative importance of religious festivals, major and minor, so that the members of no one community in government service shall have an advantage over another in this respect. There is a tendency to observe one another's holidays if only by a relaxation of effort, and this has led to the description of Palestine as the 'Land of Three Sabbaths and Four To-morrows' (Appendix F).

Complete religious freedom is safeguarded in accordance with Article 15 of the Mandate which runs:

'The Mandatory shall see that complete freedom of conscience and the free exercise of all forms of worship, subject only to the maintenance of public order and morals, are ensured to all. No discrimination of any kind shall be made between the inhabitants of Palestine on the ground of race, religion, or language. No person shall be excluded from Palestine on the sole ground of his religious belief. The right of each community to maintain its own schools for the education of its own members in its own language, while conforming to such educational requirements of a general nature as the Administration may impose, shall not be denied or impaired.'

## LAND OWNERSHIP

The system of land ownership in Palestine is very complicated. Immovable property falls into five main categories: (a) *mulk*, (b) *miri*, (c) *waqf*, (d) *metrukhi*, and (e) *mevat*. The term *mashaa* is used of land that has not been divided and is held in common. In the majority of the villages, cultivated land is held in *mashaa*, and is consequently sometimes the joint property of hundreds of people. The villager does not hold the same plot of land continuously; in some villages every child that is born acquires a share at birth, in others male children only acquire; in others, again, women who marry out of the community lose their rights. The varieties are numerous, but the basic principle is that no individual can point to a piece of land as being his own property; he can only claim to have an undivided share in all the land, and that share may be represented in the land registers as an arithmetical fraction. At intervals, varying from one to three years, according to the custom of the village, a redistribution takes place. The procedure is based on the drawing of lots, and is accompanied by a good deal of ceremony intended to guarantee fairness. A child is often selected to draw the stones on which the lots are marked. This system is obviously not the most economic, and the survey and distribution among the owners of these lands—a long process—on the part of the Government, has been in course for a number of years. *Mafruz* is land that has been divided and is owned by individuals.

(*a*) *Mulk* is in effect the equivalent of the English freehold. Land on which a man has built a house or planted vines or olive-trees thereby becomes mulk.

(*b*) *Miri* is property belonging to the State, but over which private individuals have the right of occupation or usufruct. The holder may sell, mortgage or lease the land, but not bequeath it. On the death of the holder it passes to his natural heirs; if he has no heirs it reverts to the State. It also reverts if he fails for three years to cultivate or build on the land. Most of the cultivable land of Palestine is miri.

(*c*) *Waqf* lands are mortmain property which has been dedicated to some religious or charitable object or family trust, and has been derived mainly from mulk and miri. Waqf consisting of mulk is the only true waqf; it is governed by the religious law. Such trusts can be, and generally are, dedicated on terms which secure the full use of the land to the dedicator and his descendants. The interest of the nominal owner (the Almighty) is often confined to a reversion contingent on the failure of the line; or else some charitable or religious duty of a trifling kind is imposed on the beneficiaries. Land cannot now be dedicated as waqf without the sanction of the High Commissioner.

(*d*) *Metrukhi* land is land bequeathed or given to the public, for instance for roads, or to the inhabitants of a town or village as a body, for instance for parks, communal pasture, places of worship, or markets. It cannot be alienated or used for any purpose other than that for which it was originally intended.

(e) *Mevat* is ownerless land, at a minimum distance of a mile and a half from the nearest inhabited town or village. Another system of measurement is, sufficiently distant from such a town or village that the voice of a man shouting there cannot be heard. Practically all the unoccupied land in Palestine is mevat and it cannot be occupied without the permission of the Government.

Until the law was altered in 1937, it was quite possible to own land, but not the houses or even the trees on it; or to own a tree but not its fruit.

The registration of land-ownership and consequently knowledge of the ownership was in a state of complete chaos when the British took over the administration of the country. The Ottoman Law required the registration of the title to land, but this law seems to have been more honoured in the breach than in the observance. In many cases land owned by foreigners, or foreign religious or educational establishments, had been registered in the names of nominees, Ottoman subjects, since at times it seems that foreign subjects were not entitled to hold real estate. In a very large number of instances, especially in the villages, ownership was considered to be a local matter that concerned no one outside of the village. That system may have once worked, but could no longer do so, when an increasing number of purchasers was crowding from outside. Registration, when it was effected, was in a very happy-go-lucky manner. No survey was made. Areas were sometimes expressed in the quantity of seed required to sow them, or in *dunams*, the number of which was arrived at by guesswork. In other cases there was no attempt to estimate the extent of the areas registered; indication of the boundaries by mention of the neighbouring owners or of physical features was considered sufficient. To add to the confusion, the retreating Turkish armies took with them many of the records, some of which have never been recovered. The Land Registry which was established by the British civil administration has been working ever since to bring order out of this chaos, but the very defective Ottoman records are still, in a large part of the country, the basis on which a claim to land-ownership rests. Consequently a certificate of transfer of land cannot yet in every case certify unquestionable ownership.

In view of all this, it will be realized that there is scope for special land courts which, however, are identical in personnel with the district courts. They deal with all questions of title to land, and sit also as courts of appeal (p. 205) from decisions of the magistrates' courts in land cases.

Since the British occupation there has been, especially in 'boom' periods, a considerable business in land. Consistently throughout the period the Jewish Agency, through one of its subsidiaries, has been buying land. To a large extent, and at first especially, the purchases have been from owners of large estates, farmed by tenants. The Jewish Agency has as a rule paid, in addition to the purchase money, compensation to the uprooted tenants, but the process was nevertheless creating a class of landless Arabs, whose existence was a source of some concern. More lately, when many of the large estates had passed out of the hands of the owners, purchases from small owner-cultivators were increasing. This development called for legislation, which took the form of safeguarding the cultivators. The class first to benefit was limited to that of cultivator-tenants dependent solely on their land for their maintenance. A series of ordinances to this end was enacted and these have proved effective. In short, if the tenant has paid his rent and has not grossly neglected his holding, no order for his eviction shall be made unless he has been provided with a subsistence area approved by the High Commissioner. With the increasing pressure of immigration and extension of land purchases, it became necessary, in the light of repeated expert advice, to protect the owner as well, and this was carried out in March 1940 when the Land Transfers Regulations were enacted. These regulations provide, roughly speaking, that in certain areas transfers of land from Arabs to non-Arabs shall be forbidden, in certain areas limited, and in certain areas free.

Land owned by Jews at the end of 1941 amounted to about 1,600,000 dunams or 370,000 acres, 40 per cent. of which was the property of the Jewish National Fund, a subsidiary of the Jewish Agency. The total in March 1936 was 1,231,800 dunams or 283,314 acres and the Jewish National Fund properties 30 per cent. In 1921 only 12 per cent. of the land owned by Jews in Palestine belonged to the Jewish National Fund (fig. 25).

The land acquired by the Jewish National Fund is inalienable. It is held in trust for 'the Jewish people', being leased on hereditary tenure at low uneconomic rentals to Jewish tenants. Apart from Jewish public institutions the tenants are for the most part settlers on the land. The settlements fall into two classes: *Moshav Ovdim* and

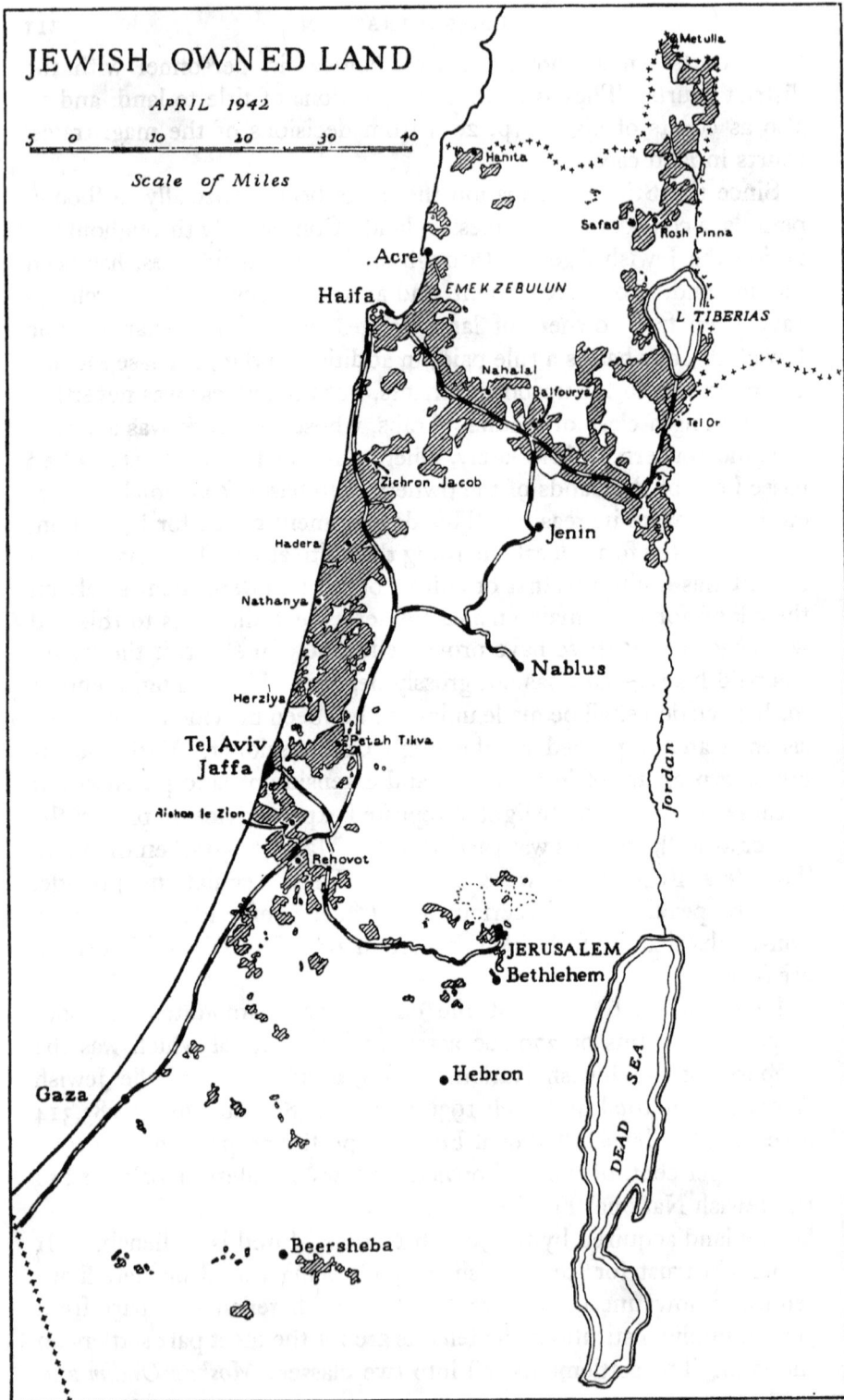

FIG. 25. *Jewish owned land, April* 1942

*Kwuzah.*[1] The *Moshav Ovdim* or Workers' Settlement consists of a group of small-holders, each living with his family in his own home, all together forming a village. The settlers must be members of the General Federation of Jewish Labour (p. 275) through which they must purchase their supplies and sell their produce co-operatively. They are not supposed to employ outside labour but to work their holdings themselves with the assistance of their families. The *Kwuzah* is a group of workers living as a community with no separate property or income. The produce of the settlement and the earnings of its members outside are shared by all the members. They also are all members of the General Federation of Jewish Labour and have also to purchase their supplies and sell their produce through it. The *Kwuzot* are as much agricultural training centres as centres of economic production and in few instances are self-supporting.

## EDUCATION

At the date of the British occupation in 1918 the public system of elementary and secondary education in Palestine was essentially that first established by the Turkish law of 1869. The secondary and higher elementary schools in the provinces were subject to provincial (*vilâyet*) control under imperial officers, and were comparatively efficient. The lower elementary schools in towns and villages were managed by special local committees, and were often little better than the old *Koran* schools. The general organization was modelled on the French school system. In theory, Ottoman public education was gratuitous and compulsory; religious instruction formed part of the curriculum, and some provision was made by law for religions other than Islam. In practice, the schools of the *millets* received little or no support. Turkish was the language of instruction in public schools down to the outbreak of war. Universal elementary education of Moslems never became a reality in any part of the empire.

Education of an elementary type was provided for Christian children by their own religious authorities or by missionary bodies of various denominations, while foreign Jewish bodies (p. 140) such as the *Hilfsverein* (German), the *Alliance Israélite* (French), and the Anglo-Jewish Association (English) conducted schools for Jewish children, employing as the chief medium of instruction the language of their country of origin. In some town schools, however, and in all

---

[1] A *Kwuzah* is a group of workers living as a community; *Kwuzot* is the plural. A *Kibbutz* is a group of *Kwuzot*, employed for collective work outside their settlements.

'settlement' schools, of which the majority were maintained by the Jewish Colonization Association, Hebrew was the medium of instruction. In 1914 the Zionist Education Council (*Vaad ha-Hinnukh*) was founded, and took over the control of twelve schools. This number had increased by 1918 to forty, and formed the nucleus of the present Hebrew public school system, now under the control of the General Council of the Jewish Community (*Vaad Leumi*).

Since 1920 two systems of national education have gradually developed, formed on a linguistic and racial basis, Arab and Hebrew. Into one or other of these systems all schools, except some of those maintained by foreign bodies, naturally fall. The Arab system includes all schools, government and non-government, where Arabic is wholly or chiefly the medium of instruction; while the Hebrew system includes all schools, whether under the *Vaad Leumi* or not, where Hebrew is the language of instruction, or at least is regarded as the predominant feature of the curriculum.

These two systems are further divided into public and non-public schools. The public schools comprise government schools on the Arab side, and, on the Jewish side, the schools controlled by the *Vaad Leumi*. The non-public schools are classified according to their religious denominations: Moslem, Christian, and Jewish. The following table shows the distribution of pupils among the various schools in 1940:

|  | No. of schools | No. of pupils |
|---|---|---|
| **ARAB:** | | |
| Public System (Government Schools) . . | 402 | 54,367 |
| Non-Public Schools: Moslem . . . | 178 | 14,204 |
| Christian[1] . . . | 195 | 25,274 |
| Total . . . . . . | 775 | 93,845 |
| **JEWISH:** | | |
| Public System (*Vaad Leumi*) . . . | 419 | 56,900 |
| Non-Public Schools . . . . . | 320 | 25,701 |
| Total . . . . . . | 739 | 82,601 |

[1] These include all schools maintained by foreign missionary bodies.

Finally there are the government Law Classes, whose primary purpose is the preparation of men and women for the examination qualifying them to practise law in Palestine. Many students, however, take the courses without that intention.

Of the Moslem children of school age, 25 per cent. attend school; of the Jewish and Christian children nearly 100 per cent. are believed to receive education of some kind or other. Most of the Christian children attend schools provided by foreign religious organizations. Almost all the Jewish and Christian children attend school for at least eight years. Both Arab and Jewish parents are equally anxious for their children to be admitted to school, and the inability of the Government, for financial reasons, to admit all who apply is one of the permanent complaints of the Arab population. In 1939, of the applications for admission to the government schools, 56 per cent. had to be rejected in the towns and 40 per cent. in the villages. The parallel figures for 1940 were 56 per cent. and 42. There is a large disparity between the number of Moslem boys and girls attending school. The percentages are:

|  | Boys | Girls |
|---|---|---|
| In towns | 80 per cent. | 50 per cent. |
| In villages | 50 ,, | 4 ,, |

The Government makes a grant for education to the General Council of the Jews of Palestine, bearing the same proportion to its expenditure on its own schools as does the number of Jewish children of school age bear to the similar number of Arab children. This grant, however, falls far short of the cost of maintaining the Jewish schools. Schools accepting a government grant are subject to inspection by government educational officers. The Department of Education can also require certain conditions to be fulfilled before a grant is paid. The co-operation of local authorities is always welcomed, and in many centres, both Arab and Jewish, there are education committees. In the government schools education is free.

Apart from the Hebrew University (p. 219), a Board of Higher Studies has been constituted consisting of official and non-official members of all communities. Its purpose is to promote education of university standard and to this end it conducts three annual examinations—Matriculation, Intermediate, and Final—leading to the Palestine Diploma. The matriculation examination can be, and is, taken in any of the three official languages.

### Arab Schools

In the government schools Arabic is the language of instruction. English is also taught in the higher classes of the urban ones, but not Hebrew. Manual training is given in all urban boys' schools, and domestic science, including needlework and embroidery, in those of the girls. In the villages the education is directed towards fitting the boys and girls for rural life. All tendency towards encouraging an exodus to the towns or the creation of a black-coated proletariat is avoided. Consequently the syllabus is different for town and for village schools. Practical horticulture, and even afforestation, are taught in many of the village schools.

In 1942 the Government established at Dura, a large village near Hebron, an advanced school in which agriculture and trades are taught. Of the 220 boys, 40 are boarders, sons of semi-nomad families.

Only one government school is directed to secondary education, but four of the other schools give a one-year secondary course and seven a two-years course. There are, however, two government Teachers' Training Colleges, one for men, the other for women. Apart from these two colleges there is a training centre attached to the Kadoorie Agricultural School at Tulkarm, where a year's course of pedagogic training for young men who have passed through the agricultural school is given. There is also, at Ramallah, a rural teachers' training centre for girls. Further, there are some twenty government scholarships tenable by prospective teachers at the American University of Beirut, technical schools in Egypt, and British universities and other educational institutions. Technical training is given in a government Trade School for Arabs at Haifa. Manual training is also provided in all town schools, and is included in the training course for teachers. Women teachers are also trained at the Jerusalem Girls' College and Schmidt's Girls' School.

## Jewish Schools

The Hebrew public school system is in the hands of the General Council of the Jews of Palestine (*Vaad Leumi*) acting through an Executive Education Committee, on which are represented the Jewish Agency, the Municipal Council of Tel Aviv, and those villages that are outside the school system of the Jewish Labour Federation. The latter has its own schools and system, which are independent of the general Jewish community, although they are mainly supported by it.[1] The budget and educational appointments of these Jewish schools have to be approved by the Government. At the end of 1939, 68 per cent. of the 78,457 Jewish schoolchildren of Palestine were attending schools of the General Council. The *Vaad Leumi* schools are classified in three groups: 'General', 'Mizrahi',[2] and 'Labour', of which the 'General' schools include about 60 per cent. of the pupils. They all impart instruction in general subjects

---

[1] Since 1938 this independence has been to a large extent modified.
[2] The Mizrahi party represents Orthodox Jewry in the Jewish Agency.

through the medium of Hebrew. In the Mizrahi schools more stress is laid on religious instruction, while in those of the Labour Federation emphasis is laid on agriculture, and the tendency is towards self-government and individual work. Of the three classes into which the schools of the General Council are grouped, 176 with 32,279 pupils are General Zionist, 82 with 13,816 pupils are Mizrahi Zionist, and 161 with 10,805 pupils Labour or Socialist-Zionist.

Outside the Hebrew public school system there are elementary schools of some importance, maintained by the Anglo-Jewish Association of London (The Evelina de Rothschild School for Girls) and by the *Alliance Israélite* of Paris (in Jerusalem and four other towns). A large number of *Talmud Torahs*, schools in which religious instruction with a certain amount of general education is given, exists in the towns. In these last, the language of instruction is, as a rule, Yiddish or Arabic. There is also a large number of theological colleges, Hebrew schools, commercial classes, &c.

Below the schools are the kindergartens, which are financially outside the Education Committee of the General Council, but are supervised by it. Most of the schools, especially the rural ones, are co-educational. In most of them English is taught; in a smaller number Arabic.

Inside the Jewish school system there are four secondary schools, at Jerusalem, Tel Aviv, Haifa, and Safad. There is also a number of smaller private Hebrew secondary schools. There are four training colleges, two for men and two for women. This duplication is due to the doubts of the Mizrahi about the orthodoxy of the other colleges. More strict is the *Agudat Israel*, which is suspicious of the orthodoxy even of the Mizrahi. It has its own schools, but they are outside the Hebrew public school system.

The schools of the Jewish community draw their support from several sources. The Government pays capitation grants (p. 215) and the Jewish Agency also grants a subvention—£40,000 in 1940. A much smaller grant is made by the Palestine Jewish Colonization Association, a private company, founded by the late Baron Edmond de Rothschild of Paris, which devotes itself to Jewish agricultural settlement. Tel Aviv and other local authorities make grants and there are also school fees. The estimated revenue of the *Vaad Leumi* Education Department for 1941–2 consisted of the Government grant, £56,000, Jewish Agency grant, £40,000, *Vaad Leumi*, £3,000, fees and municipal and community taxation, £210,000. These figures do not, however, represent the whole of the expenditure. The provision and maintenance of the school buildings is in many cases at the expense of the local communities, which in some instances also provide supplementary teachers.

## Technical and Scientific Education

Outside of the *Vaad Leumi* educational system, but yet a public institution maintained by Jews in Palestine, and to a far greater extent by those outside, is the Hebrew Technical Institute at Haifa. It now consists of a Technical High School, a Nautical School, and the College of Technology which teaches civil, mechanical, and electrical engineering, and architecture. There were 491 students in 1940. Another higher educational institution is the Daniel Sieff Research Institute, privately endowed, but maintained to some extent from other sources, which conducts scientific research especially in problems whose solution would be of advantage to local industry. It has three departments: organic chemistry, physics, and physical chemistry.

The Government maintains, with the assistance of an endowment fund bequeathed by the late Sir Ellis Kadoorie, a Jewish Agricultural School at the foot of Mount Tabor, and there is another, founded in 1870 by the *Alliance Israélite* of Paris, at Mikveh Israel near Jaffa. There is also an agricultural secondary school at Pardess Hanna, south of Haifa. For girls there are two agricultural schools, maintained by the Women's International Zionist Organization, and a semi-private training farm on the outskirts of Jerusalem. The Agricultural School at Ben Shemen for boys and girls is a German-Jewish foundation, originally an orphanage (photo. 66).

## Other Non-Government Schools

Apart from the government system there are schools for Christian children and, to a less extent, for Moslem ones. Some of these are private ventures independent of all public control: others are conducted by public organizations such as the Supreme Moslem Council and a number of British and American Christian missionary societies. The French, German, and Italian consuls-general controlled their respective national schools. The seven schools of the Supreme Moslem Council are, with two exceptions, elementary, but its orphanage teaches also trades and handicrafts. The local Christian communities have also established schools, especially in Jerusalem, Jaffa, and Haifa. The majority of the non-government schools receive small capitation grants, and are subject to inspection by the Department of Education. In these, a variety of languages is used for instruction. In the English and American schools, of which the principal ones are the Jerusalem Girls' College, St. George's School, and Bishop Gobat's School of Jerusalem, the English Girls' School and the Scots' College at Haifa, all British, and the American Friends' Mission Schools at Ramallah, English is the language of instruction. English is also used in the secondary classes of the *Terra Santa* College (Franciscan), Schmidt's Girls' School (German), and the Collège des Frères Chrétiens (French) in Jerusalem.

These higher schools are attended by children of all three communities. The Syrian Orphanage, a German foundation, is a valuable institution in which several trades are taught. The American colony in Jerusalem maintains an industrial school for girls. There is also provision on a small scale, supported by privately obtained funds, for blind, deaf, crippled, and undeveloped children, and a number of orphanages, principally for Jewish children. At Beit Jemal there is an agricultural school maintained by the Salesian Fathers.

*The Hebrew University*

The Hebrew University, on Mount Scopus overlooking Jerusalem, was opened in 1925. There are two faculties—one for humanities, the other for mathematics and natural sciences—and a medical pre-faculty. In addition the university has a College of Agriculture at Rehovot; the university staff also give extension lectures in a number of centres. The university was originally intended to be a graduate research institution, but pressure quickly compelled an alteration of its constitution and it now, though still pursuing research, grants the degrees of M.A. and M.Sc., in addition to that of Ph.D. The university itself is not so much a Palestine university as 'the University of the whole Jewish People'.[1] Its government and development have been in accordance with that principle. The university buildings have been presented by various benefactors, and there is an endowment fund of less than half a million pounds from similar sources. The income from fees is small. The remainder of the revenue is derived from contributions by Jewish well-wishers in all parts of the world. Of these contributions, as of the endowments, the greater part comes from the United States of America. The ordinary expenditure in 1939-40 was about £123,000 and the number of students 1,259, of whom 65 were research students. It has an academic staff of over 150, of whom 34 are professors, and a valuable library of over 400,000 volumes.

[1] *The Hebrew University of Jerusalem: Its History and Development*, p. 7.

# CHAPTER IX

# PUBLIC HEALTH

THE improvement in the public health of Palestine since Great Britain assumed responsibility for the mandate is a noteworthy achievement. The extent of that improvement finds expression in the vital statistics.

The population of Palestine is predominantly rural, though urbanization has proceeded apace, especially among the immigrant Jewish population. Seventy-five per cent. of the Jewish population live in the towns. Of the Arabs, however, the large majority dwells in villages and is engaged in agriculture.

The houses of Arab villages are crowded together; they are built of stone in the hills, of mud-brick in the plains (photos. 54–7). In Jewish communal village settlements the living quarters are generally in large central buildings. In the other villages the Jews mostly live in small detached houses.

## Vital Statistics

When British administration was set up, the machinery for recording births and deaths had broken down. It was immediately restarted. (For statistics *see* pp. 175-6.) Registration of births and deaths with the Health Department is now compulsory. In towns, notification of births is made by doctors or midwives, and of deaths by doctors. Burial permits are necessary where there is a District Health Office, the authority of the coroner being necessary for the issue of the permit, if the cause of death is uncertified or unknown.

In villages, births are reported by parent or midwife, and deaths by relatives or other person present at the death, to the *mukhtar* or headman, who completes the notification form for transmission to the District Health Office. Burial permits are not essential here, nor is it possible to demand medical certificates of the cause of death. *Mukhtars* receive payment for every birth or death notification sent to the District Health Office.

Registration of both births and deaths is therefore as complete as is possible in the circumstances. In normal times few such events go unrecorded, but during the disturbed period of 1936–1939 there was some interruption of notifications in certain rural areas.

In 1922 there were 116 male births recorded for every 100 female; in 1939 the ratio was 108 to 100; in 1933 it was 105. In most oriental countries, male births are much more carefully recorded than female, for they are considered far more important. Thus the sex ratio of births may indicate the completeness or otherwise of birth notifications. It is normal everywhere for male births to be more than female, an average ratio being about 105 to 100.

Even if some allowance be made for defective registration in the years of disturbance, death-rate figures give tangible evidence of improving health conditions. The death-rates of all communities for 1939 were the lowest yet recorded. In the following year there was an increase, insignificant except among the Moslems. The death-rate among Jews in Palestine is remarkably low. It should be recalled, however, that their age constitution is abnormal, and that comparisons with mortality rates of other communities are therefore not justified.

TABLE I

| | Lowest rates | | | Highest rates | |
|---|---|---|---|---|---|
| | Mean settled population | Infant mortality rate | | Mean settled population | Infant mortality rate |
| Shefa Amr . . | 3,400 | 8 | Bethlehem villages | 8,700 | 165 |
| Hadera . . | 4,800 | 41 | Mejdel . . | 7,600 | 163 |
| Jericho and villages | 4,200 | 42 | Safad villages . | 34,800 | 161 |
| Rishon le Zion . | 5,900 | 47 | Bethlehem . | 7,500 | 157 |
| Tel Aviv . . | 131,700 | 48 | Beit Jala . . | 3,200 | 154 |
| Rehovot . . | 7,400 | 57 | Jerusalem villages | 48,700 | 153 |
| Hebron villages . | 57,000 | 60 | Gaza . . | 20,200 | 150 |
| Petah Tikva . . | 16,200 | 61 | Beisan villages . | 15,200 | 148 |
| Jaffa villages . . | 77,200 | 70 | Ramallah . . | 5,200 | 146 |
| Khan Yunis . . | 4,700 | 74 | | | |
| Beersheba . . | 3,500 | 74 | | | |
| Haifa . . . | 105,900 | 82 | | | |
| Nathanya . . | 3,090 | 86 | | | |
| Jerusalem . . | 131,300 | 87 | | | |

Birth-rates among the Jewish community range between 23 and 38 per 1,000. The reduction of the Jewish infant mortality rate to 55·6 per 1,000 live births in 1941 is a noteworthy achievement. It is indicative of high hygienic standards and may be attributed not only to the measures taken by the Government Department of Health, but also to the excellent services provided by the Hadassah (Jewish Women's) Organization of U.S.A. Only twice have England and

Wales recorded lower infant mortality rates. Moslem infant mortality rates are twice as high, but they compare favourably with those of certain Balkan countries, of Spain and Portugal, and of oriental countries where the standard of living is similar. There is, moreover, a downward tendency in Moslem infant mortality rates that is testimony to improved conditions.

In 1939 the infant mortality rate in towns (total population 661,300) was 96 per 1,000 live births, and in villages (total population 743,500) 115 per 1,000. The rates varied much from place to place: the lowest and highest rates recorded in 1939 are given in Table I (p. 221).

## Causes of Death

The total number of deaths registered in Palestine in 1941 was 24,485 (1940, 27,019; 1939, 19,529). Of those in 1941, 9,077 occurred among the residents of 29 towns, where the cause of death in 8,263 cases was medically certified. The causes responsible for these deaths in 1941 were:

### TABLE II

| Cause of death | No. of deaths | Per cent. of total |
|---|---|---|
| Diarrhoea and enteritis | 1,577 | 19·0 |
| Pneumonia and broncho-pneumonia | 1,399 | 16·9 |
| Diseases of the heart | 720 | 8·7 |
| Congenital debility and malformations, premature birth, &c. | 495 | 6·0 |
| Senility | 491 | 5·9 |
| Cancer and other malignant tumours | 375 | 4·5 |
| Intra-cranial lesions of vascular origin | 373 | 4·5 |
| Nephritis | 330 | 4·0 |
| Respiratory diseases (tuberculosis and pneumonia excepted) | 219 | 2·7 |
| Accidental and violent deaths (homicide and suicide excepted) | 211 | 2·6 |
| Tuberculosis of the respiratory system | 200 | 2·4 |
| Miscellaneous, medically certified | 1,873 | 22·7 |
| | 8,263 | 99·9 |

## Infectious Diseases

All cases of notifiable diseases recorded in Palestine during 1941 are given in the following table together with the number of deaths ascribed to each disease:

## TABLE III

| Disease | 1941 Cases | 1941 Deaths | Disease | 1941 Cases | 1941 Deaths |
|---|---|---|---|---|---|
| Measles . . . | 4,861 | 687 | Tetanus . . . | 47 | 23 |
| Typhoid fever . . | 2,439 | 235 | Puerperal fever . . | 43 | 17 |
| Whooping cough . | 1,002 | 7 | Relapsing fever . . | 30 | 0 |
| Tuberculosis . . | 645 | 251 | Anthrax . . . | 21 | 2 |
| Dysentery . . | 433 | 13 | Acute poliomyelitis . | 20 | 5 |
| Mumps . . . | 402 | 0 | Leprosy . . . | 5 | 12[1] |
| Diphtheria . . | 349 | 20 | Cerebrospinal meningitis | 8 | 1 |
| Chicken pox . . | 329 | 0 | Schistosomiasis . . | 6 | 1 |
| Typhus . . . | 324 | 3 | Undulant fever . . | 5 | 0 |
| Erysipelas . . | 240 | 19 | Hydrophobia . . | 4 | 4 |
| Scarlet fever . . | 236 | 0 | Encephalitis lethargica | 3 | 2 |
| Paratyphoid fever . | 163 | 3 | German measles . | 3 | 0 |

[1] Some of these were cases from previous years.

The above list is long, but the incidence of no disease appears to be unduly high. Measles is the most prevalent, but the number of cases varies considerably from year to year: 7,594 (1937), 3,219 (1938), 237 (1939), 14,469 (1940, when there was a very severe epidemic). Scarlet fever is of a very mild type, unlike that prevalent in some of the Balkan countries. Acute poliomyelitis, or infantile paralysis, is chiefly confined to the towns of Jaffa and Tel Aviv.

Typhus fever is of the mild sporadic murine type, and most cases occur in Jaffa town and district, Haifa town and district, and Tel Aviv, generally among Jews. In this form the disease is spread from rat to man by means of the rat-flea. No case of louse-borne epidemic typhus was reported.

It is noteworthy that small-pox is entirely absent. Small-pox vaccination and revaccination receive constant attention, the total number treated being 55,422 in 1938 and 75,838 in 1939.

Cases of relapsing fever were reported from different parts of Palestine, but nowhere was there a severe outbreak. Seventeen cases were notified in Nablus and district in 1938. No death has been ascribed to this disease between 1938 and 1941.

Sporadic cases of undulant fever were reported from several towns. There were 29 cases in 1939, 20 in 1940. Both forms of the disease seem to be present. Laboratory reports for 1939 indicate that during that year 34 sera examined gave positive agglutination reactions with *Br. melitensis* and 18 with *Br. abortus*. Two of the 29 cases of undulant fever notified in 1939 were fatal, one in Jerusalem, the other in Jaffa.

Typhoid fever is prominent among the infectious diseases, but its incidence appears to be decreasing. The mortality rate is low (*c.* 10%), a fact which indicates either that notification is unusually complete or that the disease is mild in type. It is rather surprising that the incidence of the disease is as low as it is, since diarrhoea and enteritis are responsible for more deaths in the towns of Palestine than any other single cause. It is attributable to the protection afforded to a large proportion of the population by inoculation against typhoid and paratyphoid fevers, all immigrants being inoculated on arrival. Cases of typhoid fever occur throughout the year, but the incidence is generally highest in the third quarter and lowest in the first quarter. Most in recent years have been reported from Nablus and district. Jerusalem, Jaffa, Haifa, and the Jaffa district were responsible for about half the total cases notified in 1939. Of the 130 cases notified in Tel Aviv during 1938 and 1939, it is remarkable that only one terminated fatally.

Paratyphoid notifications were less than a tenth of typhoid notifications, and only three deaths were ascribed to paratyphoid fever in 1941. Laboratory reports indicate that paratyphoid bacilli A and B are about equally responsible for paratyphoid fever in Palestine: 127 positive agglutination reactions were recorded with *B. paratyphosus A* and 134 with *B. paratyphosus B* in 1939.

Dysentery is probably much more prevalent than the notifications indicate. Both bacillary and amoebic dysentery are prevalent in Palestine; laboratory findings indicate that amoebic dysentery is the more frequent, but not everywhere. A recent report on dysentery in Rehovot, population 8,300, states that there were 110 cases in 1937, of which 91 were bacillary, and 102 cases in 1938, of which 90 were bacillary. Four-fifths of the bacillary cases were associated with bacilli of the Flexner group. The *Shiga* bacillus was found in 13 per cent. of the cases.

## Malaria

Nearly the whole of Palestine was formerly intensely malarious. The experience of British troops engaged in Palestine in the war of 1914–18 showed that that country's evil reputation for malaria was not undeserved and seemed to justify the gloomy forecasts then made of the health conditions. Wisely conceived control measures and patient unremitting supervision have falsified those forebodings. The incidence of malaria throughout the country is now remarkably low. Nearly all the urban areas are free of malaria and its prevalence is almost negligible in most populated rural areas. This remarkable achievement redounds to the credit of the Palestine Department of Health. Though now unimportant as a cause of morbidity and death, malaria remains a potential menace to health: experience from time to time has shown that, if vigilance be relaxed, serious outbreaks of the disease may still occur. That the present methods of control are effective has received striking confirmation during the last few years. Disturbances during 1938 and 1939 necessitated much increased general military activity. Night patrols and pickets furnished by highly susceptible troops might be expected to provide no uncertain evidence of malaria prevalence. Yet during 1938 only 56 fresh infections were reported among the troops, and during 1939 only 203 fresh infections.

The physiography and climatic conditions of Palestine have been dealt with in Chapters II–IV, but a few facts concerning them are of special significance in relation to malaria prevalence. Sand-dunes fringe the flat, fertile coastal plain, and impede the run-off of water. Marshes and pools result, providing facilities for anopheline breeding. The central hills are limestone, covered with scanty soil, dry and barren. Winter rains erode holes in stream-beds, and seepages occur at foothills in the form of springs. Here rock-cut rain-water cisterns furnish the water-supply. Thus other important breeding-places for certain species of *Anopheles* are provided. Still farther inland, swamps and seepages are common along the whole length of the Jordan valley: this has always been one of the most malarious areas of Palestine, and the Lake Huleh marshes still have an evil reputation. The Jordan valley is but sparsely populated. Late and heavy spring rains favour malaria throughout Palestine.

The beduin population constitutes a danger from the malaria point of view. The migration of flocks from the east and the south in seasons of scanty rainfall, notably to the Jordan valley, is still a factor of importance in the epidemiology of this disease.

Nine species of *Anopheles* are to be found in Palestine: *A. bifurcatus, A. elutus, A. superpictus, A. sergenti, A. hyrcanus* var. *sinensis, A. algeriensis, A. multicolor, A. pharoensis,* and *A. mauritianus.* The last three are rare and unimportant as carriers of malaria.

*A. bifurcatus,* a domestic species, breeds in wells and cisterns and was formerly common in most towns and villages of Palestine throughout the year. It was responsible for nearly all urban malaria. Piped water-supplies, and the closing, mosquito-proofing, or oiling of wells and cisterns have almost eliminated this species from many places. Jerusalem was highly malarious; it is now free of malaria.

The Department of Health regard *A. bifurcatus* as the most dangerous species, though thanks to control it is probably now responsible for fewer cases of malaria than either *A. elutus* or *A. superpictus*.

*A. elutus* is the chief carrier of malaria in the rural plains. It is one of the varieties or 'biological races' of *A. maculipennis*, which differ from each other in their choice of breeding-places and food, and in their capacity to transmit malaria. The larvae and adults of these 'races' of *A. maculipennis* resemble each other so closely as to make identification almost impossible, and it is the well-marked characteristics of the eggs which enable differentiation to be made. *A. elutus* is the only variety of *A. maculipennis* in Palestine that is important, for it feeds on man for choice. The two other 'races' that occur, *typicus* and *messeae*, prefer the blood of cattle to that of man. *A. elutus* breeds in stagnant water, pools, swamps, reservoirs overgrown with algae, and wells. It commonly breeds in brackish water, rarely in very pure water, beginning in March and continuing until the onset of heavy November rains.

*A. superpictus* may be found breeding with various races of *A. maculipennis* in almost stagnant water, but this is exceptional. The larvae are more commonly found in eddies and backwaters of fairly rapid streams with rough rocky beds: they may be found in large numbers in small pools among boulders in streams that are nearly dry. In a general manner it may be said that *A. superpictus* is responsible for the malaria of the hills, *A. elutus* for the malaria of the plains, but the breeding-places of the two species may overlap to a slight extent. Their breeding-season is similar to that of *A. elutus*.

*A. sergenti* superficially resembles *A. superpictus*. It most commonly breeds in very slowly moving streams and in seepages under rocks and pebbles. Adults are rare in Palestine except from September to November, when they may be very numerous; this is the season of maximum malignant tertian malaria prevalence. *A. sergenti* may be an important vector of malaria.

*A. hyrcanus* var. *sinensis* breeds in marshes; it is most abundant from April to June. *A. algeriensis* is also a marsh breeder, and is the dominant species in marsh areas from January to March. Both these two species can transmit malaria, but their capacity for evil is restricted by the fact that they are usually confined to the marshland in which they breed.

All three forms of the malaria parasite are found in Palestine. *Plasmodium malariae* (quartan malaria) is rare: it is responsible for from 1 to 2 per cent. of the total malaria infections. *P. vivax*, benign tertian, infections are the most numerous; during the first half of the year they constitute the great majority of all malaria infections. During the second half of the year *P. falciparum*, malignant tertian, infections may equal, or from September to November outnumber, *P. vivax* infections.

Mosquito control in Palestine has been essentially anti-larval. In towns all possible water-holding places are catalogued and inspected. Wells necessary for a water-supply are mosquito-proofed; others are closed. Cisterns are provided with mosquito-proof tops. Other breeding-places are regularly oiled. Residents of almost all towns and of the larger villages co-operate in this work. The rural malaria problem consists of the prevention of stagnant water in summer, of drainage and irrigation schemes, and of filling and pumping operations. The annual spring cleaning by villagers and settlers under trained supervision, clearing the smaller wadis near their homes and channelling and draining small swamps and bad irrigation systems, make possible the satisfactory application of oil or Paris green. In some places rotation irrigation channels allow alternate drying of sets of channels, thus preventing the mosquito from breeding. Such a system of irrigation has been practised for generations at Nablus, which has always been free from malaria, though the disease is prevalent in surrounding villages.

The prompt and energetic co-operation of the people is perhaps the most noteworthy feature of malaria control in Palestine. The people have seen the lasting effects of swamp reclamation, and have appreciated the benefits to health resulting from proper irrigation and water tidiness. Some of the most fertile land of the country has been reclaimed and made healthy after centuries of waste.

This successful control has been carried out at very small cost. Direct anti-malarial measures cost about 1¼d. per head of population per year. The cost of major drainage schemes and reclamation is additional. The value of the free labour contributed by the beneficiaries is also very large indeed. There is no separate anti-malaria service. Malaria control is but one of the duties of the staff of the Department of Health.

The destruction of adult mosquitoes, valued highly in some countries as an anti-malaria measure, has been tried in Palestine, but is neither widely recommended nor extensively used as a practical measure, though mosquito-catching stations are widely used as a guide to breeding-conditions.

In all important drainage schemes channelling by dynamite is the method of choice, if the soil be wet: the cost is barely a tenth of that of manual labour.

The low and decreasing incidence of malaria in Palestine is shown by dispensary returns, and by the number of schoolchildren with enlargement of the spleen. The following table shows the number of malaria patients treated each year from 1927 to 1940 in the dispensaries of the country in relation to the number seeking relief for all diseases:

| Year | Total dispensary attendances | Malaria patients | Percentage |
|------|------|------|------|
| 1927 . . . | 515,147 | 16,380 | 3·2 |
| 1928 . . . | 528,166 | 12,065 | 2·3 |
| 1929 . . . | 524,977 | 18,474 | 3·5 |
| 1930 . . . | 610,140 | 16,129 | 2·6 |
| 1931 . . . | 604,308 | 15,029 | 2·5 |
| 1932 . . . | 632,531 | 4,035 | 0·6 |
| 1933 . . . | 693,833 | 4,620 | 0·7 |
| 1934 . . . | 844,324 | 10,915 | 1·3 |
| 1935 . . . | 1,036,126 | 13,679 | 1·3 |
| 1936 . . . | 857,117 | 6,295 | 0·8 |
| 1937 . . . | 1,190,787 | 7,517 | 0·6 |
| 1938 . . . | 1,169,427 | 6,709 | 0·6 |
| 1939 . . . | 1,336,219 | 9,042 | 0·7 |
| 1940 . . . | 1,379,486 | 7,008 | 0·5 |

Spleen-rates show that as early as 1925 urban malaria was well under control. The spleen-rate of Jerusalem fell from 44·3 in 1919–20 to 0·8 in 1925; in Jaffa from 16·6 to 4·9, and in Haifa from 39·0 to 5·7. Subsequent improvement has resulted in the practical eradication of malaria from towns, and it is only in certain rural areas in Samaria and Galilee that malaria continues to contribute appreciably to the morbidity of the population. The urban spleen-rate in 1925 was 4·6 and the rural spleen-rate 12·0. The spleen-rates for six recent years are tabulated below. The numbers of schoolchildren examined in 1939 were 43,232 in 19 towns and 45,691 in 454 villages.

*Spleen-rates per cent.*

| | 1935 | 1936 | 1937 | 1938 | 1939 | 1940 |
|------|------|------|------|------|------|------|
| Urban areas . . | 1·7 | 1·8 | 1·5 | 1·4 | 1·5 | 1·2 |
| Rural areas . . | 7·4 | 6·7 | 4·7 | 4·3 | 5·7 | 5·4 |

There are a few intensely malarious regions in Palestine that still remain to be dealt with. These are shown in the accompanying map

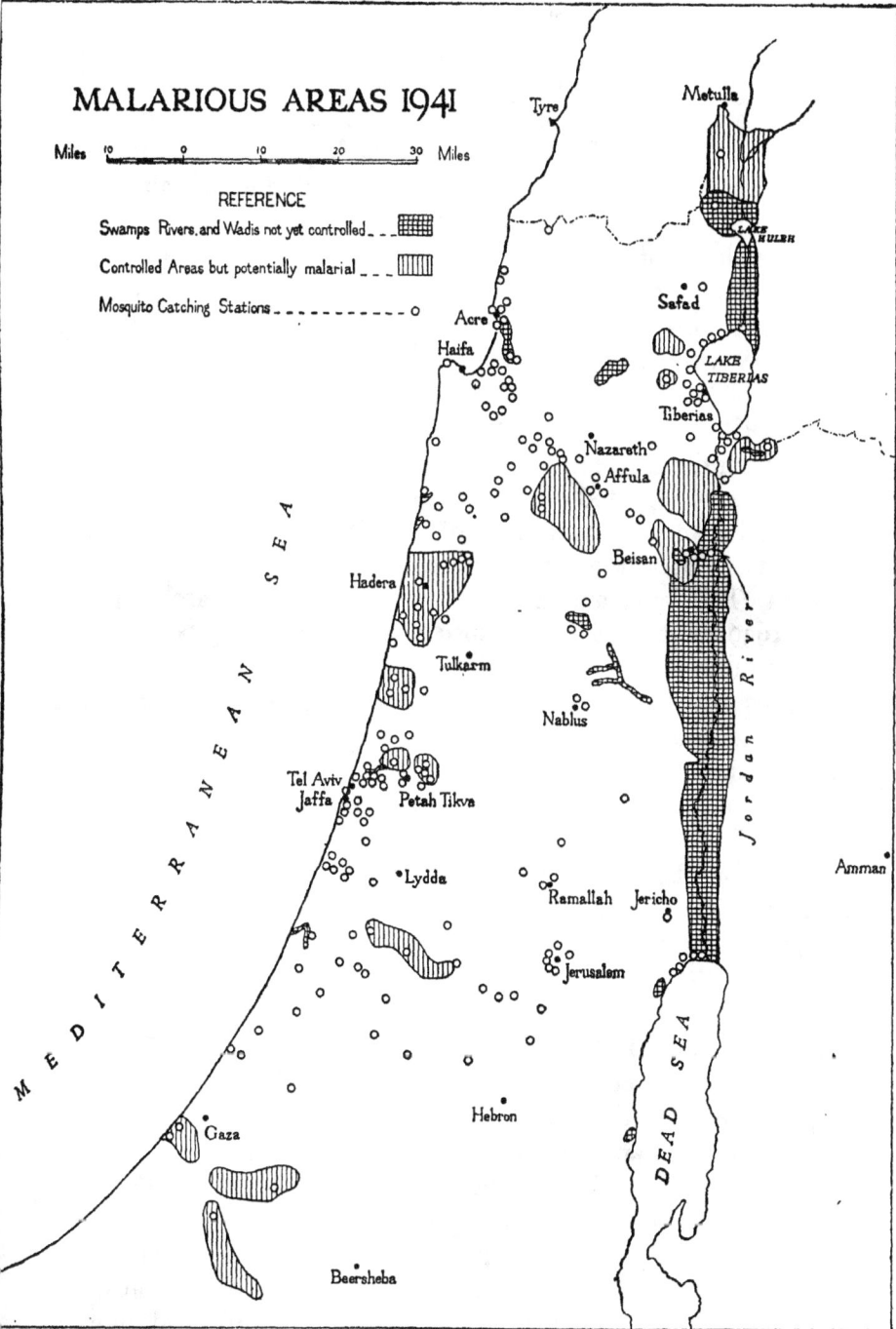

MALARIOUS AREAS 1941

Miles 10 0 10 20 30 Miles

REFERENCE

Swamps Rivers,and Wadis not yet controlled _ _ _

Controlled Areas but potentially malarial _ _ _

Mosquito Catching Stations _ _ _ _ _ _ _ _ _ o

FIG. 26. *Malarious Areas and Malarial Control*

(fig. 26). The most important of such areas are the Jordan valley, the Naamin swamps, and the Huleh marshes. These areas have a sparse population. Drainage and irrigation schemes for these areas have been prepared; their execution will make valuable additions to the agricultural wealth of the country. The experience of the Transjordan Frontier Force in 1939 demonstrated the unhealthiness of the Jordan valley. Patrol work there was responsible for a high rate of malaria infection. Of 496 admissions to hospital 41 per cent. were necessitated by malaria, and 84 primary and 117 relapsing cases of malaria were treated as out-patients. The strength of the force was 1,168 with 152 reserves.

### Kala-azar

The infantile or Mediterranean type of kala-azar occurs in Palestine: 25 cases were reported between 1920 and 1939. Six out of 11 cases reported between 1933 and 1937 died. Of the 25 cases only 2 occurred in adults. Cases have been reported from Jerusalem, Jenin, Haifa, Hadera, Tel Aviv, and Emek Jezreel. Between March 1938 and April 1939 eight cases were admitted to the Haifa hospital (7 children and 1 adult). All the children were Arab.

In this form of kala-azar dogs act as reservoirs of infection: canine visceral leishmaniasis is common in Palestine. Sandflies transmit the infection from dog to dog and from dog to man. The sandflies so far implicated in Palestine are *Phlebotomus perfilewi* (*macedonicus*) and *P. major*.

Cutaneous leishmaniasis, or 'oriental sore', is endemic in many parts of Palestine. Five British cases were treated in the Government Hospital, Jerusalem, in 1938.

### Tuberculosis

A large-scale tuberculosis survey was carried out in Palestine in 1935. This showed the disease to be very widespread, and to be responsible for a death-rate comparable to the tuberculosis death-rate of England and Wales. These facts were disquieting because the results of tuberculosis sensitivity tests indicate that the Palestinian population has not acquired a degree of immunity from, or resistance to, the disease that is generally found in countries that have been long exposed to tuberculosis infection. The health administration seem justified in anticipating increased morbidity and mortality unless adequate measures of control are instituted. Fortunately, however, death returns have not yet given any indication of such an increase. Deaths attributed to tuberculosis of the respiratory system and to other forms of tuberculosis during four recent years have been:

### Deaths from Tuberculosis

|  | Respiratory system | Other forms |
|---|---|---|
| 1936 | 153 | 32 |
| 1937 | 200 | 31 |
| 1938 | 176 | 45 |
| 1939 | 171 | 36 |

Of the 207 tuberculosis deaths recorded in 1939, 151 occurred in towns; the 56 recorded in villages are doubtless an understatement.

There are tuberculosis clinics in the larger centres. The total attendances at these government clinics in 1939 was 7,301: 292 new cases were seen. The great majority of people attending these clinics were Moslems. Most Jewish cases are cared for by the Jewish Anti-Tuberculosis League, which has a small sanatorium near Jerusalem; a few children are accommodated during the summer months at the Mount Carmel Sanatorium, Haifa. The Hadassah Tuberculosis Hospital, financially assisted by Government, has sixty beds for Jewish patients.

Bovine tuberculosis occurs very rarely in locally raised cattle. The bovine type of tubercle bacillus is thus of very little importance in the production of human tuberculosis.

### Venereal Diseases

There are main treatment centres for venereal diseases in Jerusalem, Jaffa, Haifa, and Nablus, but all medical officers treat as many cases as possible in clinics throughout the country. The progress made is reflected in the number of attendances: 9,729 (1936), 37,020 (1937), 42,730 (1938), 38,505 (1939). There is no indication that the prevalence of these diseases is increasing in Palestine, but there is more widespread recognition of the benefits conferred by modern treatment, which augurs well for the future.

*Endemic Syphilis.* A form of syphilis not contracted by sexual intercourse is endemic in villages in parts of Palestine, notably in the Hebron district: it is commonly called *firjal*. It is generally associated with communities living in very low hygienic conditions, and is very prevalent among the Euphrates Arabs. Among them the disease is known as *bejel* and is distinguished from syphilis of venereal origin which is known as *franghi*. It has not the shame and abhorrence attached to it by the afflicted population that has venereally contracted syphilis, and any suggestion that the two are connected would be resented. It is pre-eminently a disease of childhood: children may infect their parents if the latter have not previously been infected. Infection is passed by close contact in conditions of general uncleanliness. The use of a common drinking-bowl, kissing and fondling an infected child, and, possibly, flies, lice, and fleas are factors in the spread of the disease. The populations of whole villages may be affected.

This endemic syphilis has been engaging the attention of the health authorities for many years. Treatment centres have been installed in many villages, but the work was interrupted during the disturbances of 1936–1939.

### Ankylostomiasis

Ankylostomiasis, or 'hook-worm disease', is prevalent throughout the coastal plain of Palestine. Areas in the Jordan valley have also been noted as being heavily infested. It is probable that some degree of infestation with hook-worm occurs in the rural population throughout the country. The eggs of the hook-worm leave the body with human excrement. The resultant embryo gains entrance into the body through the skin, usually of the feet or ankles. Walking bare-foot on ground fouled by human excreta affords obvious facilities for contracting hook-worm disease. The degree of infestation is a measure of the lack of sanitation. As is to be expected, hook-worm disease is much more prevalent in rural than in urban communities in Palestine and the infestation rate is higher among Moslem than among the Jewish population. Jews do not commonly go unshod, and there are better methods of sanitation in most Jewish centres.

Recently nearly 4,000 persons were examined in areas on the coastal plain of the Jaffa district. Here citrus cultivation is an important industry. The percentage infestation rate varied from 2·6 to 8·0 in urban Arab districts, from 14·2 to 59·9 in the rural Arab areas, and from nil to 5·7 in the Jewish rural areas.

The measures of control that have been adopted consist of educational propaganda; the treatment and retreatment of the infested population following a preliminary survey; installation of village latrines; and a continual extension of investigation into new districts. The association of the disease with the citrus cultivation industry is noteworthy. The application of adequate sanitary control has been difficult owing to the recent depressed state of this industry.

## Schistosomiasis

Schistosomiasis, or bilharziosis, is the name given to the infection of human beings by a trematode worm, *Schistosoma*. Three definite endemic foci of the disease have been found in Palestine in the southern coastal region: the Auja basin, Wadi Rubin, and Wadi Sukreir. A small special unit of the Health Department has been engaged on a survey of this disease. From the results already reported it seems probable that a certain low degree of prevalence occurs over a wide area. The disease, however, does not constitute a serious public health problem in Palestine.

Two species of *Schistosoma* are found in Palestine, *S. haematobium* and *S. mansoni*; the latter is rare. In the endemic areas 11·4 per cent. of the population were infected with *S. haematobium* and only 0·26 per cent. with *S. mansoni*. In one area an infection rate of 31·6 per cent. has been noted.

One stage of the life-history of these parasites is passed in the body of certain species of fresh-water snails; developmental forms of the parasites called *cercariae* escape from the snail into the water. These *cercariae* are able to penetrate the skin of man: having done this they make their way to the wall of the bladder or of the lower intestinal tract, where they attain maturity. They then lay eggs which leave the body with urine or faeces. If the eggs are deposited in water containing a suitable species of snail the process may be repeated.

There is an annual Moslem festival held near the Wadi Rubin that is attended by some thousands of people for several weeks. For this reason this is the most important of the endemic centres.

Control measures include the treatment of infected individuals in hospitals; the treatment of infected waterways with copper sulphate; the collection of snails which may act as the intermediate hosts of the parasite; and propaganda regarding the dangers of bathing in endemic areas.

## Ophthalmic Diseases

The prevalence of eye diseases constitutes a serious public health problem in Palestine. The 1931 census revealed a high incidence of blindness in the southern district of Palestine. Among an estimated population of 304,532, there were 8,534 persons blind in one eye, 47 from birth, and 3,462 persons blind in both eyes, 78 from birth. Summer epidemics of acute conjunctivitis in villages, and trachoma, which is prevalent throughout Palestine, are responsible for most of this blindness.

The special government organization that has been set up to deal with this important problem includes 8 urban clinics, 3 urban special centres, and 20 first-aid units in villages. Medical Officers from central clinics supervise the work of village centres, which are in the charge of medical orderlies. These orderlies visit neighbouring villages to seek out cases for treatment. The work has expanded greatly in recent years. In 1939 the total attendances at these institutions numbered 1,048,831. The number of new cases was 72,366. Acute conjunctivitis cases numbered 35,709. A mobile ophthalmic unit operates in southern Palestine every hot-weather season: in 1939 it dealt with nine village areas outside the range of the permanent centres, and recorded 30,713 attendances.

Ophthalmic work is also done at eleven general out-patient dispensaries where 10,392 new cases were treated in 1939. The school medical service includes the treatment of eye diseases in its routine and reported attendances of 946,370 and 1,735,670 from town and village schools respectively. The British Ophthalmic Hospital of the Order of St. John of Jerusalem deserves special mention for its valuable services.

### Rabies

Rabies is widespread in Palestine. During 1939 there were 145 cases of rabies among animals, reported in 117 localities in 17 sub-districts. The sub-districts of Jaffa, Jenin, and Tulkarm reported most cases. Of 2,630 persons applying for advice about bites by rabid or suspected animals, 1,894 had been definitely exposed to risk of rabies infection and received a full course of treatment. Three-quarters of these had been bitten by dogs. Four died of hydrophobia in spite of treatment: they had all been bitten on the face, three by jackals and one by a wolf; three others died from the same cause, without presenting themselves for treatment.

A carbolized vaccine is used for anti-rabies treatment. This is prepared at the Central Laboratories in Jerusalem and issued for use in forty treatment centres. In this way the majority of persons bitten commence treatment within the four days following the infecting bite. The treatment centres are at Jerusalem, Bethlehem, Hebron, Ramallah, Beersheba, Tel Aviv, Ramleh, Mejdel, Gaza, Rehovot, Rishon le Zion, Petah Tikva, Haifa, Acre, Hadera, Nazareth, Nablus, Tulkarm, Jenin, Tiberias, Safad, and nineteen villages.

## Medical Services

*School Medical Service*

In 1939 the Department of Health looked after 482 schools with 60,882 schoolchildren. Physical examination of 37,694 pupils was made: 37 per cent. of town children and 58 per cent. of village children were suffering from trachoma. The school medical staff treat infectious conditions, ophthalmic disease, and malaria: in villages the teachers assist by carrying out routine treatment prescribed by the doctor. The Jewish school medical service, subventioned by Government, looked after 392 schools with 53,000 scholars.

*Medical and Ancillary Professions*

Palestine is well provided with doctors. At the end of 1939 there was one doctor for 625 of population, one dentist for 2,000, one pharmacist for 3,000, and one midwife for 2,500. For the Jewish community alone the provision is very much greater.

*Hospitals and Dispensaries*

Palestine is also well supplied with hospitals and dispensaries. There are government hospitals at Jerusalem, Haifa, Jaffa, Nablus, Safad, Beersheba, and Gaza, government isolation hospitals at Beit Safafa and Bnei Brak, and a municipal hospital at Tel Aviv partly supported by Government. These institutions have 574 general beds, 305 isolation beds, 109 beds for British subjects, and 89 maternity beds. During 1940 admissions totalled 24,863, of which 10,886 were Moslems and 9,525 Jews. The daily average number of patients in these hospitals was 847.

For out-patients there are 19 government general clinics and 84 special clinics (ophthalmic, tuberculosis, and venereal diseases). In twelve villages government medical officers hold weekly clinics. Attendances at the general clinics in 1940 numbered 443,105, of which 191,973 were new cases.

Voluntary hospitals and convalescent homes, of which there are a number, provided accommodation of about 2,000 beds in 1940. Prominent among these institutions is the new Rothschild Hadassah Hospital outside Jerusalem: it is extremely well equipped, has accommodation for 300 patients, and is capable of extension. Special institutions are the Ophthalmic Hospital maintained by the English Order of St. John of Jerusalem, the International Moravian Leper Hospital, the Ezrat Nashim Society's Home for the Insane and Incurable, and a government special mental hospital at Bethlehem. The voluntary hospitals include four French, two Italian, and a German (formerly two), all to some extent supported by their respective governments. In 1940 the total number of admissions to all these voluntary hospitals was 39,555, the average daily number of patients being 1,402.

The activity of voluntary dispensaries and clinics is likewise remarkable. During 1940, total attendances numbered 2,627,101, of which 785,773 were new cases. (The estimated total settled population of the country in 1940 (mean) was 1,460,923.) The out-patient clinics of the *Kupat Holim* Sick Fund of the Jewish Federation of Labour serve the needs of about 112,000 subscribers and their families, over 200,000 in all. The fund has clinics in the chief centres and employs 327 doctors and 199 nurses in towns and Jewish settlements. It has in addition 12 dental clinics and 4 X-ray laboratories. The Hadassah Medical Organization has a large polyclinic in connexion with its hospital near Jerusalem, and school ophthalmic and infant welfare services for Jews throughout the country. It also administers the Straus Health Centres in Jerusalem and Tel Aviv. The Moslem Supreme Council finances clinics in Jerusalem and in Hebron.

## Laboratory Services

The Central Laboratories of the Government in Jerusalem comprise bacteriological, chemical, entomological, agricultural, forensic, and physical laboratories, a central anti-rabies vaccine manufacturing institute, and the calf-lymph establishment. The port and quarantine laboratories at Haifa, Jaffa, and Bnei Brak undertake diagnostic work for adjacent towns and districts. The Health Department has supervisory control over laboratories and scientific institutes maintained by private funds. Standards for therapeutic substances are rigidly enforced. Palestine is thus provided with laboratory services to meet all public health needs, and much valuable research work has been done during the last twenty years. The amount of routine laboratory work carried out each year is very large.

## Infant Welfare

The remarkable improvement in infant mortality rates during the past decade has already been noted. To this infant welfare services have contributed much. During 1939 the Health Department maintained 34 infant welfare centres in towns and villages and assisted in the maintenance of 2 others. For Jewish children the Tel Aviv Municipal Council maintained 6 centres, the Hadassah Medical Organization 16, the Sick Fund of the Jewish Federation of Labour 14, and the Women's International Zionist Organization 9. Local voluntary committees maintain 3 centres for Arabs and 1 for Jews. Altogether in 1939 there were in Palestine 83 infant welfare centres, taking care of 18,444 infants, of whom 10,321 were Jewish. There is a mother-craft centre in Tel Aviv, and there are numerous day nurseries. Few countries, if any, have a more complete infant welfare service than has the Jewish community of Palestine: the total number of Jewish children born in Palestine in 1939 was 9,888.

## Quarantine Services

Four medical officers are employed in the quarantine section of the Health Department, two being stationed in Haifa and two in Tel Aviv. Haifa has complete arrangements for immigration and passenger traffic. In 1938 the Tel Aviv Jetty and Lighter Harbour section of Jaffa port was opened for passenger and immigrant traffic. In that year 28 per cent. of arrivals in Palestine by sea disembarked at Tel Aviv, 65 per cent. at Haifa. In 1939 2,050 travellers disembarked at Jaffa, of whom 12 were immigrants, 13,792 at Tel Aviv (4,954 immigrants), and 19,939 at Haifa (8,113 immigrants). In 1941, when the effects of the war had fully disclosed themselves, Jaffa and Tel Aviv were closed to passenger traffic (only ten passengers landed at Jaffa and none at Tel Aviv), and 5,869, of whom 1,916 were immigrants, landed at Haifa.

Coasting sailing-vessels are examined in the Acre and Gaza roadsteads. All immigrants are vaccinated by the Health Department against small-pox and inoculated against enteric fever. Fumigation of ships with a Clayton gas apparatus is carried out when necessary at Haifa. There are port and quarantine laboratories at Haifa, Jaffa, and Bnei Brak.

Quarantine supervision is carried out at the airports of Lydda and Haifa and the seaplane base at Lake Tiberias; 3,293 aircraft landed during 1939.

In 1939 only 64 Palestinians made the pilgrimage to Mecca, as compared with 699 Palestinians and 28 Transjordan residents in 1938. Other foreigners, however, also pass through Palestine on their way to the Hejaz, 77 in 1938, 9 in 1939. All pilgrims are vaccinated against small-pox and cholera before departure. Returning pilgrims are kept under observation at their destinations for five days.

*Lunacy*

The Government mental hospital at Bethlehem has accommodation for 157 patients, the Jewish *Ezrat Nashim* Home for 60. At the end of 1940 there were 226 patients in these institutions, and more than 300 dangerous lunatics were awaiting admission. There is also a criminal lunatic section in the Acre central prison. The provision of increased mental hospital accommodation is an urgent necessity.

## CHAPTER X

# AGRICULTURE AND INDUSTRIES

## AGRICULTURE AND FORESTRY

THE total area of Palestine is rather more than 10,000 square miles, of which 261 are water, 51 square miles are built-on areas, and 27 are forests. Of the remaining 9,740 square miles, about one-third (one-sixth in the Beersheba sub-district) are cultivable according to government estimates. The Beersheba sub-district has not been surveyed, and figures for it are estimates, but it is roughly known what water is available. Of the total cultivable area of about 2,140,000 acres 460,000 (about one-fifth) are said to be irrigable, but only about 74,000 acres are at present irrigated, though the rest is under cultivation in some form or other.

Of the cultivated area, 81 per cent. is arable land, 14·6 orchards, 2·1 forest, 1·2 meadow and pasture, and 1·1 per cent. productive waste land (moorland, heath, &c.). The proportion of arable land is very high for a Mediterranean country and is caused by the lack of grassland, for the vegetation and parched stubble of spring can hardly be reckoned as such.

Considering the low yields of cereal crops in relation to this disproportion, it would seem advisable, from the economic standpoint, to replace extensive grain-farming by intensive irrigated cropping, in which fodder crops should receive special attention. A commencement along these lines has already been made in a few of the Jewish settlements.

Of the primary factors of agricultural productivity, the climate has already been described in Chapter IV, and the geological formations, of which the soils are the debris, and on the surface of which these are spread, are broadly outlined in Chapter II. The soils themselves are next to be described; then the various crops, immemorial or recently introduced; then the redistribution of the natural water-supply by irrigation, the restoration of forests, and the control of pests. The mineral resources and industries of Palestine are then described, and the transport and commercial agencies by which agricultural and other commodities are transferred from producer to consumer, in Chapter XIII.

## Soils

For centuries the soils of Palestine have undergone progressive

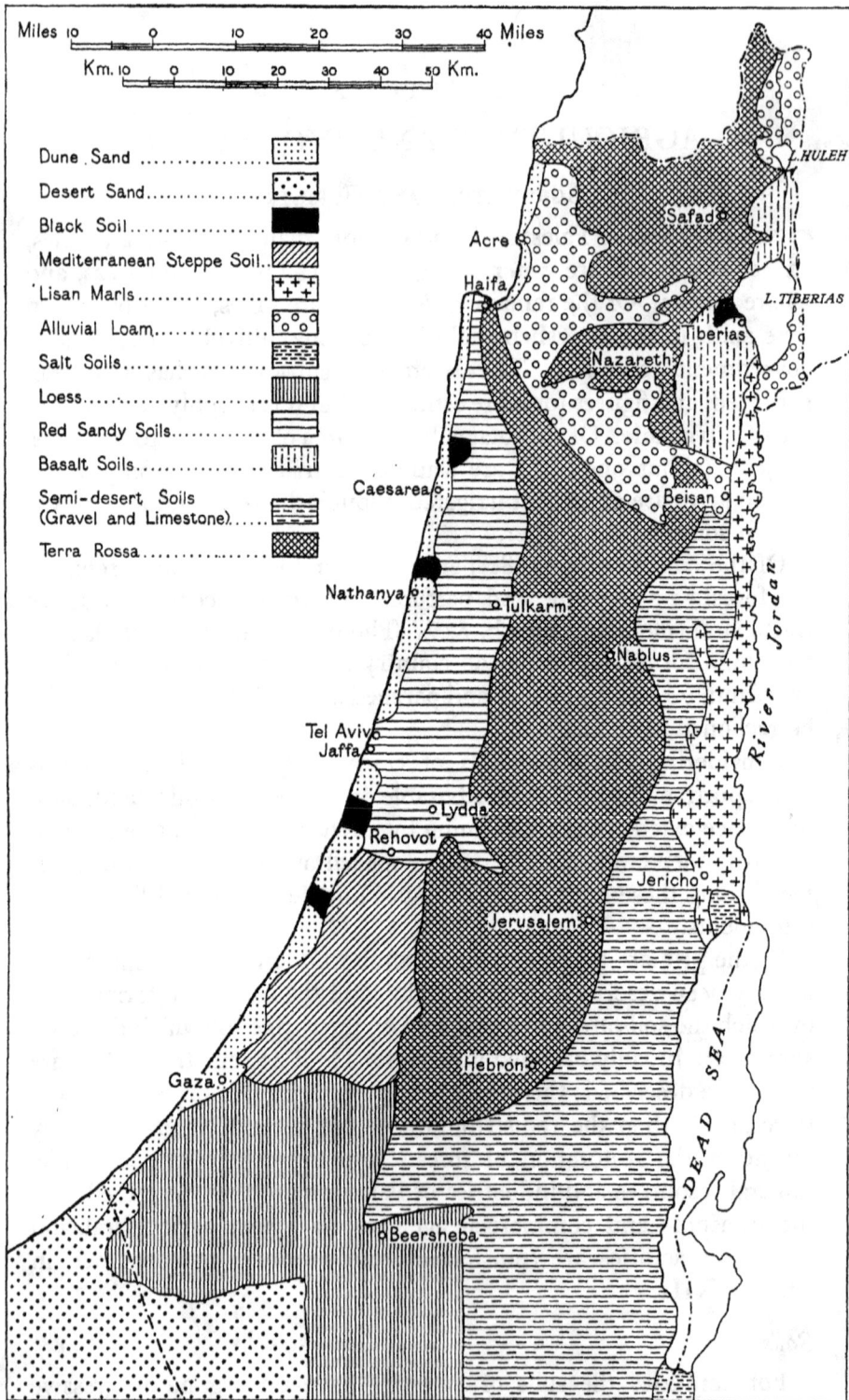

FIG. 27. *The Soils of Palestine*

impoverishment. The wholesale destruction of trees, and the abandonment of terrace cultivation, have left the soil unprotected against erosion. During the rainy season the thin layer of soil on the mountain slopes becomes loosened and is swept by violent rainstorms into the wadis. Much of this soil is spread over the plains below, but some is lost altogether, being carried out to sea, where it can be traced by discoloration for some distance from the shore. Animal dung has long been used by the villagers as fuel, not as manure, and thus soil impoverishment has been increased. This progressive exhaustion shows itself in the low yields from the non-irrigated farming areas. As in most Mediterranean countries, the soils have a low humus-content, because of the widespread calcareous substratum and intense summer insolation.

The main types of soils (fig. 27) in Palestine are as follows:

*The Coastal Plain.* Something has already been said on the soils of this region in the section on 'Vegetation' in Chapter IV. Along the coast, mobile sand-dunes, almost continuous, are a constant menace to citrus groves, vineyards, and land suitable for dry-farming. Such areas run the risk of being slowly buried. Some protection has already been given by planting suitable grasses and trees along the lee side of the dunes. The region of *kurkar* hills, with partially fossilized sand-dune deposits encrusted to a varying extent with lime, is quite unsuitable for citrus culture.

The red 'sand-clay soils', which occupy a large proportion of the light soil coastal plain, are in complete contrast to the *kurkar* soils. These deep red soils, consisting mainly of sand with a clay-content sufficient to hold the necessary moisture, are almost ideal for citrus culture, the success of which is due also to a grey impermeable sandy-clay substratum, at no great depth, known as the *sakye* layer, over which the subsoil water flows towards the sea. These soils, however, are almost entirely deficient in lime, and heavy dressings are necessary. It has been estimated, indeed, that each crop removes three-quarters of a hundredweight of calcium carbonate per acre. A local condition which may make citrus culture abortive even on these soils is the presence in many parts, especially in the plain of Sharon, of the *nazzaz* layer, a compact impermeable concretionary 'pan', slightly below the surface. Its dull grey-brown or light reddish-brown colour is brilliantly mottled with red, yellow, and black concretions of silica and oxides of iron and aluminium. Its compactness and impermeability restrict the percolation of moisture, so that the overlying soil remains wet for long periods after rain or irrigation.

*Nazzaz* occurs at an average depth of 30 inches below the surface and varies much in thickness. The roots of plants penetrate it only with difficulty, and rest in the puddled area above it, where, for lack of oxygen, they quickly decay. In districts where *nazzaz* is neither too deep nor too thick, some improvement may be brought about by deep ploughing and generous application of lime. This breaks up the layer mechanically and produces a crumb-like soil-structure.

The sandy-clay soils change somewhat in appearance southwards towards the drier *loess* soils of the Negeb (p. 23). South of Rehovot and as far as the Gaza district is a strip of Mediterranean steppe soil, consisting of brownish, greyish-brown, or bright brown loams. These soils are rich in calcareous concretions and have a satisfactory content of potash and phosphate. Irrigated crops flourish on these soils exceptionally well, provided the soil is well chosen and the irrigation water is not too saline.

Alluvial deposits brought down from the hills form the remainder of the soils of the coastal plain. These are often heavy clays, of little use for agriculture. Grape-fruit, however, less sensitive to heavy soils than oranges, may be grown on them where the alluvium is not too deep, and where irrigation is carefully controlled.

*The Mountains of Judaea and Samaria.* This hill country consists mainly of various limestones. Some are hard like marble, others are soft and chalky. The most typical soil here is *terra rossa* ('red earth'), which generally has a high content of soluble salts and a deficiency of humus. It is usually loamy in structure and reddish through abundance of iron. In the mountains *terra rossa* is very liable to erosion, which is combated by terracing. As water is scarce, only limited areas can carry crops requiring irrigation. Though it is primarily grain-country, vines and other fruits grow well. In favourable localities this soil is well suited to apples, pears, and plums, which in recent years have been grown with success by Jewish settlers.

*Esdraelon, Jezreel, and Beisan.* This plain is covered in the main with deep alluvial soils derived from the denudation of the limestone hills of Samaria and the basalt heights of Galilee. They comprise a series of calcareous clays or loams, brown or black, which are of heavier texture, and more sticky when wet, than most of the Palestine alluviums. In the absence of deep and thorough tilling these soils shrink and crack badly when dry. The colour of the surface soil varies with the rainfall, becoming progressively darker with increase in precipitation. Local drainage seems also to be correlated with colour, the better-drained soils being brown to reddish-brown, those which are excessively wet for long periods being black. Part of the plain has served as one of the granaries of Palestine for centuries; other parts as grazing ground for nomadic beduin.

*Highlands of Galilee and Carmel.* The mountains in this region are composed of various limestones, with some volcanic basalt. The landscape is very much as in the Judaean highlands. The weathered limestones produce a typical *terra rossa*, while the basalts decompose to form chocolate-brown soils. These two soils, however, in spite of their diverse origin, are chemically almost identical. This is to be ascribed to climate.

*The Jordan Depression.* The prevailing soils here consist of deposits of loose diluvial marls known as 'Lisan marl soils'. Usually pale grey, they contain an extraordinary large proportion of salts, especially chlorides, and in some places are almost completely sterile. Elsewhere, without irrigation, they support only a sparse growth of halophytes. Where water is available, however, and especially where covered by alluvium washed down from the hills, agriculture becomes possible. Jericho is so placed and is a particularly fertile oasis. But the accumulation of salt in the soil is a constant danger, and many orange plantations have been ruined by faulty irrigation.

*The Negeb.* South of the Gaza–Beersheba line large areas of southern Palestine are covered with a fine yellowish *loess* soil transported by wind from the Sinai desert. Mainly consisting of fine particles of sand (60%), it contains also silt (25%) and clay (15%); but being also calcareous, it is generally recognized as particularly good for malting-barley. Rainfall, however, is very low and variable, and one can seldom rely on a good harvest. The possibilities of irrigation, though not hitherto promising, are still being investigated. These *loess* soils pass gradually southwards into the desert sands of the southern Negeb.

## Crops

Agriculture in all Mediterranean lands is a characteristic combination of (1) annual crops, for the most part cereals, which are harvested from June to early August according to altitude and aspect, supplemented by (2) leguminous plants and marsh-side marrows and cucumbers maturing throughout the summer, with (3) deep-rooted trees, such as vine, olive, and fig, which ripen in succession through the autumn, to which have been added in modern times the orange and other citrus fruits from south-eastern Asia: to this class belong also soft fruits such as apricot and plum, indigenous in the mountain zone, or apple and pear from more northerly regions. To these food crops must be added (4) the white mulberry, for silk-growing, introduced in medieval times from China; the black mulberry indigenous in western Asia; cotton, also from farther Asia; tobacco from America, and other American food-plants—potato, tomato, egg-plant, and kindred species—and more recently and experimentally the indigenous ground-nut (*Pistacia vera*).

The relative backwardness of Palestinian agriculture is illustrated by the predominance of cereal crops; for in this regime the effect of improved methods is to increase the yield of the specialized trees, and to obtain the 'staff of life' from elsewhere in exchange for tree-fruits and their products, oil, and wine.

To the great majority of Arab cultivators cereal crops are the most important agricultural activity. The systems vary from a two-year rotation of wheat or barley with winter leguminous crops or with summer crops of durra and sesame, to a three-year rotation in which leguminous crops are normally introduced between these summer crops and the winter crops of cereals. Bare fallow is sometimes introduced between crops, to clear the land of weeds. In certain Jewish settlements where cereal-growing is important, a four-course rotation has been adopted, introducing crops of green manures or maize for the production of silage.

*Wheat and barley* are the chief cereals in Palestine, the relative proportions in a normal year being about two to one. In general, the heavier soils are devoted to wheat, the lighter to barley. In the south, where the rainfall is less, barley is more usual. Winter leguminous crops are lentils, *kersenneh (Vicia ervilia)*, beans, and peas. Vetches are occasionally sown, but it is more common to sow vetch with oats or barley, as a fodder crop, to be grazed green, or cut green for hay. Chick-peas are grown in some areas as a spring or early summer crop, but the main summer crops consist of durra (*sorghum*), sesame, melons, or in some districts tobacco. Maize is grown in Jewish settlements for silage and green fodder, but among Arab growers only in the Huleh area.

*Olives and grapes* are summer crops. These permanent plantations are found in most districts, but chiefly in the western foothills and hill-slopes of the central range. Olives normally receive some cultivation, but sufficient steps are not always taken to prevent erosion by surface water. In grape cultivation there is some terracing, but here also more could be done to prevent soil erosion.

*Vegetable-growing* increases. During the early spring good supplies

63. *Ploughing in Palestine*

64. *An Orange-grove in the Coastal Plain*

65. *Irrigation pumps on the Auja (Yarkon)*

66. *Ben Shemen, a Jewish agricultural school*

of all kinds of European vegetables are available; and as the weather becomes warmer, beans, cucumbers, vegetable marrows, pumpkins, tomatoes, egg-plants, 'ladies' fingers', &c., are produced. Late in 1941 scarcity of vegetable fats led the Government to purchase practically all the ground-nut seed in the country, sufficient to plant 15,000 dunams (3,450 acres), in the hope that by 1943 Palestine would be self-sufficient.

*Deciduous fruits* have received considerable stimulus during recent years, as the local demand for fruit, other than citrus, exceeds the supply. The limiting factor may, however, be the root-boring beetle (*Capnodis* spp.), and immune or resistant root-stocks are desirable.

*Citrus* agriculture has shown the most remarkable development in recent years. Commercial orange-groves are said to have been planted in the Acre district 170 years ago, and many of those of to-day are said to be 70 years old. The area under citrus cultivation at the end of 1939 was estimated at 75,000 acres, of which 65,070 acres were surveyed as follows:

| | | |
|---|---|---|
| Oranges | . . | 52,750 acres |
| Grape-fruit | . . | 7,430 ,, |
| Lemons | . . | 1,260 ,, |
| Other citrus fruits | . | 3,630 ,, |
| Total | . . | 65,070 ,, |

Citrus fruits form the bulk of the agricultural exports. Unfortunately, economic conditions in the industry had become so depressed by 1939, in consequence of over-production, restricted markets, and falling prices, that no further planting of citrus has been undertaken since 1938, and now it is subject to restriction under the Citrus Control Ordinance of 1940. By the end of 1941 the total area had been reduced to 68,885 acres.

In recent years, also, cultivation of a fairly large area already planted has been partially or wholly neglected. With the outbreak of war in September 1939 more foreign markets were closed or restricted, and shipping facilities were limited. Instead of the estimated 12,000,000 cases for export in 1939–40, only 7,595,646 were shipped. The following table indicates the various citrus exports for the seasons from 1937–8 to 1940–1.

| Season | 1937–8 | 1938–9 | 1939–40 | 1940–1 |
|---|---|---|---|---|
| Oranges . . | 9,573,271 | 13,055,700 | 6,448,608 | 95,099 cases |
| Grape-fruit . . | 1,794,118 | 2,066,833 | 987,528 | 14,243 ,, |
| Lemons . : | 77,019 | 142,243 | 154,329 | 461 ,, |
| Other citrus fruits . | 28,918 | 45,960 | 5,181 | . . ,, |
| Total . . | 11,473,326 | 15,310,736 | 7,595,646 | 109,803 ,, |

As a consequence of the abandonment of groves, the anticipated total crop for 1941–2 was not expected to exceed the exports of the year before, and the amount of the exports was negligible.

Since the outbreak of war the Government has come to the assistance of the citrus industry by means of loans which, as most of the borrowers have been incapable of repaying them, have become in effect grants. These subsidies were, however, limited to groves already bearing fruit and kept in good condition; the financial position of a few owners did not justify assistance. Nevertheless, in the year 1940–1 assistance was rendered to only a little more than half the area that had been in cultivation two years earlier—167,000 dunams (38,500 acres) compared with 300,000. Even the groves that received assistance showed obvious deterioration. A further measure of public assistance was the suspension of the Rural Property tax on all citrus land.

*Tobacco* is grown principally in the neighbourhood of Rosh Pinna in upper Galilee. Attempts to cultivate it elsewhere have for the most part proved failures. The area under cultivation varies from year to year, but is as a rule about 2,000 acres. The tobacco crop for the seven years 1935 to 1941 was as follows:

### Tobacco

| Crop | Tons | Crop | Tons |
|------|------|------|------|
| 1935 . . | 815 | 1939 . . | 523 |
| 1936 . . | 1,237 | 1940 . . | 985 |
| 1937 . . | 2,504 | 1941 . . | 582 |
| 1938 . . | 1,180 | | |

### Yields of the Major Crops for the years 1935 to 1941, in metric tons

| Year | Wheat | Barley | Durra | Maize (for seed) | Sesame | Kersenneh | Fodder for dairy industry |
|------|-------|--------|-------|------------------|--------|-----------|---------------------------|
| 1935 | 104,353 | 68,905 | 46,135 | 8,840 | 6,914 | 8,849 | .. |
| 1936 | 76,059 | 55,169 | 22,122 | 4,336 | 1,847 | 7,378 | .. |
| 1937 | 127,420 | 75,417 | 61,023 | 8,673 | 9,317 | 6,004 | 93,046 |
| 1938 | 44,435 | 66,736 | 63,253 | 8,010 | 6,441 | 5,374 | 102,497 |
| 1939 | 89,190 | 86,230 | 42,896 | 6,197 | 3,754 | 5,500 | 115,039 |
| 1940 | 136,082 | 102,541 | 58,301 | 9,388 | 6,624 | 11,011 | 157,035 |
| 1941 | 90,366 | 68,845 | 65,494 | 8,841* | 7,467 | 5,726* | 145,562* |

| Year | Potatoes | Tomatoes | Total vegetables | Melons and water melons | Olives | Grapes | Bananas | Other non-citrus fruits |
|------|----------|----------|------------------|-------------------------|--------|--------|---------|-------------------------|
| 1935 | 2,850 | 17,286 | 67,847 | 68,799 | 45,092 | 28,818 | .. | 20,279 |
| 1936 | 5,000 | 19,027 | 70,321 | 81,335 | 15,755 | 49,359 | 7,609 | 32,431 |
| 1937 | 9,536 | 34,907 | 120,395 | 102,859 | 47,247 | 45,673 | 2,394 | 31,861 |
| 1938 | 8,760 | 29,016 | 109,088 | 114,005 | 38,572 | 46,784 | 8,461 | 39,951 |
| 1939 | 10,480 | 36,851 | 129,373 | 86,892 | 35,232 | 45,433 | 5,615 | 44,976 |
| 1940 | 20,891 | 58,608 | 198,273 | 107,829 | 45,767 | 47,988 | 6,335 | 42,031 |
| 1941 | 20,736 | 51,500* | 189,794 | 77,906 | 13,472 | 47,417 | 7,310 | 68,199 |

* Subject to revision.

Since 1938 the cultivation of cereals, &c., by Jewish agriculturists increased. In these years Australian and Moroccan varieties of
wheat were introduced by Jewish settlers.

### Cultivation of Cereals, &c., by Jewish Agriculturists

| In dunams | 1938–9 | 1939–40 | 1940–1 |
|---|---|---|---|
| Wheat . . . | 48,400 | 66,000 | 71,600 |
| Barley . . . | 23,800 | 36,900 | 54,600 |
| Maize . . . . | 39,200 | 48,200 | 47,800 |
| Forage . . . | 2,500 | 33,200 | 35,200 |
| Legumes . . . | 1,300 | 8,500 | 9,900 |
| Other grains . . | 5,500 | 7,800 | 13,900 |
| Pasture, &c. . . | 9,300 | 15,400 | 18,900 |

Similar figures for Arab and other cultivators are not available,
but it is known that they could not show such striking increases.

### Irrigation (fig. 28)

Water-supply is one of the principal problems of agriculture in
Palestine. The amount and seasonal distribution of the rainfall have
been described in Chapter IV. Hitherto there has been a complete
lack of system in the use of the natural sources, for under the old
Ottoman law spring-water was the property of individuals, who
could sell it as they pleased. Legislation is now in draft whereby
all water-supplies, surface and underground, will be under government control for the general welfare.

There are four possible sources of irrigation: rivers, springs, wells,
and reservoirs.

*Rivers.* Palestine possesses no great watercourse that can be used
for irrigation, like the Nile or Euphrates. Of the perennial rivers,
the Jordan, with a flow of between 1,800 and 3,600 cubic feet per
second, lies so deep in its gorge and so remote from the fertile seaward slopes, that it is almost untouched for irrigation. In the north,
in the neighbourhood of Lake Huleh, Jordan water will probably be
used when the scheme for reclamation and drainage of the lake is
carried out; but south of this to Lake Tiberias the Palestine Electric
Corporation has concessionary rights.

The Yarmuk serves a very limited area in Palestine, and most of
its tributaries are in Syria. In the coastal plain the Auja (300 cub. ft.
per sec.) irrigates about 1,250 acres and might be used for another
200; but it is more likely to be required for the city of Tel Aviv.

The Crocodile river (*Nahr ez Zerka*) is expected to be used to a
greater extent than the Auja.

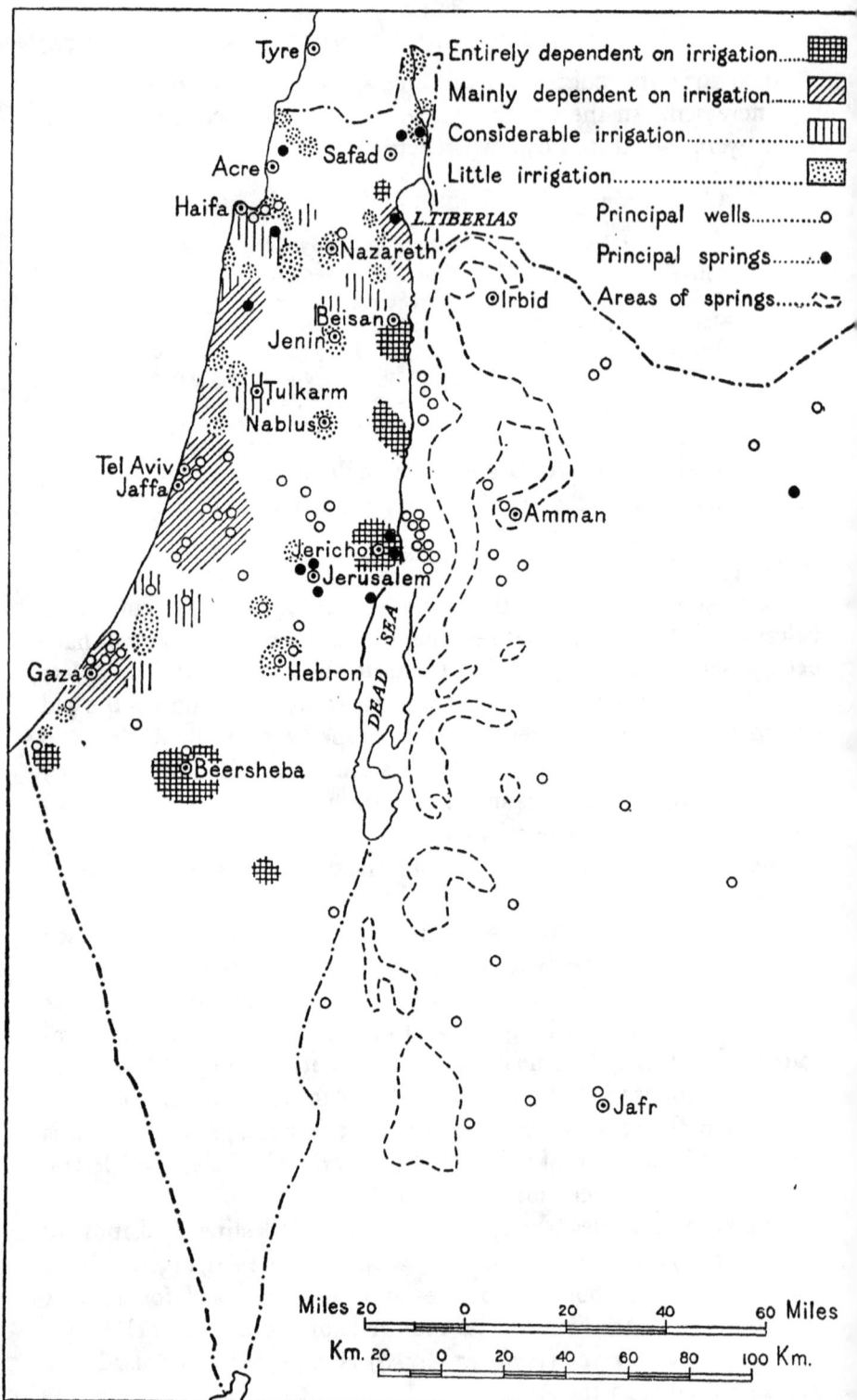

FIG. 28. *Springs, Wells, and Irrigation*

*Springs.* Irrigation from springs offers better prospects in the future than that from rivers. Owing to the amount of water sinking through the limestones, there are many springs, especially in the Beisan plain and Jordan valley, and on the lower slopes of the western Samarian and Judaean hills. Mainly through the existing property-rights in such springs, they have not yet been used extensively, and there are only two small schemes, in Beisan and in Jericho, which deserve notice.

*Wells.* Irrigation from wells is the chief method in the country, and wells are almost the only available source of irrigation water throughout the great region of citrus cultivation from Haifa to Jaffa. During the prosperous years of citrus production wells were constantly deepened and new ones were dug, because of the increasing demand made on the subsoil water by mechanical pumps. The danger of lowering the water-table has been fully recognized, and steps are to be taken to watch the water-level and to control the sinking of new wells.

The number of wells in Palestine, used for irrigation, is between 2,500 and 3,000. Much water is wasted by inadequate control over its distribution and by insufficient attention to the upkeep of channels.

*Reservoirs.* Recent investigations into the value of irrigation by reservoirs in Palestine have been disappointing. The principle is to hold up water in the valleys by dams. Two projects may be mentioned.

A gauging section constructed across the Wadi Sarar near Jerusalem showed that only 0.5 per cent. of the rainfall in the catchment ran into the wadi, while 99.5 per cent. was absorbed by the limestone rocks. Much the same happened at Beersheba, where a dam was built. Here 7 per cent. of the rain falling in the catchment passed into the reservoir, and at the end of the rainy season only one-fourteenth of this 7 per cent. remained. The rest had been absorbed by the bed, which was too large for water-proofing to be economic.

It may be concluded that irrigation must rely in the future, as in the past, almost entirely on well-water, sometimes pumped from a great depth, and in spite of the fact that both well- and spring-water alike contain large quantities of soluble salts. These waters are not merely hard waters, rich in carbonates, but they also contain chlorides. In many places waters with high and low salt-content are found close together.

The amount of chloride that may be tolerated in irrigation varies according to the presence or absence of other salts, to the nature of the soil and its natural drainage, and to the species and strength of the crop. Citrus fruits, for instance, will not tolerate a high salinity, and certain soils must be avoided. Most of the well-water in the citrus area is not too saline, though the chloride content is often considerably higher in the south than in the north. In the Gaza district a number of citrus plantations have suffered from excessive salts. The injurious action of sodium chloride is shown by a poor crop, by stunted tree-growth, and especially by the withering of the leaves, which become entirely yellow or mottled with yellow spots.

The constant use of saline irrigation water leads to progressive salting, at least on heavy soils, and there are soils at Beisan and Kinneret where the chloride-content has attained disastrous proportions.

The plain of Esdraelon has in the past suffered severely from lack of adequate water. The subsoil water is deep, and unless the market value of the crop is high, the raising of such water for irrigation must prove uneconomic.

## Research Stations

Agricultural and horticultural stations are maintained throughout Palestine by the Department of Agriculture and Fisheries. There are agricultural stations at Acre, Beisan, Jericho, Mejdel, Sarafand, Ain Arroub, and Farradiya. Their activities include the growing of selected cereals and other plants for seed distribution, the testing of indigenous and imported varieties of cereals, rotation experiments, tests of manures and fertilizers, and the growing and distribution of seedling vegetables. Each station suits its activities to the area it is designed to serve.

Horticultural stations are at Acre, Beisan, Jericho, Mejdel, Sarafand, Ain Arroub, Farradiya, Farivaneh, and Nablus. They are mainly concerned with fruit, and large numbers of fruit-trees, vines, and citrus buds are raised and distributed annually. Experimental work is also conducted on various aspects of the culture of olive, vine, citrus, banana, and other fruits.

Demonstration plots are scattered in hundreds over the country, designed to show to cultivators the value of crop rotations, cereal varieties, use of manures, the production of forage crops, potato-growing, and fruit culture.

Agricultural and horticultural research is carried on mainly by the Rehovot Agricultural Research Station of the Jewish Agency, the Hebrew University, and the Mikveh Israel Agricultural School: the Rehovot station is by far the most important. Besides the main station at Rehovot there are three sub-stations, at Kiryat Anavim (Dilb) for the hill country, at Gevat for the valley of Jezreel for non-irrigated crops, and at Geva for citrus investigations in the valley of Jezreel. Maintained mainly by the Jewish Agency, Rehovot receives also government grants for special pieces of research.

## Pests

The pests, both fungi and insects, confronting the Palestine farmer are many. The insect pests are probably the more dangerous, and much experimental work is being conducted upon them by the officers of the Plant Protection Service of the Department of Agriculture and Fisheries. This department, with its headquarters at Jerusalem, and laboratories at Acre and Tel Aviv, has done much in recent years to supply information regarding the life-histories of the insects, and has worked out many methods of control and eradication. By written word and radio-broadcasts, this service has tried to arouse a largely illiterate population to the seriousness of pests, and has endeavoured to counteract the *laissez-faire* attitude of the older generation of Arab cultivators. The number of insecticides has been reduced, by numerous trials, to three or four essential products, and arrangements have been made to bring these within the reach of all.

Many of the pests are easily controlled and are therefore of little consequence. Some, however, are more devastating in their results, and have often a complex life-history, which makes control difficult. The following are the more serious pests.

*Desert Locust* (Schistocerca gregaria). During severe visitations in 1928–1930, vigorous action was taken by the Palestine Locust Service, and some degree of success was obtained with a new flame-thrower. In 1930 a serious invasion in southern Palestine was successfully met by the zinc-sheet barrier method at a cost of £27,000. Adequate stores and personnel are always to hand to meet fresh attacks.

*Root-boring Beetle* (Capnodis sp.) causes great havoc in peaches, plums, cherries, and allied fruit. In a new method of control a layer of dried sand is applied around the tree base as a barrier to the young larvae.

*Mediterranean Fruit Fly* (Ceratitis capitata), one of the major insect pests, attacks citrus fruits in its spring generation, and in its summer phase affects all kinds of deciduous fruits. It is controlled by spraying with mixtures of copper carbonate and sugar.

*Codling Moth* (Carpocapsa Pomonella), one of the primary pests in apples, pears, quinces, and walnuts, has been recorded also in other stone fruits, and does much damage. A combination of control methods is used.

*Woolly Aphis* (Eriosoma lanigera) is an important pest of apple-trees. The service advises biological control; a small parasitic wasp (*Aphelinus mali*), which lays its eggs in the aphid's body, has been introduced from Egypt. The aphid dies as the wasp-larvae develop. Colonies of wasps are supplied to farmers by the Department. To combat the pest effectively it has been found necessary also to use chemical means.

*Grape-berry Moth* (Polychrosis botrana). The larvae take a heavy toll of an unprotected grape crop. Dusting with a mixture of equal parts of barium (or sodium) fluosilicate and sulphur (or fuller's earth) gives good protection.

*Prodenia litura.* The larvae of this moth are extremely dangerous to many crops, especially to Egyptian clover (*berseem*) and lucerne. They often cause total destruction. Barium (or sodium) fluosilicate has been used with some success.

*Plum-fruit Sawfly* (Hoplocampa flava) causes severe damage to plums in the hilly regions. A spray of quassia and soap is used.

*Scale Insects* are by far the most important pests of citrus-trees. Principal types are (1) Black Scale (*Chrysomphalus ficus*); (2) Mussel Scale (*Lepidosaphes beckii*); (3) Red Scale (*Aonidiella aurantii*); (4) Wax Scale (*Ceroplastes floridensis*); (5) Soft Scale (*Lecanium hesperidum*; (6) Olive Black Scale (*Saissetia oleae*). Various methods of fumigation or spraying with hydrogen cyanide are used. Another type of scale, the Mealy Bug (especially *Pseudococcus comstockii*), is now considered a dangerous pest of citrus, and experimental work on it is being carried out at the Rehovot Experimental Station.

*Fungous Pests*

Apart from purely physiological diseases due to the use of saline water or other factors adversely affecting growth, many diseases of agricultural crops are brought about by fungi or bacteria. Many of these are widespread and well-known disorders, against which adequate control measures have long been devised. Vines are affected, as in all vine-growing countries, by Downy Mildew (*Plasmopara viticola*). Cereal crops such as wheat, oats, barley, and rye are attacked by the same rusts and smuts as in European countries. Durra (*Sorghum*) and maize suffer from the common smuts of these crops—*Sphacelotheca Sorghi, S. Reiliana*, and *Ustilago zeae*.

Vegetable crops suffer from the usual European fungous diseases. *Sclerotinia sclerotiorum*, prevalent especially in the Jordan valley,

67. *Afforestation near Nazareth. The Balfour forest in 1929 after a few months growth*

68. *The Balfour forest in 1935*

70. *Arab women carrying papyrus for mat-making*

69. *Papyrus growing at Lake Huleh*

attacks tomato and egg-plant severely, and has also been recorded as attacking citrus and banana. Potato Blight (*Phytophthora infestans*) is epidemic is some localities. Bean Blight (*Rhizoctonia bataticola; Macrophomina phaseoli*) causes much damage over wide areas of Palestine, from Judaea to the valley of Esdraelon. Tobacco suffers from 'mosaic' and other virus diseases, and is also attacked by *Sclerotinia sclerotiorum*. The plant diseases that cause the most concern in Palestine are those that affect citrus. From seed-bed to mature fruit these plants are attacked by a series of fungous pests which demand constant vigilance.

Considerable losses are often sustained in seed-beds by the attacks of soil-fungi such as *Rhizoctonia* and *Phytophthora* on the roots and collar of seedlings. 'Blast' of nursery seedlings is due to *Pseudomonas citriputeale*. In the groves, root-rots are prevalent, one at least of which is due to the fungus *Ganoderma*. 'Gummosis' (collar and brown-rot), which causes losses of 5–50 per cent., appears to be associated with a species of *Fusarium*. Severe damage to 'sour-lemon' trees, used as a stock for orange, is caused by *Mal Secco*, due to the fungus *Deuterophoma tracheiphila*.

Fruit-rots are a constant source of anxiety to exporters. The rots of major importance are due to stem-end rot (*Diplodia natalensis*) and fruit-rots—the green moulds *Penicillium digitatum* and *P. italicum*. Both may be controlled by meticulous care in sanitation, both in the groves themselves and after picking. Mechanical injury to the fruits encourages infection.

Only a small number of the diseases affecting crops have been mentioned here. Long lists of fungous diseases recorded for Palestine have been published by the plant pathologist at Rehovot. Many of these, however, are infrequent, and probably are chance introductions from abroad. The major pests are the immediate concern of the Plant Protection Service, whose advice and help are at the disposal of cultivators at all times.

*Forestry*

Palestine has neither the altitude nor the rainfall of a forest country, and compares ill in this respect with the Lebanon immediately to the north. Biblical references to woodland, but also to great and famous trees such as the oak at Mamre, show primeval forest already broken up into groves, leaving only a few survivors among the cultivated lands.

It has been already stated in Chapter IV that true forests occupy a very small proportion of the surface of the country. Centuries of neglect and lack of forest tradition have deforested most of this small proportion in favour of meagre cereal crops. During the war of 1914–1918 much of the remaining timber was cut down for military purposes.

Such traces of forest as still persisted in the plains had then to contend with the increasing demand for agricultural land by the post-war Jewish immigrants. The draining of the Kabbara marshes, for example, exterminated an interesting forest of tamarisk. The extension of the orange-groves on the light soils of Sharon has destroyed most of the remnants of oak. A grave danger to the surviving forests and areas of *maquis* is the growth of the Arab charcoal and lime-burning industry, though the Government has tried to control this. The problem is more difficult because the inhabitants of Palestine, in general, are ignorant of the uses and value of natural vegetation in such matters as conservation of soil and production of humus. It is said, indeed, that the peasants and nomads in the south actually dislike trees.

Such natural forests as persist are mainly confined to the hills of northern Palestine. They are poorly stocked and have been repeatedly cut over, but they provide rough timber for constructional purposes, as well as firewood and charcoal, and also pasturage for sheep, goats, and cattle. They contain few straight trees suitable for planks.

These hill-forests, or forest-remnants, are widely scattered in the Acre, Nazareth, and Safad districts and on the slopes of Carmel. They also occupy small portions of the Jenin, Tulkarm, and Hebron areas. The dominant species are the deciduous oak (*Quercus ithaburensis*) and the evergreen oak (*Q. calliprinos*). Some woodlands are dominated by the deciduous oak; others are a mixed community of deciduous and evergreen oak, while in other areas the evergreen oak predominates. The commonest under-shrub is the storax (*Styrax officinalis*), but other common bushes are the thorny broom (*Calycotome villosa*), buckthorn (*Rhamnus palaestina*), and hawthorn (*Crataegus Azarolus*). Many of these degraded forests are merely transitional between oak forest and *maquis*, most of the finest trees having been cut down by man, and effective coppicing from the stumps having been prevented by grazing goats.

In a few localities there are small groups or isolated specimens of the Aleppo pine (*Pinus halepensis*).

*Olive-groves* are scattered throughout the hill regions, though very many trees were cut down for fuel in 1914–1918. A fair amount of planting has been carried out since that time; the most important groves are in the Acre, Safad, Haifa, Jenin, Nablus, Tulkarm, Jerusalem, Ramallah, and Bethlehem areas. The largest groves in the plains are around Lydda. The total area under olive-trees is about 138,000 acres, of which 118,000 acres are fruit-bearing.

The gallery forest along the banks of the Jordan has suffered much from grazing, from the lopping of branches for fodder, and from fires. The trees, therefore, are usually too ill-formed or diseased to be of much value, other than for firewood, charcoal, rough timber, or grazing (photos. 1, 27, 28).

## Afforestation (*photos. 67, 68*).

The principal aims in forest policy are to prevent erosion and to rehabilitate extensive areas of devastated land in the hills. Along the coast, also, considerable stretches of sand-dune need to be fixed. Among the problems is the great difficulty experienced by forest officers in obtaining control of the land, because of the obscurity of title-deeds and land-ownership.

The first area in which a forestry scheme started was the Tiberias slope, hot and steep, with low rainfall and maximum exposure. The experience gained in this undertaking has led to further projects in special areas urgently requiring afforestation. Under consideration is the catchment area of the Wadi Salameh, north of Tel Aviv. Other preliminary work is in progress for the Carmel range, the Nablus–Tulkarm valley, the Gaza sand-dunes, and Jebel Turan, west of Tiberias. Direct afforestation by planting is too expensive, and most of the soil is so seriously eroded that a period under grass and bush is necessary before trees can be grown at all. It is proposed also to establish village-forests to supply firewood and small timber.

At the end of 1939 there were three State forests in Palestine: (1) Khreibeh near Haifa (800 acres); (2) Beit Hanun near Gaza (42 acres); and (3) Gaza sand-dunes (445 acres). Full control of these lands is ensured, and no interests will be allowed to supersede those of the forest. Other areas known as 'Forest Reserves' have been taken under protection. On 31 March 1941 the Government forest reserves covered an area of 169,230 acres; non-government reserves covered 5,220 acres.

While indigenous species have proved superior to exotics in normal afforestation, exotics are more successful on sand-dunes. Wattle (*Acacia cyanophylla*) forms dense stands as far south as Gaza, while species of *Eucalyptus*, mainly *E. camaldulensis*, thrive in private planta-tions on alluvial plains and beside the railway. At the end of 1939, nine nurseries were being maintained, though adequate water-supply is difficult to obtain, especially in the south. The Department of Forests was formed as a separate department in 1936, but civil disturbances since that date caused such interruption that real development of the department has not been possible. The forest staff in 1939 was 116, of whom 88 were field subordinates such as forest rangers, foresters, forest-guards, and *ghaffirs* (watchmen).

Private afforestation has been undertaken, especially by the Jewish National Fund since 1918, and even before that date. Private woodlands fall into two classes. In the plains, deep soils are planted mainly with *Eucalyptus*, while in the hills are several large plantations of *Pinus halepensis, Cupressus sempervirens*, and other species of minor importance. Private afforestation, however, tends to be discouraged by the difficulties of acquiring clear titles for suitable land, and by the prevalence of vague claims to grazing and other rights. Frequent invasion by goats or camels has also to be resisted.

*Railway Tree-planting.* In the sandy stretch along the line, between Khan Yunis and the frontier at Rafa, mixed trees have been planted by the Palestine Railways for several years: in 1939, 19,300 trees were planted. It is expected that in a few years, in the absence of interruption, this stretch of line will be well wooded and protected from the encroaching sand. On the Isdud sand-dunes, where the railway occupies a large area which used to be drifting sand, there is now the beginning of a small forest. The dunes have been fixed by planting *Artemisia*, marram grass, tamarisk, &c., and there is now a good growth of pines, eucalyptus, acacias, pepper, and cypress.

### MINERAL INDUSTRIES

It is generally stated that no minerals are to be found in Palestine, and with few exceptions this is true. Prospecting for oil has been fairly thorough, but in vain. Traces of copper have been found in small quantities commercially worthless. But sulphur is worked in southern Palestine, potash and bromine are found in great quantities in the Dead Sea, and rock salt on its south-western shore; salt is obtained by evaporation at Atlit on the coast west of Carmel.

*Gypsum* is widespread, and it is believed that very large supplies could be made available, though only at Menahamiya in southern

Galilee is it produced commercially even on a small scale. Gypsum is used in the manufacture of cement and of plaster of Paris. The cost of production and of transport is high, almost £1 a ton as compared with 18s. for gypsum imported from Cyprus, including import duty of 3s.

### Production of Gypsum

| | | |
|---|---|---|
| 1938 . . | 3,984 tons | £800 |
| 1939 . . | 4,524 ,, | 1,000 |
| 1940 . . | 4,403 ,, | 900 |
| 1941 . . | 4,841 ,, | 1,745 |

*Sulphur* is extracted from deposits south of Gaza. It is estimated that there are about a million tons available.

### Production of Sulphur

| | | |
|---|---|---|
| 1938 . . | 1,215 tons | £6,417 |
| 1939 . . | 842 ,, | 4,304 |
| 1940 . . | 1,380 ,, | 11,093 |
| 1941 . . | 3,419 ,, | 37,846 |

*Rock salt* occurs in massive beds at Jebel Usdum on the south-west shore of the Dead Sea; the supply seems to be almost unlimited; but the present output, and also the salt produced by evaporation at Atlit, is absorbed entirely by the home market. The production of salt was formerly a monopoly, the Government purchasing the whole of the output. But in November 1927 the monopoly was abandoned and an excise duty substituted.

### Production of Salt

| | | | | |
|---|---|---|---|---|
| 1925 . . | 4,794 tons | 1937 . . | 9,856 tons |
| 1930 . . | 7,618 ,, | 1938 . . | 7,888 ,, |
| 1935 . . | 10,376 ,, | 1939 . . | 7,335 ,, |
| 1936 . . | 9,148 ,, | 1940 . . | 10,543 ,, |

The amount of salts in Dead Sea water is eight times that of ordinary sea-water, and in addition to the salts in solution—152,600 grains to a gallon—there is a very large but unknown quantity, mostly sodium chloride and calcium sulphate, deposited on the bottom. The most important salts in solution are potassium chloride and magnesium bromide, and their principal origin is probably the hot springs of Lake Tiberias and the Zerka-Main in Transjordan. The total amount of potash is about 2,000 million tons; of magnesium bromide, 900 million tons. The density of the brine increases with depth, and also from north to south.

## *Principal Salts in Dead Sea Water*

|  | Surface | 175 ft. depth |
|---|---|---|
| Sodium chloride (salt) . . | 7·0% | 9·3% |
| Potassium chloride . . | 1·0% | 1·5% |
| Magnesium bromide . . | 0·45% | 0·7% |
| Magnesium chloride . . | 11·0% | 17·0% |

Saturation point is reached at a depth between 250 and 300 feet.

The rate of evaporation of surface brine on the shores of the Dead Sea owing to air density and high temperature is usually high, amounting to about 1 cm. a day in the hot summer months. From brine with a surface density of 1·16 and a depth of 60 cm. almost all the sodium chloride is removed in six weeks, carnallite (potassium-magnesium chloride) begins to crystallize, and separation of this is complete in three weeks. This latter salt contains 20 per cent. of potassium chloride and from 0 to 12 per cent. sodium chloride. Recrystallization gives potassium chloride as a pure salt as the first product; later crystallizations contain more sodium chloride. Fifty per cent. of the potash content can be recovered as a salt of 80 per cent. purity. The remainder has an average quality of about 45 per cent. purity.

The solution after removal of carnallite can next be evaporated, still by solar heat, to give a very pure magnesium chloride, which is readily handled. The residual liquid contains 1·25 per cent. bromine —in the form of magnesium bromide—one of the richest known sources of bromine.

Potash is one of the three principal components of fertilizer, and about 90 per cent. of the world's production is taken by agriculture. Bromine, the other principal product of the Dead Sea, is becoming every year more necessary in industry, and enters commerce in several combinations. It is mixed with petrol to secure the smooth running of engines, and is used in the manufacture of dyes, explosives, drugs, and poison gas. The cost of production of Dead Sea potash and bromine is lower than elsewhere, but this advantage is partly offset by the high cost of transport. Palestine is the only principal producer of potash that has the advantage of solar evaporation, with all its raw material and energy on the spot—Dead Sea water, fresh water from the Jordan, and the sun. The original plant of the Palestine Potash Company was constructed at the northern end of the Dead Sea in 1929. In 1937 a second plant was constructed at the southern end.

71. *Palestine Potash Company's salt pans at the northern end of the Dead Sea*

72. *Artificial reservoir and Hydro-electric power station of the Palestine Electric Corporation at the junction of the Yarmuk and the Jordan. View north-east up the Yarmuk*

### Quantity and Value of Potash and Bromine exported from Palestine

| | Potash | | Bromine | |
|---|---|---|---|---|
| 1932 | 8,649 tons | £55,938 | 267 tons | £16,180 |
| 1933 | 10,046 ,, | 44,693 | 238 ,, | 21,560 |
| 1934 | 11,427 ,, | 56,724 | 455 ,, | 22,600 |
| 1935 | 13,124 ,, | 80,231 | 403 ,, | 18,751 |
| 1936 | 19,793 ,, | 132,857 | 478 ,, | 35,097 |
| 1937 | 29,110 ,, | 174,672 | 611 ,, | 42,026 |
| 1938 | 47,496 ,, | 284,976 | 473 ,, | 37,985 |
| 1939 | 74,700 ,, | 381,162 | 552 ,, | 46,528 |
| 1940 | 93,476 ,, | 640,396 | 929 ,, | 65,389 |
| 1941 | .. | 662,000 | .. | 37,000 |

*Bitumen* is found in the Dead Sea and in its neighbourhood, especially after earthquakes; it comes to the surface in lumps and is collected.

*Quarries.* Palestine has abundant limestones and basalts. Limestone is used in cement-making. Many houses in the hills are built of local stone and the material, usually limestone in various colours, principally yellow, red, and green, is quarried near at hand. In Galilee basalt is used. Quarrying and stone-cutting seem formerly to have long died out as industries, the stones of older buildings being used. When the Austrian Hospice was erected in Jerusalem in the middle of the nineteenth century skilled men had to be brought from Italy. These taught others from Bethlehem to quarry and to cut stone; and quarrying and masonry are still among the principal industries of Bethlehem. In northern Palestine and near Bethlehem marble is found, green, greenish-red, and white.

*Mineral Springs* in the valley of the Jordan are numerous and of wide and ancient fame, and with those of Transjordan were used by Cleopatra of Egypt and by Herod. Of those within Palestine the most valuable are near Tiberias and at El Hammeh, the village or group of buildings where the frontiers of Syria, Transjordan, and Palestine meet. The thermal springs are all highly sulphurous and some extremely saline. Most are also radio-active. The non-thermal springs are of less consequence; they are mostly in the Jordan valley, and all are highly saline. Around Haifa bay are large springs containing sodium and magnesium chloride, but these have no known therapeutic value.

The springs at Tiberias and El Hammeh are in situations ideal for health and pleasure resorts. Throughout the winter the climate is warm and mild. The natural scenery is attractive, the surroundings full of historical and biblical interest, and Tiberias has been a health and pleasure resort since its establishment at the opening of the present era. Its amenities have not, however, kept pace with the progress of those of the world at large. The water of Tiberias issues from the rock at a temperature of 160°. The baths, which are the joint property of the Government and the Municipality, were greatly neglected until the last few years, when a new concession was granted and the company introduced improvements; but even without these, the medicinal virtues of the hot baths of Tiberias were widely famous, and have been frequented by sufferers from rheumatic and skin diseases, real and imaginary, from Palestine and elsewhere.

At El Hammeh, accommodation for both visitors and residents is still very primitive, though a Palestinian company has taken steps to develop that centre also. The baths are patronized by visitors from Syria more than from Palestine. The water is too hot to be used without cooling.

The water of the Dead Sea also is said to have therapeutic value, and at Kallia on the north-west shore of the Dead Sea there is bathing accommodation.

## OTHER INDUSTRIES

Palestine is essentially an agricultural country, although there have long been a few small industries there, and in the past twenty years there has been a fair amount of industrial development, mainly on the part of new Jewish settlers. With the great expansion of Jewish immigration and the pressure on the agricultural settlements to accept new settlers irrespective of their capacity, a partial industrialization, on a small scale, of these settlements has set in and in many of the Zionist villages there have been attempts to establish small industries. Of the older industries, Arab soap-making took the first place. After it came wine-making (mainly Jewish), tanning, and the manufacture of objects of piety from local olive-wood, or imported mother-of-pearl. These objects were not so much for sale as intended (like the pressed flowers exported from Palestine) to stimulate gifts from the benevolent or religious for charitable objects.

In 1928 the Department of Customs, Excise, and Trade undertook a census of the industries. This census recorded 3,505 factories, establishments, and workshops, employing in all 17,955 persons, including owners. The average number of persons employed was thus only 5·1 per establishment, an indication of the very small scale of industry in Palestine. The total expenditure of these establishments in 1927, including raw materials, fuel, salaries, and wages, was £2,975,400, an average of £849 for each establishment. Articles valued at £3,886,150 (£1,100 per establishment) were produced, and the capital invested was £3,514,886 (c. £1,000 per establishment).

The number of very small industries is most surprising. In the Jewish villages there were over 400 enterprises in which an average of less than two persons were engaged, so that most of these were little more than home industries. In a third of the establishments counted in the census, no paid labour at all was employed, in less than a quarter were there more than three wage-earners, in less than a tenth more than five. Only twelve establishments employed over 100 wage-earners, and fifteen between 50 and 100.[1]

Since 1928 many new industrial enterprises have been started, mostly on a small scale. But the development of electric power and the immigration of Jews from Germany in 1934 and 1935 has brought a change, and several important industries on a much larger scale have been founded. These include food products, drinks, cigarettes, tobacco, building materials, metalware, furniture, textiles, leather goods, artificial teeth, matches, wearing apparel, and chemical and allied products, especially the extraction of mineral salts from the Dead Sea.

Arab industry also includes some large undertakings and numerous small ones, an appreciable and diversified contribution to the industry of Palestine. Unfortunately it has always been difficult to obtain reliable figures of these, chiefly because they are mostly of the workshop type and rather primitive. The larger Arab industries include soap manufactures; flour-milling; bricks and tiles; cigarettes and tobacco; cotton, wool, and silk-weaving; salt-quarrying; sand, stone, and lime; bedsteads; nails; wearing apparel; confectionery; and intoxicating liquors.

Generally speaking, articles are of good quality. Increase in local demand, and government assistance in the way of protective tariffs and exemption of raw materials from import duty, have enabled many factories to make some progress.

Some industries have suffered from several weaknesses: the high cost of production; insufficient attention to the potential market—generally small in comparison with the productive capacity; excessive expenditure on installation, leaving too little working capital; lack of

[1] Sir J. H. Simpson. *Palestine Report on Immigration, Land Settlement and Development*, 1930. Cmd. 3686, p. 114.

facilities for economic disposal of waste and by-products; and competition by foreign countries like Japan (with low wage standards) and
Germany (with high state-subsidies), which cannot always be met by
high protective duties.

It is noteworthy that those industries which are subject to government legislation and control—namely, tobacco, intoxicating liquors,
methylated spirits, salt, and matches—are all flourishing; also that

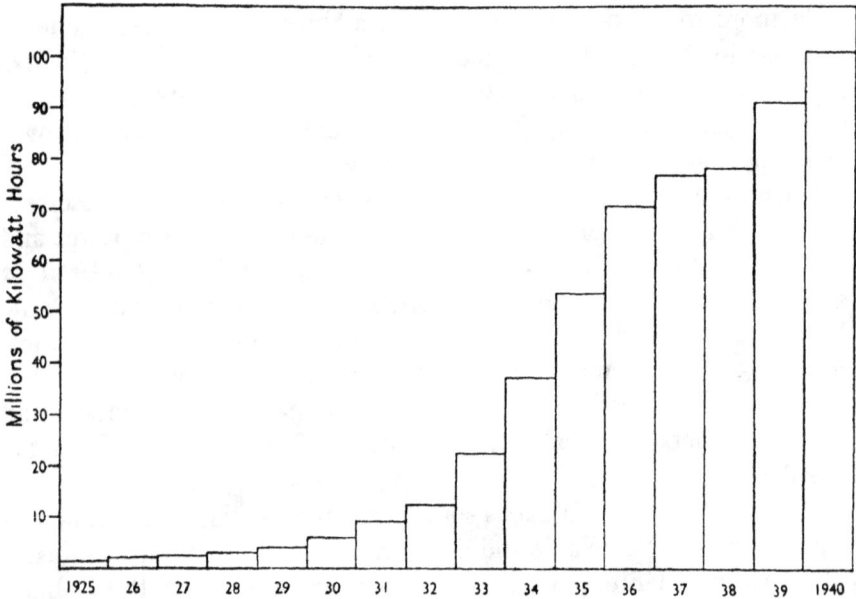

FIG. 29. *Consumption of Electricity*

all of them, except matches, depend largely on local raw materials
and unskilled labour.

### Electricity

Electricity is generated in Palestine by two undertakings, both
British. In the larger of these the greater part of the capital is Jewish,
for the most part from America and Britain. The Jerusalem Electric
and Public Service Corporation, with a capital of £500,000, has the
monopoly of the supply of electricity to Jerusalem and the surrounding
district. The Palestine Electric Corporation, with an authorized
capital of £2,500,000, has a similar monopoly for the remainder of the
country. Previous to the arrival of the British, electric power and
light were unknown in Palestine. One or two progressive indivi-

duals would have liked to install it, but their suggestions were looked on with suspicion by the Ottoman authorities.[1]

The principal generating station of the Palestine Electric Corporation is at Tel Or, where the Yarmuk flows into the Jordan south of Lake Tiberias. The machinery consists of three units, each of 6,000 kW. capacity, capable of producing 60 million kWh. per annum (photo. 72). In advance of this power-house, three oil-driven generating stations were erected, at Tel Aviv, Haifa, and Tiberias, to meet immediate needs, and eventually to serve as supplementary stations. Electricity was first supplied in 1923, but since that year, although the main power-house was completed, those at Tel Aviv and at Haifa have had to be extended. Practically the whole country, outside the Jerusalem area, is now supplied with electricity by the Palestine Electric Corporation (fig. 29).

### Consumption of Electricity since 1925

| | | |
|---|---|---|
| 1925 | . | . | 1,847,225 kWh. |
| 1926 | . | . | 2,343,764 |
| 1927 | . | . | 2,527,126 |
| 1928 | . | . | 2,973,701 |
| 1929 | . | . | 3,634,838 |
| 1930 | . | . | 6,168,198 |
| 1931 | . | . | 9,547,616 |
| 1932 | . | . | 12,643,506 |

| | | |
|---|---|---|
| 1933 | . | . | 21,526,910 kWh. |
| 1934 | . | . | 36,571,869 |
| 1935 | . | . | 53,670,371 |
| 1936 | . | . | 70,012,024 |
| 1937 | . | . | 76,990,210 |
| 1938 | . | . | 78,713,107 |
| 1939 | . | . | 91,474,839 |
| 1940 | . | . | 101,387,776 |

### Oil and Soap

The production of olive-oil from presses and the manufacture of olive-oil soap are two of the traditional industries of Palestine, and especially of the town and district of Nablus, where there are many presses and soap factories. The local olive-oil is inferior for human consumption, but is suitable for soap manufacture. The soap was formerly produced on a very large scale and marketed mainly in Egypt and other Moslem lands, where it was known to be ritually clean and therefore admissible to Moslem households (fig. 30). The industry has suffered severely from tariff restrictions in Egypt in 1931, and since then from the competition of cheap imported soaps. After Nablus, the principal centres of this industry are Jaffa and Ramleh. All the employees in these three towns are Arabs. The extraction and refining of vegetable oils and the manufacture of soap on

---

[1] A concession had indeed been granted before 1914 to a Greek financier, but he had made no move. After the war he and his supporters successfully contested the grant of a new concession to others. This is the cause of the two monopolies at present.

modern European lines are also carried on at Haifa, and to a less extent at Ramat Gan and Rishon le Zion by Jewish firms. The prosperity of the industry mainly depends on the olive harvest. A

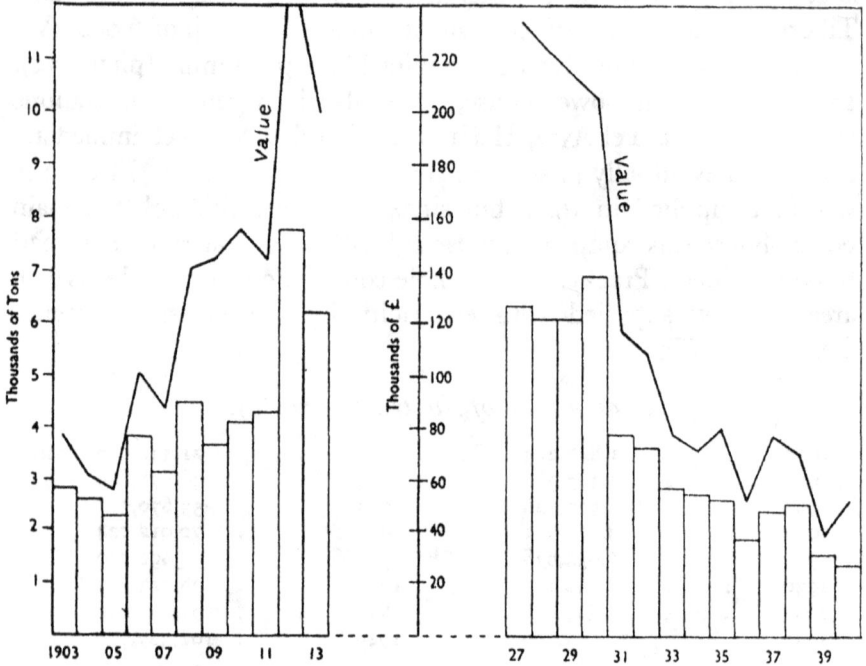

FIG. 30. *Export of Soap, 1903–1913, 1927–1940*

by-product is cattle-feeding cake. Vegetable oil is also made from sesame seed; but some of the sesame seed consumed, and all the other kinds of oil, are imported.

### Export of Soap, 1903–1940

| | | | | | | | |
|---|---|---|---|---|---|---|---|
| 1903 | . . . | 2,810 tons* | £77,650 | 1935 | . . | 2,656 tons | £79,311 |
| 1913 | . . | 6,250 ,, * | 200,000 | 1936 | . . | 1,841 ,, | 53,798 |
| 1928 | . . | 6,187 ,, | 224,496 | 1937 | . . | 2,452 ,, | 76,296 |
| 1932 | . . | 3,640 ,, | 108,101 | 1938 | . . | 2,502 ,, | 68,532 |
| 1933 | . . | 2,813 ,, | 79,342 | 1939 | . . | 1,558 ,, | 39,591 |
| 1934 | . . | 2,713 ,, | 71,532 | 1940 | . . | 1,332 ,, | 53,593 |

\* For Jaffa only.

### Wine

Wine-making is an industry with which no strict Moslem can have any connexion. Some of the Christian convents have for long made wine on a small scale, but the industry is now almost entirely Jewish and depends on an organization created by Baron Edmond de Rothschild in the 'eighties of last century to dispose of the grapes produced by the Jewish agriculturists whom he had helped to settle. Its market depended mainly on Jewish homes in all parts of the world, in which the wine—being ritually pure—was used in the domestic religious services. A very small quantity was imported into Egypt and other countries as ordinary wine and also into France to be mixed with French wines. But production beyond the capacity of the export

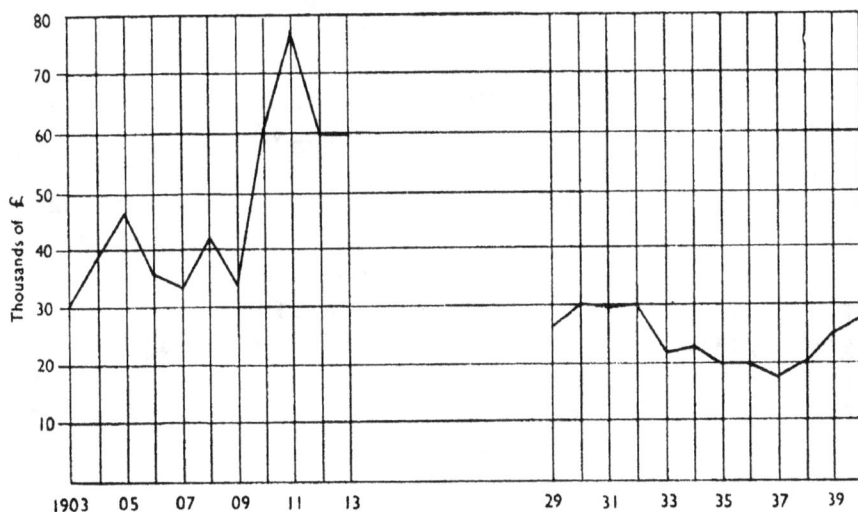

FIG. 31. *Export of Wines, 1903–1913, 1929–1940*

market, the 'prohibition' laws in the United States of America, and later the closing of Russia to imports from Palestine, dealt this industry serious blows from which it has never recovered (fig. 31).

*Export of Wines, 1903–1941*

| 1903 | . | . | £30,350 | 1936 | . | . | £20,000 |
|------|---|---|---------|------|---|---|---------|
| 1913 | . | . | 60,530 | 1937 | . | . | 18,689 |
| 1929 | . | . | 27,304 | 1938 | . | . | 21,131 |
| 1933 | . | . | 22,270 | 1939 | . | . | 26,196 |
| 1934 | . | . | 23,214 | 1940 | . | . | 28,876 |
| 1935 | . | . | 20,551 | 1941 | . | . | 16,234 |

## Tobacco

Before 1921 the cultivation of tobacco and the manufacture of cigarettes, &c., were under the control of the Turkish Tobacco Monopoly (*Régie*), and there was no tobacco-growing or manufacture in Palestine. The monopoly was abolished in 1921, production and manufacture being then permitted, subject to excise. The industry now depends both on local and on imported tobacco, and much of the demand for cigarettes is satisfied by local manufacture.

## Building

Building has been closely linked with immigration. With active immigration, building has increased, and conversely. But building activity is a cause as well as a consequence of immigration; the demand for building-labour, houses, and shops, has been made to justify more immigrants, and the presence of these immigrants has increased the demand for buildings. During the past twenty years there has also been much building for the Army and Air Force, and a Government building programme, fairly large for a country in which there were formerly very few good administrative buildings. Expansion in building has inevitably caused parallel expansion in the subsidiary industries, especially cement-making, brick-making, and woodwork.

Fig. 32 shows the investment in private building, in millions of pounds, for the period 1924–1940. The rise in 1925 was caused by the great expansion of Tel Aviv. The most marked feature is the boom in building from 1933 to 1935, caused by the influx of Jewish refugees from central Europe on Hitler's accession to power. In the early period of Nazi domination the Jews from Germany were able to bring some money with them and to invest it in Palestine. The investments in private building rose from £2,939,363 in 1932 to £5,592,377 in 1933, £6,994,258 in 1934, and £8,428,606 in 1935. The subsequent depression, caused partly by political troubles, partly by the poverty of immigrant Jews, and partly by reduced immigration, is also clearly shown. The investment in 1939 was only £1,489,830, and in 1941 £359,719.

Fig. 33 analyses the building in the four large towns of Jerusalem, Jaffa, Tel Aviv, and Haifa, during the period 1932–1941, by the area, in millions of square feet, covered by building licences. It shows the great development of Tel Aviv and Haifa during the years 1932–1935, when Tel Aviv became the largest city in Palestine, and Haifa was growing as an oil-pipe terminus, shipping and air port. The slump subsequent to 1935 is again marked for all three places, though Haifa expanded during 1938. Since that year the decline has been continuous.

Cement, said to be equal to the best English 'Portland' cement, is produced in a factory near Haifa, one of the largest industrial establishments in Palestine. It is the sole source of this commodity in the country, and benefits from a duty of 17s. a ton on imported cement.

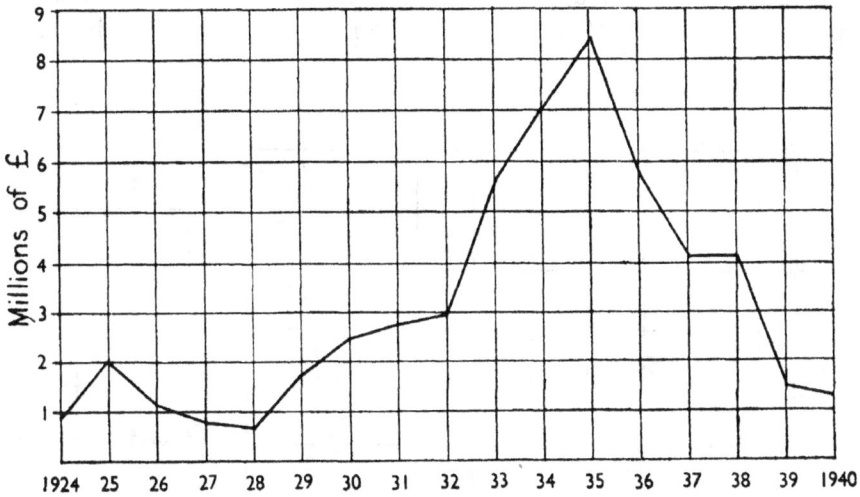

FIG. 32. *Investment in private building, 1924–1940*

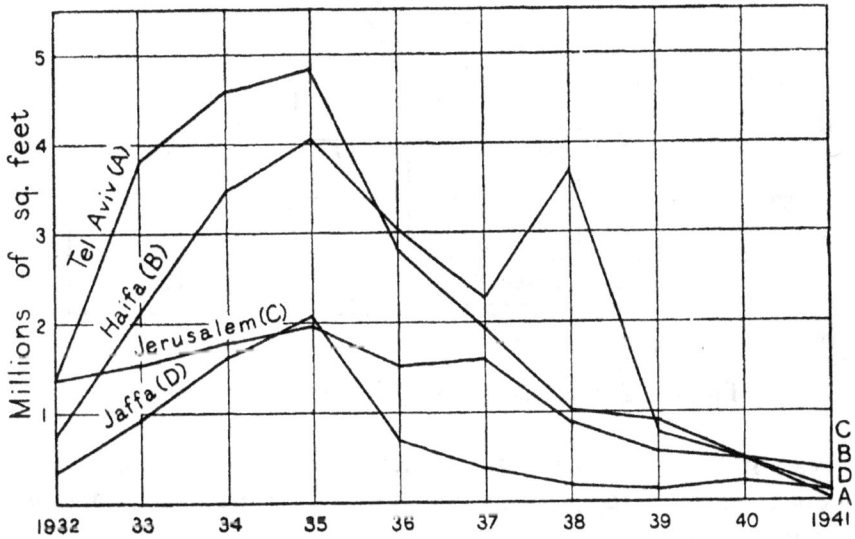

FIG. 33. *Building Licences in the four Chief Towns, 1932–1941*

Production increased steadily from 41,610 tons in 1926 to nearly 100,000 tons in 1932, keeping approximately equal to requirements, and then jumped during the building boom to 187,000 tons in 1935, fell to 98,445 tons in 1938, and then rose to 148,487 in 1940. In the boom

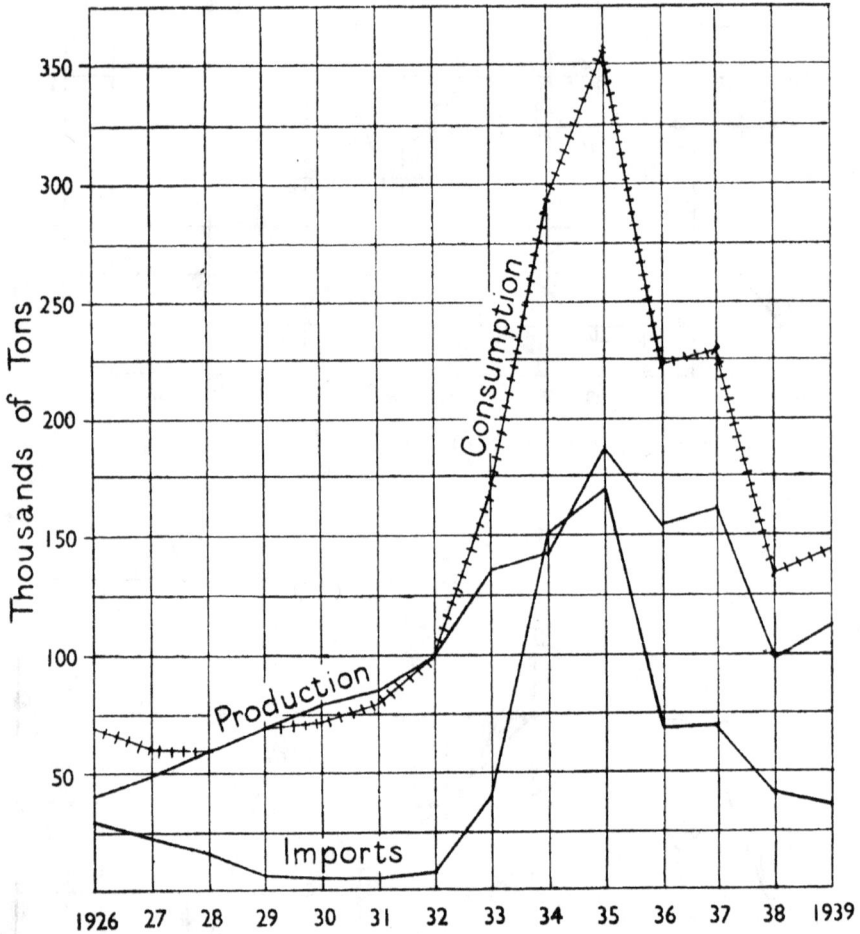

FIG. 34. *Production, Consumption, and Imports of Cement*

years it was far below requirements, which reached a maximum of 355,550 tons in 1935, so that imports in that year were also a maximum.

Fig. 34 shows the consumption, production, and import of cement from 1926 to 1939. During this period there has been a small export, averaging about 5,850 tons a year, too insignificant to show on the diagram.

## Textiles

Before the establishment of British administration, the old textile industry of Palestine was entirely in Arab hands, and all its products, clothing, carpets, and rugs, and a few minor articles, were absorbed by the home market. It was mainly carried on in the workers' homes, or in small workshops; machinery was almost unknown. Mejdel with 500 looms and Gaza with 50, both in the south, were the largest centres: but most of the industry was in the villages or the work of beduin, who made their own clothes and also carpets and small articles for sale. Coarse cotton and wool were the principal materials; but there was also some weaving in silk, and the weaving of straw mats was also widespread. All the yarns were imported, the cotton from Manchester.

This home industry continues, but on a very diminished scale. It has been supplanted by a larger industry, based on factories and workshops. The produce of this too is mostly absorbed by the country, because of the many Europeans who have settled. Development was made easy by the immigration of employers and workers from Lodz and other Polish weaving centres. By 1927 the textile industry, though still quite small, ranked fourth in the number of persons employed, leaving agriculture and building out of consideration. In 1938 about 1,600 Jews and 2,000 Arabs were employed in the manufacture of textiles—cotton-spinning, cotton and silk-weaving, knitting and dyeing, embroidery and lace-making. Of these about 1,400 worked at Mejdel. Cotton-spinning began near Haifa only in 1935, but markets in Turkey and Syria were soon secured.

### Imports of Yarn, Cotton, and Wool (tons)

|  | 1931 | 1932 | 1933 | 1934 | 1935 | 1936 | 1937 | 1938 | 1939 | 1940 |
|---|---|---|---|---|---|---|---|---|---|---|
| Silk and rayon yarn . | 12 | 23 | 45 | 76 | 110 | 134 | 166 | 118 | 138 | 185 |
| Cotton yarn . | . 326 | 477 | 580 | 629 | 752 | 430 | 558 | 548 | 615 | 887 |
| Woollen yarn . | . 22 | 47 | 101 | 107 | 90 · | 63 | 119 | 119 | 125 | 62 |
| Raw and waste cotton | 347 | 196 | 361 | 496 | 694 | 535 | 820 | 645 | 1,044 | 1,055 |
| „ „ wool | 58 | 36 | 22 | 30 | 33 | 5 | 24 | 34 | 16 | 14 |

## Oil-refining

With the completion of the oil pipe-line from Iraq in 1934, crude oil began to flow through Palestine for foreign destinations, mainly France.

### Transit of Crude Oil through Palestine

|      | | | Quantity<br>Tons | Value<br>£ |
|------|---|---|------------|--------|
| 1935 | . | . | 1,854,000 | 1,483,000 |
| 1936 | . | . | 1,954,000 | 1,563,000 |
| 1937 | . | . | 1,931,000 | 1,545,000 |
| 1938 | . | . | 2,079,000 | 1,663,000 |
| 1939 | . | . | 1,812,000 | 1,450,000 |
| 1940 | . | . | 654,929 | 523,944 |
| 1941 | . | . | 10,314 | 8,251 |

The Shell Company at Haifa can in normal circumstances make and fill 6,000 four-gallon tins of petrol per day from stocks held. Their ethyl blending plant has a capacity of 60 tons. The Socony Vacuum Company can fill 3,200 four-gallon tins per day. Their normal stocks are 12,000 tons. At the terminus of the Iraq pipe-line there are 21 storage tanks each of 12,000 tons capacity and two 12-inch steel submarine pipes, 4,200 feet long, running out to sea at Haifa. Each of these pipes can deliver from 750 to 950 tons of oil per hour. The Consolidated Refineries Ltd. commenced refining in March 1940. Its annual output is now 2 million tons of refined oil.

### Minor Industries

Some industries, minor in the number of men employed, such as diamond-cutting and -polishing, and artificial teeth manufacture, give considerable promise. The diamond-cutting and -polishing industry was introduced only in 1938, on a very small scale, but the outbreak of war and threats to Belgium and Holland led workers and employers at Antwerp and Amsterdam, hitherto the centres of the industry, to emigrate to Palestine, where they re-established their undertakings. The chief diamond-cutting centres are at Nathanya on the coast, some miles north of Jaffa, and at Tel Aviv; a subsidiary is being established in Jerusalem.

The artificial tooth industry is older, having been established by an American manufacturer at Tel Aviv soon after 1920. It is concentrated in one factory. Both the diamond and the tooth industries are dependent on foreign sources for their raw material, but the bulk being small, this is no handicap. Almost the whole product of both industries is exported.

*Fisheries* are a minor industry, despite their long history and the devotion of a branch of a government department to their encouragement. The average annual weight of sea-fish landed during the six seasons from 1934/5 to 1939/40 has been 1,400 tons (maximum, 1,640;

73. *Ain es Siyah pumping station for Mount Carmel water-supply*

74. *Oil storage tanks and workers' settlement on the Bay of Acre, east of Haifa*

75. *Arab fishermen*

76. *Fellah watering sheep and goats*

minimum, 1,286); and of fresh fish 305 tons (max. 364; min. 212). The catch mainly comprised sardine, pilchard, red-mullet, bleak (a fresh-water sardine), maigre, and sea-perch. This is an Arab occupation mainly; in 1939/40 the Jewish share was only 44 tons (3·1% of the catch) of sea-fish, and 88 tons (24·2%) of fresh-water fish.

*Tourists.* The tourist 'industry' is or should be one of the most valuable of Palestine. For many centuries Palestine has been a land of pilgrimage, and still is so to Jew, Christian, and Moslem. It has always been one of interest to the traveller, rich or poor, pious or otherwise, whether interested in history, archaeology, or in strange peoples, or merely in search of a pleasant climate. For more than a century it has attracted travellers, especially from England. In the past twenty years and longer, during which pleasure-tours have been widely developed, numbers have increased at a remarkable rate, particularly among the less prosperous class of visitors. But there are no exact statistics, and it is hard to define a tourist precisely. Many visitors come to examine the prospects of settlement or business, many of small means from Syria to visit relatives or friends from whom they have been separated; there are pilgrims and sightseers to the Holy Places. The Palestine Government does not differentiate between them: all are 'travellers' for whom figures are given; moreover, some 'travellers' settle in the country and become 'immigrants'. To give the figures for 'travellers' entering Palestine is, therefore, of little value. The Government has, however, in recent years obtained some information about temporary visitors. In 1939, 18,488 'visitors' are recorded as having departed, having spent £177,170 or nearly £10 each in the country. In the following years the figures were 33,192 and £147,826 (1940), and 40,545 and £183,310 (1941).

Until twenty years ago the only tourists or pilgrims who could come to Palestine were either the rich—almost the very rich—or the poor. The well-to-do employed the tourist agencies who provided comfort at a price. The very poor, mostly pilgrims from Russia and other lands of the Orthodox Church, or from Egypt, were more accustomed to discomfort. For them their communities provided hospices, sometimes barely furnished and with inadequate food arrangements. Since the British Occupation, however, there has been a great change. The rich still come as tourists, and the poor as pilgrims. But there is an intermediate class, larger than either, from Europe and especially from America—school teachers, clergymen, and their friends. Their means are limited, but adequate, and accommodation and other amenities, not very different from those to which they are accustomed in their own homes, are now provided to satisfy this class. A new luxury hotel has been opened in Jerusalem; several good third-class hotels have been opened in all parts of the country—Jerusalem, Haifa, Tel Aviv, even Jericho and some of the larger Jewish villages. Shipping companies also provide for this new business, with special rates for parties of visitors, and special vessels to take large parties direct to Haifa, which is also included as a port of call for many cruising parties in the eastern Mediterranean. Moreover, the journey to Palestine is much quicker than thirty years ago. By sea from England it used to take eleven or twelve days, even if the first part was made overland to Marseilles or Brindisi; now, in peace-time, it takes six days, by sea or by rail through Europe and Anatolia by the Bosporus; and those who wish to travel by air can do so at about the cost of a first-class steamship fare, by three or four different lines, in two or three days (pp. 392-5).

### Trends of Industry

One noticeable trend of industry during the past twenty years has been the almost complete disappearance of work in the home, except among the beduin, and with it the native crafts. Only embroidery and basket-weaving remain (p. 167). Industry is now concentrated in workshops, many of them very small, and in factories, none very large. Traditional methods of manufacture have almost entirely given way to machine production. The factory system, with an accompanying proletariat, has entered the national and social economy, and is extending. The Zionist aim, a large Jewish population, can only be fulfilled by increasing industrialization, without which the capacity of the country to absorb immigrants is very limited. Industrialization can only succeed if there is a wide expansion of the export trade, progress in which has hitherto been slow.

The export value of manufactured goods, apart from food, drink, and tobacco, is given below. The figures include those for potash and bromine, the increase in which is reflected in the most recent years:

| | | | | | | | |
|---|---|---|---|---|---|---|---|
| 1930 | . | . | £365,350 | 1936 | . | . | £417,078 |
| 1931 | . | . | 280,438 | 1937 | . | . | 558,753 |
| 1932 | . | . | 312,392 | 1938 | . | . | 639,604 |
| 1933 | . | . | 306,092 | 1939 | . | . | 765,255 |
| 1934 | . | . | 294,243 | 1940 | . | . | 1,715,792 |
| 1935 | . | . | 370,184 | 1941 | . | . | 1,863,602 |

But the greater part of Palestine's products is consumed within the country, and development of industry has been limited hitherto by the capacity of internal consumption.

By assistance, direct and indirect, and by general encouragement, the British administration has taken a considerable part in the development of industry. Improved means of communication, which have put an end to industrial immobility, are described in Chapter XIII. By the reform of the fiscal system, uneconomic or vexatious imposts have been abolished and taxation modified. For instance, all manufactured imports which compete with local manufactures are subject to almost prohibitive duties, but machinery and raw materials used in local industry are invariably admitted duty free. A very large range of tariffs, calculated always to benefit local industries, takes the place of the Ottoman system of a flat rate of import duty. A similar policy has been followed in dealing with taxes on agriculture, thereby lightening the burden on the land and its cultivators.

Another development during the past twenty years has been progress in mechanical engineering and transport, mainly among the new Jewish population. Some machinery was already used in Palestine in the last years of Ottoman rule, but little compared with the subsequent increase. The expansion of trade between Palestine and its neighbours, which before 1918 were parts of one state, has been attributed chiefly to motor transport. For instance, Baghdad, which used to be twenty days' journey by camel-caravan from Jerusalem, can now be reached within twenty-four hours by car.

Yet another element in industrial expansion has been the passion for economic self-sufficiency, which has shown itself especially among the Jewish population. It appears in the *Tozereth Haaretz* movement, a nationalist but short-sighted doctrine which preaches purchase only within the community, or at most only within the country, even at a higher price for an inferior article. Fortunately the practice is not universal; but it has given support, probably only temporary, to local industry. The influx of a new European population has also changed the type of goods required, and new-comers have seized the opportunity to meet the new demands by manufacture within the country. The capital invested in the country for immigrants —often in the form of machinery and raw material—and the previous experience of many in European industry, have also added incentive to local manufacture. For those without capital there was often a Jewish institution to supply it from abroad.

## Labour

Labour problems are more complicated in Palestine than in most other countries. This is perhaps inevitable in a small land with two separate peoples with distinct histories, social customs, standards of living, and outlooks on life. Among one and a half million human beings, social and cultural gradations range from those of the desert nomad to those of the Marxist socialist. In both these classes, as in those outside them, there are men and women freely offering their labour for hire, and others, though impatient of employers and of the wage system, are forced by circumstances to do so, even though they pretend to themselves that they are independent of employers.

It is impossible to estimate closely the number of wage-earners in Palestine. Very many Jews and Arabs are dependent entirely on wages, but there are also among the Arabs many cultivators, tenants, and even owners of land, whose holdings are too small to support themselves and their families, and who therefore have to enter the labour market at certain seasons. Among Jews this class is much smaller, and it is not made up by individual small holders, but by members of co-operative agricultural groups, whose land is insufficient to support the group, and whose members must therefore supplement the common earnings by work outside. Similarly, there are industrial co-operative groups, whose members accept employment only as a body, and who are in a sense co-operative contractors, though their status and earnings put them on the level of other working men.

Among the Arabs, and to a much less extent among the Jews, there are women and children who only work for hire in times of harvest or of economic necessity. This last cause also produces, especially among the Jews in the towns, a class of small shopkeepers and skilled artisans, hitherto working independently, who are compelled by circumstances to close their shops and take to labour, hoping to rise again to their former status when conditions change.

All such labour is generally paid by time, though piece-work pay has become customary in certain industries and trades. Contract-labour is widespread in the Jewish building-trade, and to a relatively small extent in factories. There is little difference between the wages of Arab and Jewish skilled artisans, and they are relatively high; but unskilled Jews are paid more highly than unskilled Arabs, and oriental Jews receive less wages than European, who are highly organized. European Jewish labour has also secured other advantages, such as the eight-hour day, and contributions have to be paid by employers to the medical fund of the General Federation of Jewish Labour. The differing rates of pay, corresponding to local standards of living, have led to much friction between Jewish employers and their men.

*Histadrut Ha-Ovdim.* The Trade Union movement, known as the *Histadrut*, or *Histadrut Ha-Ovdim* (the General Federation of Jewish Labour), is very strong and has very great control over labour conditions. Few Jewish employers are powerful enough to be independent of the Histadrut, which derives support from the Jewish Agency, in effect controls it, and is therefore strong enough to win almost every contest with the employers. There were in 1942 about 126,000 members of the Histadrut, that is, about three-quarters of the eligible population.[1] In accepting this statement it must be remembered that many who would be ineligible for membership of a British trade union, such as housewives, farmers, and professional men, are eligible to join the Histadrut, and many do so from nationalist rather than economic motives. The Histadrut in fact aims to become a nationalist-socialist commonwealth, and to that end strives to attract all the non-capitalist elements in the population. It has not yet succeeded in this, and therefore compromises at present with political elements outside. For instance, when employment is scarce and unemployment widespread it secures control of labour requirements, and distributes them among the several political parties in accordance with their size.

The Histadrut embraces both local trade unions and national trade and professional bodies. Membership is strictly limited to Jews, although the organization of Arab labour on parallel lines has been unsuccessfully attempted. Apart from the political and social difficulties, the cardinal principle of the Histadrut, that Jewish employers must employ only Jewish labourers who are members of the organization, must render any co-operation between Jewish and Arab labour impossible, although large employers and many planters still employ Arabs as well as Jews. The Histadrut is especially strong on its co-operative side: it prefers its members to combine into groups and for these groups to hire their labour *en gros*, rather than to accept employment as individuals.

[1] In 1937 about 97,000 of the 112,000 Jewish working men and women in Palestine were, according to a government memorandum, members of the Histadrut.

The approximate membership figures given by the Histadrut were as follows. These include small shopkeepers, professional men, &c.:

| | Members of workers' settlements | Jewish workers in towns | in villages |
|---|---|---|---|
| 1926 | 2,678 | 18,067 | 4,442 |
| 1937 | 14,059 | 63,283 | 26,780 |
| 1938 | 16,500 | 68,500 | 26,500 |
| 1939 | 20,000 | 74,000 | 27,000 |
| 1940 | 22,000 | 77,000 | 25,000 |

The Histadrut owns and controls marketing and trading organizations, both for sale and purchase, a bank, an insurance company, an agricultural settlement society, its own daily newspaper, theatre, sports club, and scout movement. It now has its separate school system, which enjoys considerable independence; and its own labour exchanges, through which it imposes its own conditions. The *Am Oved* is its publication society. The *Solel Boneh* is a contracting organization, the largest in Palestine, which competes successfully with private contractors, since it always has labour available to hire, if necessary at a loss which can be made good elsewhere; it has also acquired ownership of some factories which were in financial difficulty.

Funds are contributed by members, by grants from the Jewish Agency, and by sympathizers abroad. A number of employers subscribe to the *Kupat Holim*, the country-wide health organization of the Histadrut, with two hospitals, dental clinics, and laboratories. There are also separate funds for other purposes, such as unemployment relief.

Of all Jewish organizations in Palestine, therefore, the Histadrut is by far the most powerful, though it is difficult to say whether it really represents the best interests of the Jewish population. Its opponents are loosely organized or not organized at all. There are two or three other labour groups, all small, formed also more on political than on economic grounds. Of these the principal is the National Labour Organization, one of the instruments of the Revisionist or New Zionist Party, between which and the Jewish Agency and the Histadrut there is ideological war. The National Labour Organization claims to put Jewish national interests above socialist principles, and competes with the General Federation in all fields of labour activity, both rural and urban, at non-union rates of pay. In this policy they have been supported by certain influential orange-growers, organized as the Jewish Farmers' Federation, and to some extent by employers in urban districts. This support has been forthcoming chiefly as a means of defence against the General Federation, which has not hesitated to use the strike as a weapon against employers.

Disputes between workers and their employers are not infrequent, and are as a rule accompanied by suspension of work. Most have an economic basis, but some have been caused by Jewish members of the Histadrut attempting to exclude Arab labour from Jewish undertakings. In the British Government's *Report to the League of Nations, 1933*, the principal causes of strikes in Jewish undertakings are given as (1) an eight-hour day; (2) standard wage-rates; (3) recognition of the union and its claim to represent labour; (4) the union's right to recruit labour, and (5) to approve dismissal of workers; (6) annual holidays with pay; (7) accident insurance; (8) contributions by employers to workers' sick funds.

*Labour Legislation.* Labour legislation in Palestine is necessarily in an early stage. This is inevitable not only on account of the elementary standard reached by a large part of the population, and the consequent risk of legislating ahead of it, but also of the uncertain position of Palestine industry, and the consequent necessity of avoiding risk of danger to it. In two major directions the position of the worker has been safeguarded. The one covers workmen's compensation. Under the terms of the ordinance, which have been extended from time to time, compensation is payable to workmen injured or killed while employed in certain selected trades. Manual labourers earning up to £350 per annum are covered, but the ordinance does not apply to all industries. Within these limitations the lines of British legislation are generally followed.

The Industrial Employment of Women and Children Ordinance prohibits the employment of women and children in dangerous occupations, and the employment of children under 12 in any circumstances.[1] Children between 12 and 16 may be employed for not more than eight hours a day, and of these hours not more than five may be consecutive. Children may not be employed between 7 p.m. and 6 a.m. or women between 10 p.m. and 5 a.m. The Prevention of Intimidation Ordinance prohibits the intimidation of workmen, especially in the course of labour disputes. The Fencing of Machinery Ordinance requires the fencing of dangerous machinery, and the Steam Boilers Ordinance the inspection of steam boilers and prime movers. The Regulation of Trades and Industries Ordinance safeguards the health and safety of workers in certain dangerous trades.

In view of the considerable power secured by the Histadrut in Jewish industry and agriculture, and the almost universal application of the eight-hour day and six-day week, no legislation laying down the maximum hours of labour for adults has been found necessary. For the Arab section of the population, which is accustomed to work not too intensively from dawn to dusk, with a long interval at midday, there is no demand for legislation on similar

---

[1] A generous extension of this legislation has for some time been under the consideration of Government.

lines. Similarly the health insurance system of the Histadrut covers practically the whole body of Jewish workers. In times of unemployment there are the Unemployment Fund of the Histadrut and other Jewish funds in case of need, and the Government has always given assistance in the form of relief or of work. In the latter half of the year 1939, after unsuccessful attempts over a long period, 'joint labour exchanges' were established by the Jewish Agency in twenty-two villages of the coastal plain. Similar exchanges established by the Histadrut in those villages and elsewhere had long been in existence, but had been looked on with suspicion both by employers and by labour outside the Histadrut. The avowed intention of the new exchanges was to abolish the virtual monopoly of employment for members of the Histadrut. In only one of the new exchanges, however, did the employers participate. As a body they continued to look on them with suspicion. These new institutions are more than labour exchanges. They consider it their function to fix rates of wages and to ration employment when there is not sufficient for all. The labour exchange of Tel Aviv, the largest of all, which has municipal recognition, is reserved for members of the Histadrut.

In 1942 the Labour Department, which had in 1924 been merged into the Department of Migration, was reconstituted independently by the Government.

## CHAPTER XI

# BANKING, FINANCE, AND COMMERCE

## BANKING

BANKS in Palestine are classified broadly as Local Banks and Foreign Banks. The former are incorporated in Palestine, the latter abroad, though one at least of these, the Anglo-Palestine Bank, does most of its business in Palestine.

Until 1936 the local banking system was much abused. Local banks were, and still are, of three main types: (*a*) credit banks, the prime object of which is to lend money on the security of immovable property; (*b*) credit co-operative banks, which are subject to the regulations of the Co-operative Societies Ordinance, and whose main purpose is, or should be, to promote the economic interests of their members in accordance with co-operative principles; and (*c*) commercial banks, which 'carry on banking business or use the title of *bank* or any of its derivatives, as part of the title under which they carry on business'. The business dealings of the co-operative banks are mostly only with their members, although many of them accept deposits from others.

Many so-called 'banks', particularly of the commercial class, were not banks in the sense of the term as used in England. Some dealt mainly, if not entirely, in lottery-tickets; others, with little capital, loaned money at high rates of interest against little security, money collected from the issue of debentures and from deposits obtained by offering higher interest than was justified by the money market. In 1934 the average paid-up capital per local bank was less than £10,000; with many the paid-up capital, and even the nominal, was as low as £1,000. One had only £17 paid up.

In 1936 the Government stepped in with legislation. Since that year no institution has been permitted to use the title of 'bank' unless its nominal capital amounts to at least £50,000, of which £25,000 must be paid up. Frequent periodical statements of assets, liabilities, and other business information are now required. The result has been that the number of banks operating in Palestine has fallen from 76 in 1936 to 27 at the end of 1941.

The banks cover a wide field of activity, and the principal banks have branches in important trading-centres. Short-term loans to trade and industry are far more common than long-term. Relatively the credit co-operatives play a larger part than do the banks in the credit structure. Rural co-operative societies supply credit to agriculture and are themselves financed mainly by the larger banks, including a 'central bank of co-operative institutions'. Nevertheless, long-term credit for agriculture is inadequate, despite the establishment of the Agricultural Mortgage Company in 1935, which had government support.

In 1941 there were 223 registered credit co-operative societies, 115 Arab, 107 Jewish, and one other. The establishment and direction of the Jewish co-operative societies have been under the control of institutions and men with considerable experience in Europe; for the Arabs such work is undertaken by the Government.

Foreign banks which operate in Palestine often have their principal business abroad and are much more stable than local banks. The interest rates charged and paid differ as between foreign and local banks and among local banks themselves. As a rule, rates of foreign banks are lower than those of local; and the smaller the local bank, the higher the interest paid on deposits and charged for loans. The clients of such small local banks are generally those who cannot give sufficient security to obtain advances from the larger and more stable banks.

The differences are considerable. For instance, during the early months of 1936 foreign banks were paying $\frac{1}{2}$ per cent. on demand deposits and $1\frac{1}{2}$ per cent. on deposits up to six months, whereas local banks were paying $2\frac{1}{2}$ per cent. and from $3\frac{1}{2}$ to 4 per cent. respectively. At the same period foreign banks were charging 6 per cent. on loans, local banks 8 or $8\frac{1}{2}$ per cent., the maximum legal rate being 9 per cent.

A Post Office Savings Bank was opened in 1942.

## Currency

Before the British occupation Palestine was included in the Ottoman monetary system. Its currency was nominally Turkish, but the relationship between one coin and another differed in northern and southern Palestine. Thus in Jaffa 141 piastres went to one lira, in Gaza 255, and in Jerusalem only 124, though in theory the lira was equivalent to 100 piastres everywhere. With the arrival of the British army Egyptian currency was introduced—one Egyptian pound (£1. 0s. 6d. sterling) equals 100 piastres: one piastre equals 10 milliemes—and remained the legal tender in Palestine until February 1927, when a Palestine currency, based directly on sterling, was introduced. Officially the only units are the pound and the mil, and one Palestinian pound, or 1,000 mils, is equal to one pound sterling; but a 10-mil coin is generally known as a piastre. There are bronze, nickel, and silver coins. From 500 mils (10 shillings) upwards currency notes are employed.

In February 1927 the amount of Egyptian currency in Palestine was about £E1,900,000. Three years later Palestine currency was little over 2 million pounds; thereafter it rose rapidly to 4 millions in 1934, 8½ millions in 1940, £13,900,000 in July 1941, and £27,500,000 in April 1943. There were, however, some violent fluctuations in the interval. For instance, the attack by Italy on Abyssinia in September 1935, and a consequent run on the banks in Palestine, raised the currency in circulation from £5,835,135 on 31 August to £7,520,135 a month later.

The control and administration of currency is vested in the Palestine Currency Board, appointed by the Secretary of State for the Colonies and sitting in London. The value of the investments of the Currency Board, which serve as cover for the currency in circulation together with its other assets, has kept pace with the currency, and the Board has made yearly contributions to the Palestine treasury from its profits. These contributions began in 1930 with £10,000, and rose in 1936 to £115,000, but have since declined.

## PUBLIC FINANCE

Until the disturbances of 1936 Palestine was in no respect a financial burden on the British Exchequer. In one or two years revenue fell short of expenditure, but the deficit was made good out of accumulated surplus from preceding years. By 31 March 1936 there was an accumulated surplus of £6,267,810, after transferring £1,591,939 to the current account of capital expenditure, a sum originally intended to be met by borrowing. Since 1936, however, the position has changed: expenditure has always exceeded revenue, and since 1938–1939 the British Treasury has had to assist with large grants-in-aid. This situation has been caused less by reduced revenue than by increased expenditure, mostly spent on public security and ancillary objects, a direct consequence of the unsettled state of the country. The figures of revenue and expenditure since 1920–1921 and of British Treasury grants-in-aid are shown on page 282. It will be noted that the sums granted up to the year 1937–1938 were mainly for the upkeep of the Transjordan Frontier Force. The figures show the effects on revenue of the depressions of 1922–1925, 1927–1929, and 1930–1932.

*Revenue.* The principal sources of revenue inherited from the Ottoman regime were, in rural districts, the *werko* (land tax), the · tithe, and the animal tax; and in the towns the *werko* (house and land tax) and the *tamattu*, a tax on members of certain professions and callings. There were also indirect taxes on imports and exports, excise duties on wines and liquors, monopolies on salt and tobacco, and fees or stamp-duties on licences, transfers, and so on. Some of the receipts were allotted to the Ottoman Public Debt administration.

| Year | Revenue | Grants-in-aid* (included in foregoing) | Expenditure | Surplus (+) or Deficit (−) |
|---|---|---|---|---|
| 1920–1 (9 months) | 1,136,951 | .. | 1,259,587 | −122,636 |
| 1921–2 | 2,371,531 | .. | 1,929,341 | +442,190 |
| 1922–3 | 1,809,831 | 295,000 | 1,884,280 | −74,449 |
| 1923–4 | 1,675,788 | 240,622 | 1,675,105 | +683 |
| 1924–5 | 2,154,946 | 195,126 | 1,852,985 | +301,961 |
| 1925–6 | 2,809,324 | 204,878 | 2,092,647 | +716,677 |
| 1926–7 | 2,451,365 | 86,476 | 2,123,568 | +327,797 |
| 1927–8 | 2,358,365 | 30,345 (Apl.–Dec. 1927) | 2,700,414 | −342,049 |
| 1928–9 | 2,497,011 | 35,797 (1928) | 2,997,750 | −500,739 |
| 1929–30 | 2,355,623 | 24,523 (1929) | 2,245,989 | +109,634 |
| 1930–1 | 2,462,304 | 41,286 (1930) | 2,567,671 | −105,367 |
| 1931–2 | 2,354,696 | 250,643† | 2,377,625 | −22,929 |
| 1932–3 | 3,015,917 | 127,788 | 2,516,394 | +499,523 |
| 1933–4 | 3,985,492 | 137,760 | 2,704,856 | +1,280,636 |
| 1934–5 | 5,452,633 | 141,368 | 3,230,010 | +2,222,623 |
| 1935–6 | 5,770,457 | 140,345 | 4,236,202 | +1,534,255 |
| 1936–7 | 4,640,821 | 139,686 | 6,073,502 | −1,432,681 |
| 1937–8 | 4,897,356 | 140,533 | 7,331,646 | −2,434,290 |
| 1938–9 | 5,937,280 | 1,689,516 | 5,804,854 | +132,426 |
| 1939–40 | 6,868,227‡ | 2,133,392 | 6,004,738 | +863,489 |
| 1940–1 | 8,441,899 | 3,263,868 | 7,450,355 | +991,544 |
| 1941–2 | 8,325,552 | 2,098,601 | 7,463,601 | +861,951 |

\* Until and including the year 1937–8 these grants were mainly for the Transjordan Frontier Force.

† Fifteen months.

‡ Includes £99,875 for appreciation of investments.

Gradually the whole of this fiscal system has been swept away. The monopolies and the *tamattu* were the first to go. Import duties have been remodelled till the system is now unrecognizable to those acquainted with the old regime. The tithe—12½ per cent. under Ottoman rule—has been commuted or very greatly reduced; the practice of tithe-farming was abolished at once by the British military authorities. Taxation of land and real property has been revolutionized. But perhaps the most significant change has been the introduction in September 1941 of the income tax, though on a very moderate scale compared with British standards.

The largest source of revenue is the Import duty, which serves to some extent as an index of immigration, every new European or American immigrant increasing, at least temporarily, the demand for foreign goods. A more satisfactory index of financial and speculative activity is the revenue from fees for land registration and survey. These are shown graphically on fig. 35.

*Expenditure* has been classified broadly under five headings: (*a*) Defence, (*b*) Administration and Finance, (*c*) Legal Services, (*d*) Social Services, (*e*) Development and Economic Services. Defence includes, and is in practice identical with, public security, and has for some years been by far the largest single item of the five. The expenditure on defence chargeable to the Palestinian budget for the period 1931 to March 1942 has been:[1]

|  | £ |  | £ |
|---|---|---|---|
| 1931 | 591,197 | 1936–7 | 2,041,619 |
| 1932 (Jan.–Mar.) | 148,175 | 1937–8 | 1,731,713 |
| 1932 (Apr.)–1933 (Mar.) | 580,964 | 1938–9 | 1,356,246 |
| 1933–4 | 596,730 | 1939–40 | 1,647,396 |
| 1934–5 | 650,930 | 1940–1 | 1,789,000 |
| 1935–6 | 672,756 | 1941–2 (est.) | 2,211,400 |

By the terms of the Treaty of Lausanne a share of the Ottoman Public Debt was taken over by Palestine. This amounted to £T4,577,667, and the charges on it were paid in the early years of the mandatory regime out of revenue. The sum paid in Palestine currency was £813,248.

In 1927 a loan of £4,475,000, guaranteed by the British Government, was raised for the purchase of the railway constructed by the British military authorities during the occupation, for the construction of Haifa harbour, and for other capital purposes. The interest on the loan was at 5 per cent. and it was repayable between 1942 and 1967. In November 1942 this loan was redeemed, being replaced to the extent of £1,750,000 by a new 3 per cent. guaranteed stock redeemable from 1962 to 1967. A balance of £1,850,000 was offered to the public for cash. In the course of 1942 the Palestine Government

[1] The figures exclude the cost of the British army stationed in Palestine and of the Transjordan Frontier Force, which is not borne by Palestine.

issued a series of Defence Bonds in multiples of £5, bearing 3 per cent. interest and redeemable after seven years at 101 per cent. At the same time Palestine savings certificates costing 750 mils (15s.) each and valid for ten years were issued. The redemption value of these certificates is £1. 0s. 6d. and the maximum number

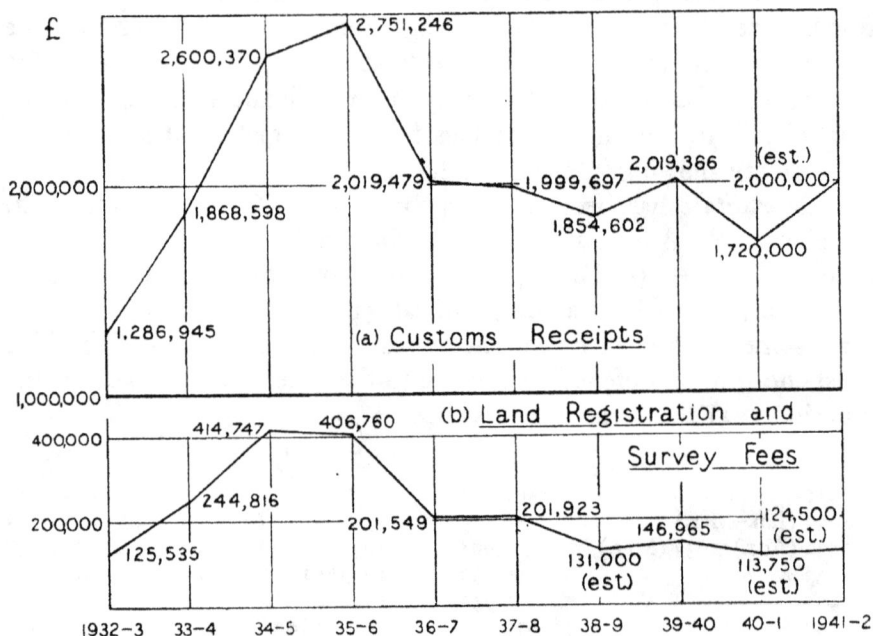

FIG. 35. *Revenue from* (a) *Customs Receipts, and* (b) *Land Fees*

that may be held by any individual is 500. The proceeds of this issue are lent to the British Government.

## COMMERCE

During the later period of the Ottoman Empire Palestine was an agricultural country and willing to remain so. Exports were from the produce of the land—oranges, wine, soap, and oil—and imports were chiefly manufactured goods for the European population, which, though not considerable, was already growing because of Jewish immigration (pp. 177–81). Separate figures for the imports and exports of Palestine during the Ottoman period are not known, but by far the greater part of this commerce passed through Jaffa, and the figures for that port are available. These show a fairly steady increase in the value of exports from £322,000 in 1903 to £745,000 in 1913, mostly to the United Kingdom and Egypt, and a similar rise in the value of imports from £440,000 in 1903 to £1,313,000 in 1913, mainly from Austria-Hungary, the United Kingdom, and to a less extent from France and Russia. In every year the value of imports exceeded that of exports, though to no very marked extent. According to one authority[1] the figures for the whole of Palestine in 1913 were: exports £1,121,025 and imports £1,657,435; but it is uncertain how this figure was reached in view of the fact that there were no land frontiers.

The development of commerce under British administration cannot be better illustrated than by quoting the corresponding figures from 1922 to 1941 (specie and re-exports are excluded).

| | Imports | Exports | | | | Imports | Exports |
|---|---|---|---|---|---|---|---|
| 1922 . | . 5,724,238 | 1,388,070 | 1932 . | | . | 7,768,920 | 2,381,491 |
| 1923 . | . 4,948,907 | 1,172,548 | 1933 . | | . | 11,123,489 | 2,591,617 |
| 1924 . | . 5,401,384 | 1,231,602 | 1934 . | | . | 15,152,781 | 3,217,562 |
| 1925 . | . 7,526,657 | 1,330,830 | 1935 . | | . | 17,853,493 | 4,215,486 |
| 1926 . | . 6,594,098 | 1,308,333 | 1936 . | | . | 13,979,023 | 3,625,233 |
| 1927 . | . 6,184,454 | 1,899,759 | 1937 . | | . | 15,903,666 | 5,813,536 |
| 1928 . | . 6,770,818 | 1,487,207 | 1938 . | | . | 11,356,963 | 5,020,368 |
| 1929 . | . 7,166,593 | 1,554,262 | 1939 . | | . | 14,632,822 | 5,117,769 |
| 1930 . | . 6,958,258 | 1,896,095 | 1940 . | | . | 11,035,454 | 4,072,823 |
| 1931 . | . 5,940,000 | 1,572,061 | 1941 . | | . | 13,324,983 | 4,216,256 |

Several factors have combined to encourage this expansion. First among them perhaps is the remarkable development of internal and external communications, and of the harbour and port of Haifa. An equally important factor is the great increase in population, with its large European element, mainly Jews, bringing with them industrial and commercial experience, energy, capital, and a greater demand for foreign products.

### The Balance of Trade

It will be seen that the adverse balance of trade has grown considerably. When Palestine was part of the Ottoman Empire the adverse balance was relatively unimportant, for the economics of Palestine were of little significance to that empire or to any other. Since 1920 Palestine has had to stand alone. The population, their needs, and also the risks of foreign trade, have considerably increased. An adverse balance of over 10 million pounds, as occurred from 1934 to 1937, often more than twice the total value of the export trade,

---

[1] A. P. C. Clark, *Annals of the American Academy of Political and Social Sciences,* vol. clxiv, p. 95.

must be a matter of deep concern, and there is no complete information as to how the gap is filled. One contribution, which may be large in times of disturbance and small in those of quiet, is the expenditure from British funds by military authorities and by officers and men from their pay. At one time it was thought that tourists made an appreciable contribution; but when the Government obtained figures of expenditure by visitors to Palestine and by Palestinian residents abroad, it was found that here again the balance was adverse; and, in fact, since the stream of rich visitors dried up about the year 1931, the tourist traffic has ceased to be generally remunerative.

A considerable item affecting favourably the balance of trade, and therefore to be classed as an 'invisible export', is the large sum contributed by Jewish, Christian, and even by Moslem bodies outside Palestine for charitable, educational, and religious objects within the country. Prominent are the contributions to various Zionist funds. There have always been many Jews in Palestine dependent on foreign charity or on assistance from relatives abroad; the total amount received by them must at times have been appreciable, but it has varied, and with robbery of European Jews by Germany in recent years it has been greatly reduced. It is even claimed that for some years past more money has gone from Jews in Palestine to impoverished relatives in Europe, sometimes in the form of ransom or blackmail, than has been received by them from abroad. Some recent settlers in Palestine still have foreign investments, to the interest or dividends on which they are entitled. But the total amount received cannot be very large, and must be diminishing, especially since the outbreak of war.

The financial and economic crisis in other countries, especially America, which occurred in the early thirties, was undoubtedly reflected by the decrease of remittances sent by Palestinian settlers abroad to their families at home, and by the smaller sums brought by them when they returned. There is now no immigration to America from Palestine, and there has been none for ten years, so that this form of capital contribution from America has ceased.

All these items, which may be classed as income, together with grants-in-aid by the British Government, and profits on investments held by the Currency Board (p. 281) and by the Government, have helped to fill the gap between imports and exports. The balance comes in the form of capital investment, which is possibly the largest single item. In the twenties there was not only an increase of immigration in the so-called 'capitalist class', but there was foreign investment in industry, in citriculture, or in loans on mortgage, which has sometimes reached a high figure, though it has not been accurately assessed. There is, or was until recently, no obligation on the immigrant to transfer his capital to Palestine, so long as he could satisfy the immigration authorities that he owned the qualifying

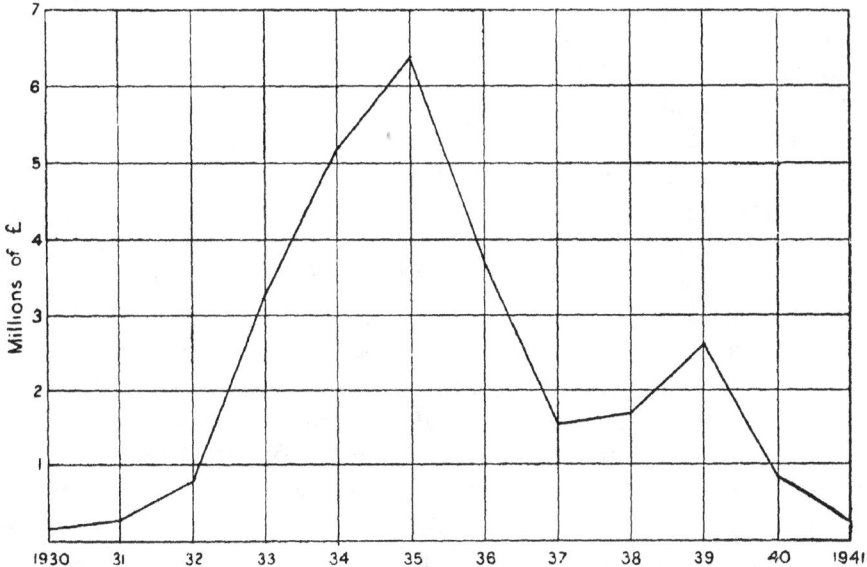

FIG. 36. *Capital brought into Palestine (average £1,000 per 'Capitalist' Immigrant Family)*

amount of capital, £1,000. Many immigrants—at one time the proportion was estimated at 25 per cent.—secured certificates as 'capitalists' without being in bona-fide possession of that sum. On the other hand, some immigrants own considerably more than £1,000, so that, by assuming this sum as an average per immigrant family, it is possible to arrive at rough totals of capital brought in during recent years. These are shown on fig. 36.

*Capital brought into Palestine by Immigrants*
*(average £1,000 per family)*

| 1930 | . | £191,000 | 1934 | . | £5,193,000 | 1938 | . | £1,771,000 |
|------|---|----------|------|---|------------|------|---|------------|
| 1931 | . | 269,000 | 1935 | . | 6,398,000 | 1939 | . | 2,623,000 |
| 1932 | . | 754,000 | 1936 | ' | 3,693,000 | 1940 | . | 819,000 |
| 1933 | . | 3,267,000 | 1937 | . | 1,545,000 | 1941 | . | 322,000 |

It is impossible to give an estimate of how much money is invested by residents or immigrants in Palestine; but it is interesting to compare fig. 36 with fig. 32 (p. 267), from which it is apparent that some at least of the capital brought in is invested in building.

*System of Foreign Trade*

The import trade of Palestine is carried on through commission agents, general import merchants, agencies and branches of foreign firms, assisted by commercial travellers. Commission agents and import merchants share most of the business, but the latter, though still important, are losing ground to Palestinian agencies of foreign firms, which are often local merchants granted the sole handling of products of a particular foreign manufacturer. Such agents are expected to refrain from dealing in competing goods. The number of branches of foreign firms is very small, the volume of trade seldom justifying them. The large number of commission agents keeps the average volume of each business low, and there is no one agent among them who would be considered rich by European standards. The terms of payment vary, but German and Italian exporters were able until 1939 to secure a growing proportion of the import trade by granting more generous terms of credit than exporters of other countries. The Government makes purchases in England mainly through the Crown Agents for the Colonies.

As regards exports, the citrus trade, which in normal times amounts to at least 75 per cent. of the total, is in the hands of citrus marketing co-operatives and shipping merchants. More than half of it is in the hands of Jewish marketing societies. Concentration into fewer businesses was attempted, but the citrus crisis of recent years, caused by over-production and more limited markets, hit the trade very hard, and problems arising from the multiplicity of societies have to some extent solved themselves by liquidations. Arab citrus-growers rely on shipping merchants, not on societies. These make advances of cash to the grower in the early part of the year, in proportion to the prospective value of the crop.

Great Britain is by far the largest buyer of Palestine citrus fruit, and with her Palestine has in consequence a favourable balance of trade, the only one of any consequence. The Government, realizing the important place the citrus industry occupies in the economy of Palestine, has taken a special interest in it, especially since the danger of over-production became acute. Measures to deal with this danger have taken the form of prohibiting the export of immature fruit, and of fruit likely to damage the reputation abroad of the 'Jaffa orange'; of imposing a small special tax on the industry, to be devoted to the advertisement of Palestinian citrus abroad and to similar benefits; and, in recent years, of remitting taxation on orange growers.

The export of agricultural products, other than citrus, is conducted as a rule through export merchants. Manufactured goods are usually shipped by the manufacturers direct without intervention. The two principal manufacturers for export, and the only ones of consequence, are the Palestine Potash Company for potash and bromine, and Consolidated Refineries Limited for fuel-oil.

*Imports.* Imports are divided into four classes: (I) Food, drink, and tobacco; (II) Raw materials and articles mainly unmanufactured; (III) Articles wholly or mainly manufactured; and (IV) Miscellaneous and unclassified. In 1937 there was some rearrangement, when many items previously included in the last class were distributed among the others.

| | Class I | II | III | IV | Total |
|---|---|---|---|---|---|
| 1937 . | £4,148,000 | £1,608,000 | £10,090,000 | £58,000 | £15,904,000 |
| 1938 . | 3,209,000 | 1,138,000 | 6,979,000 | 31,000 | 11,357,000 |
| 1939 . | 3,756,000 | 1,481,000 | 9,362,000 | 34,000 | 14,633,000 |
| 1940 . | 3,478,000 | 1,819,000 | 5,724,000 | 15,000 | 11,036,000 |
| 1941 . | 4,629,000 | 2,641,000 | 5,859,000 | 195,000 | 13,324,000 |

It will be seen that between a half and two-thirds of the imports comprise manufactured goods, and generally one-tenth are raw materials. The principal imports in Class I are wheat, flour, cattle, sheep, and goats; in Class II, wood, seeds, &c., for the extraction of oil; in Class III, industrial machinery, wearing apparel, and cotton piece-goods. The United Kingdom is the principal supplier of imports, and after her in peace-time came Germany, Syria, and Romania. An appreciable part of the goods supplied by the United Kingdom were, however, stores and equipment for the government and military services, and for the Iraq Petroleum Company, for which Britain has a monopoly. In four years, from 1934 to 1937, these averaged nearly half the imports from Britain.

### Value of Imports from Certain Countries

#### (Thousands of £)

| Country of origin | 1937 | 1938 | 1939 | 1940 | 1941 |
|---|---|---|---|---|---|
| United Kingdom . | 2,519 | 1,496 | 2,391 | 2,419 | 3,620 |
| British possessions . | 731 | 726 | 896 | 1,300 | 3,267 |
| Germany . . . | 2,628 | 1,645 | 1,622 | 166 | 14 |
| Syria . . . | 1,374 | 1,015 | 1,355 | 502 | 395 |
| Romania . . . | 1,372 | 1,253 | 1,200 | 938 | 64 |
| U.S.A. . . . | 1,099 | 969 | 1,953 | 1,152 | 1,161 |

During the earlier years quoted, imports from Germany received an artificial encouragement from the arrangement whereby Jewish immigrants from Germany were permitted to take with them capital only in the form of German goods, often only personal effects, which was the largest single item on the import list from Germany. Other imports from that country were chiefly iron girders, pipes, machinery, drugs, and medicines. Those from Romania included cattle, poultry, timber for building and for citrus packing-cases, and fuel-oil; and from the U.S.A., motor-cars, wheat flour, apples, and frigidaires.

*Exports.* These are divided into the same four classes as Imports, the figures for 1937 and subsequent years being approximately as follows:

|  | Class I | II | III | IV | Total |
|---|---|---|---|---|---|
| 1937 | 4,875,000 | 377,000 | 559,000 | 2,000 | 5,814,000 |
| 1938 | 4,172,000 | 208,000 | 640,000 | 774 | 5,020,000 |
| 1939 | 4,192,000 | 159,000 | 765,000 | 1,300 | 5,118,000 |
| 1940 | 1,702,000 | 135,000 | 277,000* | 547 | 2,115,000 |
| 1941 | 514,000 | 315,000 | 533,000* | 750 | 1,163,000 |

* The figures for 1940 and 1941 exclude those for the exports of potash, bromine, and mineral oil.

The chief markets of Palestine are the United Kingdom, Syria, and Holland. Egypt was at one time second on the list, taking more than 20 per cent. of the total exports, but a change in Egypt's fiscal policy imposing increased import duties on Palestinian products has reduced the proportion to 2 per cent. It is noticeable that the exports of products in Class I (food, drink, and tobacco) make up more than four-fifths of the exports, and citrus fruits are by far the largest item in the class. Nearly 98 per cent. of the exports into the United Kingdom are citrus fruit; Syria is the second largest exporter from Palestine; and Holland, until she was overrun by Germany, was the third.

The *transit trade* of Palestine developed appreciably with the commercial opening of the desert route to Iraq and Persia in 1935, when it rose in value to £482,000 from £239,000 in the previous year. It had already risen by about 27 per cent. in 1934, when Haifa harbour came fully into use. The average annual value of the transit trade from 1927 to 1931 was only £181,000.

## Tariff Policy

The tariff policy of Palestine is governed by Article 18 of the Mandate which lays down equality of treatment in fiscal, commercial, and similar matters for the nationals of all members of the League of Nations. Under a separate instrument, citizens of the United States of America were given similar privileges and it was found that when, for instance, Japan withdrew from the League of Nations, she was entitled under treaties previously made with the Government of the United Kingdom to 'most favoured nation treatment' wherever that Government was in control. To this rule there was one exception. Under Article 18 special customs agreements could be made 'with any state, the territory of which in 1914 was wholly included in Asiatic Turkey or Arabia'.

Under Ottoman rule there was a flat import duty of 11 per cent. on all imports from foreign countries. The Palestine Government at first retained this practice, except that a few commodities—settlers' effects, agricultural machinery, seeds—were exempted from duty, and that the import duties on certain building materials were considerably reduced and those on other items—tea, sugar, petrol, &c.— increased, but only for revenue purposes. Goods from Turkey and Egypt were placed on the same level as those from other countries. The only country that was treated exceptionally was Syria, formerly included in Asiatic Turkey. By a mutual agreement the local products of the two countries were exempted from all import duties.

In 1924, however, *ad valorem* duties were in a number of cases substituted for specific ones and the general uniformity of duties was thereby broken up, but the principle of no preference for any country was retained. The number of exempted items was increased, and where import duty was retained the specific rate was raised to 12 per cent. There had been a 1 per cent. export duty on all goods in Turkish days. This was retained until 1926, when it was abolished except for antiquities. In 1927 there were further changes, and the import tariff became definitely protective. The demand for this came from the numerous small manufacturers who had arisen in Palestine and from their supporters. The result of the changes made in that year has been (a) to relieve from duties, sometimes by means of drawbacks, all raw material used in manufacture, and (b) to impose heavy import duties on manufactured imports that compete with local manufactures. With certain articles these duties are in normal times prohibitive. The import of matches ceased altogether. Almost all import of cement was prevented, except at the period of the great building development (1932–5), when the one local factory found itself unable to satisfy the demand, forcing the building trade to pay almost any price that was asked (fig. 34). The special arrangement with Syria continued for some years, but the interests that had pressed for the introduction of a general protective tariff succeeded there also in the end, and the free trade between these two countries that had existed for centuries was brought to an end in 1939, and a system of preferential tariffs was substituted. The agreement with Iraq of February 1937, whereby imports from that country were given preferential rates and certain other concessions were granted, remained unchanged. These concessions more than doubled the trade with Iraq, which nevertheless is still not very considerable.

Despite this policy of protective tariffs, the import of manufactured goods has continued to grow. Doubtless a number of industries, for the most part small, have derived some benefit and managed to survive with the Government's assistance, but only with difficulty because of the many advantages enjoyed by competing foreign manufactures. Few of the protected industries can indeed compete with imported articles as regards price and quality, though a notable exception is the Nesher Cement Company.

The two important problems that stand out from any consideration of Palestine's economy are the large adverse balance of trade covered wholly or in part by the import of capital, a necessarily temporary expedient, and the dependence on the export of citrus fruits, forming over 70 per cent. of all exports, of which a large proportion goes to one customer. The export of Dead Sea chemicals and of refined mineral oil is growing and may be expected to relieve the situation to some extent. But an economy that could support a larger population needs more resources than oil, which is dependent on foreign raw material, and potash, bromine, and oranges, the last of which have now for some years shown signs of over-production. It is unlikely that for a long time the other industries of Palestine will be able to do more than keep themselves alive, by helping, with the assistance of protective tariffs, to provide for the local population. One means of relief would be the freedom of Palestine trade from the restrictions of Article 18 of the Mandate, and this was recommended by the Royal Commission.

### Internal Trade

Palestine is an agricultural country. It may, however, also be described as a country of petty traders. It is doubtful whether in any other country there is a larger proportion of small town and village shopkeepers and hawkers. In 1931 there were in the whole of Palestine 33·7 consumers for every person engaged in trade; among the Jews 16·5. This figure has certainly not fallen in recent years. The United States of America showed 24·8 in 1920 and 20·2 in 1930.

According to the Report on the Census of 1931, of every 10,000 members of the urban population, 1,961 were dependent on trade. If the whole of the settled population is taken into consideration, the number is 998. Among the Jews the proportion is highest (21·9 %); then come Christians (18·6 %), and lastly Moslems (13·2 %). In the towns 20 per cent. of the population is supported by trade. Of the total number of traders, 36·8 per cent. were Jewish, although Jews then formed only 18 per cent. of the population.

There is a curious specialization in the different branches of trade, among the three principal communities. Arab merchants, as would be expected, have a practical monopoly of trade with the fellahin who comprise the largest and also the poorest section of the population; they also meet most of the needs of the remainder of the Arab population. Thus the trade in rice, coffee, and cotton piece-goods is largely in their hands. To the Jews falls the trade of the European and also of the europeanized sections. European clothing, food, furniture, building materials, wine, &c., are almost their monopoly. The Arabs specialize still further among themselves, as between Moslem and Christian. The Moslems are concerned more with the necessities of life; to the Christians fall predominantly luxury and semi-luxury articles.

There are both wholesale and retail businesses, but the tendency is for them to approximate. In most cases it seems that a merchant is prepared to sell to anyone who applies to him, and in any circumstances. The Jewish Agency held a census of Jewish trade in 1931. It found that, apart from the citrus trade, the annual sales of a larger wholesale business were about £14,000, but in some cases they were as low as £1,000. The average amount of capital invested in a wholesale business was about £3,350, but the figure was a little higher for those that dealt in citrus fruits or building material. The number of employees, including owners, per wholesale establishment was only 3·7 and the annual sales about £3,810 (in citrus businesses £5,560). The yearly value of sales in Jewish retail shops was £1,120; £1,420 in Haifa, £1,357 in Tel Aviv, £970 in Jerusalem. In the other towns and villages it nowhere exceeded £1,000. In 87·7 per cent. of the Jewish shops annual sales fell below £2,000. The average capital of a Jewish shop was £436, but if partnerships and companies were excluded, £235. Most Jewish shops had no employees, the average number for all the shops being less than one. There is no parallel information regarding Arab trade, but it is safe to say that on the average this is on an equally small scale. Although there are 'speciality' shops in Jerusalem, Tel Aviv, and Haifa, the very large majority of the retail shops of Palestine are general stores, willing to sell anything for which they are asked. In the European centres a few chain-stores have been established.

The Government exercises some control over retail trade through the Trade and Industries Ordinance, under which a large number of commercial establishments, including all engaged in the sale of food, are required to be licensed by the Department of Health, and are subject to inspection. There are Chambers of Commerce in the principal towns, to watch over the interests of traders in general, but unfortunately in every town there are separate ones for Jews and Arabs.

## CHAPTER XII

# PORTS AND INLAND TOWNS

## PORTS

HAIFA, Jaffa, and Tel Aviv are the three chief ports of Palestine, but of these three only Haifa is well developed, and it is of outstanding importance; the other two are roadsteads with basins for lighters. A few vessels also call at the roadsteads of Acre and Gaza, which are mainly of historical interest.

In 1939 the totals of shipping entered for the different ports were as follows:

|  | No. | Tonnage |
|---|---|---|
| Haifa . . . . | 2,249 | 4,189,777 |
| Jaffa (with Tel Aviv) . . | 1,593 | 1,812,742 |
| Acre . . . . . | 51 | 599 |
| Gaza . . . . . | 7 | 592 |
|  | 3,900 | 6,003,710 |

The combined totals for all four ports are, however, misleading, for the same vessel calling at two or more ports is reckoned in each of them. Altogether 2,910 ships with a total tonnage of 4,411,631 called at Palestine in 1939. Since the outbreak of war in that year trade and shipping have been almost entirely confined to Haifa.

The ports are described below in order from north to south except that Tel Aviv follows Jaffa, of which as a port it is an appendage.

ACRE (*O.T.* Accho; *class.* Ptolemais; *med.* Accon *or* St. Jean d'Acre; *Arab.* Akka). 32° 55′ N., 35° 04′ E. Pop. 9,800 (*est.* 1941). Government District Office. Central Prison. Schools (2), Dispensary (but no hospital).

Acre is at the northern end of the bay of Acre, just over 8 miles north-east of Haifa. There is a roadstead and a small boat-harbour. The town stands on a triangular peninsula which projects south-westwards for about 700 yards; there is a lighthouse on the extreme south-westerly point. North and east the town is enclosed by gardens, and farther inland stretches the fertile and cultivated plain of Acre, while southwards the sandy shore of the bay is bordered by orchards and palm-groves. There are swamps on either side of the

**Key.**

1. St. Lawrence of the Knights
2. St. Lazarus
3. Hospice of the Hospital
4. Templars' Stables
5. St. Giles
6. St. Denis
7. St. Catherine
8. Franciscan quarter
9. St. Antony
10. Montmusart Street
11. Castle
12. St. Mary of the Knights
13. St. Michael
14. Dominican quarter
15. Hospital
16. Genoese quarter
17. Mount Joy
18. Temple and St. Andrew
19. Pisan quarter
20. Venetian quarter
21. Arsenal
22. Nuns of St. Lazarus
23. Patriarchate
24. St. Roman
25. German quarter
26. Germans' Tower

FIG. 37. *Acre at the time of the Crusades* (see Marino Sanudo's plan opposite)

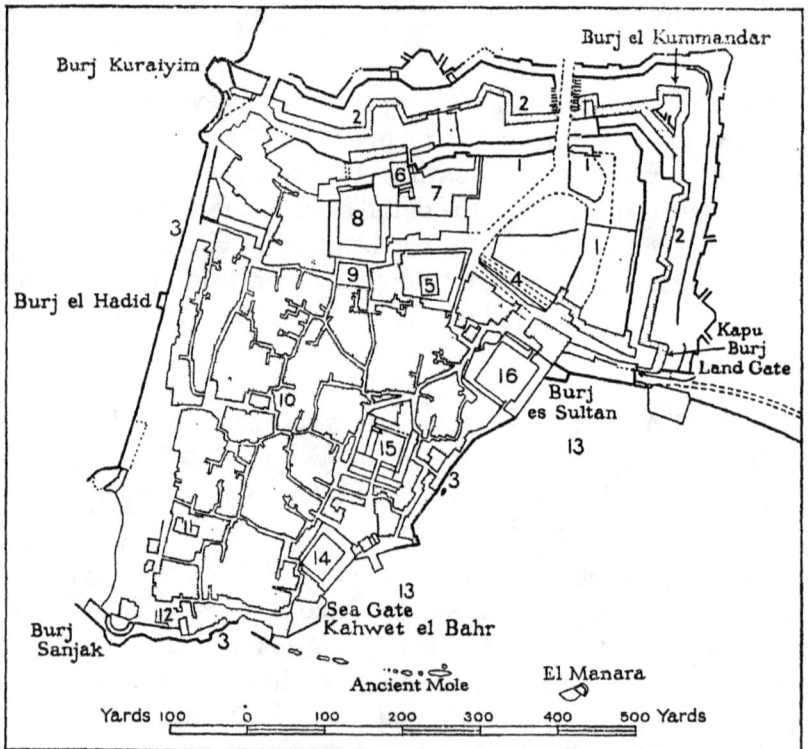

FIG. 38. *Plan of Acre*

| | | | |
|---|---|---|---|
| 1. Inner Wall | 5. Jazzar s Mosque | 9. Hammam el Basha | 13. The Harbours |
| 2. Outer Wall | 6. Citadel | 10. St. George's Church | 14. Khan el Umdan |
| 3. Sea Wall | 7. Arsenal | 11. St. Andrew's Church | 15. Khan el Faranj |
| 4. Suk el Abyad | 8. Kishla and Crusaders' Crypt | 12. St. John's Church | 16. Khan esh Shawarda |

77. *Marino Sanudo's plan of Acre at the time of the Crusades (MSS. in the Bodleian Library, Oxford)*

78. *North of Acre. Aqueduct from Kabri to Acre*

79. *Acre. Jazzar's mosque from the east*

mouth of the Nahr Naamin (*anc.* Belus), which is a mile south-east of the town. The population consists almost entirely of Moslem and Christian Arabs.

## History

Acre owes its historical importance to the fact that the bay to the south gives direct access to the great natural lowland route through the Esdraelon plain to the Jordan and Damascus. It appears first in the tribute lists of Thothmes III of Egypt and in the Tell el Amarna tablets (p. 83). In the Bible it is the port of Asher from which the Israelites were unable to drive the Canaanites. The Persians used it as a base for the conquest of Egypt in the sixth and fourth centuries B.C. After Alexander the Great's death it was within the dominions of the Ptolemies of Egypt and became a self-governing city in 261 B.C. Jonathan Maccabaeus was taken prisoner at Acre during the war with Syria in 143 B.C. St. Paul visited it as Ptolemais on his journey from Syria to Jerusalem (*Acts* xxi. 7). In A.D. 638 it fell with the rest of Palestine to the victorious Caliph Omar.

Acre grew to fame as port and fortress in medieval times. Captured in 1104 by the Crusaders after a long struggle, it was strongly fortified and held with one small break until 1291 by them or by their successors, the Knights of St. John, from whom it took its medieval name, St. Jean d'Acre. Its port, behind the ancient mole, with two inner harbours, was alive with the fleets of Italian cities, bearing not only pilgrims and Crusaders but also rich merchandise. Acre itself was a city of palaces and public buildings. Despite its wealth and strength, it surrendered without a blow on the approach of Saladin in 1187, but two years later the Crusaders again laid siege to it (p. 107), and when it was at last captured by King Richard Cœur de Lion in 1191, it became the base from which the reconquest of the Holy Land was attempted. The Templars and Knights of the Hospital of St. John established themselves in the town, which later also became the headquarters of the Teutonic Knights and of the Knights of St. Lazarus (fig. 37).

Under Christian rule new merchants and nobles from overseas settled in the town, adding to its prosperity, but the city was disturbed by faction. Pisans came to blows in its streets with Genoese, and Genoese with Venetians. The great Orders quarrelled amongst themselves and sections of the Christian population were said to be more friendly with Saracens than with their neighbours and brethren in faith. Gradually the European population adopted Levantine ways and lost their Frankish valour and virtues. On 5 April 1291 the Mamluk Melek el Ashraf appeared before Acre and in forty-three days mastered the city, which he 'sacked. Its buildings were destroyed and the whole area levelled with the ground. This was the end of Christian domination in the Holy Land until our day.

For four centuries the site of Acre remained desolate. As late as 1697 Maundrell wrote: 'Besides a large *kane* (khan) in which the French factors have taken up their quarters, and a mosque, and a few poor cottages, you see nothing here but a vast and spacious ruin.' These French factors, who represented the revival of French influence in the Levant, were interested in the cotton grown in its neighbourhood. Acre was still, however, the only good harbour, and in 1749 it was seized by Daher el Omar (Omar ez Zahir), an Arab chief of Safad, who had already extended his power south to Tiberias. He attracted a new population to the city, which became the seat of several foreign consuls, restored the seaward walls, and built a new rampart on the landward side, enclosing a town about one-third the size of the Crusaders' fortress. Henceforth Acre was the bone of contention in the wars involving Egypt and Syria, for its fortifications once more commanded the Esdraelon gateway to the route between Cairo and Damascus.

Daher was succeeded by the notorious Ahmed el Jazzar, 'the Butcher', who occupied Acre and became the leading prince in Syria, ruling from Beirut to Caesarea and inland to Baalbek (p. 110). He expelled the French merchants and, as his own engineer, built the large mosque which bears his name and the aqueduct to bring water from the hills. Under him Acre was the centre of resistance against Napoleon in 1799, and it was here that British sea-power enabled the city to repel all assaults by land and to thwart Napoleon's ambitions in Asia. It was the walls of Daher that withstood the attacks of Napoleon (p. 111). Jazzar subsequently built a new outer rampart parallel to the earlier one, consisting of bastions connected by curtain-walls about 40 feet high. Much of this is in good preservation to-day (fig. 38).

In November 1831 Ibrahim Pasha of Egypt (p. 112) laid destructive siege to the town and after six months took it by storm and sacked it. Revival was almost immediate, population and commerce returned, even the fortifications were renewed. But in 1840, when still held by Ibrahim, it was attacked by the British, Austrians, and Turks (p. 113), and fell after a few hours' bombardment from the sea.

*Description of Town*

The 'old town' (fig. 38), which dates mainly from the middle of the eighteenth century, is on the promontory and is enclosed by Jazzar's rampart on the landward side; its cobbled alleys are too narrow for motor traffic. Beyond this rampart, to the north and east, and on the destroyed site of the medieval city, is a modern quarter, built since 1920, and laid out with wide streets at right angles to one another. The sea-wall dates from the Crusades, but the only original gate, the entrance from Haifa, is on the east side. Here there is a beam from which criminals were formerly hanged. Inside the gate there is a long vaulted building known as the Suk el Abyad ('White Market'). On the north is the Citadel (*Kishla*), now used as a prison, with conspicuous tower (*Burj el Khazna*); in its walls are embedded cannon balls fired in successive sieges. Beneath the Citadel and the Girls' School are the well-preserved Crusaders' crypts. In the Citadel Tower there is a small museum containing specimens of Phoenician glass. The chief monument of the city is Jazzar's Mosque, built of ancient materials, with his tomb and that of his successor Suleiman in its court. Opposite the mosque there is the old Turkish arsenal, in which are kept large quantities of eighteenth-century ordnance. Of the four *khans* of Acre the two most interesting are the Khan esh Shahwarda and the Khan el Umdan, near the harbour. The former contains some cannon of the time of Sir Sidney Smith (p. 111).

Outside the town to the east are the Government's Experimental and Stud Farms. Close by, the garden of the Bahais contains the grave of their founder Baha-ullah (p. 144). Here also, about a mile from the walls, is the partly artificial mound of Tell el Fukh-khar, also called 'Napoleon's Mound', where King Guy and King Richard, Napoleon and Ibrahim, all pitched their tents. The road to Safad skirts its northern side.

*Water-supply* is brought by the aqueduct of Jazzar from El Kabri.

*Trade and Industry*

There are several small industries, including match, soda-water, soap, and tobacco factories, and an iron-works. Electric power is supplied from the Haifa system.

The opening of the Haifa–Damascus railway gave Acre a set-back since much of its commerce was then transferred to Haifa; the new artificial harbour at Haifa completed the ruin of Acre, which is now used only by sailing-vessels. But it is still a local market and agricultural centre.

The port is of slight importance; in 1939 only 51 sailing-vessels of 599 total tonnage entered, discharging 762 tons and loading 175 tons. In 1941 seven vessels entered of 179 total tonnage.

### Description of Port

The harbour on the south-eastern side of the town is shallow, silted, and gives shelter to small coasting-craft only. There is an anchorage in 8–9 fathoms of water about one mile south of the light and inshore of Acre Ledge, and for small vessels immediately south-east of the light, outside the ancient mole, with a depth of about 3 fathoms. Inside the boat harbour there is a jetty 50 feet long with a depth of $2\frac{1}{2}$ feet at its end. Small craft only (up to 10 tons register) can berth alongside the jetty. Larger ships discharge into lighters, which use the wharf, 90 yards long. Labour is casual.

### Communications

*Rail.* The old narrow-gauge line from Haifa has its terminus at Acre. The recently completed Haifa–Beirut–Tripoli standard-gauge line is combined with the old line to Naamin junction, where it passes a little east of the town of Acre.

*Roads.* The 'Land Gate' of Old Acre is connected by motor-road to the Haifa–Beirut coast road which skirts the eastern side of the town. A first-class road goes east to Safad. A number of fair-weather roads lead to villages in the hills.

HAIFA. 32° 49′ N., 35° 00′ E. Pop. 114,400 (*est.* 1941). District Commissioner's headquarters. Barracks. Hospitals (Government and several private), Schools, Hotels, Cinemas.

Haifa, east of Cape Carmel, is on the southern shore of the bay of Acre. It is sheltered from south, south-west, and east winds, and is the most useful anchorage on the coast of Palestine with sufficient depth of water for large vessels. Its position fulfils the same strategic purpose as did that of Acre in the past, and it was therefore well placed to become the modern port; its new harbour was completed in 1933. Sands stretch westwards along the bay and separate Carmel by little more than a narrow strip of lowland from the sea. Eastwards is the broad lowland of the Kishon and the plain of Esdraelon. Across the bay lies the picturesque city of Acre with its domes and minarets. In the farther distance east of Acre are the hills rising up to Nazareth. Farther back still are Hermon and Mount Tabor.

Of the population about 57,100 are Jews, 33,800 Moslems, and 23,500 Christians.

*History*

The remoter history of Haifa is the history of Mount Carmel, which in the Bible is the symbol of beauty, fertility, and sanctity. Carmel, in Arabic *Jebel Mar Elias*, is essentially the Mountain of the Prophet Elijah, who passed much of his life, often in hiding, within its borders. It was the scene of the famous contest with the priests of Baal, whose sanctuary it was.

Always a village and haven (*class*. Sycaminon), Haifa is a very modern city. A century ago a semi-independent Pashá of Acre removed the inhabitants of old Haifa bodily to a new site, squeezed between Carmel and the sea, built a castle to overawe them, and surrounded the village with a wall. On his death the castle fell into ruin, the wall was razed, and only an Arab village remained. About 1870 a party of German Templists (p. 155) formed their first home about a mile north-west of Haifa. Here by their industry, their observance of the law, their neatness, and other good qualities, they formed a very oasis of civilization. In their wake came a few other Europeans, among whom was prominent Laurence Oliphant, mystic, social worker, member of parliament, and wanderer, who lived there at intervals from 1879 to 1887 and was one of the earliest benefactors of the new Jewish settlement which began in his time and has continued to grow until more than half the greatly increased population of the town is now Jewish. Haifa has long since reached the German colony and passed beyond it. The population of this colony is no longer entirely German, but their work and influence have made the district the most attractive for private residence in Haifa, and perhaps in all Palestine. The modern prosperity of Haifa is, however, entirely due to its development as a major Levantine port since the British occupation in 1918.

*Description of Town* (figs. 39, 40)

Economically and commercially, though not in population, Haifa is the most important town of Palestine. The harbour, the airport, the terminus of the oil pipe-line from Iraq, the oil refinery, the railway junction, the headquarters and workshops of the Palestine

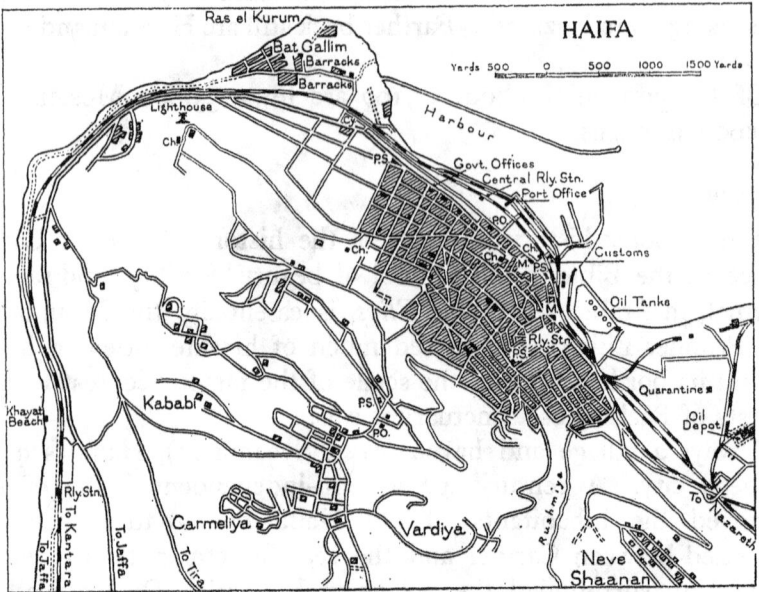

FIG. 39. *Plan of Haifa and Mount Carmel*
(Ch., Church; Cy., Cemetery; M., Mosque; P.O., Post Office;
P.S., Police Station)

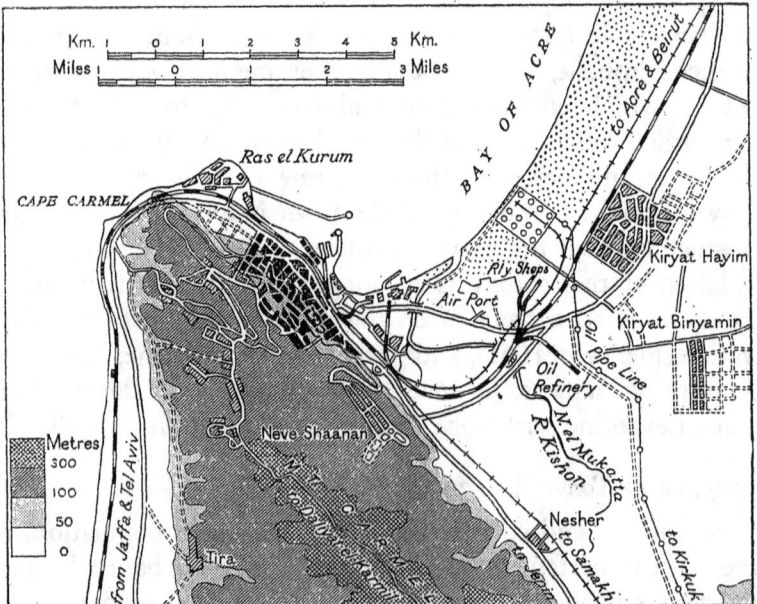

FIG. 40. *The Communications of Haifa*

Railways, all contribute to this. The town consists of three main quarters: the German colony and Bat Gallim at the north-west end, the Hadar ha-Carmel district to the south, half-way up Mount Carmel, and the old town at its foot. The best residential suburbs are on the top of Carmel. Buildings are of stone or concrete except in the old town, which is a characteristic huddle of mud houses and narrow lanes. In the past twenty years the town has extended in all directions. The small Jewish suburb of Hadar ha-Carmel has grown into a large and populous district. The principal buildings in this suburb are the Law Courts, the Municipal Buildings, and the Technical Institute, established in 1913 by a group of American and German Jewish philanthropists. Beyond Hadar ha-Carmel, farther up the mountain-side, is the temple-tomb of Sir Abbas Effendi Abdul Baha, the late head of the Bahai community, surrounded by terraced gardens in the Persian style (p. 144). From Hadar ha-Carmel the houses have spread farther to the wooded mountain top, where they are scattered among the trees and along newly laid-out roads. On Mount Carmel are also several hotels and a convalescent home.

Haifa has also spread on the narrow plain between the mountain and the sea. The first extension here since the British occupation was a small sea-side suburb south of Ras el Kurum, but the town soon passed beyond. The bathing beach is still farther west, round the cape. Towards Acre, on the eastern shore of the bay of Acre, are the various working-class suburbs, mainly Jewish, so extensive as to form, with the neighbouring railway workshops and oil refinery, a small town by itself. Between this district, known as the Emek Zebulun, and the old town are the airport and several other industrial undertakings, relatively important for Palestine.

Still more recent are the developments which the building of the harbour and the reclamation of some 109 acres of land rendered possible. This new expanse has been kept under the control of the Government. Wide streets have been laid down and certain building standards established. In other parts of the town also modern buildings have been erected. The harbour development scheme has included the opening of a spacious railway station close to the harbour, about midway between its extreme limits.

*Water-supply.* Haifa, despite its importance, has neither a modern water-supply nor a drainage system. Both have been contemplated for a number of years and a detailed survey for the provision of the former has been made. The construction of a drainage system has been commenced but is not very far advanced. With the exception of three private wells, recently acquired by the municipality from the former German owners, the whole of the water-supply of the town and port is derived from wells in private ownership. The water is somewhat saline and the supply is unsatisfactory and inadequate for the immensely increased population.

*Industry and Commerce*

Most of the principal manufacturing undertakings of Palestine are in Haifa and its neighbourhood. The Nesher cement factory is one of the most important. There are also foundries and structural steelwork firms, and factories of the Eastern Oil Industries. Power is provided by the new extensive thermo-electric power station of the Palestine Electric Corporation, close to the shore east of the town, which uses steam turbines dependent on oil fuel. Additional power comes by overhead cable from the Jordan hydro-electric works.

Exports consist mainly of citrus fruits and potash. Crude oil, which is not included in the following figures, far exceeds the total of all other exports, being 2,079,081 metric tons in 1938. The major imports include machinery, textiles, provisions, and general merchandise. Free zones for transit trade were allotted within the port area to the Iraqi and Persian governments in 1939 but have not yet been utilized.

Construction of the port began in 1929 and the main basin was opened in October 1933. The Oil Dock was completed by 1936. There is still plenty of room for extra quayage at the western end of the main basin and also in the Oil Dock. When the harbour was opened, Haifa, which had hitherto been second to Jaffa, at once forged ahead, soon surpassing Jaffa in maritime trade, though this decreased in 1941 and 1942 because of the war.

### Vessels entered

|  | Sailing | | Steam | | Total | |
|---|---|---|---|---|---|---|
|  | No. | Tonnage | No. | Tonnage | No. | Tonnage |
| 1935 | 671 | 23,509 | 1,818 | 4,900,535 | 2,489 | 4,924,044 |
| 1939 | 509 | 15,070 | 1,740 | 4,174,707 | 2,249 | 4,189,777 |
| 1941 | 799 | 37,965 | 464 | 1,153,505 | 1,263 | 1,191,470 |

### Cargo discharged and loaded
(Exclusive of crude oil)

|  | Discharged | Loaded |
|---|---|---|
| 1935 | 787,307 | 138,427 |
| 1939 | 653,171 | 343,161 |
| 1941 | 719,823 | 806,545 |

80. *Haifa. The main wharf, transit sheds, central railway station, and modern buildings lining Kingsway*

81. *Haifa and the lower slopes of Carmel. Oil dock and safety zone in the foreground. Bat Gallim in the distance to the right*

82. *Haifa port from the south, showing oil dock under construction, breakwater, and main wharf transit sheds*

83. *Haifa from the north-east, with Mount Carmel behind*

## Description of Port

The harbour (fig. 41) is protected by Mount Carmel from the south and the west winds, and to a small extent from the west-north-west. It is formed by the main breakwater on the north and the lee breakwater on the east. The former continues the shore-line from near Ras el Kurum in a general easterly direction for 7,250 feet. The lee breakwater projects northward from the shore for 2,510 feet. Between the two is an entrance, 600 feet wide and dredged to 37 feet, to the enclosed area, which consists of the main harbour and the Oil Dock.

The present accommodation in the harbour consists of a total water area of 304 acres, of which 91 acres are dredged to 37 feet, 63 acres to 30 feet, and 25 acres (in the Oil Dock) to 33 feet. Vessels of any length or beam but not exceeding 28½ feet draught can be berthed alongside the quays of the main harbour. The largest vessel hitherto berthed alongside the main wharf is the Italian S.S. *Roma* of 32,582 tons.

## Quayage

In the main harbour there are the Main Wharf and the Lighter Wharf along the shore and the Cargo Jetty projecting north from the east end of the Lighter Wharf. The West Jetty of the Oil Dock is parallel to and east of the Cargo Jetty. The Oil Dock lies between the West Jetty and the lee breakwater; its entrance is closed by a floating boom. Between the Cargo Jetty and the West Jetty is a safety zone, also closed by a floating boom. Details of quay accommodation are as follows:

| Quay | Length in ft. | Depth in ft. | Remarks |
|---|---|---|---|
| Main Wharf . . | 1,300 | 31 | Four berths for vessels of from 350 |
| | 360 | 18 | to 400 feet. Standard-gauge railway. |
| Lighter Wharf. . | 570 | 16 | Standard and narrow-gauge railway. Coal facilities. |
| Cargo Jetty . . | 700 | 31 | Standard and narrow-gauge railway. |
| | 250 | .. | |
| Oil Dock, West Jetty | 1,100 | 33 | Two berths for vessels of from 470 to 540 feet. |
| Main breakwater . | 7,250 | 23–37 | Twelve berths could be found, from 300 to 600 feet; no facilities. |

Outside the harbour there are shore installations and moorings for the loading of two tankers by pipes and also for the unloading of one tanker by pipes.

### Goods and Storage

There are 9 transit sheds, 2 of 44,950 square feet each, 1 of 39,000 square feet, 1 of 34,500, 1 of 31,000, and 4 smaller sheds. In addition there is uncovered storage space of 194,000 square feet. There is cold storage adjacent to the port with a capacity of 35,350 cubic feet above 32° and 225,220 cubic feet below freezing-point.

Some 3,000 tons of goods can be handled in a day in an emergency, and 250 standard-gauge wagons and 50 of narrow-gauge can be loaded and dispatched in a day. In addition 80 coal wagons (800 tons) can be loaded and dispatched from the eastern end of the Lighter Wharf.

General cargo is discharged on the wharf or jetty by ships' tackle and then loaded either direct to the road or rail vehicle alongside the ship for dispatch, or carried on motor-drawn trollies to the transit sheds or stacking-grounds, whence it is loaded on to vehicles. Heavy goods are discharged by ships' tackle to lighters, which are off-loaded by quay cranes at the lighter wharves and either loaded on to vehicles or transferred to a special dump area by travelling crane.

### Fuel

There is storage for 50,000 tons of fuel oil.

### Cranage

The wharves and jetties were well equipped in 1942 with steam and electric cranes, derricks, and gantry cranes of 3 tons (2), 5 tons (3), and 15 tons (2) capacity.

There is standard-gauge railway connexion to all quays, sheds, and uncovered storage space. There is also narrow-gauge railway connexion with the Lighter Wharf, the Cargo Jetty, and part of the uncovered storage space.

### Port Facilities

In the town there are workshops capable of minor repairs to vessels. The Ministry of War Transport has recently set up, as a war-time measure, a ship-repair depot capable of undertaking the heaviest hull and engine repairs, while ships remain afloat. There are no dry-docking facilities.

### Communications

*Rail.* Haifa is the railway headquarters of Palestine and the terminus of both standard-gauge and narrow-gauge railways. Run-

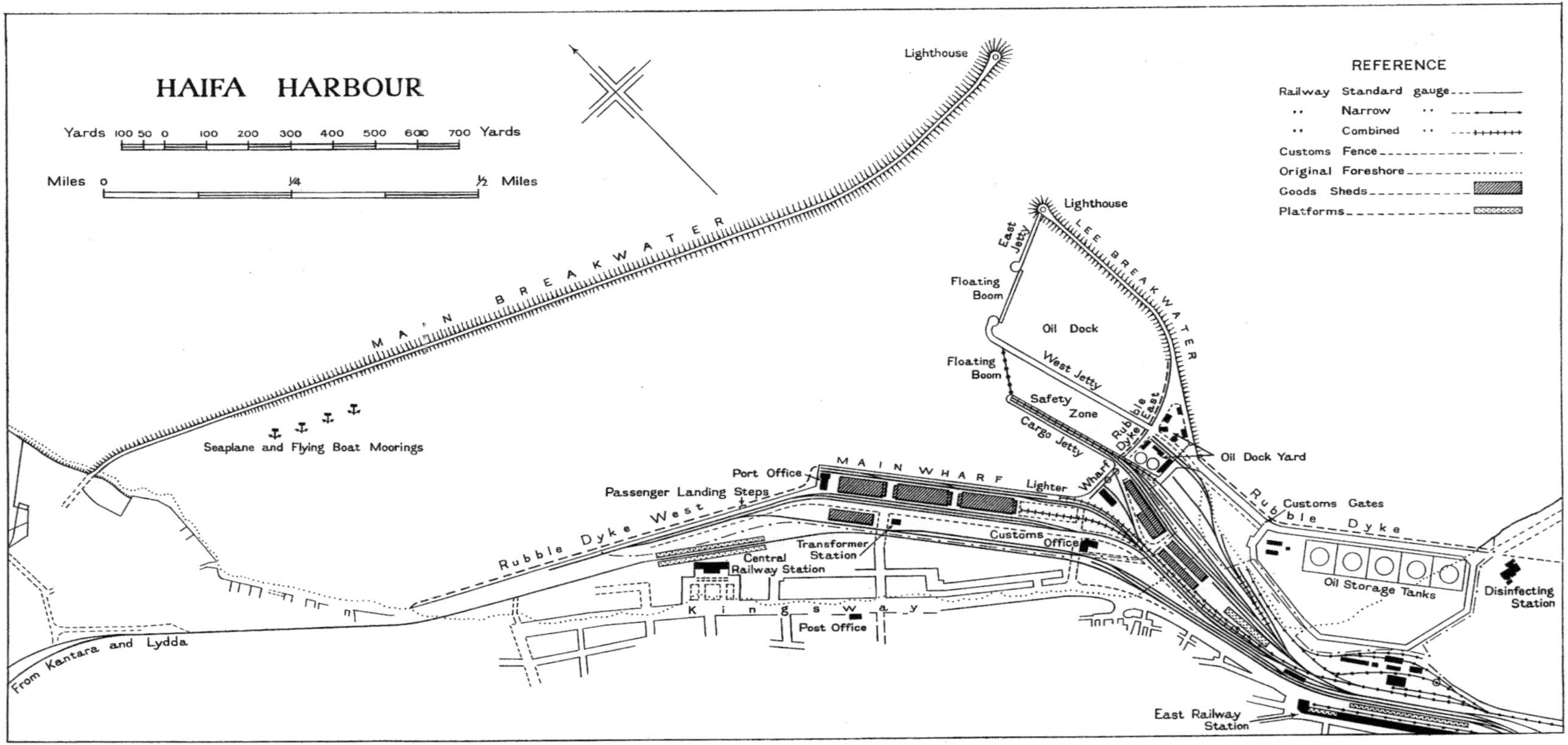
HAIFA HARBOUR
Yards 100 50 0 100 200 300 400 500 600 700 Yards
Miles 0 ¼ ½ Miles
REFERENCE
Railway Standard gauge
" Narrow "
" Combined "
Customs Fence
Original Foreshore
Goods Sheds
Platforms
Lighthouse
MAIN BREAKWATER
Lighthouse
LEE BREAKWATER
East Jetty
Floating Boom
Oil Dock
West Jetty
Floating Boom
Safety Zone
Cargo Jetty
Rubble Dyke East
Oil Dock Yard
Seaplane and Flying Boat Moorings
Port Office
MAIN WHARF
Lighter
Wharf
Passenger Landing Steps
Rubble Dyke West
Customs Office
Transformer Station
Central Railway Station
Customs Gates
Rubble Dyke
Oil Storage Tanks
Disinfecting Station
Kingsway
Post Office
From Kantara and Lydda
East Railway Station

FIG. 41. *The Port of Haifa*

ning south is the main line to Jaffa, to Jerusalem, and to Egypt, and northwards the new line to Beirut and Tripoli in Syria, and so to Turkey. A narrow-gauge railway (105 cm.) goes north to Acre and another (with a branch at Affula to Nablus) east to Deraa and thence either north to Damascus or south to Amman and Maan.

*Road.* Haifa stands where three first-class roads meet. Round the headland and then south runs the road to Jaffa and Gaza; northwards is the road to Acre, Ras en Nakura, and Syria; eastwards that to Nazareth, Tiberias, and Syria on the north, to Beisan and Transjordan on the east, and to Nablus and Jerusalem on the south.

*Air.* There are facilities for the landing of seaplanes at the western end of the harbour, and a civil airport 2 miles north-east of the town.

JAFFA (*O.T.* Jappho; *class.* Joppa; *med.* Japhe). 32° 03′ N., 34° 45′ E. Pop. 85,300 (*est.* 1941). District Commissioner's headquarters, Police Station. Prison. Hospitals (Government and private). Schools, Hotels, Cinemas.

Jaffa, 52 miles south of Cape Carmel, is an open roadstead with a lighter basin. Its chief feature is a low hill close to a flat unprotected shore. It extends along the sea-shore for about 3½ miles. The population comprises 47,000 Moslems, 23,800 Jews, and 14,500 Christians (1941).

*History*

Jaffa's first appearance is in the list of cities taken by the Egyptians in their invasion of 1472 B.C., when mention is made of the already established wealth of its inhabitants (p. 83). During the period of the Judges and later, Jaffa was a Philistine port. Mention of it in the Bible is, however, very occasional, the best known being the story of Jonah's voyage. It was there that Jonah embarked for Tarshish when he attempted to escape from his mission to Nineveh, and it was there that a few days later he was vomited forth by the monster. The story of Perseus and Andromeda is also located at Jaffa, and an aggressive and forbidding rock is still pointed out as that to which Andromeda was bound. In the New Testament (*Acts* ix. 36) Jaffa is the home of Tabitha or Dorcas, and her reputed tomb, first mentioned in the sixth century, together with the neighbouring church dedicated to her, is to-day an object of veneration to the Orthodox Church. There is also the reputed house of Simon the tanner, whence Peter proceeded to Caesarea to make the first Gentile convert to Christianity (*Acts* x. 5, 6).

In the Crusading period Jaffa passed frequently from Christian hands to Moslem and back, suffering frequent sack and destruction. Consequently when Richard Cœur de Lion marched down the coast in 1191 he found the town so ruined that he could find no shelter in it. The restoration of Jaffa dates from the year 1654, when the Franciscans received permission to build the present Latin Hospice.

FIG. 42. *Old Jaffa sea front, south of the harbour*

Napoleon in his invasion of Palestine took Jaffa, held it over a year, and sacked it on his retreat (p. 112).

### Description of Town

There are two sections: the coast ridge comprising the old town and the Ajami quarter, which rises 60 to 100 feet, and the low-lying plain behind, which comprises the commercial area, the Menshieh quarter, and orange-groves scattered with small groups of houses. A new Jewish quarter called Beit Vegan has been built on the dunes south of Jaffa, with the new Arab quarter of Holon to the east of it. Northward Jaffa merges into the very modern city of Tel Aviv (fig. 44).

The old town and the Ajami quarter hang like a squat citadel on the brow of the ridge above the harbour (fig. 42). Streets are tortuous and narrow, dark and congested. Some space was opened up during the recent extension of the harbour and also during the Arab out-

84. *Jaffa Harbour from the air, looking north-east*

85. *Jaffa Harbour from the air, looking south*

86. *Tel Aviv. The lighter basin*

87. *Tel Aviv. View south from the stadium*

break (pp. 127–9), when a section of the old town was blown up. The new town has broader streets based on a central square, and contains the banks and business houses, mainly in Bustros Street.

The town is hemmed in by Tel Aviv on the north and sand-dunes on the south, and its principal line of expansion is eastwards along the roads to Jerusalem and Gaza. Jaffa has always been the port of Jerusalem, and for the greater part of the present era it has been the gateway by which Christian pilgrims have come to Jerusalem. To accommodate them there have always been hospices, even when the place was so ruined that there were hardly any other habitable buildings.

*Water-supply* is adequate but unsatisfactory, being exposed to pollution and having no reserve pumping machinery. It comes from more than four thousand small wells, all privately owned, and four large wells which belong to the municipality. Very few of these produce a continuous supply of pure water. Three water-towers provide storage for 220,000 gallons, about a day's supply.

## Trade and Industry

Jaffa has been very unfavourably affected by the rise of Haifa, which has taken away much of its trade, and also by that of Tel Aviv, which has drawn from it all its better circumstanced Jewish residents, leaving only the very poor; Tel Aviv had also, from 1936, taken the Jewish share of its passenger and goods traffic. Local industries include soap-boiling, which has been declining of recent years, flour-mills, alcohol and cigarette factories, an iron foundry, and works concerned with stone crushing. The future of the port does not appear very promising.

*Power* is provided by the new Reading power-station north of the Auja river, built for Jaffa and Tel Aviv by the Palestine Electric Corporation, which can also supplement the supply by overhead cable from Haifa.

The principal trade consists of the import of general merchandise throughout the year and the export of citrus fruits from the southern districts between November and April. A considerable part of the citrus trade partook of the general movement to Tel Aviv. Some improvements, including the provision of special facilities for citrus handling, have been effected during the past few years.

Figures of shipping in recent years follow. The opening of Haifa harbour in 1933 caused a marked decline in the bulk of imports handled, though the export trade has remained stable. For the greater part of 1936 Jaffa Port was closed in consequence of a political strike and towards the end of that year landing of goods by lighter at Tel Aviv commenced. This caused a further decline in import trade. Since the outbreak of war the port has almost ceased to be used, except by sailing-vessels.

### Cargo discharged and loaded

#### (Metric tons)

| Year | | Discharged | Loaded |
|------|---|-----------|--------|
| 1935 | . . | 402,263 | 171,819 |
| 1937 | . . | 126,842 | 152,427 . |
| 1939 | . . | 112,711 | 153,856 |
| 1941 | . | 24,641 | 1,971 |

### Vessels entered

| | Sailing | | Steam | | Total | |
|---|-----|---------|-----|---------|-----|---------|
| | No. | Tonnage | No. | Tonnage | No. | Tonnage |
| *1937 . | . 937 | 26,732 | 929 | 1,471,373 | 1,866 | 1,498,105 |
| *1939 . | . 537 | 27,528 | 1,056 | 1,785,214 | 1,593 | 1,812,742 |
| *1941 . | . 275 | 13,765 | 4 | 1,773 | 279 | 15,538 |

* Including Tel Aviv.

### Description of Port (fig. 43)

There is only a basin for lighters. Other vessels anchor in the open roadstead about a mile from the shore, with a reef of low-lying rocks between them and the coast. In winter, owing to the absence of any protection, communication with the shore at Jaffa often ceases for several consecutive days. There is a passage through the rocks to the protected lighter-basin of 430,000 square feet. The depth of water alongside the quays is $6\frac{1}{2}$ feet. The length of the quays is 2,080 feet, with a further 2,950 feet of breakwater and sea-wall. The extreme dimensions of lighters that can be berthed alongside the quay are: length 40 feet, beam 15 feet, girth 25 feet. There are moorings in the basin for about 200 lighters and another hundred fair-weather moorings outside the basin unprotected by the reef.

### Storage and Cranage

There are five storage sheds, of a total capacity of 241,000 square feet, with an additional uncovered space for storage of 75,000 square feet. There is no cold-storage accommodation nor are there coal or oil facilities at Jaffa, except that coal for vessels is available on a small scale.

There are five electrically operated derrick cranes (from 3 to 7 tons) on the quay. General cargo is discharged into lighters alongside ship by ships' tackle. Lighters are subsequently discharged alongside the quay, and cargo is either carried into transit sheds by porters or placed on vehicles for removal. Heavy goods are also discharged by ships' tackle into lighters, but these are subsequently off-loaded by electric derrick or other cranes alongside the quay. Goods are distributed from the south quay to the uncovered storage area by decauville railway, but there is no standard-gauge railway connexion.

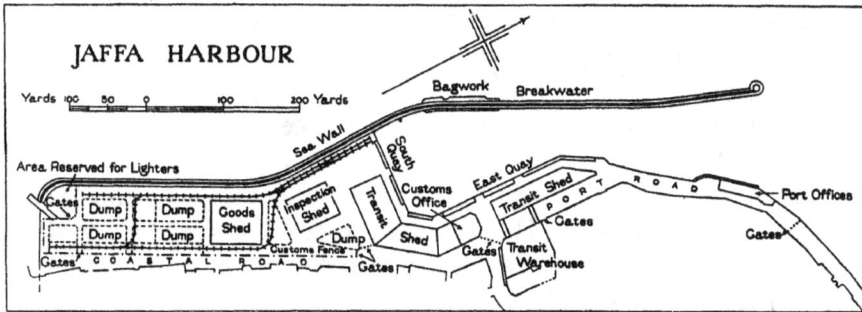

FIG. 43. *Jaffa Harbour*

*Repair facilities* with slipway for launches and lighters are provided outside the customs fence, but there are no repair facilities for steamships.

## Communications

Jaffa is the terminus of the railway line from Jerusalem; Lydda, 12 miles from Jaffa, is the junction for Haifa and Kantara. A first-class road runs through Ramleh to Jerusalem, Jericho, and Amman, and another north through Petah Tikva to Haifa and Beirut. The road south to Gaza leaves the Jerusalem road about 6 miles from Jaffa, to avoid the broad belt of sand-dunes south of the town (p. 45).

TEL AVIV. 32° 04′ N., 34° 46′ E. Pop. 141,000 (*est.* 1941). Government District Office, Police Station. Hospital (municipal and 5 private), Schools, Theatres, Cinemas, Hotels (3 large, many small).

Tel Aviv, which is the northern extension of Jaffa, is one of the two largest towns in Palestine, and of very recent growth. It arose out of the acquisition of unutilized sand-dunes north of Jaffa by some of the more prosperous Jewish inhabitants in 1907 and 1908 and the erection on them of houses with more hygienic surroundings than those of the old town. Until the British occupation, Tel Aviv remained a residential suburb of Jaffa, and its population after the War of 1914–1918 was still a matter of hundreds. Then it forged ahead, attracting the ever-increasing flow of Jewish immigrants into Palestine, and to-day about a third of the Jewish population of Palestine lives in Tel Aviv. The area of the town was doubled in 1942—from 1·9 to 3·8 square miles—and spread north of the Auja river (fig. 44). It is the cultural capital of Palestine Jewry and has an orchestra of international renown, dramatic companies, a public library, an art gallery, cinema theatres, newspapers and other periodicals, and a population pulsating with life and energy, all, with the exception of two or three hundred, Jewish.

Tel Aviv is a modern European town resembling the mushroom cities of North America. Houses are of stone or concrete two or three stories high, mostly with flat roofs. But the architecture is heterogeneous; in most cases the owner of the house designs it in the style of his native town or follows his fancy. The private residences consist for the most part of blocks of flats, many of them consisting of one room only, with small shops occupying the ground floor. Many of the streets are lined with trees, but most of them are inconveniently narrow for the volume of traffic and for the innumerable saunterers at all times of the day and much of the night.

*Water.* Tel Aviv has neither adequate water-supply nor drainage system. Water is obtained from fifteen relatively shallow bored wells, some of them badly polluted. They are under constant supervision and no serious epidemic has yet occurred, although it has been said that Tel Aviv is 'drinking its own bath water'. Moreover, the supply is inadequate; there are no private or other cisterns, and water is pumped directly into the distribution system; the total reserve in the water-towers is sufficient for only twenty minutes' consumption during a hot summer day.

*Power* and light are provided by the new large Reading power-station built by the Palestine Electric Corporation.

### Trade and Industry

Tel Aviv subsists mainly on commerce, but there are many small industries, the most important of which are textile.

The jetty and small lighter-basin date only from late in 1936 and

# JAFFA AND TEL AVIV

Yards 500    0    500    1000    1500 Yards

### Abbreviations

Gym............. Gymnasium
Hos.............Hospital
Mag.C....... ...Magistrate's Court
Mun............. Municipal
Mus........... ...Museum
P. S...............Police Station
Syn... ..........Synagogue

Municipal Boundaries ........ .... ..— —— —

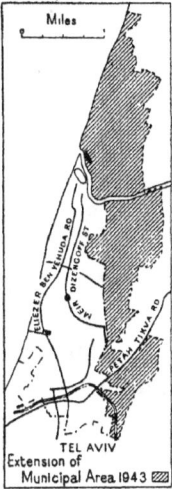

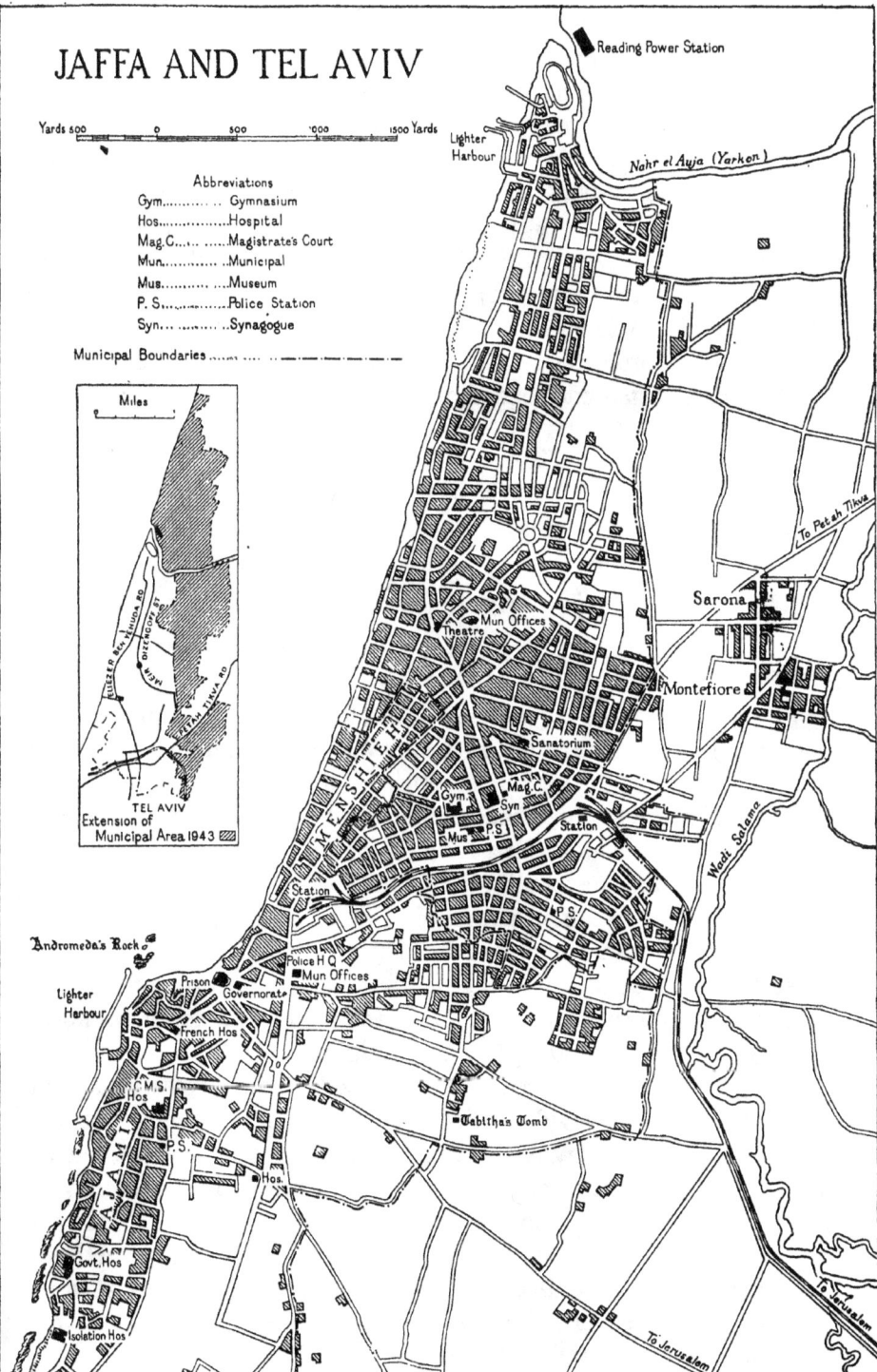

Miles

TEL AVIV
Extension of
Municipal Area 1943

Reading Power Station

Lighter Harbour

Nahr el Auja (Yarkon)

To Petah Tikva

Sarona

Montefiore

Theatre
Mun Offices

Sanatorium

Gym
Mag.C
Syn
Mus
P.S
Station

Station

P.S

MENSHIEH

Wadi Solama

Andromeda's Rock

Police H Q
Prison
Mun Offices
Governorate

Lighter Harbour

French Hos

C.M.S. Hos.

P.S.

Hos.

Tabitha's Tomb

AJAMI

Govt. Hos

Isolation Hos

To Jerusalem

To Jerusalem

FIG. 44. *Jaffa and Tel Aviv*

are a direct consequence of the Arab disturbances of that year, which made Jaffa, the normal port of Tel Aviv and Jerusalem, unsafe for Jews. Facilities were provided by a private company. For government administrative purposes Tel Aviv is a part of the Jaffa port, both places serving the one roadstead. The port has, however, functioned for little more than three years, for it was virtually closed on the outbreak of war with Italy in 1940. This period was too short for successful operation, especially in view of the relatively large expenditure on upkeep. The financial loss sustained by the sup-porters of the project was, therefore, not unexpected. The figures of cargo discharged and loaded are as follows:

### Cargo discharged and loaded

#### (In metric tons)

|        | Discharged | Loaded |
|--------|-----------|--------|
| 1938 . . | 139,448 | 57,049 |
| 1939 . . | 161,826 | 48,192 |
| 1941 . . | 2,630 | 390 |

### Description of Port

Tel Aviv has only a jetty and a lighter-basin. As at Jaffa, it is possible to work ships only in good weather, December to March (inclusive) being the worst months. But the roadstead is more distant and more exposed than at Jaffa and the lighter-basin is more open to the west winds. In a south-west wind it cannot be entered. On forty-four days, excluding Sabbaths, between October 1937 and April 1938, the weather prevented work at the port. Dredging must be continuous to prevent silting from sand brought up the coast from the south. The lighter-basin, with an area of 150,000 square feet, is protected by a breakwater and the depth of water at the quays was kept at 6½ feet by dredging.

The jetty, which was 600 feet long by 20 feet wide, was dismantled in 1941. It was provided with cranes and a decauville railway. The length of the quay is about 2,000 feet. There were five sheds, of a total floor space of about 86,000 square feet, with an additional uncovered space of 130,000 square feet for storage. There were six cranes, of which the most powerful was one of 40 tons. The methods of unloading were similar to those for Jaffa. There was a small slipway for the repair of lighters and launches inside the basin area and there were also well-equipped machine shops.

*Communications* are the same as for Jaffa.

GAZA. 31° 30′ N., 34° 28′ E. Pop. 27,400 (*est.* 1941). District Commissioner's headquarters. Police barracks. Hospitals (2), Schools.

Gaza is 41 miles south-west of Jaffa and 2 miles inland from the shore, to which it is connected by road. The town is surrounded by orchards and olive-groves, gardens and small fields, separated by tall cactus hedges, and many of them threatened by sand-dunes on the seaward side. Inland, south-east of the town, is a low ridge, Jebel Ali el Muntar, 260–300 feet high, trending from north-east to south-west. This runs almost to the Wadi Ghazza, a formidable obstacle 5 miles south of Gaza. The port consists only of an open roadstead. The population of the town is almost entirely Moslem and is slowly decreasing. *Water-supply* is from wells, of which there are over twenty and from which the importance of Gaza originates.

## History

In early times Gaza was at the junction of three great trade routes. Arabian and Asiatic trade came west by Petra or Akaba across the desert. Northward lay the 'Way of the Sea' from Damascus, which crossed the Jordan at Jisr Banat Yakub. Southward was the coastal road to Egypt. Hence Gaza was a commercial centre at the desert edge with the added advantage of direct access to the sea. But it was also intermediate between Egypt and southern Syria and was involved in all the clashes between Powers holding these two countries. In the Canaanite period, when it was one of the five cities of Canaan, it appears to have been under Egyptian control. As a Persian stronghold it resisted Alexander's advance upon Egypt for five months, and was sacked but rebuilt by him. After his death in 323 B.C. it passed with the rest of Palestine to the Ptolemies of Egypt, but was taken in 200 B.C. by the Seleucid kingdom of Syria. Later it was involved in the Maccabaean wars and was destroyed by Alexander Jannaeus in 96 B.C. After the Roman conquest of Palestine it was rebuilt on a new site in 57–56 B.C. by one of the first Roman governors, and ceased to be of military significance until the Crusader period, when it became a bone of contention between the Egyptian Mamluks and the Latin kingdom of Jerusalem; it fell to the Mamluk Sultan Beibars in 1244 (p. 108). Napoleon took it in 1799; after his defeat it reverted to Turkey, but was held by Ibrahim Pasha of Egypt when he controlled Syria. In the Great War of 1914–1918 it was the centre of Turkish resistance to the British advance on Palestine, and after resisting two assaults was captured by Allenby in November 1917 (p. 119).

Gaza is also famous in biblical history for the feats of Samson: his removal of the gates to the top of a neighbouring hill, and his destruction of the temple of Dagon, which he pulled down on himself (*Judges* xvi. 1–3, 21–31).

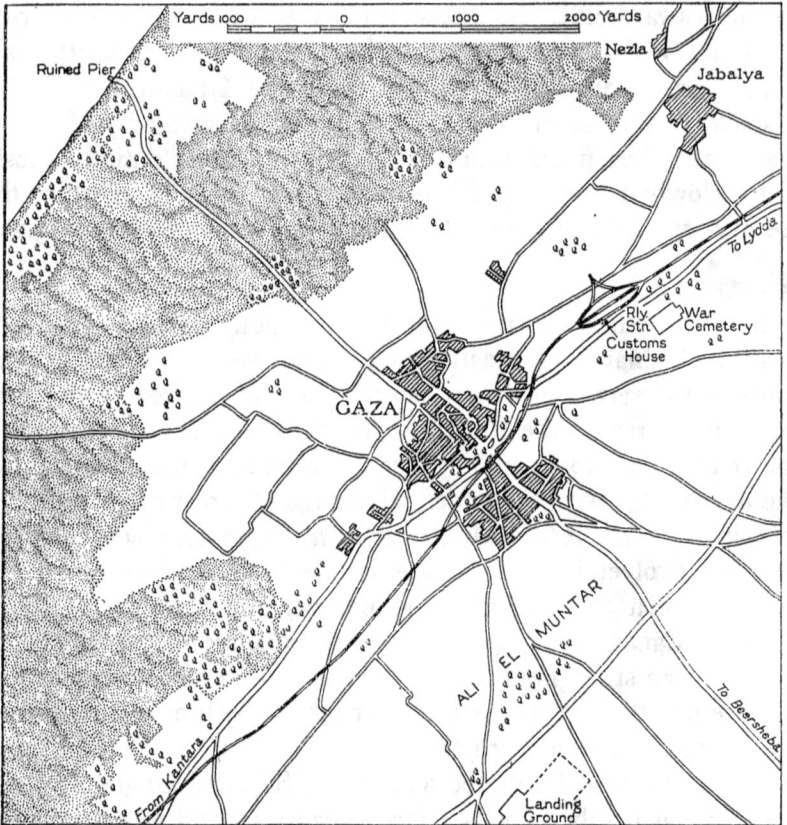

FIG. 45. *Gaza*

*Description of Town* (fig. 45)

The town is built on and around a low hill and is separated by the main road and railway into an east and a west quarter. East is the poorer quarter, composed of mud houses. 'West town' is more important and contains the administrative buildings and schools. There are busy bazaars in the Sejaiyeh quarter between the hill and Ali el Muntar. Gaza has not yet completely recovered from damage done in the 1914–1918 war. The Great Mosque, originally the Church of St. John (12th century), then hit by a bomb, also suffered in an earthquake in 1927. Other notable buildings are the Church of St. Porphyry, the mosque and the tomb of Hashim, great-grandfather of Mohammad, and the sanctuary of Abu el Azm, which is the traditional tomb of Samson. The original pre-Roman town, 4 miles to the south at Tell Ujal (Ajjul) on the brink of the Wadi Ghazza, has been excavated. The British Military Cemetery (1914–1918) is near the railway station.

## Commerce

Gaza is a local market and has some Arab hand industries. The principal exports are wheat, barley, and durra, when available. In 1938 forty-one sailing-vessels of 2,071 total tonnage entered the port, but in 1939 only seven sailing-vessels of 592 total tonnage. Steamers occasionally discharge cargo here.

## Description of Port

The open roadstead is of very little importance to-day. The anchorage, in 7 fathoms with a sandy bottom, is fairly safe between May and October. During other months when westerly winds prevail it is unsafe. The best months are August, September, and the first half of October. The landing-place affords no protection even to small craft, which are beached for safety during the winter. There are no piers or wharves.

## Communications

*Rail.* The standard-gauge line from Beirut and Haifa passes through Gaza to Khan Yunis and Egypt. The station is about ¾ mile north-east of the town.

*Road.* The coast road from Tel Aviv and Jaffa passes through Gaza with a good tarmac surface, and is continued south to Khan Yunis, whence, passing Rafa, it becomes the coastal road through El Arish to Egypt. Another first-class road strikes south-east inland to Beersheba and there are numerous seasonal tracks leading to camps and settlements. A good road connects the town with the anchorage 2 miles away. There are bus services to Rafa and Khan Yunis, to Imara and Beersheba, and to Masmiya and Jaffa.

*Air.* There is an Imperial Airways landing-ground, no longer in general use, 2 miles south of the town, reached by the metalled by-pass which crosses the Beersheba road.

## INLAND TOWNS

BEERSHEBA. 31° 14′ N., 34° 47′ E.; height *c.* 900 feet. Pop. 2,959 (1931; almost all Moslem). District Office. Rest-house. School.

Beersheba is a small compact town, little more than a village, lying at the foot of the Judaean hills and on the Wadi Bir es Saba; it stands in a wide hollow with steep rocky hills to the north. The country-side is cultivated, wheat and barley being dependent on rainfall. The town is well laid out and there are some three-storied stone buildings, but most houses are of mud brick. The road running through the town is asphalted (Photo. 89).

### History

Beersheba was the southernmost town of Palestine in the biblical period; hence the expression 'from Dan to Beersheba' described the limits of the land. Its wells receive noticeable mention in the early books of the Bible (e.g. *Genesis* xxi. 32) and it was a sanctuary later (*Amos* v. 5). During the late Roman period it was the chief town of Palaestina Tertia, and the seat of a bishopric. Later it gradually declined and was eventually deserted, except by beduin. It remained in this state for almost five centuries, but about the year 1900 the Turks began to resettle it, and by the outbreak of war in 1914 it had become a small village. Beersheba played a part in that war, serving as a base for the Turkish forces. On 31 October 1917 it was taken by the British (p. 119), and from Beersheba began the advance that ended in the capture of Jerusalem.

It now has its own Mayor and Municipal Council, and there is a district Sharia Court, presided over by the Chief Sheikh, which deals with Moslem religious affairs. The District Officer can also convene a tribal court to settle problems concerning the beduin.

*Water-supply* is inadequate, and is derived from ten wells: four outside and five inside the town, and a new one on the Hebron road.

### Communications

Beersheba is on the main first-class motor-road from Egypt through Auja el Hafir to Jerusalem. Another first-class road goes west to Gaza, and there is a seasonal motor track south-east to the Wadi Araba and Akaba. There are bus services to Hebron and Gaza. The aircraft landing-ground is just outside the town to the north-east. The narrow-gauge railway built by the Turks during the War of 1914–1918 from Beersheba by Imara has been dismantled.

BEISAN. 32° 30' N., 35° 30' E.; height 410 feet below sea-level. Pop. 5,000 (*est.* 1937; Moslem 4,600; Christian 400). District Office. Schools (2 small), Dispensary (no hospital).

Beisan is in the Jordan valley at the eastern end of the plain of Esdraelon. It is an Arab town of closely packed mud houses, rather ramshackle. Two main asphalted streets pass through it, leading to the roads to Affula and Jericho. Other streets are cobbled or mud surfaced, but wide enough for wheeled traffic (photo. 88).

Being below sea-level, the town is very hot in summer, but numerous perennial streams make the surrounding countryside very fertile. The population is mixed, and comprises Arab fellahin, beduin, Syrians, Kurds, and Druses; there are no Jews.

*History*

Beisan owes its importance to its position at the eastern entrance to the Esdraelon plain from the Jordan crossing south of Lake Tiberias. The ancient fortress, a natural mound, scarped for defence, commands a wide view from Jezreel to the Transjordan highland. Its capture was a turning-point of the Israelite invasion, and as Beth Shean it was allotted to the tribe of Manasseh, but does not seem to have been occupied at once, for it was later held by the Philistines (*1 Samuel* xxxi. 10), though recovered by David or Solomon (*1 Kings* iv. 12) to command the road to Damascus. It was in one of its temples, recently excavated, that the bodies and armour of Saul and Jonathan were exposed after their defeat at Gilboa.

From an inroad of Scythians in the seventh century B.C. it was known to the Greeks as Scythopolis. It was one of the ten foundation cities of the Decapolis on Pompey's dissolution of the Syrian kingdom in 64 B.C. (p. 91), was rebuilt by his successor Gabinius, and became an important caravan town on the route through Gerasa (Jerash) in Transjordan, between Nabataean Philadelphia (Amman) and the port of Ptolemais (Acre). On the lapse of the empire from Christianity in the time of Julian, Scythopolis was the scene of Christian martyrdoms on a large scale. From that period its importance began to diminish, but in modern times its strategic function has not changed, for its capture in September 1918 by Allenby's cavalry cut the Turkish line of retreat and completed their rout in the final campaign.

The *water-supply* is good. It is brought by pipes from the Josak springs 4½ miles distant to a water-tower recently constructed. There was no electricity supply in 1937.

### Communications

Beisan is connected by metre-gauge railway with Haifa on the west and through Samakh at the south end of Lake Tiberias with Deraa and the Hejaz railway. The railway station (351 ft. below sea-level) is about 2 miles north of the town. Roads lead to Affula, Samakh, and Jericho, and there are bus services through the first two of these to Nazareth and to Tiberias.

BETHLEHEM (*Arab.* Beit Lahm). 31° 42′ N., 35° 12′ E.; height *c.* 2,400 feet. Pop. 8,200 (*est.* 1941; mostly Christian). District Office. Women's Prison. Hospital (80 beds), Mental Hospital, Greek monastery, Armenian convent, Schools.

Bethlehem, the birth-place of David and of Jesus, is a small town on a spur running east from the Judaean watershed, about 6 miles south of Jerusalem, and a little east of the highway to Hebron. It is surrounded by terraced olive-groves; fertile valleys extend some way towards Jerusalem, producing wheat, barley, almonds, and grapes. The wine (*talhami*) is among the best in Palestine.

There are a number of stone buildings, larger and of better construction than is usual in Palestine, and the people, mostly Christians (*c.* 7,000) of the Orthodox and Latin Churches, are of superior type, little troubled by the factional and political problems of the country. The women are unusually fair, and wear high-peaked head-gear of medieval European fashion. Close touch is maintained with South America, where many of the inhabitants have relations, having themselves lived there for a time (p. 182).

The main street is macadamized and suitable for motors, but side-streets and those of the poorer quarter are narrow and impassable. There is an open square suitable for a motor-park. For the Church of the Nativity and other monuments, see Appendix C, 'The Holy Places'.

The only industry in the town is the manufacture of souvenirs in olive wood and in mother-of-pearl, for sale to pilgrims and tourists.

*Water* comes by conduit from the Pools of Solomon, and there are

*88. Beisan*

*89. Beersheba*

90. *Bethlehem. The Church of the Nativity*

91. *Bethlehem*

about 900 cisterns in the town, the three largest being in front of the church. There are springs about 800 yards south-east of the village, and also about $1\frac{1}{2}$ miles distant at Artus. The electric power for lighting comes by overhead cable from Jerusalem.

## Communications

Bethlehem is on a branch motor-road of the main Jerusalem–Hebron road, 7 miles from Jerusalem, with a frequent bus service.

HEBRON. 31° 31′ N., 35° 06′ E.; height 3,040 feet. Pop. 21,000 (*est.* 1941; almost all Moslem). District Office. Russian monastery.

Hebron is on the main road between Jerusalem and Beersheba, about half-way between the two, about 23 miles from the former. It stands on the side of a narrow valley with steep slopes, in an agricultural district which is self-supporting. It is a long straggling town with narrow roads.

Traditionally Hebron is the oldest city in Palestine (*Numbers* xiii. 22); the ancient site is a little to the west at Rumeideh. Until the capture of Jerusalem it was David's capital and the national sanctuary. Its early name Kirjath-Arba ('the City of the Four') commemorates the tombs of Adam, Abraham, Isaac, and Jacob, and the sacred Haram is built over the Cave of Machpelah, acquired by Abraham (*Genesis* xxiii. 17). From Saracen times the city has been known to the Arabs as El Khalil (or El Khalil-er-Rahman, 'the Friend of the Merciful', meaning 'Abraham, the Friend of God'); to the Crusaders it was 'St. Abraham'. The wall of the Haram appears to be Herodian, the mosque itself being originally a Christian church, which itself replaced that of Justinian.

The Moslem population is inclined to fanaticism, the small Jewish community of rabbis and students having been decimated and dispersed in the disturbances of 1929. Jews are excluded from the Haram, as were Christians until recently. Besides the tombs of the three patriarchs and their wives in the cave, those of Joseph (who is also reputed to have been buried near Nablus), Jesse, and other biblical heroes are also shown at Hebron (*see also* Appendix C, 'The Holy Places'). The traditional 'Oak of Hebron', under which Abraham 'entertained angels unawares', is in the possession of the Russian monastery.

The town has some very small but distinctive industries, tanning and glass-making, especially of a delicate blue ware; but the rearing of goats, sheep, and cattle forms the chief occupation.

*Water.* A government well just off the main road to the south supplies a reservoir 1,000 yards from the town, whence water is distributed to the houses. There are two other large wells outside the town, and most houses have a rain-water cistern.

There are four small electric plants, but no general electric supply.

### Communications

Hebron is on the main road from Jerusalem in the north to Beer-sheba in the south.

JENIN. 32° 28′ N., 35° 18′ E.; height 450 feet. Pop. 3,000 (*est.* 1938; almost all Moslem). District Office. School (in Turkish Fort), Dispensary (no hospital).

Jenin is the southernmost town of the plain of Esdraelon and lies in a narrow gap at the northern foot of the hills of Samaria, with Jebel Fakkua ('Mountains of Gilboa') rising to the north-east. It is small, has no buildings of distinction, and, except for the main thoroughfare from Affula southwards to Nablus and Jerusalem and that north-west to Megiddo, which have tarmac surfaces, the streets are cobbled and unfit for motors.

### History

Jenin is the En Gannim, or Garden-spring, mentioned in the Book of Joshua, the Beth Haggan, or House in the Garden, of the second Book of Kings, and the Ginoea of Josephus.

*Water* is supplied to two reservoirs by two pumping stations; it is adequate and good. About fifty of the houses are connected to the Palestine electricity supply.

### Communications

Jenin is on the narrow-gauge branch-line from Affula to Nablus. The roads to Affula, Haifa, and Nablus are first class. There is a dry-weather landing-ground immediately north-west of the town.

JERICHO. 31° 51′ N., 35° 27′ E.; height *c.* 820 feet below sea-level. Pop. 2,000 (*est.* 1937; nearly all Moslems). Government Agricultural Station. Hotels (2). No hospital or dispensary.

Jericho is now little more than a large village, mostly of mud-brick houses scattered over about 3 square miles, about 7 miles north-west of the northern end of the Dead Sea and deep in the Jordan valley. It is commanded by high hills 2 miles to the west and has the appear-

92. *'David's Pool' at Hebron*

93. *General view of Hebron*

94. *Jenin and the Plain of Esdraelon*

95. *Modern Jericho*

ance of an oasis, for many of its houses are scattered in orange and banana groves. In the last few years a new suburb has sprung up, with some comfortable villas, the property of the wealthier Arabs of Jerusalem.

The main road between Jerusalem and Transjordan passes through the town, bordered by small shops and rather ramshackle buildings, but there are almost no other roads.

Most of the people are very mixed, apparently with much negro blood, derived according to tradition from slaves brought by Cleopatra and her Roman friends from Africa.

### History

Jericho is famous in biblical history as the city whose walls fell to the blast of Joshua's trumpets. The mound of this ancient city, now known as Tell es Sultan, is about a mile north-west of the present settlement, and archaeological evidence points to there having been a collapse of the walls at a long distant date. By reason of its position opposite the southernmost crossing of the Jordan, it has always been strategically important (photo. 32).

*Water-supply*. The Ain es Sultan ('fountain of Elisha'), whose waters are reputed to have been 'healed' by Elisha (*2 Kings* ii. 19–22), provides 3 million gallons of water a day, which is conveyed by pipe for domestic purposes and by open channel for irrigation. Another spring in the Wadi Kelt supplies 2 million gallons entirely for irrigation.

### Communications

The main road from Jerusalem to Transjordan by the Allenby bridge is first class. The only other road, north-west to Tell es Sultan, is passable in summer but difficult during the rainy season.

There is an aircraft landing-ground between Jericho and the Jordan, north of the main road.

JERUSALEM (*Arab*. El Kuds). 31° 47′ N., 35° 13′ E.; height 2,468 feet (rly. stn.). Pop. 141,100 (*est*. 1941; Jews 85,700, Moslems 29,100, Christians 26,300). Government and District Commissioner's headquarters. Numerous public buildings, hospitals, banks, churches, hospices, convents, schools.

Jerusalem is the administrative and financial capital of Palestine, and the centre of its religions and culture; commerce it shares with Tel Aviv and Haifa; its industries are of no importance. Its history

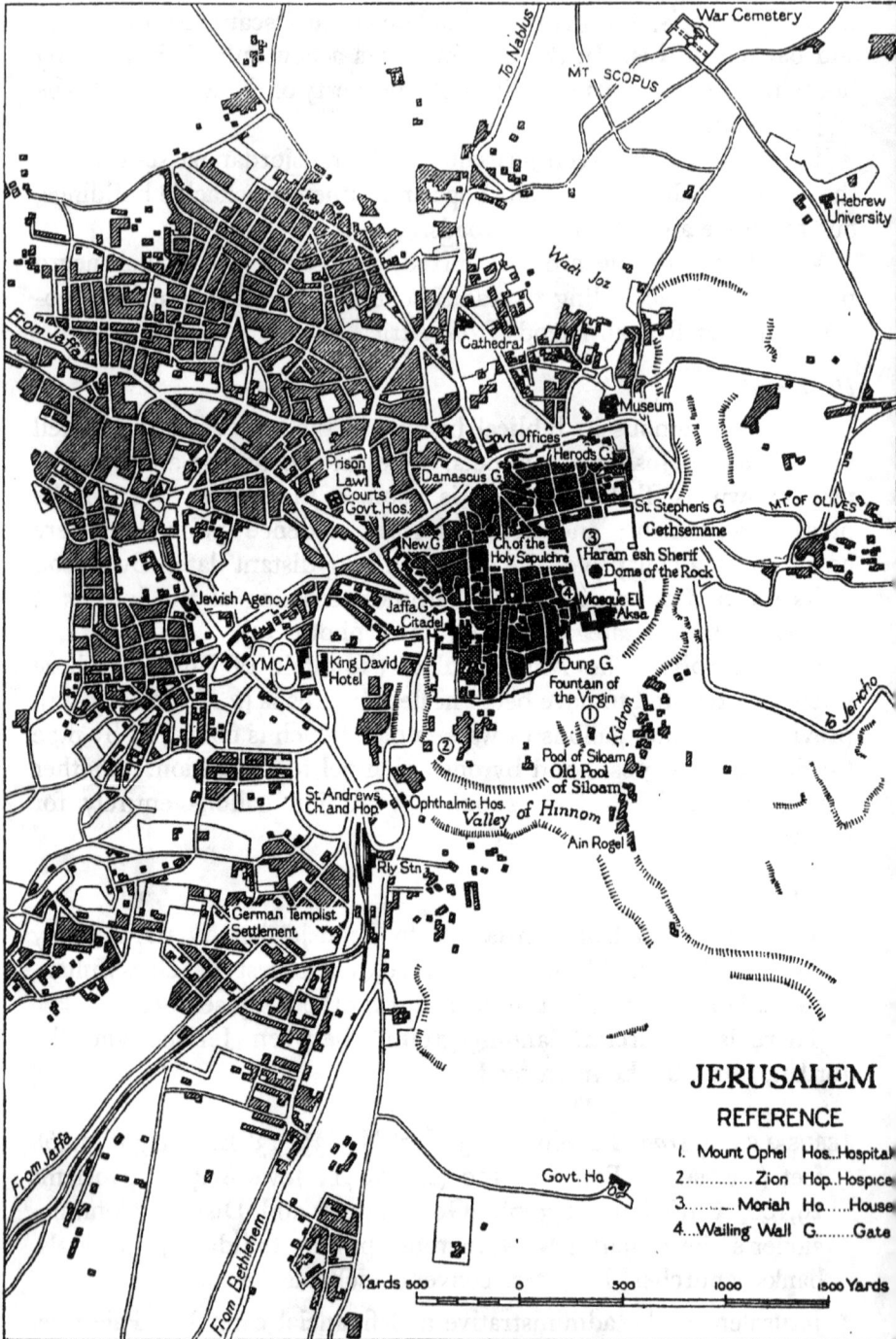

**JERUSALEM**

REFERENCE

1. Mount Ophel    Hos..Hospital
2............Zion    Hop.Hospice
3.......... Moriah    Ho....House
4...Wailing Wall    G........Gate

FIG. 46. *Plan of Jerusalem*

96. *Jerusalem. The Haram esh Sherif across the Kidron from the Garden of Gethsemane*

97. *Jerusalem. View north up the valley of Kidron from near the Pool of Siloam*

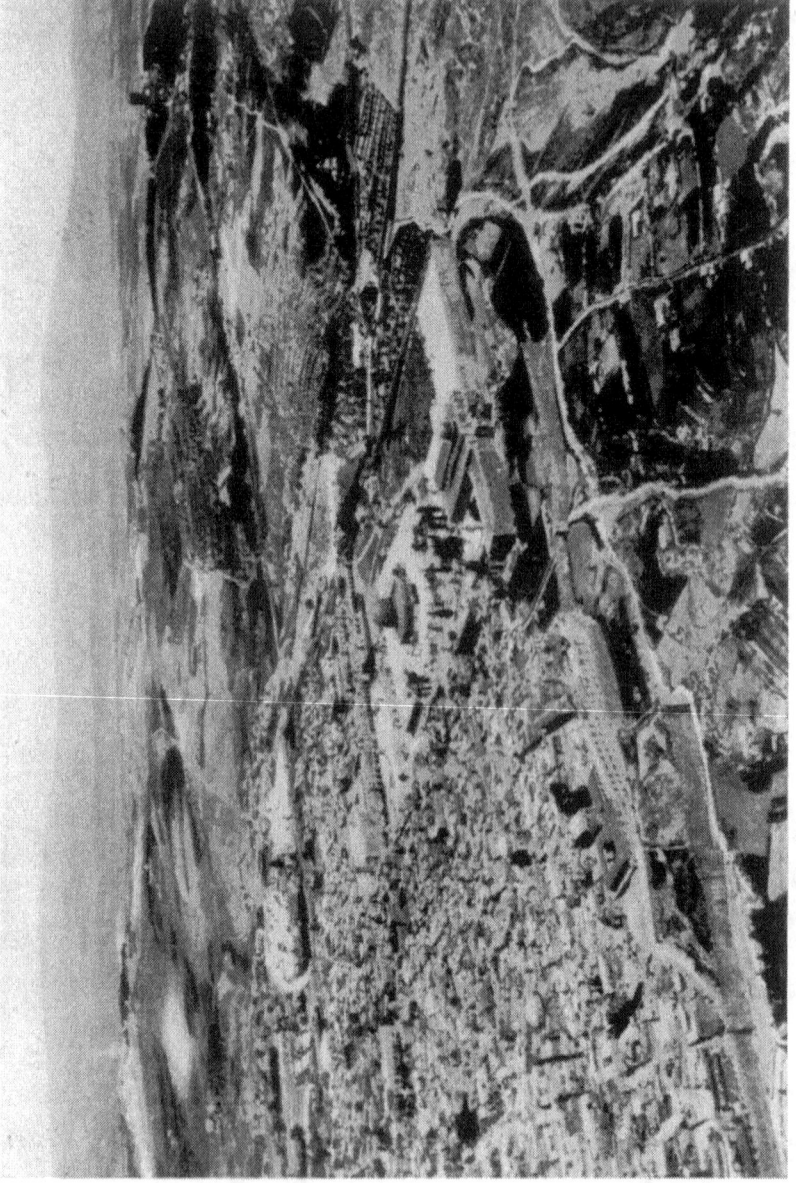

98. *Jerusalem. The old city, the Haram esh Sherif, and the Mount of Olives, seen from the air to the south*

goes back to the beginning of the biblical story, although it was only a local hill-fortress before King David made it his capital. A capital city it has remained, although its province has varied. On thirty-two occasions it has been captured, and usually devastated; but it has risen again and again from its ashes, and has been the centre of three great faiths. To-day it is the seat of the Palestinian administration, the Jewish Agency, the Supreme Moslem Council, and of three patriarchates and an Anglican bishop. The Hebrew University is on Mount Scopus, overlooking it from the north-east, and there are several other schools of learning.

There are, in a sense, two Jerusalems, both living to-day. There is the old city within the walls dating back mostly to the Middle Ages, and containing most of the buildings of antiquarian interest (*below*), the bazaars, and the old commercial centre; but its population is decreasing, the inhabitants—especially the Jewish residents—moving out to the new city beyond the walls and to the more distant suburbs (fig. 46).

## The Site and the Old City

The head-valley of the Kidron tributary of the Jordan has its source just west of the crest of the Judaean plateau, which rises here north and east of the city to 2,400 feet in Mount Scopus and the Mount of Olives. The Kidron first drains southward, parallel with this ridge, till it is joined from the west by the Wadi Rababi ('Valley of Hinnom'), a wider and shorter valley which descends likewise from the plateau parallel with the Kidron, three-quarters of a mile to the west, and then turns sharply into it south of the city. The roughly rectangular site between these two deep valleys is further defined to the north-east by a smaller valley (Wadi Joz) draining steeply into the Kidron. It is also bisected from north to south by the shallower Tyropoeon ('cheese-makers') valley, now choked with house foundations and debris, but still deep where it turns eastward into the Kidron a little north of the valley of Hinnom. All these valleys, cut in tabular limestones with hard beds of chert, are now dry, but in the Kidron bed are the two springs of the Virgin and of Ain Rogel. The primitive water-supply was the rain-fed Pool of Siloam, near the mouth of the Tyropoeon valley.

The eastern spur of the site, between Kidron and Tyropoeon, rises steep, long, and narrow, in two stages. The southern, smaller, and lower of these, Mount Ophel, rises from 2,030 feet on the valley floor to 2,300 feet, and carried the Jebusite fortress, which had an Egyptian governor about 1400 B.C., and was captured by King David about 1000 B.C. Of this 'City of David' the Jebusite wall (photo. 33) and its filling (*Millo*) (*2 Samuel* v. 9), towards the northern loftier summit, 'Mount Moriah' (2,428 ft.), was repaired by Solomon. The immemorial sanctuary on this hill was acquired by David and enclosed in Solomon's Temple and Palace. Massive substructures, preserved in the 'Wailing Wall', in parts 70–80 feet deep, greatly enlarged its area, and were connected by an 'ascent' or viaduct across the Tyropoeon valley with another Jebusite settlement, *Zion*, the 'Upper City', on the wider western summit (2,526 ft.) between the Tyropoeon and Hinnom. The 'City of David' was supplied with water from the Virgin's Spring by an aqueduct to the Upper Pool of Siloam (the 'King's Pool') and by the Lower Pool nearer Ain Rogel. Later the Upper City was supplied with pools in the upper Hinnom valley; and a new tunnel was cut by Hezekiah to augment and protect against Assyrian attack the supply from the Virgin's Spring to Siloam.[1] The Birket es Sultan reservoir in the valley of Hinnom was built much later, to supply the Crusaders' city.

Under the Kingdom, the Zion summit was fortified along its steep escarpments, and its south wall was prolonged across the lower Tyropoeon to join that of the 'City of David', enclosing the Siloam Pools. As the city grew, later kings built a 'Second Wall' farther north, in irregular sections from the north-west angle of Zion to the north-east, where the area of Moriah was enlarged on deep substructures overhanging the Kidron; and this is the extent of the city after the return from Captivity and the circuit refortified by Nehemiah in 445 B.C.

The citadel (*Acra*) overlooked the 'City of David' south of the Temple area. Within the 'First Wall' were built the palaces of the Maccabaean princes and of the Herods, and the most westerly of them became the Roman *Praetorium*, with its 'tower' (*Antonia*) on the 'Second Wall' north-west of the Temple area, dominating the whole city. Farther north still, Herod Agrippa partly enclosed with a 'Third Wall' the large new quarter *Bezetha*, with the Tombs of the Kings and the 'Bethesda' Pool. The place of the Crucifixion must have been still farther north, and quite outside the walls.

---

[1] The work was started from both ends. Instead of meeting, the workmen found themselves in parallel passages but close enough to hear one another. They then turned at an angle and met. The rough inscription cut where the two working parties met has been removed from Jerusalem to the Ottoman Museum in Istanbul. A cast is in London, in the Museum of the Palestine Exploration Fund, 2 Hinde St., W. 1.

99, 100. *Jerusalem. Streets in the old city*

101. *Jerusalem. The Jaffa Gate*

102. *Jerusalem. The Damascus Gate*

After destruction by Titus in A.D. 70 Jerusalem was rebuilt by Hadrian as a Roman city, *Aelia Capitolina*, where no Jew was allowed to live; but it was destroyed again after revolt in A.D. 135. Years later, Jewish rabbis, visiting the ruinous site, wept as they saw a fox coming out of what had once been the place of the Holy of Holies: 'Because of the mountain of Zion, which is desolate, the foxes walk upon it' (*Lamentations* v. 18).

Later the city recovered, for the recognition of the Christian 'Holy Places' by Constantine in 326 and Moslem acceptance of Moriah as the site of Abraham's sacrifice brought it prosperity and magnificence. It was devastated in 614 by Chosroes, restored in 619 by Heraclius, and captured in 637 by Omar, becoming at once a Moslem centre of pilgrimage, second only to Mecca. The 'Dome of the Rock' (*Kubbet es Sakhra*, probably on the site of Solomon's sanctuary) and the Mosque El Aksa dominate the Temple area (*Haram esh Sherif*) on Moriah, and the Constantinian Church of the Holy Sepulchre, enclosing also the traditional site of the Crucifixion (Calvary, Golgotha), stands west of the head of the Tyropoeon. Other biblical sites are the 'Golden Gate' in the east wall of the Temple area; and opposite it Gethsemane, where the road to the Mount of Olives crosses the Kidron (see Appendix C, 'The Holy Places').

*Communications.* Principal roads left the ancient city (1) for Jericho and the east, from the Sheep Gate, crossing the Mount of Olives; (2) for Beth-horon and the north, by the Fish Gate and the Old Gate in the 'Second Wall'; (3) for Joppa and the coastal plain, by the Old Gate (rebuilt as the Tower of Hippicus) at the north-west angle; (4) for Bethlehem and the south, by the Old Gate; (5) for the Dead Sea, down the Kidron valley by the Dung Gate or the Fountain Gate flanking the Tyropoeon valley. All these natural routes are still in use.

### The Medieval City

The old city was refortified by Suleiman the Magnificent in 1537, using much older material, and foundations of (at latest) Herodian date, and his walls restricted the growth of the city until modern times. Within them are the seats of the three patriarchates (Orthodox, Latin, and Armenian), and of the Supreme Moslem Council, and many churches, mosques, and synagogues. The principal entrances are Herod's Gate and the Damascus Gate in the north wall, the New Gate at the north-west angle, the Jaffa Gate in the west wall, and St. Stephen's Gate in the east wall, north of the Temple area.

Principal thoroughfares are (*a*) from the Jaffa Gate eastwards to the Via Dolorosa and St. Stephen's Gate; (*b*) southward from the Damascus Gate; but most of the city is a maze of irregular lanes, and no wheeled traffic is possible.

Among the many interesting buildings within the medieval walls two groups stand out: the Church of the Holy Sepulchre, portions of which date from the beginning of the eleventh century; and the *Haram esh Sherif* which occupies the site of Solomon's and Herod's Temples, and encloses the Dome of the Rock, commonly called the 'Mosque of Omar'—a building of outstanding beauty built by the Caliph Abd el Malik at the end of the seventh century—and the Mosque El Aksa, originally a basilica built by Justinian in A.D. 536.

In Jerusalem, as elsewhere in Palestine, religious communities and national groups tend to segregate themselves. In Jerusalem within the walls there are, and probably have long been, Moslem, Jewish, Greek Orthodox, and Armenian quarters. Even these are subdivided, for within the Jewish quarter are small groups of Karaites, Georgian Jews, Hungarian Jews, and others, living closely together.

*The Modern City*

The new city covers the high ground north and north-west of the medieval walls, and has spread southwards round the head of the valley of Hinnom beyond the railway station and the older German Templist settlement (p. 155). Its oldest buildings were erected about 1860. Under Ottoman rule there was no control or system of extension, but the British administration at once drew up a town-plan, reserving large areas adjacent to the old city, or essential to the conservation of its landscape. The greater part of the population, including all the wealthier people, live in the new city. The railway ascends from the south-west to its terminus overlooking the valley of Hinnom. The government offices, the Law Courts, the Jewish Agency, the Palestine Museum, many of the convents, the principal hotels, hospitals, and schools, are all outside the walls. The city is continually growing, and although several new suburbs have been planted some distance away from it, they are soon enveloped by it. As in the old city, there are differing quarters, but they are not exclusive. Of the newest quarters most are Jewish, and some are limited to Jews of kindred origin—Bokharan, Georgian, Kurd, Persian, and European. The Rehavia quarter has overflowed into the attractive Christian Talbieh. Some go back almost eighty years. In the best of them, Moslem as well as Christian, are to be found the finest private houses in Jerusalem. British officials and foreign consuls live in these newer quarters. The German Templists have their own comfortable village close to the railway station.

Government House, one of the finest of the modern buildings, on high ground to the south of the city, overlooks the valley of Hinnom, the old city, and beyond it the Mount of Olives and the distant mountains of Moab beyond the Dead Sea. The Palestine Museum, another fine building, built and endowed by John D. Rockefeller Jr., stands on high ground outside the north wall, and houses the Department of Antiquities; but other government offices are still in temporary accommodation. The Young Men's Christian Association has an ample and conspicuous abode, due to an American benefactor; it is designed with a stadium to bring together the younger members of all communities, and thereby foster a common Palestinian citizenship. The King David Hotel stands opposite.

The Cathedral Church of St. George the Martyr (Patron Saint of England and Palestine alike), half a mile north of the Damascus Gate, is the seat of the Anglican Bishop in Jerusalem. Its buildings also include chaplain's quarters, a pilgrim hostel, and a large school for boys. The Church of Scotland has a church and hospice dedicated to St. Andrew, close to the railway station. On the other side of the Bethlehem road is the group of buildings which includes the Ophthalmic Hospital of the Order of St. John of Jerusalem. The headquarters of the Jewish Agency for Palestine and the Zionist Organization are in a large fortress-like building on the edge of the Jewish suburb of Rehavia due west of the city.

The three summits of the Mount of Olives are occupied by the Hebrew University, with impressive but heterogeneous buildings, the Kaiserin Augusta Victoria Sanatorium, and the Tower of the Ascension. The British War Cemetery on Mount Scopus is worthy of its purpose and its surroundings: its Memorial Chapel is dedicated to men of all faiths, and holds emblems of none.

*Water-supply.* Until the advent of the British in 1917 Jerusalem was dependent for water on cisterns, some large, including the very large ancient cisterns still in use in the Haram area, others small, of which one at least was to be found under every building in the city. In normal years the supply of water from this source, although not invariably of good quality, was sufficient for domestic purposes. When the rainfall was below the normal, however, there was a shortage and much disease and suffering. One of the first undertakings of the British Army when it entered Jerusalem was to install an adequate water-supply, the source being at the village of Arrub beyond Bethlehem, where the ancient reservoir, said to have been built in the time of Pontius Pilate, was repaired. This supply was intended for military purposes only, but later the Civil Administration placed it at the disposal of all the inhabitants of the city, at first under the Public Works Department, but very soon under the Municipality. Though few houses were connected to this supply, the demand for water soon exceeded the supply, and other sources had to be found. These were at Artus, also beyond Bethlehem, the traditional site of the gardens commemorated in the *Song of Solomon*; at Ain Fara, north-east of the city; and above all at the so-called 'Solomon's Pools', a short distance beyond Bethlehem, which are certainly of Roman origin, if not older. One of the springs by which these pools are fed has been identified with the 'Sealed Fountain' of the *Song of Solomon* (iv. 12). Even these supplies proved inadequate, and a large scheme had to be undertaken by the Government, the administration within the city limits being entrusted to the Municipality. Under this scheme water is pumped up from Ras el Ain (*anc.* Antipatris), on the coastal plain 35 miles to the north-west, and almost 2,400 feet below Jerusalem. The purity of the water is controlled by weekly bacteriological examinations, but it is still inadvisable to drink unboiled water in Jerusalem or anywhere else in Palestine.

*Drainage*

Apart from a very local system within the walls of the old city, based on works that date back to Roman times, there was also no drainage system in Jerusalem when it was occupied by the British. Sewage was disposed of in cesspits, periodically emptied. The British have also taken up this problem. A plan covering the whole of the Jerusalem area has been drawn up, approved, and put in hand. Several districts in Jerusalem have already been covered, and completion is within sight.

KHAN YUNIS. 31° 20′ N., 34° 18′ E.; height *c.* 160 feet. Pop. 4,500 (*est.* 1937; mostly Moslems, a few Christians). No hospital or dispensary.

Khan Yunis is a small frontier town, 6 miles from the Egyptian boundary. It consists mainly of mud-brick houses, though a few dwellings are of stone. On the west there is a belt of sand-dunes 2 miles broad, separating the town from the sea. To the north-east, east, and south-east there is a network of small citrus, banana, and

104. *Jerusalem. The Church of the Holy Sepulchre*

103. *Jerusalem. The Ecce Homo Arch*

105. *Jerusalem. The old city*

106. *Jerusalem. The Jewish Agency in the new city*

olive groves, separated by cactus hedges. Beyond this belt on the east the ground rises inland to an open undulating plateau of firm ground.

*Water-supply.* There is a municipal well in the centre of the town which distributes water by pipes to buildings. The water-tower has a capacity of 26,400 gallons.

## Communications

Khan Yunis is on the coastal railway to Egypt; the station is about half a mile north-east of the town, with provision for end-loading, but no passenger platform. The road to Gaza is first class; that to Rafa, which passes through it, is unmetalled and rough, but passable to wheeled traffic in dry weather. The main road from Gaza to Egypt leaves the Khan Yunis road 5 miles north of the town and by-passes both Khan Yunis and Rafa.

LYDDA. 31° 57′ N., 34° 54′ E.; height *c.* 180 feet. Pop. (1941) 15,700 (11,250 in 1931; Moslems 10,002, Christians 1,210). District Office.

Lydda, like Ramleh, with which, though far older, it has shared its history, is near the northern end of the plain of Philistia. It gives its name to the important railway station, a little over a mile to the south-west, and to the airport 3 miles to the north. The neighbourhood is entirely agricultural. The population is Arab, but there are many recent Jewish settlements in the neighbourhood.

## History

Its name has been traced back to Lod of the tribe of Benjamin; for most of its earlier period, however, it was in the possession of the Philistines, and was frequented by Israelite farmers to have their implements made or sharpened (*1 Samuel* xiii. 19–22); for, under Philistine domination, 'there was no smith found throughout all the land of Israel'. After the destruction of Jerusalem it became a centre for Jewish scholars, but for many centuries few Jews have lived there.

Under the Romans it was Diospolis and under the Crusaders '*St. George*'. Later it reverted almost to its original name, Ludd, but very recently has been known as Lydda. In tradition St. George was a distinguished Roman soldier, born and buried at Lydda, where the church over his reputed grave was destroyed by Saladin. He became the patron saint of the Crusaders, of England under Edward III, of Aragon and Portugal, of the republics of Genoa and Venice, and generally of seafaring Christians. His fight with the Dragon was located at Lydda, first in the thirteenth-century *Golden Legend* of Jacobus de Voragine; but the local legend is older.

By Moslems St. George is usually identified with Elijah, but at Lydda with Christ, for an early relief of St. George and the Dragon on the church shows where Anti-Christ (*Dajjal*) will be slain at the end of the world.

## Communications

Lydda junction is the most important in Palestine, with direct main-line standard-gauge railways to Egypt, Syria, and Turkey, and to Jaffa and Jerusalem. It is also the civil airport for Jerusalem and is on the motor-road between Haifa and Jerusalem; the main coastal road passes through it, and there are good connexions with Jaffa from near Rehovot on the south and through Petah Tikva on the north.

NABLUS (*Bib.* Shechem). 32° 13' N., 35° 15' E.; height *c.* 1,900 feet. Pop. 21,900 (1941; almost all Moslems). District Commissioner's headquarters. Barracks. Latin Convent. Hotel.

Nablus is the biblical Shechem, refounded in A.D. 70–71 as Flavia Neapolis, and called Naples by the Latins. Situated in the valley between Mounts Ebal and Gerizim (Jebel Eslamiya, Jebel et Tur), it is a veritable oasis, the centre of its own small agricultural district of which it is the market town. Seventy springs irrigate its gardens and orchards. The town itself is small and its centre, the old town, is very compact with narrow streets. It was severely damaged by earthquake in 1927.

The population is almost entirely Moslem, rigid and sometimes fanatical. Except for a few Samaritans (161 at the census in 1931), the last remnant of the Jews of the time of the Captivity (p. 147), now so poor as to be safe from persecution, no Jew dares to live in Nablus. Few will even run the risk of passing through the town. This persistent anti-Jewish prejudice has its roots in the past and is traditionally ascribed to the treacherous massacre of the townsmen by Simeon and Levi, sons of Jacob (*Genesis* xxxiv). Perhaps as a consequence of this tradition Nablus has become a focus of Arab nationalism and a principal centre of anti-Zionism.

Among the chief buildings, the great mosque was once a church of Justinian; two others were Crusaders' churches; the Mosque of the Lepers was a hospital of the Templars. A little to the south of Nablus is Jacob's Well, *Bir el Yakub*, believed to have been dug in the parcel of land which Jacob purchased when he came to Shechem. There Jesus, on His way from Jerusalem, rested and conversed with the woman of Samaria (*John* iv. 6).

Until recent years Nablus had a prosperous soap-making industry, with a large trade with many parts of the Moslem world (p. 263). With the loss of this trade, mainly through the growth of Egyptian manufacture and the erection of trade-barriers, the prosperity of Nablus has declined.

The *water-supply* is adequate and good, chiefly distributed by pipe from a well 60 feet deep. There are four reservoirs with total storage capacity of 330,000 gallons. There is no public electricity supply, but both the barracks and the Latin Convent have their own plant.

### Communications

Nablus is at the end of a narrow-gauge railway (105 cm.) which connects it with Tulkarm and Affula, but the line is little used. The main first-class road from Jerusalem passes through the town, and about 6 miles north-west it branches to Tulkarm in the west and to Haifa in the north. Beisan and the Jordan valley can be reached by a dry-weather road.

NAZARETH.  32° 42' N., 35° 18' E.; height 1,600 feet. Pop. (1941) 11,300 (8,756 in 1931; Christians 5,445, Moslems 3,226). District Commissioner's headquarters. Police barracks. Hospitals (Edinburgh Mission, 70 beds; French, 56 beds). Hospices (2). Hotel.

Nazareth is a straggling town built near the top of the southern slopes of the Galilean hills and overlooking the plain of Esdraelon. It is on the ancient route between Jerusalem and Tiberias. Most houses are substantially built of stone, but streets, with the exception of the main arterial road, are narrow, steep, and winding, the surface varying from asphalt to cobble, though those in the business area are passable to motors. The town is divided into Greek, Latin, Moslem, and mixed quarters.

### History

There is no mention of the place earlier than the time of Jesus and the greater part of its history is connected with His life. Down to the time of Constantine, Nazareth was inhabited by Samaritans. After the Arab conquest it declined, but it prospered again during the Crusades, only to contract when the Franks left Palestine. In the seventeenth century the Franciscans were permitted by Fakhr ed Din, the Druse Emir of the Lebanon, to establish a church and convent on the supposed site of the 'House of the Virgin'. Since then Nazareth, like Jerusalem, has become a place of religious and charitable establishments, and the heights around it are crowned by imposing orphanages, hospitals, and schools; among them the large orphanage of the French Salesians occupies a commanding position on the ridge to the west of the town.

The inhabitants to-day include merchants, carpenters, and masons, and there are four small workshops making tiles, tobacco, silk, and pottery, but the main activities are religious.

*Water* comes from the Reina well near Reina village. In the centre of the town is the 'Virgin's Fountain' (Ain Miriam). There is, however, a shortage in summer. Electricity is obtained from the Jordan power station (220 volts A.C.). There is no proper sewerage or drainage, cesspits being used.

### Communications

Nazareth is on the main Jerusalem–Tiberias and Haifa–Tiberias motor-roads, which meet just outside. There are bus services to Tiberias and Affula and neighbouring villages.

PETAH TIKVA. 32° 05′ N., 34° 53′ E.; height *c.* 160 feet. Pop. 17,400 (*est.* 1941; all Jewish). Schools, Hospital.

Petah Tikva, 2½ miles from Ras el Ain and 7 miles from Tel Aviv on the first-class road from Tel Aviv to Haifa and the north, lies in the midst of the orange country from which it drew its prosperity. In recent years it has grown to the size of a Palestinian town and has supplemented its agricultural activities by a number of small industries. Petah Tikva was founded in 1878 by seven Jews of Jerusalem, anxious to breathe the purer air of the country and to support themselves and their families by agriculture. Without experience and lacking adequate means, these quickly failed, in part as a consequence of unhealthiness of the undrained site. Five years later there was a new settlement at Petah Tikva, of Russian Jews. Out of this has grown the town of to-day, the largest of all the Jewish agricultural settlements in Palestine.

The main road—one of the best in Palestine—from Egypt and Gaza to Haifa and the north passes through Petah Tikva.

*107. Nablus, the biblical Shechem*

*108. Nazareth in Galilee*

109. *Safad*

110. *Tiberias from the north*

RAMALLAH. 31° 54′ N., 35° 12′ E.; height 2,870 feet. Pop. 4,500 (*est.* 1937; all Christian). Broadcasting station. Schools (2 American, 1 other), Hotels (2), Dispensary (no hospital).

Ramallah is about 10 miles north of Jerusalem and about half a mile to the west of Bira, which is on the main road between Jerusalem and Nablus. It is roughly on the border between Samaria and Judaea, and in a district well cultivated with olive, fig, and vine. The town covers a considerable area for its population and is generally well built with stone houses. The main roads in it have tarmac surfaces. The whole population is composed of Christian Arabs.

### History

In Ramallah and its neighbourhood there is much Herodian and pre-Herodian masonry, to a large extent incorporated in modern structures. There are also many rock tombs. In the adjoining village of Bira also there are many architectural remains. The identification of Ramallah with Ramah, the birth-place and burial-place of the prophet Samuel, is baseless. According to legend, it was at Bira that Mary and Joseph first discovered the absence of Jesus who had stayed behind in the Temple. This was a Crusaders' centre, and the most noteworthy of their buildings is the beautiful church with pointed arches built by the Knights Templar in 1146.

*Water.* There is no piped water-supply. Water is drawn from about 400 public wells and two private springs. Most houses have cisterns, but when these run dry, water must be drawn from the wells or purchased from the spring-owners. Electricity comes from Jerusalem by overhead cable.

### Communications

There is first-class road connexion to the main Jerusalem–Nablus road, and a good second-class road to Latrun on the Jerusalem–Jaffa road.

RAMLEH. 31° 55′ N., 34° 52′ E.; height *c.* 170 feet. Pop. (1941) 13,600 (11,952 in 1937; Moslems 9,768, Christians 2,184). Police barracks. Convents (Greek, Franciscan), Schools (2), Dispensary (no hospital).)

Ramleh, 'the Sandy', is near the northern end of the plain of Philistia, 12 miles south-east of Jaffa and Tel Aviv, and 3 miles south of Lydda. The town itself is of no great importance except historically. Its buildings are mostly small, and its streets except the main

Jerusalem–Jaffa road are generally narrow and in poor repair. The neighbourhood is almost entirely agricultural. The population is very largely Arab, except for members of the Franciscan Convent. There are no Jews.

### History

The identification of Ramleh with Arimathea of the Gospels is apocryphal, for it was founded only in A.D. 716 by Suleiman, afterwards Caliph, to take the place of Lydda. Its position in the plain astride the route between Jerusalem and the port of Jaffa has always given it some strategic importance, and an early watch-tower is in fair preservation. Another, known to Christians as the 'Tower of the Forty' (the forty martyrs of Sebaste in Armenia), is claimed as a remnant of an early church and of a later Moslem building.

In the twelfth century Ramleh was, after Jerusalem, the most important Crusader city in Palestine. When Saladin razed its fortifications its decline set in, though King Richard made it his headquarters for a time. Under the Ottoman Empire even the Moslem buildings fell to ruin. Napoleon was there in 1799, and after his evacuation there was a massacre of Christians by Moslems. In the neighbourhood was Allenby's headquarters during his final campaign in 1918, and the British War Cemetery is one of the largest in the Middle East.

*Water* is pumped from a municipal well to a reservoir (110,000 gallons) and then distributed by pipe to houses. Electricity is supplied by direct current from Tel Aviv.

### Communications

Ramleh station, on the Jaffa–Jerusalem railway, is just east of the town. Lydda junction, for Egypt and Haifa, is 2 miles to the north. The R.A.F. aerodrome is about three-quarters of a mile to the southeast, and the civil airport (Lydda) 5 miles to the north. There are first-class roads to Haifa and Tel Aviv, to Lydda and its neighbourhood, and to Jerusalem.

SAFAD. 32° 58′ N., 35° 30′ E.; height *c.* 2,720 feet. Pop. (1941) 11,000 (9,441 in 1931; Moslems 6,464, Jews 2,547, Christians 426). Hospitals (2). Hotels (3).

Safad is the northernmost town of Palestine, being about 7½ miles in a direct line north-west of Lake Tiberias (14½ miles by road).

It is built round three sides of a hill, on the top of which are castle ruins. Safad is one of the highest and healthiest towns in Palestine. In summer it is a health resort, especially for the inhabitants of Tiberias, which is almost unbearable in the hot weather. The town is subject to earthquakes and suffered severely in 1837 and 1927.

## History

Safad dates from about A.D. 200, but the present town only from about 1140, when the original castle was built by the Templars. The town was held in turn by the Latins and the Saracens, and ultimately taken by the Mamluk Sultan Beibars in 1266, when, despite his promise, he massacred the garrison, razed the fortress, and built the present tower, within which was an incline wide enough for four horses abreast.

It is surprising that until the thirteenth century there is no reference to Jews in the town, since Safad is now one of their four holy cities. When the Jews were expelled from Spain at the end of the fifteenth century Safad became their principal settlement in Palestine; but it attained greater fame in their eyes when, in the middle of the sixteenth century, Isaac Luria and his disciple Haim Vital revised the Jewish mystic writings (*Cabbala*) in Safad, and Joseph Caro codified Jewish Law in the *Shulchan Aruch*. The first printing-press in Palestine was set up in Safad in 1563.

For a short time in the eighteenth century Safad was the capital of a virtually independent kingdom, under a local Arab chief, Omar ez Zahir, generally known as Taher or Daher, who seized Tiberias and made war on his overlord, the Pasha of Damascus. In 1749 he seized Acre (p. 298), and for a short time there appeared a prospect of his carving out a kingdom in southern Syria; but his sons revolted, and before he died in 1775 his plans had miscarried.

The *town* is divided into an Arab quarter with two mosques and a Jewish quarter with several synagogues. The tower built by Beibars dominates the town. In the Jewish quarter in particular the houses rise one above another, so that in some places the roofs of those of one terrace serve as approach to the houses above. Except for one road which encircles the town, streets are not passable for motors. There are no industries.

The *water-supply* is good, though insufficient in summer. It is pumped from springs and distributed by pipes. Most houses also have their own cisterns. There is no general electric supply, but the hospitals and some of the hotels generate their own electricity.

*Communications*

First-class roads connect with Acre in the west, Metulla in the north, Jisr Banat Yakub in the east, and Tiberias in the south. There are bus services on these roads.

TIBERIAS. 32° 47′ N., 35° 32′ E.; height *c.* 650 feet below sea-level. Pop. *c.* 11,000 (*est.* 1941). Hotels.

Tiberias, on the south-west shore of its lake ('the Sea of Galilee'), was built by Herod Antipas in honour of the Emperor Tiberius, and was one of the most handsome cities in Roman Palestine. It is surrounded on three sides by hills. Being about 650 feet below sea-level, it is very hot and unpleasant in summer.

*History*

Built on the site of the cemetery of an earlier city, Rakkat, there is no record of Jesus ever having set foot in it, for to a pious Jew a city built in a cemetery would be unclean. Moreover, Jews refused to settle in Herod's city, despite its attractions. Later, when the town extended a mile farther north, and after the failure of Bar Cochba's rebellion in A.D. 135, Tiberias became the headquarters of the Jewish remnant in Palestine, the seat of the *Sanhedrin* and the birth-place of the *Mishna* (Jewish legislative writings) and of the Palestinian *Talmud*. It thus rose, like Safad, to be one of the Jewish holy cities. Almost a thousand years later, in 1187, it fell to Saladin, after an historic siege. In the sixteenth century Tiberias and its neighbourhood were granted by the Sultan to Don Joseph Nasi, his Jewish adviser, for Jewish settlement, but little came of the project. Near the city are the tombs of a number of medieval European Jewish worthies who came to Palestine to die. Tiberias is now one of the four or five cities of Palestine which have a Jewish majority.

*The Town*

The Arab quarter and the Jewish commercial quarter are on the edge of the lake, while the Jewish residential quarter straggles up the hill-side to the west. There is one main street, which is the modern shopping centre. The chief roads outside the walls are asphalted and suitable for motors. The houses are mostly of basalt. A large section of the old town was badly damaged by floods in 1934.

Tiberias is a market town, with few industries or skilled labour.

There is a small iron-works, but its prosperity is dependent on neighbouring villages which have little to spend but much to sell, particularly fruit and vegetables. A mile away, close to the site of the Roman city, are mineral springs, famous for many centuries for their medicinal properties, and now enclosed by a company for baths and a spa. There is moderate prosperity during the winter as a health resort and some commercial fishing in the lake.

*Water-supplies* are ample, distributed by pipes from the lake. Electricity is obtained from the Jordan power station.

## Communications

Buses run by the main roads to Nazareth and Haifa, Safad and Samakh.

TULKARM. 32° 19' N., 35° 01' E.; height 330 feet. Pop. 6,000 (*est.* 1937; Moslems 5,500, Christians 500). Agricultural College, Schools, Dispensary (no hospital).

Tulkarm is about half-way between Haifa and Lydda, on the eastern side of the plain of Sharon; it is built on rising ground where the Zeimar tributary of the Iskanderuna leaves the hills of Samaria, and forms the main gateway to Nablus from the coastal plain. The town is compact, with stone-built houses, and is the centre of an agricultural district. The population is entirely Arab, though nearly 10 per cent. are Christians.

The *water-supply* is good and is distributed by pipes. There is storage for 7,700,000 gallons.

## Communications

Tulkarm is on the main coastal railway between Haifa and Lydda, and the junction for the metre-gauge branch-line to Nablus. First-class roads go east to Nablus, south by Kalkilya to Jaffa, and west across the plain of Sharon to the coast at Nathanya.

CHAPTER XIII

# COMMUNICATIONS

PALESTINE has occupied throughout history an important strategic position between Egypt and Mesopotamia and between Egypt and Asia Minor. Its communications, therefore, have from early times been of great importance. Two immemorial routes pass by it or through it: one, from Damascus south and west by the plains of Esdraelon and Megiddo and over the Carmel ridge to Philistia—the 'Way of the Sea' to Egypt (p. 344); the other, east of the Jordan depression to south-west Arabia (p. 435). Both were great caravan routes, linking up the trading centres of the Euphrates and southern-most Arabia with the ports of the eastern Mediterranean. Of these ports only Acre (Ptolemais) is now within the limits of Palestine and its functions have been taken over by Haifa; the ancient Phoenician ports of Tyre and Sidon, now in the State of the Lebanon, have lost their importance.

The Palestinian section of the Damascus route between Mesopotamia and Egypt received also at Gaza part of the caravan traffic from the Yemen in south-west Arabia (p. 442), the remainder passing through Transjordan to join the 'Way of the Sea' near Deraa on the Yarmuk. Less significant for trade were the cross-country routes from Gaza and from Jaffa through Jerusalem to Amman in Transjordan, and thence direct across the desert into Babylonia. All ancient, medieval, and modern roads serve more or less directly these fundamental lines of communication.

Within Palestine itself communications were no less simple. Between north and south the 'Way of the Sea' was supplemented by a ridgeway along the Judaean watershed. Evading the steep-sided valleys, it ran from highland Galilee and Acre across the plain of Esdraelon to Shechem (Nablus), Jerusalem, Hebron, and Beersheba. Transverse routes left the 'Way of the Sea' for Jerusalem at Gaza by Lachish, and at Jaffa by Ramleh; a third from Caesarea (Kisarya) reached Shechem (Nablus) through Samaria (Sebustya). Thus the topography of Palestine, with its well-marked trends, has, throughout the history of the country, strongly influenced communications.

The striking feature of the routes of Palestine is the way in which, under successive administrations, they have perpetuated the early alinements. Thus the present road system bears a well-marked relationship to that of Roman times, and of even earlier periods. This is due in part to the strong control exerted by the physical background, not only in indicating alinements, but also in influencing the situation of towns and villages. In part also it is due to the lasting effect of the road-building activities of the Romans.

Early routes were merely tracks cleared of stones to allow the passage of chariots and carts. In the plains, the valleys, and the desert the soil was firm enough to form tracks, marked out by caravan traffic, their courses fixed by the points where water could be obtained and by defensible sites. In Roman times the old network gave place to a constructed system, by which Government and Army became unified. For a long period the Romans used existing routes, while the country remained peaceful. But after the Jewish revolt of A.D. 66–70 (p. 94) they were compelled to construct roads to facilitate the movement of troops. A significant parallel occurred under the Mandate, during the disturbances of 1929–1939 (pp. 125–130), when new roads were built or old ones improved so that the authorities could more effectively control the outbreaks.

The Roman roads served the needs of the Army and of the Government, and besides their strategic functions they also brought advantages to the cities by stimulating commerce, and to the whole country through their influence on culture and the spread of ideas. They were in use during the Middle Ages, and in many places until the end of the nineteenth century, when carriage roads, so called, began to be constructed after 1890. But under Ottoman neglect great and small roads alike fell into disrepair. In 1914 only one road, from Jaffa to Jerusalem, was in fair order. Only one motor-car had been seen in Palestine, and it never left the country. On many so-called roads horse-drawn vehicles could not pass, and towns such as Nablus and Safad could be reached only by horse or donkey or on foot.

## History of Railways

The country was slightly better off for railways, although all were narrow-gauge lines (105 cm.). The first line, built between April 1890 and August 1892, linked Jaffa through Lydda with Jerusalem, a distance of 54 miles, and was owned by a French company. The Hejaz railway from Damascus to Medina had been completed, with its important branch in Palestine connecting Deraa, through Samakh, Beisan, and Affula, with Haifa. The concession, originally granted to an Anglo-Turkish syndicate, had been purchased by the Ottoman

Government, and the line was opened in 1906. A small branch from Haifa to Acre was built later, but the extension from Affula southwards to Nablus was unfinished in 1914, and there was no coastal railway south from Haifa.

During the War of 1914–1918 the railway system was hurriedly expanded by the Turks. By 1916 they had completed the line to Nablus, built a new one from Masudiya (Massoudieh) on it through Tulkarm to Hadera, a second from Tulkarm southwards to Ramleh, and a third from Wadi Sarar on the Jerusalem railway to Beersheba and Kuseimeh (Kosseima). A branch from this was built from Tina to Gaza. To do this they dismantled the lines from Haifa to Acre and from Jaffa to Lydda.

During their advance from Egypt the British Army constructed a standard-gauge double-track railway from Kantara on the Suez canal to Rafa, and thence to Beersheba. After the capture of Gaza it was extended from Rafa through Gaza to Lydda. The line from Lydda to Jerusalem was reconstructed to standard gauge, a new standard-gauge line was built from Lydda to Haifa, the small narrow-gauge line from Haifa to Acre was relaid, and a narrow-gauge (60 cm.) temporary line was built from Lydda to the port area at Jaffa.

The Civil Administration took over the Palestine railways in October 1920, the assets (fixed and otherwise) being subsequently bought by the Palestine Government. The Kantara–Rafa section, which is in Egypt, remained the property of the British Government, but it is administered by the Palestine Railways by agreement. It is now known as the Sinai (Kantara–Rafa) railway.

Under the Civil Administration there was until 1939 very little new construction. Much of the permanent way built by the military authorities was relaid on a more lasting basis. The temporary line between Lydda and Jaffa was replaced by a new standard-gauge railway, but one of the tracks from Kantara—built during the war as a double line—was removed, and the military tracks from Wadi Sarar to Beersheba and Kuseimeh, from Gaza to Tina, and from Rafa to Beersheba were dismantled for lack of traffic, the first two in 1925, the last in 1927. In 1921 the short branch from Ras el Ain to Petah Tikva was built, part of its cost of construction being contributed by Petah Tikva. With the opening of the first-class road to Tel Aviv, passengers ceased to be carried on this branch, and it was afterwards operated only for goods traffic. The section of the branch-line from Affula to Masudiya was closed in 1932 as a measure of economy for similar reasons, but the track was not removed, and it has been used since for special purposes. As part of the harbour development at Haifa, railway facilities were very greatly increased at that port from 1932 onwards, and a new large central station was built.

These railways met the needs of the country in times of peace. Traffic was only heavy on the standard-gauge line during the harvesting of the citrus crop, most of which passed through the port of Haifa. But with the outbreak of war in 1939 the temporary insecurity of sea-routes in the Mediterranean threw a greater strain on the railways than they were able to bear. This led to improvement of the railway along the ancient 'Way of the Sea' from Egypt, which became once more the main line of communications in the country, and to the extension of the standard-gauge railway from Haifa to Ez Zib, close to the 'Ladder of Tyre' on the Lebanese border.

Immediately after the Syrian campaign in 1941, which ended in the Allied occupation of the country, the different routes for a practicable standard-gauge extension to Syria were examined, and orders were given in September to build it from Ez Zib along the coast by Beirut to Tripoli, where it would link up with the standard-gauge line to Aleppo. Work was completed early in 1943 and the line opened to traffic under military control.

Apart from the great importance of connecting Egypt through Palestine with Aleppo and Turkey by standard-gauge railway, the new line will confer great benefits on Beirut, the inland communications of which were previously quite inadequate to serve its excellent harbour.

The constructional work on the main line undertaken because of the war, and the consequent insecurity of Mediterranean sea-routes, has been the installation of new passing-loops from Kantara to Lydda, improvement of terminal facilities at these two places, additional locomotive-yard space at Gaza, and extension of sidings and other facilities at Haifa East. Improvements have also been made in watering facilities at certain stations, and the capacity of the line from Kantara to Lydda has been raised to 15 trains a day.

This increased capacity has necessitated an increase of rolling-stock, some of which is on loan or hire. The most important change of all has been the gradual conversion of fuelling of all standard-gauge locomotives from coal to oil, which is refined in the country at Haifa, a change which was due for completion by the summer of 1943.

There has been less new work on the narrow-gauge lines of

Palestine than on the standard-gauge. Two interchange points[1] from standard to narrow gauge have been constructed at Nesher, near Haifa, and at Nur esh Shems, near Tulkarm; the facilities at Samakh have been improved. The lines from Nablus to Tulkarm and to Affula have at times been used, but with the great improvements on the main line they have now (1943) been placed on a 'care and maintenance' basis. The extension and improvements to the narrow-gauge line in Transjordan are given in Chapter XVII.

To what extent the changes noted above are to be considered permanent it is impossible to say. Not all will be required in times of peace. Full details are not yet available for publication, and in the description of the lines that follows they are only given in general terms.[2]

### Development of Roads

Of the ancient routes, that along the coastal plain—the 'Way of the Sea' from Egypt to Damascus—was the most important. As far as Ras el Ain its course through Gaza, Mejdel, Isdud, Yibna or by Yusur, Katia, Lydda, and Ramleh is followed by the main road of to-day (pp. 373–377). From Ras el Ain it turned inland along the foot of the Samarian highland where the ground was firmer, through Tulkarm and over the Carmel ridge to Megiddo, and thence to Damascus, either by Beisan and Fik or by Mount Tabor, lakes Tiberias and Huleh, to join the route from Tyre and Sidon. Another important route was the ridgeway, followed by Abraham, through Beisan, Nablus, Jerusalem, Hebron, and Beersheba. Among the transverse routes, that from Acre eastwards to Safad, along the fault which separates upper and lower Galilee, and that from Beisan through the vale of Jezreel, and along the plain of Esdraelon to Cape Carmel, are followed generally by first-class roads to-day. In the south the Nabataean caravan route from the Wadi Araba, through Ain Hasb, Kurnub, and Beersheba to Gaza, still forms part of the chief route between Gaza and Akaba.

The Roman roads, incorporating the ancient tracks, resolved into a pattern closely resembling that of the present day. Again the two chief roads were the coastal route and the central route. The former, from Rafa, through Gaza, Ascalon, and Jamnia, threw off a branch to Jerusalem as did its predecessor and as does its modern counter-

---

[1] Sometimes called 'transhipment points', a term which is ambiguous in such areas as Haifa, where there is transhipment from ship to ship and 'transhipment' from train to train.

[2] A brief outline of the railway to Tripoli is, however, included as this line was not completed when the Handbook on Syria (BR. No. 513) went to press.

part, then continued through Caesarea, Atlit, and round Cape Carmel to Acre for Antioch. The central road of Roman times, from Beisan through Nablus, Jerusalem, Bethlehem, and Hebron to Tell el Milh, is to-day followed by the second most important road of the country, except in the south, where Beersheba replaces Tell el Milh. Transverse roads, linking the two north–south roads, and leading east across the Jordan, were numerous, and most of them have now their modern counterparts.

Of the so-called carriage roads begun at the end of the nineteenth century—the first real attempt to replace those of Roman times—the earliest to be completed were the four linking Jaffa with Haifa, Nablus, Jerusalem, and Gaza; the two linking Jerusalem with Jericho, and with Bethlehem and Hebron; and the road from Gaza to Beersheba. But before the War of 1914–1918 Palestine had no first-class roads, and most of the routes were merely tracks, used only by animal transport and quite unsuitable for wheeled traffic. During the war, though roads received less attention than railways, some were improved by the Turkish authorities and some in the south by the British military authorities, though most were in bad repair when the war ended. Since then the Palestine Government have continued the improvements, partly in order to develop commerce and settlement, and partly for security reasons, particularly during the disturbances of the three or four years preceding the present war. This progress has not merely been maintained, but has been intensified since 1939, and to-day first-class roads connect all the principal towns and many of the villages in the country, though the main framework still follows the ancient pattern. Thus two great roads run the length of the country from south to north: (a) from Gaza in the south by the coastal plain, past Cape Carmel and Haifa to the Lebanese frontier at Ras en Nakurah; and (b) from Beersheba by the Judaean ridgeway through Hebron, Jerusalem, and Nablus to the Syrian frontier at Metulla. A number of first-class roads run from west to east, and shorter lengths of good road connect important centres. The second-class roads are as a rule motorable in the dry season only. Almost every centre of consequence in the country is now joined to its neighbour by at least one first- or second-class road.

## RAILWAYS

ALL railways now operated by the Palestine administration have single tracks, but passing-loops are numerous and, because of the great development of good motor-roads, the railways fully meet the needs of the country, certainly in peace-time. They are described in this section in the following order:

| A. *Standard Gauge* | Miles | Km. | Page |
|---|---|---|---|
| 1. Haifa–Lydda–Gaza–Kantara, . . | 257·3 | 414·1 | 351 |
| with branches, (*a*) Haifa–Nesher . | 4·6 | 7·4 | |
| (*b*) Tulkarm–Nur esh Shems . | 3·1 | 5·0 | |
| (*c*) Ras el Ain–Petah Tikva . | 4·1 | 6·6 | |
| (*d*) Kafr Yinis–Nabala . . | 3·3 | 5·3 | |
| 2. Jaffa–Lydda . . . . . | 12·4 | 20·0 | 357 |
| with Sarafand Cantonment branch . . . . | 2·5 | 4·0 | |
| 3. Lydda–Jerusalem . . . . | 41·4 | 66·7 | 358 |
| 4. Haifa–Tripoli | | | |
| Haifa–Azzib (Ez Zib) . . | 23·0 | 37·0 | 360 |
| Azzib (Ez Zib)–Tripoli . . | 119·5 | 192·4 | 362 |
| B. *Narrow Gauge (105 cm.)* | | | |
| 5. Haifa–Acre . . . . . | 12·6 | 20·2 | 365 |
| 6. Haifa–Samakh . . . . | 54·0 | 87·0 | 367 |
| 7. Tulkarm–Nablus . . . . | 23·4 | 37·7 | 369 |
| 8. Affula–Masudiya . . . . | 37·2 | 59·9 | 371 |
| C. *Narrow Gauge (105 cm.) in Syria and Transjordan* | | | |
| 9. Samakh–Deraa . . . . | 45·9 | 73·8 | 505 |
| 10. Deraa–Maan (208·6 miles, 335·7 km.) and extension . . . . | 234·1 | 376·7 | 508 |

The last two are described in Chapter XVII, which deals with the communications of Transjordan. The line between El Hammeh (5 miles beyond Samakh) and Nessib (8 miles beyond Deraa) is in Syria, but Deraa is the junction for Damascus and for Maan, so that it is more convenient to describe the lines to and from Deraa.

### Administration

All railways within Palestine are the property of the State. The Palestine Railway Administration is a department of the Government, and the General Manager is directly responsible to the High Commissioner. As stated above, the line from Rafa to Kantara in Egypt and that from Nessib to Maan in Transjordan are also, by agreement, under the same general management. The section in Syria between Samakh and Nessib is part of the *Chemin de Fer Hedjaz* and is in peace-time managed by the Syrian Railway administration. The new main line from Haifa to Tripoli is under the Palestine Railways as far as Ez Zib, but thereafter under the Military authorities.

There are nine departments under the General Manager: (i) General Management, (ii) Traffic, (iii) Commercial, (iv) Locomotive and Carriage, (v) Locomotive Running, (vi) Engineering, (vii) Stores, (viii) Medical, (ix) Accounts.

The control and administration of all railways of both gauges is centralized in Haifa. All senior officials with one exception are British. The junior grades are mostly Arabs and Jews under British supervision, but until the outbreak of war in 1939 such supervision was inadequate. Since the war additional personnel has been found from the Military services.

### Traffic

The capacity and speed limits of each line, and the time normally taken on each journey by passenger, mixed, and goods trains, are given in the detailed descriptions which follow. The figures, unless otherwise stated, are for 1939. The only regular goods train services are over the standard-gauge main line between Kantara and Haifa. Between Jaffa and Jerusalem goods trains are fitted in when required. On all others, both standard- and narrow-gauge lines, 'mixed trains' take goods wagons when necessary.

A steady flow of about 30 wagons a day was maintained before 1939 from Egypt to destinations in Palestine, freight being chiefly composed of foodstuffs, asphalt, and paraffin. Imports from Haifa, and particularly cement and building material for Tel Aviv, accounted for much of the freight southwards, but there was little export traffic by rail to Egypt. Military traffic has greatly increased the importance of this line since 1939, and the capacity has been increased to 15 trains a day.

The traffic peak period on the standard-gauge system in peace-time was the citrus season (November to March), but the density of traffic varied very much according to the crop and the external market. The citrus harvest had little effect on the narrow-gauge system, which was more influenced by the cereal season of Syria, Transjordan, and northern Palestine, particularly from June to September. Melons grown in central and southern Palestine were loaded from June to August and affected both standard gauge and narrow, some being exported to Syria. In 1937 the Masudiya–Affula section was temporarily opened expressly for the transport of melons, so that the crop loaded at Tulkarm for Syria could go through on a railway of the same gauge, to save transfer at Haifa.

### Junctions, Interchange (Transhipment) Points, and Termini

The only important junctions are Lydda and Haifa. The interchange point at the latter for the narrow-gauge line to Samakh is at Nesher. Affula, Masudiya, and Tulkarm are minor junctions, the interchange point between the two gauges for the latter being at Nur esh Shems. Jaffa, Jerusalem, Rafa, Azzib (Ez Zib), and Samakh are the official termini of Palestine railways.

### Workshops

All heavy repairs to locomotives, carriages, and wagons are carried out in the Kishon workshops, 4½ miles (7 km.) east of Haifa, which were opened in 1933 and have been expanded since 1939. General repairs to locomotives on the Hejaz line are usually done at Damascus, but since 1939 most have been effected at Haifa. The capacity of the Haifa shops at the end of 1942 was 6 heavy and 3 light repairs per month (standard gauge), and 3 heavy and 2 light repairs per month (narrow gauge).

### Fuel

Before 1940 all locomotives burnt good-quality Welsh steam coal, bought through the Crown Agents for the Colonies, and landed at Haifa. A reserve stock of about three months' supply was stored at Haifa, Lydda, Gaza, and Kantara. During the war much has been landed at Kantara and carried up the line to the other points required. But there has also been a complete change of policy. It was expected that by the middle of 1943 all standard-gauge locomotives would be converted to oil-burning, the fuel being obtained from the Haifa refineries. A similar change is projected for narrow-gauge engines, but no conversions have yet been made (Jan. 1943).

The proposals include the storage of two months' reserve stocks of oil distributed as follows:

Standard Gauge: Kantara (5,000 tons), Gaza (3,000), Lydda (5,750), Tulkarm (2,000), Haifa (1,000).

Narrow Gauge: Samakh (500), Amman (750), Maan (500).

*Water-supply*

For the standard-gauge main line, water-supplies are adequate between Gaza and Ez Zib, though the quality varies. Between Kantara and Gaza water has always been difficult. Details are given in the descriptions of the railways concerned.

Water is also sufficient but variable on the narrow-gauge line from Haifa to Samakh, and thence to Nessib; but there have always been difficulties in the Transjordan section. Latest developments are given in Chapter XVII.

### RAILWAY CONSTRUCTION

The following constructional details apply generally to the railways in Palestine.

*Standard-gauge Railways*

(*a*) *Ballast* is of crushed crystalline limestone (except on the Sinai railway (Kantara–Rafa) which is sand-ballasted), most being obtained from the railway quarries at Nur esh Shems (on a small standard-gauge branch) about 3 miles from Tulkarm. There are also private quarries east of Haifa and at Beit Nabala, from which similar ballast is purchased.

(*b*) *Sleepers.* Steel is gradually replacing timber (creosoted pine) for sleepers, but both wooden and steel sleepers are still in use on the Haifa–Kantara railway.

(*c*) *Rails.* Flat bottom rails of British standard section, weight 75 lb. per yard, are used throughout.

(*d*) *Length of running line* administered by Palestine Railways, excluding sidings, loops, and marshalling lines, but including the Kantara–Rafa section and the Haifa–Azzib line, totals about 352 miles (566 km.).[1]

(*e*) *Maximum axle-load,* 17 tons.

(*f*) *Bridges.* There are 113 bridges (excluding culverts) on the standard-gauge lines, but no tunnels.

*Narrow-gauge Railways*

(*a*) *Ballast* is mostly as for the standard-gauge lines, but east of

---

[1] This figure excludes the line from Azzib to Tripoli which is administered by the Military authorities.

Beisan black basalt from near the track is used in the Jordan valley, and in Transjordan either limestone or basalt, whichever is most convenient.

(b) *Sleepers* are of the steel 'pea-pod' type, except at crossings where creosoted pine timbers are used.

(c) *Rails.* Flat bottom rails weighing 21·5 kg. per metre (c. 43½ lb. per yard) are used throughout.

(d) *Length of running line*, within Palestine only, totals 127·2 miles (204·8 km.).

(e) *Maximum axle-load*, 10 tons.

(f) *Bridges.* There are 163 bridges within Palestine and one tunnel. From Samakh to Nessib there are 18 bridges and 7 tunnels, and from Nessib to Maan many bridges and viaducts (Chap. XVII).

## DESCRIPTION OF RAILWAYS

The description of the railways which follows is divided into three parts: (a) details of the line as a whole, distances, branch-lines, junctions, interchange points, permanent way, capacity, &c.; (b) general description of the line and the country passed; (c) details of stations and their facilities, and of chief engineering works. In the general description distances are given in miles; in the detailed description in the metric system, which is used by the railway authorities.

In the first column of the detailed description the distance is given in kilometres from the starting-point; and, where this does not conform to the kilometre posts, the distance by kilometre posts is also given.

In the second column is given the station name, sometimes an alternative name, and the distance between neighbouring passing-loops.

The third column gives the station facilities (abbreviated to save space); details of important bridges and tunnels; and remarks on alinement and gradient. Of all railway facilities, those at stations are the most liable to change, a fact particularly true of Palestine railways in time of war, when a much greater burden has been thrown on them than that for which they were maintained before 1939. While it is possible that additional facilities will be required and are in fact being provided at Haifa and Lydda, it is also probable that many will not be maintained when the war is over.

The following abbreviations are used in the last column:

| | |
|---|---|
| Alt. | Altitude of the railway station. |
| PL. | Passing-loop. The number of loops is shown in brackets. |
| W. | Watering facilities are shown in brackets after the letter W. |
| (T. 5,000 gls.). | Water tank, capacity 5,000 gallons. |
| (R.) | Water may be relied upon. |
| (UR.) | Water facilities are unreliable. |
| (C.) | Water columns; the figure gives the number of columns available. |
| (SP.); (EP.); (OP.); (HP.); (WP.). | Steam pump; Electric pump; Oil pump; Hand-pump; Wind-pump. |
| F. | Fuel (coal, oil, or both). |
| PP.; GP. | Passenger platform; goods platform. |
| GS.; C.S. | Goods shed; Citrus shed. |
| LP.; SLP.; ELP.; ELR. | Loading platform; side-loading platform; end-loading platform; end-loading ramp. |
| RpS. | Repair shops. |
| BC. | Breakdown crane. |
| Tbl. | Turntable. |
| Tr. | Turning triangle. |
| ES.(6) | Engine shed for 6 locomotives. |
| MY.(8) | Marshalling yards, 8 roads. |
| Sdg(s). | Siding(s). |

## 1. HAIFA–KANTARA

*Route*

| | | | | |
|---|---|---|---|---|
| Haifa–Tulkarm | 41·5 miles | 66·8 kilometres |
| Tulkarm–Lydda | 27·3 ,, | 44·0 ,, |
| Lydda–Gaza | 40·5 ,, | 65·2 ,, |
| Gaza–Kantara East | 148·0 ,, | 238·1 ,, |
| | 257·3 | 414·1 |

*Branch-lines*

(a) Haifa to Nesher (Interchange Point and Portland Cement Factory), 4·6 miles (7·4 km.)

(b) Tulkarm to Nur esh Shems (Interchange Point and Ballast Quarries), 3·1 miles (5·0 km.)

(c) Ras el Ain to Petah Tikva, 4·1 miles (6·6 km.)

(d) Kafr Yinis to Beit Nabala, 3·3 miles (5·3 km.)

The last three, (b), (c), and (d), are operated as sidings from the main line.

*Permanent way, stations, and kilometre posts*

Standard gauge. Single track. Ballast, crushed crystalline limestone to Rafa, thence sand-ballast. Rails, flat-bottom, 75 lb. per yd. Sleepers, wooden and steel. Maximum axle-load, 17 tons. Minimum radius of curves, 146 m. at km. 235·6. Maximum gradient: Haifa to Tulkarm, 1 in 117·5; Tulkarm to Kantara, 1 in 90. Maximum distance between passing-loops, 15 km. between Gilbaneh and Kantara. Kilometre posts are numbered from Haifa to Kantara East, 0–414 km. In the Detailed Description of the line, passing-loops with an asterisk have been constructed since 1939.

*Speed and capacity*

The times given are those taken by the old coal-burning Baldwin engines, used before 1940. Later figures are not available.

| Overall time (including stops): | *Passenger* | *Goods* |
|---|---|---|
| Haifa–Tulkarm | 1 hr. 30 min. | 2 hr. 15 min. |
| Haifa–Lydda | 2 ,, 30 ,, | 3 ,, 45 ,, |
| Haifa–Gaza | 4 ,, 15 ,, | 6 ,, 0 ,, |
| Haifa–Kantara East | 8 ,, 45 ,, | 13 ,, 15 ,, |

Maximum train speeds: Haifa to Rafa (*passenger*), 50 m.p.h.; (*goods*), 37 m.p.h. Rafa to Kantara (*passenger*), 43 m.p.h.; (*goods*), 31 m.p.h. There are permanent speed restrictions of 28 m.p.h. at curves.

Capacity of line, 10 trains each way in 24 hours, until 1940; since reported to be raised to 15 trains.

Net load, 400 tons.

*GENERAL DESCRIPTION*

This is the main line through Palestine. Only in the first few miles, where it passes round Cape Carmel, are there any difficulties, and there are no engineering works of any importance except the bridges over coastal rivers and streams.

As far as Tantura, mile 18·7, the line is never more than a mile from the shore, and often only a few hundred yards, but at Tantura it begins to cross the coastal plain, and from Hadera, mile 30·8, to Lydda junction, mile 68·9, it skirts the eastern side of the plain of Sharon, often close to the foot of the hills. The Jaffa–Jerusalem line (Rlys. 2, 3) joins at Lydda, after which the main line converges on the coast, and from Yibna, mile 77·5, to the Egyptian boundary at Rafa, mile 132·0, it follows the inland edge of the sand-dune belt fairly closely. Throughout its whole course in Palestine it never rises to 200 feet above sea-level.

In the Sinai section also there are no difficulties of alinement. The railway keeps behind the sand-dune belt, and from a few miles beyond El Arish, where it is close to the open sea, it keeps near the shore of the shallow salt lagoon, Sabkhet el Bardawil, and at Misfak is at the water's edge.

In Palestine there are no running difficulties. Water is plentiful, even at Gaza. But in the Sinai section the supply has always been inadequate, even for the restricted service in peace-time. There is no suitable water between El Arish and Kantara, and special water-trains have had to be run from Kantara to Mazar, a distance of just over 70 miles, to fill the water-tanks at this station. Under war-time conditions, with many more trains running, this is a costly operation. By January 1943 a new plan was to be in operation. This comprised the erection of a water-softening plant and 14 new tanks at El Arish, from which locomotives will be able to fill their own tenders for use between Mazar and Kantara, and from which they will also take an additional 30-ton water-tank load, half to be used for the journey to Mazar and half to be picked up for the return journey from Mazar to El Arish. The reserve storage tanks at Mazar were only to be kept filled for emergency use.

## DETAILED DESCRIPTION

| Km. from Haifa | Stations and passing-loops | Remarks |
| --- | --- | --- |
| 0·0 | HAIFA EAST[1] (1) | PL.(2); W.(town mains,50,000 gls.,R.; C.(3), EP.); F.; PP.,GP.(3); GS.; ELR.(5); RpS.; ES.(32); Tbl.; MY.; Sdgs. For description of the town and port, *see* pp. 300–307. Line passes south of the Main Wharf and Transit Sheds. |
| 1·4 | HAIFA CENTRAL (7) | PL.(1); PP.(2). One line passes to the Passenger landing wharf (with loop) rejoining the main line north-west of the station. Main line then cuts across the Bat Gallim promontory and rounds Cape Carmel, keeping close to the shore. |
| 8·5 | KAFR SEMI (6) | PL.(1). Line keeps about 400 yards or less from the shore most of the way to the Atlit promontory. |
| 14·0 | TIREH (TIRA) (7) | PL.(1). The coastal plain widens to about 1 mile. There are salt-pans near the coast just before Atlit. |

[1] Many facilities have been added since 1939. Further remodelling is in progress (1943). Details are not available for publication.

| Km. from Haifa | Stations and passing-loops | Remarks |
|---|---|---|
| 20·5 | ATLIT (ATHLIT) (10) | PL.(2); GP.; GS.; Sdg. Line keeps about ½ mile from the coast, and is separated from it by marsh. There is a ridge of low sandhills on the landward side. |
| 30·1 | TANTURA (4) | PL.(1). |
| c. 32·5 | .. | Line bends inland and crosses the Tantura river. |
| 34·3 | ZIKHRON YAKOV (ZICHRON JACOB) (7) | PL.(2); W.(T.20,000 gls. from well,R.; C.(2)); GP.; GS. Station is about 1 mile from the coast and is connected with the coastal road ¼ mile farther inland; from this there is a hill road to the village of Zichron Jacob. Line keeps round the edge of the Carmel foothills crossing the Zerka river about km. 38·8. |
| 41·2 | BINYAMINA (8) | PL.(3); GP.; GS.,CS. A rough track leads to the coast at Caesarea. Line is nearly 3 miles inland opposite Caesarea, with wide sand-dune belt between. |
| 49·6 | HADERA (8) | PL.(3); GP.; GS.,CS. Station is about 1½ miles east of the prosperous village. Line now clears the Carmel foothills and goes inland across the northern end of the plain of Sharon. |
| 49·9 | .. | Steel bridge over the Hadera river, 18 m.+3× 4·5 m. |
| 58·0 | QAQUN (KAKUN) (9) | PL.(1). Station is 1½ miles north of the small village, and is joined to it by a rough road. |
| 62·3 | .. | Steel bridge, 6×4·5 m. |
| 66·8 | TULKARM (12) | PL.(4); W.(T.4,400 gls. from well,R.; C., EP.); PP.; CS.; ELR.(2); ES.(3); Tr.; Sdgs.(3). Junction for narrow-gauge line to Nablus (Rly. 7) and for standard-gauge branch-line to the interchange point at Nur esh Shems. For town description, see p. 339. First-class roads go to Nathanya on the coast (10 miles), east to Nablus (17½ miles), and south to Tel Aviv and Jaffa. |
| 68·4 | .. | Bridge over Tin river, 10×3·65 m. (steel)+ 6×3 m. (masonry arch). |
| 78·6 | QALQILIA (KALKILYA) (13) | PL.(2); GP.; CS. Station is 1½ miles north of the village, with which it is connected by first-class branch-road to the main Tulkarm–Jaffa road. |
| 84·4 | .. | Steel bridge, single span, 18·4 m., over the Ishkar tributary of the Auja. |
| 90·9 | .. | Steel bridge, 5×6·3 m., height 4·4 m. above one of the Auja wadi-beds. |
| 91·3 | RAS EL AIN (13) | PL.(3); W.(T.20,000 gls. from well,UR.; C.(2), SP.). Short branch (6·6 km.) to Petah Tikva, operated |

| Km. from Haifa | Stations and passing-loops | Remarks |
|---|---|---|
| | | as siding. For town description of Petah Tikva, see p. 334. |
| | | First-class road from station through Petah Tikva to Tel Aviv and Jaffa. |
| 94·1 | .. | Steel bridge, 7 × 6·5 m., height 5·3 m. above Auja wadi-bed. |
| 102·5 | .. | Steel bridge, 2 × 10·5 m., over tributary of the Wadi Kebir. |
| 104·3 | KAFR YINIS (JIN-NIS) (7) | PL.(2). |
| | | Short branch (5·3 km.) to Beit Nabala, operated as siding. |
| | | Lydda airport is immediately west of the station. |
| 105·5 | .. | Steel bridge, 3 × 10 m., over the Wadi Kebir. |
| c. 108 | .. | Line enters the cultivated outskirts of Lydda, soon after crossing the bridge, and passes the built-up area about km. 108. |
| c. 109·8 | .. | Jaffa line (Rly. 2) joins in from west. |
| 110·8 | LYDDA JUNCTION (9) | PL.(8); W.(T.60,000 gls. from well,R.; C.(5)); F.; PP.(2),GP.; GS.; ELR.(2); RpS.; ES.(27); Tr.; BC.; MY.(14). |
| | | Junction for Jaffa and Tel Aviv (Rly. 2), and for Jerusalem (Rly. 3). For description of Lydda town, see pp. 331–332. |
| c. 111·3 | .. | Line leaves for Jerusalem. Main line turns west and skirts the gardens of Ramleh. |
| 115·6 | BEER YAKOV (BEER JACOB) | GP.; CS.; Sdgs.(3). A collecting centre for citrus fruit. |
| | | Line turns south-west across the richly cultivated plain of Philistia. |
| 119·9 | REHOVOT (5) | PL.(1); PP.,GP.; CS.; Sdgs.(3). |
| | | The coastal road crosses the line at Rehovot station and continues south to Rehovot village, ¾ mile distant. |
| 124·8 | YIBNA (8) | PL.(2); GP.; CS. |
| | | Station is 1½ miles north-east of the village. |
| 125·8 | .. | Steel bridge, 2 × 18 m. approx. |
| 126·9 | .. | Steel bridge, 6 × 6 m., over the Wadi Rubin. |
| c. 127·3 | .. | Line passes Yibna village. |
| c. 132·9 | SUKREIR (7) | PL.(1).* |
| 139·4 | .. | Steel bridge, 2 × 18 m. approx., height 6·5 m. above the dry bed of the Wadi Sukreir. |
| 140·3 | ISDUD (12) | PL.(1); GP. |
| | | Station is about 1½ miles north of the small village. |
| | | Line is separated from the shore by a belt of sand-dunes, nearly 3 miles wide, which begins to narrow soon after passing the village. |
| 152·8 | MAJDAL (MEJDEL) (4) | PL.(2); GP.; CS.; Sdg. |
| | | Station is about a mile east of the village, through which it is connected by a second-class road to Jura (anc. Ascalon) on the coast. |

\* Constructed since 1939 (see p. 343).

| Km. from Haifa | Stations and passing-loops | Remarks |
|---|---|---|
| c. 157·0 | EL JIYA (9) | PL.(1).* |
| 165·8 | DEIR SUNEID (10) | PL.(1); GP. |
| 166·2 | .. | Masonry viaduct, 4 × 6 m. |
| 170·2 | .. | Masonry viaduct, 4 × 6 m. |
| c. 173·5 | .. | Line enters the cultivated garden area surrounding Gaza. |
| 176·2 | GAZA (9) | PL.(3); W.(T.20,000 gls., from reservoir 110,000 gls.,R.; C.(8), SP.(2)); F.; GP.; CS.; ES.(2); Tr.; Sdgs.(2). Small repair depot. For town description, see pp. 315–317. |
| c. 182 | .. | Line leaves the cultivated area surrounding Gaza. |
| 185·0 | .. | Reinforced concrete bridge over the Wadi Ghazza, 9 × 10·5 m., height 5·5 m. above wadi bed (photo. 111). The mound Tell Ujal, the site of ancient Gaza, is visible 1 mile to the north-west. |
| c. 185·2 | RASHIDA (7) | PL.(1).* The tomb of Sheikh Rashid, from which the station takes its name, is on a hill to west, about 1 mile distant. |
| 192·5 | DEIR EL BELAH (8) | PL.(1); GP. The village, among trees, is 1 mile distant to north-west, and about the same distance from the coast. |
| 200·6 | KHAN YUNIS (12) | PL.(2); GP.; ELR. For town description, see pp. 330–331. |
| 211·3 | .. | Egyptian boundary. |
| 212·5 | RAFA (13) | PL.(3); W.; Tr.; MY. The village is about 2 miles north of the station on the Palestine side of the border. The continuation of the line is known as the Sinai Railway. |
| c. 225·5 | SHEIKH ZOWAID (11) | PL.(1).* |
| c. 236·5 | KABR AMEIR (11) | PL.(1).* |
| c. 247·5 | GERADI (11) | PL.(1).* |
| 258·6 | .. | Steel bridge over Wadi El Arish, length 160 m., 10 steel girders on pillars. |
| 258·7 | EL ARISH (11) | PL.(2); W.(softening plant);[1] Sdg.(2). |
| c. 269·7 | BARDAWIL (11) | PL.(1).* |
| c. 280·7 | EL MIDAN (11) | PL.(1).* |
| c. 291·7 | ZEBRIKA (9) | PL.(1).* |
| 300·7 | MAZAR (11) | PL.(2); W.(T.14,000 gls.,UR.; reservoir 80,000 gls. filled by water-trains from Kantara; C.(3)); Sdg. |
| c. 311·2 | EL TILUL (11) | PL.(1).* |
| 321·8 | MISFAK (8) | PL.(1). |
| c. 329·7 | SALMANAH (8) | PL.(1).* |
| 337·4 | BIR EL ABD (12) | PL.(2). |

* Constructed since 1939 (see p. 343).
[1] See General Description, p. 353.

| Km. from Haifa | Stations and passing-loops | Remarks |
|---|---|---|
| c. 349·4 | EL KHIRBA (12) | PL.(1).* |
| c. 361·4 | RABAA (11) | PL.(1).* |
| 372·5 | ROMANEH (9) | PL.(2). |
| c. 381·5 | PALUZEH (10) | PL.(1).* |
| c. 391·5 | TELL EL HEIR (8) | PL.(1).* |
| c. 399·5 | GILBANEH (15) | PL.(1).* |
| 414·1 | KANTARA EAST | PL.(1); W.(T.70,000 gls.,R.; reservoir 600,000 gls.; filtered and pumped from Sweet-water Canal; C.(6)); F.; PP.,GP.; ELR.; RpS.; ES.(6); Tr.; MY.(11). |

* Constructed since 1939 (see p. 343).

## 2. JAFFA–LYDDA

*Distance*: 12·4 miles, 20 kilometres.

*Branch-line*. Turn-out for Sarafand Military Sidings at mile 9·8 (km. 15·8).

*Permanent way, stations, and kilometre posts.*

Standard gauge. Single track. Ballast, crushed crystalline limestone. Rails, flat-bottom, 75 lb. per yd. Sleepers, steel. Maximum axle-load, 17 tons. Minimum radius of curves, 150 m. (from km. 0·08 to km. 0·14). Maximum gradient, 1 in 50 in one place. Maximum distance between passing-loops, 10 km. Kilometre posts are numbered from Jaffa, 0–20 km.

*Speed and capacity*

Overall time (including stops): *passenger*, 30 min.; *goods*, 45 min.

Maximum train speeds: Jaffa–Tel Aviv: (*passenger*), 25 m.p.h.; (*goods*), 18 m.p.h. Tel Aviv–Jaffa: (*passenger and goods*), 12 m.p.h. Lydda–Tel Aviv–Lydda: (*passenger and goods*), 43 m.p.h.

Capacity of line, 11 trains each way in 24 hours. Net load, 400 tons.

*GENERAL DESCRIPTION*

The line passes north-west out of Jaffa along the southern side of Tel Aviv, crosses the Petah Tikva road, and swings with a sharp curve southwards. Es Safiriya station is more than a mile north-west of the village of that name. The countryside is well cultivated. The large military cantonment at Sarafand, about 3 miles north-west of Ramleh, and on the first-class road between Jaffa and Ramleh, is connected by a small branch-line about 2½ miles long. With the exception of one small length of line where the gradient reaches

1 in 50, there is very little rise or fall, and the line nowhere reaches 200 feet above sea-level.

*DETAILED DESCRIPTION*

| Km. from Jaffa | Stations and passing-loops | Remarks |
| --- | --- | --- |
| 0·0 | JAFFA (2) | PL.(2); W.(T.15,000 gls. from well,R.; C.,SP.); F.; PP.,GP.; GS.; ELR.; RpS. (military); ES.; Tbl.; Sdgs.(10). For description of the town and port, *see* pp. 307–311. |
| 1·9 | TEL AVIV (10) | PL.(4); W.(direct from town mains,R.; C.); PP.,GP.; GS.,CS,; ELR.; Sdgs.(6). For town description, *see* pp. 311–314. |
| *c.* 12·0 | ES SAFIRIYA (8) | PL.(1). |
| *c.* 15·8 | .. | Turn-out for Sarafand Military Sidings (PL.; Sdg.). |
| 19·0 | .. | Line joins the main Haifa–Kantara railway (Rly. 1). |
| 20·0 | LYDDA JUNCTION | PL.(8); W.(T.60,000 gls. from well,R.; C.(5)); F.; PP.(2),GP.; GS.; ELR.(2); RpS.; ES.(27); Tr.; BC.; MY.(14). For town description, *see* pp. 331–332. |

## 3. LYDDA–JERUSALEM

*Distance*: 41·4 miles, 66·7 kilometres.

(Jaffa–Jerusalem, 53·8 miles, 86·7 kilometres)

*Branch lines*. None.

*Permanent way, stations, and kilometre posts*

Standard gauge. Single track. Ballast, crushed crystalline limestone. Rails, flat-bottom, 75 lb. per yd. Sleepers, steel and wood. Maximum axle-load, 17 tons. Minimum radius of curves, 120 m. (at kms. 56·8 and 75·9 from Jaffa). Maximum gradient, 1 in 50 frequent between Artuf and Jerusalem. Maximum distance between passing-loops, 13 km. Minimum length of loop-line at stations, 227 m. (Niana). Kilometre posts are numbered from Jaffa, 21–86 km.

*Speed and Capacity*

| Overall time (including stops): | *Passenger* | *Goods* |
| --- | --- | --- |
| Lydda–Jerusalem | 2 hr. 0 min. | 3 hr. 15 min. |
| Jerusalem–Lydda | 1 ,, 45 ,, | 2 ,, 45 ,, |

Maximum train speeds: Lydda–Artuf: (*passenger*), 43 m.p.h.; (*goods*), 31 m.p.h. Artuf–Jerusalem: (*passenger*), 28 m.p.h.; (*goods*), 22 m.p.h.

Capacity of line, 11 trains each way in 24 hours. Net load, 120 tons.

111. *Railway bridge over the Wadi Ghazza, south of Gaza*

112. *Battir station, Lydda–Jerusalem railway*

113. *Masonry bridge over the Kishon at km. 13·1 on the Haifa–Samakh railwa*

114. *Railway bridge over the Yarmuk near Naharayim*

## GENERAL DESCRIPTION

This line makes use of the narrow valley of the Wadi Sarar to reach the plateau of Judaea. From Lydda junction (alt. *c.* 200 ft.) the ascent is continuous throughout, but gradual as far as Wadi Sarar station (330 ft.), where the gradient increases. At Artuf (*c.* 720 ft.) the valley closes in and forms a narrow tortuous limestone gorge, up which the railway twists and climbs steeply, sometimes at maximum gradient of 1 in 50, past Deir esh Sheikh (*c.* 1,400 ft.) where the gorge walls rise to 2,060 feet on the north and 2,370 on the south, to Battir (*c.* 1,850 ft.). Half-way between Battir and Jerusalem station (2,468 ft.) the country begins to open out and the gradient eases, but only in the last few hundred yards does the track become level. Sand-drags are provided at Artuf, Deir esh Sheikh, and Battir.

## DETAILED DESCRIPTION

| Km. from Lydda | Jaffa | Stations and passing-loops | Remarks |
|---|---|---|---|
| 0·0 | 20·0 | LYDDA JUNC-TION (10) | Alt. *c.* 200 ft. PL.(8); W.(T.60,000 gls. from well,R.; C.(5)); F.; PP.(2),GP.; GS.; ELR. (2); RpS.; ES.(27); Tr.; BC.; MY.(14). For town description, *see* pp. 331–332. |
| | | | Line branches south-east from the main Haifa–Kantara railway immediately on clearing the junction. |
| 2·5 | 22·5 | RAMLEH | PP.,GP.; ELR.; Sdg. For town description, *see* pp. 335–336. |
| | | | Line turns south over undulating country. |
| 9·5 | 29·5 | NIANA (8) | PL.(1). |
| 16·8 | 36·8 | .. | Bridge over the Wadi Sarar, 6·2 m.+6·9 m. +7·2 m. (steel)+5·1 m. (masonry arch), height 2·3 m. |
| 17·3 | 37·3 | WADI (ES) SARAR (13) | Alt. *c.* 330 ft. PL.(2); W.(T.400 gls., from well, UR.; C.); GP. |
| | | | Line turns south-east up the Sarar valley, keeping along the steep southern slopes, and climbing steadily. |
| 30·4 | 50·4 | ARTUF (13) | Alt. *c.* 720 ft. PL.(2); W.(T.20,000 gls., reservoir filled by water trains,R.; C.(2),SP.); PP.; sand-drag; Sdgs. (2). Artuf village is 1 mile north-east, reached by a good road. |
| 31·5 | 51·5 | .. | Steel bridge over narrow tributary wadi, 2×5 m., masonry piers, height, 5·5 m. |
| | | | Sarar valley now closes in and becomes tortuous. The line conforms, crosses and re-crosses the Wadi Sarar, and climbs with maximum gradient and minimum radius of curves. |
| 36·9 | 56·9 | .. | ⌠Two steel bridges over the Sarar gorge, each |
| 38·1 | 58·1 | .. | ⌡ 5 m.+2×10 m.+5 m., high masonry piers. |

| Km. from | | Stations and | |
| Lydda | Jaffa | passing-loops | Remarks |
|---|---|---|---|
| 43·4 | 63·4 | DEIR ES SHEIKH (12) | Alt. c. 1,400 ft. PL.(1); W.(reservoir, 8,000 gls., UR.; C.(2),grav.); sand-drag; Sdg. Station is at the entrance of a narrow tributary, opening to the south. Line now keeps to the left bank of the wadi to Battir station, rising steeply with many bends (photo. 112). |
| 55·8 | 75·8 | BATTIR (11) | Alt. c. 1,850 ft. PL.(1); W.(reservoir,16,000 gls.; UR.; C.(2),grav.); PP.; sand-drag; Sdg. |
| 56·0 | 76·0 | .. | Steel bridge over the Wadi Sarar 4 m.+5 m.+ 4 m., height 5·6 m. |
| c. 61·0 | c. 81·0 | .. | Line reaches more open country. |
| 66·7 | 86·7 | JERUSALEM | Alt. 2,468 ft. PL.(6); W.(T.20,000 gls. from town mains,R.; C.(2)); F.; PP.,GP.; GS.; ELR.; ES.(3); Tbl.; Sdgs.(17). The station is south of the 'Valley of Hinnom', south of the walls of the 'Old City'. For a description of Jerusalem, see pp. 323–330. |

## 4. HAIFA–AZZIB (EZ ZIB)–BEIRUT–TRIPOLI[1]

### Route

| | | |
|---|---|---|
| Haifa–Azzib | 23·0 miles | 37·0 kilometres |
| Azzib–Beirut | 66·4 ,, | 106·9 ,, |
| Beirut–Tripoli | 53·1 ,, | 85·5 ,, |
| | 142·5 | 229·4 |

### Junctions and interchange points

Haifa East is the junction for the main line to the south (Rly. 1). The interchange point for the narrow-gauge line to Samakh is at Nesher, though the narrow-gauge leaves at Acre junction. Kishon junction is merely a junction for branch lines to workshops and stores depots. At Naamin junction the dual gauge ends, a small extension of the narrow-gauge line going on to Acre. Azzib (Ez Zib) is the terminus of Palestine Railways. Beirut is the interchange point for the narrow-gauge line to Rayak and Damascus, which serves the port of Beirut. At Tripoli the new line from the south meets the old standard-gauge line from Aleppo and Homs.

### Permanent way, stations, and kilometre posts

Standard gauge. Single track. Details of ballast, rails, and sleepers are not available. Maximum axle-load, 19 tons. Minimum radius of curves,

[1] Details compiled from information received up to March 1943. Those of the Syrian section are included here, since they were not available when the volume on Syria (BR. 513) went to press.

153 m. between Azzib and Nakurah. Maximum gradients: Haifa–Azzib, 1 in 105; Azzib to Beirut, 1 in 90; Beirut to Tripoli, 1 in 59. Maximum distance between passing-loops, 11 km.

## Speed and capacity

No details yet available.

## GENERAL DESCRIPTION

This line, though open to traffic, is not yet fully completed, some projected facilities at certain stations not yet being available. This applies particularly to sidings, which though noted in the detailed description are often very short and suitable only for laying off a few crippled trucks. For permanent running there may be some improvements in alinement. Watering details are not available. The spelling of station names differs considerably in the accounts from which the following details have been compiled.

The railway follows the coastline of Palestine and of the Lebanon very closely. As far as Naamin junction, just outside Acre, the track is dual-gauge with the narrow-gauge line (Rly. 5). Thence to Azzib station (mile 23) it traverses the coastal plain of Acre with no obstacles. Ras en Nakurah, the bold headland which marks the Lebanon boundary, presented the first formidable task for the construction engineers, and beyond it three more promontories reach seawards in the next 8 miles. Ras en Nakurah and Ras el Abyad are pierced by tunnels, the others are passed on the seaward side; all required strong walls of concrete and masonry. At mile 32 the line enters the plain of Tyre, comparatively broad and open, as far as Sidon, with no obstacles except the rivers Litani, Senik (or Zahrani), and Saitanik, all of which required major bridges.

From Sidon (mile 62·5) to Khaldeh (mile 83) the mountains again come steeply down to the shore, and there is no coastal plain. Again the line is forced to pass round the various headlands on masonry walls, and there are two large bridges over the Awali and Damour rivers. Beyond Khaldeh the railway crosses the Kafarchima stream, leaves the coast and cuts across the Beirut promontory, not far from the foot of the mountains. Near the passage of the Beirut river it crosses the narrow-gauge line from the port to Damascus, but itself does not enter the town, and there is as yet no standard-gauge link with town or port.

North of Beirut the railway continues along the shore, following the coast road closely. For a long distance the mountains rise steeply from the water's edge and again there is much masonry work. The three rivers, the Nahr el Kelb, Nahr Ibrahim, and the Nahr el Jajeh, all required major bridges. In the last few miles the line pierces the great Ras esh Shakkah by a tunnel, 1,618 yards long, and at Tripoli harbour it connects with the older standard-gauge line to Homs and Aleppo.

DETAILED DESCRIPTION

| Km. from Haifa East | Stations and passing-loops | Remarks |
|---|---|---|
| 0·0 | HAIFA EAST (2) | PL.(2); W.(town mains, 50,000 gls.,R.; C.(3), EP.); F.; PP.,GP.(3); GS.; ELR.(5); RpS.; ES.(32); Tbl.; MY.; Sdgs. For description of the town and port, see pp. 300–307. Maximum gradients to Naamin junction: 1 in 105 up, 1 in 208 down. The line is laid with the narrow-gauge line as dual track to Naamin junction (km. 19·1). |
| 2·0 | ACRE JUNCTION (7) | PL.(1). Narrow-gauge line (Rly. 6) leaves for Samakh. |
| 5·0 | .. | Steel bridge over Kishon R., 31·4 m.+2×9·1 m., masonry abutments, steel piers. |
| 5·6 | KISHON JUNCTION | Sdgs.(3) serve Post Office stores, workshops foundry, and glass factory. Branch and Sdgs.(28) serve Kishon workshops. |
| 9·1 | KIRYAT MOTZKIN (10) | PL.(2); Sdgs. to stores depot. |
| 18·7 | .. | Steel bridge over Naamin river, single span, 31·4 m., concrete abutments, masonry faced. |
| 19·1 | NAAMIN JUNCTION (2) | PL.(1); Sdgs. Other details not available. End of dual gauge; narrow-gauge line diverges for Acre (Rly. 5). Line traverses the fertile plain of Acre. Maximum gradient to Azzib, 1 in 120 up, 1 in 105 down. |
| 20·8 | MANSHIYA (8) | PL.(2). |
| 28·9 | NAHARIYA (8) | PL.(1). Sdg. |
| 31·2 | .. | Steel girder bridge, single span, 5·9 m., concrete abutments. |
| c. 34 | .. | Line passes the Arab village of Ez Zib (Azzib). |
| 34·8 | .. | Steel girder bridge over the Wadi Karn, 4× 5·7 m., concrete abutments and piers. |
| 35·0 | .. | Steel girder bridge, single span, 7·2 m., skew, concrete abutments. |
| 37·0 | AZZIB (EZ ZIB) (10) | PL.(1); W.; F.; ES.; Tr.; MY.; Sdgs. Marshalling yards sited in sand-dunes. Maximum gradient, 1 in 90 up. Line climbs to pierce Ras en Nakurah headland. There are many masonry walls. |
| 39·6 | .. | ⎧ Two tunnels through Ras en Nakurah, 110 m. |
| 39·8 | .. | ⎨ and 67 m. long. |

| Km. from Haifa East | Stations and passing-loops | Remarks |
|---|---|---|
| c. 40 | .. | Palestine–Lebanon boundary. |
| 46·6 | NAKURAH (8) | PL.(1); Sdg. |
| | | Maximum gradient, 1 in 100 up. |
| 50·2 | .. | Bayada tunnel, 1,270 m., through the Ras el Abyad (Bayada) headland. |
| c. 51·5 | .. | Line enters the plain of Tyre. There are no engineering difficulties except river crossings for the next 50 km. |
| 54·9 | MATFANA (9) | PL.(1); Sdg. |
| | | Maximum gradient, 1 in 110 up. |
| 63·7 | TYRE (SUR) (8) | PL.(1); Sdg. The station is about 1 mile inland of the town, with which it is connected by motor-road. |
| | | Maximum gradient, 1 in 110 down. |
| 72·0 | LITANI (9) | PL.(1); Sdg. |
| | | Maximum gradient, 1 in 100 up. |
| 72·8 | .. | Steel girder bridge over the Litani river, 4 × 12 m., masonry abutments, timber piers. |
| 80·7 | ADLOUN (10) | PL.(1). Phoenician caves. |
| | | Steel girder bridge, single span, 9·8 m., masonry abutments. |
| 91·1 | SENIK (9) | PL.(1); Sdg. |
| | | Maximum gradient, 1 in 90 up. |
| 93·0 | .. | Steel girder bridge over Senik river (Nahr Zahrani) 2 × 12·8 m., masonry abutments and pier. |
| 98·6 | .. | Steel girder bridge over Saitanik river, 6·1 m. + 2 × 11·1 m. + 6·1 m., masonry abutments and piers. As the line approaches Sidon it crosses the main road and passes through citrus orchards between the town and the mountains of Lebanon. |
| 100·5 | SIDON (SAIDA) (8) | PL.(2); W. |
| | | Maximum gradient, 1 in 100 up. |
| | | From Sidon to Khaldeh (km. 133·7) the country is rough, the hills coming down close to the coast. The line follows the rocky shoreline with the main road just inland. There are enormous retaining walls and sea-walls in this stretch. |
| 105·1 | .. | Steel girder bridge over Awali river, 6·1 m. + 2 × 18·3 m., masonry abutments and piers. |
| 108·3 | RMEILEH (RUMEILEH) (8) | PL.(1); Sdg. |
| | | Maximum gradient, 1 in 100 up. |
| 110·0 | .. | Steel girder bridge, single span, 6·1 m., masonry abutments. |
| 115·9 | JIYEH (9) | PL.(2). |
| | | Maximum gradient, 1 in 110 up. |
| 116·6 | .. | Steel girder bridge, as above, 6·1 m. |
| 121·4 | .. | Steel girder bridge over Damour river, 4 × 19·1 m., masonry abutments and piers. |
| 125·0 | DAMOUR (DAMUR) (9) | PL.(1); Sdg. |

| Km. from Haifa East | Stations and passing-loops | Remarks |
|---|---|---|
| | | Maximum gradient, 1 in 90 down. |
| 126·9 | .. | Steel girder bridge, single span, 6·1 m., masonry abutments. |
| 133·7 | KHALDEH (10) | PL.(2). |
| | | Maximum gradient, 1 in 90 down. |
| | | Line now swings inland across the Beirut promontory, passing through high olive-groves. |
| 137·3 | .. | Steel girder bridge over Kafarchima river, 3 × 6·1 m., masonry abutments and piers. |
| | | Line crosses a low saddle. |
| 143·9 | BEIRUT (9) | PL.(1); W.; F.; ES.; Tr.; Sdgs.; MY. Interchange depot for narrow-gauge (105 cm.) line from Beirut harbour to Damascus Station is about 3½ miles south-east of Beirut harbour. |
| | | Line immediately afterwards crosses the Nahr Beirut by steel girder bridge, 3 × 31·7 m., height 5 m. above the water, on concrete abutments and piers. |
| | | Maximum gradient, 1 in 100 down. |
| 144·0 | .. | Sdg. to stores depot. |
| | | Line keeps to the contours, crossing the Causeway road (km. 144·6), Broumana road (km. 145·7), and the main Tripoli road (km. 146·8). |
| 148·8 | .. | Steel girder bridge over the Nahr el Mott, 2 × 10·1 m., concrete abutments and pier. |
| 151·5 | .. | Steel bridge over the Nahr Antelias, 8·4 m. + 2 × 10·5 m. + 6·3 m., height 2·4 m., concrete abutments and piers. |
| 152·6 | DBAYEH (10) | PL.(1); Sdg. |
| | | Maximum gradient, 1 in 143 up. |
| 155·3 | .. | }Line crosses the Tripoli road twice. |
| 156·1 | .. | |
| 156·2 | .. | Steel bridge over Nahr Kelb, 21·3 m. + 2 × 30·5 m., height 5·5 m., concrete abutments and piers, stone-faced. |
| 162·6 | JOUNIEH (JUNEH) (7) | PL.(1); Sdg. |
| | | Maximum gradient, 1 in 166 down. |
| 164·7 | .. | Steel bridge over Maameltein, 18·3 m. + 11·0 m., height 7·6 m., reinforced concrete abutments and pier, stone-faced. |
| 164·9 | .. | Tunnel, 20 m., Ghazir (Rhazir) road over-bridge. |
| 166·1 | .. | Steel bridge, single span, 13·4 m., height 5.5 m., concrete abutments, stone-faced. |
| 169·2 | TABARJA (4) | PL.(1); Sdg. |
| | | Maximum gradient, 1 in 70 down. |
| 173·2 | .. | Steel bridge over Nahr Ibrahim, 21·3 m. + 30·5 m., height 5·5 m., concrete abutments and pier, stone-faced. |
| 173·5 | NAHR IBRAHIM (7) | PL.(1); W.(T.; C.(2)); Sdg. |
| | | Maximum gradient, 1 in 200 up. |

| Km. from Haifa East | Stations and passing-loops | Remarks |
|---|---|---|
| 177·5 | .. | Steel bridge over Nahr Fidar, 4×22·9 m., height of piers 16·8 m., concrete abutments and piers. |
| 180·4 | JEBEIL (7) | PL.(1); Sdg. Maximum gradient, 1 in 90 down. |
| 181·2 | .. | Steel bridge over Nahr el Jajeh, 3×24·4 m., height 24·4 m., concrete abutments and piers, stone-faced. |
| 187·7 | HELUEH (HENNFEH?) (10) | PL.(1); Sdg. Maximum gradient, 1 in 166 up. |
| 190·9 | .. | Tunnel (small, length not known). |
| 191·2 | .. | Steel bridge over Nahr el Fgal, single span, 24·4 m., height 15·2 m., concrete abutments, stone-faced. |
| 197·7 | BATRUN (11) | PL.(2); W.(C.2). Maximum gradient, 1 in 200 up. |
| 198·2 | .. | Steel bridge over Nahr el Joz, 2×13·5 m., concrete abutments and pier, stone-faced. |
| 201·9 | .. | Tunnel, 172 m. |
| 203·8–205·3 | .. | Tunnel, 1,480 m. through Ras esh Shakkah (Chekka). |
| 208·5 | CHEKKA (ŞHAKKAH) (4) | PL.(2); SLP.; ELR.; Stores yard. Maximum gradient, 1 in 166 up. |
| 208·8 | .. | Sdg. to cement works. |
| 209·0 | .. | Steel bridge over Nahr el Asfur, single span, 12·2 m., concrete abutments. |
| 212·0 | ENFEH (10) | PL.(1). Maximum gradient, 1 in 166 up. |
| 222·0 | KALMOUN (3) | PL.(1); Sdg. (proposed). Maximum gradient, 1 in 166 down. |
| 225·3 | BAHSA (BARSA) (4) | PL.(1); W.(C.); SLP.; ELP.; Tr.; MY.(5). Maximum gradient, 1 in 59 down. |
| 225·8 | .. | Steel bridge over Nahr el Kalta, single span, 12·2 m., height 4·6 m., concrete abutments. |
| 229·4 | TRIPOLI | .. |

## 5. HAIFA-ACRE

*Distance*: 12·6 miles, 20·2 kilometres.

*Branch-lines.* None.

*Permanent way, stations, and kilometre posts*

Narrow gauge (105 cm.). Single track. Ballast, crushed crystalline limestone. Rails, flat-bottom 43·5 lb. per yd. Sleepers, steel. Maximum axle-load, 10 tons. Minimum radius of curves, 270 m. Maximum gradient, 1 in 125. Maximum distance between passing-loops, 10 km. Minimum length of loop-line at stations, 240 m. Kilometre posts are numbered from Haifa East (narrow gauge), 0–20 km.

*Speed and capacity*

Overall time (including stops): mixed trains, 30 min., goods, 45 min. Maximum train speeds: 37 m.p.h. (with restrictions).

Capacity is dependent on requirements of new standard-gauge line to the north, with which it is dual-gauged. Net load, 120 tons.

## GENERAL DESCRIPTION

This narrow-gauge line leaves the Haifa–Samakh railway (Rly. 6) at Acre junction, bends north, and crosses the Kishon river. At Kishon junction a siding serves the Railway workshops. Kiryat Haim, Kiryat Motzkin, Kiryat Shemuel, and Kiryat Bialik form a compact group of industrial suburbs immediately east of the Iraq Petroleum Company's storage tanks, and are served by this railway. The line then traverses the Emek Zebulun with sand-dunes on the seaward side and the marshes of the Naamin to the east.

As far as Naamin junction this railway runs as dual gauge with the new main line to Beirut and Tripoli (Rly. 4). Both are at present used.

## DETAILED DESCRIPTION

| Km. from Haifa East | Stations and passing-loops | Remarks |
|---|---|---|
| 0·0 | HAIFA EAST (N.G.)* (9) | W.(town mains, 50,000 gls.,R.; C.(3), EP.); Tbl.; Sdgs. For description of the town and port, *see* pp. 300–307. |
| 2·0 | ACRE JUNCTION | PL.(1). Narrow-gauge line (Rly. 6) leaves for Samakh. |
| 5·0 | .. | Steel bridge over Kishon river, 31·4 m.+2× 9·1 m., masonry abutments, steel piers. |
| 5·6 | KISHON JUNCTION | Sdgs. from junction serve Railway workshops. The airport adjoins the workshops. |
| 6·2 | KISHON HALT | .. |
| 8·2 | KIRYAT HAIM | Sdgs. serve Iraq Petroleum Company. |
| 9·1 | KIRYAT MOTZKIN (10) | PL.(2). |
| 18·7 | .. | Steel bridge over Naamin river, single span, 31·4 m., concrete abutments, masonry faced. |
| 19·1 | NAAMIN JUNCTION (1) | PL.(1); Sdgs. Other details not available. End of dual gauge. Standard-gauge line diverges for Beirut. |
| 20·2 | ACRE | PL.(1); W.(T.4,400 gls., from town mains, R.; C., EP.) Sdg. The station is near the Land Gate in the south-east corner of the ramparts. For description of the town, *see* pp. 295–300. |

* Many facilities have been added since 1939. It is not known to what extent these apply to the narrow-gauge line.

## 6. HAIFA–SAMAKH

*Route*

| Haifa–Affula | 22·6 miles | 36·4 kilometres |
|---|---|---|
| Affula–Samakh | 31·4 ,, | 50·6 ,, |
| | 54·0 | 87·0 |

*Branch-line*

Affula–Masudiya, 37·2 miles (59·9 km.), for Nablus, 48·3 miles (77·8 km.), and Tulkarm, 49·5 miles (79·7 m.); see Rlys. 7, 8.

*Permanent way, stations, and kilometre posts*

Narrow gauge (105 cm.). Single track. Ballast, crushed crystalline limestone to Beisan; thereafter black basalt obtained locally. Rails, flat-bottom, 43·5 lb. per yd. Sleepers, steel. Maximum axle-load, 10 tons. Minimum radius of curves, 125 m. (at km. 65·0, 80·0, 80·1, 80·3). Maximum gradient, 1 in 70. Maximum distance between passing-loops, 26 km. Minimum length of loop-line at stations, 280 m. Kilometre posts are numbered from Haifa to Samakh, 0–87 km.

*Speed and capacity*

Overall time (including stops): mixed trains, 2 hr. 30 min.; goods, 3 hr. 30 min.

Train speeds: 30 m.p.h. (except between Beisan and Delhamiya, 25 m.p.h.).

Capacity, 10 trains each way in 24 hours. Net load of trains, 120 tons.

## GENERAL DESCRIPTION

This railway, originally built as a branch of the Hejaz railway, is still important as the only direct line of communication between Transjordan and the Mediterranean coast. It follows the ancient route through the plain of Acre to the defile of Haritiya ('Harosheth of the Gentiles') and thence to the broad fertile plain of Esdraelon. The line rises very gently to a maximum of about 175 feet at the watershed near Affula. Thence it begins to descend, but the valley of the Jalud affords an easy route, and its gradient never exceeds 1 in 125. As far as Beisan it meets with no difficulties, excepting the single crossing of the Mukatta branch of the Kishon at mile 8·1. After Beisan it keeps along the western escarpment of the Jordan trough, gradually losing height, and crosses the Jordan at Jisr el Majami, about 800 feet below sea-level. The continuation of the line from Samakh is described in Chapter XVII, which deals with the communications of Transjordan.

DETAILED DESCRIPTION

| Km. from Haifa East | Stations and passing-loops | Remarks |
|---|---|---|
| 0·0 | HAIFA EAST (N.G.)* (7) | PL.(1); W.(town mains, 50,000 gls.,R.; C.(3), EP.); Tbl.; Sdgs. For description of the town and port, see pp. 300–307. |
| 2·0 | ACRE JUNCTION | Narrow-gauge line (Rly. 5) leaves for Acre. Line passes up the Kishon valley, keeping close to the Carmel foot. |
| 4·5 | .. | Quarry siding. |
| 7·4 | NESHER (15) | PL.(2); Sdgs.(2), serving the Nesher cement works. |
| 10·2 | MESHEK YAJUR | Halt only. Road and railway run alongside each other. |
| 13·1 | .. | Masonry bridge at Haritiya over Kishon river, 6 × 6·75 m. arches (photo. 113). Here the plain of Acre ends, and the hills of Samaria approach Carmel. Road and railway pass up opposite sides of the narrow valley to Megiddo. |
| 15·0 | EL ROY | Halt only. |
| 17·0 | KIRYAT HAROSHET | GP. The hills now recede on both sides, the line turning south-east across the open plain of Esdraelon. |
| 21·9 | KEFAR (KEFR) YEHOSHUA (15) | PL.(2); W.(T. 4,400 gls. from well, R.; C.(2), SP.). The Jewish settlement of Nahalal is about 3 miles north-east. The line continues dead straight across the open plain. |
| 26·7 | KEFAR (KEFR) BARUKH | .. |
| 30·4 | AFFULA (15) | PL.(4); W. (from town mains, R.; C.); GP.; GS.; Tr.; Sdg. Junction for Masudiya, Nablus, and Tulkarm. The main road from Jerusalem to Nazareth crosses the line here. Affula, alt. c. 175 feet, is the highest station on the line, which now begins to descend the Jordan watershed, between Jebel Dahi (Little Hermon) and Jebel Fakkua (the mountains of Gilboa), reaching sea-level at about km. 42·8. |
| 45·8 | AIN HAROD | Sdg. |
| 48·7 | TEL YOSEF (YUSUF) | .. |
| 51·0 | SHATTA (26) | PL.(1); GP.; GS.; Sdg. |
| c. 57·0 | HASSADEH | .. |
| 59·2 | BEISAN | W.(T. 4,400 gls. from town mains, R.; C.(2), OP., & grav.); Sdgs.(2). One siding goes to quarry. For description of the town, see pp. 319–320. The station is 351 feet below sea-level. The town is about 2 miles to the south, across the Jalud river. |

* Many facilities have been added since 1939. It is not known to what extent these apply to the narrow-gauge line.

| Km. from Haifa East | Stations and passing-loops | Remarks |
|---|---|---|
| | | Line turns north up the Jordan valley, gradually losing height. |
| 61·5 | .. | Quarry and siding (P.W.D.). |
| 69·9 | BEIT YOSEF (YUSUF) | GP.; GS. |
| 74·5 | .. | Masonry bridge over Wadi Bira, 5×5·75 m. arches. |
| 76·5 | JISR EL MAJAMI (10) | PL.(2). |
| 77·1 | .. | Masonry bridge over Jordan, 5×11 m. arches, about 800 feet below sea-level. |
| 78·0 | .. | Palestine Electric Corporation siding. |
| 78·7 | .. | Reinforced concrete girder bridge over canal leading to P.E.C. power house, single span, 8 m. |
| 79·0 | NAHARAYIM | Station is west of the Yarmuk reservoir. |
| 79·8 | .. | Steel bridge over Yarmuk, 50 m. (photo. 114). |
| 79·9 | .. | Steel bridge over P.E.C. canal, single span, 16 m. |
| 81·4 | DELHAMIYA | Quarry and siding. |
| 84·2 | EMEK YAHARDEN | .. |
| 87·0 | SAMAKH | PL.(4); W.(T. 8,800 gls., pumped from lake, R.; C.(2), SP.); F.; GP.; GS.; ES.; Tbl.; BC. The station is 617 feet below sea-level and immediately south of the town, which lines the edge of Lake Tiberias. |

## 7. TULKARM–NABLUS

*Route*

| | | |
|---|---|---|
| Tulkarm–Masudiya | 12·3 miles | 19·8 kilometres |
| Masudiya–Nablus | 11·1 ,, | 17·9 ,, |
| | 23·4 | 37·7 |

*Junction* at Masudiya for Affula. Interchange point with main standard-gauge line at Nur esh Shems, 3·1 miles (5·0 km.).

*Permanent way, stations, and kilometre posts*

Narrow gauge (105 cm.). Single track. Ballast, crushed crystalline limestone. Rails, flat-bottom, 43·5 lb. per yd. Sleepers, steel. Maximum axle-load, 10 tons. Minimum radius of curves, 125 m. (many between Masudiya and Nablus). Maximum gradient, 1 in 53 between Sebastiya (Sebustya) and Nablus. Maximum distance between passing-loops, 18 km. Minimum length of loop-line at stations, 261 m. Kilometre posts are numbered from Masudiya to Tulkarm (0–19 km.) for the first section, and from Affula (60–77 km.) for the section from Masudiya to Nablus.

*Speed and capacity*

Overall time (including stops): mixed trains.

Tulkarm–Masudiya (either way),  1 hr.  0 min.
Masudiya–Nablus               1 „   15  „
Nablus–Masudiya              0 „   45  „

Train speeds: Tulkarm–Masudiya, 30 m.p.h., Masudiya–Nablus, 25 m.p.h.

Capacity, 7 trains each way in 24 hours. Net load of trains, 90 tons.

## GENERAL DESCRIPTION

This line is now little used, except for goods traffic, the first-class road being much quicker. The railway crosses the Wadi Zeimar about 1½ miles north-east of Tulkarm and then ascends the Zeimar valley. There are no great difficulties in alinement before Anabta is reached, though the line crosses the Zeimar before reaching that station, and there are a number of small bridges over tributaries. About 3½ miles beyond Anabta the line recrosses the Zeimar and ascends the left bank of a ravine descending from the north flank of the hill of Sebustya. Immediately before Masudiya station it crosses the ravine and enters the station from the east. For the journey onwards to Nablus the train reverses direction, ascends the ravine, crosses it again higher up, makes a semicircle round the hill of Sebustya, and with steep gradients and curves climbs to Nablus.

## DETAILED DESCRIPTION

| Km. from Tulkarm | Stations and passing-loops | Remarks |
|---|---|---|
| 0·0 (19·8)* | TULKARM (5) | PL.(2); GP.; GS.; Sdg. For Tulkarm standard-gauge station, *see* p. 354; for town description, *see* p. 339. |
| 5·0 (14·8)* | NUR ESH SHEMS (15) | Alt. *c.* 330 ft. PL.(1); Sdg.; ballast quarries. Interchange point. |
| 10·6 (9·2)* | ANABTA | Alt. *c.* 500 ft. Sdg. |
| 19·8 (59·9)† | MASUDIYA JUNCTION (18) | Alt. *c.* 850 ft. PL.(1); W. (pipe-line from Sebastiya, R.; C., grav.); PP., GP.; GS. Junction for Affula. |
| 25·6 (65·7)† | SEBASTIYA (SEBUSTYA) | Alt. *c.* 1,180 ft. W. (reservoir fed by gravity from springs; C.); GP.; GS. |
| 37·7 (77·8)† | NABLUS | Alt. *c.* 1,880 ft. PL.(2); PP.; GS.; Tbl. For town description, *see* pp. 332–333. |

* Figure in brackets is distance from Masudiya (kilometre posts).
† Figure in brackets is distance from Affula (kilometre posts).

## 8. AFFULA–MASUDIYA

*Distance*: 37·2 miles, 59·9 kilometres.

*Permanent way, stations, and kilometre posts*

Narrow gauge (105 cm.). Single track. Ballast, crushed crystalline lime-stone. Rails, flat-bottom, 43·5 lb. per yd. Sleepers, steel. Maximum axle-load, 10 tons. Minimum radius of curves, 125 m. (many between Arraba and Masudiya). Maximum gradient, 1 in 60. Maximum distance between passing-loops, 20 km. Minimum length of loop-line at stations 337 m. Kilometre posts are numbered from Affula (0–59 km.).

*Speed and capacity*

Overall time (including stops) of goods trains, 3 hr. 15 min., either way.
Maximum train speeds, 30 m.p.h. (trains must always proceed with caution in view of the condition of the track).
Capacity, 7 trains each way in 24 hours. Net load of trains, 90 tons.

*GENERAL DESCRIPTION*

This line is now placed on a 'care and maintenance' basis and is only opened for special purposes. From Affula it runs due south across the open plain of Esdraelon, crossing the Kishon (Mukatta) at about mile 2½ near the aircraft landing-ground. There is only a very gentle rise for most of the way to Jenin, which stands at the northern entrance of the hills of Samaria. South of Jenin the line passes up a narrow valley and crosses the plain of Arraba, with Arraba station at the southern exit of the plain, where the hills again close in. The alinement is well graded, and from Arraba to Sileh it keeps below 1,000 feet. From Arraba to Masudiya there are many bends as the line climbs to 1,300 feet to pass through a tunnel at Khan Rashin. Here it enters the valley of the Wadi Zeimar, high up on the northern slopes, and with sharp curves it gradually loses height to reach Masudiya junction (alt. *c.* 850 ft.).

*DETAILED DESCRIPTION*

| Km. from Affula | Stations and passing-loops | Remarks |
| --- | --- | --- |
| 0·0 | AFFULA (17) | Alt. *c.* 175 ft. PL.(4); W. (from town mains, R.; C.); GP.; GS.; Tr. Junction for Haifa and Samakh. |
| 16·8 | JENIN (11) | Alt. *c.* 500 ft. PL.(2); W. (municipal supply from well, R.; C.); GP.; GS. For town, *see* p. 322. |
| 28·2 | ARRABA (12) | Alt. *c.* 880 ft. PL.(2); GP.; GS. |

| Km. from Affula | Stations and passing-laops | Remarks |
|---|---|---|
| 40·3 | SILEH (20) | Alt. *c.* 980 ft. PL.(2); W.(T. 10,000 gls., UR.; C., grav.); GP.; GS. |
| 48·1 | .. | Masonry tunnel, 221·5 m., on slight curve. |
| 59·9 | MASUDIYA JUNCTION | Alt. *c.* 850 ft. PL.(1); W. (pipe-line from Sebastiya, R.; C.); PP.,GP.; GS. Junction for Nablus and Tulkarm. |

# ROADS

ALL road development is now in the hands of the Department of Public Works; revenue is obtained from licence fees under the Road Transport Ordinance and from import duties on petrol, oil, and automobiles. In 1940 there were 1,454 miles (2,340 km.) of all-weather roads, and 987 miles (1,588 km.) of seasonal tracks in Palestine. Regular communication, serving both passengers and goods, is now established between all the chief towns, effected by omnibuses and motor cars licensed as public vehicles, for Palestine has no tramways. All motor vehicles entering the country have first to be registered by the Traffic offices under the Department of Police and Prisons, and thereafter must be licensed annually.

The cost of construction of roads varies considerably as a result of the geological structure and relief of the country, and in the plains, where transport expenses for road material are high, the cost of road construction may be twice as much as in the hill districts where local stone is available. Only in the coastal plain is local material lacking, and here in the north metalling is brought down from the hills, while in the south concrete is frequently used for new roads. Elsewhere the abundance of limestone in the hills is an asset; in the Beisan–Tiberias district basalt can be used, and in the Beersheba area surface flints supply material. Asphalt is imported mainly from Suez. Modern bridges are mostly of reinforced concrete.

Donkeys and camels are still widely used for transport, and while the total number of camels in the country has decreased from 32,317 in 1932 to 28,085 in 1937, the number of donkeys has increased (74,177 in 1932; 92,205 in 1937). Since 1933 the number of motor vehicles has increased rapidly, and by 1936, 9,182 vehicles were licensed (11,847 in 1940). With this increase has gone a decrease in the number of road accidents, from 1,730 in 1935 to 1,675 in 1940.

The present road pattern is simple. As of old, two important roads, linking Egypt with Syria, traverse the country from south to north, one following the coastal plain from Rafa on the Egyptian frontier to the Lebanese frontier at Ras en Nakurah, the other along the central hill belt from the Egyptian frontier near El Auja el Hafir to Metulla on the Syrian frontier. These are described below as roads 1 and 2. Nine main transverse roads (Nos. 3–11) link the coastal road with the central road, and four of these, from the ports of Jaffa with Tel Aviv, Haifa, and Acre, continue east to the five bridges across the Jordan—Allenby bridge, Jisr Damiya, Jisresh Sheikh Hussein, Jisr el Majami, and Jisr Banat Yakub. Excepting a small stretch near Rafa and the road from Nablus to Jisr Damiya, the whole of this basic network is of first-class standard, and there are in addition many branch-roads equally good, particularly in the coastal plain and inland from the ports. The road along the Jordan depression, which was never of much historical importance, but now serves as the frontier road between two states, is the last to be described (No. 12). The many branch-roads and tracks are only briefly mentioned.

## DESCRIPTION OF ROADS

[1]. THE COASTAL ROAD

*Rafa–Ras en Nakurah* (through distance,[1] 170 miles; 274 kilometres)

This is an important road leading north from Egypt to Syria. The section between El Arish in Egypt and the branch to Khan Yunis is not yet completed. Its surface is tar-macadam, in good condition except at a few points between Rafa and Gaza, where it is liable to flooding after heavy rainstorms, and between Ramleh and the cross-roads at Beit Lid, where it is bumpy. There are about 40 bridges, most of them concrete, but few of them over 100 feet long. The country traversed is cultivated and generally undulating, though the road does not rise or fall to any great extent, and except for the Carmel ridge, which forces the road round its seaward flank, the landscape is open. The Haifa–Kantara railway runs generally parallel to the road, at varying distances from it, throughout its course. The road is described below in six sections: Rafa–Gaza–Masmiya-el-Kebira–Ramleh–Zichron-Jacob–Haifa–Ras-en-Nakurah. It has a minimum width of 19 feet, but between Ramleh and Beit Lid is generally 25 feet wide.

[1] The through distance is the shortest between the two terminals, not including small branches into towns off the road as Rafa, Zichron Jacob, and Acre.

## ITINERARY

### Rafa–Gaza (25 miles; 40 kilometres: by the new road)

There are two roads, the old and the new, from El Arish to Khan Yunis. The new main road, in 1942 still under construction at its southern end, passes neither through Rafa, where it is about 3 miles to the east, nor through Khan Yunis; but it is connected with Rafa by a second-class road from Khirbet abu Kashta, and with Khan Yunis by a short branch (1¼ miles) from Beni Suheila. Beyond Khan Yunis it joins the older road, which from El Arish runs close to Rafa and passes through Khan Yunis, where it becomes first-class and runs parallel with the coast and the railway to Gaza.

Between the junction of the Khan Yunis road with the new main road, 5 miles from Khan Yunis, and Gaza, 15 miles from Khan Yunis, the coast road crosses the railway twice, by level crossings at miles 9 and 12½ from Khan Yunis. It passes over the Wadi Ghazza by a bridge 10 miles from Khan Yunis, but is liable to flooding here after heavy rain. Gaza may be by-passed by a road which branches from the main road 3 miles south-west of the town, avoids the gardens, and passes the airfield to cross the Gaza–Beersheba road [4] a mile south-east of Gaza, and to rejoin the main road 3 miles beyond the town. The direct distance between Rafa on the Egyptian frontier and Gaza is 20 miles, but by the new main road it is 25 miles, and by the old road 23.

### Gaza–Masmiya el Kebira (27·3 miles; 44·0 kilometres)

The road leaves Gaza over a level crossing, and goes north-east, avoiding the edge of the sand-dunes, to Beit Hanun (mile 4½). From the cross-roads a mile from Gaza a branch goes west to Jabal village and east to the Gaza by-pass. The by-pass joins the main road 3 miles from Gaza. Between Beit Hanun and the branch-road to Mejdel the main road keeps close to the railway, through Deir Suneid and Barbara, passing through cultivated country and occasional orange-groves. There are two level crossings of the railway at miles 6 and 14 from Gaza, and several temporary military camps along the road. A mile before the second level crossing a first-class branch-road goes west through the village of Mejdel and continues as a second-class road to El Jura on the coast near ancient Ascalon. A new road [1 g] following the railway parallel to the coast to beyond Rishon le Zion has recently been completed from the Mejdel road junction, 15 miles from Gaza, but the main road bears north-east away from the coast and the railway, and passes through Julis (17½ miles), Sawafir el Gharbiya (21 m.), Sawafir esh Sharkiya (21½ m.), Kiryat Shemuel (24 m.), and Kastina (25 m.), to Masmiya el Kebira (27½ m.). There are reinforced-concrete bridges at miles 16 (length 41 ft.), 17½ (53 ft.), 21 (50 ft.), 22 (108 ft.), 25 (40 ft.), and 27 (no details).

Branch-roads and connexions are as follows: a good new tarmac road—the Bureir by-pass—averaging 16–18 feet leaves the Gaza by-pass and turns inland of the coast road through Bureir [1 *f*] to rejoin near Julis; from mile 15½ a track across the new coast road leads to Hamama, where there is a break in the sand-dunes; from Julis a track goes south-east to the first-class road [5] from Mejdel through Faluja to Hebron; from mile 19 another track joins the Hebron road [5]; from Sawafir el Gharbiya a track through broken country north-west to Beit Deras, thence to the new coastal road at Isdud; from Kiryat Shemuel a road north-west to Beer Tuviya village; from Kastina a track west through Beer Tuviya and Beit Deras to the new coastal road, also south to Faluja, and south-east to Beit Jibrin, both on the Hebron road. Masmiya el Kebira is also a road junction, for besides the main road through it, a first-class road continues north-east to Latrun [1 *k*], and tracks lead west to Barka and south-east through Tell es Safi to the Hebron road.

## Masmiya el Kebira–Ramleh (14·3 miles; 23·0 kilometres)

From Masmiya el Kebira (c. 200 ft.) to Ramleh (230 ft.) the road passes through gently rolling, well-watered agricultural land, with citrus-groves on either side as far as Kefar Bilu road-junction (mile 9½ from Masmiya el Kebira). These give place to scattered and then thick orange plantations, with olive-groves round Ramleh. There are two reinforced-concrete bridges, one over a tributary of the Sukreir on the outskirts of Masmiya el Kebira, and the other over the Rubin 5 miles beyond. Neither stream is perennial. The road passes the villages of Gedera (4 miles), Katra (4½ m.), and El Mughar (6 m.). From El Mughar it follows the east flank of a low ridge for 1¼ miles, then passes through unbroken groves of orange-trees to the Kefar Bilu road-junction, where the Rehovot road [1 *h*] branches north to Jaffa. Beyond the junction the main road runs on through orange- and olive-groves to Ramleh, passing Ramleh airfield on the right and the town buildings on the left.

Ramleh is an important centre, on the Jaffa–Jerusalem road [6], and on the Jerusalem railway between Lydda junction and Niana (Naaneh).

The most important branch-roads and tracks in this section are as follows: from mile 3 west to Gan Yavneh; tracks from El Mughar north-west to Yibna and north to Zarnuka, and a bitumen road to Akir airfield on the east; from mile 8½ tracks to Zarnuka on the left and Akir village on the right; from Kefar Bilu good roads south to Akir and north through

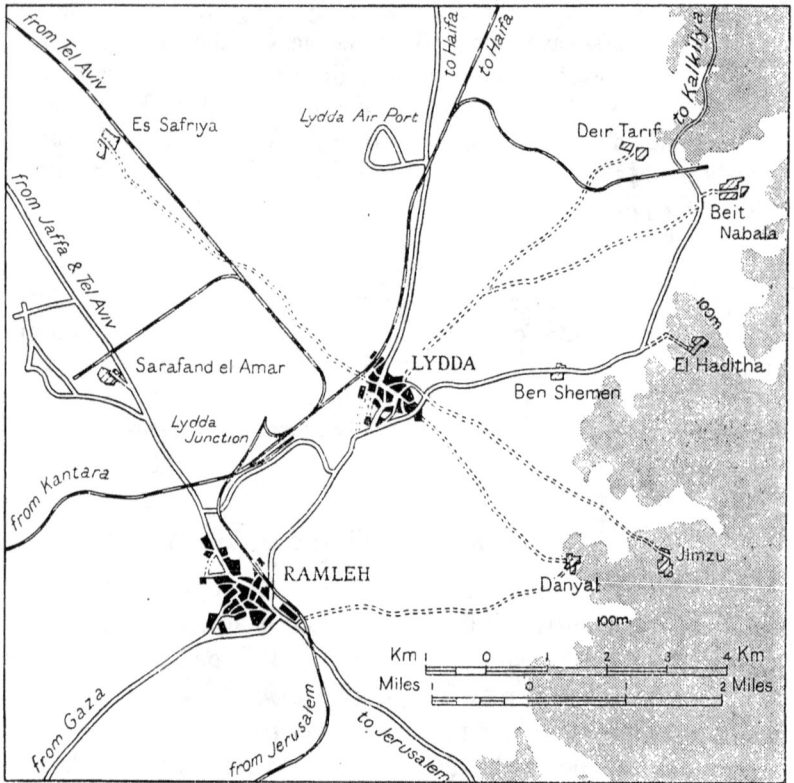

FIG. 47. *Ràmleh road-centre.*

Rehovot, Nes Ziona (Siyona), Rishon le Zion, and Nahalat Yehuda to the Jaffa–Jerusalem road 5 miles from Jaffa.

*Ramleh–Zichron Jacob* (55·5 miles, 89·3 km.; to Zichron Jacob road-junction 53·5 miles, 86·1 km.)

As far as Kefar Malal, 18½ miles from Ramleh, the road passes through the most densely populated part of Palestine, and branch-roads are numerous. Four perennial rivers, the Auja, Iskanderuna, Hadera (Mifjir), and Zerka, are crossed by bridges at miles 15, 33, 40, and 51, and there are a number of smaller bridges.

On leaving Ramleh the road crosses the Lydda–Jerusalem railway by a level crossing, then passes between olive-groves and fields of vegetable and cereal crops to Lydda (alt. 180 ft.) at mile 3, sending a short branch west to the station half-way between the two towns. From Lydda it keeps close to the Haifa main line, which it crosses at mile 5 with a sharp westward bend close to Lydda airport, the most important in the country; eastwards a first-class road is almost completed to Beit Nabala. The main road continues north, diverging from the railway, to the German agricultural settlement of Wilhelma (mile 7½). Here a first-class branch [1 *i*] leads west to Jaffa and also connects with the Jaffa–Jerusalem road. From Wilhelma to the dilapidated Arab village of Fajja (mile 12), groves of orange and banana trees and some arable fields line the road. Beyond Fajja the road meets the first-class road [1 *j*] from Jaffa through Petah Tikva to Ras el Ain on the Haifa railway, and makes use of it for a quarter of a mile, then continues north, crossing in succession a 3-span bridge over an Auja tributary, the Petah Tikva branch of the railway, and a single-span iron bridge over the Auja river itself (mile 15). A number of Jewish settlements are then passed, and about mile 19½ several roads branch off—to Raanana and Herzlya (Herseliya) on the west, to Tira on the north-east, and across the Haifa railway to Kalkilya for Tulkarm on the east [1 *n*], [1 *m*]. From this junction the road keeps straight, parallel to the coast and less than 4 miles away, through level country to the Beit Lid cross-roads at mile 30, where a first-class road [7] leads west to the coast at Nathanya, and east through Tulkarm to Nablus. The main road continues straight to Hadera (mile 38½), partly through open arable land, partly through enclosed orange-groves, and at one point, about mile 35½, through sand-dunes planted with eucalyptus trees. The Iskanderuna is crossed at mile 33 by two bridges 80 feet apart, the second being over the main channel. At Hadera road-junction (mile 38) a road branches west through the dunes to the coast, the main road turning east sharply into the village. Beyond the bridge over the Mifjir or Hadera river (mile 40), where the road again turns east, there is a level crossing over the Haifa railway at Hadera station (mile 41). Khirbet es Sarkas, at mile 42, is a road-junction for Affula [1 *o*], and the main road swings north-west through citrus-groves to Binyamina, passing Pardes Hanna at mile 45, then crossing the Haifa railway at Binyamina station (mile 48). From Binyamina a branch-road goes off over rising ground to Zichron Jacob and the main road passes through flat open country to the bridge over the Zerka at mile 51, after which it

again crosses the railway. From this point to Haifa the road is dominated on the east by the high limestone cliffs of the Carmel ridge. At
mile 53½ a first-class branch-road leads to Zichron Jacob, 2 miles
away, whence it continues as a first-class road over the Carmel ridge
to the plain of Esdraelon.

### Zichron Jacob road-junction–Haifa central (21·0 miles; 33·8 kilometres)

This straight section of the road runs north along the coastal plain,
hemmed in on the east by the Carmel ridge. Cultivated land extends
up the slopes, and a string of villages lies off the road to the east where
valleys open to the plain. There are no perennial streams in this
section, though bridges are numerous. A narrow ridge 1½ miles west
of the road separates the road from the railway between El Fureidis
(mile 2) and the prison camp at mile 10. At mile 3 a new road goes
west to the coast at Tantura and there is a first-class road south-
east to Zichron Jacob. Beyond Jaba, mile 6, there are several tracks
leading west to the coast at Atlit. From mile 12 the road passes
through country thickly wooded with olive-trees for 3½ miles, and
beyond them is forced, with the railway, to keep close to the sea
round the Carmel promontory into Haifa. The municipal boundary
is passed at mile 17, near Khayat beach, but Cape Carmel is not
passed for another 2 miles. Haifa port and central station are at
mile 21.

### Haifa–Ras en Nakurah (26 miles; 42·1 kilometres)

On leaving the built-up area of Haifa the road crosses the single-
track Acre railway and the Kishon river (mile 2), and then, after
passing the airfield, recrosses the railway beyond the Kishon railway
bridge. It runs between oil refineries and the railway workshops, and
through a small factory district to Kiryat Haiyim (Hayim) (mile 4),
then follows the Emek Zebulun round the bay of Acre. Cultivation
is sparse, and there are marshy areas on the outskirts of Acre. At
mile 3½ a second-class branch-road goes east to Kefr Ata, and at
mile 6½ another [1 t] leads through Shefa Amr to Nazareth. The
coastal road by-passes immediately east of Acre (mile 12), sending
a branch to the Land Gate of the town, and a first-class road [10]
eastwards for Safad. It then continues north traversing flat agricultural country, with an aqueduct alongside on the east as far as
Mazraa (mile 18). The Jewish resort of Nahariya lies to the west of
the road at mile 20, and 3 miles farther on, the perennial Wadi Karn
is crossed by a concrete bridge at Ez Zib. The road follows the cliffs

for a little way, then bends inland to skirt the dunes. About mile 25 hills close in on the east, and the road climbs fairly steeply up the rocky hill-side to round the promontory of Ras en Nakurah at 240 feet above sea-level, where the boundary between Palestine and the Lebanon reaches the sea (photo. 115). Where the climb begins a first-class branch-road [11] has recently been constructed parallel to the frontier through Tarbikha and Kadas to the central road [2]. A second-class branch [1 *u*] eastward from Nahariya forks to link this with the Acre–Safad road [10].

## [2]. THE CENTRAL ROAD

### El Auja el Hafir–Metulla (253 miles; 406 kilometres)

This is the main road from Egypt to Syria, though its course is more difficult than the coastal road since it traverses the central highland belt where topography causes many detours to avoid steep slopes. The surface of the road, generally tar-macadam, is throughout in first-class condition. There are about 30 bridges, none of them large. After crossing the Negeb desert and then its fringe of wild, rocky hills, the road runs over the plateau of Judaea, the highland of Samaria, and Galilee, where bare, stony hills, and steep valleys alternate with cultivated and terraced fields and gardens. In its last section the road descends past the Horns of Hattin to the Jordan valley at Tiberias, thence making use of the lowland almost to the frontier. The road crosses only one railway—the narrow-gauge line from Haifa to Samakh at Affula—but it links the ends of several roads and the termini of two transverse railways leading from the coast to the interior at Jerusalem and Nablus.

### ITINERARY

### Egyptian frontier–Beersheba (50 miles; 80 kilometres)

The road starts at Cairo and has an asphalt surface as far as the boundary, where tar-macadam begins. Between the boundary and Beersheba the road is at least 18 feet wide with earth verges up to 6 feet on either side; there are 140 culverts and 6 bridges, yet traffic may still be interrupted by floods after the heavy rain-storms which are characteristic of this region. None of the wadis contain perennial water. The country traversed—the Negeb desert—is arid and rocky, with occasional patches of sand-dunes and low-lying alluvial plains. El Auja el Hafir is reached at mile 4 from the boundary, where broken limestone country gives place to an alluvial belt with some cultivation in patches. The Wadi Abyad is crossed by a bridge of ten 8-foot spans at mile 11, and the road continues through occasional fields of barley to El Mushrifeh (mile 18; Mishrafa on some maps), whence an open plain extends to Bir Asluj (mile 30). Thence for $8\frac{1}{2}$ miles to Bir el Mishash the road runs between limestone hills which rise on either side to over 1,320 feet, with patches of cultivation on the lower slopes, before crossing a narrow belt of sand-dunes with some scrub. Then cultivation begins to line both sides of the road, and undulating alluvial country, occasionally cultivated, continues to Beersheba, which is entered over a small bridge. In this section the alinement of the dismantled railway, built by the Turks through Beersheba to Kuseimeh during the War of 1914–1918, is crossed several times.

Branches in this section are as follows: from El Auja el Hafir a road [3] is believed to be under construction, mainly on the Egyptian side of the frontier, to the new coastal road [1] south of Rafa, a distance of 34 miles, and the old main road to Egypt branches south across the frontier to Kuseimeh; from El Auja el Hafir also a good track [2 a] takes a direct route through El Khalasa to Beersheba; another track [1 d] links Beersheba with Gaza; at Beersheba the road [4] from the coast through Gaza to Ain Hasb for Akaba and the Dead Sea crosses the central road, with a branch east to Ras ez Zuweira.

## Beersheba–Jerusalem (54·0 miles; 87·0 kilometres)

The road in this section is from 15 to 18 feet wide. From Beersheba (900 ft.) it follows the Wadi Khelil for $11\frac{1}{2}$ miles through flat steppe-desert, with some sparse cultivation; then it enters the foothills of the Judaean highlands, climbing a narrow defile to the village of Dhahiriya at 2,190 feet (mile 19). It crosses a small plateau, descends in sharp zigzags, and then winds across several valleys and ridges to rise again to 3,040 feet at Hebron (mile 31). After a sharp turn north-west in the town the road continues, winding steeply over the hills, past Solomon's Pools (mile $45\frac{1}{2}$) to Bethlehem (2,460 ft.), which lies just off the road to the east at mile 48. Jerusalem, at 2,985 feet, is reached after 6 miles through gently rolling upland with terraced hill-sides.

Branches in this section are as follows: from Beersheba a good track [2 b] leads north through Faluja, on the Mejdel–Hebron road [5], to Kastina: parts of it have been newly constructed as a good stone-surfaced road; from Hebron a first-class road [5] passes west through Beit Jibrin to the coastal road near Mejdel, and several short tracks lead to the surrounding

115. *The coast road into Syria at Ras en Nakurah 12 miles north of Acre. View southwards*

116. *On the road from Jerusalem to Jericho*

117. *Old Jisr Banat Yakub from the Syrian side*

118. *Lydda airport. View eastwards from the air*

villages; from Solomon's Pools (mile 45½) a first-class road [2 *d*] goes west, then forks south to Beit Jibrin on the Mejdel–Hebron road and north to the Jaffa–Jerusalem road [6]; Jerusalem, besides being the terminus of the Jaffa railway, is on the road from Jaffa to Jericho and thence across the Allenby bridge to Amman in Transjordan (p. 514).

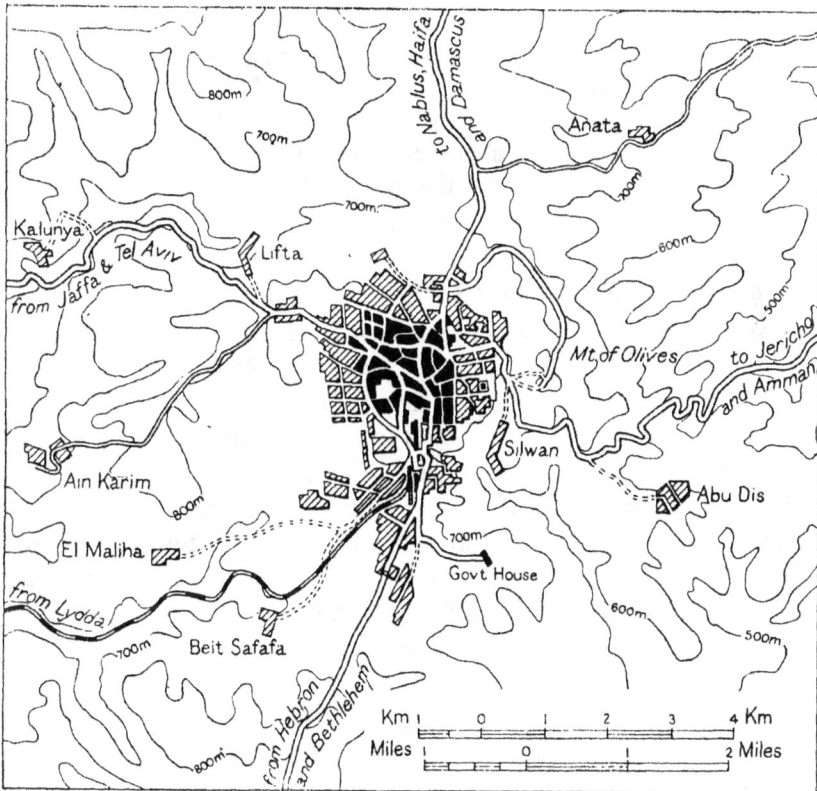

FIG. 48. *Jerusalem road-centre*

*Jerusalem–Nablus* (42·5 miles; 68·0 kilometres)

The minimum width of the road from Jerusalem northwards to the frontier at Metulla is 15 feet. From Jerusalem the road winds northwards over bare, stony hills, then after passing through the twin town of Ramallah-Bira (mile 10; alt. 2,790 ft.) it ascends a steep-sided, wooded valley. About mile 22 the trees give place to sparse pasture and the road descends past Khan el Lubban with five sharp loops (mile 26). After 6 miles alternately rising and falling over crest and valley the road enters the plain of Sahl Mukhnah and follows its western edge through cultivated country to Jacob's Well (mile 40). Here it bends north-west and ascends through orchards and gardens to Nablus between Mounts Ebal (3,084 ft.) and Gerizim (2,890 ft.).

Branches in this section are as follows: from Ramallah a first-class road [2 *e*] winds west to Latrun on the Jaffa–Jerusalem road [6]; from Nablus a second-class road [2 *f*] leads west to Kalkilya on the road [1 *m*] from Petah Tikva to Tulkarm; Nablus is on the transverse road [7] from Nathanya through Tulkarm to the Jordan at Jisr Damiya, which makes use of the central road between Nablus and Jacob's Well. In this section also there are many tracks branching off to nearby villages. On the west some of these tracks cross the watershed and descend to the coastal plain, where they join the coastal road. On the east they penetrate the hills for short distances, but none reach the Jordan.

*Nablus–Affula* (39·1 miles; 63·0 kilometres)

From Nablus to Jenin (mile 27½) the road traverses mountainous country with some olive-groves. As far as Deir Sharaf (mile 6) it makes use of a valley which is also followed for part of the way by the Tulkarm–Nablus railway, and in this stretch it forms part of the road [7] between the same places. The railway winds considerably more than the road and is much higher up the hill-side; before Deir Sharaf is reached the railway has turned north towards Sebustya (*anc.* Samaria). The road bends north from Deir Sharaf and passes round the west side of the hill on which stands Sebustya. There is a level crossing of the Tulkarm–Nablus railway at mile 9, near Masudiya station, where the line from Affula comes in. The road then winds north through the hills, with the Affula railway at varying distances to the west, until at about mile 19 both road and railway descend a narrow gully to the Sahl Arraba, an alluvial basin at 750 feet drained by the Wadi Abu Nar, which in the coastal plain becomes the Hadera or Mifjir river. After following the south-east margin of the plain, road and railway descend a narrow defile to Jenin, at 410 feet (mile 27½). From Jenin the road, with the railway about 1½ miles to the west, crosses the plain of Esdraelon, and is here almost straight. The Nablus railway is crossed just over a mile south of Affula.

Branches in this section are as follows: from Deir Sharaf at mile 6 the Tulkarm road [7] branches west; from mile 15 an unmetalled road [2 *g*], impassable in wet weather, leads east through Meithalun and across the Merj Sannur to Kufeir (10 miles); from mile 21 a road [2 *h*] branches west through Arraba, Fahma, and Kefr Rai to Illar (9½ miles), metalled as far as Kefr Rai; from the same point another road [2 *i*] branches north-west, then forks to Ain Ibrahim on the Karkur–Affula road [1 *o*] and to Baka on the Tulkarm–Karkur road [1 *p*]; from mile 25 an all-weather road [2 *j*] leads south through Kabatya, Kufeir, and Tubas to the Nablus–Jisr Damiya road [7]; from Jenin a first-class road [8] goes north-west to Haifa; at Affula the central road is crossed by the Haifa–Beisan road [9], which makes use of it for about 3 miles north of Affula; from Affula a first-class road [2 *k*] goes north-east to Samakh (31 miles).

## *Affula–Tiberias* (26·7 miles; 43·0 kilometres)

From Affula the road, set in an avenue of trees, goes straight north over the plain of Esdraelon, past Balfourya and other Jewish settlements, crosses the pipe-line from Iraq at Mizra (mile 3), zigzags steeply up the flanks of Jebel Kafza (1,320 ft.), and descends for half a mile into Nazareth (mile 7½). Crossing a narrow valley it winds with sharp bends up through the hills past the Arab village of Reina and on through olive-groves to Kefr Kenna (mile 13½). Bending gradually eastward over level ground, it reaches the edge of the highland at mile 23, descends gently for a mile and drops steeply through Mizpah (Mitspa) to Tiberias, on the edge of the lake at 650 feet below sea-level.

Branches in this section are as follows: near Mizra (mile 3) the Haifa–Beisan road [9] comes in from the west; from Nazareth a first-class road [2 *l*] runs west through the Balfour and King George V forests to Shimron (8 miles), on the Haifa–Beisan road; and a second-class road [1 *t*] leads north-west through Shefa Amr to the coastal road between Haifa and Acre (16 miles); from mile 18 a good tarmac road [2 *m*] goes north to the Acre–Safad road [10] and another [2 *k*] goes south to the Affula–Samakh road; from Tiberias a first-class road [2 *n*] follows the south-west shore of the lake to Samakh, across the Jordan (7 miles).

## *Tiberias—the frontier near Metulla* (40·4 miles; 65·0 kilometres)

In this section the road keeps to the Jordan trench almost throughout, until it bends north-west beyond Metulla to cross into the Litani valley in the Lebanon. For 3 miles it runs between Lake Tiberias and the rocky escarpment to the west, closely following the water's edge at about 650 feet below sea-level. At Mejdel (mile 3) the hills recede westward and the road traverses a small alluvial plain (photo. 13), crossing the wadis Hamam, Rubadiya, and Amud, the last two of which have perennial water and stone bridges. The plain ends at Tabgha (mile 8), and the road leaves the lake where the hills close in and climbs 1,300 feet with hairpin bends to 660 feet above sea-level, then rises more gradually to 1,300 feet near Rosh Pinna (mile 17). It then descends gradually northwards to cross the Huleh plain at a height of about 500 feet, and after crossing the Wadi Hindaj follows closely the foot of the escarpment. At the north end of the plain the road is hemmed in between the escarpment on the west and the marshes round the Jordan and other streams which drain south into Lake Huleh. Near Khalisa (mile 33) the hills stretch farther east, and the road climbs to 1,000 feet near Kefar Giladi, then ascends a small valley to Metulla at 1,722 feet (mile 39) close to the Syrian boundary. Here the road turns west and crosses the northernmost tip of Palestine to the frontier with the Lebanon.

Branches in this section are as follows: near Rosh Pinna (mile 17) the first-class Acre–Safad road [10] comes in from the west; it leaves at mile 18½ eastwards for the Jordan at Jisr Banat Yakub and for Damascus; from mile 23½ a second-class road [2 o] branches east to Lake Huleh (3 miles); at mile 26½ the frontier road [11] from Ez Zib through Kadas winds down the escarpment and joins; from mile 34 a metalled road [2 p] branches east across the Jordan to Banyas (Dan), near the Syrian frontier (6 miles).

## The Transverse Roads

[3]. *Rafa–El Auja el Hafir* (34 miles app.; 55 kilometres)

No information is available for publication.

[4]. *Gaza–Beersheba–Ain Hasb–Akaba* (175·5 miles; 282·4 kilometres)

The first section of this road, as far as Beersheba (29 miles), is a good tarmac road. A short stretch (2½ miles) connects Gaza beach with Gaza, crossing sand-dunes sparsely covered with cactus and stunted trees (fig. 45).

From Gaza to Beersheba the road lies in open, undulating country, and has three bridges and many culverts. Wet weather may completely interrupt traffic. After crossing the new coastal by-pass just outside Gaza the airfield is passed (mile 1½ from the level crossing), and the wireless station is on a hill north of the road at mile 4½. The Wadi Sharia is crossed by a 5-arch masonry bridge at mile 13; the concrete bridge over the Wadi Abu Semara at mile 16½ was unfinished in October 1942 and a metalled deviation over the wadi bed was used; a 4-arch masonry bridge (18 ft. long with 12-ft. roadway) spans the Wadi Zumeili at mile 22. Gradually ascending, the road reaches Beersheba at 900 feet.

East of Beersheba the road becomes an earthen track which breaks down into dust very quickly; it follows the general line of the Wadi Sab for 9½ miles, then turns south-south-east and climbs over rolling hills to Kurnub (mile 57). From Kurnub it keeps fairly level, through mountain gorges, until at about mile 72 it reaches the Nakb es Safi pass in the hills overlooking Ain Hasb. The road descends the pass from about 1,000 feet to sea-level in 2 miles, cut out of the earth and rock on the steep face of the escarpment, with 12 hairpin bends and 15 others, and with a gradient of about 1 in 8, though steeper in places. The surface is reasonably good and the alinement sufficiently well made not to require renewal after heavy rain. The gradient is more gradual to Ain Hasb, at about 330 feet below sea-level (mile 82). Here the track turns south along the Wadi Araba, crossing 93 miles of sand-dunes, rolling gravel, and soft mud-flats to Akaba. For 20 miles beyond Ain Hasb it is below sea-level, but in the next 25 miles it rises to over 600 feet above, and thereafter descends gradually to sea-level at the gulf of Akaba. The motor track follows the western side of the depression, generally skirting the Palestine foothills; it is sited where possible on hard ground, but going is slow, for many wadis drain down from the hills on the west and cross the track at right angles, flowing to the lowest part of the trough. The track is therefore impassable after heavy rain, which is not unknown in this region.

Branch-tracks from this route not already mentioned are: from mile 39 through Tell el Milh to Ras ez Zuweira (c. 18 miles) overlooking the Dead Sea [4 c]; and from Ain Hasb [4 a] north along the Wadi Araba, a made road for about 13 miles and then poor track past the south end of Jebel Usdum to the south-west shore of the Dead Sea, where are the potash works and a timbered wharf and jetty (25 miles); it sends a branch round the south-east side of the Dead Sea to Kerak in Transjordan (p. 518). This track, only recently completed, is one of the only two routes passable for wheeled traffic from Akaba to the Transjordan plateau, the other being the road to Maan.

## [5]. *El Jura–Hebron* (c. 40 miles; 64 kilometres)

This road connects the coast and the coastal road with the Judaean highlands and the central road, through a region without railways. From El Jura, near the site of the ancient port of Ascalon, it goes east through Mejdel (mile 2), across the coastal road and the Haifa–Kantara railway, climbing gradually past Faluja (mile 12½) to Irak el Menshiya at 410 feet. It passes up the Wadi Kubeiba for 4 miles, then turns north-east through the hills to Beit Jibrin at 980 feet (mile 23). Ascending a small valley, it reaches Tarkumiya (1,550 ft., mile 31) and winds up through broken country to the central road at 3,100 feet, 1½ miles north of Hebron. The chief branch connexions, [1 f], [2 b], and [2 d], have already been mentioned as subsidiaries to roads [1] and [2].

[6]. *Jaffa–Jerusalem–Jericho–Allenby Bridge* (68·5 miles; 110·2 kilometres)

This is the main road from the Palestine coast across the Jordan to Amman. Within Palestine it is a first-class tar-macadam road throughout, and has very recently been realined to avoid the steep, winding descent of the 'Seven Sisters' hill west of Jerusalem. There are only a few small bridges, apart from the Allenby bridge over the Jordan.

From Jaffa to Ramleh (mile 11) it traverses the coastal plain through citrus-groves, crossing the Sarafand branch of the Jaffa–Lydda railway at mile 8½ and the main Haifa–Kantara line at mile 10. After passing through open country parallel to a tributary of the Auja river it reaches Latrun (650 ft.) at mile 21 and enters the hills, climbing through a narrow gorge from Bab el Wad at 1,000 feet (mile 24). Fir-trees cover the slopes for about 4 miles, but before the top of the rise is reached at mile 30 the hills are bare. Kiryat el Inab (mile 30½) lies on a watershed (2,540 ft.) and at El Kastal, 2½ miles farther on, the descent of the 'Seven Sisters' hill began. This took the road down to 1,960 feet at Kalunya (mile 35), where the final climb to Jerusalem (2,985 ft.) began. Details of the new alinement are not yet available. From Jerusalem (mile 39) to Jericho (mile 62) the road winds north-east through desolate, rocky hills, generally descending. It leaves Jerusalem by the junction with the central road on the northern outskirts of the city, rounding the head of the Kidron valley and passing along the western slope of the Mount of Olives near Et Tur. A mile or two beyond Kalat ed Damm (mile 53) the main road makes a wide loop southwards down a dry valley where the descent is less steep and less tortuous than the former Roman road. Sea-level is reached at mile 55½ (16½ miles from Jerusalem), and from the mouth of the valley the road turns north up the flat Jordan plain to Jericho at 850 feet below sea-level. Continuing east across the floor of the depression, Allenby Bridge is reached after 6 miles, and the road crosses the river, here 26 yards wide, into Transjordan (p. 514). The new bridge, opened for traffic in May 1938, is a steel structure built to the design of the Crown Agents for the Colonies; it has two spans of 59 feet and one of 118 feet, a concrete deck, and a clear width of 20 feet allowing for two-way traffic. The old bridge is to be dismantled and moved north to Jisr el Majami.

The chief branches and connexions of this road, most of which have already been mentioned, are: the new road [1 g] from mile 5½ through Rishon le Zion to Mejdel on the coastal road for Gaza; from the same point north the connexion [1 h] with the coastal road near Wilhelma; at Ramleh the coastal road north and south; [1 k] from Latrun goes south-west to Masmiya on the coastal road; from Latrun a first-class road [2 e] goes north-east to Ramallah, on the central road; from Bab el Wad a second-class road [2 d] goes south for Beit Jibrin on the El Jura–Hebron road [5], and east as a first-class road to the central road south of Bethlehem; a first-class macadam road [6 b], 6 miles long, branches off at mile 59 and goes south-east to the north shore of the Dead Sea at Kallia and the potash works; a metalled road [6 a], 25½ miles long, branches north from Jericho to the Nablus–Jisr Damiya road [7] at Jiftlik.

[7]. *Nathanya–Tulkarm–Nablus–Jisr Damiya* (55·5 miles; 89·3 kilometres)

This road, a first-class tar-macadam road as far as Nablus, thereafter a rough, metalled road, connects the coast, through the railway junctions at Tulkarm and Masudiya, with Amman in Transjordan. From Nathanya to the Beit Lid cross-roads (mile 3) it runs due east from the cliffs through cultivated land. It continues across the coastal plain, here the fertile plain of Sharon, with orange-groves and fields of cereal crops on either side, to Tulkarm (mile 10½), crossing the Wadi Nahr by a concrete bridge at mile 7, and the Haifa–Kantara railway by a level crossing at mile 9½. At Tulkarm (330 ft.) it begins its ascent through the hills, following with the Tulkarm–Nablus railway the constricted valley of the Wadi Zeimar, past Anabta (mile 17) where it crosses the railway, and Ramin (mile 20), where the railway crosses it by a bridge, to Deir Sharaf (mile 23). Here it joins the central road, which takes it to Jacob's Well (mile 31), east of Nablus. From Jacob's Well it turns north-east, as a metalled all-weather road for 6 miles, then bends south-east down the Wadi Faria to the Jordan valley. For the greater part of the way the road is on a ledge cut into the rock side and is rough and uneven in places. Jisr Damiya, where the Jordan is crossed at the end of this 19-mile stretch, is at 950 feet below sea-level.

Branches and connexions of this road, all of which have already been mentioned, are: at Beit Lid (mile 3) the coastal road [1]; from Tulkarm first-class [1 m] south to Kalkilya for Lydda, Petah Tikva, and Jaffa, north [1 p] to the Hadera–Affula road [1 o]; from Nablus second-class [2 f] west to Kalkilya; from mile 37 second-class [2 j] north to the central road near Jenin; from Jiftlik [6 a] south along the Jordan trench to Jericho, and north to Beisan.

## [8]. *Haifa–Jenin* (29 miles; 46·7 kilometres)

This is a short road, linking the coast with the Samarian highland, across the plain of Esdraelon and through Megiddo. It is a good tar-macadam road throughout, and keeps practically level. In its first section, as far as Jalama (mile 6½), where it follows closely the foot of the Carmel ridge with the Haifa–Samakh railway, the Kishon river, and the oil pipe-line from Iraq to its left, it is part of the Haifa–Jisr el Majami road [9]. At Jalama it crosses the railway, and both pass through a narrow defile with the Kishon river between them, and the pipe-line east of the railway. The defile, where the mountains of Galilee send off spurs south-westward almost to the Carmel ridge, leads from the plain of Acre to that of Esdraelon. The road enters the latter plain near Kiryat Haroshet (mile 8½), diverges from the railway, and continues south to Tell Kamun (mile 10½), then follows the south-west margin of the plain, flanked by the Carmel ridge, past Megiddo to Jenin, on the central road and on the Affula–Masudiya railway. The road crosses this railway by a level-crossing at mile 27½, just before reaching Jenin.

Branches from this road, already referred to elsewhere, are: the new first-class road [1 q] from Tell Kamun south-west over the Carmel ridge to Zichron Jacob and the coastal road (14 miles); at mile 19, near Megiddo, the first-class Karkur–Affula road [1 o] crosses, linking the railway junction at Affula with the coast near Hadera.

## [9]. *Haifa–Affula–Beisan–Jisr el Majami* (53½ miles; 86·1 kilometres)

This is a good tar-macadam road throughout, with average width 18 feet, connecting the port of Haifa with the Jordan valley, and across the river, through Irbid, with the northern road through Transjordan (p. 515). From Haifa it goes south-east across the plain of Acre, passing under the concrete viaduct which carries the Acre railway on the outskirts of Haifa. It follows the foot of the Carmel ridge, with the Haifa–Samakh railway close beside it, past the Nesher cement factory (mile 2½) to Jalama (mile 6½). Here it leaves the rail-way and the Jenin road, crosses the Kishon and the pipe-line, then climbs over a rocky, wooded spur past Kiryat Amal (mile 8½) to Jeida (mile 11½). Following the northern edge of the plain of Esdraelon through cornfields and olive-groves, it reaches Shimron (mile 14), then branches south past Nahalal towards the pipe-line, avoiding the hills which close in on the Nazareth road, and joining the central road at mile 22. It makes use of the central road [2] to Affula (mile 26½), then follows the Nahr Jalud (Vale of Jezreel) down to Beisan (mile 42), reaching sea-level at mile 30½. The vale is about 1½ miles wide, and almost flat, with the mountains of Little Hermon rising to the north, and Jebel Fakkua (Mountains of Gilboa) to the south. The road closely follows the Samakh railway, and crosses it by a level crossing at Beisan station, 351 feet below sea-level. Beisan itself is 410 feet below sea-level. On leaving Beisan the Nahr Jalud is crossed by a 2-span stone bridge, and the road follows the railway northwards up the Jordan valley, keeping about a mile west of the meander belt of the river, and crossing the pipe-line at mile 51. The bridge at Jisr el Majami has two spans, and is to be replaced by the old Allenby bridge so that the bottleneck in traffic with Transjordan may be lessened, for it is from this point that the new road across Transjordan and the desert to Baghdad has been constructed (p. 515).

Branches and connexions of this road are: the coastal road from mile 0·6 to Acre and the north; from mile 5 a new first-class road [1 s] goes north to Birwa on the Acre–Safad road [10], thus relieving the coastal road of some of its traffic; from Jalama (mile 6½) the Jenin road [8] leads southeast; from Shimron (mile 14) a first-class road [2 l] goes east to Nazareth, on the central road; from Affula first-class roads lead south-west to the coast near Hadera [1 o], north-east to Samakh [2 k],[1] and south to Jenin [2]; from Beisan the second-class metalled road [6 a] goes south along the Jordan valley to Jericho (61½ miles) and a track [9 b] goes east to the Jordan at Jisr Sheikh Hussein for Irbid; from Jisr el Majami a first-class tar-macadam road [2 n] goes north to Samakh (6 miles) at the south end of Lake Tiberias.

## [10]. *Acre–Jisr Banat Yakub* (45 miles; 72·4 kilometres)

This is a good tar-macadam road, averaging 18 feet wide but occasionally narrowing to 13 feet, which links the coast with the central road and the Jordan valley, through a region without railways. From Acre it crosses the new railway to Tripoli, then goes through 6 miles of the coastal plain. After leaving Birwa on the south at mile 6, it continues east through rolling hills to Rama (mile 17½), beyond

---

[1] The section between Kefar Tavor and Kinneret on Lake Tiberias is only 14 feet wide, with steep gradients and sharp bends; it is metalled and in good condition but barely up to first-class standard.

which it enters the mountains of Galilee, winding north to Meirun (mile 27) at 2,460 feet. Turning east again, and then south-east, it loops up past Safad (mile 32) at 2,620 feet, and then winds obliquely down Jebel Canaan (Kanan) to Rosh Pinna (mile 37½) at 1,312 feet. At mile 38 it reaches the central road and makes use of this for 1½ miles, then branches north-east over the Jordan plain to Jisr Banat Yakub (mile 44½) at 328 feet, where there is a single-span girder bridge across the Jordan. The road crosses the Syrian boundary at mile 45 and goes on to Damascus.

Branches from this road are: from near Birwa first-class [1 s] south to the Haifa–Affula road [9] near its junction with the Jenin road [8]; from Rama second-class [1 u] north-west to the Ez Zib–Kadas road [11] at Sasa, and to the coastal road at Nahariya; from mile 20 a good but narrow second-class tar-macadam road [2 m] south to the central road.

[11]. *Frontier road: north of Ez Zib–Kadas–Ain Beisamun* (38 miles; 61·5 kilometres)

This is the newly constructed northern frontier road (p. 379). As far as Sasa (mile 21½) it has a tar-macadam surface. Beyond that it has a broken tar or gravel surface. The Frontier Fence, with gates at intervals, runs along its north side almost for the whole way. Leaving the coastal road from a point half-way between Ez Zib and Ras en Nakurah, it proceeds eastward across a short stretch of plain, then over undulating country past El Bassa until it enters the hills about mile 4½. Continuing eastward through rocky hill-country, it passes Ikrit at mile 10½ and Tarbikha at mile 11, then winds south-east to Sasa (mile 21½). Beyond Sasa it swings generally north-east to Malikiya (mile 31½), then turns abruptly east, over a concrete bridge to Kadas (mile 34½). After passing the new aircraft landing-ground the road, cut in the mountain-side, drops down the escarpment in hairpin bends to the Huleh plain. In this section it falls from 1,230 feet to 320 feet in about 1½ miles, and has four bridges. At Ain Beisamun it joins the central road, here passing the extensive area of marsh at the northern end of Lake Huleh.

The chief branch is the second-class road [1 u] from Sasa which forks south-west to the coastal road at Nahariya, and south to the Acre–Safad road [10] at Rama.

[12]. *The Jordan valley road: Kallia–Tiberias* (96 miles; 154·5 kilometres)

This road has been referred to as branches or parts of the main roads [6 *b*, 6 *a*, 9, 2 *n*, 2], but it has some significance as a continuous road, for it follows the eastern frontier of Palestine and makes use of the most striking topographical feature of the country, despite the difficulties caused by depth below sea-level and the consequently numerous wadis which have to be crossed by any north–south road in the trough. The road has a good metalled surface throughout, has many small bridges and culverts, but some of the wadis are only crossed by causeways.

From Kallia, on the north shore of the Dead Sea, the main road goes west to the Jerusalem road [6] which takes it into Jericho (mile 9½). Thence to Beisan (mile 71) it winds as a second-class road through the foothills of the escarpment, crossing the Nablus–Jisr Damiya road [7] at Jiftlik where the vale of Jezreel opens to the Jordan valley, then joining the Haifa–Jisr el Majami road [9] at Beisan. This road takes it another 11½ miles to Jisr el Majami, where it crosses the Jordan and continues north to Samakh (mile 88½) and Tiberias (mile 96), where it joins the central road which extends the Jordan valley route to Metulla.

## SHIPPING SERVICES

THERE were four shipping lines (two Italian[1] and two French) that used to bring passengers regularly to Palestine. Of these the *Servizi Marittimi* or Sitmar called twice a month at Jaffa, coming from Italy or Alexandria, and twice on the return journey from the Piraeus, Istanbul, and Beirut. The *Lloyd Triestino* called at Jaffa, Tel Aviv, and Haifa, weekly from Italy, weekly from Greece and Beirut, and in alternate weeks from Alexandria or Cyprus. Of the French lines the *Fabre* made two calls a month and the *Messageries Maritimes* four. Two of the *Messageries Maritimes* vessels came by Naples, the Piraeus, Istanbul, and Beirut, the rest from Marseilles by Alexandria to Jaffa. There was no regular British passenger line, but the vessels of the Prince Line came to Palestine frequently, especially during the orange season, with accommodation for a small number of passengers, and the Orient Line occasionally brought passengers direct from Southampton. Russian and Romanian ships also brought passengers from Black Sea ports, but irregularly. A small Palestinian line, the Atid Navigation Company, carried goods and passengers irregularly between Egypt, Palestine, Syria, and Turkey.

[1] In 1937 the east European services of the *Servizi Marittimi* and the *Lloyd Triestino* lines were amalgamated to form the *Adriatica*.

## CIVIL AVIATION

WITH the conquest of the air, Palestine and Transjordan have re-sumed their historic importance between Europe and the East. The Great Circle between London and Karachi passes north of Vienna, over the Crimea, the Caucasus, and the Dasht-i-Lut of Persia; long distances of this route are sparsely inhabited and, certainly in the early days of flying, to establish an air-route would have been impossible, quite apart from political considerations.

For a British air-route to the East the obvious stopping-place was Egypt. Thence to India the route over Palestine, Iraq, and the Persian Gulf was enforced by the deserts of Arabia.

The pioneers of the route were British, and it was opened in sections. Early in 1919 the first reconnaissances were made between Baghdad and Damascus and between Baghdad and Lake Tiberias. Alternative routes were examined on the ground by car, and in 1920 the selected line was marked across the desert by a shallow trench cut by motor-plough. Then the line was reconnoitred from the air; but it was not till January 1927 that the first regular service from Britain to Baghdad was opened; early in 1928 the first mails by air were carried to India.

By the summer of 1939 there were five trunk air services passing through Palestine. Two were operated by Imperial Airways (British), one by K.L.M. (Dutch), one by Ala Littoria (Italian), and one by L.O.T. (Polish). Lydda had become the junction for regular air services to Europe, to Egypt for South Africa, to Syria, and to India, Australia, and the Far East. At Haifa there is a smaller airport, and there are seaplane stations at Haifa and Tiberias. There were also five local services, between Palestine and Syria, Egypt, Cyprus, or Iraq. A few planes were owned privately, and others could be chartered. Civil Aviation was controlled by the Director of Civil Aviation. The trunk and local routes in service in the summer of 1939 were as follows:

(i) *Trunk Routes*

  *Imperial Airways Ltd. (British)*

  1. Southampton—Alexandria – Tiberias (Palestine) – Habbaniya (Iraq)——Singapore. Three times weekly, with flying-boats. At Singapore there was connexion by air with Australia.

2. Southampton—Alexandria–Lydda (Palestine)–Baghdad (Iraq)
—Calcutta. Twice weekly, with flying-boats as far as Alexandria and thence by land-planes to Calcutta.

*K.L.M. (Koninklijke Lucktvaart Maatschappij Voor Nederland en
Kolonien) (Dutch)*

1. Amsterdam—Alexandria–Lydda–Baghdad (Iraq)—Bandoeng
(N.E.I.). Three times weekly, with land-planes.

*Ala Littoria, S.A. (Italian)*

1. Rome—Rhodes (Dodecanese)–Haifa (Palestine)–Baghdad (Iraq)
–Basra (Iraq). Three times weekly, with land-planes.

*L.O.T. (Polskie Linje Lotnieze) (Polish)*

1. Warsaw–Athens–Lydda–Beirut (Syria). Twice weekly, with
land-planes.

(ii) *Local Routes*

*Palestine Airways Ltd. (Palestinian)*

1. Lydda–Tel Aviv–Haifa–Beirut (Syria). Twice daily, with land-
planes.

*Misr Airwork S.A.E. (Egyptian)*

1. Cairo–Port Said–Lydda–Larnaka (Cyprus). Once weekly, with
land-planes.
2. Cairo–Port Said–Lydda–Haifa. Once daily, with land-planes.
3. Cairo–Lydda–Baghdad. Twice weekly, with land-planes.

The war has necessarily brought many changes. The Polish, Dutch,
and Italian services have ceased to operate; Imperial Airways has
been reorganized as the British Overseas Airways Corporation
(B.O.A.C.), and the trunk services are now operated by this corporation alone. Fewer scheduled services are available, but far more
journeys are made. The Egyptian company still operates, between
Egypt, Palestine, and Syria; but the Palestinian company has been
merged with B.O.A.C. and the local services have been extended to
Adana in Turkey and to Teheran in Persia. The services in operation
in August 1943 were the following:

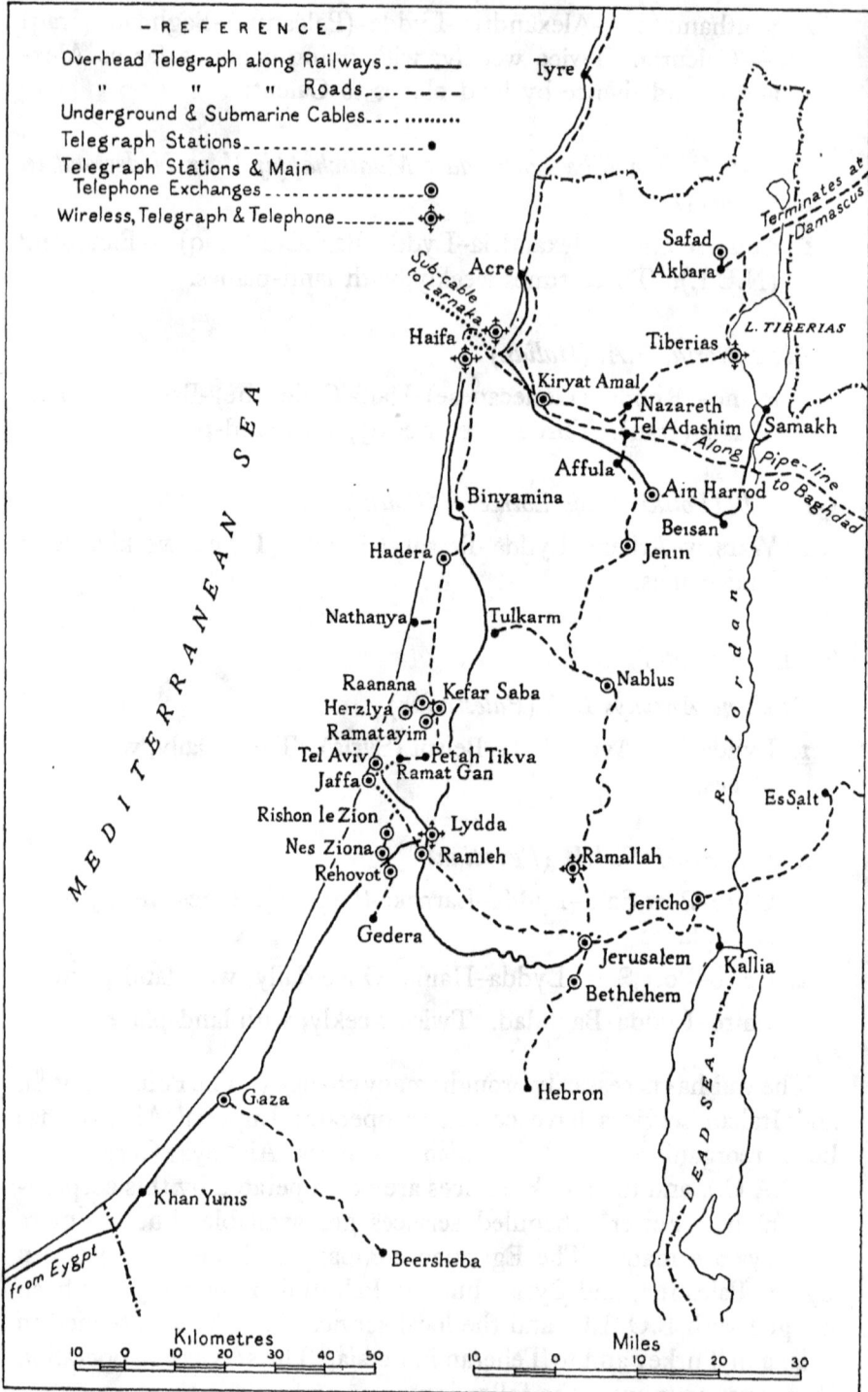

- REFERENCE -

Overhead Telegraph along Railways.. ——
       "    "    "   Roads.... – – –
Underground & Submarine Cables.... ·········
Telegraph Stations.................. •
Telegraph Stations & Main
    Telephone Exchanges ............... ◎
Wireless, Telegraph & Telephone.......... ◈

FIG. 49. *Telegraphs, Telephones, and Wireless Stations*

(i) *Trunk Routes*

B.O.A.C. (*British Overseas Airways Corporation*) (*British*)

1. Durban—Cairo–Kallia(Palestine)–Habbaniya—Calcutta. Twice weekly, with flying-boats.
2. Cairo–Lydda (Palestine)–Habbaniya——Karachi. With landplanes.

(ii) *Local Routes*

Misr Airwork S.A.E. (*Egyptian*)

1. Cairo–Port Said–Lydda–Beirut. With land-planes.
2. Cairo–Port Said–Lydda. With land-planes.
3. Cairo–Port Said–Lydda–Beirut–Larnaka (Cyprus). With landplanes.

B.O.A.C. (*British Overseas Airways Corporation*) (*British*)

1. Cairo–Lydda–Adana (Turkey). Once weekly, with land-planes.
2. Cairo–Lydda–Habbaniya (Iraq)–Teheran (Persia). With landplanes.

By far the most important airfield in Palestine is the airport of Lydda (photo. 118); next is Haifa, which was used by the Italian company until 1940. There are also a number of local landing-grounds and military landing-grounds throughout the country.

Fig. 62 shows the airfields, landing grounds, and seaplane bases in Palestine. In 1939, passengers arriving from abroad numbered 5,240; in ten months, from March to December, 43,882 kg. of freight, and in the whole year 54,018 kg. of mail were discharged. Lydda airport and Haifa seaplane port were by far the most important for passenger traffic; but Tiberias shared with Lydda almost all the loading and unloading of mails.

## SIGNAL COMMUNICATIONS

There were telegraphs along the railways of Palestine before 1914, but it might almost be said that signal communications were introduced during the War of 1914–1918 by the British Army. In 1924 over a quarter of a million telegrams were sent and there were 7,400,000 local telephone calls and 316,000 trunk calls; in 1939 there were 462,128 telegrams and over 35,675,000 local and 2,252,000 trunk calls, a remarkable increase. The country is now covered with a network of lines along the railways and roads, and it is possible to telephone to other countries. There are also nine main wireless stations, four aircraft wireless stations, and over a hundred smaller sets. At Jerusalem 20-kW. output is available for the broadcasting station.

*Telegraphs and Telephones* (overhead, underground, and submarine)

In 1939 the telegraph and telephone trunk lines totalled 13,000 miles. Telephone and telegraphic services are available in all towns and larger villages, and the inhabitants make full use of them. There are eighteen automatic exchanges with over 3,000 subscribers at Haifa, Jerusalem, and Tel Aviv and a number of manual exchanges. Besides the normal telegraph system there are teleprinter circuits from Jerusalem to Haifa, Jaffa to Lydda airport, and Lydda airport to Haifa and Tiberias.

The international trunk circuits are Jerusalem–Amman, Haifa–Baghdad, Ramleh–Beirut, Ramleh–Cairo, Ramleh–Ismailia.

Cables and Wireless Ltd. own and operate a submarine cable from Haifa to Larnaka where it is joined through to Alexandria (thus being connected with the main system). Larnaka breaks in at stated times with its own traffic.

*Wireless*

The main wireless stations belong to the Department of Posts and Telegraphs, to the Department of Civil Aviation, to Imperial Airways, and to the Iraq Petroleum Company. Details are given below. In addition, there were in 1939 seventy-five wireless sets used by the Palestine Police Force, eighteen by the Arab Legion, and others by the Transjordan Frontier Force, Palestine Electric Corporation, Palestine Potash Limited, and Sulphur Quarries Limited. These are all low-power sets, and many are temporary or provisional. The Palestine Police Force has stations at district headquarters: Gaza, Haifa, Jerusalem, Lydda, Nablus, and Nazareth; at divisional headquarter stations: Acre, Beersheba, Jenin, Safad, Tiberias, and Tulkarm; and under their control there are sets in certain towns and villages, and mobile sets in cars. The headquarters of the Arab Legion at Amman has wireless sets at certain villages working under it, and the Transjordan Frontier Force has wireless communication with Irbid, Jisr el Majami, Maan, Samakh, and Zerka.

The chief broadcasting station is at Ramallah, 10 miles north of

Jerusalem. Posts, telegraphs, telephones, wireless, and broadcasting are organized in one government department under the Postmaster General.

## Principal Wireless Stations

| Station | Position | Wave-length, long, medium or short | Power in kW | Remarks |
|---|---|---|---|---|
| **DEPARTMENT OF POSTS AND TELEGRAPHS** | | | | |
| JERUSALEM broadcasting station at Ramallah | 31° 55′ N. 35° 12′ E. | 1 medium | 20 | Palestine Government. |
| | | 2 medium | { 1 0·7 | Palestine Government. |
| **DEPARTMENT OF CIVIL AVIATION** | | | | |
| HAIFA AIRPORT | 32° 49′ N. 35° 03′ E. | 1 medium | 0·5 | Palestine Government. Temporarily closed in 1940. |
| LYDDA AIRPORT | 31° 55′ N. 35° 12′ E. | 5 medium 3 short | { 1 0·7 { 0·25 0·12 | Palestine Government. Meteorological report. |
| TIBERIAS AIRPORT | 32° 47′ N. 35° 32′ E. | 1 medium | 0·25 | Imperial Airways (now B.O.A.C.). |
| **IMPERIAL AIRWAYS (B.O.A.C.)** | | | | |
| TIBERIAS AERADIO | 32° 47′ N. 35° 32′ E. | 2 medium 1 short | 0·25 .. | Works to Haifa, Habbaniya, Lydda, Rutba, Alexandria, Cairo. Meteorological report. |
| **IRAQ PETROLEUM COMPANY** | | | | |
| I.P.C. HAIFA | 32° 50′ N. 35° 03′ E. | 3 medium 1 short | { 0·5 0·25 0·15 | At I.P.C. Building, Catoni Street, Haifa. |
| I.P.C. | 32° 11′ N. 37° 07′ E. and 32° 30′ N. 38° 12′ E. | 3 medium 1 short } ditto | 0·25 0·15 ditto | In Transjordan, Pumping-Station No. 5, Landing-ground 21. In Transjordan, Pumping-Station No. 4. |
| Four Aircraft mobile stations | .. | 1 medium | 0·6 | Trailing Aerial 200′ to the aircraft in Transjordan and Iraq. |

# PART II. TRANSJORDAN

## CHAPTER XIV

## PHYSICAL GEOGRAPHY

*Introduction*

THE Amirate of Transjordan lies between latitudes 29° 20′ N. at Kalat Mudauwara in the south and 33° 25′ N. near Jebel Tinf in the north-east; and between longitudes 35° E. at Akaba in the south-west and 39° E. near Jebel Aneiza in the east. These are the extreme limits, for south of Jebel Aneiza the breadth from west to east contracts considerably. On the west the frontier marches with Palestine; on the north with Syria; on the north-east, between Jebel Tinf and Jebel Aneiza, a distance of about 75 miles, with Iraq; on the south-east and south with Saudi Arabia.

The length from north to south along the crest of the Jordan–Araba escarpment is about 230 miles, the greatest breadth, from the western boundary to Jebel Aneiza, about 200 miles. The country has never been accurately surveyed, and existing maps are based mainly on route traverses and travellers' accounts, though maps on the scale of 1 : 50,000 have been compiled from air photographs of the eastern approaches to the Jordan valley and part of the lava belt east of Kasr Azrak. The total area of Transjordan is roughly estimated at 33,750 square miles.

The western boundary with Palestine has been described on p. 1. The northern boundary towards Syria is that defined by the Anglo-French Convention of 1920. It follows the general course of the river Yarmuk to Mezerib (the railway being in Syria), passes immediately south-west of Deraa to Nessib (Nasib) on the Hejaz railway, thence to Imtan near the Jebel Druse. From here to the outskirts of Abu Kemal on the Euphrates the Syrian boundary is a straight line, or, more strictly speaking, a great circle, but the boundary between Transjordan and Iraq leaves it from the nearest point to Jebel Tinf, and is defined by an approximately straight line to the intersection of the 32nd parallel and the 39th meridian (south-west of Jebel Aneiza). The boundary when demarcated may be defined by prominent physical features which must not, however, be more than 5 kilometres from the great circle passing through the two terminal points.

The boundary with Saudi Arabia, also undemarcated, is similarly defined by straight lines passing through particular points: from latitude 32° N., longitude 39° E., roughly west-south-west to latitude 31° 30′ N., longitude 37° E.; thence due south to latitude 31° 25′ N. and south-east to latitude 30° N., longitude 38° E.; but some divergence is allowed so that the western tributaries of the Wadi Sirhan shall be in Saudi Arabia, a consideration which could only be decided by survey on the ground, in the event of dispute. From the point last defined the boundary follows the 38th meridian south to latitude 29° 35′ N.

The southern boundary is subject to no formal agreement (p. 463), but in a note dated 19 May 1927, addressed to the King of the Hejaz and Nejd (*Cmd.* 2951), Sir Gilbert Clayton stated that H.M. Government regarded the boundary as starting from latitude 29° 35′ N., longitude 38° E., proceeding in a straight line to a point on the Hejaz railway 2 miles south of Mudauwara, and thence in a straight line to a point on the gulf of Akaba 2 miles south of the town of Akaba.

Transjordan is still a country little known to the West. The north-west settled region is mapped, but most of the country east of the railway and south of Maan is unsurveyed, and until the War of 1914–1918 had few travellers. The construction of the pipe-line to Iraq and of the motor-road adjacent to it has added to our knowledge of the north-eastern part. A few British officers of the Arab Legion and of the Royal Air Force have motored or flown over the rest. West of the railway, Amman and Jerash are now easily accessible to visitors from Palestine, but few visit them. European and American residents are very few. Still fewer have written on the country or its people. The principal sources of information are therefore the narratives of travellers, spread at intervals over a century and a half, and the Annual Reports of H.M. Government to the Council of the League of Nations, mostly dealing with administration. The latest of these to be published relates to the year 1939, but some more recent developments are briefly mentioned in this book.

The northern part of habitable Transjordan has often been incorporated with Palestine in the past. In early biblical times Moab and Ammon were separate from Canaan, but Gilead was included in the Promised Land, and the region occupied by Reuben, Gad, and half of Manasseh, which comprised the Hauran of Syria and the Ajlun highland of Transjordan, was an integral part of the kingdom of Israel. Later, under new and sometimes identical masters their destinies and roles were often dissimilar. The country west of Jordan remained Jewish even during the Captivity, but Transjordan no longer formed part of it. Under the Nabataeans its role changed and the Transjordan towns won prosperity because of their geographical position on the caravan routes between Egypt, Syria, the Persian gulf, and Arabia. Only the small Transjordan frontage of Peraea belonged to Palestine under the Herods. In Roman times after the annexation Transjordan was never Jewish. Its role again changed, and it became the hellenized right flank of the frontier facing east to the desert. Beyond the line of *castella* from Bostra to the gulf of Akaba, most of the Roman province of Arabia Petraea was loosely held for the West by subsidized desert chieftains who had brought their tribesmen from the south and who in later contact with Byzantine culture became Christians.

Thus, though the movements of the Edomites, Israelites, Nabataeans, Ghassanids, and later Arabian tribes were mostly part of a single process, the Israelites are the only people known to have passed directly into Palestine in organized tribal state without tarrying in Transjordan. The boundary between the settled and the nomad peoples runs north and south through Transjordan, and it is here, and not in Palestine, that there is the clash between the settled people and the beduin.

The Jordan valley has never been a definite political boundary until 1923, when the Ottoman Empire came to an end, because the rival Powers who claimed the mastery of these regions generally faced each other north and south, or because the whole area, including Egypt and Syria, was in Roman, Arab, or Ottoman hands. In Roman times the frontier was at the desert's edge from north to south in Transjordan; in Moslem times none was needed. Thus at the Treaty of Lausanne the settlement of boundaries between the three newly created states of Syria, Palestine, and Transjordan had no historical basis and was an attempt to find the best solution of war-time pacts and pledges. It should be remembered that there was no real Arab unity at that time. Iraq was by no means desirous of union with Syria nor with Arabia, and there were rivalries between the Arabian Emirs, and particularly between the Hashimites of Mecca and Ibn Saud. The Jordan boundary was accepted as the best at the time, and it was only with the growth of Arab nationalism and active Jewish Zionism that the boundary has been considered 'unnatural'; this attitude is not a valid criticism of the line taken by the boundary, but echoes a fundamental objection to the separation of the three states of Syria, Palestine, and Transjordan. Some such view appears to have been held by the Royal Commission on Palestine, whose recommendations, though rejected by both peoples, Arab and Jew, attempted to satisfy them by cutting Palestine in two and by incorporating the Arab portion in the Amirate of Transjordan. If this compromise had been accepted there would have been a united Arab Palestine on both sides of the Jordan, but a portion of Palestine would have been excluded to become a separate non-Arab State.

Since the outbreak of war in 1939 the settlement of these difficult problems has been in abeyance. Transjordan was the least affected of the Arab States by the prospect of a German victory following the events of 1940 and 1941. The fall of France with the consequent campaign in Syria and rising in Iraq show, however, that the spirit of Arab nationalism is very much alive. Since then Arab policy has moved towards federation, rather than union, between Palestine, Transjordan, Syria, the Lebanon, and Iraq, though Saudi Arabia at present stands aloof, and it may be that eventual solution will follow some such course.

The Arab world has been likened by Ibn Khaldun, a Berber writer, to a stormy sea breaking against the shore. One strong tribe after another billows in from the desert to break and lose its virility on the cultivation. This has been markedly true of Transjordan, where many of the villagers are descendants of some great fighting Arabian tribe of the past which gradually settled down in the land which they had raided and conquered. Even to-day new tribes are gradually moving north through Arabia, and practically none of the larger tribes now in Transjordan have been there for more than 300 years.

The population at the present time is little more than 300,000, not more than one-third of the number which were in the country during the prosperous Roman period from A.D. 200 to 500. The much greater population of those times is shown by the ruins of the Roman towns, and particularly of public buildings. Amman and Petra each had very large amphitheatres, and Jerash had three. The reason for the decline of population was the lack of public security, particularly during the Ottoman period. In Roman times no nomad could own land or graze west of the line of *castella* along the Akaba–Amman road, a wise rule dictated by the necessity to protect the vineyards and olive-groves. With the withdrawal of Roman troops, raiding and insecurity increased, and the nomad has gradually encroached on the cultivable land. It is this conflict between the desert and the sown that creates the chief difficulty of the administrator in Transjordan to-day.

The cultivated part of Transjordan to-day is, roughly, all the north-western part, the ancient Gilead, between Amman and the Jordan, and also the districts near the villages west of the Hejaz railway as far as the southern end of the Dead Sea. Wheat and barley are grown extensively, lentils, *sim-sim* for oil, and in some parts maize as summer crop with irrigation. Olives, figs, vines, apricots, and other fruit flourish, and citrus cultivation is being introduced. With more settled conditions the area under cultivation is being gradually increased; there is still much cultivable land not yet used except for grazing. Nevertheless Transjordan must remain both a pastoral and an agricultural country. There are no metals or raw materials of sufficient importance with which to build up any large-scale industries, and no need for them.

Much of the progress in the last twenty years is due to Colonel F. G. Peake, who first commanded the Egyptian Camel Corps which operated east of the Jordan with Feisal's Arab army during the final stages of the campaign, and then raised the Arab Legion in October 1920 and became the Amir Abdulla's right-hand man and chief military adviser.

## TOPOGRAPHY

Transjordan occupies part of the high north-western edge of the great Arabian slab which is tilted gently from west to east until it is submerged in the Persian gulf. The structure is simple, for the slab is covered by stratified limestones and sandstones, only slightly bent or dislocated during the tilting movement, and overspread in places by vast sheets of lava which have welled up through fissures to heights of over 6,000 feet. Within Transjordan, however, the only lava sheets are those on the southern margin of the Jebel Druse, and farther east and south where a broad belt extends across Transjordan from Syria into Saudi Arabia.

On the western side of this belt, mostly in Arabia, is a wide shallow depression, the Wadi Sirhan, with drainage towards the marsh and pools south of Kasr Azrak in Transjordan at the northern end. Other marshes extend north-westwards along the south-west margin of Jebel Druse towards the low watershed of the Yarmuk river (c. 2,400 ft.), east of Mafrak station on the Hejaz railway.

Transjordan contains three main regions, each extending through the country from north to south: (*a*) the eastern half of the Jordan depression on the western border of the country; (*b*) the western highlands lying east of (*a*); and (*c*) the desert, east of the Hejaz railway. Each of these can be subdivided on a basis of local topography.

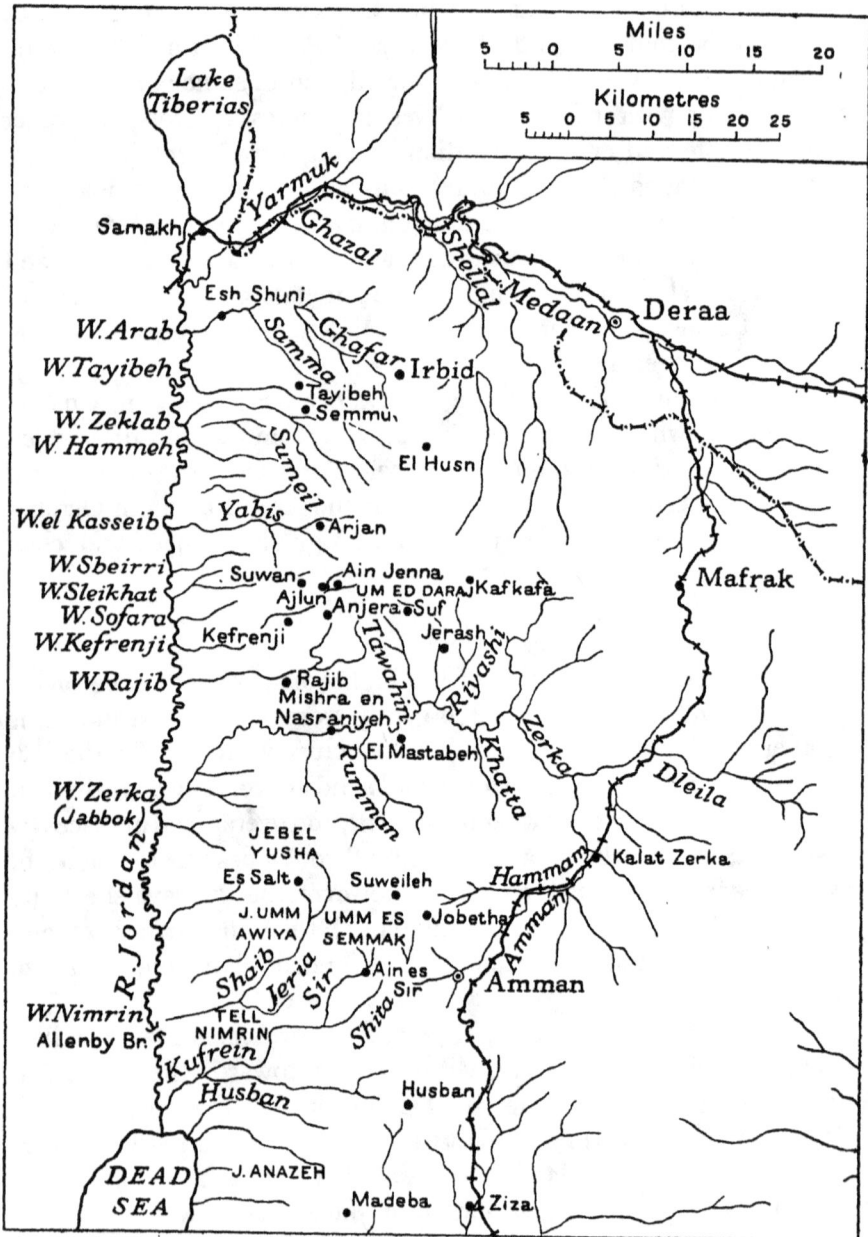

FIG. 50. *The Highlands of Ajlun and the Northern Belka*

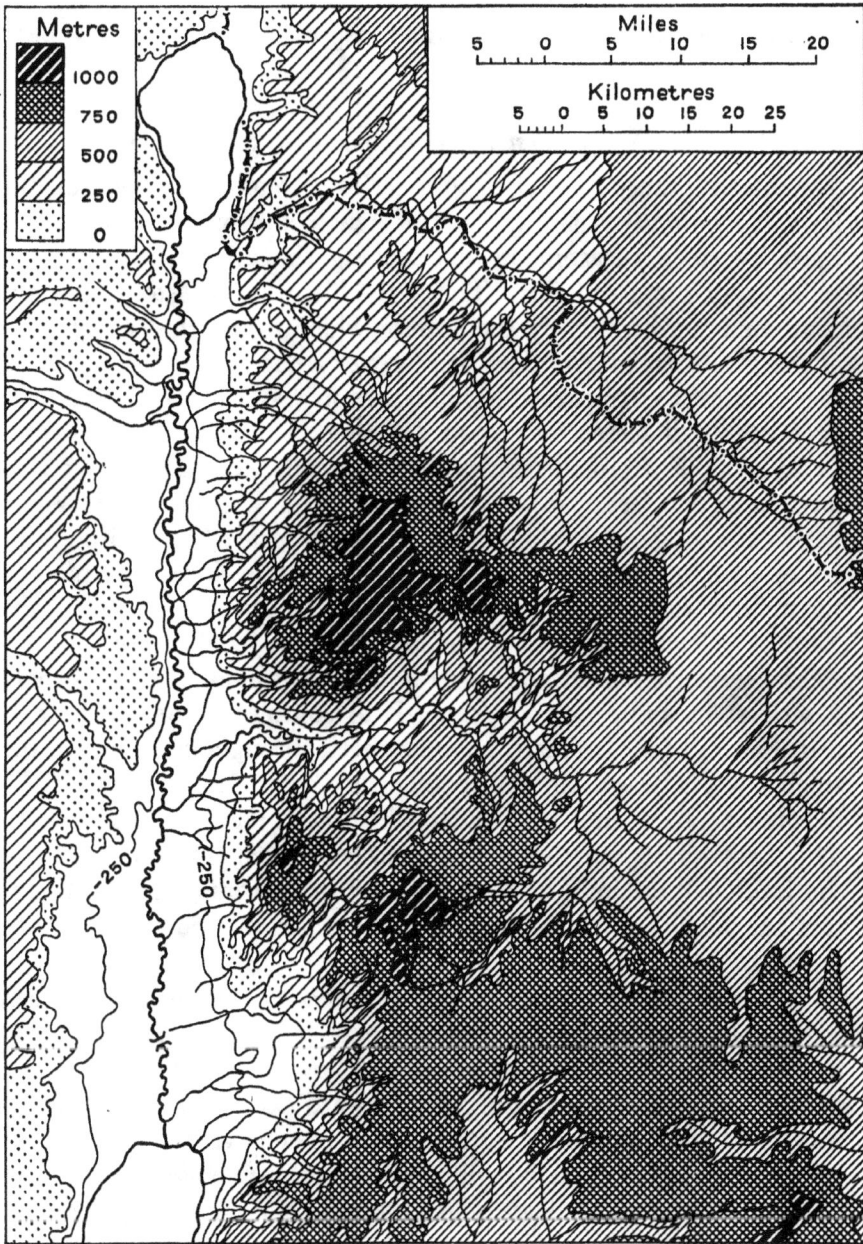

FIG. 51. *The Highlands of Ajlun and the Northern Belka*

### (a) The Jordan Depression

The main features of the Jordan depression have already been described on pages 21–23.

### (b) The Western Highlands (figs. 50–54)

Western Transjordan rises to a series of highlands, between the lower Yarmuk valley and the gulf of Akaba, abruptly bounded westward by steep escarpments overlooking the Ghor (lower Jordan valley) and the Dead Sea. They are chiefly of limestone, but are continued southwards by the granite which forms the eastern wall of the Wadi Araba. As they rise to over 4,000 feet above sea-level, they intercept an appreciable rainfall from westerly winds and have been deeply dissected by torrent drainage. The watershed lies from 15 to 40 miles from the escarpment at about 3,000 feet above sea-level and 4,000 feet or more above the Jordan. East of the watershed begins the long gentle slope of the Arabian plateau, with little rainfall or erosion, except where the Yarmuk and the Zerka have pierced the main watershed and annexed some of the drainage east of it, the Yarmuk collecting some western streams from Jebel Druse.

The western plateaux are therefore discontinuous, and are here described in succession from north to south, together with their principal valleys. It must be remembered throughout that even the smaller wadis bear a different name every few miles, and are usually denoted here by the name under which each joins a larger stream. The discontinuity of the plateaux makes movement from north to south difficult except near the sources of the streams, and it is therefore the highland which forms the great natural route from north to south.

The *Yarmuk* river and the railway mark the boundary between Syria and Transjordan from near Deraa (which is itself in Syria) to its outlet into the Jordan valley. It flows first north-west, then west, then south-west, skirting a northward extension of the plateau watershed, both slopes of which it drains in open valleys. The headwaters of the Nahr Shellal tributary lie some 30 miles south of its junction with Wadi Medaan, which rises south of Deraa, near Mafrak. Thereafter it has cut a deep narrow channel through the plateau, and has therefore always been a formidable obstacle, though the wide district which it drains is comparatively open country. The large tributaries from the north, on its right bank, the river itself, and the railway are in Syrian territory (photos. 119, 120).

119. *The Yarmuk valley between Samakh and El Hammeh. Railway bridge at km. 6·2 from Samakh*

120. *The Yarmuk valley between the railway stations of Wadi Khaled and Esh Shajara. Bridge at km. 26·6*

121. *Es Salt*

122. *Amman*

*The Ajlun Highland* (anc. *Gilead*, later *Galaaditis*) (figs. 50, 51)

Between the Yarmuk and Wadi Zerka is a roughly triangular plateau, with its highest point, Umm ed Daraj (4,070 ft.), between Ajlun and Jerash. The westward escarpment and the southern face above the lower Zerka are very steep and deeply dissected. The lower slopes overlooking the Yarmuk are abrupt, but not so high (*c.* 1,200 ft. above sea-level), and above these the plateau drainage is more open. North-eastward the plateau only reaches 2,000 feet near El Husn, and east of Kafkafa north of Jerash, on the long east–west ridge between the head-waters of the Yarmuk and of the Zerka. Most of this Ajlun highland is broken plateau, deeply furrowed by narrow valleys. It is more thickly wooded than the districts farther south (p. 426), but on its gentler slopes are many small valleys and cultivated plains.

Most parts of Ajlun are rich in springs and brooks with good drinking-water. The exceptions are the east side of the watershed and the high plateaux west and south-west of Irbid, where cisterns are used. The five principal villages in the south, Suf, Ain Jenna, Ajlun, Kefrenji, and Rajib, have abundance from springs and streams, and there are copious springs in and north of Jerash.

The drainage, west of the watershed, is distributed as follows:

*Wadi Arab*, south of the Ghazal tributary of the Yarmuk, drains a triangular fertile basin through a deep outlet gorge at the western angle, with rapid stream between steep limestone walls 800–900 feet high. The main wadi has its source north of Irbid, 15 miles east of the outlet; it falls over 1,300 feet from its first spring, 620 feet above sea-level, to the bridge near Esh Shuni (−720 ft.) below the gorge, and 150 feet more to its confluence with the Jordan 3 miles below. Its main tributary, Wadi Ghafar, with many affluents, rises 8 miles south of Irbid, close to the source of Wadi Tayibeh (*below*). Just above the gorge of the Wadi Arab comes in Wadi Zahar (Samma), down a long narrow valley from the south-east, separated only by a narrow ridge from the middle course of Wadi Tayibeh. In its last 2 miles it is fed by many springs of good, clear water, and is perennial. Below the gorge, Wadi Arab is bordered by meadows and water-mills, and is full of fish. Here, too, are many springs of excellent water.

*Wadi Tayibeh* cuts a single nearly straight trench from the south-east, as much as 500 feet below the plateau near the village of Semmu. It has many local names, but no tributaries. Torrential in winter, it is perennial only in its last 6 miles. Tayibeh village is on the ridge overlooking the Wadi Samma branch of the Wadi Arab.

*Wadi Zeklab* also flows from the south-east alongside Wadi Tayibeh, with narrow lower course, and only one northern affluent, Wadi Semmu. From the south it receives Wadi Sumeil, which has beheaded the Wadis Zeiyad, Hammeh (with hot springs), Neheil, and Yesna, but is itself cut short by Wadi Yabis. Wadi Zeklab is perennial only in its last 6 miles.

*Wadi Kasseib* (*Yabis* upstream) has a deep narrow gorge but a large upper basin. The main stream rises in the same high water-shed as Wadi Tayibeh and Wadi Ghafar. It has one parallel affluent on the north and a long southward tributary rising near Khirbet es Suwan, north-west of Ajlun. It is perennial from Ain el Beidha, $1\frac{1}{2}$ miles above Arjan village.

*Wadis Sheirri* (*Libbeh*), *Sleikhat*, and *Sofara* issue independently from the escarpment, but are confined between the Kasseib and upper Kefrenji, and are only perennial for short distances.

*Wadi Kefrenji* (*Ajlun*) flows south-west from several headstreams east of Ajlun and north of Umm ed Daraj. It has small tributaries on both banks, above its deep narrow gorge; on its banks are three large villages: Ain Jenna, Ajlun, and Kefrenji. It begins to carry water above Ain Jenna, about 4 miles from its head, and receives more at Ajlun from Wadi Ain et Teis coming in from the north, and lower from the perennial Wadi Deir from the south-east. Round Ajlun its valley is well wooded and healthy. At its outlet into the Ghor are the ruins of an aqueduct.

*Wadi Rajib* also rises on Umm ed Daraj, 3 miles west of Suf, and flows at first south. Its deep narrow valley is well wooded and rich in waterside growth: perennial almost from its head, it has copious water—much diverted, however, for irrigation—and is most open and best cultivated near Rajib village, whence an irrigation channel runs along the north bank for more than a mile. From the south it receives no perennial tributary, but a northern affluent rises 1 mile south of Anjera on the Wadi Deir tributary of the Kefrenji.

*Wadi Zerka* (anc. *Jabbok*) is, after the Yarmuk, the principal tributary of the Jordan. It has a narrow twisting gorge about 2 miles east of its outlet into the Ghor. Above this is a long, nearly straight valley which cuts through the plateau in a tortuous upper gorge, the bottom of which is still below sea-level 6 miles from the Jordan trench and 10 miles from the Jordan river. Above the upper gorge it collects the drainage from a long section of the watershed from

Amman nearly to Mafrak station on the Hejaz railway, beyond which is the upper basin of the Yarmuk. Of the two southern headstreams, Wadi Hammam has perennial flow from several miles above its' junction with the feebler Wadi Amman, which has water in it from about a mile upstream of Amman but is discontinuous below in the dry season. At Kalat Zerka the combined stream, now called Nahr Zerka from its grey-blue (*zerka*) shingle bed, turns north and then cuts north-west into higher ground, receiving from the east Wadi Dleila, from the north-north-east Wadi Kharasan, from the north Wadi Ras el Ain, Wadi Riyashi, and Wadi Jerash—which rises a little west of Suf—Wadi Tawahin (Ghedeir) from the southern spur of Umm ed Daraj, and several smaller wadis from the steep ridge which divides it from the upper Rajib. From the southern uplands, which are inhospitable and ill explored, come only two considerable affluents, Wadi Khatta and Wadi Rumman (Rumeimin). The latter rises east of Jebel Yusha and drains the saddle between it and the main Amman highland, as far south as the road from Es Salt to Suweileh: its lower course is perennial, and its right-bank tributary, Wadi Selileh, has a waterfall.

At most seasons the Zerka is a brook flowing over a stony bed; but after heavy rain it runs rapidly with great volume. Its valley is a gateway from the east and an obstacle to traffic between the highlands of Ajlun and the northern Belka. The number of fords is large, but the chief are at points where tracks link the two highlands: (*a*) on the easterly Amman–Jerash road by Yaguz, 10 feet by 1 foot in autumn; (*b*) at the confluence with the Wadi Jerash, 25–30 feet by 2 feet in spring, but much wider and deeper early in the year and after rain; (*c*) at Mishra en Nasraniyeh, up to horse-girth as late as May. Now, the high road from Es Salt or Amman to Jerash descends 1,500 feet to the new Jerash bridge (460 ft.), north-west of Mastabeh village, and there are stone bridges also at Amman and Kalat Zerka.

The total fall of the Zerka is *c.* 3,580 feet; about 1,500 feet in the first 30 miles, then a steeper descent of 1,350 feet in 18 miles to Tulul ed Dahab; 300 feet in 4 miles to Deir Alla in the Ghor, and 430 feet in the remaining 10½ miles south-westward across the Jordan plain.

The upper valley is open and fertile throughout, with a good track and small cultivated plains, orchards, and gardens, irrigated by ancient channels between Kalat Zerka and the Jerash fords. The Hejaz railway follows it from Kalat Zerka to Amman. Within the plateau the sides are steeper and wooded. Below the fords the valley narrows to 100 yards, and from the sandstone sides there are frequent landslips; but even here there are cultivated patches and a track along the stream. Out on the Ghor the banks are lined with trees, shrubs, and other vegetation, with dense thicket at the Jordan confluence, where winter floods form the lake Watut el Khatalin (*frontispiece*).

### The Northern Belka or Highland of Amman (anc. *Heshbon* and *Ammon*, later *Esbonitis* and *Ammanitis* (p. 438))

South of the lower Zerka the land rises gradually to a detached peak, Jebel Yusha (3,640 ft.), connected by an open ridge with the larger mass south of Suweileh, of which the highest point, Umm es Semmak, reaches 3,580 feet. The plateau now widens from north-east to south-west and extends some 40 miles to the south-east, retaining this greater breadth and a height of over 2,000 feet southward to the Arabian border.

The Ghor frontage from the Zerka southwards to the southern spurs of Jebel Yusha is on the same north–south alinement as farther north, but from Jebel Umm Awiya, south of Es Salt, it has been deeply disintegrated by its wadis, and makes a 20-mile bay, returning gradually to the east shore of the Dead Sea at Jebel Anazeh. But since the watershed follows a north-east to south-west alinement—marked by the Amman–Madeba road—the westward valleys become shorter and are also more open.

There are few parts of the northern Belka in which drinking-water cannot be obtained within moderate distances. The two chief exceptions are the slope towards the Jordan valley between the Zerka and the Wadi Nimrin, and the interior slope north of Husban, draining to the south and east. Like the plateau of Moab to the south, the highland between Es Salt and Amman is superficially poor in water; but there is abundance round its edges, and its north-eastern angle is enclosed by two perennial streams.

Of the streams entering the Ghor between the Zerka and the northern end of the Dead Sea, the principal are Wadi Nimrin and Wadi Kufrein.

*Wadi Nimrin* (*Shaib* upstream), which is followed by the motor-road from the Allenby bridge to Es Salt and Amman, rises near Es Salt and runs first southwards through an open valley with rich garden cultivation; perennial from the source, it is soon enlarged by springs. After about 4 miles it bears south-west and then south-south-west, the banks rising more steeply and to a greater height; they are not wooded, but the brook is lined with large oleanders, willows, and reeds. About 7 miles from its south-westerly bend it bears almost west and in another mile enters the Ghor at Tell Nimrin. Chief affluents come from the north-east, from the border of the upland between Es Salt and Semmak. Of these, Wadi Azrak, rising south of the road from Es Salt to Suweileh, has a permanent brook between high rocky banks, partly wooded, with several water-mills. Wadi Jeria rises a mile or so east of Wadi Shaib about 5 miles above their point of junction; it runs more or less parallel and has springs along its course; then bears round a spur towards Tell Nimrin. It is not wooded, and has no perennial stream; the road from the Jordan to Amman via Arak el Emir follows part of its lower course.

*Wadi Kufrein* is formed by the confluence of Wadi Sir and Wadi Naur. They both rise in the mountainous region west of Amman. Wadi Naur becomes perennial below Khirbet Naur, where there are a spring and a waterfall. Below this point its banks are high and often wooded, and it receives additional springs. About 3 miles farther down it receives on the right Wadi Shita, with a brook in its lower course. After another 2 miles it is joined by Wadi Sir. This tributary, beginning not far east of Fuheis village, is perennial from Ain es Sir, whence its valley is wooded for 5 miles to Arak el Emir; thence it descends rapidly to its junction with Wadi Naur, forming numerous cascades.

Below the confluence the joint stream, known as Wadi Kufrein, runs south-west for 8 miles to Tell Kufrein on the edge of the Jordan valley, where a long irrigation channel diverges to the north-west. From Tell Kufrein it runs south-west across the Ghor Seiseban ('valley of Shittim') opposite Jericho, and after 3–4 miles joins the Wadi Husban.

*Wadi Husban*, the southernmost tributary of the Jordan, rises near Husban (*anc.* Heshbon), close to the Amman–Madeba road. It drains the southern part of the 20-mile break in the escarpment, its green sides, abutting rocks, and fallen boulders giving it the appearance of a Scottish glen.

## The Southern Belka (anc. *Moab*, later *Esbonitis* and *Moabitis*)

South of the Amman highland the plateau is lower: no height compares with Umm es Semmak (3,580 ft.) till Jebel Thomma (3,790 ft.) and Jebel Jafar (3,900 ft.) between Wadi Mojib and Wadi Hasa are reached. The escarpment is again steep and continuous, and falls abruptly to the Dead Sea; for long stretches it is not possible to ride or even walk along the shore. There are, however, many little

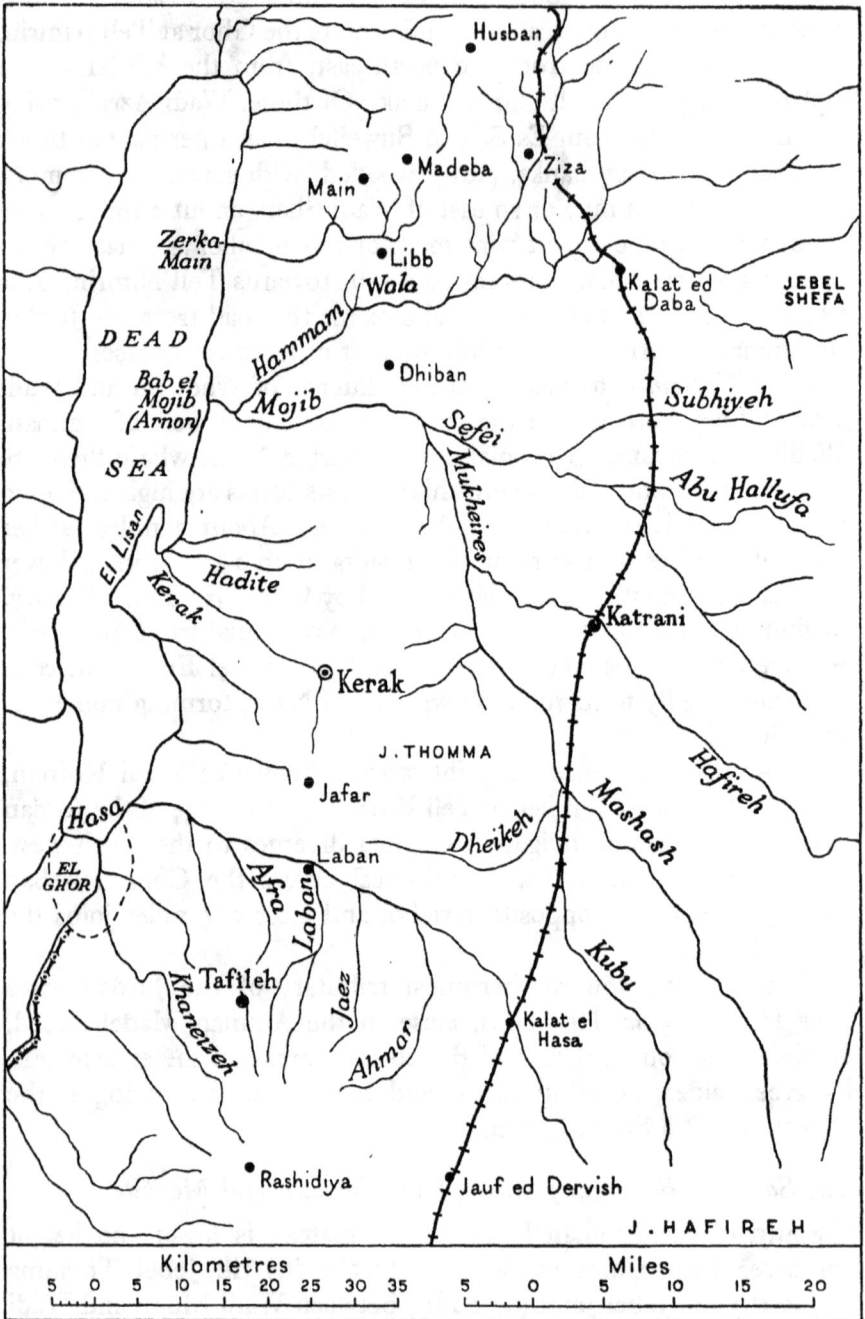

FIG. 52. *The Southern Belka*

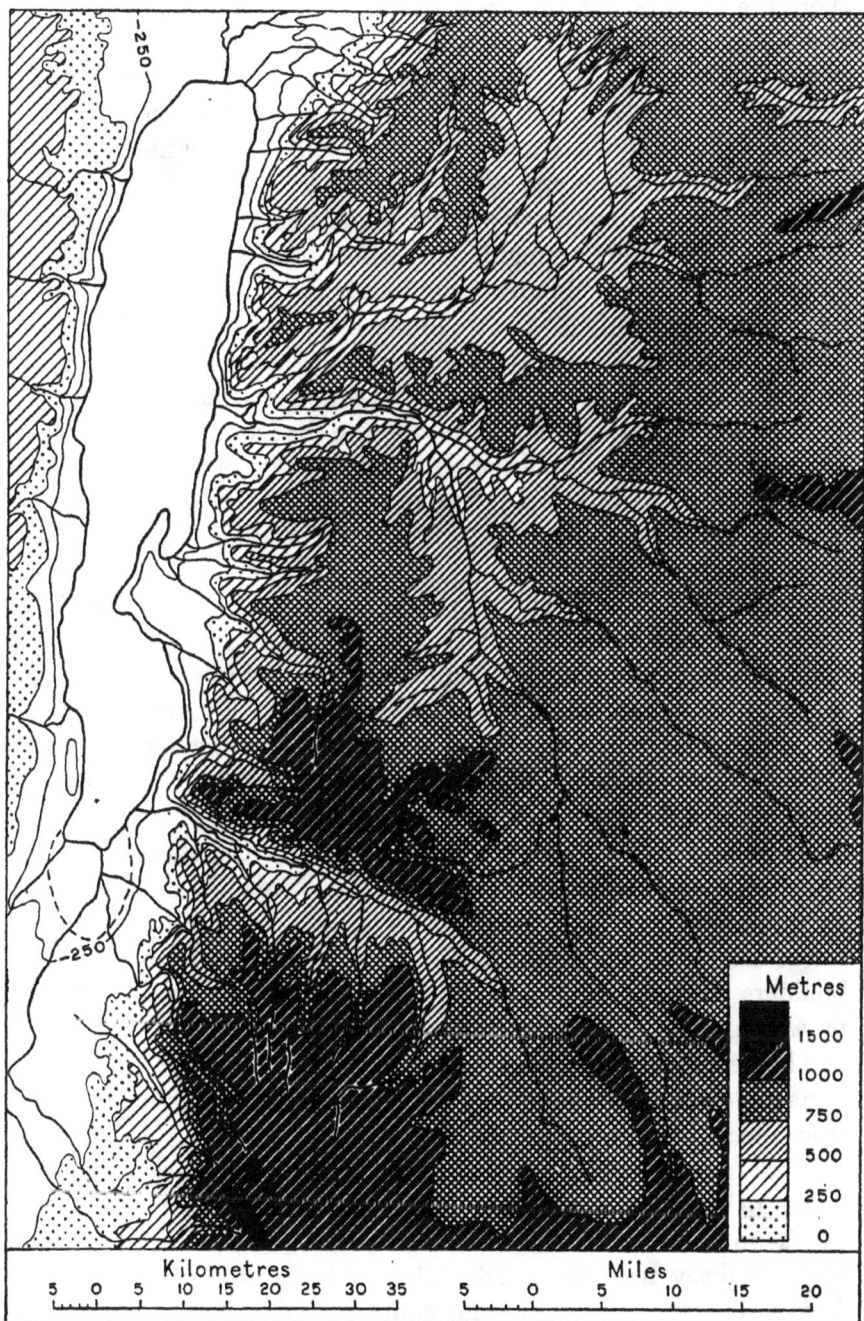

FIG. 53. *The Southern Belka*

watercourses, with alluvial patches at their outlets, and here and there the cliffs recede for a few miles. Only where the Seil Hadite and Seil Kerak flow into a bay sheltered by the north promontory of the Lisan peninsula does the foreshore widen and connect with the low Lisan plateau (400–500 ft. above water-level). South of this neck are similar smaller beaches (*ghors*), and it is possible to follow the shore to the south end of the Dead Sea.

Within the plateau itself a new feature is the wide depression round Ziza, roughly triangular, 25 miles from north to south and 20 from east to west. It sinks below 2,000 feet above sea-level, and is drained at its south-west corner to the Dead Sea by Wadi Hammam (Wala). It is traversed by the high road to Maan, and by the Hejaz railway, as far as Kalat ed Daba on its south-east margin.

Of the rivers that flow from the east into the Dead Sea the principal are Wadi Zerka-Main (Nahaliel), Wadi Mojib (Sefei, *anc.* Arnon), Wadi Kerak (Seil Buksaseh), and, at the extreme south, Wadi Hasa; there are several smaller streams between Wadi Husban and Wadi Zerka-Main.

*Wadi Zerka-Main* rises south-west of Husban and runs as Wadi Habis, almost due south, for 13 miles. It then turns west not far north of Libb, making a great loop, to the spring Ain ez Zerka, 3 miles south-south-west of Main. It is now perennial, and turns south again for 3 or 4 miles, with the name Zerka-Main, in an impassable ravine; then westward down to the Dead Sea through a deep but more open gorge of sandstone and volcanic rock. The well-known hot springs of Hammam ez Zerka are about 3 miles from the shore. It issues into the Dead Sea through a cleft in dark sandstone not more than 25 yards across, the cliffs rising for some 300 feet on either side. Still warm from the hot springs, the rapid stream runs out through boulders and vegetation to a small beach of gravel, sand, and rock, on which are tamarisks, willows, and reeds.

The next break in the escarpment is the Bab el Mojib, the narrow joint outlet of Wadi Hammam and Wadi Mojib, which meet 2 miles from the sea (photo. 123).

*Wadi Hammam* (Heidan, Wala) with its many tributaries drains the whole of the Ziza depression. The main stream rises under Jebel Shefa on the eastern watershed, is crossed by the high road and Hejaz railway near Kalat ed Daba, and receives large tributaries from north-east and north rising south-east of Amman. West of the railway the bed becomes deep and there are springs. After confluence with the Wadi But it is called Wadi Wala, and becomes perennial

1½ miles east of the Madeba–Kerak road. Lower, the valley deepens, and turning south-west, as Seil Hammam and then Seil Heidan, cuts through volcanic rock, with gentler slopes and fertile affluents from Jebel Arus, with a pass into Wadi Zerka-Main, and joins Wadi Mojib near their common mouth.

*Wadi Mojib (anc.* Arnon), the largest and most important river of Transjordan after the Jordan, the Yarmuk, and the Zerka, rises on Jebel Hafireh, 70 miles south-south-east of its mouth and 60 miles from the southern end of the Dead Sea. Known first as Ghadir Sultan and Wadi Kubu, it receives as chief tributaries, on the left bank Ghadir Abyad (Wadi Shermeh), a seasonal stream with several branches, and on the right bank Wadi Mashash and others. Traversing broken limestone hills, it receives on the left, some 30 miles from its head, Wadi Dheikeh, from the south-west near Jafar, which becomes perennial as Wadi Hanakein. As Seil Mojib it is crossed at Lejjun by the Katrani–Kerak road; this important ford is used by caravans from the north in preference to the direct route across the Wala and lower Mojib gorges. North of Lejjun the stream (there called Seil Mukheires) can be crossed only in one or two places. It flows in a deep gorge through plateau-country, between fertile land on the west and barren on the east. On the desert side it receives one large tributary, Wadi Tarfawiyat (or Hafireh), from Jebel Mughar on the eastern watershed, which is crossed by the railway and pilgrim road at Katrani. Two left-bank tributaries, Wadi Ghuweiteh and Seil Shukeifat, have running water; a little lower Seil Sefei (Saideh or Subhiyeh) comes in on the right from far to the east, falling 600 feet in 5 miles through a rocky gorge 300 feet deep, and joining the Mojib through a second inaccessible gorge with 600-foot walls. Seil Mojib now runs west about 2,000 feet below the plateau, and passes the crest-line of the escarpment, receiving short tributaries on both sides. The gorge soon narrows, and the cliffs rise to a great height, but the wadi can be passed by way of the tributary wadis Sideir and Masammat; though the track is steep and rough, the crossing is less tedious than at the ford on the main road. Finally the river cuts its way through sandstone cliffs into the Dead Sea about 2 miles below its junction with Wadi Wala (Hammam); the outlet, only 40 yards wide, known as Bab el Mojib, is now invaded by the Dead Sea, though as recently as 1874 there was a delta in front of the cliffs. The water at the entrance is shallow, and even in mid-winter small boats can go only as far as the first bend, beyond which the sides are inaccessible. The Mojib could never

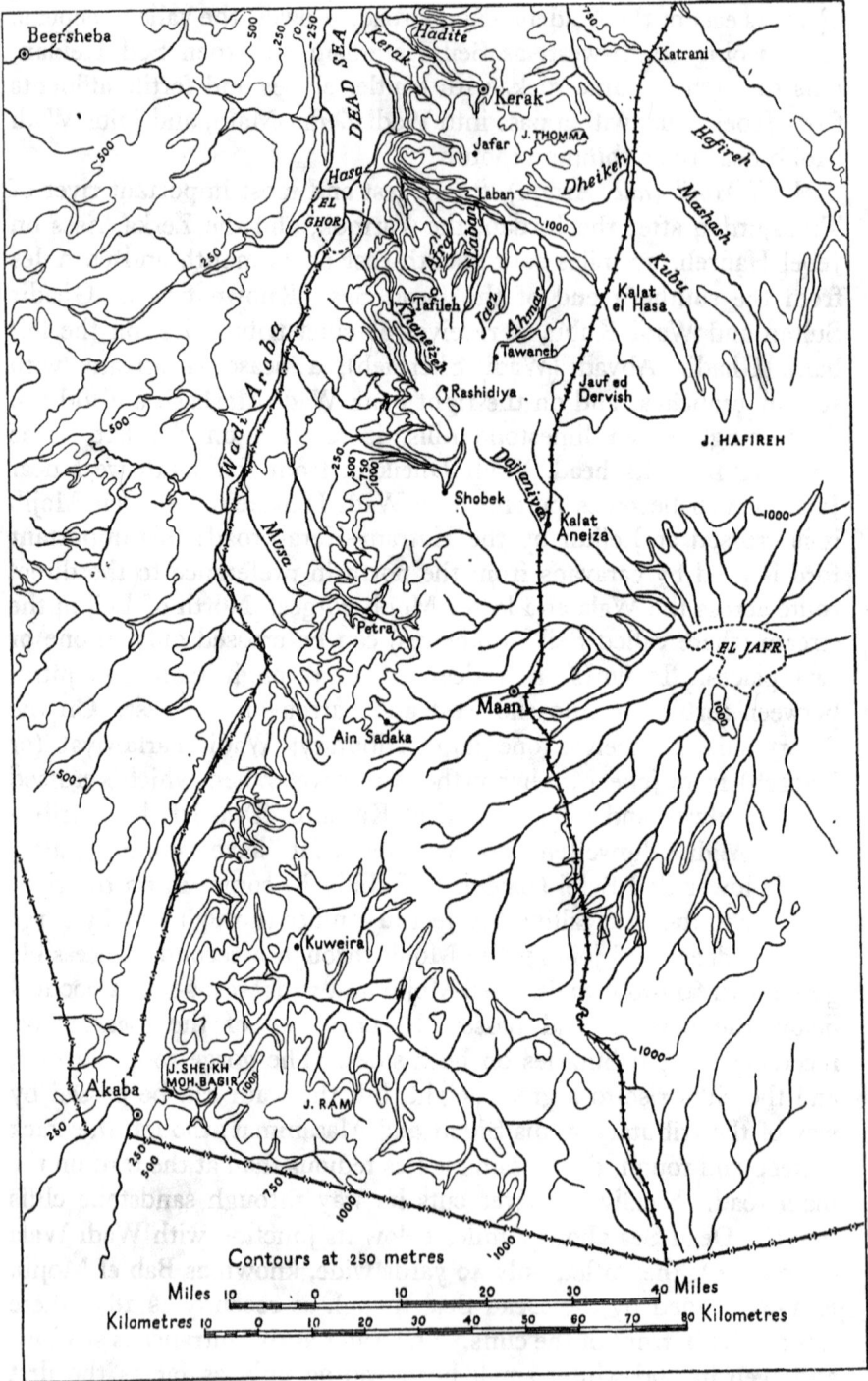

FIG. 54. *The Highland of Maan*

be a navigable stream even for small craft, since in 13 miles between the Kerak–Madeba road and the sea it falls no less than 1,600 feet.

*Wadi Kerak* rises in the fertile tract of Khor Mezar, near Jafar, 10 miles due south of Kerak town. In its upper course it is known as Wadi Senineh; as Wadi Hanish it deepens its channel to 150 feet, receives several affluents, and from the large spring, Ain el Franj, becomes perennial as Seil Medabegh. North-west of Kerak it is joined on the right by Wadi Malilheh, from Middin, round the north and east of the fortress hill. The valley now widens, with the fertile Kubbet Abd es Seyyid slope on the right, to the perennial Seil Duweihek. Here are springs on both banks. Through an inaccessible gorge, where limestone overlies sandstone, it finally issues through sandstone rocks in alluvial ground at Mezra. Here it is known as Seil Buksaseh, and receives on the left the perennial Seil Dhra, which flows almost parallel with it for $5\frac{1}{2}$ miles (photos. 124, 125).

Several short wadis descend into the same bay as Wadi Kerak, north of the Lisan isthmus, and two others into the bay south of it.

*Wadi Hasa* rises in hills far to the south-east and is crossed by the railway at Kalat Hasa and by the Maan high road at Laban, half-way between Kerak and Tafileh. Its general course is from the south-east, and it enters the Dead Sea a little east of the shallow south end (*El Ghor*). From Ain el Baziyeh it is said to be perennial; the valley is fairly broad, with cultivable strips, though the banks are steep. Chief southern affluents are the Wadi Ahmar, the Seil Jaez, the Wadi Laban, and the Seil Afra. The Laban has a broad valley with strips of cultivation, and running water in its middle and lower courses. The depth of Wadi Hasa is only exceeded in Moab by that of Wadi Mojib; it is the broad and deep natural boundary of Moab, to cross which takes some two hours.

## The Highland of Maan or Mountains of Seir (anc. Edom) (fig. 54)

South of the Mojib basin, and east of the straight escarpment from the Mojib outlet to Akaba, the highland of Maan rises above 4,000 feet, and extends eastward in Jebel Ithriyat to the north margin of the Jafr[1] depression (p. 420). West of Tafileh and Rashidiya the escarpment is broken and gradual, but it becomes abrupt again 40 miles north of Akaba where the granite outcrop begins, and so continues east of the gulf into Saudi Arabia.

The highland is open plateau dissected by deep wadis draining to

---

[1] Distinguish Jafr east of Maan from Jebel Jafar south of Kerak and from the more important Jauf south-east of the Wadi Sirhan depression in Arabia.

the south end of the Dead Sea and into the dry Wadi Araba. The
northern part, as far as the Wadi Hasa, is known to the Arabs as *El
Jibal*, a term connected with the Nabataean district of Gabalitis (p.
438). The southern part, known as *Esh Shera*, is identified with the
biblical Seir. Its higher western edge forms the watershed between
the Wadi Araba and the Jafr depression, and curves eastward in the
south to separate that depression from the plains of the Wadi Yutm
Nijad (or Wadi Itm) and Mazhlum. It was the boundary between
Edom and the territory of the Midianites in early biblical times, and
between Turkish Syria and the Hejaz in modern times. In the north,
from the Wadi Hasa to a line between Kalat Aneiza on the Hejaz
railway and Jebel Dana, it is volcanic country, broken by valleys and
extinct craters. The rest of Esh Shera is a broad flat-topped ridge
rising westwards, and covered with coarse gravel and rough pasture.
Maan, on the eastern slope, with its many springs and cultivable
limestone soil, forms an oasis on the western edge of the desert.

From about 30 miles south-west of Maan, where the ridge of Esh
Shera begins to curve eastwards, away from the Wadi Araba, the
escarpment is formed of granite, and rises to 4,500 feet in the rocky
peaks of Jebel Turban and Jebel Umm Gadid. The lower peaks of
Jebel Sor, Jebel Taba, and Jebel Bagir rise above the flat-topped upland which blocks the western end of the Wadi Yutm Nijad and bends
eastwards through Jebel Ram and Jebel Riga along the southern border.

*Seil Khaneizeh*, the last perennial stream to enter the Dead Sea,
has a tortuous outlet gorge, and thence runs nearly north through
El Ghor, where it is joined by the Seil Tileh, which descends the
plateau from Tafileh. The watershed of the plateau is still about
40 miles eastward, and beyond it the land sinks gently towards the
Wadi Sirhan depression, which is in Saudi Arabia (p. 420).

The first two wadis entering the Araba from the east are the
Ghuweir, up which there is a track to Buseira, and the Ifdan, which
comes down from Shobek and joins the Seil Dana at Feinan (Punon,
*Numbers* xxxiii. 42). South of this are the Bweirda, the Musa, and the
Kusheibeh, the last-named draining the southern slopes of Jebel
Harun (the traditional Mount Hor), south of Petra, which stands on
the Wadi Musa (photo. 127). The southernmost wadi of the Dead
Sea catchment is the Dilagha, the Gharaudel draining south-west
into the Sabkhet Ghudian, which is dry except in winter.

Wadi Yutm Nijad drains a wide depression on the south margin of
the ridge of Esh Shera, north-westwards from Mudauwara on the
border of Saudi Arabia. It does not appear ever to have a continuous

123. *Bab el Mojib. Junction of the Wadi Mojib (Arnon) with the Dead Sea*

124. *View westwards down the Wadi Kerak*

125. *The Seil Kerak in flood*

flow, but dries out into mud-flats in summer. On either side of its lower course the escarpment rises to Jebel Bagir (5,220 ft.) and Jebel Ram (5,400 ft.). Its gorge forms the main route up from Akaba to the highland of Maan.

### (c) The Desert

East of the 'Hejaz' or 'Pilgrim' railway as far as Iraq, and south from the Syrian frontier to the Nefud district of Saudi Arabia, is a great triangle stretching from latitude 32° 30′ N. to 29° 30′ N. In the north a projection to the north-east (longitude 37° E.–39° E.) separates Saudi Arabia from Syria and at the same time connects Transjordan and Iraq; it is a parallelogram about 150 miles long from north-east to south-west, with an average width of 72 miles, and is crossed by the oil pipe-line from Kirkuk and the motor-road from Baghdad (fig. 59). The Syrian desert, of which geographically this district is a part, extends to Iraq and in the south into Arabia. Saudi Arabia, however, projecting northwards, has taken from Transjordan about 22,500 square miles of the desert, including the Wadi Sirhan depression except for its northernmost section around Kasr Azrak. The desert region of Transjordan is uninhabited except for a few oases, and practically unknown, except along the Syrian border, the pipe-line, and the new Haifa–Baghdad motor-road.

The *north-eastern desert* is occupied over two-thirds of its area by volcanic country—the lava-belt mentioned above (p. 403). The lava stretches for 106 miles between Kasr Azrak and Kasr Burka. It is one of the most desolate and forbidding areas on the surface of the earth, a region of extinct volcanoes and weathered lava-flows, broken by gullies and undulations, and covered with black basalt rocks. The rocks may be several feet in diameter and extend about 500 feet below the surface; the interstices are filled with loose, abrasive volcanic ash. Wheeled transport is impossible away from the new road. The wadis flood after heavy rain, and those which come from the Jebel Druse flow also when the snow melts. Otherwise it is waterless country. The highest points are in the north-west on the flanks of the Jebel Druse, and in the east in Jebel Ashakif and Jebel Jethum. A point on the Syrian boundary near Umrkaa reaches 3,576 feet, and Tell Shabah and Jebel Ashkaf in the Jebel Ashakif reach 3,435 feet and 3,412 feet respectively. Between the flanks of the Jebel Druse in the north-west and Jebel Ashakif and Jebel Jethum in the east is a wide depression with an average height of 2,400 feet in the north-east, sloping towards the marshes round Kasr Azrak and Jiyashi in the south-west, where the height is only 1,680 feet. ' This depression collects most of the drainage from the lava-belt and contains many mud-flats.

East of the lava-belt the desert is of limestone, overlaid with alluvial clay. Large stretches are covered with a reddish loam strewn with flints. The surface rises towards the east in wide swells and valleys with barren slopes, and the only vegetation is in low-lying hollows where soil can accumulate. The western edge of this region is marked by a string of mud-flats and rain-pools, beyond which rises the sombre precipice of the lava-belt. The most extensive mud-flats are round Kasr Burka in the north and Khabra Abil Husein near the Arabian border in the south.

The *desert east of the Hejaz railway* is an undulating region everywhere over 1,650 feet in altitude except for the Azrak district in the north. It rises in the south to over 3,300 feet in the broken hills of Jebel Tubeik, along which the Arabian boundary lies. The principal oases are at Kasr Azrak in the Wadi Sirhan depression, at Bayir in the south, half-way between the railway and the Arabian frontier, and at Jafr, 30 miles east-north-east of Maan.

The *Wadi Sirhan depression* (p. 403), most of which is in Saudi Arabia, is relatively fertile. The important Ruwalla tribe of Syria claims watering rights, and some of the Transjordan tribes also water there in winter. The Transjordan section of the wadi is centred on Kasr Azrak (36° 50' E., 31° 50' N.), where there is an aircraft landing-ground. Much of the depression is a grey, rolling plain, covered with flints and barren of vegetation, but the northern end contains the rain-pools and marshes of Jiyashi, south of Kasr Azrak and between the volcanic district of Jebel Uweinid and the Wadi Rajel where the lava-belt begins. There is some pasture in the district, and the marshes of Jiyashi are surrounded by lowland covered with high reeds and thickets. The pools abound in fish and crabs.

The *Jafr depression*, east of Maan (fig. 54), is a circular hollow about 50 miles in diameter, surrounded by hills except on the east where the ground slopes down beyond the frontier towards the Wadi Sirhan. The plain, in places covered with coarse grey sand and cut by twisting wadis, slopes inwards towards the salt marshes round Jafr. The surface is broken by clumps of vegetation, with bushes and low trees in the lower portions of the wadis. In the south the plain of Shubaicha is covered with coarse brown gravel on which grows *semh*, an annual with green, fleshy leaves and small green flowers, whose seeds provide food for the inhabitants of the oasis. On the southern border the isolated hill of Chabd merges westwards into the plain of Ratiya, where the soil has been swept away, exposing the desert pavement.

South of the Ratiya plain is the lower plain of Mazhlum, which drains south-westwards towards Mudauwara on the Arabian border and joins with the wide depression of Wadi Yutm Nijad (p. 418) on the southern margin of the Maan highland.

## CLIMATE

The climate of Transjordan is very similar to that of the uplands of Palestine, but mean temperatures are lower, and the range is wider; rainfall is considerably less and probably more variable, and the climate is altogether harsher, because Transjordan is farther from the sea and nearer to the great desert. Very few stations in Transjordan have records of climate, and the only full records are maintained by the R.A.F. at the Amman meteorological station (2,548 ft.).

### Pressure

Pressure conditions are similar to those in Palestine. In winter, when the eastern Mediterranean is a region of relatively low pressure, a series of depressions passes eastwards from the coast to the Persian gulf. In summer the region of low pressure is centred over the Persian gulf, pressure conditions are very stable, and the passage of depressions is rare. The pressure in the Jordan rift is described on p. 48.

### Winds

(a) General. Throughout the year winds from the west and south-west predominate. The south-west direction is more pronounced during the winter months when the depressions originating in the Mediterranean pass over Transjordan. East winds from the desert occur during winter and spring, but are very rare in summer. They are responsible for the highest and lowest temperatures, being cold and dry in winter, but hot, dusty, and scorching in spring. South winds also are hot and dry in winter, but north winds are cold and bring clear skies and a fresh atmosphere. During the summer, west winds blow with remarkable regularity (on an average one day in three at Amman), and the number of calm days in July is less than in any other month of the year. Coming from the sea, west winds exercise a strong moderating influence on the climate in summer, which, on the Transjordan plateau, is seldom uncomfortably hot. North-west winds blow on about one day in four, and south-west winds are much less frequent. In the Jordan valley the influence of topography is marked, and there is great local variation at all seasons (p. 49).

The number of calm days is fairly high throughout the year, particularly from autumn to early spring (27 to 37%), and is least in July. Strong winds occur occasionally in winter during the passage of depressions, when they may reach gale force (force 8). At Amman such gales occur on an average seven times a year, principally in January, February, and March.

(b) *Local.* For scirocco and dust-bearing winds see p. 50.

### Temperature

Altitude and topographical dissimilarity are the causes of the great difference of temperature between the Jordan depression and the Transjordan plateau. In many respects the temperature on the plateau is similar to that of the hill-stations in Judaea and Samaria, but owing to distance from the sea and proximity to the desert the average maxima, though less than in the Ghor, are greater than in the uplands of Palestine, and the average minima tend to be lower. The figures quoted below are for Amman alone, which is fairly representative of the northern part of the plateau, but in villages in the south the temperature is generally higher, and to the east the annual range is greater.    Temperatures are in Fahrenheit.

In winter the mean daily temperature is about 48°, but the mean daily minimum lies around 39°, and frosts are not unknown. The lowest monthly minima recorded at Amman, are: December 25°, January 21°, February 23°.

In the summer months the mean daily maximum is a few degrees higher than in the uplands of Palestine, but absolute maxima are very similar. Farther east and in the south, the heat is greater. At Amman the daily maximum is about 90° in summer, and the temperature often rises above 100°. In the Jordan valley the heat is stifling, and from June to September the daily temperatures are over 100° (*see* Table II for Beisan, Jericho, and Dead Sea).

In spring and autumn the normal temperature-trend may be interrupted, as in Palestine and Syria, by spells of exceptionally hot, dry weather, and the scirocco may bring these at any time between May and October. September is usually as warm as June, but the temperature generally drops rapidly from October to December (Amman mean daily max.: 82° October, 59° December).

### Humidity

Humidity is low in Transjordan as in Palestine. It is greatest (70%) on the plateau in January, the month of heaviest rainfall. It decreases fairly rapidly to a minimum in May or June, when it is as low as 30 per cent. at Amman. It is probable that in eastern Trans-jordan the relative humidity is similar to that of the west in winter, but lower still in summer, and resembles that of eastern Syria (Deir ez Zor minimum 29% in July). In the Ghor (p. 53) the relative humidity is roughly the same as that of the plateau in winter (Jericho, maximum in January 70%), but higher in summer (minimum in May 43%).

## Visibility

(a) *Fog and Mist.* Fog and mist are rare, occurring on an average only three days in a year. Fog is most frequent in January, and never occurs between May and September inclusive. In the Ghor, fog and mist are more common (p. 55). During spring and autumn local visibility may be considerably affected by the scirocco or by dust-storms.

(b) *Mirage* is commoner than in Palestine, particularly in summer and in eastern Transjordan, where conditions approximate to those of Arabia and Iraq.

## Cloud

The only statistics available for cloud are for Amman, but on the whole the amount of cloud is probably very similar to the highlands of Palestine (p. 55).

### Cloud at Amman (1924–1941)

| | Scale 0 (cloudless) to 10 (completely overcast) | | | Number of days[*] | |
|---|---|---|---|---|---|
| | 0800 hrs. | 1400 hrs. | 2000 hrs. | Clear | Overcast |
| Jan. . . . | 5·3 | 5·5 | 3·8 | 8 | 5 |
| Feb. . . . | 5·3 | 5·5 | 3·5 | 7 | 5 |
| March . . | 4·2 | 4·7 | 2·5 | 12 | 2 |
| April . . . | 3·6 | 4·1 | 2·3 | 12 | 2 |
| May . . . | 2·9 | 3·2 | 1·9 | 16 | 1 |
| June . . . | 0·7 | 0·9 | 0·4 | 27 | 0·1 |
| July . . . | 0·6 | 0·5 | 0·1 | 30 | 0 |
| Aug. . . . | 0·6 | 0·5 | 0·2 | 29 | 0 |
| Sept. . . . | 1·0 | 0·8 | 0·2 | 26 | 0 |
| Oct. . . . | 2·3 | 2·9 | 1·6 | 20 | 0·8 |
| Nov. . . . | 3·9 | 4·6 | 2·8 | 11 | 4 |
| Dec. . . . | 4·9 | 5·3 | 3·3 | 9 | 5 |
| Year . . . | 2·9 | 3·2 | 1·9 | 207 | 25 |

[*] 11 years' observations. Clear is defined as one-tenth covered or less, overcast as nine-tenths covered or more.

*Rainfall*

The division of the year into a rainy and a dry season is the ruling feature of the climate of Transjordan as in Palestine (p. 56), and the habitability of the' country is directly governed by it. The rainy season usually starts a little later than in Palestine.

As in Palestine, there are three phases in the rainy season, the 'Former' rains, the 'Main' rains, and the 'Latter' rains. The Former and the Latter rains are most important for the agriculturist, the first for ploughing and sowing, and the second for the ripening crops. If the Latter rains fail, the spring harvest and the summer crops are endangered.

Rain generally begins to fall at the end of October, but its quantity is usually insignificant until early November. The heaviest rains occur in January and February, after which they decrease rapidly until April, when the Latter rains occur. From June to September inclusive there is complete drought.

Even during the heaviest rains in January and February, rainfall is not continuous, but storms which may last for two or three days are followed by a week of sunny weather, then succeeded by another downpour. Although the intensity of rain varies considerably, there are few years when there is no rain heavy enough to disrupt the country's traffic for days, and even to cause floods. In the course of twenty-four hours 3 to 4 inches of rain may fall, and even more in the higher regions of Transjordan, such as Kitte, 2 miles west of Jerash (5·1 in. on 4 February 1935). In the east, and south of Maan, the maximum fall in twenty-four hours is much lower (0·7 in.).

There is considerable variation in the amount of rainfall throughout the country (fig. 14). The westerly rain-bearing winds lose most of their moisture while passing over Palestine, and the remainder falls within a hundred miles of the western boundary of Transjordan. The rainfall is higher in the north (Irbid 19·2 in., Kefr Yuba[1] 25·7 in., and Tayibeh 22·0 in.) than in the south (Maan 3·1 in. and Jafr 1·9 in.), where rainfall in any year is uncertain. The western highlands have the heaviest rainfall (Es Salt 39·2 in., Kefrenji 32·1 in., and Kitte 27·3 in.), but this decreases rapidly eastwards, particularly in the south. The greater part of Transjordan east of the Hejaz railway has an average annual rainfall of less than 4 inches (100 mm.). For rainfall in the Jordan valley *see* p. 59.

[1]  3 miles west of Irbid.

## Snow

Snow is more common, and lasts longer, in Transjordan than in Palestine. In the higher parts of the country, such as Ajlun, and in the higher mountains farther south, it is usual to have a fall every year, mostly in February. In the Ghor, snow is unknown.

## Thunder

At Amman, the only station for which information is available, thunder is liable to occur in any month of the year, excepting from June to September inclusive. The maximum incidence is in November, at the beginning of the rainy season. Thunder is more common in the Jordan valley than in the rest of the country.

For hail there is no information.

### VEGETATION

Knowledge of the indigenous vegetation of Transjordan is much more limited than for Palestine. The narrow strip of territory to the west of the Hejaz railway has been partially investigated, notably by the late Aaron Aaronsohn, but many districts in the interior and towards the eastern boundaries have never been visited by a botanist; knowledge of the vegetation in these areas is therefore based on observations of travellers, such as Alois Musil, who collected specimens during his travels, and whose books, *Arabia Deserta* and *The Northern Hejaz*, contain some useful descriptions of plant communities.

The country may be divided into three main zones (fig. 17): (*a*) Mediterranean, (*b*) Steppe, and (*c*) Desert. The boundaries of these areas at present must be regarded as tentative. No orographical factors delimit the zones as in Palestine, and climatic factors only, principally rainfall, determine the vegetation.

Towards the west, in the neighbourhood of the Jordan and its tributaries, hydrophytic vegetation is richly developed. A large part of the country, however, has no perennial watercourses, but only valleys and wadis which run dry across steppe or desert. Where evaporation results in salt marsh, the flora is halophytic. Many wadis are thus the only centres of vegetation in immense barren areas, distributing and preserving the steppe and desert floras. In the south, vegetation is limited to those depressions where periodical rain-water accumulates.

*Soils*

There are five main types of soil in Transjordan:

(1) *Steppe soil* is the commonest, and results from weathered limestone. It is soft and light grey, of high lime-content (30–72%), and almost completely without humus. Water penetrates easily and it is well aerated.

(2) *Hammada.* The surface of these areas results from selective weathering and is usually composed of black flint pebbles or gravel. This type is found between Amman and El Azrak in west-central Transjordan and east of the Wadi Araba. Vegetation is very poor.

(3) *Terra Rossa* (p. 242), a reddish-brown soil with a lime-content of 10–40 per cent. and some humus, is more compact, less aerated, less permeable, but moister and more sticky than (1). It is limited to the Mediterranean zone.

(4) *Sandy Soils.* Large sandy areas, produced by the weathering of Nubian sandstone, are found east of the Wadi Araba. Plants of the steppe sand-dune type are found here. Sandy soils are also widely distributed in dry wadis, e.g. Wadi Sirhan.

(5) *Harra.* These surfaces consist of black basalt boulders and are extremely barren: they occur only in north-east Transjordan, e.g. in the Harrat er Rujeila.

## Botanical Divisions

### (a) The Mediterranean Zone

The narrow strip west of the Hejaz railway from the Syrian boundary southwards almost to Maan has 'Mediterranean' vegetation. Its average breadth south of Amman is about 9 miles; farther north and including the Amman district it widens abruptly and so continues into Syria, where it meets the Mediterranean regions of upper Galilee and the Lebanon. Three sub-regions can be distinguished: (i) the southern part between Ain Musa and Wadi Hasa, fairly well covered by Mediterranean forest growth or its remnants; (ii) west-central Transjordan northwards to Amman, with only vestiges of Mediterranean vegetation; (iii) northern Transjordan, the richest in woods and scrub-land (*maquis*).

This Mediterranean strip is frequently interrupted, especially in the middle sub-region, by wadis draining into the Jordan valley and by lowlands now bearing a different vegetation, and the primary growth has been devastated by the pastoral inhabitants of the neighbouring steppes and deserts for hundreds, perhaps thousands, of years. Natural regeneration has been retarded or prevented because the belt is on the extreme eastern edge of the Mediterranean vegetation region.

The flora of this part of Transjordan differs greatly from that of Palestine and is more closely related to that of Syria and Lebanon. Several hundreds of species found in the mountainous parts of Palestine are absent from Transjordan. These include the lentisk, Syrian pear, buckthorn, Spanish broom, Palestine woundwort, and others. On the other hand, a number of east Mediterranean species which occur in Transjordan are common to Syria and Lebanon, though lacking in Palestine. The reasons are probably, (1) the lower rainfall compared with Palestine; (2) the small size of 'Mediterranean' Transjordan; (3) the presence of steppe and desert on two sides, and of Jebel Druse and Hermon, with their poor Mediterranean vegetation to the north.

Nevertheless, the Mediterranean zone is fairly rich in species. Near Amman 200 plant species have been found in an area of $1\frac{1}{2}$ square miles. This comparatively well-watered strip, especially towards the north, has long been cultivated and the natural vegetation of large tracts has given way through the centuries to communities of plants known as 'weeds of cultivation', comprising field weeds, wayside plants, and other species that follow the activities of man.

*Forest Communities.* Although there has been much indiscriminate felling of forests, such communities have in general been better preserved and are in better condition than the ancient forests of Palestine. There are still fine forests of Aleppo pine (*Pinus halepensis*). Destruction by man and the pine's lack of regenerative powers have resulted in the widespread disappearance of many. Some remain, with the thyme-leaved St. Johns-wort (*Hypericum serpyllifolium*) as the principal shrub, but they are now found only in the districts of Ajlun (Gilead) and Amman, the best stands being in the neighbourhood of Jerash. Another type of forest which was formerly abundant is that of the deciduous oak (*Quercus ithaburensis*). Found only as remnants in parts of northern Gilead, it is described by Tristram and other travellers as having once covered extensive areas with an open park-like covering of beautiful trees. These oak forests chiefly occupied the lower altitudes, especially on level ground where the soil was deep, whereas the pine forests clothed the higher ranges. Little is known of the present distribution of oak in Transjordan.

At the southern extremity of the Mediterranean zone, in the former Edom, the Phoenician cedar (*Juniperus phoenicia*) is the principal constituent of a well-developed tree-community. It may be found throughout the Mediterranean zone, but only in dry, somewhat high localities, and is known in the neighbourhood of Petra, on the summit of Jebel Harun (Mount Hor), and between Shobek and Tafileh. An occasional feature of the undergrowth of this community is wormwood (*Artemisia herba-alba*) which invades from the contiguous steppe.

Although forest covers only a small proportion of the Mediterranean zone, scrub-land (*maquis*, p. 72) and other degraded forms of vegetation are much commoner. On the western slopes of the Amman mountains and farther north is found a type of maquis in which the evergreen oak[1] and the terebinth[2] are dominant. Other shrubs include strawberry-trees,[3] hawthorn,[4] storax,[5] buckthorn,[6] and sometimes wild almond,[7] wild olives,[8] and such woody climbers as honeysuckle[9] and clematis.[10] This type of maquis is said to occur also farther south.

The next retrograde stage, *garigue* (p. 73), is less easily recognizable in Transjordan than in Palestine, but occurs in the Amman district which is transitional between the more tree-clad Gilead and the denuded plateau of Moab; the shrub constituents are similar to those of maquis, but more degenerate.

Dwarf-shrub communities known as *batha*, so characteristic of Palestine (p. 74), are found in Transjordan, mainly in the northern and central districts, but they are less widespread. As in Palestine, the shrubby burnet[11] is the dominant plant together with rock-roses.[12] Typical batha in Transjordan tends to be invaded by steppe elements in the east, which often produces a mixed community intermediate between a strictly Mediterranean batha and the more eastern 'rocky soil steppe'. It has been seen, at Ain Hummar, east of Es Salt, where rock-roses, shrubby burnets, and sun-roses[13] were common, the first two typically Mediterranean, the last-named an inhabitant of drier regions. Mesophytic grasses, such as cocksfoot, were found side by side with the strongly xerophytic *Stipa Fontanesii*. Many other contrasting species belonging to other families were seen, though, on balance, the dominant character of the vegetation was Mediterranean.

---

[1] *Quercus calliprinus.*
[2] *Pistacia Terebinthus.*
[3] *Arbutus Andrachne.*
[4] *Crataegus Azarolus.*
[5] *Styrax officinalis.*
[6] *Thamnus palaestina.*
[7] *Amygdalus communis.*
[8] *Olea europaea* var. *oleaster.*
[9] *Lonicera etrusca.*
[10] *Clematis cirrhosa.*
[11] *Poterium spinosum.*
[12] *Cistus villosus.*
[13] *Helianthemum vesicarium.*

In a type of batha confined to rocky habitat, the common *Varthemia*,[1] a low shrubby member of the *Compositae*, is dominant.

*Annual Vegetation.* During the rainy season the mountains are covered by a rich but fleeting carpet of annuals. They persist only for a few months and represent many families: grasses, buttercups, poppies, peas, carrots, cabbages, and others.

*Hydrophytic Vegetation.* This specialized community is found only in the valleys of the permanent and temporary tributaries of the Jordan and in other depressions capable of holding rain-water for sufficient periods. On the banks of streams, sometimes growing in the water, are reeds, tall grasses, sedges, rushes, irises, and the like; trees and shrubs, commonly associated with running water, are tamarisks, oleanders, and willows. Annuals and perennials growing in damp places include horsetail,[2] mints, and watercress.[3]

Towards the drier southern extremity of the Mediterranean zone, steppe communities intrude and are directly encouraged by man's destruction of the primary Mediterranean vegetation.

## (b) Steppe Zone

This cannot be delimited from the desert zone for lack of distinguishing orographical features. Climatic boundaries, the only criteria, can scarcely be represented by a line on a map. Included in it are certain desert areas, but their vegetation conforms to the steppe type of flora.

*Rocky Soil Steppe.* This vegetation type is found on the high parts of western Transjordan. It is distinctly drought-resisting (xerophytic) and resembles in many respects the flora of the eastern slopes of the Samarian and Judaean mountains on the opposite side of the Ghor. Characteristic plants include a number of xerophytic grasses[4] which are often found in rock crevices baked by the sun. Among the rocky soil and stones there is a fairly rich flora comprising dwarf shrubs such as *Gymnocarpus decandrus* with its zigzag whitish branches, and sun-roses,[5] several species of milk-vetch, and other xerophytic perennials. A series of other well-distinguished plant communities has been recognized in parts of the steppe. They are as follows:

(i) *Pistacia atlantica* forest community. This is the most important arboreal community in Transjordan and is characteristic of its more

---

[1] *Varthemia iphionoides.*
[2] *Equisetum ramosissimum.*
[3] *Nasturtium officinale.*
[4] *Stipa tortilis, Stipa Fontanesii, Hordeum spontaneum.*
[5] *Helianthemum salicifolium, H. vesicarium.*

favourable conditions. *Pistacia atlantica* (*P. Mutica* of some authors) is a large deciduous tree found nowhere else in Asia except in Sinai, though it occurs also in north Africa. Under natural conditions it produces a park-land of herbaceous plants and scattered trees. Solitary but well-developed trees have been found in and around Petra, while farther north in the Jordan valley and on the mountain slopes facing it, some stands and remnants of *pistacia* forests have been seen. In eastern Gilead, also near Khirbet Tmeiri, well-developed stands have been recorded. Farther east, on the northern fringe of the Wadi Sirhan near Kasr Amra, Musil records a *pistacia* stand, probably *Pistacia atlantica*. The composition of these forest-stands in Transjordan is little known, but in some Syrian communities *pistacia* is accompanied by a few shrubs such as buckthorn[1] and prunus,[2] while certain dwarf shrubs, such as wormwood and thorny-saltwort,[3] are also present. *Pistacia* itself is of economic significance, since its seeds are used in tanning, its wood for fuel, and the red berries are eaten by the beduin.

(ii) *Zizyphus Lotus* community. The Lotus-tree has a similar distribution to that of *pistacia*, but unlike the latter is thermophylous, preferring hot plains, valleys, and depressions, where it is protected against low temperature. In Transjordan the lotus-tree appears to be limited to the upper Jordan valley and the mountain slopes facing it.

Non-arboreal steppe communities include:

(iii) *Artemisia herba-alba* (Wormwood) community, important and widely spread, and a true indicator of steppe. It prefers the greyish-white, somewhat compact steppe-soil and completely shuns saline or rocky soils. In spring this community is generally very rich in annuals and is often characterized by a grass, *Poa sinaica*; in summer it is governed by the late-flowering wormwood accompanied by other perennials of the goosefoot family (*Chenopodiaceae*). This community is the first to invade Mediterranean arboreal communities disturbed by man and contributes to the undergrowth of cleared woods.

(iv) *Haloxylon articulatum* community, also common and characteristic of stony and gravel soils, is particularly resistant to drought, and penetrates also into the desert regions. It is well represented on the high plateau west and south-west of Maan. A low bush, up to 20 inches high, it possesses jointed stems, minute leaves, and small whitish flowers.

(v) *Anabasis articulata* community is widely distributed, although

---

[1] *Rhamnus palaestina.*    [2] *Prunus microcarpa.*    [3] *Noaea mucronata.*

126. *Lake deposits of salt and clay of the Lisan peninsula, Dead Sea*

127. *View eastwards from the Deir plateau near Petra*

*128. Oleanders in full bloom in the Sik gorge at Petra*

*129. Vegetation at Amman*

less common than *Haloxylon* (iv). In depressions and somewhat wet places it displaces wormwood (iii) and occurs as a weed of irrigated fields. Though not a true halophyte, it will tolerate saline soils to some extent. It is a bush 3 feet high or less, with jointed brittle branches and small leaves.

Other less important plant-communities have been recognized in Transjordan, some very uncommon and limited often to specialized localities. South of Maan, at the extremity of the steppe zone, soil conditions are very favourable. The shallow broad valleys are well covered with annuals and perennials, and since there is a fair quantity of water—nearly every watercourse contains a spring—much of the area might be transformed into fertile fields. On the slopes of the gullies an abundance of grass and other plants affords fine pasture. Conditions in the Harrat er Rujeila, in the north of the lava-belt, however, form a vivid contrast. Sombre and arid, the volcanic rocks support little vegetation. Scrubby, grey, or prickly bushes occur here and there in depressions, more especially in the neighbourhood of rain-water pools.

*Hydrophytic Communities.* The *Populus euphratica* community is arboreal and restricted, as in Palestine, to the banks of the Jordan and its tributaries. Forming a narrow gallery forest along these water-courses, the community includes willows[1] and tamarisk[2] besides the dominant poplar. Hydrophytes are sensitive to soil-composition and less affected by variations of climate; consequently these communities are similar in each of the three regions, the governing criterion being sufficient moisture. The species found in Mediterranean hydrophytic associations (p. 429) occur also in similar habitats in the steppe.

*Halophytic (Salt-steppe) Communities.* These, like hydrophytes, are sensitive to soils, and are restricted to the *sabkhas* which either (*a*) occur in the immediate vicinity of salt lakes and are periodically inundated by them, e.g. those of the Dead Sea, or (*b*) are left in flat depressions by the rapid evaporation of rain-water after the rainy season. Characteristic of these saline areas are certain species of the goosefoot family and the *Zygophyllaceae*. Among the first-named are *Suaeda monoica*, a large showy shrub with fleshy leaves, the silvery white *Atriplex Halimus*, the white *Salsola tetrandra*, and *Arthrocnemum glaucum*. The last-named is generally found in association with one of the tamarisks.[3] Another large shrub with fleshy leaves is *Nitraria retusa*. A grass, *Aeluropus repens*, and a rush, *Juncus maritimus*, are also found in saline areas.

---

[1] *Salix safsaf, S. acmophylla.*    [2] *Tamarix Jordanis.*    [3] *Tamarix mannifera.*

## (c) Desert Zone

This occupies the greatest area of Transjordan, but only the part west of the Hejaz railway is well known botanically. Farther east the scanty records are mainly contributed by Musil and other travellers. The flora as a whole is poor, though well-marked plant-communities can be recognized.

*Haloxylon salicornicum* is the most important and most characteristic community, as much indicative of desert conditions as wormwood is of steppe. The plant is a typical goosefoot shrub with jointed branches and minute leaves. It is usually confined to sandy, though not necessarily loose, soils. From Musil's records it seems to be a common species throughout the desert zone.

*Rhanterium epapposum* community is characteristic of eastern desert conditions and is probably found only in the eastern districts, though isolated plants have been seen on the northern edge of the Wadi Sirhan. It is a branching, rather shrubby, yellow-flowered 'Composite' known to the beduin as *Arfaj* and is used by them for fuel and camel-food. Little known to botanists, it is probably *Musilia arabica*.

*Haloxylon persicum* community, confined to sandy soils, is mainly characteristic of dunes and valleys. The tree-like shrub attains 20 feet, with white bark and brittle branches, and resembles the tamarisk. The beduin use it in the desert for camel-food, timber, and fuel. It has been noted in Edom (south of Kuweira), in Ghor es Safi (southeast end of Dead Sea), and in Ghor Feifeh (east of Wadi Araba); also by Musil in the neighbourhood of Wadi Sirhan.

*Calligonum comosum*, fairly common but restricted to sandy habitats and mainly to sand-dunes, is a large, whitish, many-branched shrub attaining 16 feet.

Many other plant communities are less common. The white broom (*Retama Raetam*) has been found in the vicinity of Kasr Azrak in the north of Wadi Sirhan and on mountain-sides facing the Jordan valley; both are limestone districts. One of the wormwoods (*Artemisia judaica*) has been seen between Kuweira and Akaba. The gravel plain 35 miles south-east of Maan produces, after a good rain, a rich covering of *Mesembryanthemum Forsskalii*. This plant, which grows thickly, never exceeds $1\frac{1}{2}$ inches in height, is yellowish-green in colour, soft and fleshy, and bears small whitish flowers. The tiny seeds are used by the beduin for food.

Included in the vegetation of Transjordan are a few tropical species whose soil requirements can be satisfied only in the Jordan valley and the Wadi Araba. They require a somewhat high temperature and sufficient moisture to produce a savanna community, comprising a few trees with usually, though not always, a grassy or herbaceous layer below them. The conditions are well represented in the Ghor es Safi, where two-thirds of these tropical elements are found. The grass *Desmostachya bipinnata*, which is often present as an undergrowth, is a tall tough species, giving the savanna a vivid appearance. The most widespread tree of this community is the Christ-thorn,[1] while other constituents include salvadora,[2] balsam,[3] acacias,[4] and Sodom Apple.[5] Solitary members of this tropical group are found occasionally in favourable spots in wadis and oases.

## FAUNA

The fauna of Transjordan west of the Hejaz railway is for the most part similar to that of Palestine (pp. 78–80). In the highlands of Ajlun and Belka, fish abound in the perennial watercourses, and boars are found in the wadis. Ibex haunt the rocky gorges round the Dead Sea. Farther south, in the Maan highlands (El Jibal and Esh Shera), the wolf, fox, hyena, jackal, hare, wild cat, and boar are found, with panthers in the gorges on the edge of the Wadi Araba. Bees are numerous in the highland of Esh Shera. In addition, bustards and land-tortoises are plentiful in the desert of southern Transjordan, and gazelles are occasionally met.

Wild fowl, especially pigeons and partridges, are plentiful. In four days of the winter of 1924–5 Air Force officers at Azrak killed 2,742 head, including 1,103 green teal, 313 shoveller, 233 widgeon, 253 snipe, 215 mallard, 170 pin-tail, 146 gadwall, and 101 sheldrake.

---

[1] *Zizyphus Spina-Christi.*
[2] *Salvadora persica.*
[3] *Balanites aegyptiaca.*
[4] *Acacia Seval, A. tortilis.*
[5] *Calotropis procera.*

# CHAPTER XV
# HISTORY OF TRANSJORDAN

## 1. EARLIEST TIMES TO ALEXANDER THE GREAT

TRANSJORDAN, like western Palestine, contains traces of palaeolithic occupation, and at Kilwa in eastern Transjordan a large number of very ancient (*Natufian*) rock-drawings are superimposed on still earlier ones, while there are also others of chalcolithic date. At Tuleilat Ghassul frescoes of chalcolithic origin, having similarities with predynastic Egyptian culture, have been discovered, and megalithic structures (*dolmens*) and stone-circles (*gilgals*) are more common than west of the Jordan (photos. 130, 131).

The ancient history of Transjordan is clearly divided into prosperous periods, when its sedentary population shared the culture of Palestine, separated by pauses of several centuries, during which the land seems to have been inhabited only by primitive nomadic tribes from the eastern desert fringe.

The first prosperous period occurred in the Early Bronze Age, when large fortified cities such as Feinan, Khirbet Iskander, Lejjun, Baluah, and Ader were city-states, each politically independent and mostly situated along the great highway from Damascus and southward along the Transjordan watershed which has transmitted trade and wealth between Syria, Arabia, Babylonia, and Egypt throughout the centuries. Agriculture in terraced fields was widespread and prosperous. In general culture there is no great difference from Bronze-Age Palestine. Who these Early Bronze-Age people were is not known, though they must have been akin to the people of Palestine (p. 82), probably also to the Horites or Hurrians of Syria.

Somewhere about 1800 B.C. this flourishing civilization came to an abrupt end. Weakened by political disunity, the sedentary people seem to have fallen a prey to fierce nomads who so devastated both the cities and the countryside that for 500 years Transjordan was occupied only by primitive beduin. The Egyptian conquest of Palestine by Thothmes III about 1500 (p. 83), and subsequent conflicts between Egypt and Hittite aggressors, had little direct influence on Transjordan. But in the thirteenth century B.C. came new people, more civilized and better organized, who drove out the nomads, refortified the old cities, and built new ones, introducing the second prosperous period, an Iron Age like that of contemporary Palestine.

130. *Dolmen between Dana and Shobek*

131. *Gilgal (stone circle) near Petra*

132. *Amman, from south-east of the theatre*

133. *Kerak. East face of the castle battlements*

In the north, the country was once more temporarily in Egyptian control. In the south the Edomites established a kingdom about 1170 B.C.; Moab did likewise along the eastern shores and valleys of the Dead Sea north to the Arnon (Mojib); the Amorites took the land of Gilead from Lake Huleh southwards to the Arnon; and the kingdom of Ammon was formed east of the Belka highland. An intricate system of forts was erected on all frontiers. Terrace culture was reintroduced, and painted pottery with Cypro-Phoenician affinities shows a high cultural level more or less common to all.

Religion also was similar throughout Transjordan. Fertility deities were prominent, and crude pottery images are found in the houses. A pottery fragment shows a horse and rider; pottery heads of rams and bulls suggest that these animals were used for ritual purposes as in Palestine. The head of a Semitic king found at Mudeiyineh has a squat nose, bulging cheek, thick full lips, prominent eyes, large ears, and a pointed beard. His plaited hair hangs down each side of his face, and his head-dress is held in place by a kerchief (*ukkal*) tied in front with a bow knot.

Foreign influences came from Arabia and from Syria with the caravans which now began to pass north and south, and the Transjordan kingdoms grew rich. There is early evidence of the historical role of Transjordan as a caravan route between Mesopotamian markets and both Egypt and Arabia, alternative to the 'Way of the Sea' through the coast plain and Esdraelon (p. 344). This caravan route was the biblical 'Kings' high-road' (*Num.* xx. 17). In quiet times the caravanserais and caravan-cities along this route prospered, and created a chain of principalities, but always at the cost of feud not only with nomad raiders from the desert but with the Palestinian kingdoms which exploited the 'Way of the Sea' and also attempted to control the Transjordan routes. The danger from the desert was illustrated when the wandering Israelites were prevented from crossing the Negeb (*Num.* xxi. 1) and were forced to turn east of Edom and the 'Kings' high-road' to reach the Jordan through the weaker Amorite kingdom of Sihon.

## The Israelite Occupation

The date of the Israelite migration is disputed (p. 83), and there may have been an earlier and a later incursion. But it was in any event through Transjordan that the invaders came. Moab, Ammon, and the Amorite tribes were subdued, and Israelite tribes, Reuben, Gad, and half of Manasseh, remained east of Jordan to occupy the greater part of Gilead and the country eastwards to Bostra (*mod.* Bosra eski Sham), over the present Syrian border. Under King Solomon the Transjordan territory extended south to the river Arnon and included the former kingdom of Ammon, but later, under the Kings of Israel, the eastern frontier was withdrawn closer to the 36th meridian.

It was during the Iron Age, if not earlier, that the numerous copper and iron mines of Transjordan were actively worked. At Khirbet Nahas, Khirbet Meneiyeh, Feinan, and elsewhere Iron-Age fortresses guard adjacent mines. Within the massive walls are smelting furnaces, slag heaps, and large buildings which appear to have been prison-camps, suggesting that the mines were worked by slave labour. The custom lasted long, for Solomon introduced the corvée, and there are references in early Christian literature to gangs of Christians and criminals used at Feinan for mining.

It seems to have been during Solomon's reign that the mines were most fully worked. Though Simeon's heritage in the Negeb in southern Palestine passed from his control, King Solomon protected the caravan route to the gulf of Akaba and built the port of Ezion-Geber 'beside Eloth' (later Aela or Aelana, *mod.* Akaba) at the northern end of the gulf, whence his 'ships of Tarshish', with Phoenician crews from Tyre, carried copper and caravan-goods to other lands, bringing back gold, silver, 'ivory, apes, and peacocks', red sandalwood, precious stones, and incense, from Arabia, Africa, and even India, taking three years on the round voyage. The town has been excavated, and large smelters have been found, worked on a natural-draught principle which was afterwards forgotten and re-discovered in modern times. Caravan trade by western Arabia to the south also flourished, and the visit of the Queen of Sheba probably had more to do with business and trade treaties than with learned curiosity.

After the death of Solomon, Ammon recovered its independence and Moab extended its boundaries. With the rise of the Israelite monarchy, on the other hand, the power of Moab fell, and in the ninth century B.C. Omri reduced it to a vassal state (2 *Kings* iii. 4). But after the death of Ahab, Mesha, king of Moab, once more regained independence and recorded the full story upon the 'Moabite Stone', as well as details of the cities he built and the roads he con-structed. The attempt of Jehoshaphat to revive Solomon's port of Ezion-Geber failed. Before the end of the kingdom of Judah all its territory east of Jordan had been lost.

*The Assyrian and Persian Empires* (883 B.C.–334 B.C.)

During the period of the Assyrian Empire Transjordan had little peace. The Syrian kingdom of Benhadad and Hazael threatened it from Damascus; from the rear of Syria came Assyrian invasions. Between 741 and 732 B.C. Tiglath-Pileser IV fought five campaigns in the course of which he sent his armies as far south as Arabia, subduing all the tribes with whom he came in contact, including the Nabathu or Nabataeans (biblical Nebajoth, *Gen.* xxv. 13). About 711 Sargon II carried war into Moab and Edom; twenty-one years later Sennacherib made a similar attempt; then came Esarhaddon in 673, and Assurbanipal in 648. With the fall of Assyria, the desert tribes rose about 600 B.C., and seem to have displaced the old Edomites, who moved southward to the city later known as Petra, and westward into the Negeb and southern Palestine. In their old country they were succeeded about 587 B.C. by the Nabataeans. In Ammon, a half-Jewish dynasty, the Tobiads (to whom reference is made in the biblical story of Nehemiah: ii. 10, iv. 7, xiii. 1–8) carved out a princedom, and ruled there as vassals of Persia (*c.* 530–335).

Throughout the two hundred years of the Persian Empire Transjordan appears to have had little history. There is little doubt that already under the Assyrians and Neo-Babylonians there had been a great development of caravan trade. The union of all the civilized states of the Middle East, from the Bosporus and eastern shores of the Mediterranean to the Indus, gave great impetus to this overland trade, for the empire tapped the riches of Asia at their source. Most of it must have passed through Persia and Mesopotamia to the Greek cities of Asia Minor and to the Phoenician ports of the Mediterranean coast through Syria, as is shown by the continuous growth at this period of the four great inland cities, Damascus, Emesa (Homs), Hamath (Hama), and Aleppo, facing the Syrian desert and the Euphrates. There is nothing in the south to compare with this growth; in fact, the western Arabian route probably declined in consequence. Greek Naucratis in Egypt, the forerunner of Alexandria, tapped the Egyptian terminal of the west Arabian trade and acted as entrepôt between the Mediterranean and the East, but was chiefly concerned with the corn of Egypt and did little to compete with the northern trade-routes. Transjordan, throughout this period, was off the highways of Egyptian and Syrian trade; it was not till the break-up of the Persian Empire by the conquest of Alexander the Great that the country again appears in history.

## 2. From Nabataeans to Ghassanids

The Nabataeans first appear in history (p. 437) as Nabathu, an Arabian tribe subdued by Tiglath-Pileser between 741 and 732 B.C. On the fall of Assyria they regained independence and moved westward into Edom, east of the Wadi Araba and south of Moab. Living for long a simple tent life with tribal organization, they gradually extended their hold astride the northern end of the west Arabian routes, establishing their caravan city at Petra, the biblical Sela. Towards the end of the Persian Empire the west Arabian and Red Sea trade with Egypt and southern Palestine increased in importance, Petra at first sharing its profits with Aela at the head of the gulf of Akaba near Ezion-Geber, the ancient port of Solomon. It is reasonable to deduce from the plans of Alexander the Great before his death in 323 for expeditions by sea from the Persian gulf to the Red Sea, and vice versa, a wish to develop and control this trade.

### The Hellenistic Period (c. 320 B.C.–68 B.C.)

The division of the Persian Empire among the successors of Alexander and the constant warfare in the generations after his death disorganized the northern trade-routes and gave impetus to those from Gerrha, on the Persian gulf opposite the island of Bahrein, and by western Arabia and the Red Sea. These met at Petra. An early hellenistic attempt to secure this trade and to control the Nabataeans was made by Antigonus the One-eyed, and his son Demetrius, who led an unsuccessful expedition against Petra in 312 B.C. The whole of Palestine, Transjordan, and Syria south of the Eleutherus river (Nahr el Kebir) was held from 302 to 198 B.C. by the Ptolemies of Egypt, under whom Transjordan was divided into five administrative subdivisions, Gabalitis, Moabitis (Moab), Esbonitis (Heshbon), Ammanitis (Ammon), and Galaaditis (Gilead), names which can be traced back to the second century B.C. and which are mostly recognizable in biblical history.

Unlike the Seleucids in northern Syria, the Ptolemies colonized Transjordan very little, preferring to settle their immigrants in more fertile Egypt. They looked upon Palestine and Transjordan more as a buffer between them and the Seleucids, and held the harbours of Ptolemais-Ake, Tyre, and Sidon rather as naval outposts than as commercial ports. They occupied Aela, renaming it Berenice—thus controlling most of the Red Sea trade and fostering the prosperity of Alexandria—and Rabbath Ammon (Rabbatammana) in northern

Transjordan. Gerasa (*mod.* Jerash) may already have had a small Macedonian colony, placed there earlier by Perdiccas; Abila and Gadara, in Gilead, are first mentioned in 217 B.C., but had probably grown up in the late Persian period.

An interesting glimpse of Ptolemaic Transjordan is afforded by the archives of Zenon (*c.* 259 B.C.), who spent a year in Palestine and Transjordan as the agent and afterwards secretary-general of Apollonius, the finance minister of Ptolemy Philadelphus. These archives reveal that Tobias, Emir of the Ammonites, was in close touch with Ptolemy, and had at his disposal Ptolemaic soldiers quartered at Rabbath Ammon, which was renamed Philadelphia either by Ptolemy himself or in his honour by Tobias. The relations between king and emir were friendly, the latter sending presents of horses, wild asses, mules, and donkeys to the king, and slaves to Apollonius.

Other Egyptian citizens are known to have travelled in Palestine and Transjordan. Starting from Gaza, the Ptolemaic harbour in southern Palestine, they visited the chief markets and caravan cities, coming in touch with the Nabataeans of Petra in the south and with the Aramaeans of Damascus in the north. Their purpose was to buy goods for export: slaves and horses, raided by Ammonites and Nabataeans from the territory of the Seleucid rivals of the Ptolemies, and incense and myrrh brought overland from southern Arabia.

It must be assumed therefore that the Ptolemies of Egypt had a friendly, though loose, control in northern Transjordan, but that they never fully mastered Petra or the confederacy of Nabataean tribes astride the land routes of northern Arabia. There was little hellenization among the people, though the letters of Tobias are written in excellent Greek. Control of the trade-routes through Palestine and Transjordan became a main cause of rivalry between Seleucid Syria and Ptolemaic Egypt. By neutralizing Petra the Ptolemies attempted to divert the trade to Alexandria, while the Seleucids by expansion southwards tried to draw it by the land routes through Palestine and Transjordan to Phoenicia and Damascus.

Petra refused to be subjected either by Syria or by Egypt. She played off one against the other, her clever merchants benefiting by the weaknesses and rivalry of both, and drawing more firmly into their own hands control of the caravan routes. Towards the end of the second century or beginning of the first, the Nabataeans regained Aela on the gulf of Akaba and took Leuce Come, a port some 200 miles to the south on the Arabian coast. This failure to gain control of the land routes across the Sinai peninsula explains the policy of Ptolemy II.

It was he who reopened the canal between the Nile and the Red Sea, founded a number of ports on the Egyptian coast, possibly helped to create a Greek port on the Arabian side, and established Egyptian control over the Lihyanitic kingdom in western Arabia, south of Leuce Come. The Nabataeans in turn took to the sea and raided the Egyptian ships, thus earning for themselves an undeserved reputation in history as pirates.

Meanwhile the Seleucids under Antiochus III, after defeating the Egyptians at Paneas in 198, and expelling them from Palestine (p. 89), gradually hellenized the country to the east by founding a chain of colonies along the caravan road from Damascus southward. These settlements now became, in fact, fortified caravan towns with Greek culture, and it is probable that under Seleucid rule Philadelphia (*mod.* Amman) grew into a real Greek city. Gerasa (*mod.* Jerash) also became a fortified Greek colony, under the name of 'Antioch of the Gerasenes', from the semi-nomadic tribe which had previously occupied the village, or 'Antioch on the Chrysorhoas' from the stream (now W. Suf or W. Jerash, tributary to the Zerka) running through it.

Throughout ancient times, and also later, there was a rather marked distinction between the population of the countryside and of the cities. At first each habitable area was occupied by a tribe or group of related or associated tribes living on the land, either with their flocks or as cultivators of the soil in villages with water supply and defensive position, under the very simple, and usually patriarchal, rule of a chief and a council of elders. Cities, throughout the Near and Middle East, came into being to serve more specific needs, which were of several kinds, though some of the greater cities served more than one of them.

A *fortress-city* occupied a place of natural security, often at some strategic route-centre, and became the refuge, rallying-point, and political capital of such neighbourhood as it could defend. It was usually in the hands of a military chief and governed by force. A *bazaar-city* at the economic centre of a natural district served its material needs, and being also at the junction of routes, exchanged commodities with neighbouring districts or similar trade-centres at a distance. A *caravan-city* was a bazaar-city which conducted long-distance traffic by organized and periodical convoys. A *sanctuary-city* satisfied needs not material but spiritual, by the maintenance of a place of worship, often supplemented by an oracle or a healing-shrine, which attracted votaries from afar, and enriched the priesthood which administered the holy place.

In Transjordan, bazaar-cities, such as Damascus, Homs, Hama, and Aleppo of Syria, were absent, for except in Gilead there were no large districts of cultivation. Except in the immediate neighbourhood of cities, the habits of the countryside were mainly pastoral and semi-nomadic. The only fortress-city of any note was Philadelphia. Most were caravan-cities pure and simple, strung like beads on a line along the caravan route from south to north, usually at long intervals. Of these the most important were Petra in the south, which was also the sanctuary-city of the Nabataeans, and Gerasa in the north. Philadelphia also functioned as a caravan-city.

The effect of hellenization on Palestine has already been mentioned (p. 89). Resistance to it came to a head among the Jews during the reign of Antiochus IV Epiphanes, whose attempt to suppress Judaism led to the revolt of the Maccabees (168 B.C.). Across the Jordan the new civilization spread more slowly but peaceably, and was more acceptable, especially as the Palestine revolt rendered unsafe the 'Way of the Sea'. The Nabataeans took advantage of these troubles in Palestine to expand northwards under Aretas I, their first known 'king'. During the second half of the second century their power was extended by Erotimus; at the beginning of the first century B.C. Aretas II assisted the men of Gaza against the Maccabaean Alexander Jannaeus, and for a short time Aretas III even occupied Damascus.

Alexander Jannaeus (103–76 B.C.) was almost the last independent ruler of Palestine (p. 91). He subdued Galaaditis (Gilead) but failed to take Philadelphia, which was ruled by a tyrant, Zeno Cotylas, whose son Theodorus later held both Philadelphia and Gerasa, and thus stood astride the Nabataean trade-route to the north.

## Roman Rule

Transjordan at the time of Pompey's dissolution of the Syrian kingdom in 64 B.C. was thus Jewish in the north and Nabataean in the south, Philadelphia and Gerasa being under the independent tyrant Theodorus. Gilead, much of whose Greek culture had been destroyed during the short Jewish occupation, together with Ituraea to the north of it, was 'annexed' to the new Roman province of Syria; the 'free' and self-governing cities with Greek cultures united as the Decapolis for defence against their nomad neighbours and against the Jews. The ten foundation cities of this league probably included Scythopolis (Beisan) and Pella on either side of the Jordan in the Beisan lowland, Gadara near the mouth of the Yarmuk, Hippos immediately east of Lake Tiberias, Dium in the Gilead highland—

all formerly in the possession of Alexander Jannaeus—Philadelphia and Gerasa, freed from Theodorus, and Canatha in Auranitis (*mod.* Hauran), formerly in the Ituraean principality (fig. 55).

The Ituraeans and the Nabataeans suffered less than Judaea in the Pompeian settlement, for they had been far less troublesome. The territory of the former, though brought under Roman vassalage, was actually enlarged at the expense of Judaea, recent conquests by Alexander Jannaeus being handed back. Aretas of the Nabataeans, by formal submission to Pompey, retained his territory up to the Zerka river, including Esbus (*anc.* Heshbon, *mod.* Husban) and Medeba, which had recently been ceded to him by Jannaeus. Only a narrow frontage on to the Jordan valley and Dead Sea, south to the river Arnon, and the immediate approaches to the Jordan from the east—the district known as Peraea—were left to the Judaean kingdom of Herod and his successors (p. 91).

Rome inherited from both Seleucids and Ptolemies the task of organizing the eastern commerce. The rivalries of Syria and Egypt were now at an end. All the caravan routes which Petra controlled remained little affected, because the change was political, not commercial. The caravan-cities found a greater prosperity, and from their profits adorned themselves in Roman fashion with theatres and baths, and temples rededicated to Graeco-Roman gods. Such at least were Philadelphia, Gerasa, Canatha, and Bostra, the last-named once a small settlement of Nabataeans from Petra, now an ever-expanding centre of caravan trade.

At this period some of the merchandise of India and all from South Arabia passed up the eastern shores of the Red Sea, or along the Arabian highlands where Egra (*mod.* Medayin Salih) was the frontier town, or by sea to Leuce Come or Aela, both Nabataean ports. From Aela it went west across the Sinai peninsula to Pelusium, or north by west to Gaza, both routes being controlled by Petra. Other merchandise from Egra and Aela passed direct to Petra, the junction with a great north-Arabian caravan route from Gerrha on the Persian gulf. From Petra the main route ran north to Esbus, Philadelphia, Bostra, and Damascus. Gerasa was on a branch-road from Philadelphia to Ptolemais, which crossed the Jordan between Pella and Scythopolis (Beisan) and passed along the Esdraelon plain. All roads east of the Jordan were controlled by Nabataean merchants; for though Damascus had only been occupied by Aretas III for a brief period before the Roman conquest, it was again ceded to the Nabataeans by Augustus (A.D. 4), was ruled by a Nabataean ethnarch when

St. Paul visited the city about A.D. 40, and was still under Nabataean influence up to 94.

The Nabataean kingdom was the last of the border states to be annexed by Rome and brought into the defence system of the Roman Empire. After submission to Pompey it continued for a century and a half in semi-independence. Throughout this period of peace and security—broken only by the civil wars of Caesar, Antony, and Cleopatra (49–30 B.C.)—the demand for eastern goods and luxuries continually increased throughout the Mediterranean, and brought great wealth to the cities on the trade-routes.

## Administration and Culture

Little is known of the internal administration of the Nabataeans. Caligula, Claudius, and Nero maintained Pompey's policy of ruling difficult areas of the east by means of vassal kings. It is in this garb of a vassal state that the Nabataeans appear in control at Damascus. The division of the country into regions under the supervision of a *strategus* or general—first introduced by the Ptolemies—was maintained by the Nabataean kings. Yet their 'generals' were only sheikhs in disguise. When the daughter of Aretas, wife of Herod Antipas, escaped from the fortress city of Machaerus (*mod*. Khirbet el Mekawar) in southern Peraea to Petra, her father's capital, she was escorted by the *strategi* of each district in succession. This is normal desert custom anywhere in Arabia to-day, and indicates that tribal customs prevailed under Nabataean rule, though the name of 'king' gave semblance of civilized authority to local sheikhs. On the other hand, the Nabataean merchants in the towns seem to have shed their tribal status and to have adopted Graeco-Roman civilization. Petraean merchants of this type were found in the ports of Syria and of the Aegean, and even in Italy, where they formed a wealthy community.

As desert-dwellers the Nabataeans had an expert knowledge of water conservation; natural clefts were provided with stone dams, so that winter and spring rains supplied the cities with water throughout the dry season. Aqueducts carried water from springs to areas otherwise dry, and small areas of agriculture around the settlements reached a high excellence. The art, architecture, and ceramics of the Nabataeans, especially in the Roman period, rivalled the best that either Palestine or Transjordan has ever produced. Much of it shows the effect of hellenistic contact with desert folk.

Desert influence is more apparent in religion than in architecture. Petra's chief deities, Dushara the sun-god and Allat the moon-goddess, were worshipped on the hill-tops outside the city, where from time immemorial beduin had paid homage to their emblems. Dushara's symbol was a phallic obelisk, a black meteor fallen from the sky, like the ancient stone in the *kaaba* at Mecca. Bloody sacrifices were performed in these mountains on rough rock-hewn altars, and it was not only the semi-nomadic desert tribes and the camel-men who came here to worship, but also the merchants and people of the town. The city temples represented a tribute to fashion paid by the rich and their retinue; but the hearts of the people were still in the desert, and their real prayers were said on the hill-tops. Even to-day a solemn rite is performed on the Altar-hill of Petra.

This desert influence was never eradicated in Transjordan. There was no fanatical faith, such as Judaism in Palestine. Roman gods were accepted, and Roman temples were afterwards replaced by Christian churches, but Christianity here had no deep roots and was as easily replaced by Islam.

## Roman Arabia

Trajan annexed the Nabataean kingdom in A.D. 105, and from then onwards western Transjordan was part of the Roman province of Arabia Petraea. One of his first acts was to remove the administrative capital from Petra to Bostra (Bosra), which became the chief city of the fertile lands of what is now the Hauran district of southern Syria. The Roman province extended eastward, north of Amman, to the eastern flank of Jebel Druse; southward to Maan the frontier seems to have followed the line now taken by the Hejaz railway.

Meanwhile the function of the Transjordanian region was changing. It continued to be a focus of trade-routes, but it was also developed as a frontier region, a buttress against the turbulent tribes of 'Arabia proper, linked to the more complicated defence system of eastern Syria. To this end the Romans established a garrison of one legion, the Third Cyrenaic, at Bostra and built a paved road from Bostra to Aelana (Aela) to give the army mobility. A system of forts and strong-points assured the control of the key positions of the country, and formed an interconnected defended frontier or *limes* which enabled the Romans to control all beduin movement into Syria from the Arabian peninsula. Some of these *castella* are still well preserved, notably the fortresses of Odruh and Kasr Bjer. In the fourth century a second legion, the Tenth Fretensis, was brought to Philadelphia (Amman) to reinforce the Arabian garrison. Its memory is still echoed in the name of one of its fortresses, Lejjun. The two fortresses

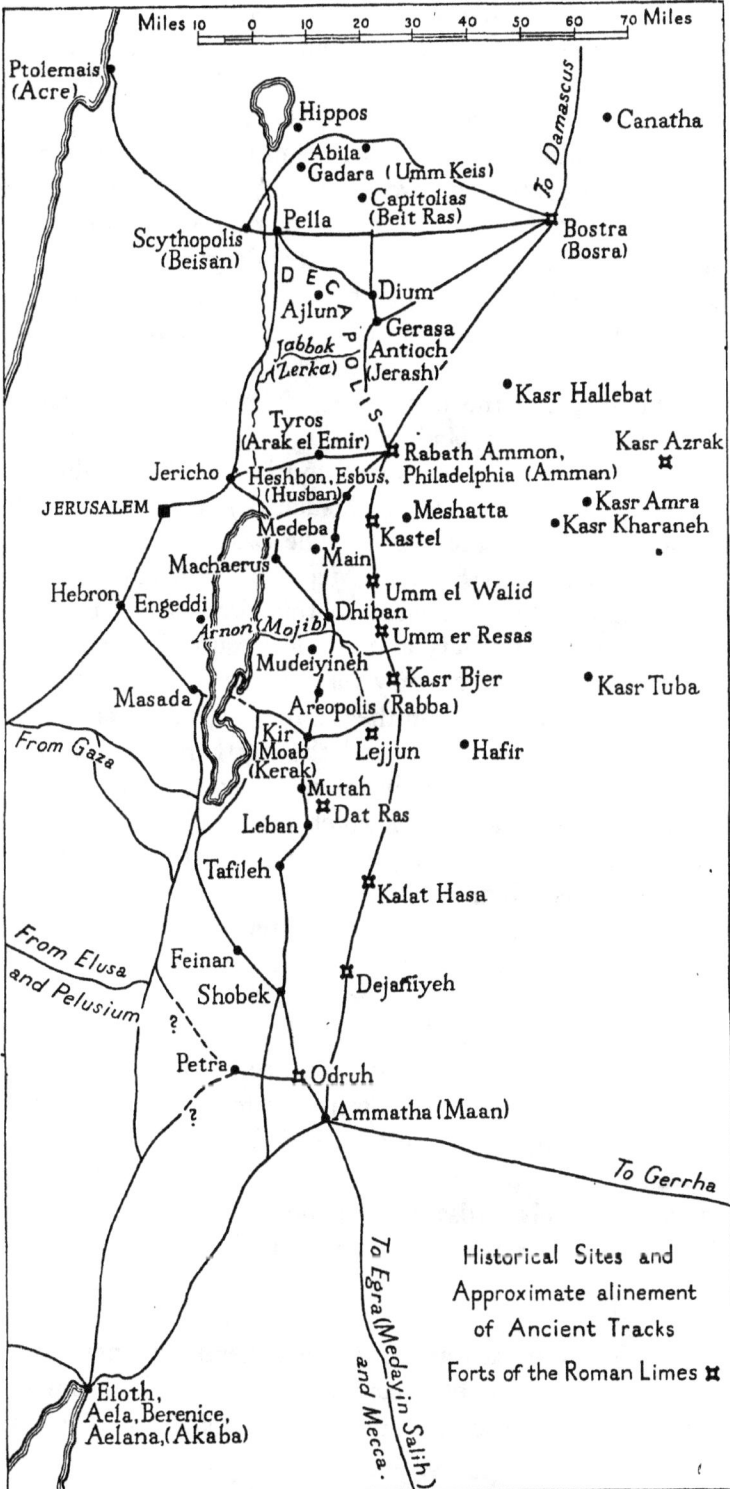

FIG. 55. *Roman Sites and Roads*

of Bostra and Philadelphia controlled the northern and westward exits
of the Wadi Sirhan. At this period the southern part of the old province south of the Wadi Hasa was detached from Arabia Petraea to
form part of the small province of Palaestina Tertia.

For five centuries, from the annexation to the Arab conquest, the
country enjoyed continuous prosperity and underwent a remarkable
urban development based on successful agriculture around the towns
and villages. Under Roman rule the Graeco-Roman civilization and the
Greek language strengthened their hold upon the upper classes, and in
the later centuries the whole country seemed to have been christianized.

It is to this period that the remarkable ruins of Amman and Jerash
(Gerasa) belong, and the later ruins of Petra; the last-named was
visited by the Emperor Hadrian in 130. But these were only the
largest of a number of small towns and large villages which sprang
up wherever circumstances allowed, such as Areopolis (Rabba) in the
south and Medeba in the north. The oases to the south-east of
Transjordan such as El Ela and Medayin Salih along the caravan
route to southern Arabia shared in this prosperity. But with the
establishment of the military and political centre in the fertile north
the whole balance of the country was changed. Trade too showed a
decided tendency to pass from the sea routes by Aelana and Petra to
the inland routes by Palmyra and the northern desert. This was
mainly due to the virtual establishment of peace between the Roman
Empire and the Parthian power which ruled in Mesopotamia.

In the third century Parthia was replaced by the aggressive Persian
power of the Sassanids and wars became frequent between Rome and
Persia. Palmyra itself was destroyed after a rebellion in 256. Yet
Petra did not recover its old primacy, and in fact became a place of
banishment. Trade continued to pass mainly overland through
Mesopotamia, though the Akaba route continued to be used to some
extent till the fifth century. By the sixth century, before the Moslem
conquest, Petra seems to have been deserted by its old population,
and the former commercial mart—which had also been a 'holy city'
in its time—was replaced by a great Christian monastery. The
Nabataeans themselves disappeared and a nomadic tribe of southern
Arabian origin, the Thamudaeans, took their place.

### The Ghassanids

This latter movement was part of the general tendency throughout
Roman Arabia. In the fifth century A.D. the Roman emperors of
Byzantium began to lose their direct control of Arabia Petraea. The

134. *View south down the depression from Azrak*

135. *The keep at Kasr Azrak*

136. *Camels grazing at Kasr Azrak. View from the south*

137. *Camel caravan in southern Transjordan*

whole area gradually fell into the hands of the Ghassanid Arabs, who were recognized as vassals of the emperor and were paid to maintain peace in the Syrian desert. Their particular duty was to hold in check the Lakhmid Arabs of Hira, vassals of Persia, who performed similar services on the Euphrates side of the desert. The Ghassanids were the first important tribe to emigrate from southern Arabia, thereby foreshadowing the later Islamic movement. Though they seem to have left Yemen in the third or fourth century A.D., it was not till the sixth century that they played a major part in Transjordan, in the reign of El Harith II (A.D. 529–569), who overwhelmed his Lakhmid rival of Hira, and was given the high rank of patrician by Justinian and appointed supreme ruler over all the tribes of the Syrian borderland.

The Ghassanid kingdom differed from that of the Nabataeans— though likewise greatly enriched by control of the desert trade-routes —in that its power was based not on trade but on the sword, and that the Ghassanids remained a beduin tribe. Their capital tended to shift from place to place and was in essence a military camp. The small fortress towns and forts became rallying points with reserve garrisons. Some of the larger towns undertook the forging of weapons for desert warfare. The centre of gravity was no longer Petra and the south, but the Belka highland and the Hauran district of modern Syria. Under their rule the life of the now christianized cities of Transjordan continued to flourish. The Ghassanids, like most of the Arab tribes of the Syrian borderlands, were themselves Christians of the monophysite belief, a doctrine with a tendency to pure monotheism which particularly appealed to Semitic peoples. El Harith was a strong supporter of Jacob Bardaeus, the founder of the Syrian Jacobite Church, and it was through the Ghassanid Arabs that, before the rise of Islam, monophysite Christianity spread southward into the Hejaz.

The Ghassanids were thus an Arab people who adopted the culture of the Byzantine Empire while retaining their beduin way of life, and speaking both Aramaic, the language of Syria, and their native Arabic. The Lakhmids were also Christians, but of the Nestorian sect, and this form of Christianity which spread from Anatolia and Armenia influenced the beduin tribes farther east. Moreover, after the adoption of Christianity by Constantine in 324 and the increased dispersal of the Jews from Palestine, Judaism was brought into the oases of the northern Hejaz. There was a large colony at Medina by the end of the sixth century, and for a short time Judaism became almost the state religion in the Yemen.

Though neither the Christianity of the Monophysite Church nor of the Nestorian was vital enough to strike deep roots anywhere in Arabia, pre-Islamic poets became familiar with Christian ideas, and Aramaic words passed into the Arabic vocabulary. Transjordan was the chief of many routes along which these intellectual, religious, and material influences were passing to Arabia, where the ancient paganism and polytheism no longer met the spiritual demands of the people. Organized national life in the south was disrupted, vague monotheistic ideas were spreading, and the stage was set for the rise of Islam.

### 3. Arab and Turkish Rule

As long as the Ghassanid confederation of Arab tribes was united, no serious danger could arise from the peninsula. But by the seventh century the power of the Ghassanid kings had become split up among a number of minor sheikhs. Worse still, the Emperor Heraclius withdrew the subsidies which were regularly paid to the north Arabian tribes beyond the Ghassanid region. In 611 the Syrian defences collapsed before Chosroes II of Persia, Jerusalem was sacked in 614, and it was not till 628 that Heraclius recovered both Syria and Palestine (p. 99).

### The Rise of Islam

During these critical years, while the two northern Powers were exhausting their strength, the teaching of Mohammad was gaining ground throughout Arabia.[1] Scorned and persecuted in Mecca, he settled in 622 in Medina, where he gained adherents and waylaid Meccan caravans. Native Jews and Christians of the northern tribes came under the protection of the new faith by payment of *jizya*, a land and capitation tax; delegations from Arab tribes came to offer allegiance, which was accepted on easy terms by a verbal profession of faith and payment of the *zakah* or 'poor tax'. Prospects of booty added to the ranks of the new faith.

It was about the time when Heraclius, newly arrived from victory over the Persians, was celebrating at Jerusalem the recovery of the Holy Cross, that word came of a raid by Arabs on the frontier post of Mutah (*mod.* Moteh) east of the southern end of the Dead Sea. It was interpreted as one of the usual raids to which the border forts had long been accustomed, and none suspected that it was the first active aggression of a new Power which within a decade would successfully challenge the might of both Persia and Byzantium.

[1] A brief summary of the teaching of Islam is given on page 100.

This northern raid was the only one carried out during the lifetime of Mohammad. It was led by his adopted son, Zaid ibn Harithah, with the ostensible object of avenging the death of the Prophet's emissary at the hands of the Ghassanid prince of Bostra, though the real purpose was to secure swords manufactured at Mutah and neighbouring towns for an impending attack on Mecca. The raid was unsuccessful, Zaid was killed, and the defeated remnants of his 3,000 men were withdrawn to Medina by Khalid ibn Walid, who assumed command.

Before Mohammad's death in 632, peace was restored between Mecca and Medina; but conversion to Islam among the tribes beyond the Hejaz was too recent to be lasting, and the first few months of the caliphate of Abu Bekr were occupied with the reconquest of Arabia. It was Khalid, the survivor of Mutah, who was entrusted with this task, and he reduced the tribes of central Arabia to submission in a campaign lasting six months. Islam now acted as a cement to the Arab tribes. Campaigns which started as raids provided new outlets for the warring spirit of tribes who were now prevented by the teaching of Islam from engaging in fratricidal combats. As booty was gained, the movement gathered momentum, and the desert warriors passed from victory to victory.

The conquest of Syria began in much the same way. In recruiting for this campaign the Islamic tribes were summoned to a 'holy war', and their desire for it was increased by promises of booty from the enemy. But vast forces were not employed. In the autumn of 633 three detachments each of about 3,000 men marched northwards and began operations in southern Palestine and Transjordan. Two took the direct route from Tebuk to Maan, the third went by the coast through Aylah (*class.* Aela). In the first encounter, in the Wadi Araba, Yezid defeated Sergius, the patrician of Palestine, whose force of several thousand troops were pursued and almost annihilated at Dathin on its retreat towards Gaza in February 634. East of the Dead Sea the invaders made little headway against the frontier forts, and Heraclius had time to dispatch into Palestine a fresh army under his brother Theodorus.

Meanwhile Khalid ibn Walid, who became known as 'the Sword of Allah', and who was operating in Iraq near Hira with some 500 veterans of his Arabian campaigns and with local tribesmen, received orders to race to the assistance of the Moslems operating in Transjordan. Having received the submission of Hira, Khalid crossed the desert to Jauf, skirted the eastern edge of the Wadi Sirhan, avoided the easiest natural route between Amman and Bostra to the Yarmuk, which was well guarded with forts, and led his force mounted on camels north through the lava belt to Suwa (*mod.* Saba Biar), the oasis of 'the Seven Wells', 85 miles east-north-east of Damascus. The journey from Hira had occupied eighteen days. With dramatic suddenness he appeared before Damascus, defeated the Ghassanid levies near Adhra, 14 miles from the city, and turned south to take Bostra, the Syrian fortress, from the rear. Having effected a junction with other Moslem forces which had broken into Palestine, Khalid assumed supreme command. Bostra fell almost at once, and a great victory was won over Theodorus at Ajnadain in July 634. Next year the fortress of Fihl (*anc.* Pella), which commanded the Beisan crossing of the Jordan, was secured on 23 January 635 and held. With his western flank secure Khalid turned north again to Damascus, winning another victory at Merj es Suffar, and the city, abandoned by its Byzantine garrison, surrendered in September after a siege of six months. Baalbek, Homs, Hama, and Aleppo followed suit in quick succession, and it appeared that the Byzantine Empire had lost all Syria except Antioch.

But the emperor made a determined effort to recover Syria, and, gathering yet another army of 50,000 men—again under his brother Theodorus—prepared to take the offensive. Khalid withdrew southwards, abandoning his recent conquests, and took up his position with about 25,000 men on the Yarmuk, near the modern Deraa. Months of skirmishing came to a climax on 20 August 636, when on a day chosen for its intense heat Khalid launched his attack in a sandstorm, and overwhelmed the Byzantines. Theodorus was killed, and the remnants of the imperial army became a routed and panic-stricken mob.

No further serious resistance stood in the way of Arab arms until the natural limits of Syria, the Taurus mountains, were reached. Few cities failed to open their gates: most welcomed the invaders. In the south only Jerusalem and Caesarea held out stubbornly, the former till 638, the latter till October 640. Caesarea received help from the sea which the Arabs had no means of intercepting, but after a siege of seven years it fell to attack, aided by treachery from within. Between 633 and 640 all Syria was subdued.

### Moslem Rule to 1914

After the Arab conquest the role of Transjordan changed again. The frontier between the Arabs and the Byzantine Empire shifted north to the Taurus, and Arab aggression reached out eastwards into Persia and westwards along the north coast of Africa. The administrative centres of the Arabs were outside Arabia proper, first at Damascus, then at Baghdad and in Egypt. The 'Way of the Sea' became the main line of communication between Syria and Egypt, and the ancient highway through Transjordan became one of many roads trodden by pilgrims to the shrine at Mecca. Many of the old forts along the route were occupied for a new purpose, the protection of pilgrim caravans. For a short time also the country continued to charm the early caliphs at Damascus, who still maintained their inbred love of the desert and its pursuits. To this period belong the country palace of Yezid at Muwakkar in the Belka highland, the hunting-lodges rebuilt by Walid II on the sites of Roman forts at Kastel and Azrak (photo. 135), and the best known of all, the Kasr Amra, possibly a Ghassanid foundation but rebuilt and decorated between A.D. 712 and 715 by Walid I, and since famous for its magnificent frescoes, the earliest known examples of Moslem pictorial art. The Kasr at Meshatta, almost as famous, is now attributed to Walid II (p. 545).

Once for a period of two hundred years in the succeeding centuries Transjordan emerges from obscurity into the light of history, playing the role that made it famous in earlier times.

After the capture of Jerusalem (A.D. 1099) by the Crusading leader Godfrey de Bouillon (p. 106), the Latin kingdom was extended eastwards of the Dead Sea and the Wadi Araba. Opposition to the Crusaders was centred at Aleppo and Damascus, neither of which were they able to capture; Damascus was the terminus of Moslem routes to the Hejaz and to Egypt, the latter of which was forced to pass through Transjordan, because of the loss of the Palestinian coast. Baldwin's first raid in 1100 across the Wadi Araba to the Wadi Musa was a failure. But between 1114 and 1116, based on Hebron, whence he could command the roads through the Negeb, Baldwin struck east again and established himself across the Wadi Araba at Shawbak (*mod.* Shobek), where he built the formidable fortress known as *Crac de Montroyal* or *Montréal*. Pushing southwards, he built another castle at El Aswit, in the neighbourhood of Petra and the Wadi Musa—generally referred to in the chronicles as *Li Vaux Moyse*. The exact site of this castle, known as Airé to the chroniclers, sometimes as *Selem*, an echo of ancient Sela, is uncertain, but it may be the modern Waira.

From Petra he reached Ailat (*arab.* Aylah, *class.* Aela) on the Akaba gulf. Later the Crusaders occupied the old Roman fortress of Odruh, built other smaller castles at Ahamant—possibly in the neighbourhood of Maan—and at Tafileh; and in 1142, on the site of the biblical Kir Moab, on ruins known as *Petra Deserti*, they built the great fortress of *Crac des Moabites* or *Krak* (*mod.* Kerak) (photo. 133). Airé was lost for a time but recaptured after siege in 1144.

This important seigneurie of Krak-et-Montréal did not extend into northern Transjordan, where the Saracens built the fortress of Ajlun to command the Jordan crossings (p. 540). It was governed in the twelfth century by feudal lords, dependants of the King of Jerusalem, Krak becoming the chief fortress and key to military and caravan routes through Transjordan (p. 544). Its most famous seigneur was Renaud de Châtillon, who not only plundered caravans as they passed within reach of the castle walls of Krak, but also occupied the island of Jeziret Firaun—L'île de Graye—off Ailat, fitted out a fleet, like Solomon of old and the Nabataeans, and harassed the coasts of the Hejaz, preying on the pilgrims by land and sea. He earned the personal hatred of Saladin, and was killed by Saladin's own hand in accordance with his oath, after being captured at the battle of Hattin in 1187, which put a virtual end to the kingdom of Jerusalem. The castle of Krak held out for a year after the fall of Jerusalem; that of Montréal fell in 1189.

The sultanate founded by the Kurdish leader Saladin, from Mesopotamia to Egypt, was divided in 1193 among his various heirs, of whom his younger brother Saif ed Din—Saphadin of Latin chronicles—received Krak-et-Montréal. But between 1196 and 1199 Saif ed Din acquired sovereignty over Egypt and most of Syria.

In the next century Tatar invaders from the Asiatic steppes hastened the regrouping of the Moslem world. The Mamluks, who rose from being slaves to be palace favourites of the former dynasty, seized power in Egypt. In 1228 the Tatars, invited by the Emir of Damascus, turned on him and ravaged Syria and Palestine, but were expelled, leaving these countries in the hands of the Egyptian Mamluks. In 1260 the Mongols, after the capture of Baghdad, attacked Syria and Palestine, but were likewise repelled by the Mamluks. Three years later Beibars, the Mamluk Sultan, established his eastern frontier along the desert edge through Transjordan, with its defence once more centred at Krak. But with the end of the Crusades (1294), Transjordan disappears from history and was forgotten by the western world until the nineteenth century.

It was probably the Latin kingdom that dealt the death-blow to the

Transjordan caravan trade. During the Mamluk sultanate of Egypt, eastern trade passed more and more by the Red Sea to Alexandria and, except when Tatar and Mongol invasions caused temporary dislocation, by the northern routes from the Euphrates to northern Syria. In 1401 Syria was invaded by Tamerlane; Aleppo, Hama, Baalbek, and Damascus were sacked, but Transjordan was no longer a competitor for the transit trade, and these north Syrian towns soon recovered. A hundred years later the deflexion of Far Eastern trade round the Cape of Good Hope put an end to any possible recovery. Even in the Arabian Sea in 1509 the Egyptian fleet failed to check Portuguese sea-power, which was only finally halted off Jidda, the port of Mecca, in 1514.

In 1516 the Ottoman Sultan Selim I seized the possessions of the Eastern Caliphate west of the Euphrates, and a year later defeated the last Mamluk sultan and became master of Egypt. His successor, Suleiman the Magnificent, made a last effort to wrest the sea-power of the Indian Ocean from the Portuguese in 1538, but failed. Thenceforward the Ottoman Empire was heavily involved in Europe. Transjordan, like Syria and Palestine, became a backwater, closed to the West. Portuguese occupation of coastal forts in Oman for a century and a half, and of Aden or its islets intermittently, closed the Middle East and Arabia effectively from the Indian side. Ancient shrines and holy cities caused the old routes to be trodden by countless pilgrims, but control was lax, and the administration degenerated into quarrels between disfavoured Turkish governors and truculent local sheikhs, and of these with one another. The Transjordan fortresses were not deliberately dismantled by the Ottoman Turks, but became deserted when they had no longer a protective role to play. They gradually fell to ruin, and only Krak was still sufficiently formidable about 1840 to deserve the attention of Ibrahim (p. 112), the son of Mehemet Ali.

### Exploration in the Nineteenth Century

After about 400 years of obscurity Transjordan became suddenly 'rediscovered' by the West. In 1812 the Swiss explorer J. L. Burckhardt, under the auspices of the African Association, the forerunner of the Royal Geographical Society of London, travelled from Syria to Egypt. Intent on visiting Mecca, in which he succeeded two years later, he had embraced Islam and passed as 'Sheikh Ibrahim' in Moslem dress. At that time the Dead Sea was not known to be below sea-level and Burckhardt thought that the Wadi Araba, which he discovered, was the extension of the Jordan course to the Akaba gulf. The sanctity surrounding Jebel Harun, traditionally believed by Moslems to be Mount Hor and to contain the tomb of Aaron, increased Arab suspicion of strangers, but Burckhardt penetrated the Sik gorge to discover the ancient city of Petra, which he made known once more to the Western world. Publication of the account of his discoveries brought other explorers, the two British naval officers Irby and Mangles in 1818, the Frenchmen Laborde and Linant in 1828, and about thirty in all had visited Petra by 1850. Among the best-known British travellers were the Assyriologist Layard (1840), Viscount Castlereagh (1842), Ross, Frazer, Lord Hamilton, Palmer, and Maugham. But not till 1896 did the site attract scholars and orientalists, and the pre-eminence of Petra for long led to the neglect of other historical sites in Transjordan and of the topographical study of its early history. This was first undertaken in detail by the Czech scholar Alois Musil between 1896 and 1908, though a few notable travellers passed through to Arabia and described their routes: the meticulous Swedish scientist G. A. Wallin about 1842, and the less reliable English Jesuit of Jewish extraction, W. G. Palgrave, twenty years later, went by Maan to Jauf; the French Alsatian Charles Huber in 1878 journeyed to Jauf from Damascus by Bosra, Kaf, and the Wadi Sirhan; and the greatest of all, C. M. Doughty, in 1875 accompanied a pilgrim caravan under the protection of a Kurdish pasha all the way to Medayin Salih, the ancient Egra, on the old Nabataean border by the Hejaz proper. Most of these explorers traversed Transjordan to explore northern and central Arabia—the Great Nefud, the Jebel Shammar, Nejd, and the pilgrim route as far as Medina—and it was through their writings that the organization of the north Arabian tribes (p. 467) was understood by a small band of orientalists and Arabic scholars of the West at the outbreak of war in 1914.

Meanwhile traffic to India by way of the Suez canal, cut between 1860 and 1869, had greatly stimulated Ottoman interest in Arabia. Turkish troops arrived in the Hejaz, and Ottoman influence was increased by bribe and intrigue. In the closing years of the nineteenth century proposals were made for a railway from Damascus by the old Syrian pilgrim route through Transjordan to the Hejaz. Funds were raised by public subscription and special stamp tax. Work was begun in 1900, completed to Maan by September 1904, and later extended to Medina; Deraa was linked by branch-line to Haifa in 1905.

Even in its projected stage this railway, ostensibly built for pilgrim traffic, had considerable political and economic significance. It enabled the Sultan Abdul Hamid to assert himself more forcibly at Mecca, where he interposed by appointing a successor to the Emir, and by removing to Constantinople some of the influential Hashimite family, including Sherif Hussein ibn Ali and his four sons, Ali, Abdulla, Feisal, and Zeid. When Abdul Hamid fell in 1909, however, the Young Turks reversed his policy and sent Hussein back to Mecca as Emir.

## 4. THE WAR OF 1914–1918

Arab nationalism had its roots in the closing years of the nineteenth century when secret Arab societies were formed in Syria. Before 1914 there were similar movements in Mesopotamia, Palestine, and Egypt, and in the spring of that year Abdulla, son of Sherif Hussein, went to Cairo intending to sound Lord Kitchener, then Agent-General at Cairo, on the subject of Arab hopes.

The outbreak of war between Britain and Turkey brought difficulties to the Hejaz. The pilgrimage and the revenues connected with it ceased, and the Hejaz now depended for its existence either on the single line of railway and the goodwill of the Turks, or on Indian food-ships to the Red Sea, controlled by the British Navy. The declaration of a Holy War by the Sultan required the sanction of Mecca to be popularly effective throughout Islam. Hussein was shrewd and obstinate, but deeply pious. To him a Holy War was incompatible with alliance with Germany in an aggressive war; he therefore refused the Sultan's demand, and appealed to Britain not to starve his province for what was not his people's fault. The Turks thereupon instituted a partial blockade by controlling supplies on the Hejaz railway; the British left the coast open to regulated food-ships.

About the same time, in January 1915, the chief Arab nationalists in Syria and Mesopotamia appealed to Hussein, as the 'Father of the Arabs', to save them from the ruthlessness of the 'Young Turks', Enver, Jemal, and Talaat. From that date Hussein and his sons planned the liberation of the Arab states from Ottoman rule, though delays were caused by the failure of the Dardanelles campaign, by British difficulties in Mesopotamia, and by the executions of Arab supporters in Syria, before the standard of revolt was raised.

The early operations in the Hejaz only indirectly concern the history of Transjordan, inasmuch as the Turkish 12th Army Corps under Fakhri Pasha at Medina was supplied by the Hejaz railway. But it is necessary to outline them in order to understand the later stages of the campaign. At the outbreak of the revolt Hussein drove the Turks from Mecca and the surrounding hills, but his sons Feisal and Ali failed to take Medina through lack of modern arms and ammunition. The resulting rape and massacre of the women and children in the Awali suburb of Medina sent a shock of anger across Arabia, which did more than anything else to unite the Arabian people.

It was at this time that T. E. Lawrence, a young graduate from Oxford, who had undertaken archaeological work in Syria before the war and was now attached to Intelligence at Army Headquarters in Cairo, reached Feisal's headquarters, south-west of Medina. In close collaboration with D. G. Hogarth and a small group of men in Egypt who understood Arab hopes, Lawrence had been sent to organize the Arab revolt. In Feisal, third son of Hussein, he found a 'national' leader, whom he persuaded to move up the Arabian coast and occupy Wejh in January 1917, the same month that Sir Archibald Murray crossed the Egyptian frontier and captured Rafa (p. 118). Up till the arrival of Lawrence the revolt had not prospered, and the Arabs were in danger of being decisively defeated before Mecca. From then onwards he was the mainspring of the Arab cause.

The move to Wejh was an attempt to seize the initiative. From here Feisal set marching an intense movement for freedom among the tribes to the north and east. He enrolled most of the Billi and the Moahib, thus making himself master of the country between the railway and the sea; he made contact with the semi-sedentary coastal Howeitat tribesmen towards Akaba, and received emissaries from the tribes to the east and north-east, including the Jazi Howeitat from near Maan and several owing obedience to Nuri Shaalan, head of the Anazeh clan and Emir of the Ruwalla, fourth among the precarious princes of the desert. Most of the northern clans were at perpetual blood-feud: Feisal brought the chiefs face to face, composed their differences, and inspired them to co-operate in the Arab cause.

The object of these preliminaries was twofold. First they enabled the Arabs to harass the Turkish communications by the Hejaz railway north of Medina; secondly, they prepared the way for a possible move northwards into Transjordan.

It was while engaged from Wejh in cutting the Hejaz railway about 80 miles north of Medina that Lawrence conceived his strategy for the future of the revolt. The subsequent operations bear a curious resemblance to those of Khalid ibn Walid thirteen hundred years earlier, but with striking differences. The resemblance is caused by the similarity in the general situation, and by the qualities of speed, endurance, secrecy, and independence of fixed communications which the Arabs possessed. At both periods also there were Arab sympathizers in the alien rear, who could be counted upon to welcome success, though not openly to show their hand too soon. To Feisal, the 'ideal of freedom' supplanted the nascent Islam of earlier days as the binding and motive force behind the movement. Freedom meant not merely the nationalism of Arabs in Baghdad, Damascus, and Cairo: it was the freedom to live their lives in the Arab way throughout the whole Arab world, including Syria and Palestine, free of Turkish and Western restraint. If Hussein went farther than this and viewed himself as head of a nationalist Arabia, it must not be assumed that Arabs in Syria and Iraq, or even throughout Arabia, were prepared to accept Hussein as king. Later events have indeed proved that this was not so (pp. 462, 463).

To understand fully the complex part played by Lawrence in the following operations, it is necessary to state the different outlooks of the British and Arab leaders. To the British, Turkey was a vassal of Germany; Palestine was still a 'side-show'; Murray's mission was still the 'defence of Egypt', though on political grounds he had been urged by the War Cabinet to advance into Palestine (p. 118). With forces too weak for this, he sought Arab help to contain as many Turks as possible in the neighbourhood of Medina. To the Arabs, who planned their revolt of their own free will with no British promises, the British were there to help them gain their independence and win freedom. Even at a later stage the Arab revolt was to the British in Palestine, and even to Allenby, only the right flank of their army striving to overthrow the Turks. But to Feisal, though he accepted military subordination, the Palestine campaign was the left wing of Arab freedom.

While at Wejh Lawrence dissuaded an attempt to take Akaba from the sea, which after landing would have meant attacking the covering hills and forcing a way north against a strong defensive position. The Turks would have been in the element for which they were best fitted by character and training. Instead, he planned a wide detour and a descent on Akaba through the Howeitat country on the north.

With Auda, chief of the Abu Tayi clan of the eastern Howeitat, and a small party of other chiefs and followers, Lawrence crossed the railway and the Hul desert north-eastwards, descending the Wadi Fejr to the neighbourhood of Jauf, the capital of Nuri Shaalan, Emir of the Ruwalla. Thence he passed north-west along the wells of the Wadi Sirhan to Nebk. It was here that Nesib el Bekri, one of the leaders, who knew the Druses covering Damascus from the south-east, proposed an immediate attack on the city with their help. But the British could not instantly attack in Palestine—they had already in April been checked before Gaza—and even if the Arabs took Damascus, they would be unable to hold it, and Arab support would dissipate. Akaba must be taken first, Nuri's role was to cover the desert flank at a later stage, and the northern Arabs were to come in only on the tide of victory. Nesib left the party and went north to the Jebel Druse, but the rest turned west to the wells of Bayir. It was during this period that Lawrence rode north to Saba Biar, Ras Baalbek, and Damascus, and back through the Hauran, to make contact with the leaders among the Arabs in these parts.

Thence to Jafr, the pastures of Auda's clan, where wells had been damaged by the Turks, and on to a brisk fight at Abu Lisan, where a raw Turkish battalion was cut to pieces with the loss of only two Arabs. The local tribes came in as success followed success, the small Turkish garrisons surrendered, and Akaba was taken on 6 July 1917. Its capture both closed the Hejaz campaign, though the Turks still held Medina, and established confidence between Lawrence and Allenby, the new Commander-in-Chief in Egypt. Feisal, with his Arab army, moved from Wejh to Akaba, and was transferred to Allenby's command, which became responsible for his equipment and supply, Akaba being organized as base for further operations.

In the next stage, during the winter of 1917–18, Allenby turned the Turkish left flank at Beersheba (31 October) and occupied Jerusalem in December and Jericho in February (p. 119). The Arabs were a shield to his right flank and a menace to the Turkish left and rear. A small force was established at Kasr Azrak at the northern end of the Wadi Sirhan, and was a constant threat, though an early attempt to destroy the Yarmuk railway bridge at Shehab failed through treachery, and later the severe winter kept the Azrak force immobile. Farther south between Amman and Mudauwara frequent attacks on the railway, and more particularly on running trains, were made by Arab parties trained to demolition work by Lawrence and others. The line was not permanently interrupted: enough trains to Medina were allowed to run to make the task worth while and to feed

the Arab appetite for loot. Most of these attacks were made from the
Wadi Itm in the south and from the line of Roman, Crusader, and
Moslem posts on the escarpment edge west of the railway: Kuweira,
Petra, Odruh, Shobek, and Tafileh, the last-named being taken on
20 January 1918 and held after a stiff counter-attack. Tafileh commanded the southern approaches to the Dead Sea, whence a small
Turkish flotilla had been used to convoy supplies. The supply depot
was burnt, the ships were sunk, and all traffic by the Dead Sea was
stopped.

January and February were months of snowfall and bitter winds.
The Arab detachments on the escarpment suffered severely from the
cold, and it was difficult to get them to undertake active operations
or to exploit success. In the advance to Damascus, planned for the
spring, Feisal's task was to capture Maan and to roll up the Turkish
posts thence to Amman, where he would join hands with the British
from Jericho. Before these plans could be consummated, however,
the German offensive in France caused Allenby's force to be depleted
and the role of the Arabs changed. Maan was invested but not
seriously attacked, Turkish attention was distracted for its relief,
Allenby reinforcing his Arab right with armoured cars and air
support, and constant attacks on the Turkish communications prevented concentration from Damascus and Deraa against the depleted
force in Palestine.

With the arrival of reinforcements from Mesopotamia and India
the autumn offensive was planned. There was little time left before
winter set in. Allenby's objectives were the destruction of the
Turkish armies in Palestine and the capture of Damascus. The role
of Feisal's army was to hold the Turkish 4th Army south of Deraa,
the junction of the railways north to Damascus, west to Palestine,
and south to Maan, and to rivet Turkish attention east of the Jordan.

Early in September Lawrence concentrated Feisal's army at Azrak,
the old castle at the northern end of the Wadi Sirhan, and key to the
Yarmuk south of Jebel Druse. Arab regulars, camel caravans of
supplies, and armoured cars moved by Jafr and Bayir; two aeroplanes
flew from Palestine; the beduin collected: Nuri Shaalan and the
Ruwalla tribes, Auda and other Howeitat from the south, clans from
the west, Talal with Hauran peasants from the north. Several
British officers, experts in Arab tactics or in demolition, were included.

By the 12th all was ready. Between the 14th and 16th a long section
of the southern line near Mafrak station was demolished, isolating
Deraa from Amman; the northern line was cut at Arar; on the

western, Mezerib station was destroyed and the line west of Shehab demolished, though the Yarmuk bridges were too strongly held to be attacked.

These activities had the desired effect, and caused the Turks to fear for the safety of the 4th Army, strung out between Deraa and Tafileh. On the 19th Allenby struck and broke the Turkish line in the plain of Sharon; his cavalry poured through the gap and over the Carmel ridge to the plain of Megiddo, herding the Turks into the hills of Samaria, where they became a rabble of fugitives. Three columns were formed for the pursuit across the Jordan: the New Zealanders to Amman, the Indians to Deraa, and the Australians north of the sea of Galilee to Kuneitra.

By the 27th the Arabs were astride the roads north of Deraa and the 4th Turkish Army was in full retreat. Deraa fell to Lawrence before the Indians arrived. The disorganized columns crowded northwards, harassed all the way through the now hostile country-side. They were cut to pieces, the final action taking place near Jebel Maani about 15 miles south of Damascus, where the last remnants were caught between the Middlesex Yeomanry and Auda's Howeitat tribesmen. Damascus was entered on 2 October.

## 5. AFTER THE WAR: 1919–1939

*The Settlement*

With the consent of the British Government Feisal hoisted the Arab flag at Damascus on 3 October, proclaimed Syrian independence, and appointed Syrian advisers. This was followed by a joint Anglo-French declaration of policy from General Headquarters, which was issued in Palestine, Syria, and Iraq on 7 November. The whole country was placed for the time under the Occupied Enemy Territory Administration, the eastern half of Syria, including Damascus, Homs, Hama, and Aleppo, the Hauran and Transjordan, being under Feisal's administration; western Syria, Cilicia, and a large district north of the Baghdad railway under the French; Palestine and Iraq under the British. These were primarily military arrangements and the boundaries were not fixed.

The sudden end of the Great War left the victors totally unprepared with plans for peace. The future of Transjordan was a very small part of the Middle East problem, caused by the break-up of the Ottoman Empire.

In the north there was conflict between Arab hopes and French ambitions; in the west between Jewish hopes and Arab fears; in the south and east between Hussein, Ibn Rashid, and Ibn Saud, Emirs of the Hejaz, the Jebel Shammar, and Nejd (p. 462). These interests had to be balanced in London and at the Peace Conference, on advice given by political officers who saw too clearly the problems in their own areas but not always the problem as a whole, nor the wider repercussions of a false move.

The claims and interests of all the Allies, great and small, had to be met by negotiation and compromise. It was impossible immediately to fulfil all the conflicting hopes which had been raised by the interpretation of indefinite clauses in agreements made during the stress of war. The outcome of the conference was to define the Arab sphere on the west by the Lebanon, the Jordan, and the Dead Sea, with the Yarmuk as the dividing line between regions placed under mandate to France and to Britain until such time as the Arab State could stand alone. Thus for a few months after September 1919 Transjordan was part of Feisal's uneasy state of Syria. Those who knew best the trend of French ambitions foresaw the dangers of this settlement, though few realized how quickly it would end.

Feisal accepted the Versailles settlement and threw himself into the task of organizing his state. There were difficulties on the borders, particularly in the north, caused by the passions roused by war, but none which could not have been overcome with patience on the French side. But in July 1920 General Gouraud, the French Commander-in-Chief in western Syria, on the excuse of constant friction, sent an ultimatum to Feisal and backed it up by force. Rather than plunge the country again into war, Feisal withdrew from Syria, and the region of the French mandate was broken up into fragments more directly under French rule.[1]

Transjordan was, however, in the British sphere, and the British High Commissioner at once called a meeting of sheikhs and notables at Es Salt in August 1920, where he declared that H.M. Government favoured self-government for them, with the assistance of a few British officers and advisers. That policy, taken boldly in fulfilment of war-time pledges, has been consistently followed ever since, unaffected by difficulties in Syria and elsewhere.

Three months later the Emir Abdulla, brother of Feisal, appeared in Transjordan with a small force from the Hejaz, intent on raising the tribes and marching into Syria against the French. His movements

[1] For a more detailed account of these events and the subsequent history of Syria, see *Syria* (N.I.D. B.R. 513, pp. 140 seqq.).

were slow, and in March 1921 he was still at Amman. Winston Churchill, then Secretary of State for the Colonies, with Lawrence as adviser, was in Cairo, attending a conference on Middle East affairs. At a meeting in Jerusalem between Churchill, Sir Herbert Samuel (High Commissioner for Palestine), Abdulla, and Lawrence, Abdulla agreed to abandon his Syrian project and to accept the Amirate of Transjordan under British mandate, with a grant-in-aid from the British. The lines along which the new Arab state of Iraq was to be organized had already been decided. Feisal, who had done so much for the Allied cause and who had been so humiliated by Gouraud in 1920, was put forward by the British as a candidate for the Iraqi throne, and was elected king the following June by an overwhelming majority of the people. Thus the British fulfilled their pledges to Feisal, so far as was within their power. When the mandate for Palestine was confirmed by the Council of the League of Nations, the clauses relating to the establishment of a proposed Jewish National Home were expressly excluded from application to Transjordan.

The Organic Law of 1928, following agreement between Britain and Transjordan, laid down the constitution and set up an independent government, 'provided that such Government is constitutional and places His Britannic Majesty in a position to fulfil his international obligations' (Cmd. 3069 (1928)). This was accepted by an elected Legislative Council in April 1929 and from that date self-government in Transjordan has been effective. The status of the Amirate[1] was further advanced in 1939 by a new agreement with the British Government, whereby a cabinet, responsible to the Amir, took the place of an Executive Council, and the Amir was authorized to raise military forces and to appoint consuls in neighbouring states. The British Government has only retained the right to maintain armed forces in Transjordan.

In the early days of Abdulla's regime difficulties were naturally caused by raids of beduin tribes from the east and south, and by ancient feuds, so long composed by Feisal's prestige. Unrest was increased by rival claims in southern Transjordan.

At the end of the war, control of central Arabia was in the rival hands of Ibn Rashid of Jebel Shammar, of Ibn Saud, Emir of Nejd, who had initiated the Wahhabi revival in 1910, and of Hussein, now recognized as King of the Hejaz, though self-styled 'King of the

---

[1] Throughout history Arab 'Emirs' appear in English literature. Since 1920 the official spelling is *Amir*, though the 'Emir Abdulla' is still commonly used.

Arabs'. Ibn Saud, like Hussein, had allied himself with Britain during the war, but after defeat by Ibn Rashid, who was loyal to the Turks, he had remained inactive. Rival claims to the oasis of Khurma on the borders of Nejd and the Hejaz led to hostilities, in which Hussein joined with Ibn Rashid in the north, and with the Idrisi of Asir in the south against Ibn Saud. In May 1919 Ibn Saud defeated Hussein's troops, sent to occupy Khurma; the following year he annexed upland Asir; in August 1921 he captured Hail and annexed the Jebel Shammar; and in July 1922 he captured the Jauf district from the Shaalan dynasty of the Ruwalla. This brought him to the Wadi Sirhan and the confines of Transjordan; in August some three or four thousand Wahhabi camel-men raided to within 12 miles south of Amman, but they were defeated with heavy loss at Umm el Amad by the armoured cars and air force of Abdulla's British allies.

An attempt was made by the British at a meeting in Kuwait on the Persian Gulf at the beginning of 1924 to settle the differences between Ibn Saud and the Hashimite rulers of the Hejaz, Transjordan, and Iraq, but with no success. In August that year a Wahhabi force captured Taif, the summer capital of the Hejaz, and in October entered Mecca. Hussein abdicated, his son Ali who succeeded him shut himself up in Jidda for a year, but by 1925 all opposition was at an end. Ibn Saud was proclaimed king in Mecca, with the title of 'King of Hejaz and Sultan of Nejd and its dependencies'.

In these early days marauders from Transjordan raided into Syria, and even while the Wahhabi incursion was being defeated at Umm el Amad, a band of raiders was over the Syrian border. But they were in no sense invasions; and the Transjordan government took suitable steps to deal with the culprits. Gradually the country settled down. In May 1927 Great Britain signed a treaty with Ibn Saud, formally recognizing the complete independence of his dominions; Ibn Saud agreeing to continue the *status quo* by which the Maan and Akaba districts were administered by Transjordan. Relations between Abdulla and Ibn Saud remained unhappy until 1933, when they also signed a treaty of friendship and good neighbourliness. Since then friendship has been more cordial, though agreement concerning the province of Maan and the port of Akaba has not been sealed by formal treaty. The dominions of Ibn Saud were unified into the kingdom of Saudi Arabia in 1932.

The periodic outbreaks in Palestine have had their reactions in Transjordan, where the sympathy of the people has been unanimously with the Arabs in Palestine. No colonization or settlement by immigrant Jews in Transjordan is permitted. The proposal made by the Royal Commission in 1937 to unite an Arab State in Palestine with the Amirate of Transjordan (p. 130) at first secured the support of Abdulla; but when he found that in this attitude he stood almost alone, both among his own people and among the rulers and people of neighbouring states, his support of the project was withdrawn.

## CHAPTER XVI

# THE PEOPLE AND THEIR GOVERNMENT

## THE PEOPLE

THERE has been no census of Transjordan. The population is estimated at from 300,000 to 350,000, although in 1940 a figure as high as 440,000 was suggested.[1] It is overwhelmingly Arab, but has small groups of Circassians, Chechens, Turkomans, Bahai, Armenians, and Druses, of whom only the Druses (p. 143) are Arab in origin. There are also a few Europeans, almost all of them British officers and officials. The great majority of the people are Moslems, of the orthodox Sunni sect, and in accordance with Article 10 of the Organic Law, Islam is the state religion. There are, however, about 20,000 Christian Arabs, and the Armenians and Europeans are of course Christians, while the Druses and Bahai are heretical offshoots of Islam.

The *Arabs* of Transjordan are the descendants of tribes which have come northwards in the nomadic state, by a process of slow migration which has been continuing from time immemorial. These tribes were not always nomadic, but were composed of families originally settled in the south, driven by economic pressure and over-population into the desert, where they adopted the way of life best suited to desert conditions, families forming themselves into clans, and clans into tribes under patriarchal discipline. Pressure from behind drove them on from one oasis to another. Some succumbed; others combined into larger confederations under leaders or warriors of character, and held their ground for a while or were driven to more northern wells, whence they raided centres of settlement on the desert's edge and caravans passing between them. The fittest survived to reach Syria and Iraq, where they came up against those who had gone before them, halted, and settled down. Under this contact they become less nomadic but still tented communities, less dependent on their flocks and cultivating the land, and in course of time they lose their cohesion and organization, and eventually their tribal status. Tribes break away from confederations, clans from tribes, and

---

[1] Estimates vary greatly: the *Encyclopaedia Britannica* gives 30,000 Circassians and Chechens and 40,000 Christians. According to the High Commissioner's Report of 1924, these figures should be 10,000 and 15,000 respectively, but his report of 1935 reduces the former figure to 7,000.

H h

families from clans, till the units become absorbed into the villages and towns, only to combine again in time of stress.

This reinforcement of Arabian stock in Palestine and Syria is going on to-day. Transjordan, at the frontier between the desert and the sown, shows well the latest stage. All three types of community are represented: the sedentary or settled, the semi-nomads, and the beduin—the first living in fear of the second and the second of the third.

The settled inhabitants (130,000–150,000), who include also all the non-Arab peoples, live in houses in the towns and in many of the villages. They are concentrated in the north-west. Almost all the population of the Ajlun district, the ancient Gilead, is sedentary, the chief centres being Husn, Irbid, and Jerash. In the Belka and Amman districts, farther south, about half are sedentary, Es Salt and Amman being the chief towns. Elsewhere there is no fully settled population except in the towns of Kerak, Maan, and Akaba.

The semi-nomads (130,000–150,000) are organized by clans and tribes, and dwell in tents, but cultivate the land. They comprise the other half of the Belka and Amman highland populations, most of the inhabitants of the Kerak district, and a small part of those in the Maan district.

The nomad beduin (40,000–50,000) are found scattered throughout the rest of the country. They are entirely dependent on their flocks, and cultivate no land. They live on the fringe of the desert on both sides of the Hejaz railway, based on certain groups of wells, and in varying states of allegiance, alliance, or feud with one another. There is a continual ebb and flow of seasonal nomadism, some clans moving across into Palestine, others into Arabia and back again. In winter and in a favourable year when the desert pastures can maintain them the movement is eastwards; in summer and in drier winters the movement is westwards, to profit from the rain. Some regularly winter in the Jordan valley, and it is impossible to assign them as inhabitants of either Palestine or Transjordan. Some move into Palestine or Syria in times of drought, or at harvest time for temporary employment, though there is a bigger influx for this purpose from the Negeb and Sinai than from Transjordan. Most of this movement is seasonal, and when the drought is broken or the harvest gathered, all of these nomads return.

*Beduin Tribes*

The wholly nomadic tribes of Transjordan are broadly divisible into two groups: 'the people of the north' and 'the people of the south'. This division is officially recognized in the Electoral Law of 1928, the beduin of the north comprising the Beni Sukhr, Sirhan, Beni Khalid, Issa, and Sleit, with the tribes and clans under their protection, and those of the south being the Howeitat, the Manaiyoun, and the Hajaya, also with their protected communities. The Beduin Control Law of 1929 adds the Kaabna, Najadat, and the Rasheida to those of the south, but the Najadat have since acknowledged the supremacy of the Ibn Jazi section of the Howeitat (*see below*). No details are available concerning the Kaabna and the Rasheida, but they may be sub-tribes either protected by or broken away from a larger group. In Musil's time (*c.* 1900), the Manaiyoun (Mannaiyyin) appear to have been a branch of the Hajaya, but have since become independent.

The two tribes which have played the greatest part in recent Transjordan history and politics are the Howeitat of the southern group and the Beni Sukhr of the northern.

The Howeitat of Transjordan are the Howeitat Ibn Jazi, one of the three branches of the tribe. They include both nomads and semi-nomads. In 1918 authority over this branch was divided between Hamad Ibn Jazi, representing the old line of paramount sheikhs, and Auda abu Tayi, the fierce old warrior who accompanied Lawrence on many of his exploits (p. 456). Auda took a leading part in the disturbances of 1921, connected with Syrian troubles, and was also suspected of intriguing with the Wahhabis (p. 463). After arrest and imprisonment at Es Salt in 1922, he escaped to Baghdad, but was pardoned and returned to Transjordan in January 1924. He died in Amman after a surgical operation the following summer. Throughout these years Hamad remained a strong supporter of Abdulla, and after Auda's death the whole of the Howeitat recognized him as paramount sheikh. He has since become a leading landowner of the country, with estates at Rashidiya.

The Beni Sukhr bore the brunt of the Wahhabi attack in August 1922 (p. 463), but are said to have threatened to secede to the Wahhabis unless the Amir's government could protect them. When victory was won, however, they received a subsidy for their services, and have since remained loyal.

The Wahhabi attack had its roots deep in Arabia, but frontier troubles of local significance are not uncommon. Many feuds that had been composed by Feisal during the years of liberation were renewed afterwards. Some were fostered by Syrian agitators, others were of longer standing, and yet others arose directly from disputes over wells or pastures. It is difficult for the beduin to respect a political boundary, especially when it exists only on a map. Seasonal nomadism eastwards or westwards over the border is common to Iraq, Syria, and Palestine and is not a military aggression. The clans of the Ruwalla based on Jauf in Nejd may be in alliance or at feud with Transjordan clans. In 1930 the Transjordan Howeitat and the Beni Sukhr clashed with the Mashhur clan of the Ruwalla who pasture in the Wadi Sirhan. The trouble was probably caused by some incident which occurred when the Tawayiha clan of the Ibn Jazi Howeitat, formerly under Auda abu Tayi and based at Jafr, was pasturing across the frontier in the same area. Few casualties are caused in such affrays, but they are troublesome and may lead to wider issues. As the result of this campaign the Tawayiha clan no longer crosses the frontier.

There have also been minor troubles with the settled Arabs at times, particularly in the early 'twenties, but they have been of less consequence during the last ten years. The most serious occurred in 1923 when the settled Adwan Arabs, led by their chief, Sultan Adwan, and supported by the Beni Hasan and other semi-nomad tribes of the Belka, revolted and cut the road and telephone communications between Es Salt and Amman. Prompt action by government troops quickly quelled the rising; Sultan Adwan took refuge with the Syrian Druses, but was subsequently pardoned.

Gradually the country has settled down, and such clashes, both internal and external, are now less frequent. The election to the Legislative Council of the two leading beduin chiefs, Mithkal Pasha el Faiz of the Beni Sukhr for the north and Hamad Ibn Jazi of the Howeitat for the south, has led to a growth of nationalism, and in 1937 these two chiefs founded the Party of National Fraternity (*Hizb el Akha el Watani*), with which were associated Rufeifan Pasha and Majid Pasha, heads of two of the largest settled tribes, the Majali and the Adwan. The party was nationalist and ostensibly formed to support the Amir.

## Non-Arab Communities

None of the non-Arab communities are numerous. The *Circassians* formerly lived on the western slopes of the Caucasus leading down to the Black Sea and were settled by Sultan Abdul Hamid in Transjordan after the loss of their homes as the result of the Russo-

Turkish war of 1877–1878. They occupy eight villages in the Belka district, with their principal centres at Wadi Sir, Jerash, Naur, and Suweileh. Circassians formerly predominated in Amman, but as it grew to become the capital it attracted a larger Arab population, though there are still about 1,700 Circassians there.

*Chechens* also settled in Transjordan as a result of Russian encroachment. They used to live in the mountains of Daghistan at the eastern end of the Caucasus, and withstood the Russian advance until their country was ultimately conquered in 1864. Many then emigrated to other parts of the Ottoman Empire; some, as well as the later emigrant Circassians, were placed by the Sultan on the eastern fringe of the settled land, partly as a counterpoise to the Arab communities who were none too loyal and equally warlike. The Chechens are found mostly in the villages of Suweileh, Zerka, Rusaifa, and Sukhneh.

*Turkomans* also settled in the country during the Ottoman period, but most of them withdrew with the Ottoman troops. Only one Turkoman settlement remains, at Rumman south of Jerash. The few *Bahai* at Adassia, a hamlet south of Lake Tiberias, are part of the Bahai community of Haifa (p. 144). After the suppression of the Druse rebellion against the French in Syria in 1927, a number of *Druses* took refuge in Transjordan; most of them subsequently returned to Jebel Druse, though some remained and settled down. In 1936 there were said to be 312 *Armenians*, of whom only 172 were Transjordanian subjects.

In the same year there were listed about 1,900 foreigners, of whom 855 were Syrians, 515 Palestinians, 56 British subjects—excluding British troops—and 37 other Europeans and Americans. All but about 300 of the foreigners were Arab by blood. There is now no appreciable emigration, and no immigration since the Druse country settled down, but a few shopkeepers, mostly from Nablus, make homes in Amman, and there is the seasonal nomadism to and fro across the frontiers which has already been mentioned (p. 466).

## Births and Deaths

Though there are no census figures, births and deaths have been registered annually since 1926. As in all Moslem countries the figures cannot be considered complete, though they probably approximate to the truth in recent years. They are said to include all classes of the population—settled, semi-nomads, and beduin.

## Registered Number of Births and Deaths

| Year | Births | Deaths | Natural increase | Infant mortality per 1,000 |
|------|--------|--------|------------------|----------------------------|
| 1926 | 3,483  | 2,939  | 544    | 131 |
| 1930 | 10,340 | 6,661  | 3,679  | 222 |
| 1934 | 10,742 | 7,925  | 2,817  | 242 |
| 1938 | 12,746 | 5,627  | 7,119  | 181 |
| 1939 | 13,969 | 5,473  | 8,496  | 171 |
| 1940 | 13,135 | 5,273  | 7,862  | .. |

Assuming a total population of 300,000 in 1938—a government estimate was 300,214 in that year—the rates per 1,000 for that year were: births, 42·5; deaths, 18·8; net increase 23·7. The estimated population at the end of 1941 would therefore be approximately 330,000 (p. 465).

### Religion

There is little to be added on the subject of religion to what has already been written in Part I. The great majority are Sunni Moslems and there is no religious problem in Transjordan as there is in Palestine. The hostility of certain tribes to European Christians, particularly in the neighbourhood of Petra, is much less than it used to be (p. 454), but care must always be taken not to offend Moslem susceptibilities.

Christianity in Transjordan goes back to a very early period (p. 444). At the Arab conquest a great part of the population embraced Islam, and almost all of the later arrivals from the south have been Moslems. But Christianity has survived, not only in the towns but also among a few semi-nomadic tribes. In the Kerak district there are Christian clans, only distinguishable from their Moslem fellow-tribesmen by their religion, their priests who are beduin, and their churches which are tents. Most are Orthodox Christians under the Orthodox Patriarch of Jerusalem (p. 148), with principal centres at Es Salt, Kerak, and Husn. The Latin Patriarch of Jerusalem and the Melkite Archbishop of Galilee also have small congregations in Transjordan under a Vicar-General and a bishop respectively. The spiritual needs of the small Anglican community, which is under the Anglican Bishop in Jerusalem, are served mainly by the Church Missionary Society. Other communities are the Armenians and the Greek Catholics.

*Education*

Arabic is the language of the country and of instruction, but English is taught in all the government schools and in most of those of the Christian communities. Education is free. The Government Department of Education has established elementary or secondary schools for boys in all the towns and for girls in the six principal ones. There are village schools in all parts of the country. Two schools have been established at desert wells for sons of beduin sheikhs. But it is not easy in such a country to find employment for these boys, born to be the natural leaders of tribal raids and desert life. Some are being trained as wireless operators, others as motor mechanics. Most schools have gardens where pupils are taught horticulture. There is a government school of Arts and Crafts at Amman. Some boys attend the American university at Beirut, the government Arab College and St. George's School in Jerusalem, and three girls were recently in the Women's Training College and the English Girls' College, Jerusalem. British Council scholarships are also occasionally held by young men of Transjordan at British universities. Outside the government system the Christian communities maintain schools in their towns and villages. Of these there are seven—two Church of England, two Roman Catholic, and three administered by American churches.

The number of pupils in the schools of Transjordan in 1940 are given in the following table:

### Government Schools

| Type | Schools Boys | Schools Girls | Pupils Boys | Pupils Girls |
|------|------|------|------|------|
| Town elementary | 12 | 9 | 3,828 | 1,840 |
| Village elementary | 45 | 1 | 3,821 | 55 |
| Desert | 2 | .. | 113 | .. |
| Arts and crafts | 1 | .. | 70 | .. |
| Secondary | 4 | .. | 423 | .. |
| Total | 64 | 10 | 8,255 | 1,895 |

These figures show increases of 1,423 boys and 215 girls on the previous year. The number of government schools was unchanged. Of the pupils in the government schools 9,043 (7,569 in 1939) are Moslems and 1,107 (943 in 1939) Christians.

Of 6,605 pupils in 116 private schools in 1940 there were 4,155 boys and 2,450 girls (2,086 Moslems and 4,519 Christians), an increase of 1,263 pupils (613 Moslems and 650 Christians) on the previous year.

*Culture*

Of art, music, literature, and the drama in Transjordan nothing can be said. There is only one newspaper—a small sheet that appears intermittently. There is a central library available to the public in Amman, where some steps have been taken by the Government to promote urban development.

The many sites of antiquity do not interest the villagers except as illicit sources of stone work; but they are conserved by a government inspector, visited by a growing number of students and tourists, and excavated by archaeological missions under government licence and supervision. Movable antiquities are national property in law, and the more important finds are claimed for the Department of Antiquities, but there is surreptitious traffic with foreign visitors and dealers.

## GOVERNMENT

*Central Government*

TRANSJORDAN is subject to the Mandate of the League of Nations, entrusted to Great Britain, for both Palestine and Transjordan. The terms for the two countries are identical, excepting that those clauses relating to the Jewish National Home are expressly excluded from application to Transjordan. Until 1928 one High Commissioner acted for both countries on behalf of Great Britain. Separate high commissionerships were then formed, though the two offices are still held by the same official, who resides in Jerusalem. The High Commissioner for Transjordan is represented in the country by a British Resident.

The ruler of Transjordan (1943) is His Highness the Amir Abdulla Ibn Hussein, G.C.M.G., G.B.E., born in Mecca in 1882, whose rights and powers as Amir are set out in the Organic Law. This instrument declares the equality of Transjordanian subjects, irrespective of race, religion, and language; and guarantees their personal freedom and right of access to courts of law, and their rights of ownership. Islam is recognized as the state religion, Arabic as the official language; but communities have the right to establish and maintain schools where teaching may be in their own language. The Amir may appoint consuls in foreign territories, but all communication with foreign governments is in the hands of the High Commissioner or of the British Government. Advisers appointed by the High Commissioner control judicial and fiscal matters, and public finance.

The British Government is authorized to maintain armed forces in the country.

Until 1939 the Amir was assisted by an Executive Council and a Legislative Assembly. In that year the Executive Council was replaced by a Cabinet of six ministers. The Legislative Assembly is composed of these ministers and sixteen other members elected for five years. The latter are made up of nine settled Moslem Arabs, three Christians, two Caucasians, and two Beduin. At the head of this administration is the Prime Minister.

All male Transjordan residents of eighteen years and upwards are entitled to vote. There is a special procedure for the appointment of the beduin representatives. The Judicial and Financial Advisers, who are British officials, attend meetings of the Cabinet and the Legislative Assembly, but are not entitled to vote.

A Beduin Control Board with statutory powers was set up in 1929 to control the movements of the beduin, to check raids, and to settle inter-tribal disputes. It consisted of a member of the Amir's family, the British Officer in command of the Arab Legion (p. 475), and a beduin sheikh.

*Divisional Government*

Transjordan is divided into the Desert Area, and four administrative divisions, known as *Montakas* or *Liwas* (Ajlun, Belka, Kerak, and Maan), each under a governor. The settled parts of these divisions are subdivided into districts, under officers who have the help of administrative councils consisting each of two official and four unofficial members, in addition to the Administrative officer who is chairman. If the Christian population exceeds 500, one of the unofficial members must be a Christian, and if this population exceeds 1,000 a second Christian member is appointed. The Desert Area is under the jurisdiction of the Beduin Control Board.

*Municipal Government*

There are municipal councils at Amman, Es Salt, Irbid, Kerak, Maan, Madeba, Ajlun, Jerash, and Tafileh, several of which are villages rather than towns. Most members are elected by the local male residents, but provision is made for the representation of all important communities, and technical members are appointed by the Prime Minister. The presidents of these councils are selected by the Government from among the elected members, except at Amman, where the president may be chosen from any of the members.

Municipal estimates are framed by the councils, but are subject to approval by the Prime Minister. Revenues are derived chiefly from a local octroi tax on goods imported from abroad, and from government grants apportioned to the municipalities from central funds. The councils also have the power to levy rates for general purposes and for education.

## ADMINISTRATION

The departments of the Government are Justice, Finance, Customs, Education, Lands, Agriculture and Forestry, Public Works, Antiquities, Public Security, Public Health, Development, and Posts and Telegraphs. Some account of education has been given above (p. 471). Antiquities are noted upon on p. 472, and certain historical sites are described in Appendix D. Below are given brief notes on Justice, Lands, Public Security, and Public Health (p. 476). Finance, Customs, Agriculture and Forestry, Public Works, Development, and Communications are dealt with in Chapter XVII.

### JUSTICE

The laws in force in Transjordan were, until April 1940, comprised in the Ottoman codes unless altered by local legislation. Since that date local legislation has prevailed in all spheres, and the Ottoman legislation has been repealed. There is a Court of Appeal at Amman, Courts of First Instance at Amman, Irbid, and Kerak, and Magistrates' Courts in these three towns and also at Es Salt, Madeba, Jerash, Ajlun, Maan, and Tafileh. The trial of foreigners is subject to special agreement with His Majesty's Government.

The Religious Courts consist of (a) *Sharia* or Moslem Courts, and (b) Religious Community Councils. The Sharia courts have exclusive jurisdiction in matters of the personal status of Moslems and are guided by Moslem law. They have also jurisdiction in matters connected with the constitution or internal administration of Moslem Waqfs (p. 203). In cases of mixed suits the Civil Courts have jurisdiction unless both parties accept that of the Sharia courts. The Religious Community Councils deal with the non-Moslem religious communities, and each has similar jurisdiction over members of its own community.

Among the beduin tribal law prevails, one of the oldest systems of law still existing, and closely akin to that which formed the basis of both Jewish and Moslem law. It is framed to suit a primitive nomadic people and differs from the systems of long-settled peoples by regarding the tribe or family, not the individual, as the unit. For instance, if a man wrongs a relative, it is for the family to decide the matter; if he wrongs a member of his own tribe, it is a tribal affair; but if he wrongs a beduin of another tribe, the central authority must promptly intervene if inter-tribal bloodshed is to be avoided. Punishment among beduin for the most part takes the form of retaliation. Among them the Mosaic law of retribution, 'an eye for an eye, a tooth for a tooth', is still widely followed. Until 1936 the settlement of inter-tribal disputes was the duty of the Beduin Control Board, but on the death of the representative of the Amir's family a change was made. Since then, tribal courts, composed of judges selected from a panel of sheikhs by the contending tribes, have been set up. There is a Tribal Court of Appeal.

The Land Settlement Court is the only 'special' court so far established.

## LANDS

The system of land tenure follows generally that of Palestine (pp. 208–10), except that in Transjordan, where so large a part is practically uninhabited, the beduin tribes virtually possess very large tracts over which their members pasture their flocks and herds. In the settled districts the Turkish registers of ownership are, as in Palestine, practically useless and a new cadastral survey of properties and of village boundaries is being made. At the same time *mashaa* land, hitherto held in common, is gradually being divided among the villagers.

## PUBLIC SECURITY

The Arab Legion of 47 officers and 1,577 men forms the police force, both urban and rural. It is also charged with transport, passport, and prison control, and with the protection of the oil pipe-line in Transjordan territory (p. 516), the additional cost of which is defrayed by the Iraq Petroleum Company. The Desert Patrol, a special section of the Arab Legion, is recruited from beduin, for the purpose of maintaining security in the desert.

The Transjordan Frontier Force is a military body of some 700 men, recruited in Palestine and Transjordan, and commanded by selected British officers. Based at Zerka, Maan, and Tel Or in Transjordan and at Rosh Pinna in Palestine, it forms, with detachments of the Royal Air Force stationed at Amman and Maan, the standing garrison for the protection of the country; and because the safety of Palestine is dependent on that of Transjordan, as it has been throughout the centuries, five-sixths of the cost of maintaining the military force is defrayed out of Palestine funds (pp. 281–2).

## PUBLIC HEALTH

### Medical Organization

The Department of Health maintains hospitals of 20 beds at Amman and 12 beds at Irbid. There are epidemic posts at Irbid, Amman, Kerak, and Maan, and small posts (4 beds) at Jerash, Tafileh, and Akaba. A most interesting and valuable development has been the Desert Mobile Medical Unit, which generally moves about east of the railway, conducting clinics and nursing small numbers of sick under canvas. The department is in close touch with the Palestine Department of Health and is dependent on that organization for certain specialist help, particularly in laboratory diagnosis; with a personnel almost entirely Arab, it suffices for the needs of a small and rather poor country. There are as yet no vital statistics of any value, even in the settled areas.

In addition to the government hospitals, there is a Royal Air Force sick quarters at Amman with accommodation for 2 officers and 8 airmen, and at Es Salt a long-established hospital with 30 beds and an X-ray apparatus is maintained by the Church Missionary Society. The latter with its out-stations deals yearly with some 20,000 out-patient attendances and 800 in-patients, and performs about 200 major operations. A small mission hospital, mainly for women, is privately supported in Amman, and until the outbreak of war the Italian Government maintained charitable hospitals at Amman (40 beds) and Kerak (36 beds). At the two stations of the Iraq Petroleum Company there are four-bed dressing-stations, and at one of them is stationed an assistant medical officer with motor-ambulance.

### Principal Diseases

There is no precise information about the incidence of intestinal diseases, nor about the deaths caused by them. But they are, as elsewhere, especially prevalent among young children. Among children under two years of age in Transjordan the death-rate for towns only is as high as 178 per thousand, which may be compared with figures of from 40 to 100 for cities of western Europe or North

America. It is also known, from the surrounding territories, that a large proportion of these deaths in infants are due to diarrhoea and enteritis, the death-rate from these diseases being often a hundred-fold greater than in Europe. These intestinal diseases are infectious, and the question arises whether these very high rates could be prevented, or whether they are due in part to climatic or other unavoidable causes. That they can be prevented is suggested by figures for infant mortality in Palestine (pp. 221-2).

Dysentery and enteric (typhoid and paratyphoid) in people of all ages are very frequent. The local Department of Health has been active in the improvement of water-supplies in villages and towns, an important part of the control of all intestinal infections. Diarrhoea and dysentery may be considered inevitable, especially during the warm months, but the incidence could be greatly reduced by familiar measures: the chlorinating or boiling of water; cleanliness in the preparation of food and its protection from flies and dust; avoidance of most types of uncooked food; careful construction and use of latrines; destruction of house-flies and of their breeding-places. Enteric (typhoid and paratyphoid) particularly should be almost entirely eliminated by the general measures outlined above and by protective inoculation.

Though cholera has been absent from the Arab countries for some years, Transjordan must be regarded as a country where it could occur, particularly under conditions which may prevail in war-time.

## Malaria

Malaria only accounts for 3-4 per cent. of all out-patients visiting government dispensaries, and except in the Jordan valley and its tributaries, it is generally a less serious menace than in Palestine (p. 224). An extensive survey, carried out in Transjordan in 1927, revealed a spleen rate of under 10 per cent. in many parts, though no place was found entirely immune. In the most malarious highland places, Zerka, Jerash, Ajlun, and Irbid, the spleen rates were only between 20 and 40 per cent. Figures for the year 1937 show that malaria is still found in the districts of Amman and Es Salt, though spleen rates are lower because of successful local measures for the control of *Anopheles*.

The whole Jordan valley is extremely malarious (pp. 225, 229) and only limited anti-malarial measures are taken by the Public Health Department annually on the eastern tributaries, wadis, springs, and irrigation channels. The slopes of the hills and mountains are malaria-free, but all river valleys and marsh areas between the Jordan and the Hejaz railway may be malarious.

The district east of the railway is free, except the Azrak marshes, about 60 miles east of Amman, and the Chechen settlements of Zerka and Rusaifa. Zerka is well controlled but Rusaifa is dangerous, because of insufficient labour and funds for adequate anti-malarial work. The following are the spleen rates of school children in towns in 1937: Jerash (24·8), Ajlun (7·7), Tafileh (3·6); Es Salt, Madeba, Kerak, Amman, and Maan (all under 1); Irbid and Akaba were free.

The distribution of the *Anopheles* mosquito in Transjordan is complex. In the hill country of the north *Anopheles superpictus* breeds abundantly in summer in small trickles and pools in almost dry stream-beds, and causes the 'hill malaria' which is prevalent in such places as Jerash and Ajlun. Where there is more water, stagnant or moving slowly, there may be *Anopheles elutus*. Some towns and villages which are very far from surface water in summer rely on water stored in cisterns beneath houses. In these cisterns *Anopheles bifurcatus* breeds, or did so until recently, producing that unusual condition 'urban malaria', formerly widespread.

Malaria in Transjordan is complicated by the migratory habits of the people. For instance, many of the beduin camp for the summer on bleak waterless plains, where they are almost safe from the disease. But in winter they move down into the Jordan valley or the Ghor es Safi, where *Anopheles* are active and transmit the disease even in the cool months. Elsewhere malaria is mostly acquired in summer and autumn, though attacks may recur at any time of the year in those who have previously suffered from the disease. Benign tertian malaria is probably dominant in early summer, malignant tertian becoming more frequent from August to November. The frequency of the disease differs greatly from year to year, for if the winter rains are much above the normal, and particularly if heavy rain occurs late in the spring, there will be much surface water and the springs will remain full even until the late summer, thus yielding particularly favourable breeding-places for the *Anopheles*.

## Typhus Group

Both the Mediterranean types of typhus, epidemic (exanthematous) and murine, occur in Transjordan, which notifies between 20 and 70 cases yearly. But it is known that louse-carried epidemics have occurred, as they would doubtless do again in the event of war or famine. Typhus may be epidemic not only in towns and villages but also among nomads.

The eruptive fever of the Mediterranean (*fièvre boutonneuse*) may be expected to occur in Transjordan. The infection is transmitted to man by the dog tick, *Rhipicephalus sanguineus*, which is abundant in summer.

## Relapsing Fever

Two distinct types of relapsing fever probably occur. The tick-carried type is properly an infection of rats and wild rodents. It is known to occur in several different parts of Palestine, and presumably occurs in Transjordan. Occasionally an infected tick bites a man, particularly one whose work brings him into close contact with rats or wild rodents. The disease is therefore sporadic and uncommon. The second type, which is transmitted by lice, occurs only in human beings, and may produce widespread epidemics. The louse-carried epidemic relapsing fever has not been recorded from Transjordan for some years, but it is no doubt present. Control of the disease is by destruction of lice, especially body lice.

## Leishmaniasis

A small number of cases of oriental sore or dermal leishmaniasis have been seen in Amman and Jerash. In Transjordan it is probable that oriental sore is transmitted by sand-flies (*Phlebotomus papatasii*).

## Deficiency Diseases

Malnutrition and deficiency diseases rank high as a cause of sickness, incapacity, and death, at least among the nomads, though it is difficult to assess their importance and distinguish their effects among the other infections and diseases which are so rife among these people. According to a report by the medical officer in charge of the Desert Mobile Medical Unit, xerophthalmia is common, as a consequence of the lack of vitamin A, and even in a normal year scurvy, caused by lack of vitamin C, is serious and not rare. In the spring, following the winter rain, the grazing is good and milk is abundant, but in autumn and winter these people are very close to starvation. Their life becomes much more severe if rain is deficient, for this may lead to a lack of wheat and barley, and also of grazing for the sheep and camels.

The whole position of the beduin in the Arab lands, both in Asia and Africa, is now critical. In the old days they made their livelihood partly by hiring camels for transport. Lorries and motor-cars are replacing the camel; raiding is suppressed, and beduin find it very difficult to obtain a livelihood.

The lot of the villagers is much better than that of the nomads, for, judged by local standards, they are well housed and well fed, because of their domestic animals and of their variety of cereals, fruits, and vegetables, some of which are grown under irrigation. But even the villagers may come near to starvation owing to failure of rain, or outbreaks of locusts, field mice, and other pests.

### Venereal Diseases

It is often said, on most inadequate grounds, that venereal diseases are particularly common. A very mild form of syphilis, known as *bejel*, occurs in country districts. It is held by some that this infection is most commonly transmitted by close contact, such as the use of coffee cups and tobacco pipes in common, or the treatment of an ulcer with an old clout removed from another man's sores. On the clinical side *bejel* most commonly attacks the soft structures in the mouth and pharynx.

### Diseases of the Eye

Diseases of the lids and conjunctiva are extremely prevalent throughout the Arab world. Among the nomads it is thought possible that malnutrition, and particularly the deficiency of vitamin A, may be a predisposing cause to conjunctivitis, even if it is not so severe as to produce xerophthalmia.

### Other Fevers

European troops spending their first summer in the Mediterranean would almost certainly suffer from epidemics of *sand-fly fever*, which might incapacitate whole units for periods of a few weeks. At the peak of an epidemic 30 or even 50 per cent. of new arrivals might be sick or convalescent at the same time. The epidemic season is from May to October inclusive. Sand-flies (*Phlebotomus papatasii* and other species) are very widely distributed and prevalent.

Epidemics of *dengue*, transmitted by *Aëdes aegypti*, might also occur, but only in summer and only in towns or large villages.

Small-pox has been greatly reduced by systematic vaccination, which is well understood and highly valued.

*Other Diseases*

Among the diseases which are less important (or perhaps less studied) *tuberculosis* must not be overlooked. In all countries it is a difficult matter to obtain an accurate conception of its occurrence: in Palestine and Transjordan it is generally held to be a common and serious cause of sickness and death. *Hookworm* is absent, or so rare as to be insignificant. The common intestinal worms (*Ascaris*, *Trichuris*, &c.) are doubtless prevalent.

In times of scarcity, for instance if locusts are numerous and rain deficient, the people may be driven to eat the pea *Lathyrus sativus* which is grown for oxen and camels. A considerable number of unfortunates are then afflicted by an incurable paralysis of the limbs, their general health remaining good.

Water at nearly all the stations along the oil pipe-lines (from Kirkuk to Tripoli and Haifa) contains over one part in one million of fluorides. The figure is rather high, but it is probable that adults could drink this water for long periods without harm.

*Pests*

Many of the biting insects have already been referred to, in connexion with the diseases which they transmit. Those not previously mentioned include domestic mosquitoes, of which the most troublesome is *Culex pipiens*: it very commonly breeds in cesspits. Bed bugs are extremely common in towns and villages, and fleas are troublesome in April and May. Scorpions are probably common and most active in summer. The sting is extremely painful, but not very serious. The black spider, *Latrodectus 13-guttata*, almost certainly occurs in Transjordan: the bite may produce intense pain and loss of consciousness. A mite (*Pediculoides*, related to the itch-mite) which occurs in barley and straw attacks the human skin, and causes serious eruptions in people who handle these materials. It is common in many subtropical lands, and in the eastern Mediterranean area is particularly troublesome. The large grey fly *Wohlfahrtia magnifica* puts its maggots in wounds and cuts, on men or animals. The maggots destroy tissues with great rapidity, and spread sepsis. This insect may occasion a considerable amount of serious injury.

## CHAPTER XVII

# ECONOMIC GEOGRAPHY

TRANSJORDAN has few economic activities, mainly because the population depends almost entirely on subsistence agriculture and nomadic pastoral pursuits. Possibilities of development are limited by scarcity of natural resources, by climatic difficulties, and by lack of capital. Communications, though ill developed, are adequate for the needs of the country in its present condition. The chief incentives to further progress in economic organization arise from the pressure of population on the land and from the position of Transjordan in relation to neighbouring countries. The former requires better control of the use of the land, which would lead to an increase in production and commerce. The latter indicates that greater provision might be made for through communications by railway as well as by road.

In this chapter are described the mineral resources, industry, labour supply and organization, agriculture and forestry, commerce and finance, and communications. Notes are included on the Departments of Development and Public Works, and the only port, Akaba, is described at the end with the coasts of Palestine and Transjordan on the gulf of Akaba.

## MINERALS

No mines are worked in Transjordan, and the existence of minerals on a scale justifying commercial exploitation in present circumstances has not yet been proved. Under the amended Organic Law, all rights in mines and minerals, subject to prior concessionary rights, are vested in and may be exercised by the Amir in trust for the Transjordan Government, and grants or leases for the exploitation of mineral resources are made under the Mining Law of 1926, which follows generally the terms of the Palestine Mining Ordinance of 1925. Exploration for oil in commercial quantities has so far given only negative results. There is one seepage of liquid petroleum at the base of the Nubian sandstone at Ain Umma, on the east of the Dead Sea about 2½ miles south of the Wadi Mojib; the oil is asphaltic, with about 23 per cent. sulphur, and in some respects is similar to 'Heavy Mexican Crude'. Elsewhere, extensive scope for investigation and possible development is indicated by the occurrence of bituminous limestone and of bitumen and oil in the Nubian sandstone. Bituminous limestone is fairly widespread in northern and central Transjordan, though it does not occur in the south. Near the Yarmuk river and the Syrian frontier it is over 300 feet in thickness, with considerable variation in bitumen content. In central Transjordan, on the other hand, the bituminous limestone appears to be found only in basins or troughs, separated by chalk beds. Bitumen occurs also in the Nubian sandstone south of Draa (10 miles north-west of Kerak) and is occasionally dislodged by earthquakes from the bed of the Dead Sea.

Iron ore was worked in the Crusading period near Jerash, and slag-heaps are still to be seen at Ajlun. Commercial exploitation of the Zerka district ores is at present hindered not so much by lack of a market as by transport and fuel difficulties. About 22 miles of rope railway would be necessary to link the mine with Samakh, and there is no fuel available for smelting on the spot, nor is water power sufficient for electricity. A vein of pure haematite has been discovered south of Petra; it varies from 2 to 12 inches in thickness, but is not thought to be deep. Great copper slag-heaps are widespread in the ill-explored districts of southern Transjordan, especially at Feinan, and there is evidence of early copper smelting near Akaba. This ancient activity has been attributed to King Solomon, as a source of his mineral riches (p. 436), but modern investigation of these old workings has revealed only cupriferous sandstone deposits and no rich mineral veins. In the Wadi Dana south of Tafileh there are manganese deposits, estimated at about 5,000 tons, but probably more extensive. Ochre and alum have been found near the hot springs of the Wadi Zerka-Main and at Khabara on a tributary of the Wadi Jerash, but neither of these deposits is thought to be of much consequence.

Rich phosphate beds have been discovered at Rusaifa, 7 miles north-east of Amman, and in 1936 a local company was formed .to exploit them. In 1942 it was announced that rock phosphate, quarried there, was being used in the manufacture of fertilizers in Palestine. There are extensive deposits of gypsum in the south-west of Transjordan, near the Dead Sea. The first bed suitable for development was found in the Wadi Hasa, and a second is exposed on the sides of the Wadi Kerak on the road between Kerak and Draa. Gypsum also occurs in workable quantities in the Wadi Mojib to the north and near the Wadi Huni in the Wadi Zerka; but compared with the Kerak deposits, which are linked by road to Mezra on the Dead Sea and could be fitted with a rope railway, these deposits are likely to remain undeveloped for lack of transport.

The chief building-stones are limestones, of which those of the Amman and Jerash districts have in the past been most widely used. The most important of these in the Amman district is a yellowish marble, from quarries within 5 miles of Amman on the Suweileh and Naur roads; most of the recent buildings in Amman, as well as the Amir's palace, the Residency, and the Ottoman Bank, are built of this stone. In the Jerash district, besides a hard crystalline limestone used mainly for important buildings where its strength was particularly suitable for columns and façades, there is a softer stone, used for bridges and domes because of its lightness, and a brown limestone peculiar to the district and specially suitable for quarrying by ancient methods because it is soft and easily dressed. The present village of Jerash is largely built from the stones of the Graeco-Roman ruins. Sandstones, though there are several exposures hard enough to make good building-stone, have not often been used, and buildings of Nubian sandstone are limited to the Petra and Nabataean culture periods.

Other mineral resources in Transjordan include salt deposits at Azrak, the chemical content of the Dead Sea, and a number of mineral springs. The southern works of the Palestine Potash Company (p. 258) are in Transjordan territory, and the Transjordan Government participates in the royalties. Of the mineral springs, the largest issues at a high temperature from basaltic rocks about $2\frac{1}{2}$ miles up the Wadi Zerka-Main, mixes with the water of an adjoining cold spring, and flows down to the Dead Sea through a gorge of striking beauty. In composition the water is similar to that of Tiberias (p. 259), but is also sulphurous; it is so hot that it is only just bearable to the human body. Three miles south of the Zerka-Main are several thermal springs, sulphurous and saline, which have been identified with the classical Callirrhoe, visited by Herod the Great on the advice of his physicians during his last illness. Modern baths have recently revived the function of their ancient counterpart, and a road has been built by the Government to link the spring in the Wadi Zerka-Main through Madeba with Amman. There is also a small chalybeate spring near the mouth of the Zerka river. For mineral springs at El Hammeh on the Palestine–Transjordan–Syrian border see p. 259.

## INDUSTRIES

Transjordan is a pastoral and agricultural country, and except for some tailoring and dyeing, two small tobacco factories at Amman, and three small distilleries near Es Salt it has no industries. Wines, spirits, tobacco, and cigarettes are the only industrial products. Production figures for these are as follows:

| Year | Wines and spirits (gals.) | | | | | Cigarettes (lb.) | Cut tobacco (lb.) |
| | Cognac | Arak | Wine | Methylated spirit | Alcohol | | |
|---|---|---|---|---|---|---|---|
| 1933 | 2,944 | 6,120 | 1,392 | .. | .. | 57,180 | 65,408 |
| 1934 | 2,279 | 6,237 | 1,486 | .. | .. | 51,080 | 54,314 |
| 1935 | 2,368 | 5,428 | 1,535 | .. | .. | 45,814 | 49,027 |
| 1936 | 2,436 | 5,631 | 1,588 | 427 | 17 | 48,166 | 88,989 |
| 1937 | 2,356 | 5,778 | 1,247 | 380 | 8 | 44,765 | 104,643 |
| 1938 | 2,527 | 6,611 | 1,319 | 292 | 4 | 52,090 | 94,059 |
| 1939 | 3,856 | 8,674 | 1,818 | 457 | 4 | 70,634 | 87,209 |
| 1940 | 5,329 | 8,760 | 1,065 | 687 | 13 | 79,849 | 56,966 |

Pastoral industries include the manufacture of *samne*, a clarified butter made from the milk of sheep and goats, some of which is exported to Palestine, and the domestic manufacture of rugs and sacks from home-produced wool when prices are low. When prices are high most of the wool is sold to merchants for export, mainly to Syria. Among the beduin, livestock are bred on a commercial scale, especially camels and sheep, though the market is fast disappearing.

Fish is very plentiful at Akaba (p. 523), and with better transport and marketing arrangements the fishing industry could be made a source of some profit to the country. Two or three Palestinian companies were formed for the sale of Akaba fish in Palestine, but transport is the chief difficulty, and between October 1940 and March 1941 only 25 tons net weight of fish in ice reached Palestine markets from Transjordan.

*Labour*

Agriculture is practically the only employer of labour, and finds no difficulty in meeting its needs. At the end of harvest and of the ploughing season there is usually a surplus of labour which was formerly absorbed temporarily in Palestine. The two tobacco factories employ only 65 men, and 37 boys between the ages of 15 and 17 years, and the three distilleries employ only 6 men regularly, with some casual and seasonal help. The hours of work in these factories vary from six to nine hours a day. Since Transjordan is mainly a primitive pastoral and agricultural country, with society conducted on patriarchal lines, no legislation is called for by the conditions governing employment, but the International Convention

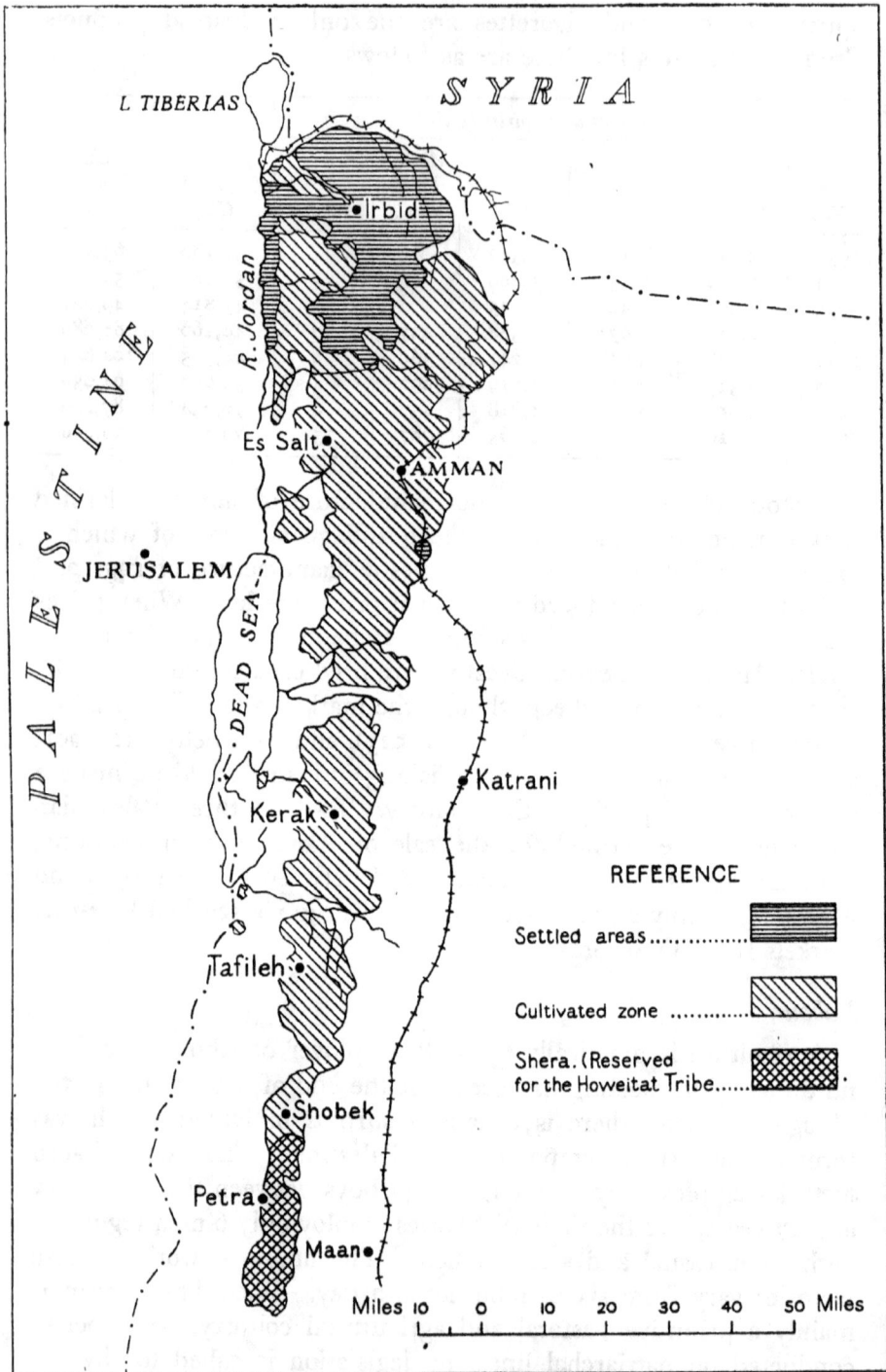

FIG. 56. *The Cultivated Zone of Transjordan.*

prohibiting forced or compulsory labour has been adopted and the necessary legislation passed. Care has also been taken that local legislation shall not be contradictory or repugnant to the terms of the International Labour Conventions on other matters. In the few factories undertakings have been given and are carried out to conform to the draft conventions and recommendations of the International Labour Conference regarding the employment of children. Women and girls do not work outside their homes, except to a small extent in domestic service; boys work with their families in the fields. Dangerous and unhealthy trades are controlled by the Department of Health.

### AGRICULTURE

From the scattered remains of ancient towns, and traces of terraced fields in many districts, it is evident that Transjordan was once far more productive than it is to-day. This decay of ancient prosperity is due largely to the neglect of former elaborate systems of water and soil conservation. In places the surface soil has been washed away, leaving sterile rock exposed, and soil erosion has continued unchecked for so long that in some areas little can now be done to restore former fertility. Over most of the country erosion has reduced the land to its lowest level of productivity, and apart from rock erosion, has ceased altogether. A higher level can only be attained by a progressive policy of soil conservation, carried out through the individual farmer, for Transjordan has no capital to devote to the clearing and terracing of land on a large scale.

The steppe and desert areas east of the Hejaz railway are unsuitable for cultivation except in isolated localities. Unfavourable factors are the lack of permanent watercourses, the low and irregular rainfall, and soils which are often strongly saline. In such inhospitable country only nomads can exist, grazing their camels and flocks on the sparse vegetation which springs up in winter.

Rainfall is thus of the utmost importance to Transjordan, though as shown in Chapter XIV the amount is everywhere small, even when compared with that of other countries with a Mediterranean type of climate. This importance is further intensified by topography, for, with so much of the plateau deeply cut by wadis draining to very low levels, the water-table generally is far below the surface. Thus ground-water cannot be used to any appreciable extent to supplement inadequate rainfall, nor are there many perennial streams. An annual total of 8 inches of rain is taken as the absolute minimum with which dry farming is possible, and even then, only with favourable soils. This low limit is possible only because the standard of living of the cultivators is low (compare the accepted limits for cereal-growing of 12 inches in the Great Plains of the United States of America, in Canada, and in Australia). The area over which the rainfall exceeds 8 inches is estimated at 2,265,250 acres,[1] but of this only about half is cultivable land, the rest being denuded hill-side, bare rock, forest, or scrub. Towards the western edge of the plateau particularly, soil erosion has been severe, and here too topography is unfavourable to cultivation, with deeply incised valleys, steep gorges, and precipitous slopes, dropping away to the floor of the Jordan rift valley.

The cultivated area (fig. 56) thus corresponds roughly with the Mediterranean and steppe regions west of the railway, and is more or less defined by the 8-inch rainfall line (fig. 14). The area is estimated at 1,122,500 acres, of which 65,000 acres are irrigated and the rest dry-farmed. Most of the cultivated land lies at an altitude of from 2,300 to 3,300 feet above sea-level, and here rainfall is normally sufficient for cereal crops. Agriculture is principally centred in the north-west, where rainfall is comparatively high and the land less hilly, particularly between Lake Tiberias and Irbid, where much of the ground is well watered by perennial streams draining to the Yarmuk and Jordan rivers. The width of the cultivated zone is about 30 miles at its widest in the north, but this decreases rapidly southwards and eventually tapers off into the desert south of Maan. The proportion of uncultivated land increases towards the desert, since lower rainfall demands better soils before cultivation is possible, and these are frequently lacking. In the final stage, only land in hollows or in the beds of shallow wadis, which has a slight accumulation of rain-water, can be cultivated. The whole transition is well marked and occupies only 2–3 miles, with the 8-inch rainfall line on its eastern edge.

The average annual rainfall in the cultivable region is about 14 inches compared with 20 inches in Palestine, and the cultivable area is small when compared with the total area of Transjordan. Only about 225,000 acres have a rainfall of over 20 inches; 687,500 acres have over 12 inches, and the rest, 435,000 acres, has between 8 and 12 inches. With a population which is assumed to be increasing, and with no scope for expansion eastwards where dry-farming already extends to the lowest limit of rainfall, land-hunger is showing signs of

[1] A rough approximation of 1 acre = 4 dunams has been used throughout this chapter.

becoming a serious problem. The average holding per agricultural family in Transjordan is estimated at 21 acres, whereas in Palestine, where dry-farmed land receives half as much again of rainfall, a corresponding plot is reckoned to be 32 acres. The position was summed up by the Palestine Partition Commission which visited Transjordan in 1938 and reported: 'In our opinion Transjordan offers small scope for intensive settlement on the land. We do not suggest that it cannot carry a larger agricultural population than it does, but we are convinced that the additional agricultural population which the land can support is small.'

In the northern part of the cultivated zone an area of 100,000 acres stands apart from the rest, lying at an average altitude of 3,000 feet and with rainfall sufficient to ensure a good cereal crop. The rest of the rain-fed cereal area is less favoured. For instance, the Husn–Remtha plain, east of Irbid, and the Madeba plain, south of Amman, where the soil is very fertile, frequently suffer from inadequate rain and disastrously high temperatures. At the southern end of the cultivated zone, the highland of Esh Shera rises from 3,000 feet near Maan to nearly 5,000 feet in the west and south, and only on the higher ground is rainfall occasionally enough to produce cereal crops. The chief use of Esh Shera is for summer grazing by the Howeitat tribe. The lands bordering the eastern desert, and in the Jordan valley or on its slopes, which are usually uncultivable, may cease to be so in years of ample and well-distributed rainfall. The use of this land adds 515,900 acres to the area of the cultivable zone, making in favourable years a total of 1,638,400 acres.

In the desert area there are oases at Azrak and Jafr, but apart from rain-pools there are few other water-points. After a year of good rainfall the grazing will support the camels, sheep, and goats of the nomads who spend their time between the highlands to the west in summer and the Wadi Sirhan and the Ghor in winter.

## Soils

For the soils of Transjordan, see p. 426. In the cultivated zone the most important soil is *Terra Rossa*, which has been derived from the weathering of limestone rocks; it is a deep red, loamy soil with low humus content but rich in mineral salts. Occasionally, where the rocks are softer and more chalky, the soil is modified by the yellow clay found with these rocks, and the grey 'steppe soil' is produced. This has a higher content of lime than Terra Rossa, even less humus, and much more clay, being rather a marl than a loam.

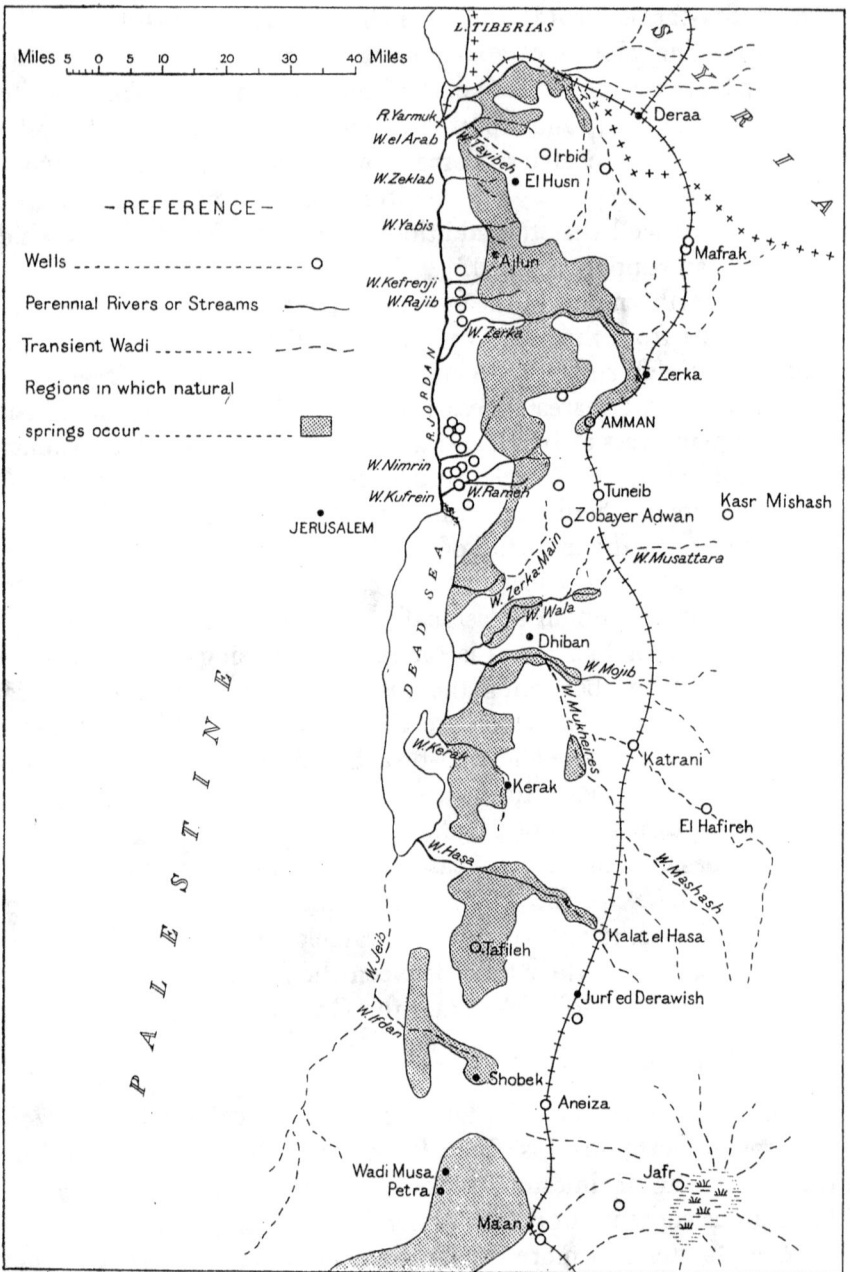

FIG. 57. *Water-supply of Transjordan.*

In the *Jordan valley* the lower terrace of the river is covered with rich soil washed down from the hills, and is usually from 5 to 10 furlongs wide, much of it liable to flood. Between the lower and upper terraces is a precipitous slope of saline marls, incapable of supporting vegetation. In Transjordan no records are available of soil analyses for the Jordan valley, but some facts may be deduced from the Palestine survey on the opposite side. Though generally classed as loams, the soils are really marls, and may have a chlorine content of up to 2 per cent. In considering irrigation projects, therefore, chemical and physical analyses should be undertaken before plantations are opened up. The soils of the upper terrace vary in constitution from one end to the other. Predominantly marly, they vary from fine-textured to rougher types containing fine gravel and stones. Where more clay is present they become true loams, and on Nubian sandstone exposures they become sandy and rather saline. All the soils become thinner and more saline towards the river, but all have a high potash-content.

In the *hill country* most soils are light or heavy loams of the Terra Rossa type. Those of the small alluvial plains among the hills, almost free of stones and gravel and consisting mainly of fine sand and clay, are classed as heavy loams. In the Ajlun district, on the steep slopes leading down to the Jordan from near Tayibeh, soils are black, due to a high humus content. Although they overlie beds of chalk and flint they contain no lime, and the abundant humus is probably due to former oak forests, traces of which still exist. The semi-desert soils of Esh Shera have a high content of clay, silt, and fine sand, with less lime. They appear also to be rich in potash and phosphates. In spite of a high percentage of silt and clay, percolation is good, and with adequate water such soils should respond well to cultivation.

## Irrigation

Most of the 65,000 acres classed as irrigated land is in the Ghor, where the climate is otherwise too arid for cultivation to be successful. In the hills, irrigation is on a very small scale, chiefly in order to supply the villages with fruit and vegetables. Only the perennial supply of streams and springs is used, seasonal run-off being allowed to run to waste.

The total annual flow of springs and streams (fig. 57) which can be used for irrigation on the plateau and in the Ghor is about 52,580 million gallons, and little of this is not already used, though the systems of distribution make some waste inevitable under present conditions. The need for improvement is obvious when it is considered that it takes about 440,000 gallons to mature an acre of cereals, the staple crops of the country.

An extension in the use of irrigation offers the only hope of increasing the cultivated area and the yield per acre, since the pressure of population on the land is already severe and likely to become more so. Soil conservation should be encouraged, though nothing can at present be done to replace soils which have been swept away by erosion, for such a policy requires a very long period before results become apparent. Thus an increase of irrigation, to make better use of the soils which remain, is an urgent necessity.

The storage of seasonal run-off could never be a profitable undertaking for the Government, nor would it substantially affect the development of the country. Only towards the desert east of the dry-farmed zone would it be justifiable, and even here, after allowing for loss by evaporation and for reserves in years of poor rainfall, when there might be little or no run-off available for storage, the supply would probably not exceed 2,200 million gallons a year.

In the hills practically all the water available is already used, and there is little scope for government schemes since most of the springs and wells are owned by separate villages, and the cost of large-scale pumping and storage works would vastly outweigh any benefits which might arise therefrom. The efforts of individual farmers, however, would be far from insignificant, and here the Government could assist to some purpose by introducing legislation to give security of title to water, which is just as important to the landowner as his title to land. Few farmers are prepared to spend money on improvements until confidence is established in the regularity of water-supply. Hitherto, the use of water for irrigation has been controlled by Ottoman law, unamended, but by the end of 1938 a new law had been drafted, and was under consideration by the Department of Development. It included provision for water settlement and for control of distribution in areas proclaimed as Irrigation Areas.

In the Ghor, where the land is fertile and the climate warm and almost free from frost, there is much scope for development. Most of the irrigated land of Transjordan is concentrated in the valley, and further improvement, designed to effect a better distribution of water-supply and a decrease in waste through percolation, would certainly justify its cost. Several schemes, including a diversion canal from the Yarmuk river and control of the water of the wadis

Arab and Zeklab, have been considered, but have had to be postponed owing to the Palestine disturbances. Other possibilities in the Ghor are pumping from the Jordan and from wells, saving absorption losses by the construction of impervious canals, and control of the existing systems.

## Crops

Within the cultivated area of Transjordan, rain-fed cereals occupy an area of about 1,037,500 acres, almost entirely on the plateau. Wheat and barley, with some leguminous crops especially in the north, are the chief winter crops, and durra the chief summer crop. A two-year rotation is practised, one year of winter cereals being followed by leguminous winter crops on one third of the land, by summer crops on another third, and by bare fallow on the remaining third. In some years irregular rainfall causes disappointment both in quantity and quality of crops. Such a season occurred in 1938, though total rainfall was above the average, and an added complication was a serious and widespread outbreak of 'rust' disease.

The leguminous crops are chiefly vetches and *kersenneh* peas, though lentils are also grown. Summer crops, besides durra, include melons and cucumbers. In the valleys sloping towards the Jordan, and at a few places on the plateau, fruit-growing is increasing, since besides the demand for fruit in Transjordan itself, there is a ready market in Palestine. Deciduous fruits thrive well if protected from the wind, and on lower land, particularly in the Ghor, bananas and other tropical fruits are grown with irrigation. In the hills of the Ajlun and Es Salt districts, where rainfall is greatest, vineyards produce excellent grapes and raisins. Altogether there are about 20,000 acres of vineyards in Transjordan. Large areas are given over to vegetables; in 1938 there were 2,000 acres of winter vegetables and 9,250 acres of summer vegetables. Irrigation is used for some fruit and vegetables. *Tombac* and *hisheh* tobacco are also grown, mainly for home consumption.

Agricultural produce makes up most of the export trade, though the chief concern of the peasantry is to grow enough cereals for their own needs. Any excess that can be spared is sold to pay for their very modest import requirements. Thus exports vary from year to year with the weather. The following table shows the production and export of the chief crops in 1938:

|  | Production | Exports |
|---|---|---|
| Wheat  .  .  .  . | 85,000 tons | 33,000 tons |
| Barley  .  .  . | 45,000 ,, | 4,000 ,, |
| Durra  .  .  .  . | 8,900 ,, | 800 ,, |
| Kersenneh peas.  . | 7,500 ,, | 1,200 ,, |
| Lentils  .  .  . | 4,600 ,, | 1,000 ,, |
| Fresh vegetables  . | .. | 3,000 ,, |
| Grapes  .  .  .  . | .. | 1,200 ,, |
| Raisins  .  .  .  . | .. | 350 ,, |
| Fresh fruit  .  .  . | .. | 1,530 ,, |

The Department of Agriculture has for some years supplied seed to cultivators of wheat, barley, kersenneh, jibbaneh, and lentils. This has resulted in higher average yields and better prices. Besides encouraging the establishment of school gardens, of which there are many, the Department maintains the following nursery stations:

1. Horticultural station at Rusaifa, near Amman, where fruit-trees such as apples, apricots, peaches, plums, and cherries, suitable to the altitude of the plateau, are grown and grafted for distribution.

2. Horticultural station at Bagoora in the northern Jordan valley, for citrus and other fruit-trees, date-palms, and vegetables. Grafted citrus trees are issued, planted, and maintained until established, free of charge to the inhabitants of the Jordan valley.

3. Horticultural station at Jerash in the Ajlun hills, chiefly concerned with the growing of olives.

4. A demonstration plot of 20 acres at Mejdel, also in the Ajlun hills, for carobs.

5. The Wadi Zahar nursery, in the foothills west of Irbid, confined to the production of seedlings of forest trees for afforestation of areas in the north of the country selected for that purpose during settlement operations. All other stations maintain some forest seedlings.

6. Agricultural station at Jubeiha, 6 miles north-west of Amman, which started practical experiments in 1938 when test-crops sown included 48 varieties of wheat, 40 of barley, 4 of lentils, 1 of oats, 3 of kersenneh, and 2 of potatoes. A quantity of vines, fruit and forest trees were planted.

## Livestock

There are no adequate records of the domestic animals of Transjordan. Camels are bred, but no longer on so large a scale as formerly.

Cattle are numerous, and sheep and goats are also bred for export. Of the agricultural produce exported, samne (ghee) is the most valuable, though wool is exported according to the state of world markets. Exports of livestock and animal produce for 1938 are given below:

|  | Quantity | Value |
|---|---|---|
| Sheep . . . . | 28,602 (Nos.) | £P.25,010 |
| Goats . . . . | 7,769 ,, | 5,000 |
| Cattle . . . . | 679 ,, | 2,673 |
| Samne . . . . | 108 tons | 12,356 |
| Wool . . . . | 33 ,, | 1,149 |

## FORESTRY

There are still a few good forests left in Transjordan, in spite of a long history of uncontrolled felling. As in Palestine, the value of forests has never been appreciated, and the landowner's chief concern has been to convert them into cultivable land or to use the timber as fuel. Financial stringency in the past has prevented control of wood-cutting, and supply has always been greater than demand. Stricter government control has now caused fuel and timber prices to rise, and the economic value of trees is thus being stabilized.

Most of the good forests are to be found in the Ajlun district on the slopes of the higher hills. The Aleppo pine (*Pinus halepensis*) has disappeared from large areas, having suffered much at the hand of man, but there are still some fine stands. More common is the ever-green oak (*Quercus calliprinos*) which, though typically a maquis species, can become a large tree when protected and thinned out. The deciduous oak (*Quercus ithaburensis*) is now not common, and little is known of its present distribution, though not so long ago it formed park-like forests in the northern districts. Forests of *Pistacia atlantica* or their remnants are restricted to the steppe region. The northern and western parts of the Ajlun district are better wooded than the rest of the country, but the trees are too widely separated by areas of cultivation to justify the term 'forest area'. The exact constitution of these forests has not been recorded, but they are almost certainly of the park type, with undergrowth of shrubs and herbaceous plants.

The chief forest areas are:

1. The Heisheh forest, between Wadi Musa and Shobek in the Maan district.

2. The Feinan forest, south-west of Tafileh in the Kerak district.

3. The Ben Hamideh forest, north-west of Kerak and south of the Wadi Mojib.

4. The Aluk and Howeish forest, south-east of Jerash.

5. The Ardah el Abbad forest, north of Es Salt in the Belka district.

6. The Jebel Ajlun forests, which cover much of the district of Ajlun.

*State Forests*

Until 1 April 1938 all forests, except those acquired by the Government in the course of settlement operations, were under the care of the Department of Agriculture and Forests. Those acquired by the Government during settlement were placed under the control of the Director of Lands and Surveys immediately after registration. By the end of 1937 the area of forests to which the Government had a clear title was 16,500 acres, and this amount was rapidly increasing as settlement proceeded. The whole administration of forests owned or controlled by the Government was therefore placed under the Director of Lands, the transfer taking place on 1 April 1938, and at the end of the year, 28,200 acres of forest and scrub land were owned by the Government. A sub-department of Forests has been formed to take charge of this land, and the administration has been decentralized. Forest officials have been attached to the six district offices of the Department of Lands and Surveys, and are now responsible for the supervision of forest guards, issue of licenses, and prosecutions for forest offences.

The total of 28,200 acres controlled by the Government is constituted as follows:

|                          | Number | Area   |
|--------------------------|--------|--------|
| Reserves over 250 acres  | 12     | 6,510  |
| ,,    125–250 acres       | 27     | 4,593  |
| ,,     25–125 acres       | 217    | 12,670 |
| ,,    under 25 acres      | 471    | 4,427  |

Of these reserves, 54 per cent. are classed as thick forests, 18 per cent. as well-timbered, 10 per cent. as scattered trees, and 18 per cent. scrub land.

A beginning has been made with reafforestation in State forests where root stocks have survived in spite of past despoliation. At the end of 1938 a total of 745 acres had been fenced and reafforested and 30,000 trees had been planted; 857 acres had been fenced to permit natural regeneration, and seeds of juniper, pistachio, and other indigenous scrub sown throughout the enclosure.

The real value of forests to Transjordan lies in the direct economic and aesthetic value of the trees themselves, in addition to their function as wind- and water-breaks. There is no positive evidence to show that a greater area of forest would augment the available water resources of the country; the indirect benefit of forests should be considered in relation to the ground immediately in their lee, and this effect is determined by their form and position rather than by their superficial area.

## COMMERCE

Transjordan's share in world trade is very small, and foreign commerce is almost entirely confined to the neighbouring countries, Palestine, Syria, Iraq, and Saudi Arabia. This is to be expected in a small country, already experiencing difficulty in supporting a population which, though increasing, still depends largely on very limited agricultural resources. Only in favourable years is there any appreciable surplus of produce to exchange for the essential imports, and trade therefore fluctuates with the weather. The balance of trade cannot be assessed with certainty, for customs posts in the central and southern areas are too few for complete statistics to be recorded, and it is known that cereals are freely exported from these areas to Palestine and Nejd. There is also a relatively large re-export of foreign goods to Nejd. From such figures as are available it appears that the value of imports is usually at least twice that of exports.

*Total recorded Trade, excluding Re-exports, 1936–1940*

|  | | | | | Imports £P. | Exports £P. |
|---|---|---|---|---|---|---|
| 1936 | . | . | . | . | . 935,305 | 228,376 |
| 1937 | . | . | . | . | . 1,054,286 | 510,968 |
| 1938 | . | . | . | . | . 1,306,179 | 472,399 |
| 1939 | . | . | . | . | . 1,309,090 | 517,295 |
| 1940 | . | . | . | . | . 1,492,850 | 770,451 |

No duty is payable on exports from Transjordan. The import tariff is on a 12 per cent. *ad valorem* basis, but there are specific rates for a few items. In addition there is an examination fee of ½ per cent. on the c.i.f. value. By agreement, there are no import duties on the products of Palestine and Syria, apart from tobacco and alcohol, and in practice no duties are levied on those from Saudi Arabia.

A 908

The principal articles of trade are as follows:

### Imports

| | 1936 £P. | 1937 £P. | 1938 £P. | 1939 £P. | 1940 £P. |
|---|---|---|---|---|---|
| Cotton goods | 131,801 | 103,717 | 130,229 | 202,073 | 174,988 |
| Art. silk goods | 73,045 | 97,891 | 50,000 | 31,941 | 69,528 |
| Benzine | 46,881 | 35,665 | 39,410 | 49,902 | 71,794 |
| Sugar | 45,597 | 47,277 | 46,951 | 50,675 | 135,578 |
| Rice | 41,637 | 40,377 | 24,758 | 28,522 | 45,651 |
| Kerosene | 21,700 | 24,820 | 25,001 | 17,660 | 36,859 |
| Animals | 16,277 | 23,256 | 126,075 | 117,846 | 104,524 |
| Confectionery | 11,554 | 17,328 | 21,394 | 18,125 | 18,145 |

### Exports *

| | 1936 £P. | 1937 £P. | 1938 £P. | 1939 £P. | 1940 £P. |
|---|---|---|---|---|---|
| Wheat | 108,623 | 274,656 | 324,103 | 303,433 | 488,308 |
| Sheep | 32,322 | 11,240 | 25,010 | 26,497 | 41,519 |
| Barley | 4,679 | 40,317 | 20,473 | 61,268 | 53,792 |
| Fresh fruit | 4,754 | 10,212 | 15,656 | 14,178 | 15,801 |
| Dyed goods | 3,194 | 31,558 | 4,312 | 2,435 | .. |

\* Actual exports are known to be considerably greater.

The striking increase in the import of animals since 1938 was due to the construction of the Haifa–Baghdad road which was started in that year. Many animals were imported for this work since little transport was otherwise available.

Other imports include clothing, woollen goods, timber, coffee and tea, paperware, iron goods, samne, soap, and olive-oil. Other exports have been referred to on page 494.

Syria and Palestine are the most important of the countries which share in Transjordan's trade. In the years immediately preceding the outbreak of war the trend of foreign trade was away from Palestine to Syria. There were two reasons for this: one, political, was a repercussion of the Arab-Jewish differences in Palestine which led to a mutual boycott between the two communities; the other, economic, was the fall in value of the franc and the reduction of freight rates on the Syrian railway. Trade with Palestine is so much affected by the political situation that the greater part of purchases made by Transjordan consists not of Palestinian goods but of foreign goods on which duty is paid in Palestine.

The published figures of foreign trade with the four neighbouring countries, though far from complete, are given below:

### Imports, irrespective of goods in transit

| Year | Palestine £P. | Via Palestine* £P. | Syria £P. | Via Syria* £P. | Saudi Arabia £P. | Iraq £P. |
|---|---|---|---|---|---|---|
| 1933 | .. | .. | 68,532 | 12,718 | 6,821 | .. |
| 1934 | .. | .. | 79,425 | 13,627 | 2,730 | .. |
| 1935 | .. | .. | 81,048 | 12,320 | 7,550 | .. |
| 1936 | 36,088 | 121,453 | 153,963 | 22,863 | 11,115 | 9,508 |
| 1937 | 60,390 | 200,683 | 156,853 | 20,299 | 14,898 | 7,141 |
| 1938 | 46,347 | 373,055 | 175,670 | 30,831 | 4,410 | 106,316 |
| 1939 | 65,181 | 249,475 | 221,561 | 34,964 | 372 | 106,597 |
| 1940 | 154,576 | 303,486 | 175,840 | 19,791 | 1,118 | 120,641 |

* Foreign goods re-exported to Transjordan.

### Exports

| Year | Palestine £P. | Re-exports to Palestine £P. | Syria £P. | Re-export to Syria £P. | Iraq £P. |
|---|---|---|---|---|---|
| 1933 | .. | .. | 7,043 | .. | .. |
| 1934 | .. | .. | 9,220 | .. | .. |
| 1935 | .. | .. | 21,487 | .. | .. |
| 1936 | 198,215 | 2,678 | 29,781 | 564 | 380 |
| 1937 | 404,107 | 12,239 | 106,861 | 2,173 | .. |
| 1938 | 444,523 | 77,597 | 27,677 | 11,967 | 199 |
| 1939 | 477,438 | 51,211 | 39,837 | 8,878 | .. |
| 1940 | 750,888 | 48,150 | 17,419 | 21,421 | 6 |

The other countries which supply imports to Transjordan through Palestine, Syria, or Iraq are:

| | Egypt £P. | Japan £P. | Romania £P. | United Kingdom £P. | U.S.A. £P. |
|---|---|---|---|---|---|
| 1939 | 512,600 | 198,598 | 64,757 | 42,944 | .. |
| 1940 | 125,614 | 176,076 | 28,309 | 28,162 | 54,933 |

### Transit Trade

Geographical position makes transit trade relatively important among the economic activities of Transjordan. Figures for the value of this trade between Iraq and Palestine are given below; those for trade between Nejd and Syria are not known.

| | 1935 £P. | 1936 £P. | 1937 £P. | 1938 £P. |
|---|---|---|---|---|
| From Iraq to Palestine | 407,262 | 243,123 | 390,321 | 365,920 |
| From Palestine to Iraq | 280,728 | 193,886 | 313,465 | 161,338 |
| Via I.P.C. Pipe-line, Iraq to Palestine. Crude oil * | | 1,537,998 | 1,619,292 | 1,628,854 |

* Arbitrary value at 16 shillings per ton.

## FINANCE

The main source of the revenue of the Government of Transjordan is Licences and Taxes; next come Customs and Excise. The other receipts, apart from the grants-in-aid, are of little importance.

Revenue receipts since the financial year 1924/5 follow:

| Year | Licences and Taxes | Customs and Excise | Grants-in-Aid | Total |
|---|---|---|---|---|
| | £P.. | £P. | £P. | £P. |
| 1924/5 | 110,342 | 52,412 | 77,572 | 280,673 |
| 1925/6 | 101,308 | 48,964 | 103,957 | 282,459 |
| 1926/7 | 138,688 | 54,123 | 66,000 | 302,520 |
| 1927/8 | 138,197 | 61,237 | 45,000 | 282,073 |
| 1928/9 | 118,583 | 82,390* | 67,644 | 307,555 |
| 1929/30 | 129,587 | 64,168 | 76,975 | 316,147 |
| 1930/1 | 133,381 | 64,956 | 117,452 | 367,516 |
| 1931/2 | 111,384 | 65,039 | 115,144 | 338,046 |
| 1932/3 | 117,159 | 82,397 | 101,139 | 354,888 |
| 1933/4 | 101,611 | 103,530* | 119,905 | 381,412 |
| 1934/5 | 113,057 | 98,627 | 101,259 | 377,517 |
| 1935/6 | 140,637 | 104,567 | 81,783 | 395,630 |
| 1936/7 | 89,121 | 133,884* | 130,510 | 418,650 |
| 1937/8 | 149,397 | 125,351 | 110,990 | 459,150 |
| 1938/9 | 137,650 | 127,704 | 180,412 | 529,611 |
| 1939/40 | 158,226 | 142,386 | 220,069 | 623,040 |

\* The contribution of Palestine was increased in this year.

The revenue from licences and taxes varies as a rule with the yield of the harvest since in bad harvest years taxation has to be remitted. Excise duties are levied on wine, spirits, and tobacco manufactured in the country, but the sum thus received is small. The grants-in-aid are for several purposes—for the maintenance of the Transjordan Frontier Force, for the repayment of Transjordan's share of the Ottoman Debt, for the hydrographic survey, and for the general public finances of the country. This last named item has been of recent years very considerably reduced, in view of the general improvement in the government finances.

The totals of expenditure over the same period are given in the following table. By far the largest item of expenditure is that of Police.

| | £P. | | £P. | | £P. |
|---|---|---|---|---|---|
| 1924/5 | 274,868 | 1930/1 | 350,532 | 1935/6 | 381,300 |
| 1925/6 | 274,573 | 1931/2 | 344,983 | 1936/7 | 435,039 |
| 1926/7 | 274,920 | 1932/3 | 340,883 | 1937/8 | 462,710 |
| 1927/8 | 318,260 | 1933/4 | 374,769 | 1938/9 | 547,546 |
| 1928/9 | 318,950 | 1934/5 | 369,395 | 1939/40 | 599,338 |
| 1929/30 | 338,461 | | | | |

The Public Debt of Transjordan stood on 31 December 1940 at £P.155,043, the whole being Transjordan's share of the Ottoman Debt under the Treaty of Lausanne. Half of that share had been paid by that date out of grants by the British Government. Until 1933 the old Ottoman taxes were practically unchanged. In that year, however, fiscal reforms were introduced. The former *tamattu* tax on trades and professions was abolished and an income tax on members of those classes, and licences, were substituted for it. The former Tithe, House, Land, and Road taxes were abolished at the same time and one consolidated Land Tax substituted without reducing the total received. The reform resulted in more equitable distribution of taxation between the richer and poorer taxpayers. A new stamp-duty was imposed in 1936.

*Specie and Currency Notes.* This item of import and export statistics, furnished in the Transjordan Government publications, is more proper to this section than to that of commerce. The Arab revolt of 1915 to 1918 brought a large amount of gold coin into Transjordan and in the quarter of a century since the War of 1914–1918 much of this has filtered out. In years of agricultural depression the expatriation of capital in the form of specie and currency notes has been more evident than in other years. However, there is still a movement in the other direction which at times rises to large proportions. Figures are given for the five years 1936–1940. The import of a large amount of gold coin, possibly in exchange for currency notes, in 1940 is exceptional. It is probably connected with the financial panic in Palestine that accompanied the outbreak of war with Italy.

### Exports

|  | 1936 £P. | 1937 £P. | 1938 £P. | 1939 £P. | 1940 £P. |
|---|---|---|---|---|---|
| Gold coin | .. | .. | .. | .. | .. |
| Silver coin | 45,800 | 27,000 | 21,700 | 24,400 | 33,500 |
| Other metal coins | 4,320 | 700 | 1,200 | 2,180 | 1,600 |
| Currency notes | 160,355 | 154,850 | 90,050 | 214,759 | 656,459 |
| Total | 210,475 | 182,550 | 112,950 | 241,339 | 691,559 |

### Imports

|  | 1936 £P. | 1937 £P. | 1938 £P. | 1939 £P. | 1940 £P. |
|---|---|---|---|---|---|
| Gold coin | .. | .. | .. | .. | 309,720 |
| Silver coin | 4,847 | 4,530 | 77,232 | 14,303 | 6,076 |
| Other metal coins | .. | .. | .. | .. | .. |
| Currency notes | 4,000 | .. | 18,800 | 11,500 | 41,100 |
| Total | 8,847 | 4,530 | 96,032 | 25,803 | 356,896 |

*Currency*

Transjordan has no currency of its own, but uses that of Palestine, receiving from the Palestine Currency Board (p. 281) an appropriate share of the profits every year. The relatively high cost of living in Transjordan is partly due to the fact that although the Palestine pound is divided into 1,000 mils, the lowest spending unit is really the 5-mil piece.

*Banking*

The only ordinary bank operating in Transjordan is the Ottoman Bank, which has a branch at Amman. It is the Government banker and the agent for the issue of currency. There is, however, also an Agricultural Bank, a relic of the Ottoman period. It was founded with the object of promoting agriculture by providing credit facilities to cultivators of limited means at reasonable rates of interest. Its capital was originally provided by a special tax on the agricultural community. Since 1924 the Transjordan Government has made an annual grant out of its revenues for the same purpose. The bank is governed by a board consisting of five senior government officers, with a manager and assistant manager, and three elected members. Recently the Agricultural Bank has practically limited its activities to long-term loans and to the financing of co-operative societies. The establishment and encouragement of these societies have been undertaken by the Government through the Director of Development. The capital of this bank on 31 March 1938 was £P.69,000, having increased from £P.15,500 when the Transjordan Government first took it over.

## DEPARTMENT OF DEVELOPMENT

The Department of Development was established in May 1937, under a British Director, and is maintained by a grant from the Colonial Development Fund. Before a programme could be drawn up, the circumstances of the Department were changed by the decision to undertake a hydrographic survey of the country, to be executed by the Department of Lands and Surveys under a grant from the British Government. This work, the outcome of the Royal Commission Report on Palestine, absorbed most of the activities of the new Department of Development, and by the end of 1938 the systematic compilation of the results of the survey was in hand. Besides this, the Department prepared and examined several irrigation control schemes (p. 492), and drafted a new law to control irrigation and land drainage water.

## PUBLIC WORKS

This department has charge of road-building and road-reconstruction, erection and maintenance of Government buildings, and water-supplies (in conjunction with the Department of Public Health). In 1938, 516 miles of road were continuously maintained and 444 miles partially maintained. Work on the Haifa–Baghdad road (p. 515) between Jisr el Majami and Irbid was carried out by this Department.

## RAILWAYS

The only railway within Transjordan is that part of the old Hejaz railway, south of Nessib on the Syrian border, which has survived to Maan, and a small extension recently built to Nakb Shtar, $25\frac{1}{2}$ miles beyond (fig. 58). It is administered by Palestine Railways at Haifa, and as the only connexion with the lines in Palestine is by the old branch of the Hejaz railway from Samakh to Deraa, which is now in Syria, it is convenient to include a brief description of this line in this account.

### History

As stated in Chapter XIII (p. 341), the Hejaz railway from Damascus to Medina, and its branch from Deraa to Haifa, were completed before 1914. The line from Damascus to Maan was opened in September 1904, that from Samakh to Deraa a year later. Their original purpose was ostensibly to serve the pilgrim traffic to Mecca, but their completion served a strategic purpose as well, for it enabled Ottoman influence to be exercised at Mecca (p. 455). During the War of 1914–1918 the line to Medina became rather a snare, for while it enabled the Turks to threaten Mecca in the early stages of the Arab revolt, from 1917 onwards long stretches of it were so vulnerable to attack by Arab irregulars based on Akaba that the Turkish troops in Medina could neither be supplied with more than the bare necessities of existence nor withdrawn to reinforce the Turkish front in Palestine.

At the end of the war several of the smaller bridges had been demolished and long sections of the line had been broken. The line was soon re-established from Samakh to Deraa and from Deraa to Amman; but it was only when some measure of security was established and when the ancient sites, notably Petra, began to draw visitors, that the line was repaired as far as Maan, though traffic never became sufficient to justify more than one train a week beyond the

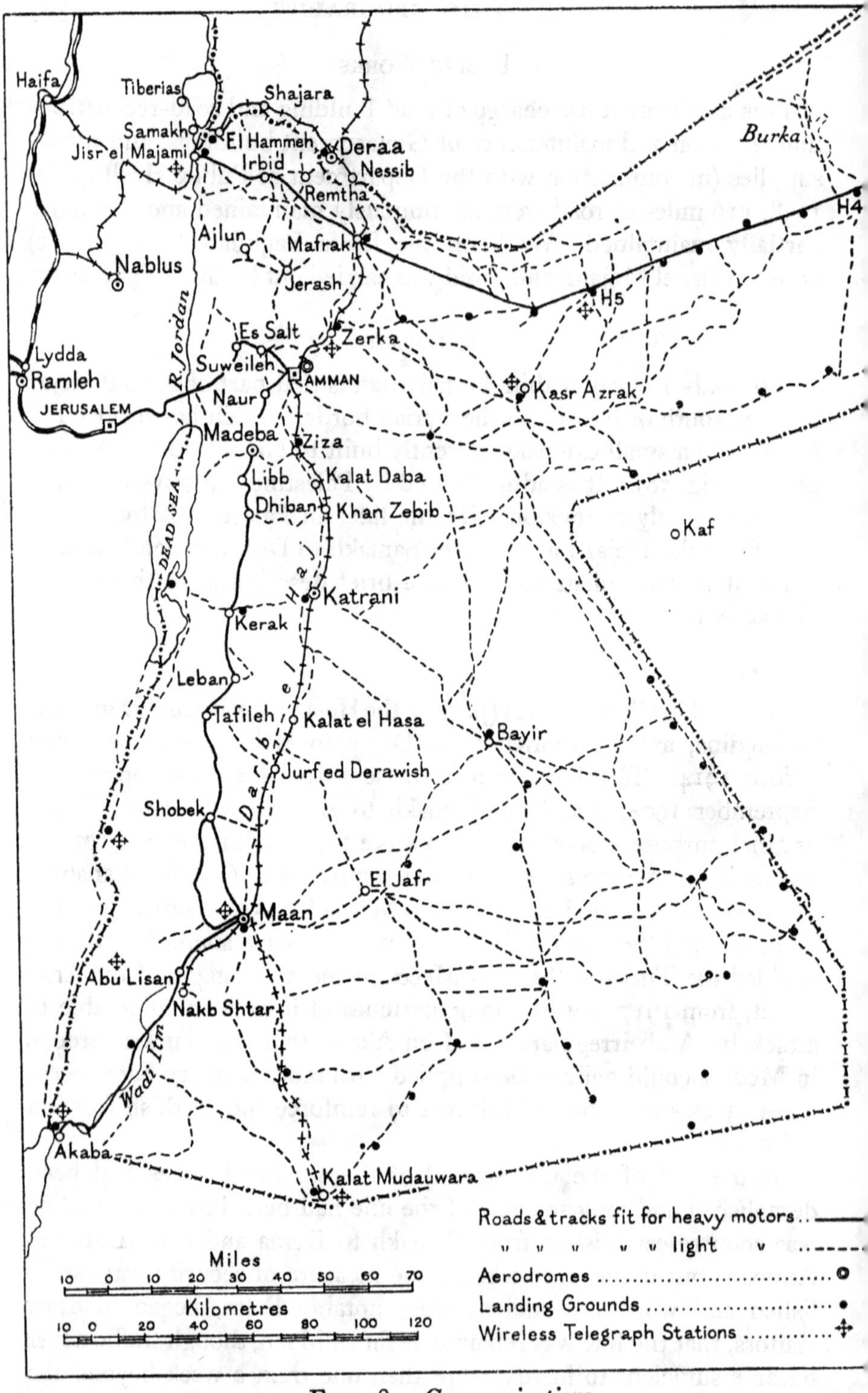

FIG. 58. *Communications*

capital. There was only one signal on the line—all having disappeared during the Arab revolt and the years of unrest that followed—but there was no need for them. The signal that was erected just outside Amman required no signal box nor operator. As the weekly train drew out of the station it halted, the engine-driver descended, lowered the signal arm, returned to his cab, drove the train on for perhaps a hundred yards, returned on foot to raise the signal, and then repaired to his engine. The Maan 'express' was then able to continue its journey to the south in safety.

In 1939 the line south of Maan was still derelict. It had not been repaired, but broken stretches of line were still in place. The effect of the outbreak of war on the railways of Palestine has already been noted (p. 343). As the Mediterranean sea-route to Haifa became insecure, the route round Africa came into use, and Suez and Kantara became the sea bases of Palestine. When the threat to Egypt from the west became pronounced, preparations were made to develop the port of Akaba and the communications inland to Maan. The route by the Wadi Itm was made fit for motors, and an extension of the line from Maan towards Akaba was begun, the derelict rails of the old railway to Medina being used. New passing-loops were laid along the line to increase its capacity to eight trains a day, and no doubt signals have now been erected. Thus for a short period at least this ancient route has once more come into its own; though it is too soon to say whether the new facilities provided will be maintained in post-war years.

## Detailed Account of Railways

In the detailed account of the two lines which follows, the same arrangement as that for the railways of Palestine has been adopted, and the same abbreviations are used (p. 351).

## 1. SAMAKH–DERAA

*Distance:* 45·9 miles, 73·8 kilometres.

*Permanent way, stations, and kilometre posts*

Narrow gauge (105 cm.). Single track. Ballast, crushed crystalline limestone or black basalt. Rails, flat-bottom, 43·5 lb. per yard. Sleepers, steel (pea-pod). Maximum axle-load, 10 tons. Minimum radius of curves, 100 m. (several throughout the line after El Hammeh). Maximum gradient, 1 in 50 (frequent between Makaren and Mezerib). Maximum distance between passing-loops, 13 km. Minimum length of loop-line at stations,

115 m. at Zeizun (elsewhere 225 m.). Kilometre posts are numbered from Haifa, 87–160 km.

## Speed and capacity

Overall time (including stops): mixed trains (3 hr.); goods trains (4 hr. 15 min.).

Maximum train speeds: mixed, 25 m.p.h.; goods, 20 m.p.h.

Capacity, 8 trains each way in 24 hours. Net load of trains, 120 tons.

## GENERAL DESCRIPTION

From Samakh the line traverses the plain to the entrance of the Yarmuk defile, which is only a mile wide, with steep hills on either side. The river flows in a narrow rocky bed with steep banks 40–50 feet high. The line follows the right bank to about mile 4 from Samakh, where it crosses and soon afterwards recrosses the Yarmuk before reaching El Hammeh (photo. 119). Here the line crosses the Palestine border into Syria. After again crossing and recrossing the river the line keeps for several miles to the right bank, passing through a tunnel, and crossing again to the left bank before Wadi Khaled. Similar country is passed as far as Makaren at mile 22, where there were great difficulties in construction, the line having to cross the Yarmuk to the right bank, ascend the Wadi Ehrer, cross and recross this tributary, and tunnel through spurs to regain the Yarmuk. About mile 35 there are further difficulties, the line having to double back on itself and descend the right bank in order to pass round a spur.

The line throughout passes through very enclosed country. There are no fewer than 14 major bridges over the Yarmuk or its principal tributaries and 7 tunnels of 90 yards or more.

## DETAILED DESCRIPTION

| Km. from Samakh | Stations and passing-loops | Remarks |
|---|---|---|
| 0·0 | SAMAKH (9) | Alt. −617 ft. PL.(4); W.(T.8,800 gls., pumped from lake, R.; C.(2), SP.); F.; GP.; GS.; ES.; Tbl.; BC. |
| | | Line crosses open plain to the entrance of the Yarmuk defile. |
| | | Yarmuk defile is narrow with precipitous sides. |
| 6·2 | .. | Steel girder bridge over Yarmuk, 30 m. +50 m.+30 m.; masonry piers; height 20 m. (photo. 119). |
| 7·5 | .. | Steel girder bridge over Yarmuk, 30 m. +50 m.+30 m.; masonry piers; height 15 m. |

| Km. from Samakh | Stations and passing-loops | Remarks |
|---|---|---|
| 8·5 | EL HAMMEH (12) | Alt.−479 ft. PL.(2); GP. Station is on the right bank of the Yarmuk. Line cuts across loop of the Yarmuk river and then crosses to the left bank. |
| 9·1 | .. | Steel girder bridge over Yarmuk, 30 m. +50 m.+30 m.; masonry piers; height 15 m. |
| 13·2 | .. | Steel girder bridge over Yarmuk, 30 m. +50 m.+30 m.; masonry piers; height 15 m. The bridge is near the junction of the tributary Wadi Samar. |
| 16·6 | .. | Tunnel, 220 m. |
| 18·6 | .. | Masonry bridge over Yarmuk, 6 × 12 m. arches; height 12 m. |
| 20·5 | WADI KHALED (12) | Alt.−177 ft. PL.(1); W.(reservoir, R.; C.(2),grav.); GP.; Sdg. Station is on the left bank of the Yarmuk. |
| 26·6 | .. | Masonry bridge over Yarmuk, 5 × 12 m. arches; height 10 m. (photo. 120). |
| 29·0 | .. | Line reaches sea-level. |
| 32·5 | ESH SHAJARA (CHEJERE) (5) | Alt.+89 ft. PL.(1); GP. Station is on the right bank of the Yarmuk. |
| 33·2 | .. | Masonry bridge over side valley, 6 × 12 m. arches;[1] height 12 m. |
| 34·3 | .. | Masonry bridge over Yarmuk, 5 × 5 m. arches; height 10 m. |
| 37·5 | MAKAREN (11) | Alt.+236 ft. PL.(2); W.(reservoir, R.; C.(2),grav.); GP. Station is on the left bank of the Yarmuk. |
| 38·3 | .. | Steel girder bridge, 15 m.+10 m.; masonry piers; height 10 m. This bridge is just above the junction of the Ehrer, a right-bank tributary of the Yarmuk. |
| 40·0 | .. | Tunnel, 144 m., through the promontory separating the Yarmuk from the Ehrer. Line now ascends left bank of the Ehrer valley. |
| 41·4 | .. | Masonry bridge over Ehrer, 3 × 12 m. arches; height 10 m. Line ascends the right bank of the Ehrer valley. |
| 43·5 | .. | Masonry bridge over the Ehrer, 3 × 12 m.; height 12 m. Line descends the left bank of the Ehrer. |
| 44·7 | .. | Tunnel, 94 m., through spur in the Ehrer valley. |
| 46·1 | .. | Tunnel, 125 m., through promontory, into the Yarmuk valley. |

[1] Official records give 6 arches. An old photograph purporting to be of this bridge distinctly shows 7 arches.

| Km. from Samakh | Stations and passing-loops | Remarks |
|---|---|---|
| | | Line ascends the right bank of the Yarmuk. |
| 48·8 | ZEIZUN (13) | Alt. 860 ft. PL.(1); W.(reservoir, R.; C.(2),grav.). Station is on the right bank of the Yarmuk. |
| 50·5 | .. | Tunnel, 160 m. |
| 51·8 | .. | Tunnel, 90 m. |
| 54·2 | .. | Masonry bridge over the Wadi Bajeh, 3×6 m.+12 m.+3×6 m. arches; height 15 m. |
| 54·4 | .. | Masonry and girder bridge over the Wadi Zeidi (Yarmuk), 2 × 5 m. (masonry arches)+50 m. (girder)+3 × 5 m. (masonry arches); height, 20 m. Line ascends the left bank of the Wadi Zeidi. |
| 56·3 | .. | Masonry bridge over the Wadi Zeidi, 6 m.+12 m.+6 m. arches; height 10 m. |
| 56.4 | .. | Tunnel, 178 m. The line descends the valley, climbing steadily up the hill-side on to the plateau crest. |
| 62·1 | MEZERIB (12) | Alt. 1,527 ft. PL.(1); W.(T.; SP.); GP. Line crosses open plateau country. |
| 73·8 | DERAA | Alt. 1,742 ft. PL.(10); W.(T.16,000 gls.,R.; C.,SP.); GP.; GS.(2); ES.; Tr.; Sdgs.(4). · |

## 2. DERAA–MAAN–NAKB SHTAR

| | | | | | |
|---|---|---|---|---|---|
| Deraa–Nessib | . | 8·0 miles, | 12·8 | kilometres | |
| Nessib–Amman | . | 53·7 ,, | 86·5 | ,, | |
| Amman–Maan | . | 146·9 ,, | 236·4 | ,, | |
| Maan–Nakb Shtar | . | 25·5 ,, | 41·0 | ,, | |
| | | 234·1 | 376·7 | | |

*Permanent way, stations, and kilometre posts*

Narrow gauge (105 cm.). Single track. Ballast, crushed crystalline limestone and black basalt. Rails, flat-bottom, 43·5 lb. per yard. Sleepers, steel (pea-pod). Maximum axle-load, 10 tons. Minimum radius of curves, 100 m. (many between Amman and Kassir, and near Suwaga). There are also many 125-m. curves near Deraa and south of El Hasa. Maximum gradient, 1 in 50 (frequent between Amman and Kassir). Other steep gradients between 1 in 52 and 1 in 60 are near Zerka, Rusaifa, Kalat ed Daba, and Suwaga. Maximum distance between passing-loops, 25 km. Kilometre posts are numbered from Damascus, 124–459 (at Maan).

*Speed and capacity*

Journey times with the latest station facilities are not available. Before 1939 the weekly train was scheduled to take about 11 hours to cover the 209 miles to Maan. Goods trains took 14 or 15 hours. With additional stops and increased traffic these times would be increased. Train speeds are between 20 and 30 m.p.h. There are several section speed restrictions because of the gradients and sharp curves. With the new passing-loops added since 1939, the capacity is said to have been increased to 8 trains a day. Net load of trains, 125 tons.

## GENERAL DESCRIPTION

The line passes through open undulating cultivated country as far as Amman, mile 62, with no engineering difficulties or steep gradients except near Zerka, where the descent to the depression is steep, and beyond where there are occasional severe gradients. From Amman to Kassir the line climbs steeply in a series of sharp curves to over 3,000 feet to pass the Ziza watershed and then descends more gradually into the pasture-land of the Beni Sukhr. Cultivation gradually disappears south of Libban, pasture becomes more sparse, and from El Hasa to Maan broken volcanic country is traversed. Beyond Kassir gradients and curves are not usually severe, except where the line has to leave the general level of the plateau to cross one of the larger wadis.

No details of the extension from Maan to Nakb Shtar, which was built in 1942, are available.

## DETAILED DESCRIPTION

| Km. from Deraa | Damascus | Stations and passing-loops | Remarks |
|---|---|---|---|
| 0·0 | 123·3 | DERAA | Alt. 1,742 ft. PL.(10); W.(T.16,000 gls.,R.; C.,SP.); GP.(2); ES.; Tr.; Sdgs.(4). |
| | | | The station is on the north side of the Wadi Zeidi (Yarmuk), the town on the south. |
| | | | Line ascends steadily over open cultivated country. Gradient reaches 1 in 66 at one place. |
| 4·7 | 128·0 | KUM GHARZ (KHUM GARZ) (8) | Alt. *c.* 1,800 ft. PL.(2); GP. Junction for Bosra branch. |
| 6·2 | 129·5 | .. | Masonry bridge over the Wadi Zeidi, 6 × 6 m. arches; height 12 m. |
| 11·4 | 134·7 | .. | Steel bridge over the Wadi Butm, 4 × 5 m., height 5 m. |

| Km. from | | Stations and | |
| Deraa | Damascus | passing-loops | Remarks |
| --- | --- | --- | --- |
| 12·8 | 136·1 | NESSIB (NASIB) (13) | Alt. *c.* 1,880 ft. PL.(1).<br>Station is on the east side of the Wadi Butm. The Transjordan section of the Hejaz railway begins at Nessib. Transjordan boundary.<br>Country is undulating and cultivated. |
| *c.* 26.2 | *c.* 149·5 | *Ghadir el Abyad* (12) | PL.(1).* |
| 38·6 | 161·9 | MAFRAK (16) | Alt. *c.* 1,960 ft. PL.(1); GP. Station acts as the base for the I.P.C. pipeline engineers, and starting-point for the trans-desert road to Baghdad. It is on the watershed between the Yarmuk and the inland basin to the south. Line passes over open undulating country. |
| *c.* 54·6 | *c.* 177·9 | *Toghra* (8) | PL.(1).* |
| 62·2 | 185·5 | SAMRA (18) | Alt. *c.* 1,830 ft. PL.(1). |
| 63·6 | 186·9 | .. | Masonry viaduct, 7 × 5 m. arches; height 5 m.<br>Line crosses the plateau east of the Wadi Zerka. |
| 70·7 | 194·0 | .. | Masonry viaduct, 6 × 6 m. arches; height 12 m. |
| 79·7 | 203·0 | ZERKA (8) | Alt. *c.* 2,030 ft. PL.(1); W.(T.8,000 gls., UR.; HP.); LP.<br>The Circassian village is about ¼ mile to the west.<br>Line descends into the wide depression of the Wadi Zerka, with gradient of 1 in 62, increasing to 1 in 55. The valley is well cultivated.<br>Line ascends the Zerka valley with gradient of 1 in 80. |
| 82·3 | 205·6 | .. | Masonry viaduct, 6 × 6 m. arches; height 12 m. |
| 83·9 | 207·2 | .. | Masonry viaduct, 6 × 6 m. arches; height 7 m. |
| 88·1 | 211·4 | *Rusaifa* (11) | PL.(1).*<br>Gradient near Rusaifa is 1 in 52. |
| 95·8 | 219·1 | .. | Masonry viaduct, 5 × 6 m. arches; height 5 m. |
| 99·3 | 222·6 | AMMAN (12) | Alt. *c.* 2,420 ft. PL.(5); W.(T.8,800 gls. from well, R.; C.(2),SP.); F.; GP; GS.; ES.(6); Tbl.; Sdgs.(6).<br>Line turns out of the Amman valley, with many sharp curves of 100 to 150 m. radius and maximum gradient of 1 in 50 at several places. |

* The stations in italics are new since 1939. It is uncertain whether passing-loops have been laid at all of them.

| Km. from Deraa | Damascus | Stations and passing-loops | Remarks |
|---|---|---|---|
| 104·9 | 228·2[1] | .. | Masonry viaduct, 10×5 m. arches; height 25 m. |
| 105·1 | 228·4[1] | .. | Tunnel, 140 m., on sharp curve, at maximum gradient (photo. 138). Line passes through a deep cutting and reaches the watershed between the Zerka basin and the Ziza depression, drained by the tributaries of the Hammam (Wala). Country is open. |
| 111·1 | 234·4 | Kassir (15) | Alt. c. 3,090 ft. PL.(1); Sdg. Line descends steadily through undulating open country towards the Ziza depression with gradient reaching 1 in 70. |
| 125·8 | 249·1 | Libban (11) | Alt. c. 2,540 ft. PL.(1); LP. Good grazing in spring by Beni Sukhr tribesmen; some cultivation. |
| 135·2 | 258·5 | .. | Masonry bridge, 5×4 m. arches; height 5 m. |
| 136·7 | 260·0 | Ziza (19) | Alt. c. 2,390 ft. PL.(2); LP. Line winds over undulating semidesert country, crossing head wadis of the Hammam, most of them dry and stony. |
| 145·3 | 268·6 | .. | Masonry bridge, 4×6 m. arches; height 7 m. |
| 146·6 | 269·9 | .. | Masonry bridge, 5×5 m. arches; height 3 m. |
| 147·4 | 270·7 | .. | Masonry bridge, 6×6 m. arches; height 4 m. There is a long ascent of 1 in 55 towards Kalat ed Daba, then descent. |
| 155·6 | 278·9 | Kalat ed Daba (17) | Alt. c. 2,460 ft. PL.(1).* Line traverses bare undulating country, but with no serious gradient. |
| 156·5 | 279·8 | .. | Masonry bridge, 3×5 m. arches; height 5 m. |
| 172·4 | 295·7 | Khan Zebib (14) | Alt. 2,570 ft. PL.(1); LP. Line enters the catchment of the Wadi Mojib. |
| 181·5 | 304·8 | .. | Masonry bridge, 3×6 m. arches; height 5 m. |
| 181·6 | 304·9 | .. | Masonry bridge, 3×6 m. arches; height 5 m. |
| 183·4 | 306·7 | .. | Masonry viaduct, 6×6 m. arches; height 8 m. |
| 186·4 | 309·7 | Suwaga (17) | PL.(1).* |
| 186·7 | 310·0 | .. | Masonry viaduct over dry stony bed of a wadi, 6×6 m. arches; height 7 m. |

[1] One account gives these distances as 232·2 and 232·4 km.

| Km. from Deraa | Damascus | Stations and passing-loops | Remarks |
|---|---|---|---|
| | | | The line climbs with gradient of 1 in 60 up the left bank of the wadi. |
| 203·3 | 326·6 | KATRANI (22) | PL.(2). W.(T.4,400 gls. from rainwater reservoir, UR.;[1] C.,SP.); LP.; Tr. Katrani is the station for Kerak which is reached by the motor-road through Lejjun, and is 20 miles distant to the west. |
| 203·7 | 327·0 | .. | Masonry viaduct over the Wadi Hafireh, 6 × 5 m. arches; height 3 m. |
| 216·1 | 339·4 | .. | Masonry bridge, 6 × 3 m. arches; height 3 m. |
| 225·5 | 348·8 | MENZIL (19) | PL.(1). |
| 227·6 | 350·9 | .. | Masonry viaduct, 5 × 6 m. arches; height 10 m. |
| c. 244·2 | c. 367·5 | *Fareifra* (11) | PL.(1).* Line ascends at 1 in 50 for a short distance, then crosses undulating desert country. There is a long descent of 1 in 55 into the Wadi Hasa. |
| 254·9• | 378·2 | KALAT EL HASA (19) | Alt. c. 2,700 ft. PL.(1); W.(T.6,600 gls. from well, R.; C.,SP.); LP. Line crosses the dry bed of the Wadi Hasa (details of bridge not available) and ascends tributary ravine southwards with gradient of 1 in 66. |
| 273·8 | 397·1 | .. | Masonry viaduct, 6 × 6 m. arches; height 12 m. |
| 274·5 | 397·8 | JEROUF (JURF ED DERAWISH) (25) | Alt. c. 3,220 ft. W.(T.8,000 gls.,UR; C.,WP.). Road leads north-west to Tafileh. Line climbs gradient of 1 in 80 and crosses the watershed of Wadi Hasa into the catchment of the Jafr depression, leaving the low watershed range 3 miles to the west. |
| 294·6 | 417·9 | .. | Masonry viaduct, 15 × 3 m. arches. |
| 299·7 | 423·0 | ANEIZA (KALAT ANEIZA) (17) | Alt. 3,450 ft. PL.(1). Track leads west to Shobek. |
| c. 317·0 | c. 440·3 | WADI JARDUN (19) | PL.(3); GP.; GS. |
| 321·5 | 444·8 | .. | Masonry viaduct, 6 × 5 m. arches; height 6 m. |
| 331·6 | 454·9 | .. | Masonry viaduct, 10 × 6 m. arches; height 10 m. (photo. 139). |
| 333·2 | 456·5 | .. | Masonry bridge, 4 × 5 m. arches; height 5 m. |

[1] The well at Katrani has dried up. A new bore is being sunk to get a fresh well. Rainwater is now accumulated in a reservoir capable of holding 6½ million gallons, and pumped to overhead tanks.

138. *Tunnel on the railway south of Amman* (km. *105·1*)

139. *Railway bridge over dry wadi near Maan* (km. *331·6*)

140. *The desert near pumping station H4 in wet weather*

141. *Auto-patrol laying the surface mat over a desert culvert*

142. *Motor-mechanical angle-dozer clearing a track in the lava belt*

| Km. from | | Stations and | |
| Deraa | Damascus | passing-loops | Remarks |
|---|---|---|---|
| 335·7 | 459·0 | Maan (14) | Alt. 3,540 ft.  PL.(3); W.(T.8,800 gls. from well,[1] R.; C.,SP., WP.); F.; GP.; GS.; ES.(3); Sdgs.(7). Line follows tributary wadi westwards. |
| c. 349·7 | c. 473·0 | Ain Waheida (17) | PL.(1).* |
| c. 366·7 | c. 490·0 | Ain Abu Lisan (Lusan) (10) | PL.(1).* |
| c. 376·7 | c. 500·0 | Nakb Shtar | PL.(1).*  W.(from newly bored well; details not available). Heavy motor transport can reach Nakb Shtar from the port of Akaba, by way of the Wadi Itm (Yutm Nijad). |

## ROADS

There are very few metalled roads in Transjordan, but much of the desert is passable for motors and a number of tracks have been improved to take light or heavy motors; these are only impassable for short periods after heavy rain. Generally speaking, the roads to-day follow the historical pattern, for the old pilgrim road, *Darb el Haj*, still runs along the desert's edge from north to south, though its alinement is now also taken by the Hejaz railway, and though a better and much more interesting road to the west of it has recently been improved from Amman southwards through Madeba, Kerak, and Tafileh. Moreover this follows an old Roman alinement for much of its way. In the south also the ancient route by which the Israelites are traditionally supposed to have reached the Transjordan plateau from Ezion-Geber at the head of the gulf of Akaba has now been improved through the defile of the Wadi Itm to take heavy lorries to the railway terminus south of Maan, and the route by the Wadi Araba has been made fit for light motors to the south end of the Dead Sea and the Lisan peninsula, whence a passable track has been made by the Seil Kerak to Kerak, an ancient route that must have been used in Crusading times.

Farther north the ancient campaigning route from Jerusalem by Jericho to Amman is now a first-class metalled road. It crosses the Jordan by the Allenby Bridge, and, as would be expected, there are many roads fit for cars in fine weather which link it and the capital to the fertile settlements of the Ajlun highland to the north. Only one modern road in Transjordan can claim no historical basis. This

[1] A new well with a good supply has been bored since 1939.

is the new trunk road between Haifa and Baghdad which crosses the Jordan at Jisr el Majami to Irbid, an ancient alinement perhaps to this place, but thereafter striking east through Mafrak and across the desolate lava belt and waterless desert beyond to the wells of Rutba in Iraq. In the past the lava belt was never easy of passage, and great labour with motor-mechanical angle-dozers and heavy rooters was required to clear the basalt blocks, before the trans-desert road to Baghdad was fit for heavy lorries in almost all weather (photo. 142).

Brief notes on some of the roads are given below, but since most of them are unmetalled, no attempt is made to assess their actual surface condition. They are described in the following order (fig. 58):

1. The main metalled road from the Allenby Bridge to Amman, which is part of the Jerusalem–Amman road.
2. The main metalled road from Jisr el Majami along the general alinement of the oil pipe-line, part of the through trunk road between Haifa and Baghdad.
3. The unmetalled pilgrim road, *Darb el Haj*, from Deraa through Amman to Maan.
4. The reconstructed road west of the pilgrim road, from Amman through Madeba, Dhiban, Kerak, Tafileh, and Shobek, to Maan.
5. The reconstructed road from Akaba through the defile of the Wadi Itm to Abu Lisan and Maan.
6. The track from Akaba by the Wadi Araba to the Dead Sea and by the Seil Kerak to Kerak.
7. The unmetalled roads in the north linking the chief villages with Amman.
8. The principal links joining the pilgrim road and railway to the western road through Madeba and Kerak.
9. The principal tracks east of the Hejaz railway.

1. *Allenby Bridge to Amman* (43 miles, 69 km.)

This is a well-graded metalled road, fully bridged and with culverts throughout, and fit for continuous heavy traffic. The Allenby Bridge, 28½ miles (46 km.) from Jerusalem, is about 1,140 feet below sea-level. The road keeps close to the Wadi Nimrin across the open floor of the Ghor and enters the Jordan escarpment near the small village of Shunet Nimrin and immediately north of Tell Nimrin. It climbs steadily with well-engineered gradient up the left bank of the Wadi Nimrin (Wadi Shaib), which is lined with wild oleanders, and crosses to the right bank by a stone bridge (Jisr Wadi Shaib) about 1,000 feet above sea-level. Here the gradient becomes steeper and as the town of Es Salt is approached there are orchards of figs and pomegranates, and some cultivation.

Es Salt (*c.* 2,750 ft.), which is reached at mile 24, is a busy market-town with a population of about 20,000, of whom 6,000 are Christians (photo. 121). It specializes in the production of raisins, from grapes grown on the neighbouring slopes. The town is built round both sides of a hill at the junction of two narrow tributaries of the Wadi Shaib. Jebel Yusha (3,640 ft.), immediately to the north, commands a wide view of the Jordan valley and has a small Moslem shrine traditionally holding the tomb of the prophet Hosea.

Beyond Es Salt the road continues north to the watershed between the Shaib and the Zerka and then turns east-south-east along the undulating plateau, climbing gradually towards Suweileh, a large village inhabited by Circassians and Chechens, which is reached at about mile 34 from Allenby Bridge (km.-post 14 from Amman). It is the main road-junction for unmetalled roads to the Ajlun highland to the north (routes 7 below). A mile and a half beyond Suweileh the road reaches its highest point, about 3,400 feet above sea-level, and then descends gradually to Amman (*see* Appendix D, 'Some Historical Sites in Transjordan').

2. *Trunk road Jisr el Majami–Irbid–Mafrak–H5 Pumping station–Iraq boundary* (220 miles, 354 km.) (photos. 140–2)

This road was completed in 1940 and is now passable throughout its length for heavy motor traffic except for short periods after heavy rain. It will take axle-loads up to 8 tons and motor traffic with tyre pressures up to 80 lb. per sq. inch. Bridges and culverts are built to this specification, but heavier traffic is allowed, provided it uses the causeways and not the bridges. Mails use this road from Baghdad to Haifa and there is growing commercial lorry traffic. The road is dealt with in four sections.

(*a*) *Jisr el Majami to Irbid* (24 miles, 38 km.). The road rises from 820 feet below sea-level at the Jordan crossing to 1,840 feet at Irbid. After crossing the Wadi Arab at Esh Shuni it ascends the Awaj tributary, crosses the Wadi Samma, and climbs over the plateau to cross other tributaries of the Wadi Arab near their sources. The Transjordan Public Works Department has recently improved this section of the road, widening it to a 16-foot surface on a 23-foot formation, and it is now fully bridged and is complete with culverts.

The alinement and gradients are good, but there are some sharp bends. There is a road connexion from the Jordan crossing at Jisr esh Sheikh Hussein to the main road near Esh Shuni.

(b) *Irbid to Mafrak* (26 miles, 42 km.). The road follows an entirely new alinement and is not yet shown on maps. For the first 6 miles it is some 3 miles north of the pipe-line and traverses good agricultural land with cotton soil and red clay, then over loam with limestone outcrops. Desert is reached about mile 10, the road crossing a low pass. The maximum gradient is 1 in 20; the formation is raised about

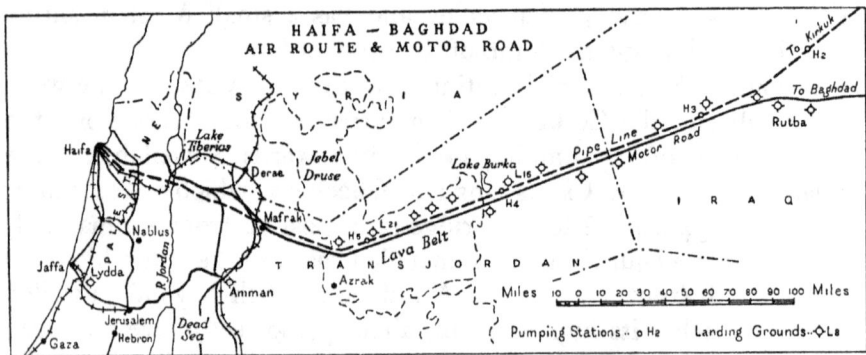

FIG. 59. *The Pipe-line and desert motor-road*

18 inches and has base and surface courses of crushed limestone metalling, consolidated, sealed, and surfaced with bitumen.

(c) *Mafrak to the east end of the Lava Belt* (114 miles, 184 km.). Mafrak is a station on the Hejaz railway, the stores railhead for the Iraq Petroleum Company, and grew to importance during the construction of the oil pipe-line. It has a good tube well, an electric-light plant, rail-sidings, and a small I.P.C. staff. It now forms an important stage on the new road, and the last permanently inhabited spot before the desert crossing.

From a little west of Mafrak to the lava belt, 9½ miles beyond, the road is over hard flat desert passable in all weathers for a limited number of vehicles. The lava belt stretches for over a hundred miles and is broken by gullies and closely packed with black basalt boulders. The I.P.C. had cleared a track through the lava and soled it to make a road 18 feet wide, but the surface was rough and became impassable in wet weather. The whole section has been reconstructed, three major realinements of the old road have been made, and about one-quarter of the old road has been regraded. After cutting through the rock and clearing a level surface, the new road was soled with lava ash, metalled with crushed lava, and consolidated and surfaced with bitumen. The road passes H5 Pumping station at about mile 62 (km. 100) from Mafrak.

(d) *Desert east of the Lava Belt to the Iraq frontier* (56 miles, 90 km.). The road beyond the lava belt runs over slightly undulating desert of alluvial clay, passing H4 Pumping station at about mile 124 (km. 200) from Mafrak. The clay is underlaid with limestone at shallow depth and has often a surface of flints. As in the section between Irbid and Mafrak, the road formation has been raised and consolidated about 18 inches above desert level with a surface width of 26 feet and with base course and surface metalling of crushed stone, consolidated, sealed, and surfaced with bitumen. One major wadi, the Wadi Burka, had to be bridged. Piers and abutments are of concrete faced with masonry and there are six 30-foot spans (standard heavy-bridge spans of Crown Agents' type).

3. *The Pilgrim Road* (Darb el Haj) *from Deraa through Amman to Maan*

The old pilgrim road has been largely superseded by the railway and by the new route on the west (route 4). It has never been reconstructed throughout to take heavy motor traffic, but is generally passable for motors in fine weather. Its general alinement is slightly west of the Hejaz railway throughout, though it takes a rather straighter alinement north and south of Mafrak and avoids many of the twists of the railway south of Amman. Improvements have been made on the road south of Amman, and it is a good unmetalled road as far as Katrani. It passes through Kastel (20 miles from Amman) and Ziza (mile 23), where there are ruins of an Arab castle. At Kalat ed Daba (2,463 ft.) road and railway are side by side, and afterwards are never far apart. There is a large rain reservoir 70 yards long by 50 yards wide at Katrani, but water-supply is unreliable, and is indeed the principal difficulty throughout this route.

4. *Amman–Madeba–Dhiban–Kerak–Tafileh–Shobek–Maan*

This road has been greatly improved in recent years and has become more important than the pilgrim road, for it passes through most of the inhabited places of the highlands and is comparatively well supplied with water. It is said to be fit now for medium motor lorries throughout, but it is uncertain whether it is yet fully bridged.

It runs south-west from Amman through the villages of Naur, El Al, and Husban (*anc.* Heshbon) which is passed at mile 17½, whence it takes the alinement of the old Roman road to Madeba (mile 23) (*see* Appendix D).

Madeba is the junction of a number of tracks passable to light cars in fine weather: north to Suweileh, north-west to Shuni, and south-west to the Wadi Zerka-Main and the warm sulphur springs at Hammam ez Zerka (p. 484). On a spur about 4 miles north of the Zerka-Main is Mukaur, the ruins of the ancient castle of Machaerus, where John the Baptist was imprisoned.

South of Madeba the new road continues south through Libb and Dhiban, where the 'Moabite Stone' was discovered (p. 436). Thence it crosses the gorge of the Wadi Mojib (Arnon) and traverses fine mountain country to Kerak, where there is an improved road down the Seil Kerak to the Lisan peninsula on the Dead Sea (route 6), and eastwards to Katrani on the Hejaz railway (*see also* Appendix D).

At Leban the road crosses the Wadi Hasa, then climbs over the crest of the plateau to Tafileh, and passes the ruined walls of Shobek castle before joining the older road from Maan to the Wadi Musa, not far from the ruins of Petra.

### 5. *Akaba–Abu Lisan–Maan* (*c.* 75 miles, 121 km.)

No details of the work recently carried out on this old Roman road are yet available for publication, but the track through the Wadi Itm and up to the plateau has been made fit for heavy lorries, which can now travel from Akaba to Maan, passing the new railhead (Nakb Shtar) at mile 50.

### 6. *Akaba–Ain Hasb–Ghor es Safi–Kerak.*

This is an earthen track which has had a made-up formation for much of the way, but is often in very bad repair. It is the only route from Akaba to the plateau fit for motor vehicles alternative to that by the Wadi Itm mentioned above (route 5), but it can at present only take light motors. All wheeled traffic is completely interrupted in wet weather when the wadis are in flood, but may be resumed with care when the waters subside (p. 385).

For the first hundred miles the track follows the western side of the Wadi Araba depression, which is enclosed on both sides by impassable escarpments; it crosses the watershed between the Red Sea and the Dead Sea near Jebel Rishi. Some improvements have recently been carried out in this section and ditches have been dug in some places to prevent flooding, but it is not known whether such work is likely to be permanent. Beyond Ain Hasb (mile 93, km. 150) the track was in need of extensive reconstruction for use by lorries in January 1943 and, though passable with difficulty, much of the formation had been washed away. The track crosses the Ghor at the south end of the Dead Sea to the Palestine Potash Company's works at Ghor es Safi, and then skirts the south-east shore to the mouth of the Seil Kerak at the north end of the Lisan peninsula. From here there is a recently constructed unmetalled road fit for light motors up the Seil Kerak to Kerak on route 4, whence Katrani on the railway may also be reached by a good unmetalled road, fit in fine weather for heavy motor traffic (route 8 (b)).

7. *The unmetalled roads in the Ajlun highland linking the chief villages with Amman*

(a) *Amman to Jerash* (35·5 miles, 57 km.). Suweileh, about 9 miles (14 km.) from Amman, on the Jerusalem–Amman motor-road, is the chief road junction for the roads to the Ajlun highland. A good unmetalled road leaves Suweileh and descends a broad open valley northwards. After following the bottom of the valley for some distance it climbs gradually to a high ridge from which it descends 1,500 feet abruptly with hairpin bends to the bottom of the Wadi Zerka. After crossing the stream by the new Jerash bridge (alt. 460 ft.), the road climbs a spur on the northern bank keeping to the western slopes of the Wadi Tawahin, which it crosses about mile 32 (km. 51·5). Beyond the crossing there is a branch to Ajlun and the north-west, the main road turning east to Jerash, now a small Circassian village on the east bank of the Wadi Suf (*see* Appendix D).

(b) *Amman to Ajlun* (direct, 43·5 miles, 70 km.; by Jerash, 51 miles, 82 km.). The direct road to Ajlun, which is the better of the two, leaves the road last described after crossing the Wadi Tawahin (mile 32 from Amman), passes through the hamlets of Kitte and Reimon to Sakib (mile 36), climbs steadily the southern slopes of Umm ed Daraj to 3,675 feet, and descends to Anjera (mile 41) and Ajlun (mile 43½), near the head of the Wadi Kefrenji.

The alternative road through Jerash leads north-west from there through Suf (mile 41) and just beyond the village of Ibbin (or Abbin) joins the road from Ajlun to Irbid (*below*). The country passed through is pleasantly wooded with dwarf oak and pines. Ajlun is a small village with the ruined castle of the Saracen emirs, built on the hill to the west to watch the Jordan crossings (Appendix D).

(c) *Ajlun to Irbid* (20 miles, 32 km.). This also is a good unmetalled road running north-east up the Kefrenji and along the plateau watershed east of the Yabis and Zeklab headstreams through El Husn (mile 15). Irbid is the chief town of the northern district and an important stage on the new trunk road between Palestine and Iraq.

A number of other unmetalled roads connect with Irbid, among which may be mentioned the road north and then north-west to Umm Keis, the ancient Gadara, 19 miles from Irbid, and that east through Remtha (14 miles) to Deraa (23 miles). Remtha can also be reached direct from Amman through Jerash (72 miles), and there is a motorable road from Remtha to Mafrak (26 miles). The distances given above are approximate. (*For* Gadara, *see* Appendix D.)

8. *Principal links joining the pilgrim road and railway to the western road through Madeba and Kerak:*

(a) *From Ziza to Madeba* (*c.* 13 miles, 21 km.). The track goes south-west to Umm Kuseir (mile 5), climbs to the watershed between the Wadi Wala and Wadi Zerka-Main (Habis), crosses this stream (mile 10), and climbs to Madeba.

(b) *Katrani to Kerak* (*c.* 20 miles, 32 km.). The track is good and passable for heavy motor traffic in fine weather, but the Wadi Mukheires forms an obstacle which is crossed close to Lejjun. This was the usual route to Kerak before the Madeba–Kerak road was reconstructed.

(c) *Jurf ed Derawish to Tafileh* (*c.* 22 miles, 35 km.). The track leads north-west over the plateau watershed south of the Wadi Hasa.

(d) *Kalat Aneiza to Shobek* (*c.* 12 miles, 19 km.). This is a short track direct over the desert with no obstacles.

9. *Desert tracks east of the Hejaz Railway*

The desert east of the railway south of Amman offers few obstacles to motor travel except at the crossings of wadi beds, where delay may be caused by having to make ramps down to the bed of the stream. The chief tracks from the railway are Amman to Kasr Azrak, Katrani to Bayir, and Maan through Jafr to Bayir.

## AIR ROUTES

The Alexandria–Baghdad air-route of Imperial Airways (p. 393) traverses the country from west to east, the Lydda airport being the last station in Palestine, and Rutba the first halt in Iraq. The mail planes do not stop in Transjordan, but there is a Royal Air Force airfield with a R.A.F. detachment at Amman, and a number of intermediate landing-grounds along the pipe-line; these are numbered L.G. 14, 15, 16, &c., to L.G. 22 north of Kasr Azrak and there are two intermediate ones between L.G. 22 and Amman. Lights are shown at Amman, Kalat Zerka, L.G. 20, and the I.P.C. airfield at H 4 Pumping station, where there is also radio-communication.

Other landing-grounds used for administrative purposes are at Ziza, Katrani, the Lisan peninsula, Maan, Bayir Wells, and Akaba, and the Iraq Petroleum Company have a landing-ground at Mafrak.

*For* SIGNAL COMMUNICATIONS *see* Chapter XIII, pp. 395–7.

## THE PORT OF AKABA AND THE ADJACENT COASTS OF PALESTINE AND TRANSJORDAN

The gulf of Akaba is about 100 miles long from north-north-east to south-south-west, and varies in width from 7 to 14 miles. The entrance is obstructed by extensive reefs round Tiran island, and the shores are steep-to. The only anchorages are at Sherm Mujawan, Sherm Dhaba, Bir el Mashiya, and between Humaidha island and the mainland on the east side of the gulf; at Mersa Dahab, Ras Arser, Wasit, Nawibi, Abu Ramlah, and off Firaun island on the west side. Akaba is the only anchorage on the Palestine or Transjordan coasts of the gulf.

North-north-easterly winds, sometimes of considerable force but generally moderate in April and May, prevail for the greater part of the year, with an occasional change to southerly winds. The northerly winds raise a considerable swell, and the gulf is therefore almost devoid of native craft. All the anchorages, except Sherm Mujawan and Humaidha island, are exposed to the southerly winds, which sometimes begin suddenly and blow hard.

*Coast*

The head of the gulf is a semicircular bay about 3 miles wide. Its northern side is low and flat, being the end of the Wadi Araba, a wide, sandy valley which is part of the depression occupied farther north by the Dead Sea and the Jordan river. The eastern and western sides of the gulf are backed by mountains which continue northward to form the walls of the Wadi Araba and over which passes are few and difficult. Akaba is on the east side of the bay, and the beach for about 3 miles north-west of the village is sandy, clear of reefs, and suitable for landing, with low sandhills and scrub immediately inshore. From about half a mile inland, up the Wadi Araba, the land is flat and devoid of cover apart from occasional scrub. Farther round the bay to the west the low shore is backed by a narrow sandy plain behind which the mountains rise to over 2,300 feet. On the east side of the bay foul ground lies off shore for a mile south of Akaba, but farther south still, for another mile to El Burg point, the beach is suitable for landing, opening to a flat, swampy plain. The plain is commanded by precipitous mountains which run in an arc from Jebel Shahabi to Jebel Maaruf, and there is no cover between them and the shore. South of El Burg point the coast is steep-to and unsuitable for landing. The nearest anchorages to Akaba are off Jeziret Firaun (Pharaoh's island), about 2 miles south of the Palestine–Sinai frontier at Bir Taba, 8 miles from Akaba; and between Humaidha island and the mainland, 23 miles south of Akaba on the east side of the gulf.

AKABA.   29° 31′ N., 35° 00′ E.   (*Bib.* Ezion-Geber, Eloth; *Class.* Aelana.)   Pop. *c.* 200 (permanent inhabitants in 1941).

Akaba (photo. 143) is a small village on the east side of the head of the gulf, surrounded by groves of date-palms which conceal it from the sea. North of it lies the broad valley of the Wadi Araba, leading to the Dead Sea. East of it, and bending south-west to the coast at El Burg, steep, barren mountains form a strong defensive position in the rear, broken by the Wadi Itm, which takes the road to Maan, and immediately east of the village by the Wadi Shallala, which contains a well-concealed line of trenches built by the Turks during the War of 1914–1918.

From a naval point of view it is the most important place in Transjordan, because of its strategic situation near the frontiers of Sinai–Palestine, Palestine–Transjordan, and Transjordan–Saudi Arabia. The Sinai–Palestine frontier runs north-west from Bir Taba, about 8 miles south-west of Akaba round the coast of the gulf; the Palestine–Transjordan frontier runs up the Wadi Araba from a point 2 miles west of the village, and the Transjordan–Saudi Arabia frontier runs east-south-east from El Burg point, 2 miles south of the village. Akaba is still claimed by King Ibn Saud. It commands routes alternative to that of the Suez canal, has sheltered waters which make good seaplane anchorages, and has a natural airfield west of the village on a plateau overlooking the gulf.

*History*

As Ezion-Geber, the port from which Solomon's fleet sailed to

143. *Akaba from the sea*

144. *Akaba. View up the Araba depression*

145. *Akaba wireless post*

146. *Akaba Customs House and Fort from the west*

Ophir (*1 Kings* ix. 26), Akaba is famous, and it continued to be commercially important under the Romans, when it was once the headquarters of the tenth legion. The ruins of the biblical Eloth, classical Aelana, lie a little to the north of the present village, on the seashore. The fort is believed to have been built in 1588 by the Sultan Murad III, to protect the pilgrim route between Egypt and Mecca. The village lost its importance as a supply depot when the pilgrims turned to the sea-route. During the War of 1914–1918 it was an essential base of operations for Feisal's army, to which were attached a flight of Royal Flying Corps and British technical personnel. The present war, with the threat to the Suez canal and to the ports of Palestine, revived its function as a port of supply, and considerable improvement, though possibly temporary, has taken place in its port facilities and communications.

The *village* is merely a collection of roughly built huts of granite masonry, extending for 800 yards along the shore, among palm-groves owned from time immemorial by the Howeitat beduin. It still shows the effect of occupation during the War of 1914–1918, and the ruined buildings have been partly replaced by mud huts, chiefly occupied by fishermen. Some military huts overlook the bay from the slopes to the east. The old square fort, at the south end of the village, is not visible from the sea, and the white, well-built customhouse is the only conspicuous building. It is used as a general-purpose government office. The village headman is subordinate to the C.O. of the Arab Legion post, who acts as military commandant. The chief occupation of the inhabitants is fishing, but the attempt to develop the industry in recent years has not been successful, and the remains of the refrigerating plant now stand idle. An experimental fisheries station has recently been set up on the Palestine coast of the gulf by the Palestine Government, to discover whether a dried-fish industry can be organized.

Water-supply, though it varies with the season, is ample. There is a large deep well, formerly used for supplying pilgrim caravans, in the fort; another well near Chatham pier provides fair drinking-water, and there are springs north-west of the village. New wells have recently been drilled, and about 400 cubic metres of water per day are now available.

## The Port

There is anchorage in about 20 fathoms, sand and coral, from 2 to 2½ cables off shore near the village, and in 17–20 fathoms from

$2\frac{1}{4}$ to 3 cables off shore in the north of the bay. Both are exposed to southerly winds, which raise a heavy sea.

Chatham pier, which was in ruins in 1941, extends 200 feet west and north-west from the shore off the village west of the old fort. It is 1 foot above water-level, has a depth of about 3 feet on its south side, and is 500 yards from the nearest point of anchorage. The head and north side are foul, and there is a reef 50 feet south of it. It could be rebuilt to take lighters and boats, though the nearest available stone is on Firaun island. Victoria pier, now derelict, is 4 cables farther north. The white custom-house stands at the landward end of Chatham pier, conspicuous when approaching Akaba from the sea. During 1942 a new lighter basin was under construction north of the village, and by June of that year the wharf was three-quarters completed. A temporary wharf (Imperia wharf) has been built at the south end of the village. In September 1941 there were no lifting appliances, warehouses, or power plant, and at this date the capacity of the port was about 100 d.w. tons per day. In February 1943 this had increased to 600 tons as a result of the new port works.

### Communications

To increase the capacity of the port it has been necessary to improve communications inland. The track from Akaba by the Wadi Itm to Maan has been macadamized, and meets the new railhead of the Hejaz railway at Nakb Shtar, 50 miles from Akaba, 25 miles from Maan. This road is now fit for heavy lorries, and takes most of the traffic. The track up the Wadi Araba can only take light motors and is impassable in wet weather when the wadis are in flood, but it is the only alternative route to Transjordan, leading up the wadi to the south end of the Dead Sea with a branch east to Kerak (p. 518) and another west through Ain Hasb to Beersheba (p. 384) in Palestine. Another track follows the shore of the gulf westward past the police post to Bir Taba, with a branch across the frontier into Sinai for Nekhl.

There is an emergency landing-ground for aircraft about a quarter of a mile inland from the head of the gulf, where the Akaba–Nekhl track meets the one up the Wadi Araba to Ain Hasb and Kerak.

In 1941 there was no telegraph or telephone system, but the Arab Legion post has a wireless-telegraphy station in touch with Amman.

# APPENDIX A

# TABLE OF STRATA AND IGNEOUS ROCKS

## (*Palestine and Transjordan*)

| Period | Strata | Thickness (feet) |
|---|---|---|
| *Recent* | Dunes, beach deposits, blue marly clay, green clay, gypsum with chalky sands. Jordan Valley clays. | Various |
| *Pliocene* | False-bedded calcareous sandstones. Silts, sandstones, and conglomerates with basalt pebbles. In the west, silts and sandstones with abundant marine fossils. | Up to 1,900 |
| | White chalky and gypseous marls with veins and beds of gypsum. Basal conglomerate with basalt pebbles. | 160 |
| | Variegated bright-coloured chalky marls with gypsum veins. Conglomerates without basalt pebbles. | 590 |
| | Repetitions of cycles of conglomerates, sandstones, marls, and limestone containing melanopsis. | 1,980 |
| *Miocene and Oligocene* | Fossiliferous limestones and foraminiferal marls and clays only present in the west along the coastal slopes. | Up to 200 |
| *Eocene* | Marls and nummulitic limestones, as one facies; chalky limestones with nodules and beds of chert, as another. | Up to 1,080 |
| *Upper Cretaceous* | Chalk with flints and flint breccia, bituminous limestone. Phosphate rock interbedded with the chalks. Fossiliferous and rudist limestones, gypsum and gypseous limestone. | Up to 800 |
| *Middle Cretaceous* | Grey, red, and brown fossiliferous limestones with red and green shales associated with gypsum beds. Grey, yellow, white, and brown limestones and dolomites with fossiliferous horizons. Marls below. | Increasing north-westwards from 600 to 2,500 |
| *Lower Cretaceous* | White, red, and purple sandstones in the south, part of the Nubian sandstone. | About 2,000 |
| | Sandstone with shale, limestone, and marls to the north, also oolitic and ferruginous limestones with some gypsum. | 550 to 1,360 |
| *Jurassic* | Sandstones with beds of ash in the south, part of the Nubian sandstone. Variegated limestones with interbedded dolomites. | About 800 |
| *Triassic* | Marly limestone with chalky, red and rusty-coloured limestones with gypsum veins. Green, purple, and brown micaceous sandstones, purple shales with yellow sandstones. Local gypsum and red shale. | 250 to 300 |

| Period | Strata | Thickness (feet) |
|---|---|---|
| Carboniferous | Red shales and purple sandstones, passing down to calcareous shales and sandstone with manganese ore, part of the Nubian sandstone (age inferred from similarity to beds of this age in Sinai). | 80 to 150 |
| Cambrian | Black quartzite and grit with dark limestones containing fossils, associated with red and white sandstones. | 20 to 800 |
| Pre-Cambrian | Coarse conglomerates, quartzites, and schists. | .. |

### Igneous Rocks

| | | |
|---|---|---|
| Sub-Recent | Basalt and basanite flows. | .. |
| Pliocene | Basalt interbedded with conglomerates. | .. |
| | Intrusive nepheline syenite. | .. |
| Middle Cretaceous | Olivine basalts and tuffs. | .. |
| Jurassic | Olivine basalts and tuffs near the top. | .. |
| Pre-Cambrian | Granodiorites, rhyolite, trachytes, augite, nepheline, syenite, dolerite. | .. |

# APPENDIX B

# CHRONOLOGICAL TABLE

## (The earlier dates are approximate)

| Year | Palestine | General History | Year |
|------|-----------|-----------------|------|
| B.C. | | | B.C. |
| **EARLIEST CULTURE** | | | |
| 3000 | Settlements of Stone Age | .. | |
| 2500 | Semitic immigration into Canaan | Beginnings of Assyria | 2300 |
| | .. | Hammurabi of Babylon | 2280 |
| | .. | Hyksos invasion of Egypt | 1800 |
| | .. | Eighteenth Dynasty of Egypt | 1600 |
| 1479 | Conquest of Thothmes III: Battle of Megiddo | | |
| 1450 | Israelite Invasion (*earlier date*) | .. | |
| 1400 | Tell el Amarna Letters | .. | |
| 1350–1270 | Wars between Hittites and Egyptians | Rameses II (? the Pharaoh of the Oppression). Meneptah (? the Pharaoh of the Exodus) | 1292–1225 |
| **ISRAELITE KINGDOMS** | | | |
| 1200 | Israelite Invasion (*later date*) and 'Sea-raiders' (Philistines) | End of Hittite Empire | 1200 |
| 1025 | Accession of Saul | .. | |
| 1000 | King David captures Jerusalem | .. | |
| 935 | Separation of Israel and Judah | .. | |
| 930 | Jerusalem sacked by Pharaoh Shishak | Rise of Assyrian Empire | 883 |
| 880 | Omri founds Samaria | .. | |
| 876–853 | Ahab, King of Israel | .. | |
| 727–699 | Hezekiah, King of Judah | .. | |
| 722 | End of the Kingdom of Israel: First Exile | .. | |
| 701 | Sennacherib besieges Jerusalem | .. | |
| 637–608 | Josiah, King of Judah | .. | |
| 620–580 | Jeremiah | .. | |
| **BABYLONIAN AND PERSIAN RULE** | | | |
| 608 | Battle of Megiddo: Egyptian Conquest | Fall of Assyria: Rise of Babylonia | 606 |
| | .. | Nebuchadnezzar defeats the Egyptians at Carchemish | 604 |
| 597 | Nebuchadnezzar takes Jerusalem: | .. | |
| 586 | Second Exile | Cyrus the Persian conquers the Medes | 549 |
| 539 | Persian rule replaces Babylonian | Cyrus conquers Babylonia | 539 |
| 537 | Return of the Jews under Zerubbabel | Cambyses conquers Egypt | 525 |
| 520–516 | Rebuilding of the Temple | Darius invades Europe | 515 |
| | .. | Xerxes succeeds Darius | 486 |
| | .. | Xerxes defeated at Thermopylae and Salamis | 480 |
| 457 | Ezra arrives in Jerusalem | .. | |
| 445 | Nehemiah arrives in Jerusalem | .. | |
| 444 | Re-establishment of the Law | .. | |
| 431 | Pentateuch completed | .. | |
| 360 | Samaritan Temple on Mt. Gerizim | Philip of Macedon unites Greece | 337 |
| | .. | Alexander invades Asia | 334 |
| **HELLENISTIC PERIOD** | | | |
| 332 | Alexander in Palestine | Death of Alexander | 323 |
| 320–301 | Wars of the Successors | .. | |
| 301 | Ptolemaic sovereignty established | Foundation of Kingdom of Parthia | 250 |
| | .. | Antiochus III the Great | 223 |
| 217 | Antiochus defeated at Raphia | .. | |

| Year | Palestine | General History | Year |
|---|---|---|---|
| B.C. | | | B.C. |
| 198 | Battle of Paneas: Antiochus establishes Seleucid sovereignty | Romans defeat Antiochus at Magnesia | 190 |
| 169 | Temple plundered by Antiochus IV Epiphanes | .. | |
| 168 | Revolt of the Maccabees | .. | |
| 165 | Recovery and cleansing of the Temple | .. | |
| 161 | Death of Judas Maccabaeus | .. | |
| 153 | Jonathan, High Priest (150, Ethnarch) | .. | |
| 143 | Simon Maccabaeus: Judaea independent | .. | |
| 103–76 | Alexander Jannaeus | .. | |

ROMAN PERIOD

| Year | Palestine | General History | Year |
|---|---|---|---|
| 64 | Rise of the Pharisees | Syria a Roman province | 64 |
| 63 | Pompey takes Jerusalem | .. | |
| 62 | Hyrcanus becomes a Roman vassal | Caesar invades Gaul | 58 |
| 42 | Mark Antony in Palestine | Battle of Philippi | 42 |
| | .. | Parthian invasion | 40 |
| 37 | Herod becomes Roman client king | Battle of Actium | 31 |
| | .. | Augustus becomes Roman Emperor | 27 |
| 4 | Birth of Jesus: Death of Herod | | |
| A.D. | | | A.D. |
| 6 | Judaea a Roman province | .. | |
| 26 | Beginnings of Christ's ministry | .. | |
| 26–36 | Pontius Pilate, Procurator of Judaea | .. | |
| 31 | The Crucifixion | .. | |
| 37–44 | Herod Agrippa I, King of Palestine | .. | |
| 45 | Roman province re-established | .. | |
| 59–60 | St. Paul's voyage to Rome | .. | |
| 66–73 | Jewish insurrection | .. | |
| 70 | Destruction of Jerusalem by Titus | .. | |
| 73 | Fall of Masada | .. | |
| 130 | Jerusalem rebuilt by Hadrian | .. | |
| 132–5 | Revolt of Bar Cochba | .. | |
| 136 | Aelia Capitolina (Roman Jerusalem) | .. | |
| 200 | Compilation of the *Mishna* | Coming of the Goths | 250 |
| | | Constantine recognizes Christianity | 323 |
| 326 | Empress Helena discovers the Holy Sepulchre | Foundation of Constantinople | 330 |
| | .. | Baptism and death of Constantine | 337 |
| | .. | Final division of the Empire | 395 |
| | .. | End of the Western Empire | 476 |
| 527–65 | Justinian's buildings | Birth of Mohammad | c. 569 |
| 614 | Sack of Jerusalem by Persians | The Hejira | 622 |
| 628 | Recovery of Jerusalem | Arabs raid Mutah | 628 |
| | .. | Death of Mohammad | 632 |
| | .. | Death of Abu Bekr: Succession of Omar | 634 |

RISE OF ISLAM

| Year | Palestine | General History | Year |
|---|---|---|---|
| 636 | Battle of the Yarmuk | Arabs capture Damascus | 636 |
| 638 | Fall of Jerusalem | Damascus, capital of the Ommayad Caliphate | 661 |
| 691 | The Dome of the Rock completed | Moslem conquest of Spain | 713 |
| | .. | Battle of Tours | 732 |
| | .. | Transfer of Caliphate to Baghdad | 750 |
| 831 | Church of the Holy Sepulchre restored | .. | |
| 969–70 | Fatimid conquest of Palestine | Fatimids conquer Egypt | 970 |
| c. 996 | Destruction of churches | Invasion of the Seljuk Turks | 1070–85 |
| | .. | Preaching of Peter the Hermit | 1096 |

THE CRUSADES

| Year | Palestine | General History | Year |
|---|---|---|---|
| 1097–9 | *First Crusade* | .. | |
| 1099–1187 | Latin Kingdom of Jerusalem | .. | |
| 1100 | Baldwin I, King of Jerusalem | .. | |
| c. 1118 | Order of the Temple founded | Rise of Saladin | 1173 |
| | .. | Saladin's conquest of Syria | 1183 |
| 1187 | Battle of Hattin and Fall of Jerusalem | Division of Saladin's conquests among his heirs | 1193 |

| Year | Palestine | General History | Year |
|------|-----------|-----------------|------|
| A.D. | | | A.D. |
| 1189–92 | *Third Crusade*: Richard Cœur de Lion | Frank occupation of Constantinople | 1202–4 |
| 1229 | Emperor Frederick II recovers Jerusalem | .. | |
| 1253 | Jerusalem taken by the Mamluks | Mongols under Hulagu capture Baghdad | 1258 |
| 1260 | Jerusalem destroyed by Mongols | .. | |
| 1271 | Prince Edward relieves Acre | .. | |
| 1291 | Fall of Acre and Atlit: end of Frank occupation | .. | |
| 1400 | Invasion by Timur | Sultan Mohammad II takes Constantinople | 1453 |
| 1492 | Expulsion of the Jews from Spain and settlement in Palestine | Portuguese defeat Mamluk fleet off Diu in the Arabian Sea | 1509 |

## OTTOMAN RULE

| Year | Palestine | General History | Year |
|------|-----------|-----------------|------|
| 1517 | Ottoman Turks seize Palestine | End of Mamluk rule in Egypt | 1517 |
| 1537 | Suleiman the Magnificent rebuilds the walls of Jerusalem | Portuguese defeat Suleiman's fleet off Diu | 1538 |
| 1570 | Joseph Nasi rebuilds Tiberias | .. | |
| 1700 | Fakr ed Din rules northern Palestine | Clive Governor of Bengal (1758–60; 1765–7) | 1758–67 |
| 1799 | Napoleon invades Palestine | .. | |
| 1831–40 | Mehemet Ali invades Palestine | .. | |
| 1839 | British intervention | .. | |
| 1841 | Anglican Bishopric in Jerusalem | Crimean War (1854–6); Indian Mutiny (1857) | 1854–7 |
| .. | | Indian government transferred to British Crown | 1858 |
| .. | | Druse Revolt in Syria | 1860 |
| .. | | Opening of Suez Canal | 1869 |
| | | German Empire created | 1871 |
| | | The Berlin Congress | 1878 |
| .. | | 'Young Turk' Revolution | 1908 |
| 1897 | First Zionist Congress | .. | |
| | | First World War: British Protectorate in Egypt: British land in Iraq | 1914 |
| 1916 | British invade Palestine | Arab Revolt in the Hejaz | 1916 |
| 1917 | Balfour Declaration: British capture Jerusalem | Bolshevik Revolution: Collapse of Russia: British capture Baghdad | 1917 |
| 1918 | British occupy Palestine and Syria | Defeat of Germany: the Armistices | 1918 |
| 1921 | British Civil Administration | Abdulla, Emir of Transjordan; Feisal, King of Iraq | 1921 |

## MANDATORY PERIOD

| Year | Palestine | General History | Year |
|------|-----------|-----------------|------|
| 1922 | British Mandate for Palestine and Transjordan | Mandates for Iraq (British) and Syria (French); Independence of Egypt recognized | 1922 |
| .. | | Treaty of Lausanne signed | 1923 |
| 1925 | Opening of Hebrew University | Ibn Saud King of Hejaz | 1925 |
| .. | | Anglo-Iraq Treaty: Anglo-Hejaz treaty | 1927 |
| 1929 | Foundation of Jewish Agency: Civil disturbances | .. | |
| 1930 | Shaw Commission Report | Mandate for Iraq ends: Kingdom of Saudi Arabia formed | 1932 |
| .. | | Rise of Hitler | 1933 |
| 1936–9 | Arab Rebellion | Anglo-Egyptian Alliance | 1936 |
| 1937 | Royal Commission's Report | .. | |
| 1939 | Statement of British Policy (Macdonald 'White Paper') | Second World War: Anglo-French-Turkish Treaty | 1939 |
| 1941 | Allies occupy Syria | Allies occupy Iraq and Persia: Declaration of Syrian independence: | 1941 |
| .. | | Anglo-Soviet Treaty | 1942 |
| .. | | Germans and Italians driven out of North Africa: Arab Governments confer on Arab federation | 1943 |

# APPENDIX C

# THE HOLY PLACES

PALESTINE'S principal title to fame is its place in the Bible narrative. To Jews and to Christians it is 'The Holy Land', and to Moslems Jerusalem is third in holiness after Mecca and Medina; the end of Mohammad's miraculous ride, and the first step on his journey to heaven. The country is consequently a land of pilgrimage to members of all three faiths, and by many such a pilgrimage is supposed to ascribe special sanctity to the pilgrim.

## CHRISTIAN SITES

Of the Christian sites the principal are in Jerusalem, Bethlehem, and Nazareth.

### JERUSALEM (pp. 323–30)

*The Church of the Holy Sepulchre* in Jerusalem encloses not only the reputed Tomb of Christ and consequently the site of the Resurrection but also the Place of the Crucifixion (photo. 147). The authenticity of these sites is not accepted by all Christians. It depends largely on the line of the Second Wall of Jerusalem (p. 326), since a tomb within that wall—that is, inside the city—is inconceivable. Until recent years the present North Wall, under which there are remains of an earlier one, was accepted as the Third Wall. The First Wall is known to have been in the neighbourhood of the Jaffa Gate. The Second Wall, therefore, lay between the two, on a line which could not be identified because of later buildings. But as another wall of the Roman period, found recently some distance north of the present North Wall, would appear to be the Third Wall, the present North Wall should lie on the Second Wall and there need be no buried wall between it and the Jaffa Gate.[1]

The discovery or selection of this site occurred during the pilgrimage of Helena, mother of Constantine, in the course of whose excavations a tomb was discovered, and then the wood and the nails of the Cross. At once two churches were erected on the site: the *Anastasis* or Church of the Holy Sepulchre, surrounding the tomb; and another dedicated to the Sign of the Cross. Of the latter only a part of the *atrium* remains. These churches were consecrated in A.D. 336. They were destroyed by the Persians three centuries later, but new churches, as well as a new church of Calvary, were erected within a few years by the Abbot Modestus. Not many years later

---

[1] This view was in part anticipated by the advocates of the 'Garden Tomb' (called 'Gordon's Tomb' from a remark attributed to General Charles George Gordon), for which there is no serious evidence.

147. *The Church of the Holy Sepulchre, Jerusalem*

148. *Interior of the Church of the Nativity, Bethlehem*

149. *The Mosque El Aksa, Jerusalem*

150. *Kubbet es Sakhra, the Dome of the Rock, Jerusalem*

a fourth church was dedicated to the Virgin. From time to time these buildings suffered damage by fire or enemy violence. The Crusaders at the beginning of the twelfth century erected a great building which enclosed all previous ones. Although much of this building was destroyed in 1187 and 1244, a large part of it is incorporated in the present church. In 1808 it suffered severely from fire, and was rebuilt two years later by the Greeks and the Armenians, who by now owned most of the buildings. Disputes as to ownership hindered repairs until 1868, when the Turkish Government, as neutral, intervened to reconstruct the dome, the condition of which was dangerous. In recent years the fabric has suffered seriously from earthquake and natural decay, and in 1938 it had to be closed while temporary repairs were effected at the expense of the Government of Palestine. Permanent repairs will be costly; the Christian communities of Palestine who are interested have not the means of paying for them; and, until the war ends, the temporary and precarious safeguards have to remain, concealing parts of the buildings.

The principal sacred sites within the church are the Tomb of Christ and the Place of Crucifixion. There are also many minor ones such as the Tomb of Adam.[1]

Almost all of the Christian communities have some share in the church, and their rights are very closely defined for the guidance of the Palestine Government, which is guardian of them all. As these rights often impinge on one another, tact and diplomacy have to be exercised to reconcile rival claims and keep the peace, for quarrels over apparently trivial matters have sometimes led to bloodshed.

The principal buildings are in Orthodox and Latin ownership: the *Catholicon*, formerly the nave of the Crusaders' church, said to have been built on the Garden of Joseph of Arimathaea, belongs to the Orthodox. But these properties are much mixed: the Chapel of the Invention of the Cross belongs to the Orthodox, but its altar is Latin property. Godfrey de Bouillon and Baldwin the first King of Jerusalem were buried within the church, but their tombs were destroyed by the Orthodox in the hope of eradicating all Latin claim to ownership.

Until very recent times Jews could enter the Church of the Holy Sepulchre only at the risk of their lives; some have even been murdered for passing near the sacred building. To-day, in their own interests, Jews are not admitted on the major festivals, such as the Orthodox Easter when the Miracle of the Holy Fire occurs annually. Occasionally an American or European Jew, or one not obviously Jewish, having gained admission, has had to be guarded and removed by the Moslem police who are always on duty within the Christian building; but at ordinary times European and

---

[1] More authentic is the grave of Sir Philip d'Aubigny, one of the signatories of Magna Carta, Governor of the Channel Islands and tutor of King Henry III, in the courtyard close to the entrance to the church. He went to Palestine as a Crusader and died in Jerusalem in 1236 (p. 108).

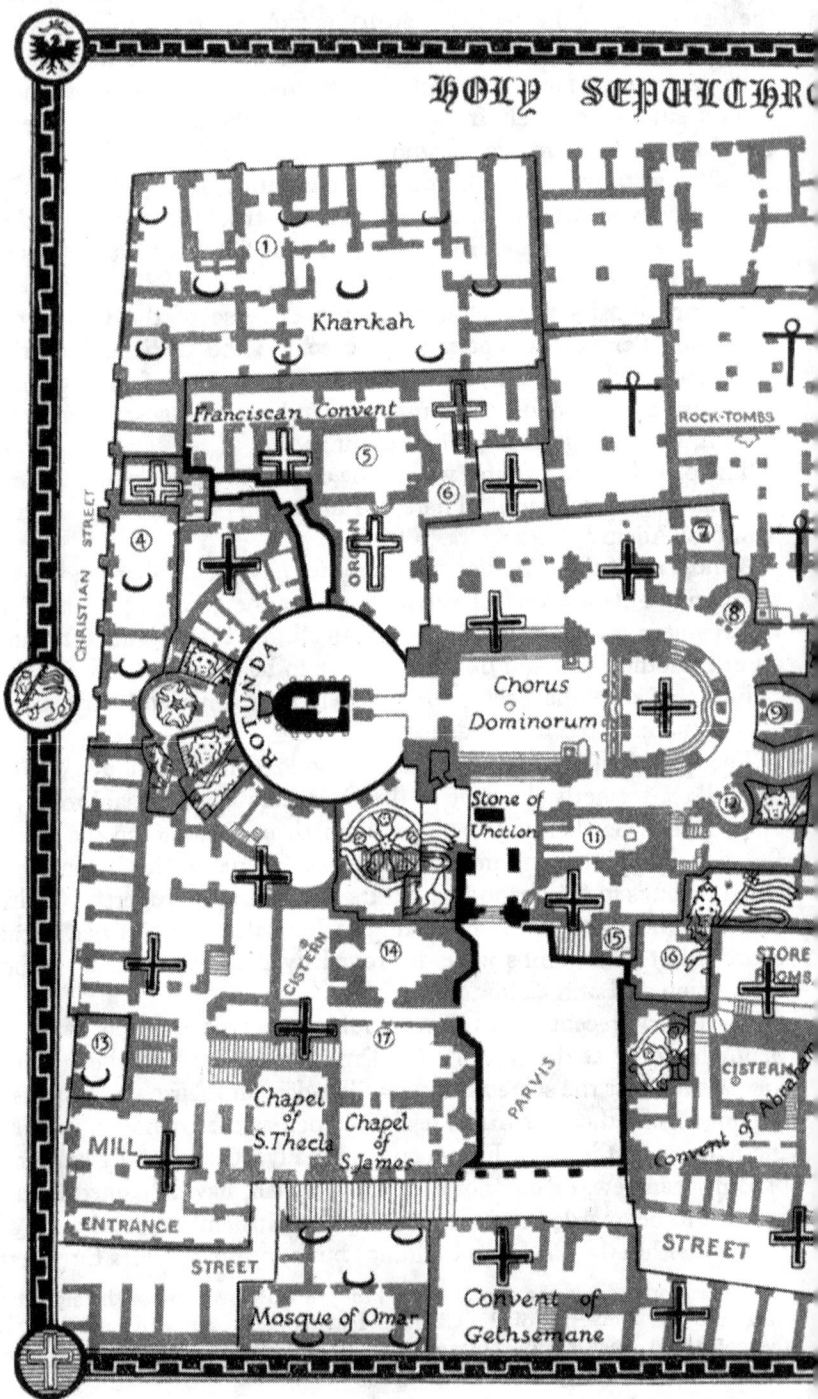

FIG. 60. *Plan of the Church of the Holy*

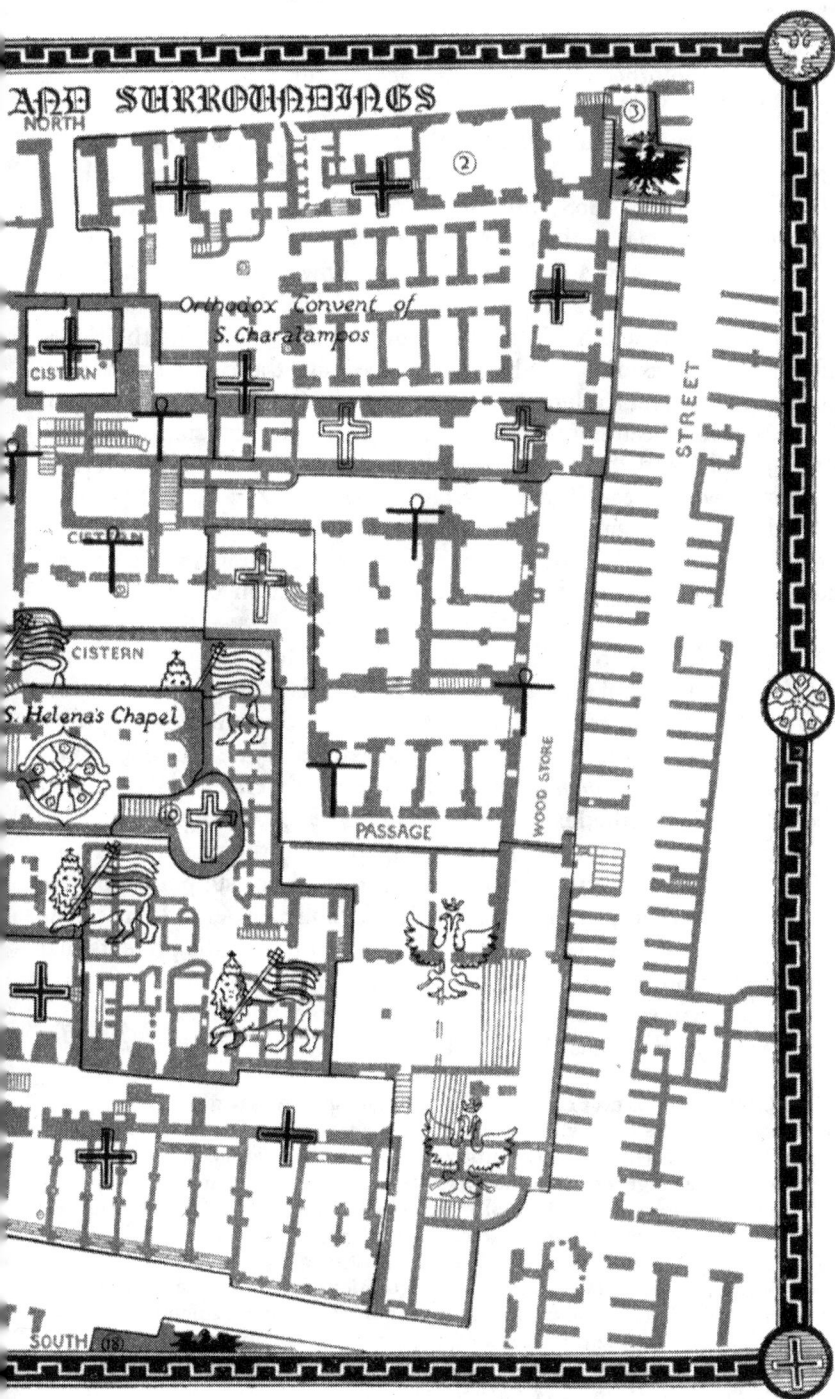

AND SURROUNDINGS

NORTH

②

③

Orthodox Convent of
S. Charalampos

CISTERN

CISTERN

STREET

CISTERN

S. Helena's Chapel

WOOD STORE

PASSAGE

SOUTH

*Sepulchre.* (For key see bottom of page 535)

American Jews are unlikely to be molested so long as they conduct themselves reverently.

The rights of the several communities in the Church of the Holy Sepulchre and the other sacred sites are governed by Article LXII of the Treaty of Berlin (1878), which lays down that the *status quo* must in every instance be observed. There had been similar rulings on several previous occasions, by the Sultan, and at international conferences, after a declaration by the Sultan in 1808; but the firman of Sultan Abdul Mejid in 1852 is the first formal declaration of the *status quo*. Article XIII of the Mandate for Palestine lays on the Mandatory Power the responsibility of seeing that the *status quo* is observed until the special Commission to be appointed, under Article XIV, 'to study, define, and determine the rights and claims in connexion with the Holy Places and the rights and claims relating to the different religious communities in Palestine' has reported, and its report has been adopted. But this special Commission has never been appointed,[1] and the relations of the communities are still governed by the *status quo*. By the *Palestine (Holy Places) Order in Council* (25 July 1924) all disputes or claims in regard to the Holy Places or religious buildings or sites in Palestine, or disputes or claims relating to the several religious communities, are taken out of the jurisdiction of the courts of Palestine.

The *Via Dolorosa*, from the Church of the Holy Sepulchre to St. Stephen's Gate, is full of sacred sites. Here there is more room for differences in identification, and as both the principal communities desire to secure all the sacred sites, every Latin site is matched by an Orthodox rival.

The *Garden of Gethsemane*, outside St. Stephen's Gate, is also shared between Latin and Orthodox. Near it is the *Tomb of the Virgin*, identified in the fourth century at latest. The Latins, although they lost their rights in this church in 1757, still demand its return and are supported by the Government of France, in the name of the Catholic Powers. In 1850 the rejection of this claim at the instance of Russia was one of the pretexts that led to the Crimean War. The Copts have the right to hold two services a week on the Armenian altars, and the Syrian Jacobites one.

The *Mount of Olives* has the traditional site of the Ascension which is

---

[1] If the Commission is ever constituted it will not have an easy task. In the words of Sir Harry Luke, the history of the Holy Sepulchre by itself 'will involve, when it comes to be undertaken, not only a study of the countless works, both manuscript and printed, of the pilgrims and other travellers, who in the course of seven centuries have written accounts of the Holy Sepulchre; it will also necessitate a critical examination of many *firmans* in Arabic, in Turkish, and in the Tataro-Arabic jargon employed by some of the Caucasian Mamelukes of Egypt which the Moslem rulers of Palestine granted to the several communities of the Holy Sepulchre. The circumstance that these *firmans* are not infrequently in contradiction with one another will not lighten the difficulties of the Holy Places Commission, when that body is constituted and has begun to address itself to the prosecution of its task.' H. C. Luke, *Prophets, Priests, and Patriarchs*, p. 38.

venerated by all the communities that hold rights in the Holy Places. The building is Moslem property, but all the Christian communities are permitted to hold services there on Ascension Day, the date of which fortunately does not coincide for all of them.

## BETHLEHEM (pp. 320–1)

*The Church of the Nativity* in Bethlehem is the second most sacred Christian site in Palestine (photos. 90, 148). It is the oldest building that has been continuously used as a church. Built by the Emperor Constantine in 330, it is in the centre of the town. Its two great festivals are the Latin Christmas Eve and the Greek, when the services are magnificent. Besides the reputed scene of the Nativity, the church encloses the altar of the Magi, the tomb of Eusebius, the cave in which St. Jerome translated the Bible into Latin, and his tomb. Adjacent are Greek, Latin, and Armenian convents.

## NAZARETH (pp. 333–4)

The third holy city of the Christians is situated on the southern slope of the mountains of Galilee near the crest, so that the visitor coming from the south or the west ascends among houses and streets until he has passed out of the city. The Latin Monastery in the south of the town encloses the fine Church of the Annunciation, on the site of the House of the Virgin. Only a cave or cistern remains, the house itself having been miraculously transferred (so it is said) to Loretto in Italy, at a time when Palestine was closed to Christian pilgrims. The present church dates from 1730, but two columns belong to an earlier building. The Column of Mary, a fragment of red granite, pendent from the roof, is supposed to mark the spot at which the angel appeared to announce the coming birth of Christ.

---

## KEY TO PLAN OF HOLY SEPULCHRE

✠ ORTHODOX

† COPTS

✝ LATINS

⌣ MOSLEM

RUSSIANS

ABYSSINIANS

JACOBITES

ARMENIANS

GERMAN

■ COMMON PROPERTY OF ALL CHURCHES

① Khankah Mosque
② Church of Saint Charalampos
③ Hospice of German Knights of Saint John
④ Maghsan el Belik
⑤ Chapel of the Apparition of the Virgin
⑥ Sacristy
⑦ Prison of Christ
⑧ Chapel of Saint Longinus
⑨ Parting of the Raiment

⑩ Chapel of the Invention of the Cross
⑪ Chapel of Adam
⑫ Chapel of Derision
⑬ Mosque
⑭ Chapel of the Martyrs
⑮ Chapel of S. Mary of Egypt
⑯ Chapel of Saint Michael
⑰ Chapel of S. Mary Magdalen
⑱ Lutheran Church

The only spring within the city, Ain Miriam, known also as the spring of Jesus or of Gabriel, is within the Church of Gabriel, the Orthodox 'Church of the Annunciation'. The water flows through a short conduit into the centre of the city, where it fills a little reservoir under an arch, and is the main water-supply (photo. 60). The Orthodox church, about 230 years old, is partly underground. South-west of the city is a little Maronite church close to a precipice, which has been identified with that over which the townspeople threatened to cast Jesus. This is, however, not the traditional 'Mount of Precipitation' of popular opinion, a precipice overlooking the plain of Esdraelon two miles south-east of the city (photo. 4).

## MOSLEM SITES

The sacred sites of the Moslems are also very numerous, and include wayside wells, shrines, and tombs of unknown holy men whose tradition goes back sometimes before the rise of Islam.

The *Haram esh Sherif* ('august sanctuary'), outstanding among Moslem holy places, occupies the site of the Temple of Jerusalem and the surrounding enclosure. Within this enclosure are the Dome of the Rock (*Kubbet es Sakhra*), wrongly termed the 'Mosque of Omar', and the Mosque *El Aksa*. The latter, built by Justinian in 536, is one of the earliest buildings still devoted to the worship of God, though under a different name (pp. 327–8).

There is no doubt that the *Haram esh Sherif*, the great open platform, in part natural, in part artificial, on which these two mosques stand, includes the site of the Temple of the Jews. The exact part of the platform on which the Temple was erected is disputed; but here stood the Temples of Solomon, of Zerubbabel, and of Herod, and here the last of the three was destroyed by the soldiers of Titus. Here also Hadrian erected his Temple of Jupiter. Then for centuries the site lay desolate, the receptacle of rubbish and of filth, purposely desecrated on account of its sanctity to the Jews, a state in which the Caliph Omar was so overcome to find it, that he began to cleanse it with his own hands. Omar erected a temporary place of worship over the central rock from which, according to Moslem tradition, Mohammad ascended with his steed to heaven. In 691 the present central building, the Dome of the Rock, was completed by the Caliph Abd el Malik, and two years later El Aksa at the far end of the platform was completed as a mosque. In the ninth and tenth centuries the Dome of the Rock was restored (photos. 149, 150).

In 1099, when Jerusalem passed into the hands of the Christians, the enclosure and its buildings were retained for religious purposes; the Dome of the Rock became a Church, the altar being placed on the sacred rock; and to maintain this 'Temple of the Lord' the Order of Knights Templar was founded. It thus became an architectural type which was followed by Christian architects throughout Europe, as in the Temple Church in London, and in churches at Cambridge, Northampton, Aix-la-Chapelle,

Metz, and elsewhere. El Aksa was transformed into the palace of the Templars, and was known as the 'Palace of Solomon'.

In 1187 the Christians were driven from Jerusalem, and Saladin immediately restored both buildings to their former Moslem use. All traces of Christian occupation were removed except the wrought-iron screen within the Dome of the Rock, and new decorations were introduced. Both buildings have since remained in Moslem use, the Dome of the Rock being renovated by Suleiman the Magnificent. Many biblical stories and Moslem traditions have long been attached to this site: the creation of Adam, the altars of Adam and Noah, the sacrifice of Isaac, Jacob's vision, the threshing-floor of Araunah the Jebusite, and Mohammad's ascent to heaven.

The Dome of the Rock, on a platform 10 feet high, in the centre of the enclosure is one of the most beautiful of buildings, in its proportions, its symmetry, the simplicity of its style, and the rich colours of its tiles, glass, and mosaics. Under the centre of the Dome is the *Sakhra* or Holy Rock, the actual mountain top, 58 feet long by 44 feet wide, projecting between 4 and 6½ feet above the pavement. This could not, on account of its size, have been the altar within Solomon's 'Holy of Holies', but it may have been his 'Altar of Burnt Sacrifice'—a theory that seems to be supported by reputed traces of a channel for draining away the blood. Underneath is a cave, approached by eleven steps, which may once have been a cistern or granary. The 'Well of Souls' (*Bir el Arwah*, the descent to Hades) is underneath. North of the Dome a jasper slab, said to cover the tomb of Solomon, is probably the grave of a Knight Templar.

Until the British occupation Christians and Jews were admitted to the *Haram esh Sherif* only exceptionally; now no discrimination is made, but they are expected to withdraw at prayer time.

*The Wailing Wall.* The Western Wall of the *Haram esh Sherif* is known as *El Burak* from the name of the miraculous steed of Mohammad; and this part of the enclosure and wall is exceptionally sacred to Moslems. The lower courses of this wall are, however, the one and only surviving remnant of Herod's Temple, and in consequence a most sacred site of the Jews; even when the Jews were excluded by the Romans from the city and its site, the prohibition was raised once a year so that they might pray at the Western Wall (*Kotel Maaravi*), now known as the 'Wailing Wall'. Since the return of the Jews to Jerusalem the side of this wall outside the *Haram* has been a place of continuous worship and of lamentation on sabbaths, festivals, and fasts, by the Jews of the city, and on special occasions by Jews from the remainder of the country, and by pilgrims from abroad. The Jews hold no property there, but they have the prescriptive right to worship (photo. 40).

In the last two years of the Ottoman period there were occasional disputes as to the extent of Jewish rights, but they were never serious. After the British occupation, however, the claims of the Jews became more insistent, and the resistance of the Moslems more determined. Political elements introduced from both sides culminated in demonstrations and bloodshed; and the 'Wailing Wall' question was one of the causes of the outbreak of 1929 (p. 126). With the approval of the Council of the League of Nations, the British Government appointed in 1930 a commission consisting entirely of foreign jurists 'to determine the rights and claims of Moslems and Jews'. The following conclusions were reached:

(*a*) The sole ownership of the Wall and its immediate approaches rests with the Moslems.

(*b*) The owners are not entitled to construct, demolish, or repair any of their property so as to interfere with the access of Jews to the Wall or their devotions there.

(*c*) The Jews should have free access to the Wall for the purpose of devotion at all times, subject to the conditions that had been laid down by the Government, with one additional right.

(*d*) Apart from a few ritual objects, no permanent or temporary structure or piece of furniture should be placed by the Jews on the pavement near the Wall.

(*e*) On the other hand, animals should not be driven across the pavement at certain stated periods, but the right of way by non-Jews at all times should be retained.

(*f*) The blowing of the ram's horn (*shofar*) by Jews and the carrying out of the *zikr* ceremony by Moslems in the neighbourhood of the Wall should both be prohibited.

(*g*) No person should use the place in front of the Wall or its surroundings for political speeches, utterances, or demonstrations.

The report was at once accepted by the Government and put into force.

*The Haram at Hebron.* Next in importance to the Moslems is the *Haram* at Hebron, which encloses the reputed Cave of Machpelah and the tombs of the Patriarchs, the ancestors of both the Jews and the Arabs. The present building was a Crusaders' Church, on the site of a church of Justinian, but the surrounding wall is apparently Herodian. The mosque is approached by two flights of steps, once jealously guarded against all unbelievers, though now Jews alone are prohibited from ascending. Even Jews, however, are permitted to mount seven of these steps; but one who placed his foot on the eighth would endanger his life. By the side of the fifth step is an aperture which is believed to lead to the Tombs of the Patriarchs, and into this aperture the Jews—those of Hebron are especially superstitious—are accustomed to drop messages to their ancestors. On Fridays the Jews pray and lament, as at the 'Wailing Wall' at Jerusalem. Inside the mosque—beautiful like other Moslem places of worship in its proportions and its simplicity—are six cenotaphs which are reputed to stand directly over the tombs of the Patriarchs and their wives in the cave below, to which no one is admitted. Joseph is said to have been buried in Hebron, but outside the sacred enclosure—though there is an alternative burial site at Nablus—but Rachel is buried on the high road close to Bethlehem (*below*). The tomb of Adam is shown at Hebron, but according to legend his grave stretches from Hebron to Jerusalem.

*Mount Carmel.* The proximity of Moslem and Jewish holy places usually leads to contest. But the group of shrines that pertain to Elijah, who is holy to both communities, and also to Christians, is an important exception. These centre on Mount Carmel, the 'Mountain of the Prophet Elijah' (*Jebel Mar Elias*) to the Arabs. From the hermits who clustered in the mountain arose the Order of Carmelites, more familiar in London as the 'White Friars'. By tradition this Order was instituted by Elijah out of the 'sons of the prophets', but it is now accepted that it dates only from 1156. The principal shrine on Mount Carmel is the cave in which Elijah is said to have dwelt; here is celebrated the Feast of St. Elias, a Maronite, Melkite, and Carmelite festival; all creeds and sects participate in it, and all are welcomed. Not far from Elijah's Cave is the 'Place of Burning' where fire from heaven consumed Elijah's offering, and at the foot of the mount, within sight of those celebrating the Feast of St. Elias on its summit, is the 'River of Slaughter' (*Nahr el Mukatta*) where the false prophets of Baal were slaughtered. Elijah may be said to be the patron saint of Palestine. To the Jews he is *Eliahu Hanavi*, 'Elijah the Prophet'; to the Christians *Mar Jirgis*, St. George; to the Moslems *El Khudr*, 'the Evergreen'.

## JEWISH SITES

The *Western Wall of the Temple* and the *Tombs of the Patriarchs*, both mentioned above as Moslem sites, are the principal holy places of the Jews. Third in importance is the *Tomb of Rachel*, at the point where the road to Bethlehem leaves the main road from Jerusalem to Hebron. This site has been accepted for many centuries by tradition, and is consistent with Genesis, xxxv. 19, 20. The present structure, a small domed building, was restored by Sir Moses Montefiore about 1840, but there was an earlier structure at least as far back as the fifteenth century, and for long before that the site was marked by a heap of stones. The tomb is Jewish property, but revered by both Jews and Moslems, who share ownership of the portico.

There are the reputed graves of many Jewish holy men in Palestine, especially near Safad and Tiberias, two holy cities of the Jews. These are places of pilgrimage, especially on reputed anniversaries of their deaths.

## APPENDIX D

# SOME HISTORICAL SITES IN TRANSJORDAN

THE sites described in the following pages have been selected as the best illustrations of different phases in the history of the country between the third century B.C. and the twelfth century A.D. All of them were places or buildings of some importance in their day. The mixed Hellenistic-Oriental culture of the earliest phase is exemplified at Petra and Arak el Emir; the Roman phase at Amman, Petra, Jerash and Umm Keis; the Christian phase at Jerash and Madeba, the Omayyad or early Muslim at Meshatta and Amman. Ajlun and Kerak illustrate a later stage, Ajlun the type of castle built by Muslim rulers to control marauding beduin, Kerak one of a series of Crusader fortresses. All these places are within easy access of Amman.

AJLUN

Ajlun is connected by road with Irbid in the north and Jerash to the east. The castle (*Kalat er Rabad*) occupies a magnificent position on a summit 3,363 feet above sea-level dominating the Jordan valley—800 feet below sea-level—and is visible as a landmark from many parts of Palestine; it is reached by a track from the village 750 feet below. It was begun in A.D. 1184–5 by Izz ed Din Usama, one of Saladin's emirs, partly to threaten the Crusaders in northern Palestine and in Transjordan to the south, partly to control the local Arabs of the Beni Auf. Thirty years later important additions were made by an emir called Aibak. The whole castle is surrounded by a scarped fosse; the principal buildings of Usama are a quadrilateral of four square towers connected by curtain walls on the high north-west side of the hill, and two baileys on the lower platforms; Aibak's chief work is the great tower to the south-east. The castle was partly ruined by the Mongols in 1260 but subsequently repaired: one of Usama's towers is still standing to its full height.

AMMAN

The name Amman has survived from the early period when this place, then called Rabbath Ammon, was the capital of the Ammonite kingdom (p. 438), but in the classical period it was known as Philadelphia, after Ptolemy Philadelphus of Egypt (p. 439). It is one of the places where Circassians were settled in 1878 and the ruins have suffered greatly since that date. By the river banks, where most of the modern houses stand, old travellers described a number of ancient buildings of which little or nothing remains, a colonnaded street, a temple, a *nymphaeum*, and a mosque of the Abbasid age; the great theatre (photo. 151), at the east end of the town opposite the Philadelphia Hotel, and a small *odeum* near it are the only impressive antiquities in this quarter; both date from the second or third century A.D. The ruins of a sixth-century basilica have been found in a garden at the west end; the ruins of another church underlie the government offices in the middle of the town. On the acropolis immediately to the north there are remains of at least three periods. Parts of the fortifications and the reservoir are certainly pre-Hellenistic. The foundations of two temples and a vast colonnaded court, which have been excavated by Italian archaeologists, are Roman, one of the temples containing an inscription of Marcus Aurelius. More interesting than any of these is a small cruciform building, called the *Kasr* by the people and fancifully identified by them as the tomb of Uriah 'the Hittite'; the walls inside are decorated with panels delicately carved with arabesques, vine, and palmette motives. The building was originally domed; its date and purpose have been much debated, but it is now generally assigned to the eighth century and regarded as the vestibule to an Omayyad palace.

## Arak el Emir

Arak el Emir is about 12 miles west-south-west of Amman, some two hours' ride beyond the terminus of a road from Amman to the Circassian village of Wadi Sir. It is the ancient Tyros, a name preserved in that of the wadi. Josephus (*c*. A.D. 70) has given a good description of it: a strong castle, built entirely of white stone with 'animals of a prodigious magnitude engraven upon it' and water round it, and near by caves 'of many furlongs in length' cut in the rocks. The existing ramifications of caves and the ruins of a palace with a great frieze of lions passant support the account of Josephus, but it is generally held now that he was wrong in attributing the remains to Hyrcanus who was expelled from Jerusalem in 175 B.C.; they were the work probably of a local dynast named Tobias who is mentioned in Greek papyri about 259 B.C. (p. 439), and whose name is carved in Hebrew letters on the rock façade. The ruins are impressive and particularly significant because they date from a period from which nothing comparable has survived, but they have not yet received the attention they deserve.

## Gadara

Umm Keis—also written Umm Qeis and Mukeis—is the site of the ancient Gadara, one of the foundation cities of the Decapolis (p. 441), the birth-place of the poet Meleager and of the cynic and satirist Menippus, and the scene of the famous episode of the swine in the Gospels. It is 1,200 feet above sea-level, and nearly 1,900 feet above the Jordan. It may be reached in a car either from Irbid, by taking a track north-westwards a little north of Beit Ras, the site of Capitolias, another city of the Decapolis, or from the Yarmuk by a steep climb from El Hammeh, on the

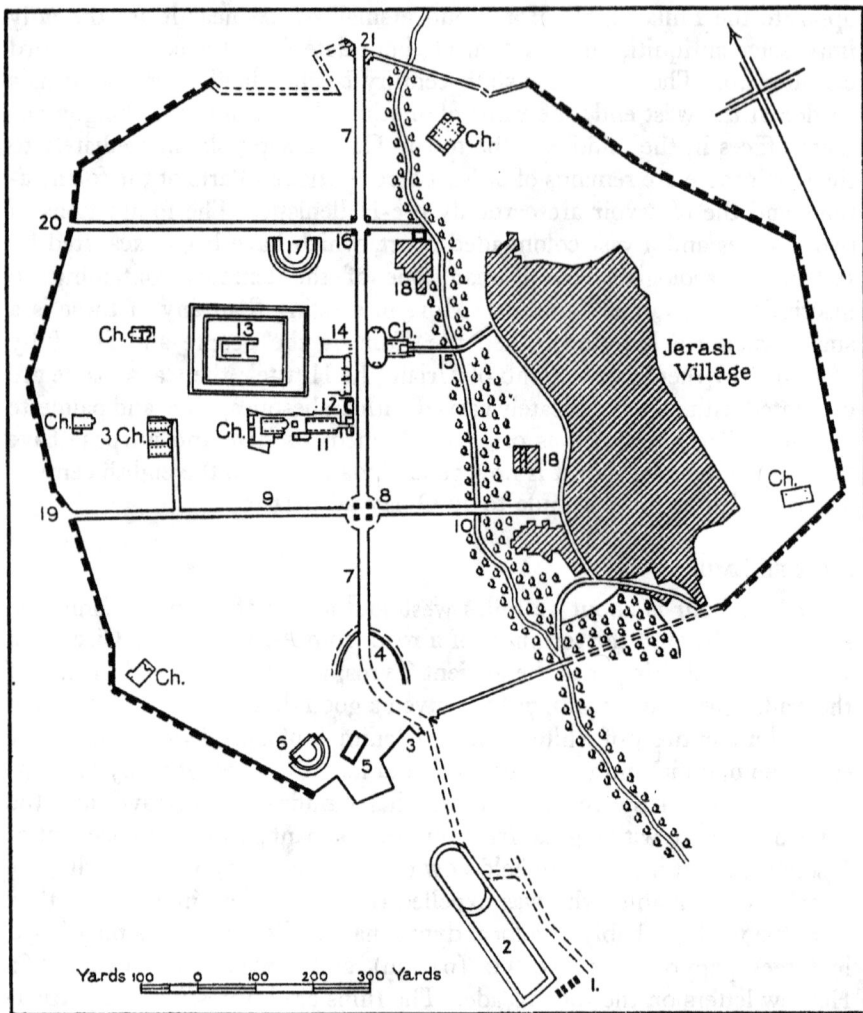

FIG. 61. *Plan of Jerash*

1. Triumphal Arch (Hadrian)
2. Hippodrome
3. Philadelphia Gate
4. Forum
5. Temple of Zeus
6. South Theatre
7. Antonine Street
8. South Tetrapylon
9. Pella Street
10. Pella Bridge
11. Cathedral of Theodore Stratelites
12. Nymphaeum
13. Temple of Artemis
14. Propylaea
15. Artemis bridge
16. North Tetrapylon
17. North Theatre
18. Baths
19. Pella Gate
20. Gadara Gate
21. Damascus Gate
Ch. Churches

151. *The Roman Theatre at Amman*

152. *Jerash. Monumental gateway (propylae) leading to the Temple of Artemis*

153. *Meshatta from the Air*

154. *Petra. The Khazna Firaun or 'Pharaoh's Treasury'*

Syrian border. It has not been excavated, but the remains of tombs, limestone colonnades, and theatres built of basalt are still visible. The site commands a magnificent view of the Sea of Galilee with Mount Hermon in the distance.

JERASH (fig. 61; photo. 152)

The road to Jerash branches from the Amman–Jerusalem road about 8 miles from Amman at the Circassian village of Suweileh and runs north from Suweileh for 28 miles through beautiful country. The old name of Jerash was Gerasa, but it was called for some centuries ' Antioch on the Chrysorhoas ' after one of the Seleucid kings, possibly Antiochus IV. The town, 1,760 feet above sea-level, lay on both banks of a permanent stream, the ancient Chrysorhoas (*mod.* Wadi Suf), which is a tributary of the Zerka (Jabbok). After having been long deserted it was reoccupied in the last century by Circassians, who settled on the east bank where the less important ruins stood.

The walled area covers more than 200 acres, but 400 yards south of the south or Philadelphia gate are a triumphal arch built in honour of a visit of the Roman Emperor Hadrian in A.D. 129–130 and a hippodrome converted into a polo ground in early Arab days. Inside the gate the first building is an oval enclosure surrounded by Ionic columns, perhaps a sort of forum or market-place; on high ground to the south-west is a temple of Zeus begun in the first century A.D. and completed in the second; north-west of the temple is a finely preserved theatre. From the Forum a paved and colonnaded street runs straight through the town to the north gate, the colonnades, except at the north end, having been built or rebuilt in the Corinthian order in the second century A.D. About 200 yards north of the Forum this street is crossed at right angles by another leading eastwards to the Pella bridge over the river, which has been only recently destroyed; a roundabout and four monumental gateways, known as the South Tetrapylon, were built where the two streets crossed. The chief religious centre of the Roman town, a temple to Artemis, stood on a high platform west of the main street about 250 yards farther north; the temple was approached from the street by a magnificent stairway, and across the street two courts led to a second bridge (Artemis bridge) over the river. This 'sacred way' (*Via Sacra*) was laid out about A.D. 150 and forty years later a richly decorated *nymphaeum* or public fountain was built just south of the great stairway. North of the Artemis precinct was a second theatre and, on the opposite side of the main street, some baths of the second or third century, which contain one of the earliest domes on pendentives. The ruins of other baths on an even larger scale lie on the east bank.

This series of buildings in the fine limestone of the country, exuberantly decorated with florid detail, illustrates town planning and building in a city of lesser importance in the second century A.D. Besides these classical works there are the remains of nearly a dozen churches and a synagogue, dating from the fourth to the seventh centuries; they include a great complex which rose just south of the Artemis temple round a sacred fountain which was made to run wine on the anniversary of the miracle of Cana in Galilee. In the Omayyad period the district was famous for its gardens and vineyards, and the churches remained in use, but a succession of earthquakes and the insecurity of the country after the fall of the Omayyads led to the gradual desertion of the site.

## KERAK

Kerak is connected with Amman by a road branching off the pilgrim (Mecca) road and railway at Katrani, about 65 miles south of Amman. It is the ancient Kir Moab or Kerak Moab, once the capital of the Moabite kingdom and one of the few inhabited places in Transjordan which have never been wholly abandoned: for many centuries the local Christians took refuge here. It lies at the head of a wadi falling into the Dead Sea just north of the Lisan peninsula. The site is surrounded by wadis on three sides; on it the Crusaders built a great castle (photo. 133); at the south end, where it was connected with the plateau by a tongue of rock, they cut a broad fosse more than 100 feet deep; a second fosse separated their citadel from the rest of the hill. It was from this castle that Renaud de Châtillon, the fiercest of all the Crusaders, organized his famous expedition against Mecca (p. 452). After Renaud's execution by Saladin, after the battle of Hattin in 1187, Kerak was defended by his widow for a year, but it was starved into surrender and passed into Moslem hands. The chief remains are the tower of Beibars (1264) at the north end, the Crusaders' citadel at the south, and various underground passages, cisterns, and dungeons.

## MADEBA (*anc.* Medeba)

Madeba can easily be reached by road from Amman, the distance being about 22 miles. It is the site of an ancient city which is mentioned several times in the Old Testament, but it was deserted for centuries and only reoccupied, mainly by Christians from Kerak, about 1880, when the countryside began to become more secure. In the process of building houses and churches the new-comers uncovered numbers of mosaics dating mostly from the sixth and seventh centuries. The most famous of these is a map of Palestine and Transjordan which lies under the floor of a modern Greek church. The mosaic, which was badly damaged when the church was built, is now carefully protected and shown to visitors. The map was evidently compiled for the use of pilgrims to the places mentioned in the Bible, and it contains a plan of Jerusalem which is of historical value. The town, like many others in these arid parts, contains a large open reservoir and several other mosaics worth seeing. Interesting churches and mosaics have been found also in many of the surrounding villages, as for example Khirbet Mukhayyat, Main, and Ras Siagha, the last being a supposed burial-place of Moses.

## MESHATTA (photo. 153)

The palace of Meshatta lies in the desert about 4 miles north-east of the station of Ziza. The south wall of the palace, about 150 yards long, was originally decorated on either side of the entrance with a great band of carved stone some 15 feet high; heavy mouldings covered with lace-like scrolls ran above and below the band, and between these mouldings the stone was carved with zigzags and rosettes filled with fantastic tree motives, conventionalized vines and palmettes, animal and bird forms, cornucopiae, a rich and varied version in stone of the mosaic designs in the Dome of the Rock. The whole façade was presented to the Emperor William II by the late Sultan and all but one section carried off to Berlin. In spite of this loss the remains of the palace with its lofty audience halls, which were built of brick, are still well worth visiting. The date of this building, like that of the Kasr at Amman, was long in dispute, but most scholars now attribute it to the Omayyad Caliph Walid II, A.D. 743, a prince who like many of his house was passionately addicted to hunting in the desert (p. 451).

## PETRA

The route from Amman to Petra leaves the railway line at Maan, whence a motor-road leads 16 miles past Ain Musa to El Ji. Thence travellers must proceed on foot or on horseback. Petra ranks with Baalbek and Palmyra as one of the wonders of the ancient world, but it owes far more than its rivals to unique natural surroundings. From El Ji a valley with rock tombs cut in the cliffs on either side, the most famous of them a tomb with four obelisks, leads to the entrance of a ravine called the Sik. This is the bed of a winding watercourse, rarely more than 15 feet wide, between cliffs which tower perpendicularly 300 feet or more; progress is slow because the bed of the watercourse, once paved, is now rough, and it is only after marching for about 45 minutes that one emerges into broad daylight in front of 'Pharaoh's Treasury', the Khazna Firaun. This is a stupendous shrine facing the mouth of the Sik, a façade of Corinthian columns with a pediment crowned by an urn about 100 feet above ground-level, all carved out of the rose-coloured rock in the rich style of the late Hellenistic period (photo. 154); the building has been identified by some as a temple of Isis. The great theatre lies about 660 yards from the Khazna and beyond this the valley widens; the public buildings of the city, the markets, a gymnasium, a *nymphaeum*, a decorated gateway, temples, and palaces stood here on either side of the stream, in a sort of avenue. Beyond them were city walls, but though both walls and buildings have been cleared in the last few decades, only the remains of the gateway and one temple, called sometimes the Kasr Firaun, sometimes the Kasr el Bint, are still visible. To the west rises a precipitous cliff, the Habis, honeycombed with rock-cut houses and tombs, rising tier above tier, in every state of preservation, some of the more ambitious never completed. Other monuments have been constructed in the valleys north and south. The Deir, the greatest of all, lies to the north-west; it is a huge façade surmounted by an urn which is nearly 30 feet high; to the south-east is El Farasa and the Garden tomb, to the north-east El Khubza and the tomb of a former governor of the Roman province of Arabia, named Florentinus, with a Latin inscription bearing the date A.D. 117. In the decoration of the tombs Hellenistic elements, derived no doubt from Alexandria, are dominant, mainly classical pediments carved above Corinthian or Doric columns, but they are mingled with oriental features, obelisks and crow-step crenellations. The briefest visit to Petra will leave an ineffaceable impression, but it would take days to explore all the scattered monuments and 'high places'.

# APPENDIX E

# THE ROYAL NAVY IN PALESTINE, 1936–1938

*(These notes refer only to the work of the Royal Navy in connexion with Palestine, and are not concerned with any other part of the very extensive naval operations which were taking place in the Mediterranean both before and after the period under review).*

THE Palestine troubles provided interesting evidence of the versatility of the Royal Navy and of the different tasks which it may be called upon to perform in an emergency. In April 1936 there were only two battalions in Palestine, and these with the help of the Navy succeeded in keeping the situation under control until they were reinforced by a division in September.

As soon as the rioting started, two cruisers (at Haifa) were brought to short notice for steam in case they should be required at Jaffa, and all ships prepared to land parties at short notice to assist the army and police, if required, in restoring law and order. The rioting became a serious menace, and from April onwards the Haifa Naval Force was primarily concerned with shore commitments. The following gives some idea of the different tasks undertaken by the Navy in this area during 1936:

*Arms Traffic.* On 26 June a patrol of the whole coast was instituted. As many as 150 vessels a week were sometimes searched and, although no arms were found, it was considered that as a preventive measure the patrols were effective.

*Landing Parties.* Towards the end of July, at the request of the Army, naval platoons were landed on several occasions to reinforce either the police or military forces. They operated at first, not only in Haifa town, but also in surrounding country districts, undertaking the protection of Jewish settlements in the plain of Acre, and on the south side of Mount Carmel. From the end of July, however, their duties and those of marine units were restricted to the support of the military and police in Haifa, where their presence had a considerable moral effect in maintaining law and order. When the general strike broke out in August the Navy took over the control of Haifa town, in order to release troops for mobile operations in the country. Nine naval platoons were landed and formed into the 'Haifa Town Force' under the command of the Squadron Royal Marine Officer, 3rd Cruiser Squadron. At the end of the month arrangements were made to withdraw this force, but disturbance in the town continued and three Royal Marine platoons were again landed at the special request of the police.

*Pom-pom and Searchlight Lorries.* Armed lorries, fitted and manned by naval ratings, were first used in June to combat the sniping of Arab bands.

The first pair of pom-pom and searchlight lorries proved so effective that during the following three months six more were brought into use.

*Artillery Assistance.* Two howitzers, manned by naval crews, were stationed at the military camp at Nablus. Rebel snipers, who had begun to be troublesome, were successfully dispersed by them from the surrounding hills.

*Fire-fighting.* Several big fires, all in timber yards, occurred at Haifa in April, May, August, and September, and on each occasion large parties were landed from H.M. ships to fight them. The work was often dangerous, as there was usually no chance to do more than isolate the blaze, and on one occasion several bombs were found concealed among the burning timber.

*Railways.* On the outbreak of the general strike thirteen crews, each consisting of a driver and fireman, were sent ashore daily from H.M. ships for training on the railways. In three weeks they were passed by the railway authorities as fit to take charge of trains. When Arab engine-drivers and railwaymen were forced to leave their jobs because of concentrated and serious intimidation by Arab extremists, the Navy immediately took charge, and with twelve traffic-control ratings, maintained service for about 10 days. This had the desired effect, a serious dislocation was avoided, and the railwaymen resumed work. Naval personnel also manned an armoured train which began to work on the standard-gauge line from Haifa to Lydda and Jerusalem in July. When troops were available for picketing the line the following month this train was dismantled, but another was constructed and operated in a similar manner on the narrow-gauge line between Haifa and Samakh. These naval armoured trains did much to counteract the attempts at sabotage on the railways. Men from H.M. ships also occasionally manned signal boxes.

Other shore duties included assistance in demolition work at Jaffa in June 1936, and in customs control, which became a regular task from that month onwards.

The early months of 1937 were comparatively quiet, but terrorism broke out again in the summer. The murder of the District Commissioner of Galilee and of a British constable (26 Sept. 1937) called for drastic action, and it was decided, with naval aid, to remove the root of the trouble by arresting and deporting the members of the Arab Higher Committee. On 1 October public announcement was made of the intended arrest of six members of the Arab Higher Committee and two other prominent disturbers of the peace. Five arrests were made, and the men concerned were deported in a British warship. The Mufti, however, managed to evade arrest, and eventually escaped to Syria.

It was not until July 1938, however, that naval assistance was again required, following a new series of bomb outrages at Haifa. By this time there was every possibility of serious rebellion, or even of civil war. There was no immediate prospect of military reinforcement, so that the arrival of a capital ship at Haifa had an important effect on the general situation. The landing of five naval platoons and the visible presence of a man-of-war at Haifa once again had a steadying influence on the populace. Landing-parties were soon busy on duties similar to those undertaken in 1936, and the Navy again assisted in the control of the town. A Town Security Com-- mittee, with a naval officer as Town Commander, was formed on 29 July, by which time naval platoons were working regularly as search parties. A naval detachment was providing howitzer crews, thus freeing troops for inland operations, including a successful round-up of bandits south-west of Carmel (26 July). Other naval assistance given to the army included the taking over of the camp at Lydda (31 August), the manning of a mobile howitzer detachment on the northern frontier, the walling up of several streets which had been the scenes of some of the worst disorders, and the demolition of the Arab 'Tin Town' district in Haifa—a squalid but necessary task. The combined operations of 1936–1938 provided an inter-esting inversion of the usual roles of the Army and the Navy. Normally the Army is responsible for the defences of naval bases. Here the positions were reversed; for the Navy, in providing landing-parties, secured the safety of the Army base, thereby freeing troops for operations in the surrounding districts.

# APPENDIX F

## TIME, CALENDARS, FESTIVALS, WEIGHTS AND MEASURES

### Time

The system of time adopted in Palestine is Eastern European time, which is two hours in advance of Greenwich mean time.

### Calendars

Four principal calendars are in use in Palestine and receive official recognition: two Christian, one Moslem, and one Jewish.

The *Gregorian Calendar*, used in all Western lands, has in recent years extended to the East, and is observed by European and American residents, and by the Latin Church.

The older *Julian Calendar*, now thirteen days behind the Gregorian, is still used by the Orthodox Church, and by the Syrian and Palestinian Patriarchates, though the Holy Synod of the Oecumenical Patriarchate adopted the Gregorian calendar a few years ago. The lack of uniformity between the Latin and Orthodox Churches has some advantages, for it ensures that their major festivals—always a period of considerable anxiety to those responsible for order—fall on different dates.

The *Moslem Calendar* comprises twelve lunar months; the Moslem year is therefore ten or eleven days shorter than the Gregorian or Julian, and festivals gradually rotate round the seasons, describing a complete cycle in about 33 years. The calendar is made more complicated by grouping the Moslem years into cycles of thirty, of which nineteen are 'common years' of 354 days each, and eleven 'intercalary years' each with an additional day in the last month. The *Hejira*, the 'flight' of Mohammad from Mecca, is reckoned to have taken place on the night of 20 June, A.D. 622, but the Moslem era, instituted 17 years later by the Caliph Omar, dates from the first day of the first lunar month, Moharram (Thursday, 15 July, A.D. 622). Moslem years are prefixed with the letters A.H. The formula for the identification of the Gregorian year from the Moslem is:

$$\text{A.D.} = \text{A.H.} - \frac{3 \times \text{A.H.}}{100} + 621\cdot54$$

Thus 1 January, A.D. 1944, falls in A.H. 1363

### Moslem Lunar Months

| | | | | | |
|---|---|---|---|---|---|
| 1. Moharram | . | . 30 days | 7. Rajab | . | . 30 days |
| 2. Safar | . | . 29 „ | 8. Shaban | . | . 29 „ |
| 3. Rabi el Awal | . | . 30 „ | 9. Ramadan | . | . 30 „ |
| 4. Rabi eth Thani | . | . 29 „ | 10. Shawal | . | . 29 „ |
| 5. Jumada el Awal | . | . 30 „ | 11. Zul Kadeh | . | . 30 „ |
| 6. Jumada eth Thani | . | . 29 „ | 12. Zul Hija | . | . 29 „ (30 in intercalary years) |

The *Jewish Calendar* is also essentially lunar, but it is much more modified than the Moslem. It varies from the Gregorian Calendar within a range of about three weeks. The Jewish year has twelve lunar months each of 29 or 30 days, but to bring it periodically into line with the solar year an additional month of 30 days (Adar Sheni) is inserted seven times in every series of 19 years. There are, however, other complications; for instance, two days are observed for the festival of the New Year, and the first of these must not fall on the first, fourth, or sixth day of the week: the calendar has to be manipulated accordingly. The Jewish year 5704 (from the Creation of the Universe) began on 30 September 1943.

*Jewish Lunar Months*[1]

|  |  |  |  |  |  |
|---|---|---|---|---|---|
| 1. Tishri . | . 30 days | | 7. Nisan | . | . 30 days |
| 2. Heshvan | . 29 ,, | | 8. Iyyar | . | . 29 ,, |
| 3. Kislev . | . 30 ,, | | 9. Sivan | . | . 30 ,, |
| 4. Tevet . | . 29 ,, | | 10. Tamuz . | | . 29 ,, |
| 5. Shevat . | . 30 ,, | | 11. Ab | . | . 30 ,, |
| 6. Adar . | . 29 ,, | | 12. Elul | . | . 29 ,, |

The small sect of the Samaritans has a calendar of its own.

*Days of the Week*

Both the Moslem day and the Jewish day are reckoned from sunset to sunset; they therefore vary in length with the season, and what a European would call the night of Friday the 6th is the night of the Saturday the 7th in Moslem or Jewish style.

There is, however, an additional complication. With Moslems there is both a civil month and a religious month, which may differ by one or two days. The latter begins at sunset of the day when the new moon is first seen after sunset, or at latest on the third evening after the astronomical new moon. This is a matter of considerable importance at the end of the fast-month of Ramadan. To avoid confusion, official documents should always be dated by the day of the week as well as the day of the month.

*Moslem Days of the Week*

| Sunset Saturday to sunset Sunday | Yom el Ahad (*lit.* 'first day') |
|---|---|
| ,, Sunday ,, Monday | Yom el Ithnain (*lit.* 'second day') |
| ,, Monday ,, Tuesday | Yom eth Thalatha (*lit.* 'third day') |
| ,, Tuesday ,, Wednesday | Yom el Arbaa (*lit.* 'fourth day') |
| ,, Wednesday ,, Thursday | Yom el Khamis (*lit.* 'fifth day') |
| ,, Thursday ,, Friday | Yom el Jumaa (*lit.* 'day of reunion') |
| ,, Friday ,, Saturday | Yom es Sabt (*lit.* 'seventh day') |

[1] In enumerating the months it is usual to begin with Nisan, the month in which the Passover occurs, in accordance with God's command to Moses (*Exodus* xii. 2), though the New Year falls on 1 Tishri.

## Days of Rest, Holidays, and Festivals

Christians, Moslems, and Jews observe different 'sabbaths' or days of rest. A strict Jew must abstain from all work on Saturday (sunset Friday to sunset Saturday); non-observant Jews in Palestine, almost without exception, will also refuse to work on that day, though for political or nationalist reasons rather than religious. Moslems are less punctilious and are generally satisfied if they are given an hour or two to attend their mosque on Friday, but a strict Moslem will require time to pray at noon on every day of the week, and in the month of Ramadan, when he fasts from dawn to sunset, he needs a shorter working day. Sunday is the official day of rest for Christians, as elsewhere, but all the religious communities observe a large number of festivals, and are often not disinclined to abstain from work on the occasion of the festival of a different community. Palestine has, indeed, been described not inappropriately as the 'Land of Three Sabbaths and Four To-morrows'.

*Moslem Festivals.* The principal Moslem festivals are: (official holidays are marked with an asterisk)

| Festival | Date |
|---|---|
| New Year . . . . . . . | 1 Moharram |
| *Yom Ashura* (date of Noah leaving the Ark, and of the death of Hussein at Kerbela) . . . | 10 Moharram |
| *Muled en Nebi* or *M. esh Sherif* (Mohammad's birthday) . . . . . . . | 12 Rabi el Awal |
| *Muled el Hussein* . . . . . . | 6–29 Rabi eth Thani |
| *Lailat er Raghaib* (night of Mohammad's conception) . . . . . . . | Eve of first Friday in Rajab |
| *Muled es Sayida Zenab* (festival of this granddaughter of Mohammad) . . . . | 15 Rajab |
| *Lailat el Maraj* or *el Isra* (night of Mohammad's ascent to heaven) . . . . . | 27 Rajab |
| *Lailat el Baraat* ('Night of Decrees', when the guardian angels receive from the Almighty tablets recording the fate of their charges in the coming year) . . . . . . | 15 Shaban |
| *Ramadan* . . . . . . . | 1–30 Ramadan |
| *Lailat el Kader* ('Night of Power', on which the requests of all worshippers are believed to be granted) . . . . . . . | 27 Ramadan |
| *Id el Feter* (*Sheker Bairam*—3 days) . . . | 1–3 Shawal |
| Procession of the *Kiswa* (the inner covering of the Kaaba shrine at Mecca) . . . . | 25 Shawal |
| *Arafeh* (the eve of *En Nahar*) . . . . | 9 Zul Hija |

| Festival | Date |
|---|---|

*Id el Adha* or *En Nahar* (*Kurban Bairam*—3 days.
Lamb festival, marked by sacrifices; amongst
beduin a camel is the victim, if possible, elsewhere a sheep or goat) .  .  .  .  . 10–12 Zul Hija

There are two additional Moslem Festivals, peculiar to Palestine, dated
by the Orthodox Calendar: the Descent of the Holy Banner (*Sanjak esh
Sherif*) to Nebi Musa, on the Friday before the Orthodox Good Friday;
and the Return of the Banner from Nebi Musa, on the Orthodox Maundy
Thursday.*

*Jewish Festivals* are divided into three categories: (i) days of rest,
(ii) festivals on which work is permitted, and (iii) fasts. The chief are as
follows: (official holidays are marked with an asterisk)

|  | Date |
|---|---|
| (i) *Rosh Hashana** (New Year: 2 days) .  . | 1–2 Tishri |
| (i) (iii) *Yom Kippur** (Day of Atonement)  . | 10 Tishri |
| (i) *Sukkot** (1st Day of Tabernacles)  .  . | 15 Tishri |
| (i) *Simhat Tora** (8th Day of Tabernacles and Festival of the Rejoicing of the Law)  . | 22 Tishri |
| (ii) *Hanuka* (Recovery of the Temple by Judas Maccabaeus).  .  .  .  .  . | 25 Kislev to 2 Tevet |
| (iii) *Asara Betevet* (Siege of Jerusalem)  .  . | 10 Tevet |
| (iii) *Taanit Esther* (Fast of Esther)  .  .  . | 13 Adar |
| (ii) *Purim* (Feast of Lots)  .  .  .  . | 14 Adar (15 in Jerusalem) |
| (i) *Pesach* (Passover: 1st* and 7th* days only are days of rest; 2nd to 6th days are in category (ii)) | 15–21 Nisan |
| (i) *Shavuot** (Pentecost) .  .  .  .  . | 6 Sivan. |
| (iii) *Shiva Asar Betamuz* (Capitulation of Jerusalem) .  .  .  .  .  .  . | 17 Tamuz |
| (iii) *Tisha Beav* (Destruction of the Temple)  . | 9 Ab |

*Christian holidays* which are officially recognized, and observed accord-
ing to the Gregorian or Julian Calendars, are New Year's Day, Epiphany,
Good Friday, Easter Monday, Ascension Day, Whit Monday, Christmas
Day, and Boxing Day.

## Weights and Measures

There are several systems of measures and weights in Palestine, varying
in different parts of the country. They are a survival from the Ottoman
period. The British Administration has on more than one occasion
endeavoured to bring order out of chaos, chiefly by the introduction of
the metric system which alone is now officially recognized. Recently, in

the autumn of 1942, a determined effort was made to suppress all its rivals, but some still persist in popular use. Thus, in measures of length and area the unit is the *pic* or *draa*, but in 'cloth measure' a pic is 26·38 inches long and in building and land measure 29·53 inches. A *dunam* equals 1,600 square pics, or 919 square metres (0·23 acre). But this is the official dunam, and in practice the size of the dunam ranges between 900 and 1,000 square metres.

Measures of weight include the *dirhem* (3·205 grammes), 400 of which constitute an *okka* or 'oke'. In northern Palestine two okka amount to a *rotl*, but in southern Palestine 2·25 of them are required to reach the same weight. In consequence, the *kantar* (100 rotl) weighs 564 lb. in northern Palestine and 634 lb. in the south. For capacity the *tabbeh* is complicated by being the equivalent of 50·6 lb. for barley, but of 44 lb. for wheat. In southern Palestine a *jarra* contains 22 litres of olive oil (20·2 kilograms), but in the north olive oil is measured by the rotl (2·5 kg.).

A tabbeh of wheat in Jerusalem measures 8 rotl (23 kg.), in Hebron 9 rotl, in Nablus 13·33 rotl. In Nablus a tabbeh of other agricultural products varies from 9·75 rotl (sesame) to 13·75 (kersenneh), with six intermediate weights. Similarly a *kail* at Haifa is either 18 rotl of barley or sesame, or 28·5 rotl of other products. In Hebron, however, a kail of barley is only 6·25 rotl, and in other places and for other products it varies within a wide range.

This system of weights must be sufficiently difficult for the purchaser, if not for the vendor. But the complications do not end here. The long list of standard weights is for many a small shopkeeper and hawker of no interest. A recent correspondent in a Palestine periodical suggested that the prohibition in *Deuteronomy* (xxv. 13) is still appropriate. 'Thou shalt not have in thy bag divers weights, a great and a small.' He continued: 'Since those words were written, nothing has changed. When you want to buy something from one of these hawkers, he puts a stone on one side of the scales, your purchase on the other, and he says, " That's what it weighs; pay your money and take your goods ", and you are unable to know exactly what you have bought.' A piece of old iron or other object collected out of the gutter sometimes takes the place of the stone.

# METEOROLOGICAL TABLES*

TABLE I. *Frequency of Wind Direction*
Percentages of Total Observations

| | | Jan. | Feb. | Mar. | Apr. | May | June | July | Aug. | Sept. | Oct. | Nov. | Dec. | Year |
|---|---|---|---|---|---|---|---|---|---|---|---|---|---|---|
| **1. Coast** | | | | | | | | | | | | | | |
| Haifa | N. | 2 | 2 | 3 | 6 | 8 | 6 | 3 | 2 | 6 | 5 | 3 | 2 | 4 |
| (10 yrs.' | NE. | 4 | 3 | 6 | 3 | 6 | 3 | 1 | 4 | 6 | 4 | 5 | 4 | 4 |
| obsns.) | E. | 14 | 12 | 13 | 7 | 7 | 4 | 2 | 2 | 5 | 10 | 18 | 14 | 9 |
| (Obsns. 0800 | SE. | 20 | 17 | 17 | 9 | 8 | 4 | 3 | 2 | 4 | 10 | 17 | 23 | 11 |
| and 1400 hrs.) | S. | 20 | 19 | 14 | 13 | 9 | 16 | 16 | 15 | 12 | 11 | 15 | 24 | 15 |
| | SW. | 14 | 18 | 14 | 16 | 10 | 19 | 27 | 23 | 18 | 12 | 14 | 15 | 17 |
| | W. | 4 | 8 | 5 | 12 | 9 | 11 | 17 | 17 | 12 | 7 | 5 | 3 | 9 |
| | NW. | 2 | 7 | 9 | 12 | 15 | 13 | 9 | 9 | 12 | 10 | 7 | 2 | 9 |
| | Calm | 20 | 14 | 19 | 22 | 28 | 24 | 22 | 26 | 25 | 31 | 16 | 13 | 22 |
| Jaffa (1880–89) | | | | | | | | | | | | | | |
| (Obsns. 0700 | N. | 5 | 4 | 3 | 2 | 5 | 2 | 0 | 0 | 6 | 6 | 1 | 2 | |
| hrs.) | NE. | 8 | 6 | 5 | 3 | 2 | 1 | 0 | 0 | 2 | 4 | 6 | 9 | |
| | E. | 8 | 3 | 3 | 2 | 2 | 1 | 1 | 0 | 0 | 5 | 5 | 6 | |
| | SE. | 15 | 16 | 9 | 4 | 1 | 1 | 0 | 1 | 1 | 5 | 12 | 17 | |
| | S. | 32 | 23 | 19 | 12 | 3 | 3 | 0 | 5 | 5 | 10 | 22 | 25 | |
| | SW. | 7 | 14 | 15 | 19 | 24 | 34 | 56 | 48 | 35 | 15 | 12 | 8 | |
| | W. | 2 | 5 | 12 | 19 | 26 | 33 | 30 | 23 | 13 | 5 | 2 | 4 | |
| | NW. | 4 | 2 | 5 | 9 | 19 | 14 | 3 | 8 | 12 | 8 | 2 | 1 | |
| | Calm | 20 | 27 | 28 | 29 | 17 | 12 | 8 | 14 | 25 | 43 | 37 | 29 | |
| Gaza (1921–34) | | | | | | | | | | | | | | |
| (Obsns. 0800 | N. | 0 | 1 | 2 | 3 | 5 | 2 | 3 | 4 | 2 | 3 | 1 | 0 | 2 |
| hrs.) | NE. | 2 | 1 | 2 | 3 | 3 | 3 | 0 | 1 | 1 | 3 | 1 | 1 | 2 |
| | E. | 2 | 1 | 4 | 2 | 2 | 1 | 1 | 1 | 3 | 1 | 5 | 3 | 2 |
| | SE. | 5 | 8 | 6 | 4 | 3 | 3 | 1 | 1 | 3 | 3 | 5 | 7 | 4 |
| | S. | 34 | 29 | 24 | 18 | 11 | 10 | 14 | 19 | 16 | 25 | 26 | 32 | 21 |
| | SW. | 14 | 15 | 8 | 11 | 8 | 8 | 11 | 7 | 5 | 7 | 8 | 11 | 9 |
| | W. | 2 | 4 | 5 | 5 | 8 | 11 | 12 | 8 | 4 | 1 | 3 | 2 | 5 |
| | NW. | 1 | 3 | 4 | 7 | 8 | 10 | 11 | 6 | 3 | 0 | 1 | 1 | 5 |
| | Calm | 40 | 38 | 45 | 47 | 52 | 52 | 47 | 53 | 63 | 57 | 50 | 43 | 49 |
| **2. Inland** | | | | | | | | | | | | | | |
| Nazareth | | | | | | | | | | | | | | |
| (1891–1906) | N. | 5 | 11 | 10 | 12 | 22 | 13 | 7 | 11 | 22 | 31 | 12 | 3 | |
| | NE. | 19 | 21 | 13 | 10 | 9 | 6 | 0 | 1 | 6 | 21 | 29 | 18 | |
| | E. | 27 | 23 | 17 | 20 | 6 | 4 | 2 | 0 | 6 | 14 | 23 | 29 | |
| | SE. | 14 | 10 | 11 | 9 | 10 | 2 | 0 | 1 | 2 | 8 | 8 | 20 | |
| | S. | 9 | 6 | 3 | 1 | 2 | 0 | 0 | 0 | 1 | 2 | 6 | 7 | |
| | SW. | 7 | 9 | 15 | 10 | 22 | 24 | 40 | 21 | 15 | 4 | 7 | 15 | |
| | W. | 10 | 11 | 19 | 22 | 15 | 26 | 32 | 39 | 24 | 6 | 6 | 2 | |
| | NW. | 9 | 9 | 12 | 16 | 13 | 25 | 18 | 26 | 24 | 14 | 9 | 6 | |
| | Calm | 0 | 0 | 0 | 0 | 0 | 0 | 0 | 0 | 0 | 0 | 0 | 0 | |
| Jenin (1921–34) | | | | | | | | | | | | | | |
| (Obsns. 0800, | N. | 3 | 3 | 3 | 3 | 7 | 3 | 2 | 2 | 4 | 3 | 5 | 4 | 3 |
| 1400, and | NE. | 5 | 3 | 4 | 2 | 3 | 1 | 1 | 0 | 1 | 3 | 7 | 4 | 3 |
| 2000 hrs.) | E. | 10 | 7 | 7 | 4 | 2 | 1 | 0 | 0 | 1 | 4 | 11 | 9 | 5 |
| | SE. | 10 | 8 | 7 | 6 | 3 | 1 | 0 | 0 | 2 | 5 | 11 | 12 | 5 |
| | S. | 11 | 11 | 8 | 11 | 8 | 8 | 6 | 3 | 3 | 8 | 13 | 16 | 9 |
| | SW. | 30 | 34 | 32 | 34 | 31 | 38 | 43 | 40 | 34 | 30 | 25 | 29 | 33 |
| | W. | 25 | 29 | 32 | 32 | 32 | 38 | 42 | 45 | 43 | 36 | 21 | 21 | 33 |
| | NW. | 6 | 5 | 7 | 8 | 13 | 10 | 6 | 10 | 12 | 11 | 7 | 5 | 8 |
| | Calm | 0 | 0 | 0 | 0 | 1 | 0 | 0 | 0 | 0 | 0 | 0 | 0 | 0 |

\* In all these tables figures in heavy type denote maxima, those in italic minima.

## TABLE I—continued

| | | Jan. | Feb. | Mar. | Apr. | May | June | July | Aug. | Sept. | Oct. | Nov. | Dec. | Year |
|---|---|---|---|---|---|---|---|---|---|---|---|---|---|---|
| **Jerusalem** | | | | | | | | | | | | | | |
| (1918–34) | N. | 1 | 1 | 2 | 4 | 1 | 4 | 2 | 3 | 3 | 3 | 2 | 0 | 2 |
| (Obsns. | NE. | 3 | 2 | 3 | 2 | 4 | 1 | 0 | 1 | 1 | 3 | 3 | 3 | 2 |
| 0800 hrs.) | E. | 9 | 5 | 10 | 10 | 8 | 3 | 0 | 0 | 2 | 6 | 9 | 10 | 6 |
| | SE. | 7 | 7 | 6 | 5 | 5 | 2 | 1 | 0 | 3 | 3 | 6 | 6 | 4 |
| | S. | 13 | 14 | 9 | 8 | 9 | 8 | 10 | 11 | 6 | 6 | 4 | 8 | 9 |
| | SW. | 12 | 21 | 14 | 11 | 13 | 15 | 17 | 15 | 14 | 12 | 9 | 11 | 14 |
| | W. | 13 | 14 | 12 | 19 | 16 | 25 | 26 | 22 | 18 | 12 | 7 | 12 | 16 |
| | NW. | 3 | 6 | 9 | 9 | 9 | 14 | 15 | 18 | 17 | 12 | 5 | 5 | 10 |
| | Calm | 39 | 30 | 35 | 32 | 35 | 28 | 29 | 30 | 36 | 43 | 55 | 45 | 36 |
| **El Latrun** | | | | | | | | | | | | | | |
| (1905–12) | N. | 4 | 2 | 4 | 4 | 4 | 3 | 1 | 6 | 10 | 10 | 5 | 4 | |
| | NE. | 3 | 1 | 1 | 2 | 2 | 0 | 0 | 0 | 1 | 1 | 1 | 2 | |
| | E. | 17 | 11 | 10 | 8 | 4 | 1 | 1 | 2 | 4 | 11 | 16 | 22 | |
| | SE. | 14 | 15 | 16 | 17 | 14 | 12 | 14 | 18 | 16 | 16 | 15 | 15 | |
| | S. | 6 | 7 | 6 | 5 | 5 | 5 | 5 | 2 | 2 | 3 | 5 | 4 | |
| | SW. | 17 | 18 | 10 | 7 | 3 | 3 | 3 | 1 | 1 | 4 | 10 | 19 | |
| | W. | 11 | 20 | 18 | 14 | 9 | 9 | 11 | 9 | 6 | 8 | 12 | 10 | |
| | NW. | 17 | 16 | 25 | 31 | 42 | 51 | 49 | 49 | 47 | 36 | 21 | 14 | |
| | Calm | 11 | 10 | 9 | 13 | 17 | 15 | 15 | 13 | 13 | 11 | 14 | 10 | |
| **Hebron** | | | | | | | | | | | | | | |
| (1896–1914) | N. | 7 | 7 | 6 | 10 | 12 | 12 | 11 | 14 | 16 | 14 | 11 | 7 | |
| | NE. | 7 | 6 | 5 | 5 | 4 | 3 | 1 | 1 | 3 | 8 | 8 | 7 | |
| | E. | 10 | 6 | 8 | 10 | 8 | 3 | 1 | 1 | 3 | 8 | 12 | 13 | |
| | SE. | 10 | 11 | 12 | 11 | 10 | 2 | 1 | 2 | 3 | 8 | 8 | 11 | |
| | S. | 3 | 4 | 3 | 4 | 5 | 1 | 1 | 1 | 2 | 2 | 2 | 3 | |
| | SW. | 6 | 4 | 4 | 3 | 4 | 2 | 1 | 1 | 1 | 2 | 3 | 5 | |
| | W. | 30 | 32 | 30 | 23 | 16 | 18 | 17 | 11 | 12 | 14 | 22 | 27 | |
| | NW. | 27 | 29 | 32 | 34 | 41 | 59 | 67 | 68 | 61 | 42 | 34 | 26 | |
| | Calm | 0 | 0 | 0 | 0 | 0 | 0 | 0 | 1 | 0 | 2 | 0 | 0 | |
| **Beersheba** | | | | | | | | | | | | | | |
| (1921–34) | N. | 5 | 6 | 7 | 7 | 4 | 3 | 1 | 2 | 1 | 3 | 7 | 3 | 4 |
| (Obsns. | NE. | 6 | 5 | 4 | 4 | 7 | 1 | 1 | 1 | 0 | 2 | 10 | 3 | 4 |
| 0800 hrs.) | E. | 21 | 12 | 17 | 12 | 10 | 5 | 5 | 2 | 5 | 16 | 25 | 24 | 13 |
| | SE. | 26 | 19 | 15 | 13 | 8 | 5 | 2 | 1 | 4 | 7 | 12 | 22 | 11 |
| | S. | 12 | 18 | 8 | 7 | 4 | 4 | 4 | 4 | 1 | 4 | 8 | 12 | 7 |
| | SW. | 11 | 13 | 5 | 7 | 6 | 7 | 7 | 5 | 1 | 5 | 3 | 8 | 7 |
| | W. | 11 | 14 | 16 | 21 | 21 | 37 | 45 | 44 | 46 | 37 | 20 | 15 | 27 |
| | NW. | 2 | 3 | 3 | 6 | 7 | 7 | 3 | 5 | 9 | 5 | 3 | 3 | 5 |
| | Calm | 6 | 10 | 25 | 23 | 33 | 31 | 32 | 36 | 33 | 21 | 12 | 10 | 23 |
| **3. Jordan Valley** | | | | | | | | | | | | | | |
| Tiberias | N. | 6 | 0 | 6 | 0 | 0 | 0 | 0 | 0 | 0 | 0 | 0 | 0 | |
| | NE. | 0 | 0 | 0 | 0 | 0 | 0 | 0 | 0 | 0 | 0 | 0 | 0 | |
| | E. | 3 | 11 | 0 | 0 | 0 | 0 | 0 | 0 | 0 | 0 | 10 | 29 | |
| | SE. | 0 | 0 | 0 | 0 | 0 | 0 | 0 | 0 | 0 | 0 | 0 | 0 | |
| | S. | 0 | 0 | 10 | 0 | 0 | 0 | 0 | 0 | 0 | 3 | 0 | 3 | |
| | SW. | 0 | 0 | 0 | 0 | 0 | 0 | 0 | 0 | 0 | 0 | 0 | 0 | |
| | W. | 10 | 7 | 6 | 33 | 71 | 93 | 100 | 58 | 23 | 42 | 13 | 0 | |
| | NW. | 0 | 0 | 0 | 0 | 0 | 0 | 0 | 0 | 0 | 0 | 0 | 0 | |
| | Calm | 81 | 82 | 78 | 67 | 29 | 7 | 0 | 42 | 77 | 55 | 77 | 68 | |
| **Jericho** | | | | | | | | | | | | | | |
| (1921–34) | N. | 19 | 14 | 18 | 17 | 20 | 18 | 13 | 13 | 19 | 22 | 20 | 18 | 18 |
| (Obsns. 0800, | NE. | 15 | 13 | 22 | 23 | 27 | 24 | 19 | 24 | 23 | 25 | 20 | 14 | 21 |
| 1400, and | E. | 3 | 4 | 6 | 7 | 5 | 6 | 6 | 7 | 8 | 7 | 5 | 2 | 6 |
| 2000 hrs.) | SE. | 4 | 5 | 6 | 10 | 12 | 15 | 19 | 16 | 14 | 10 | 7 | 7 | 10 |
| | S. | 9 | 9 | 5 | 7 | 9 | 8 | 12 | 11 | 8 | 7 | 6 | 7 | 8 |
| | SW. | 11 | 15 | 7 | 5 | 4 | 5 | 7 | 8 | 5 | 4 | 7 | 10 | 7 |
| | W. | 12 | 14 | 10 | 8 | 6 | 6 | 6 | 4 | 3 | 5 | 8 | 13 | 8 |
| | NW. | 23 | 21 | 22 | 20 | 13 | 14 | 14 | 13 | 12 | 14 | 21 | 25 | 18 |
| | Calm | 4 | 5 | 4 | 3 | 4 | 4 | 4 | 4 | 8 | 6 | 6 | 4 | 5 |

## TABLE I—*continued*

| | | Jan. | Feb. | Mar. | Apr. | May | June | July | Aug. | Sept. | Oct. | Nov. | Dec. | Year |
|---|---|---|---|---|---|---|---|---|---|---|---|---|---|---|
| 4. *Dead Sea** | | | | | | | | | | | | | | |
| North end | N. | 25 | 10 | 35 | 25 | 50 | 38 | 39 | 16 | 21 | 32 | 34 | 15 | |
| | NE. | 2 | 3 | 1 | 1 | — | 1 | 8 | 3 | 1 | — | 3 | — | |
| | E. | 1 | 2 | — | 1 | — | — | — | — | — | 1 | 2 | — | |
| | SE. | 3 | 2 | 3 | 4 | 2 | 3 | 10 | 2 | 2 | 3 | 1 | 2 | |
| | S. | 25 | 41 | 28 | 37 | 35 | 47 | 80 | 51 | 34 | 30 | 25 | 18 | |
| | SW. | 4 | 5 | 5 | 1 | 3 | 3 | 4 | 3 | — | 6 | 7 | 5 | |
| | W. | 5 | 6 | 5 | 6 | 2 | 3 | 1 | 1 | 1 | 2 | 8 | 3 | |
| | NW. | 30 | 36 | 34 | 22 | 24 | 20 | 40 | 46 | 31 | 37 | 19 | 6 | |
| 5. *Transjordan* | | | | | | | | | | | | | | |
| Amman | N. | 3 | 2 | 3 | 4 | 5 | 7 | 4 | 5 | 6 | 4 | 3 | 4 | 4 |
| (14 yrs.' | NE. | 5 | 3 | 4 | 2 | 2 | 1 | <1 | 1 | 2 | 4 | 5 | 6 | 3 |
| obsns.) | E. | 9 | 3 | 5 | 4 | 4 | 1 | <1 | 1 | 2 | 6 | 9 | 10 | 5 |
| (Obsns. 0500, | SE. | 7 | 5 | 4 | 4 | 2 | <1 | <1 | <1 | 1 | 4 | 5 | 8 | 3 |
| 0800, 1400, | S. | 5 | 7 | 6 | 5 | 6 | 4 | 3 | 3 | 3 | 7 | 7 | 8 | 5 |
| and 2000 hrs.) | SW. | 27 | 30 | 25 | 25 | 20 | 16 | 18 | 17 | 19 | 24 | 30 | 28 | 23 |
| | W. | 25 | 33 | 28 | 30 | 30 | 35 | 44 | 37 | 28 | 20 | 19 | 17 | 29 |
| | NW. | 5 | 4 | 8 | 11 | 16 | 25 | 24 | 24 | 20 | 10 | 4 | 3 | 13 |
| | Calm | 14 | 13 | 17 | 15 | 15 | 11 | 7 | 12 | 19 | 21 | 18 | 16 | 15 |

* The figures for the Dead Sea are relative only and are not percentages (Novemeysky: ' The Dead Sea: a storehouse of chemicals ').

## TABLE II. *Temperature*

### (Degrees Fahrenheit)

| | Jan. | Feb. | Mar. | Apr. | May | June | July | Aug. | Sept. | Oct. | Nov. | Dec. | Year |
|---|---|---|---|---|---|---|---|---|---|---|---|---|---|
| 1. *Coast* | | | | | | | | | | | | | |
| Acre (1928–40) | | | | | | | | | | | | | |
| Mean | 56 | 56 | 59 | 64 | 69 | 73 | 80 | 81 | 77 | 73 | 68 | 59 | 70 |
| M.D. max. | 66 | 66 | 70 | 75 | 80 | 83 | 86 | 88 | 87 | 85 | 78 | 69 | 78 |
| M.D. min. | 47 | 47 | 49 | 51 | 58 | 64 | 72 | 71 | 68 | 62 | 56 | 50 | 58 |
| Absolute max. | 81 | 82 | 94 | 109 | 110 | 100 | 91 | 92 | 110 | 108 | 97 | 84 | — |
| Absolute min. | 35 | 35 | 34 | 40 | 46 | 54 | 60 | 59 | 55 | 51 | 41 | 36 | — |
| Haifa (1921–34) | | | | | | | | | | | | | |
| Mean | 57 | 58 | 62 | 67 | 74 | 78 | 82 | 83 | 81 | 76 | 69 | 60 | 71 |
| M.D. max. | 65 | 66 | 72 | 76 | 83 | 86 | 88 | 90 | 88 | 85 | 79 | 68 | 79 |
| M.D. min. | 49 | 50 | 52 | 58 | 65 | 70 | 75 | 76 | 74 | 68 | 60 | 52 | 62 |
| M.M. max. | 72 | 77 | 89 | 93 | 99 | 95 | 92 | 93 | 94 | 92 | 90 | 77 | 103 |
| M.M. min. | 43 | 44 | 45 | 50 | 57 | 65 | 70 | 72 | 68 | 61 | 51 | 45 | 41 |
| Absolute max. | 79 | 87 | 104 | 108 | 108 | 107 | 96 | 99 | 107 | 100 | 97 | 83 | — |
| Absolute min. | 38 | 37 | 36 | 44 | 53 | 58 | 67 | 69 | 64 | 57 | 48 | 38 | — |
| Jaffa (1907–12) | | | | | | | | | | | | | |
| Mean | 55 | 57 | 60 | 65 | 70 | 74 | 78 | 79 | 77 | 72 | 65 | 59 | 68 |
| M.D. max. | 64 | 66 | 70 | 75 | 80 | 84 | 87 | 89 | 87 | 83 | 74 | 68 | 77 |
| M.D. min. | 47 | 48 | 50 | 54 | 60 | 64 | 68 | 69 | 67 | 62 | 55 | 50 | 58 |
| M.M. max. | 76 | 80 | 87 | 95 | 94 | 88 | 91 | 91 | 90 | 92 | 83 | 77 | — |
| M.M. min. | 37 | 41 | 43 | 45 | 52 | 58 | 62 | 65 | 62 | 55 | 46 | 42 | — |
| Absolute max. | 86 | 87 | 93 | 98 | 102 | 91 | 97 | 93 | 91 | 96 | 88 | 84 | — |
| Absolute min. | 32 | 39 | 39 | 44 | 48 | 57 | 59 | 63 | 60 | 53 | 40 | 38 | — |

## TABLE II—continued

| | Jan. | Feb. | Mar. | Apr. | May | June | July | Aug. | Sept. | Oct. | Nov. | Dec. | Year |
|---|---|---|---|---|---|---|---|---|---|---|---|---|---|
| **Tel Aviv (1928–40)** | | | | | | | | | | | | | |
| Mean | 55 | 58 | 61 | 66 | 71 | 76 | 80 | 81 | 78 | 73 | 66 | 58 | 69 |
| M.D. max. | 63 | 65 | 70 | 75 | 80 | 85 | 89 | 90 | 86 | 81 | 74 | 66 | 77 |
| M.D. min. | 48 | 48 | 51 | 56 | 62 | 67 | 71 | 73 | 70 | 65 | 57 | 50 | 60 |
| Absolute max. | 80 | 88 | 90 | 100 | 115 | 100 | 95 | 96 | 103 | 105 | 90 | 80 | — |
| Absolute min. | 37 | 38 | 38 | 45 | 52 | 59 | 65 | 66 | 62 | 55 | 47 | 38 | — |
| **Gaza (1921–34)** | | | | | | | | | | | | | |
| Mean | 55 | 56 | 60 | 64 | 70 | 74 | 77 | 78 | 76 | 72 | 67 | 59 | 67 |
| M.D. max. | 65 | 65 | 70 | 75 | 81 | 84 | 86 | 87 | 86 | 82 | 77 | 69 | 77 |
| M.D. min. | 46 | 46 | 49 | 53 | 59 | 64 | 68 | 69 | 67 | 62 | 56 | 49 | 57 |
| Absolute max. | 84 | 94 | 102 | 110 | 108 | 112 | 101 | 96 | 108 | 99 | 97 | 87 | — |
| Absolute min. | 30 | 35 | 37 | 42 | 47 | 54 | 62 | 63 | 59 | 51 | 44 | 35 | — |
| **2. Inland** | | | | | | | | | | | | | |
| **Nazareth (1891–1906)** | | | | | | | | | | | | | |
| Mean | 49 | 54 | 56 | 63 | 68 | 74 | 78 | 79 | 77 | 75 | 65 | 54 | 66 |
| M.D. max. | 57 | 62 | 65 | 74 | 79 | 86 | 89 | 90 | 89 | 88 | 76 | 62 | 77 |
| M.D. min. | 41 | 43 | 46 | 52 | 57 | 62 | 67 | 68 | 65 | 62 | 53 | 46 | 55 |
| M.M. max. | 68 | 73 | 82 | 92 | 98 | 99 | 97 | 95 | 100 | 99 | 88 | 77 | — |
| M.M. min. | 33 | 36 | 38 | 43 | 49 | 55 | 62 | 64 | 57 | 55 | 45 | 36 | — |
| Absolute max. | 75 | 79 | 93 | 96 | 105 | 111 | 100 | 100 | 110 | 108 | 98 | 85 | — |
| Absolute min. | 28 | 31 | 35 | 40 | 46 | 50 | 59 | 63 | 54 | 50 | 35 | 25 | — |
| **Jenin (1921–34)** | | | | | | | | | | | | | |
| Mean | 51 | 52 | 58 | 63 | 72 | 77 | 80 | 81 | 79 | 74 | 65 | 55 | 67 |
| M.D. max. | 62 | 63 | 71 | 78 | 88 | 91 | 93 | 95 | 93 | 88 | 79 | 66 | 81 |
| M.D. min. | 45 | 45 | 49 | 53 | 60 | 65 | 69 | 70 | 69 | 63 | 56 | 48 | 58 |
| Absolute max. | 82 | 88 | 94 | 109 | 109 | 110 | 108 | 107 | 109 | 105 | 98 | 84 | — |
| Absolute min. | 31 | 33 | 32 | 41 | 45 | 50 | 52 | 61 | 59 | 51 | 41 | 33 | — |
| **Beit Jemal (1930–40)** | | | | | | | | | | | | | |
| Mean | 55 | 55 | 61 | 67 | 73 | 76 | 79 | 80 | 78 | 76 | 67 | 59 | 69 |
| M.D. max. | 62 | 64 | 71 | 78 | 85 | 89 | 90 | 91 | 89 | 86 | 75 | 66 | 77 |
| M.D. min. | 48 | 48 | 51 | 56 | 61 | 65 | 68 | 69 | 67 | 65 | 57 | 52 | 59 |
| Absolute max. | 84 | 84 | 95 | 105 | 109 | 113 | 102 | 100 | 111 | 102 | 100 | 85 | — |
| Absolute min. | 33 | 33 | 38 | 44 | 51 | 56 | 61 | 64 | 57 | 56 | 46 | 38 | — |
| **Jerusalem (1918–34)** | | | | | | | | | | | | | |
| Mean | 47 | 48 | 55 | 61 | 69 | 73 | 75 | 75 | 73 | 69 | 62 | 52 | 63 |
| M.D. max. | 54 | 55 | 65 | 72 | 81 | 85 | 87 | 88 | 85 | 80 | 70 | 59 | 73 |
| M.D. min. | 41 | 41 | 45 | 50 | 56 | 60 | 63 | 63 | 62 | 58 | 53 | 45 | 53 |
| *M.M. max. | 60 | 67 | 80 | 85 | 92 | 98 | 96 | 97 | 96 | 90 | 78 | 68 | — |
| *M.M. min. | 32 | 33 | 34 | 41 | 46 | 53 | 58 | 59 | 56 | 51 | 42 | 34 | — |
| Absolute max. | 70 | 80 | 87 | 102 | 101 | 107 | 100 | 103 | 103 | 96 | 88 | 79 | — |
| Absolute min. | 26 | 27 | 30 | 36 | 42 | 47 | 50 | 52 | 50 | 47 | 39 | 27 | — |
| **El Latrun (1901–12)** | | | | | | | | | | | | | |
| Mean | 54 | 57 | 60 | 67 | 74 | 77 | 80 | 82 | 79 | 75 | 67 | 59 | 69 |
| M.D. max. | 62 | 67 | 70 | 80 | 88 | 91 | 95 | 95 | 92 | 88 | 77 | 68 | 81 |
| M.D. min. | 46 | 48 | 49 | 55 | 59 | 63 | 66 | 68 | 66 | 63 | 57 | 51 | 58 |
| †M.M. max. | 78 | 82 | 86 | 100 | 106 | 104 | 102 | 102 | 100 | 98 | 93 | 80 | — |
| †M.M. min. | 36 | 42 | 43 | 46 | 52 | 59 | 63 | 65 | 62 | 57 | 49 | 42 | — |
| †Absolute max. | 85 | 91 | 91 | 104 | 109 | 112 | 114 | 109 | 109 | 107 | 99 | 87 | — |
| †Absolute min. | 27 | 37 | 40 | 43 | 49 | 57 | 61 | 62 | 60 | 51 | 42 | 36 | — |
| **Hebron (1896–1914)** | | | | | | | | | | | | | |
| Mean | 45 | 48 | 51 | 58 | 66 | 69 | 72 | 73 | 71 | 67 | 57 | 49 | 60 |
| M.D. max. | 52 | 56 | 61 | 71 | 80 | 84 | 86 | 87 | 85 | 80 | 67 | 57 | 72 |
| M.D. min. | 37 | 39 | 41 | 46 | 51 | 55 | 57 | 59 | 57 | 54 | 46 | 40 | 48 |
| M.M. max. | 68 | 70 | 76 | 89 | 95 | 97 | 94 | 96 | 94 | 91 | 80 | 71 | — |
| M.M. min. | 28 | 31 | 31 | 34 | 40 | 46 | 50 | 51 | 48 | 44 | 37 | 32 | — |
| Absolute max. | 76 | 78 | 84 | 91 | 101 | 103 | 102 | 103 | 102 | 98 | 85 | 77 | — |
| Absolute min. | 19 | 26 | 25 | 31 | 34 | 45 | 45 | 48 | 45 | 42 | 32 | 27 | — |

## TABLE II—*continued*

| | *Jan.* | *Feb.* | *Mar.* | *Apr.* | *May* | *June* | *July* | *Aug.* | *Sept.* | *Oct.* | *Nov.* | *Dec.* | *Year* |
|---|---|---|---|---|---|---|---|---|---|---|---|---|---|
| **Beersheba (1921–34)** | | | | | | | | | | | | | |
| Mean | 54 | 54 | 60 | 66 | 73 | 77 | 79 | 80 | 77 | 73 | 67 | 58 | 68 |
| M.D. max. | 65 | 66 | 75 | 82 | 90 | 93 | 94 | 94 | 92 | 88 | 80 | 69 | 82 |
| M.D. min. | 42 | 43 | 45 | 50 | 56 | 60 | 64 | 64 | 61 | 57 | 52 | 46 | 53 |
| Absolute max. | 83 | 90 | 98 | 104 | 110 | 115 | 108 | 107 | 111 | 103 | 96 | 86 | — |
| Absolute min. | 23 | 32 | 34 | 36 | 40 | 46 | 54 | 54 | 49 | 45 | 39 | 33 | — |
| **3. Jordan Valley** | | | | | | | | | | | | | |
| **Tiberias (1890–1905)** | | | | | | | | | | | | | |
| Mean | 56 | 58 | 63 | 69 | 77 | 84 | 87 | 88 | 84 | 80 | 70 | 61 | 73 |
| M.D. max. | 65 | 68 | 73 | 81 | 90 | 97 | 100 | 100 | 96 | 91 | 79 | 69 | 84 |
| M.D. min. | 47 | 49 | 52 | 58 | 65 | 70 | 74 | 76 | 72 | 69 | 60 | 53 | 63 |
| M.M. max. | 73 | 77 | 88 | 96 | 103 | 108 | 108 | 107 | 106 | 101 | 92 | 82 | — |
| M.M. min. | 39 | 43 | 44 | 50 | 56 | 64 | 70 | 72 | 66 | 62 | 53 | 44 | — |
| ‡Absolute max. | 78 | 82 | 97 | 101 | 109 | 114 | 111 | 112 | 111 | 104 | 100 | 88 | — |
| ‡Absolute min. | 34 | 37 | 40 | 43 | 50 | 59 | 67 | 67 | 50 | 57 | 48 | 39 | — |
| **Beisan (1930–40)** | | | | | | | | | | | | | |
| Mean | 56 | 58 | 63 | 69 | 76 | 81 | 83 | 87 | 82 | 79 | 70 | 59 | 72 |
| M.D. max. | 66 | 69 | 77 | 84 | 92 | 97 | 99 | 100 | 98 | 94 | 79 | 71 | 86 |
| M.D. min. | 45 | 46 | 48 | 52 | 59 | 66 | 71 | 72 | 68 | 64 | 56 | 48 | 58 |
| Absolute max. | 81 | 87 | 97 | 108 | 114 | 113 | 111 | 109 | 118 | 108 | 100 | 85 | — |
| Absolute min. | 31 | 34 | 33 | 40 | 48 | 54 | 63 | 64 | 56 | 51 | 42 | 33 | — |
| **Jericho (1921–34)** | | | | | | | | | | | | | |
| Mean | 57 | 59 | 65 | 72 | 80 | 85 | 88 | 88 | 85 | 80 | 71 | 60 | 74 |
| M.D. max. | 68 | 71 | 79 | 87 | 97 | 101 | 103 | 103 | 100 | 94 | 84 | 72 | 88 |
| M.D. min. | 50 | 51 | 55 | 60 | 67 | 73 | 75 | 76 | 74 | 69 | 61 | 53 | 64 |
| Absolute max. | 84 | 88 | 100 | 117 | 120 | 118 | 114 | 117 | 117 | 107 | 99 | 85 | — |
| Absolute min. | 37 | 37 | 35 | 47 | 50 | 59 | 66 | 70 | 63 | 57 | 46 | 36 | — |
| **4. Dead Sea** | | | | | | | | | | | | | |
| **North End (4 yrs.' obsns.)** | | | | | | | | | | | | | |
| Mean | 58 | 60 | 67 | 73 | 81 | 86 | 88 | 88 | 84 | 79 | 69 | 61 | 75 |
| M.D. max. | 66 | 70 | 79 | 84 | 93 | 97 | 99 | 99 | 94 | 90 | 82 | 71 | 85 |
| M.D. min. | 50 | 52 | 56 | 61 | 67 | 75 | 76 | 78 | 74 | 69 | 59 | 52 | 64 |
| Absolute max. | 75 | 87 | 97 | 106 | 111 | 116 | 108 | 108 | 109 | 102 | 93 | 84 | — |
| Absolute min. | 37 | 36 | 43 | 49 | 59 | 61 | 64 | 72 | 66 | 59 | 43 | 37 | — |
| **5. Transjordan** | | | | | | | | | | | | | |
| **Amman (1924–41)** | | | | | | | | | | | | | |
| §Mean | 46 | 48 | 55 | 61 | 69 | 75 | 77 | 78 | 75 | 69 | 60 | 50 | 64 |
| §M.D. max. | 54 | 56 | 65 | 73 | 83 | 88 | 89 | 91 | 88 | 82 | 70 | 59 | 75 |
| §M.D. min. | 39 | 40 | 44 | 49 | 56 | 61 | 65 | 65 | 62 | 57 | 50 | 41 | 52 |
| M.M. max. | 65 | 70 | 82 | 91 | 99 | 99 | 98 | 101 | 99 | 92 | 82 | 69 | 103 |
| M.M. min. | 31 | 32 | 34 | 38 | 46 | 52 | 58 | 58 | 55 | 50 | 40 | 34 | 29 |
| Absolute max. | 76 | 85 | 90 | 103 | 105 | 104 | 103 | 109 | 103 | 99 | 91 | 77 | — |
| Absolute min. | 21 | 23 | 26 | 34 | 43 | 46 | 56 | 55 | 52 | 44 | 35 | 25 | — |

\* 1882–1901.
† Less 1903–4.
‡ 1890–9.
§ 15 years' observations.

## TABLE III. *Relative Humidity* (%)

| | *Jan.* | *Feb.* | *Mar.* | *Apr.* | *May* | *June* | *July* | *Aug.* | *Sept.* | *Oct.* | *Nov.* | *Dec.* | *Year* |
|---|---|---|---|---|---|---|---|---|---|---|---|---|---|
| **1. Coast** | | | | | | | | | | | | | |
| Acre (1928–38) | 72 | 77 | 68 | 67 | 66 | 70 | 74 | 73 | 68 | 62 | 65 | 70 | 70 |
| Haifa (9 yrs.' obsns.) | 72 | 71 | 69 | 69 | 70 | 72 | 71 | 68 | 67 | 66 | 69 | 72 | 69 |
| (Obsns. 0700, 1400, and 2200 hrs.) | | | | | | | | | | | | | |
| Jaffa (Sarona) | 76 | 75 | 71 | 71 | 71 | 73 | 74 | 72 | 70 | 70 | 71 | 73 | 72 |
| (1896–1905) (Obsns. 0700, 1300, and 2100 hrs.) | | | | | | | | | | | | | |
| Gaza (1921–34) | 77 | 75 | 69 | 65 | 63 | 67 | 72 | 72 | 71 | 70 | 69 | 73 | 70 |
| (Obsns. 0800 hrs.) | | | | | | | | | | | | | |
| **2. Inland** | | | | | | | | | | | | | |
| Jenin (1926–7 and 1937–8) | 62 | 64 | 62 | 61 | 61 | 63 | 64 | 66 | 67 | 66 | 61 | 59 | 63 |
| Beit Jemal (9 yrs.' obsns.) | 74 | 74 | 67 | 59 | 56 | 63 | 68 | 73 | 73 | 67 | 66 | 69 | 67 |
| Jerusalem (1918–34) | 78 | 72 | 60 | 52 | 44 | 46 | 50 | 55 | 60 | 58 | 62 | 73 | 59 |
| (Obsns. 0800 hrs.) | | | | | | | | | | | | | |
| El Latrun (1903–12) | 65 | 63 | 62 | 57 | 49 | 53 | 53 | 55 | 57 | 55 | 55 | 61 | 57 |
| (Obsns. 0600, 1200, and 1800 hrs.) | | | | | | | | | | | | | |
| Hebron (1896–1914) | 83 | 78 | 74 | 62 | 53 | 54 | 55 | 59 | 63 | 62 | 72 | 80 | 66 |
| Beersheba (1921–34) | 78 | 75 | 67 | 57 | 53 | 59 | 67 | 67 | 70 | 66 | 67 | 72 | 66 |
| (Obsns. 0800 hrs.) | | | | | | | | | | | | | |
| **3. Jordan Valley** | | | | | | | | | | | | | |
| Tiberias (1896–1905) | 70 | 67 | 63 | 58 | 50 | 46 | 50 | 52 | 50 | 49 | 60 | 68 | 57 |
| (Obsns. 0800 and 1600 hrs.) | | | | | | | | | | | | | |
| Beisan (9 yrs.' obsns.) | 73 | 76 | 68 | 58 | 58 | 56 | 55 | 55 | 59 | 53 | 66 | 54 | 60 |
| Jericho (1921–34) | 70 | 68 | 56 | 48 | 43 | 44 | 45 | 46 | 52 | 54 | 59 | 66 | 54 |
| (Obsns. 0800, 1400, and 2000 hrs.) | | | | | | | | | | | | | |
| **4. Transjordan** | | | | | | | | | | | | | |
| Amman (1924–41) | 68 | 64 | 52 | 42 | 30 | 31 | 33 | 36 | 40 | 39 | 53 | 63 | 46 |
| (Obsns. 0800 and 1400 hrs.) | | | | | | | | | | | | | |

## TABLE IV. *Mean Monthly Evaporation*
### (In inches, Piche method)[1]

| | *Jan.* | *Feb.* | *Mar.* | *Apr.* | *May* | *June* | *July* | *Aug.* | *Sept.* | *Oct.* | *Nov.* | *Dec.* | *Total* |
|---|---|---|---|---|---|---|---|---|---|---|---|---|---|
| **1. Coast** | | | | | | | | | | | | | |
| Acre . . . | 5·9 | 5·2 | 6·3 | 6·9 | 6·7 | 5·8 | 6·3 | 7·0 | 7·4 | 7·9 | 7·0 | 6·9 | 79 |
| Haifa . . . | 5·0 | 4·9 | 6·0 | 6·0 | 7·0 | 6·6 | 7·0 | 7·2 | 7·4 | 6·9 | 5·9 | 5·2 | 75 |
| Tel Aviv . . | 2·1 | 2·4 | 3·1 | 3·7 | 3·5 | 3·3 | 3·7 | 3·8 | 3·8 | 3·4 | 2·4 | 2·2 | 37 |
| Gaza . . . | 3·4 | 3·9 | 5·0 | 6·4 | 7·3 | 7·2 | 7·2 | 7·1 | 6·5 | 5·9 | 4·6 | 3·9 | 68 |
| **2. Inland** | | | | | | | | | | | | | |
| Jenin . . . | 3·5 | 3·8 | 4·6 | 7·9 | 10·0 | 11·1 | 11·2 | 11·7 | 10·5 | 9·5 | 6·1 | 4·5 | 94 |
| Beit Jemal . | 4·4 | 5·1 | 6·0 | 7·3 | 8·5 | 8·2 | 8·2 | 7·2 | 6·5 | 7·3 | 6·4 | 6·0 | 81 |
| Jerusalem . . | 2·8 | 2·9 | 6·0 | 7·6 | 10·9 | 10·1 | 10·6 | 9·3 | 7·6 | 7·8 | 4·8 | 3·5 | 83 |
| Beersheba . ' . | 5·0 | 3·9 | 7·7 | 10·6 | 12·9 | 12·2 | 12·2 | 10·9 | 8·5 | 8·4 | 7·1 | 5·9 | 105 |
| **3. Jordan Valley** | | | | | | | | | | | | | |
| Beisan . . . | 3·5 | 3·4 | 6·0 | 7·7 | 10·7 | 12·0 | 12·1 | 11·4 | 9·8 | 8·7 | 5·2 | 4·6 | 95 |
| Jericho . . | 4·7 | 4·9 | 8·1 | 8·7 | 14·7 | 13·8 | 14·5 | 13·4 | 11·7 | 10·4 | 7·1 | 5·3 | 117 |
| Dead Sea . . | 7·5 | 6·8 | 11·7 | 13·9 | 16·8 | 17·2 | 17·3 | 18·2 | 14·7 | 13·3 | 11·9 | 8·8 | 157 |

[1] 10 years' observations within the period 1926–38, except Tel Aviv (1934–8) and Dead Sea (1933–6)

TABLE V. *Mean Number of Days with Fog* [1]

| | Jan. | Feb. | Mar. | Apr. | May | June | July | Aug. | Sept. | Oct. | Nov. | Dec. | Year |
|---|---|---|---|---|---|---|---|---|---|---|---|---|---|
| **1. Coast** | | | | | | | | | | | | | |
| Jaffa (Sarona) (1896–1905) | 0·0 | 0·8 | 1·8 | 2·2 | 2·0 | 1·2 | 0·8 | 0·3 | 0·0 | 1·0 | 0·0 | 2·0 | 12·1 |
| Gaza (1896–1905) | 0·0 | 0·7 | 0·4 | 1·1 | 1·5 | 2·5 | 2·6 | 0·9 | 0·7 | 2·1 | 0·3 | 0·1 | 12·9 |
| **2. Inland** | | | | | | | | | | | | | |
| Jerusalem (1896–1905) | 2·4 | 1·7 | 1·4 | 0·6 | 0·4 | 0·8 | 0·6 | 1·4 | 2·1 | 0·8 | 1·4 | 1·6 | 15·2 |
| El Latrun (1906–12) | 0·1 | 0·6 | 0·3 | 2·1 | 2·4 | 2·6 | 3·3 | 3·3 | 0·7 | 0·6 | 0·6 | 0·1 | 16·7 |
| **3. Jordan Valley** | | | | | | | | | | | | | |
| Tabgha (1909–12 and 1915) | 4·0 | 3·5 | 4·0 | 3·7 | 3·5 | 2·0 | 1·3 | 1·3 | 3·3 | 1·0 | 1·5 | 3·7 | 32·8 |
| **4. Transjordan** | | | | | | | | | | | | | |
| Amman (1924–41) | 1·0 | 1·0 | 0·2 | 0·0 | 0·1 | 0·0 | 0·0 | 0·0 | 0·0 | 0·0 | 0·2 | 0·5 | 3·0 |

[1] Fog is undefined, except for Amman, where observations refer to visibility of 1,100 yards or less.

TABLE VI. *Cloud* [1]

Scale 0 (cloudless) to 10 (completely overcast)

| | Jan. | Feb. | Mar. | Apr. | May | June | July | Aug. | Sept. | Oct. | Nov. | Dec. | Year |
|---|---|---|---|---|---|---|---|---|---|---|---|---|---|
| **1. Coast** | | | | | | | | | | | | | |
| Acre (10 yrs.' obsns.) | 4·5 | 4·6 | 2·9 | 2·5 | 2·0 | 1·6 | 2·4 | 2·3 | 2·2 | 2·3 | 3·2 | 4·3 | 2·9 |
| Haifa (1897–1905) | 5·2 | 4·6 | 4·7 | 3·7 | 3·0 | 2·5 | 2·6 | 2·5 | 2·1 | 2·6 | 4·2 | 5·1 | 3·6 |
| Jaffa (1907–12) | 4·6 | 4·0 | 3·7 | 3·4 | 2·3 | 1·4 | 1·8 | 2·2 | 2·3 | 2·4 | 3·0 | 3·6 | 2·9 |
| Gaza (1921–34) | 4·1 | 4·2 | 3·0 | 2·4 | 2·0 | 1·6 | 2·2 | 1·7 | 1·7 | 1·6 | 2·7 | 3·7 | 2·6 |
| **2. Inland** | | | | | | | | | | | | | |
| Nazareth (1891–1904) | 4·9 | 4·6 | 5·4 | 4·3 | 3·5 | 2·2 | 3·5 | 3·6 | 2·3 | 2·5 | 4·5 | 5·1 | 3·9 |
| Jenin (1921–34) | 4·4 | 4·3 | 2·8 | 2·2 | 1·3 | 0·5 | 0·3 | 0·4 | 0·7 | 1·1 | 2·2 | 3·8 | 2·0 |
| Beit Jemal (1930–8) | 5·2 | 4·9 | 3·8 | 3·8 | 2·7 | 1·3 | 1·2 | 1·4 | 1·7 | 2·5 | 3·8 | 4·1 | 3·0 |
| Jerusalem (1918–34) | 4·7 | 4·8 | 3·1 | 3·1 | 1·8 | 0·8 | 0·6 | 0·7 | 1·1 | 1·6 | 2·6 | 4·0 | 2·4 |
| El Latrun (1901–12) | 4·0 | 3·4 | 3·6 | 2·8 | 1·5 | 0·6 | 0·4 | 0·4 | 0·8 | 1·8 | 2·7 | 3·4 | 2·1 |
| Hebron (1896–1914) | 5·9 | 5·5 | 5·3 | 4·0 | 1·6 | 0·6 | 0·6 | 0·5 | 1·4 | 2·8 | 4·1 | 4·6 | 3·1 |
| Beersheba (1921–34) | 4·0 | 4·0 | 3·0 | 2·4 | 1·5 | 1·0 | 1·3 | 1·3 | 1·4 | 1·6 | 2·0 | 3·6 | 2·3 |
| **3. Jordan Valley** | | | | | | | | | | | | | |
| Tiberias (2 yrs.' obsns.) | 6·2 | 4·6 | 4·3 | 3·1 | 1·2 | 0·5 | 0·6 | 0·6 | 1·1 | 1·0 | 4·1 | 4·5 | 2·7 |
| Beisan (1930–8) | 4·5 | 6·5 | 2·7 | 2·5 | 2·1 | 0·7 | 0·9 | 1·0 | 1·0 | 2·3 | 2·4 | 3·1 | 2·5 |
| Jericho (1921–34) | 4·1 | 4·2 | 2·5 | 2·2 | 1·6 | 0·6 | 0·4 | 0·4 | 0·7 | 1·5 | 2·4 | 3·8 | 2·0 |
| **4. Transjordan** | | | | | | | | | | | | | |
| Amman (1924–41) | 4·9 | 4·8 | 3·8 | 3·3 | 2·7 | 0·7 | 0·4 | 0·4 | 0·7 | 2·3 | 3·8 | 4·5 | 2·7 |

[1] Mean of day, except at Gaza, Jerusalem, and Beersheba (0800 hrs. only), and Jaffa (0700 hrs. only).

TABLE VII.  *Mean Duration of Sunshine at North End of Dead Sea*
Monthly Mean for 1932–1933

|  | Hours | Minutes |
|---|---|---|
| January . . . . . | 4 | 29 |
| February . . . . . | 6 | 26 |
| March . . . . . | 8 | 3 |
| April . . . . . . | 10 | 52 |
| May . . . . . . | 11 | 2 |
| June . . . . . . | 12 | 4 |
| July . . . . . . | 12 | 28 |
| August . . . . . | 12 | 20 |
| September . . . . | 10 | 17 |
| October . . . . . | 10 | 15 |
| November . . . . | 8 | 20 |
| December . . . . | 7 | 2 |
| Average for the year . . | 9 | 28 |

TABLE VIII.  *Precipitation (in inches)*

|  | Jan. | Feb. | Mar. | Apr. | May | June | July | Aug. | Sept. | Oct. | Nov. | Dec. | Year |
|---|---|---|---|---|---|---|---|---|---|---|---|---|---|
| **1. Coast** | | | | | | | | | | | | | |
| **Acre (1928–38)** | | | | | | | | | | | | | |
| Mean | 5·5 | 7·9 | 0·9 | 0·7 | 0·2 | trace | 0·0 | 0·0 | 0·2 | 1·3 | 4·1 | 3·7 | 24·5 |
| Max. in 24 hrs. | 1·2 | 1·1 | 0·5 | 0·4 | 0·1 | trace | 0·0 | 0·0 | 0·1 | 0·3 | 0·9 | 1·4 | — |
| **Haifa (1921–34)** | | | | | | | | | | | | | |
| Mean | 7·1 | 5·7 | 0·9 | 0·7 | 0·1 | 0·0 | 0·0 | 0·0 | 0·0 | 0·5 | 2·7 | 6·7 | 24·4 |
| Max. in 24 hrs. | 3·4 | 2·2 | 1·0 | 1·0 | 0·4 | 0·2 | 0·3 | 0·1 | 0·1 | 1·9 | 2·6 | 7·2 | — |
| *Max. in month and year | 12·1 | 10·5 | 6·0 | 3·5 | 2·1 | 0·6 | 0·0 | <0·1 | 0·5 | 3·3 | 13·6 | 13·9 | 39·5 |
| *Min. in month and year | 0·7 | 0·2 | 0·9 | <0·1 | 0·0 | 0·0 | 0·0 | 0·0 | 0·0 | 0·0 | <0·1 | 0·0 | 16·8 |
| **Jaffa (1902–12)** | | | | | | | | | | | | | |
| Mean | 5·6 | 3·9 | 2·7 | 0·9 | 0·1 | <0·1 | 0·0 | 0·0 | 0·2 | 1·4 | 3·2 | 5·6 | 23·6 |
| Max. in month and year | 8·6 | 5·9 | 7·6 | 2·0 | 0·6 | 0·2 | 0·0 | 0·0 | 1·1 | 3·9 | 5·5 | 12·5 | 28·4 |
| †Min. in month and year | 4·0 | 1·0 | <0·1 | <0·1 | 0·0 | 0·0 | 0·0 | 0·0 | 0·0 | 0·0 | 0·4 | 1·9 | 17·3 |
| **Gaza (1921–34)** | | | | | | | | | | | | | |
| Mean | 3·6 | 3·4 | 0·7 | 0·7 | 0·1 | 0·0 | 0·0 | 0·0 | 0·0 | 0·3 | 1·4 | 3·6 | 13·8 |
| Max. in 24 hrs. | 2·7 | 1·8 | 0·8 | 2·7 | 0·4 | 0·1 | 0·0 | 0·0 | 0·0 | 1·3 | 2·1 | 2·9 | — |
| **2. Inland** | | | | | | | | | | | | | |
| **Jenin (1921–34)** | | | | | | | | | | | | | |
| Mean | 5·1 | 5·4 | 1·1 | 1·2 | 0·1 | 0·0 | 0·0 | 0·0 | 0·0 | 0·3 | 1·7 | 4·1 | 19·0 |
| Max. in 24 hrs. | 2·2 | 2·6 | 1·1 | 2·5 | 0·5 | 0·1 | 0·0 | 0·1 | 0·0 | 1·1 | 2·8 | 2·1 | — |
| **Nazareth (1891–1907)** | | | | | | | | | | | | | |
| Mean | 6·3 | 4·6 | 3·7 | 1·0 | 0·2 | 0·0 | 0·0 | 0·0 | 0·0 | 0·8 | 3·4 | 7·1 | 27·1 |
| Max. in month and year | 14·2 | 10·3 | 5·9 | 2·8 | 1·0 | 0·0 | <0·1 | 0·0 | <0·1 | 2·5 | 9·1 | 12·8 | 37·9 |
| Min. in month and year | 1·2 | 1·7 | <0·1 | 0·0 | 0·0 | 0·0 | 0·0 | 0·0 | 0·0 | 0·0 | 0·3 | 0·7 | 18·5 |

## TABLE VIII—continued

| | Jan. | Feb. | Mar. | Apr. | May | June | July | Aug. | Sept. | Oct. | Nov. | Dec. | Year |
|---|---|---|---|---|---|---|---|---|---|---|---|---|---|
| **Beit Jemal (1930–8)** | | | | | | | | | | | | | |
| Mean | 4·3 | 4·0 | 1·1 | 0·7 | 0·1 | 0·0 | 0·0 | 0·0 | trace | 0·6 | 2·8 | 2·5 | 16·1 |
| Max. in 24 hrs. | 1·2 | 1·5 | 0·8 | 0·5 | 0·1 | 0·0 | 0·0 | 0·0 | trace | 0·3 | 1·4 | 0·8 | — |
| **Jerusalem (1918–34)** | | | | | | | | | | | | | |
| Mean | 4·1 | 5·3 | 1·1 | 1·0 | 0·1 | 0·0 | 0·0 | 0·0 | 0·0 | 0·2 | 1·2 | 2·9 | 15·9 |
| Max. in 24 hrs. | 3·9 | 3·4 | 1·4 | 1·5 | 0·5 | 0·1 | 0·0 | trace | 0·4 | 0·9 | 2·2 | 3·0 | — |
| ‡Max. in month and year | 14·5 | 12·6 | 12·4 | 6·5 | 1·3 | 0·2 | 0·0 | 0·1 | 0·8 | 2·3 | 8·0 | 16·5 | 41·6 |
| ‡Min. in month and year | 0·1 | 0·2 | 0·4 | 0·0 | 0·0 | 0·0 | 0·0 | 0·0 | 0·0 | 0·0 | <0·1 | 0·5 | 13·3 |
| **El Latrun (1901–12)** | | | | | | | | | | | | | |
| Mean | 6·5 | 3·3 | 2·8 | 1·3 | 0·3 | <0·1 | 0·0 | 0·0 | <0·1 | 0·9 | 2·4 | 5·2 | 22·8 |
| §Max. in 24 hrs. | 4·6 | 2·1 | 1·6 | 1·9 | 0·5 | 0·0 | 0·0 | 0·0 | 0·3 | 1·4 | 1·6 | 3·1 | — |
| Max. in month and year | 8·9 | 7·7 | 6·9 | 4·0 | 1·6 | 0·2 | 0·0 | 0·0 | 0·1 | 4·5 | 7·0 | 12·5 | 32·5 |
| Min. in month and year | 3·4 | 0·0 | 0·6 | 0·2 | 0·0 | 0·0 | 00· | 0·0 | 0·0 | 0·0 | 0·0 | 1·9 | 15·8 |
| **Hebron (1896–1914)** | | | | | | | | | | | | | |
| Mean | 6·2 | 4·6 | 3·4 | 2·0 | 0·3 | <0·1 | 0·0 | 0·0 | <0·1 | 0·5 | 2·1 | 5·1 | 24·3 |
| Max. in 24 hrs. | 13·9 | 12·4 | 8·6 | 8·3 | 2·2 | 1·3 | 0·0 | 0·0 | 0·2 | 2·5 | 6·1 | 14·1 | 39·8 |
| Min. in month and year | 1·6 | 0·2 | 0·2 | <0·1 | 0·0 | 0·0 | 0·0 | 0·0 | 0·0 | 0·0 | 0·0 | 1·1 | 16·3 |
| **Beersheba (1921–34)** | | | | | | | | | | | | | |
| Mean | 1·9 | 2·2 | 0·7 | 0·4 | 0·1 | 0·0 | 0·0 | 0·0 | 0·0 | 0·1 | 0·8 | 1·6 | 7·8 |
| Max. in 24 hrs. | 2·0 | 1·6 | 1·0 | 1·0 | 1·0 | 0·0 | 0·0 | 0·0 | trace | 0·4 | 1·4 | 2·5 | — |
| **3. Jordan Valley** | | | | | | | | | | | | | |
| **Tiberias (1890–1907)** | | | | | | | | | | | | | |
| Mean | 4·7 | 3·2 | 2·6 | 1·1 | 0·2 | 0·0 | 0·0 | 0·0 | <0·1 | 0·6 | 2·9 | 5·1 | 20·2 |
| ‖Max. in 24 hrs. | 2·7 | 1·2 | 2·0 | 1·5 | 0·4 | 0·0 | 0·0 | 0·0 | <0·1 | 0·5 | 1·6 | 2·4 | — |
| Max. in month and year | 11·2 | 6·5 | 5·0 | 3·0 | 0·9 | 0·0 | 0·0 | 0·0 | <0·1 | 2·1 | 6·7 | 8·8 | 27·7 |
| Min. in month and year | 0·5 | <0·1 | 0·4 | 0·0 | 0·0 | 0·0 | 0·0 | 0·0 | 0·0 | 0·0 | 0·0 | 1·7 | 14·4 |
| **Beisan (1930–8)** | | | | | | | | | | | | | |
| Mean | 3·1 | 2·8 | 0·7 | 0·4 | 0·2 | 0·0 | 0·0 | 0·0 | 0·0 | 0·7 | 1·2 | 1·4 | 10·5 |
| Max. in 24 hrs. | 0·9 | 0·9 | 0·4 | 0·3 | 0·1 | 0·0 | 0·0 | 0·0 | trace | 0·5 | 0·4 | 0·6 | — |
| **Jericho (1921–34)** | | | | | | | | | | | | | |
| Mean | 1·3 | 1·3 | 0·2 | 0·4 | 0·1 | 0·0 | 0·0 | 0·0 | 0·0 | 0·1 | 0·4 | 1·2 | 5·0 |
| Max. in 24 hrs. | 1·0 | 1·3 | 0·6 | 0·7 | 1·0 | 0·2 | 0·1 | 0·0 | trace | 0·2 | 1·0 | 1·6 | — |
| **Dead Sea, North end (1934–7)** | | | | | | | | | | | | | |
| Mean | 0·6 | 0·4 | <0·1 | <0·1 | <0·1 | 0·0 | 0·0 | 0·0 | 0·0 | 0·4 | <0·1 | 0·4 | 1·9 |
| **Dead Sea, South end (1935–6)** | | | | | | | | | | | | | |
| Mean | 0·1 | 0·1 | 0·0 | 0·0 | 0·0 | 0·0 | 0·0 | 0·0 | 0·0 | 0·3 | 0·3 | 0·4 | 1·2 |
| **4. Transjordan** | | | | | | | | | | | | | |
| **Amman (1924–41)** | | | | | | | | | | | | | |
| ¶Mean | 2·5 | 3·3 | 0·8 | 0·8 | 0·1 | 0·0 | 0·0 | 0·0 | 0·0 | 0·1 | 1·3 | 1·6 | 10·5 |
| Max. in 24 hrs. | 2·0 | 2·8 | 1·4 | 1·6 | 0·9 | 0·0 | 0·0 | 0·0 | 0·0 | 0·4 | 3·1 | 2·1 | — |

\* 1884–1905.
† 1907–12.
‡ 1860–99.
§ 1906–12.
‖ 1890–9.
¶ 15 years' obsns.

## TABLE IX. *Mean Number of Rain-days**

| | Jan. | Feb. | Mar. | Apr. | May | June | July | Aug. | Sept. | Oct. | Nov. | Dec. | Year |
|---|---|---|---|---|---|---|---|---|---|---|---|---|---|
| **1. Coast** | | | | | | | | | | | | | |
| Haifa (1921–34) | 14 | 13 | 5 | 4 | 1 | 0 | 0 | 0 | 0 | 2 | 6 | 11 | 56 |
| Jaffa (1907–12) | 15·2 | 10·0 | 7·4 | 5·0 | 1·2 | 0·2 | 0·0 | 0·0 | 1·0 | 4·4 | 7·5 | 10·6 | 63 |
| Gaza (1921–34) | 11 | 10 | 3 | 2 | 0·5 | 0·2 | 0·1 | 0·1 | 0·1 | 1 | 4 | 8 | 40 |
| **2. Inland** | | | | | | | | | | | | | |
| Nazareth (1891–1907) | 12·4 | 12·0 | 9·9 | 4·5 | 1·9 | 0·0 | 0·0 | 0·0 | 0·2 | 2·5 | 8·1 | 11·8 | 63 |
| Jenin (1921–34) | 14 | 12 | 5 | 4 | 0·7 | 0·5 | 0·0 | 0·1 | 0·0 | 1 | 5 | 10 | 52 |
| Beit Jemal (1930–8) | 9 | 6 | 3 | 3 | 0·3 | 0 | 0 | 0 | 0 | 1 | 4 | 5 | 31 |
| Jerusalem (1918–34) | 11 | 11 | 4 | 4 | 0·6 | 0·1 | 0 | 0 | 0·3 | 2 | 5 | 8 | 46 |
| El Latrun (1901–12) | 14·2 | 9·0 | 9·6 | 6·5 | 2·3 | 0·4 | 0·1 | 0·3 | 0·8 | 3·3 | 7·3 | 10·5 | 64 |
| Hebron (1896–1914) | 12·9 | 10·6 | 9·4 | 5·4 | 1·4 | 0·1 | 0·0 | 0·0 | 0·3 | 2·6 | 6·8 | 8·9 | 58 |
| Beersheba (1921–34) | 7 | 7 | 3 | 2 | 0·2 | 0·1 | 0 | 0 | 0 | 0·4 | 3 | 4 | 27 |
| **3. Jordan Valley** | | | | | | | | | | | | | |
| Tiberias (1890–1907) | 10·9 | 10·3 | 8·8 | 3·8 | 1·3 | 0·0 | 0·0 | 0·0 | 0·0 | 1·6 | 6·4 | 10·4 | 54 |
| Beisan (1930–8) | 9 | 8 | 3 | 2 | 1 | 0 | 0 | 0 | 0·2 | 1 | 4 | 6 | 34 |
| Jericho (1921–34) | 7 | 7 | 2 | 2 | 0·3 | 0·1 | 0·1 | 0 | 0 | 0·8 | 3 | 5 | 27 |
| Dead Sea (N. end) (1934–7) | 4 | 3 | 1 | 0·4 | 0·02 | 0 | 0 | 0 | 0 | 0·6 | 1 | 2 | 12 |
| Dead Sea (S. end) (1935–6) | 2 | 2 | 0 | 0 | 0 | 0 | 0 | 0 | 0· | 2 | 2 | 1 | 9 |
| **4. Transjordan** | | | | | | | | | | | | | |
| Amman (1924–41) (15 yrs. obsns.) | 11 | 10 | 5 | 3 | 1 | 0 | 0 | 0 | 0 | 2 | 5 | 7 | 44 |

\* A rain-day is one with a trace (0·004 in.) or more of precipitation.

## TABLE X. *Number of Days with Dew in 1938*

| | Jan. | Feb. | Mar. | Apr. | May | June | July | Aug. | Sept. | Oct. | Nov. | Dec. | Year |
|---|---|---|---|---|---|---|---|---|---|---|---|---|---|
| **1. Coast** | | | | | | | | | | | | | |
| Acre | 0 | 0 | 9 | 11 | 10 | 14 | 3 | 2 | 5 | 4 | 8 | 6 | 72 |
| Haifa | 0 | 3 | 1 | 11 | 17 | 25 | 18 | 19 | 22 | 19 | 0 | 0 | 135 |
| Tel Aviv | 5 | 9 | 5 | 0 | 2 | 1 | 0 | 0 | 0 | 1 | 15 | 16 | 54 |
| Gaza | 0 | 3 | 2 | 3 | 3 | 8 | 3 | 4 | 5 | 0 | 10 | 10 | 51 |
| **2. Inland** | | | | | | | | | | | | | |
| Beit Jemal | 0 | 8 | 13 | 10 | 17 | 18 | 8 | 22 | 11 | 14 | 14 | 12 | 147 |
| Beersheba (8 months only) | 4 | 8 | 8 | 6 | 8 | 7 | 17 | 7 | — | — | — | — | (65 |
| **3. Jordan Valley** | | | | | | | | | | | | | |
| Beisan (6 months only) | 6 | 0 | 9 | 13 | 12 | 7 | — | — | — | — | — | — | (47 |

## TABLE XI. *Mean Number of Days with Snow-fall*

| | Jan. | Feb. | Mar. | Apr. | May | June | July | Aug. | Sept. | Oct. | Nov. | Dec. | Year |
|---|---|---|---|---|---|---|---|---|---|---|---|---|---|
| Jerusalem (1896–1905) | 1·4 | 0·5 | 0·2 | 0 | 0 | 0 | 0 | 0 | 0 | 0 | 0·1 | 0·7 | 2·9 |
| El Latrun (1906–12) | 0 | 0·1 | 0 | 0 | 0 | 0 | 0 | 0 | 0 | 0 | 0 | 0 | 0·1 |
| Bethlehem | 1·2 | 0·4 | 0 | 0 | 0 | 0 | 0 | 0 | 0 | 0 | 0 | 0·4 | 2·0 |
| Amman (1924–41) | 0·4 | 1·0 | 0 | 0 | 0 | 0 | 0 | 0 | 0 | 0 | 0 | 0·2 | 1·6 |

TABLE XII. *Mean Number of Days with Thunder*

| | Jan. | Feb. | Mar. | Apr. | May | June | July | Aug. | Sept. | Oct. | Nov. | Dec. | Year |
|---|---|---|---|---|---|---|---|---|---|---|---|---|---|
| **1. Coast** | | | | | | | | | | | | | |
| Acre (1938) | 0 | 0 | 0 | 1 | 0 | 0 | 0 | 0 | 0 | 1 | 5 | 3 | 10 |
| Haifa (1938) | 2 | 1 | 0 | 2 | 0 | 0 | 0 | 0 | 0 | 1 | 0 | 0 | 6 |
| Jaffa (Sarona) (1896–1905) | 2·0 | 1·4 | 1·0 | 0·3 | 0·3 | 0 | 0 | 0 | 0 | 1·0 | 2·8 | 3·5 | 12·3 |
| Gaza (1896–1905) | 0·7 | 0·9 | 0·9 | 0·3 | 0·2 | 0 | 0 | 0 | 0 | 0·7 | 2·1 | 1·4 | 7·2 |
| **2. Inland** | | | | | | | | | | | | | |
| Jerusalem (1896–1905) | 0·4 | 0·7 | 1·2 | 1·0 | 0·8 | 0·1 | 0 | 0 | 0 | 0·8 | 1·4 | 1·0 | 7·4 |
| Beit Jemal (1938) | 0 | 3 | 0 | 0 | 0 | 0 | 0 | 0 | 1 | 1 | 4 | 1 | 10 |
| El Latrun (1906–12) | 0·4 | 0·7 | 0·7 | 0·7 | 0·6 | 0 | 0 | 0 | 0 | 2·0 | 1·6 | 1·4 | 8·1 |
| Bethlehem | 0·2 | 0·6 | 0·6 | 0·2 | 1·0 | 0 | 0 | 0 | 0 | 0·7 | 0·7 | 0 | 4·0 |
| Hebron | 0·3 | 1·4 | 1·0 | 0·2 | 0·8 | 0 | 0 | 0 | 0 | 0·8 | 1·3 | 0·2 | 6·0 |
| **3. Jordan Valley** | | | | | | | | | | | | | |
| Tabgha (1909–12, and 1915) | 2·5 | 3·0 | 2·5 | 1·0 | 1·5 | 0 | 0 | 0 | 0·2 | 2·5 | 2·2 | 3·0 | 18·4 |
| **4. Transjordan** | | | | | | | | | | | | | |
| Amman (1924–41) | 0·4 | 0·4 | 0·3 | 0·6 | 0·6 | 0·1 | 0 | 0·1 | 0·1 | 0·9 | 1 | 0·5 | 5·0 |

TABLE XIII. *Mean Number of Days with Hail*

| | Jan. | Feb. | Mar. | Apr. | May | June | July | Aug. | Sept. | Oct. | Nov. | Dec. | Year |
|---|---|---|---|---|---|---|---|---|---|---|---|---|---|
| **1. Coast** | | | | | | | | | | | | | |
| Acre (1938) | 2 | 3 | 0 | 0 | 0 | 0 | 0 | 0 | 0 | 0 | 1 | 0 | 6 |
| Jaffa (Sarona) (1896–1905) | 1·0 | 0 | 0 | 0 | 0 | 0 | 0 | 0 | 0 | 0 | 0·3 | 1·3 | 2·6 |
| **2. Inland** | | | | | | | | | | | | | |
| Jerusalem (1896–1905) | 0·3 | 0·8 | 0·6 | 0·1 | 0·1 | 0 | 0 | 0 | 0 | 0 | 0·1 | 0·7 | 2·7 |
| Beit Jemal (1938) | 0 | 2 | 1 | 0 | 0 | 0 | 0 | 0 | 0 | 0 | 0 | 0 | 3 |
| El Latrun (1906–12) | 0·3 | 0·7 | 0·6 | 0·3 | 0 | 0 | 0 | 0 | 0 | 0 | 0·1 | 0·6 | 2·6 |
| Bethlehem | 0·4 | 0·6 | 0·8 | 0·2 | 0 | 0 | 0 | 0 | 0 | 0 | 0 | 0·2 | 2·2 |

# APPENDIX H

# CONVERSION TABLES
## METRIC AND BRITISH UNITS

All metallic standards are subject to molecular change. Tables differ according to the date of the comparison on which they rest. These are based on the 1896 comparison between Yard and Metre, which gives:

$$1 \text{ metre} = 39 \cdot 370113 \text{ inches.}$$

Tables 1 to 6 give the ratios between units of the same sort.

Space, and printing, deny the use of many decimal figures. Therefore such a figure as 0·00000032 is given as $3 \cdot 2 \times 10^{-7}$ (which means that the first significant figure is the seventh after the decimal point: 0·0001925 becomes $1 \cdot 925 \times 10^{-4}$, and 0·0000734 is $7 \cdot 34 \times 10^{-5}$).

Tables 7 to 20 give ratios *in extenso* between single units.
These deal with conversions from metric into the equivalent British units.

Figures referring to metric units are given in italics; metric units (1 to 9) are given at the top of each table, reading horizontally from left to right; metric tens read vertically from top to bottom on extreme right and left of the table.

Thus in Table 8, if *87* centimetres are to be converted to inches, the *8* is read on the left edge, and following the horizontal line until it comes in the 7 unit column the answer 34·252 is read.

## LIST OF TABLES

1. Units of Length
2. Units of Area
3. Units of Volume
4. Units of Weight
5. Units of Pressure
6. Yields per Area
7. Metres to Feet
8. Centimetres to Inches
9. Kilometres to Statute Miles
10. Square Metres to Square Feet
11. Hectares to Acres
12. Square Kilometres to Square Miles
13. Cubic Metres to Cubic Feet
14. Kilogrammes to Pounds
15. Litres to Gallons
16. Metric Tons to Tons
17. Quintals per Hectare to Tons per Acre
18. Numbers per Square Kilometre to Numbers per Square Mile
19. Degrees Centigrade to Degrees Fahrenheit
20. Millibars, Millimetres of Mercury, and Inches of Mercury

## TABLE 1. UNITS OF LENGTH

| Nautical mile | Statute mile | Kilometre | Metre | Yard | Foot | Inch | Centimetre |
|---|---|---|---|---|---|---|---|
| 1 | 1·152 | 1·853 | 1853 | 2027 | †6080 | 72,960 | 185,300 |
| $8·684 \times 10^{-1}$ | 1 | 1·60934 | 1609·34 | 1760 | 5280 | 63,360 | 160,934 |
| $5·396 \times 10^{-1}$ | $6·21372 \times 10^{-1}$ | 1 | 1000 | 1093·61 | 3280·84 | 39,370·1 | 100,000 |
| $5·396 \times 10^{-4}$ | $6·21372 \times 10^{-4}$ | $1·0 \times 10^{-3}$ | 1 | 1·09361 | 3·28084 | 39·3701 | 100 |
| $4·934 \times 10^{-4}$ | $5·68182 \times 10^{-4}$ | $9·14399 \times 10^{-4}$ | $9·14399 \times 10^{-1}$ | 1 | 3 | 36 | 91·4399 |
| $1·645 \times 10^{-4}$ | $1·89394 \times 10^{-4}$ | $3·048 \times 10^{-4}$ | $3·048 \times 10^{-1}$ | $3·33333 \times 10^{-1}$ | 1 | 12 | 30·48(00) |
| $1·371 \times 10^{-5}$ | $1·57828 \times 10^{-5}$ | $2·54 \times 10^{-5}$ | $2·54 \times 10^{-2}$ | $2·77778 \times 10^{-2}$ | $8·33333 \times 10^{-2}$ | 1 | 2·54(000) |
| $5·396 \times 10^{-6}$ | $6·21372 \times 10^{-6}$ | $1·0 \times 10^{-5}$ | $1·0 \times 10^{-2}$ | $1·09361 \times 10^{-2}$ | $3·28084 \times 10^{-2}$ | $3·93701 \times 10^{-1}$ | 1 |

† This is the customary British practice, and not the international nautical mile, of 1852 metres, which Great Britain has not adopted.

*Rough rules:* 1 millimetre = 0·04 inch.
1 metre = $\frac{10}{9}$ feet.
1 kilometre = $\frac{5}{8}$ of a mile.

## TABLE 2. UNITS OF AREA

| Square mile | Square kilometre | Hectare | Acre | Square metre | Square yard | Square foot |
|---|---|---|---|---|---|---|
| 1 | 2·58998 | 258·998 | 640 | $258,998 \times 10$ | $30,976 \times 10^{2}$ | $278,784 \times 10^{2}$ |
| $3·86103 \times 10^{-1}$ | 1 | 100 | 247·106 | 1,000,000 | $119,599 \times 10$ | $107,639 \times 10^{2}$ |
| $3·86103 \times 10^{-3}$ | $1·0 \times 10^{-2}$ | 1 | 2·47106 | 10,000 | 11,959·9 | 107,639 |
| $1·5625 \times 10^{-3}$ | $4·04685 \times 10^{-3}$ | $4·04685 \times 10^{-1}$ | 1 | 4046·85 | 4840 | 43,560 |
| $3·86103 \times 10^{-7}$ | $1·0 \times 10^{-6}$ | $1·0 \times 10^{-4}$ | $2·47106 \times 10^{-4}$ | 1 | 1·19599 | 10·7639 |
| $3·22831 \times 10^{-7}$ | $8·36126 \times 10^{-7}$ | $8·36126 \times 10^{-5}$ | $2·06612 \times 10^{-4}$ | $8·36126 \times 10^{-1}$ | 1 | 9 |
| $3·58701 \times 10^{-8}$ | $9·29029 \times 10^{-8}$ | $9·29029 \times 10^{-6}$ | $2·29568 \times 10^{-5}$ | $9·29029 \times 10^{-2}$ | $1·11111 \times 10^{-1}$ | 1 |

*Rough rules:* 1 square kilometre = $\frac{3}{8}$ square mile.
1 hectare = $2\frac{1}{2}$ acres.

## TABLE 3. UNITS OF VOLUME

| Kilolitre | Cubic metre | Cubic yard | Bushel | Cubic feet | Imp. gall. | Litre | Pint |
|---|---|---|---|---|---|---|---|
| 1 | 1·000027 | 1·30799 | 27·4969 | 35·3157 | 219·976 | 1000 | 1759·80 |
| $9·99973 \times 10^{-1}$ | 1 | 1·30795 | 27·4962 | 35·3148 | 219·970 | 999·973 | 1759·75 |
| $7·64532 \times 10^{-1}$ | $7·64553 \times 10^{-1}$ | 1 | 21·0223 | 27 | 168·178 | 764·532 | 1345·43 |
| $3·63677 \times 10^{-2}$ | $3·63687 \times 10^{-2}$ | $4·75685 \times 10^{-2}$ | 1 | 1·28435 | 8 | 36·3677 | 64 |
| $2·83160 \times 10^{-2}$ | $2·83167 \times 10^{-2}$ | $3·70370 \times 10^{-2}$ | $7·78602 \times 10^{-1}$ | 1 | 6·22882 | 28·3160 | 49·8306 |
| $4·54596 \times 10^{-3}$ | $4·54608 \times 10^{-3}$ | $5·94607 \times 10^{-3}$ | $1·25 \times 10^{-1}$ | $1·60544 \times 10^{-1}$ | 1 | 4·54596 | 8 |
| $1·0 \times 10^{-3}$ | $1·000027 \times 10^{-3}$ | $1·30799 \times 10^{-3}$ | $2·74969 \times 10^{-2}$ | $3·53157 \times 10^{-2}$ | $2·19976 \times 10^{-1}$ | 1 | 1·75980 |
| $5·68245 \times 10^{-4}$ | $5·68260 \times 10^{-4}$ | $7·43258 \times 10^{-4}$ | $1·5625 \times 10^{-2}$ | $2·00680 \times 10^{-2}$ | $1·25 \times 10^{-1}$ | $5·68245 \times 10^{-1}$ | 1 |

## TABLE 4. UNITS OF WEIGHT

| Ton | Millier or metric ton | Quintal | Kilogram | lb. |
|---|---|---|---|---|
| 1 | 1·01605 | 10·1605 | 1016·05 | 2240 |
| $9·84207 \times 10^{-1}$ | 1 | 10 | 1000 | 2204·62 |
| $9·84207 \times 10^{-2}$ | $1·0 \times 10^{-1}$ | 1 | 100 | 220·462 |
| $9·84207 \times 10^{-4}$ | $1·0 \times 10^{-3}$ | $1·0 \times 10^{-2}$ | 1 | 2·20462 |
| $4·46429 \times 10^{-4}$ | $4·53592 \times 10^{-4}$ | $4·53592 \times 10^{-3}$ | $4·53592 \times 10^{-1}$ | 1 |

*Rough rule:* To turn metric into British tons deduct 1½ per cent.

## TABLE 5. UNITS OF PRESSURE

| Atmosphere normal 760 mm. Hg at 0° C. ($g = 980\cdot665$ cm. per sec. per sec.) | Bar (= $10^6$ dynes per sq. cm.) | lb. per sq. inch ($g = 980\cdot665$ cm. per sec. per sec.) | Inches of mercury at 32° F. ($g = 980\cdot665$ cm. per sec. per sec.) | Millibars (1,000 dynes per sq. cm.) |
|---|---|---|---|---|
| 1 | $1\cdot01325$ | $14\cdot6959$ | $29\cdot9213$ | $1013\cdot25$ |
| $9\cdot86923 \times 10^{-1}$ | 1 | $14\cdot5037$ | $29\cdot5300$ | 1000 |
| $6\cdot80461 \times 10^{-2}$ | $6\cdot89477 \times 10^{-2}$ | 1 | $2\cdot03603$ | $68\cdot9477$ |
| $3\cdot34210 \times 10^{-2}$ | $3\cdot38639 \times 10^{-2}$ | $4\cdot91153 \times 10^{-1}$ | 1 | $33\cdot8639$ |
| $9\cdot86923 \times 10^{-4}$ | $1\cdot0 \times 10^{-3}$ | $1\cdot45037 \times 10^{-2}$ | $2\cdot95300 \times 10^{-2}$ | 1 |

## TABLE 6. YIELD PER AREA

| Ton per acre | Metric ton per hectare | Quintal per hectare |
|---|---|---|
| 1 | $2\cdot51071$ | $25\cdot1071$ |
| $3\cdot98294 \times 10^{-1}$ | 1 | 10 |
| $3\cdot98294 \times 10^{-2}$ | $1\cdot0 \times 10^{-1}$ | 1 |

## TABLE 7. METRES TO FEET. 1 metre = 3·28084 feet

|  | 0 | 1 | 2 | 3 | 4 | 5 | 6 | 7 | 8 | 9 |  |
|---|---|---|---|---|---|---|---|---|---|---|---|
|  | ·· | 3·3 | 6·6 | 9·8 | 13·1 | 16·4 | 19·7 | 23·0 | 26·3 | 29·5 |  |
| 1 | 32·8 | 36·1 | 39·4 | 42·7 | 45·9 | 49·2 | 52·5 | 55·8 | 59·1 | 62·3 | 1 |
| 2 | 65·6 | 68·9 | 72·2 | 75·5 | 78·7 | 82·0 | 85·3 | 88·6 | 91·9 | 95·1 | 2 |
| 3 | 98·4 | 101·7 | 105·0 | 108·3 | 111·6 | 114·8 | 118·1 | 121·4 | 124·7 | 128·0 | 3 |
| 4 | 131·2 | 134·5 | 137·8 | 141·1 | 144·4 | 147·6 | 150·9 | 154·2 | 157·5 | 160·8 | 4 |
| 5 | 164·0 | 167·3 | 170·6 | 173·9 | 177·2 | 180·5 | 183·7 | 187·0 | 190·3 | 193·6 | 5 |
| 6 | 196·9 | 200·1 | 203·4 | 206·7 | 210·0 | 213·3 | 216·5 | 219·8 | 223·1 | 226·4 | 6 |
| 7 | 229·7 | 232·9 | 236·2 | 239·5 | 242·8 | 246·1 | 249·3 | 252·6 | 255·9 | 259·2 | 7 |
| 8 | 262·5 | 265·8 | 269·0 | 272·3 | 275·6 | 278·9 | 282·2 | 285·4 | 288·7 | 292·0 | 8 |
| 9 | 295·3 | 298·6 | 301·8 | 305·1 | 308·4 | 311·7 | 315·0 | 318·2 | 321·5 | 324·8 | 9 |
| 10 | 328·1 | 331·4 | 334·6 | 337·9 | 341·2 | 344·5 | 347·8 | 351·0 | 354·3 | 357·6 | 10 |
| 11 | 360·9 | 364·2 | 367·5 | 370·7 | 374·0 | 377·3 | 380·6 | 383·9 | 387·1 | 390·4 | 11 |
| 12 | 393·7 | 397·0 | 400·3 | 403·5 | 406·8 | 410·1 | 413·4 | 416·7 | 419·9 | 423·2 | 12 |
| 13 | 426·5 | 429·8 | 433·1 | 436·4 | 439·6 | 442·9 | 446·2 | 449·5 | 452·8 | 456·0 | 13 |
| 14 | 459·3 | 462·6 | 465·9 | 469·2 | 472·4 | 475·7 | 479·0 | 482·3 | 485·6 | 488·8 | 14 |
| 15 | 492·1 | 495·4 | 498·7 | 502·0 | 505·2 | 508·5 | 511·8 | 515·1 | 518·4 | 521·7 | 15 |
| 16 | 524·9 | 528·2 | 531·5 | 534·8 | 538·1 | 541·3 | 544·6 | 547·9 | 551·2 | 554·5 | 16 |
| 17 | 557·7 | 561·0 | 564·3 | 567·6 | 570·9 | 574·1 | 577·4 | 580·7 | 584·0 | 587·3 | 17 |
| 18 | 590·6 | 593·8 | 597·1 | 600·4 | 603·7 | 607·0 | 610·2 | 613·5 | 616·8 | 620·1 | 18 |
| 19 | 623·4 | 626·6 | 629·9 | 633·2 | 636·5 | 639·8 | 643·0 | 646·3 | 649·6 | 652·9 | 19 |
| 20 | 656·2 | 659·4 | 662·7 | 666·0 | 669·3 | 672·6 | 675·9 | 679·1 | 682·4 | 685·7 | 20 |
| 21 | 689·0 | 692·3 | 695·5 | 698·8 | 702·1 | 705·4 | 708·7 | 711·9 | 715·2 | 718·5 | 21 |
| 22 | 721·8 | 725·1 | 728·3 | 731·6 | 734·9 | 738·2 | 741·5 | 744·8 | 748·0 | 751·3 | 22 |
| 23 | 754·6 | 757·9 | 761·2 | 764·4 | 767·7 | 771·0 | 774·3 | 777·6 | 780·8 | 784·1 | 23 |
| 24 | 787·4 | 790·7 | 794·0 | 797·2 | 800·5 | 803·8 | 807·1 | 810·4 | 813·7 | 816·9 | 24 |
| 25 | 820·2 | 823·5 | 826·8 | 830·1 | 833·3 | 836·6 | 839·9 | 843·2 | 846·5 | 849·7 | 25 |
| 26 | 853·0 | 856·3 | 859·6 | 862·9 | 866·1 | 869·4 | 872·7 | 876·0 | 879·3 | 882·5 | 26 |
| 27 | 885·8 | 889·1 | 892·4 | 895·7 | 899·0 | 902·2 | 905·5 | 908·8 | 912·1 | 915·4 | 27 |
| 28 | 918·6 | 921·9 | 925·2 | 928·5 | 931·8 | 935·0 | 938·3 | 941·6 | 944·9 | 948·2 | 28 |
| 29 | 951·4 | 954·7 | 958·0 | 961·3 | 964·6 | 967·8 | 971·1 | 974·4 | 977·7 | 981·0 | 29 |
| 30 | 984·3 | 987·5 | 990·8 | 994·1 | 997·4 | 1000·7 | 1003·9 | 1007·2 | 1010·5 | 1013·8 | 30 |
| 31 | 1017·1 | 1020·3 | 1023·6 | 1026·9 | 1030·2 | 1033·5 | 1036·7 | 1040·0 | 1043·3 | 1046·6 | 31 |

| | 0 | 1 | 2 | 3 | 4 | 5 | 6 | 7 | 8 | 9 | |
|---|---|---|---|---|---|---|---|---|---|---|---|
| 33 | 1082·7 | 1086·0 | 1089·2 | 1092·5 | 1095·8 | 1099·1 | 1102·4 | 1105·6 | 1108·9 | 1112·2 | 33 |
| 34 | 1115·5 | 1118·8 | 1122·0 | 1125·3 | 1128·6 | 1131·9 | 1135·2 | 1138·5 | 1141·7 | 1145·0 | 34 |
| 35 | 1148·3 | 1151·6 | 1154·9 | 1158·1 | 1161·4 | 1164·7 | 1168·0 | 1171·3 | 1174·5 | 1177·8 | 35 |
| 36 | 1181·1 | 1184·4 | 1187·7 | 1190·9 | 1194·2 | 1197·5 | 1200·8 | 1204·1 | 1207·3 | 1210·6 | 36 |
| 37 | 1213·9 | 1217·2 | 1220·5 | 1223·8 | 1227·0 | 1230·3 | 1233·6 | 1236·9 | 1240·2 | 1243·4 | 37 |
| 38 | 1246·7 | 1250·0 | 1253·3 | 1256·6 | 1259·8 | 1263·1 | 1266·4 | 1269·7 | 1273·0 | 1276·2 | 38 |
| 39 | 1279·5 | 1282·8 | 1286·1 | 1289·4 | 1292·7 | 1295·9 | 1299·2 | 1302·5 | 1305·8 | 1309·1 | 39 |
| 40 | 1312·3 | 1315·6 | 1318·9 | 1322·2 | 1325·5 | 1328·7 | 1332·0 | 1335·3 | 1338·6 | 1341·9 | 40 |
| 41 | 1345·1 | 1348·4 | 1351·7 | 1355·0 | 1358·3 | 1361·5 | 1364·8 | 1368·1 | 1371·4 | 1374·7 | 41 |
| 42 | 1378·0 | 1381·2 | 1384·5 | 1387·8 | 1391·1 | 1394·4 | 1397·6 | 1400·9 | 1404·2 | 1407·5 | 42 |
| 43 | 1410·8 | 1414·0 | 1417·3 | 1420·6 | 1423·9 | 1427·2 | 1430·4 | 1433·7 | 1437·0 | 1440·3 | 43 |
| 44 | 1443·6 | 1446·9 | 1450·1 | 1453·4 | 1456·7 | 1460·0 | 1463·3 | 1466·5 | 1469·8 | 1473·1 | 44 |
| 45 | 1476·4 | 1479·7 | 1482·9 | 1486·2 | 1489·5 | 1492·8 | 1496·1 | 1499·3 | 1502·6 | 1505·9 | 45 |
| 46 | 1509·2 | 1512·5 | 1515·7 | 1519·0 | 1522·3 | 1525·6 | 1528·9 | 1532·2 | 1535·4 | 1538·7 | 46 |
| 47 | 1542·0 | 1545·3 | 1548·6 | 1551·8 | 1555·1 | 1558·4 | 1561·7 | 1565·0 | 1568·2 | 1571·5 | 47 |
| 48 | 1574·8 | 1578·1 | 1581·4 | 1584·6 | 1587·9 | 1591·2 | 1594·5 | 1597·8 | 1601·0 | 1604·3 | 48 |
| 49 | 1607·6 | 1610·9 | 1614·2 | 1617·5 | 1620·7 | 1624·0 | 1627·3 | 1630·6 | 1633·9 | 1637·1 | 49 |
| 50 | 1640·4 | 1643·7 | 1647·0 | 1650·3 | 1653·6 | 1656·8 | 1660·1 | 1663·4 | 1666·7 | 1669·9 | 50 |
| 51 | 1673·2 | 1676·5 | 1679·8 | 1683·1 | 1686·4 | 1689·6 | 1692·9 | 1696·2 | 1699·5 | 1702·8 | 51 |
| 52 | 1706·0 | 1709·3 | 1712·6 | 1715·9 | 1719·2 | 1722·4 | 1725·7 | 1729·0 | 1732·3 | 1735·6 | 52 |
| 53 | 1738·8 | 1742·1 | 1745·4 | 1748·7 | 1752·0 | 1755·2 | 1758·5 | 1761·8 | 1765·1 | 1768·4 | 53 |
| 54 | 1771·7 | 1774·9 | 1778·2 | 1781·5 | 1784·8 | 1788·1 | 1791·3 | 1794·6 | 1797·9 | 1801·2 | 54 |
| 55 | 1804·5 | 1807·8 | 1811·0 | 1814·3 | 1817·6 | 1820·9 | 1824·1 | 1827·4 | 1830·7 | 1834·0 | 55 |
| 56 | 1837·3 | 1840·6 | 1843·8 | 1847·1 | 1850·4 | 1853·7 | 1857·0 | 1860·2 | 1863·5 | 1866·8 | 56 |
| 57 | 1870·1 | 1873·4 | 1876·6 | 1879·9 | 1883·2 | 1886·5 | 1889·8 | 1893·0 | 1896·3 | 1899·6 | 57 |
| 58 | 1902·9 | 1906·2 | 1909·4 | 1912·7 | 1916·0 | 1919·3 | 1922·6 | 1925·9 | 1929·1 | 1932·4 | 58 |
| 59 | 1935·7 | 1939·0 | 1942·3 | 1945·5 | 1948·8 | 1952·1 | 1955·4 | 1958·7 | 1961·9 | 1965·2 | 59 |
| 60 | 1968·5 | 1971·8 | 1975·1 | 1978·3 | 1981·6 | 1984·9 | 1988·2 | 1991·5 | 1994·8 | 1998·0 | 60 |
| 61 | 2001·3 | 2004·6 | 2007·9 | 2011·1 | 2014·4 | 2017·7 | 2021·0 | 2024·3 | 2027·6 | 2030·8 | 61 |
| 62 | 2034·1 | 2037·4 | 2040·7 | 2044·0 | 2047·2 | 2050·5 | 2053·8 | 2057·1 | 2060·4 | 2063·6 | 62 |
| 63 | 2066·9 | 2070·2 | 2073·5 | 2076·8 | 2080·1 | 2083·3 | 2086·6 | 2089·9 | 2093·2 | 2096·5 | 63 |
| 64 | 2099·7 | 2103·0 | 2106·3 | 2109·6 | 2112·9 | 2116·1 | 2119·4 | 2122·7 | 2126·0 | 2129·3 | 64 |
| 65 | 2132·5 | 2135·8 | 2139·1 | 2142·4 | 2145·7 | 2149·0 | 2152·3 | 2155·5 | 2158·8 | 2162·1 | 65 |
| 66 | 2165·4 | 2168·6 | 2171·9 | 2175·2 | 2178·5 | 2181·8 | 2185·1 | 2188·3 | 2191·6 | 2194·9 | 66 |

| | 0 | 1 | 2 | 3 | 4 | 5 | 6 | 7 | 8 | 9 | |
|---|---|---|---|---|---|---|---|---|---|---|---|
| 67 | 2198·2 | 2201·5 | 2204·7 | 2208·0 | 2211·3 | 2214·6 | 2217·9 | 2221·1 | 2224·4 | 2227·7 | 67 |
| 68 | 2231·0 | 2234·3 | 2237·5 | 2240·8 | 2244·1 | 2247·4 | 2250·7 | 2253·8 | 2257·2 | 2260·5 | 68 |
| 69 | 2263·8 | 2267·1 | 2270·4 | 2273·6 | 2276·9 | 2280·2 | 2283·5 | 2286·8 | 2290·0 | 2293·3 | 69 |
| 70 | 2296·6 | 2299·9 | 2303·2 | 2306·4 | 2309·7 | 2313·0 | 2316·3 | 2319·6 | 2322·8 | 2326·1 | 70 |
| 71 | 2329·4 | 2332·7 | 2336·0 | 2339·2 | 2342·5 | 2345·8 | 2349·1 | 2352·4 | 2355·6 | 2358·9 | 71 |
| 72 | 2362·2 | 2365·5 | 2368·8 | 2372·0 | 2375·3 | 2378·6 | 2381·9 | 2385·2 | 2388·5 | 2391·7 | 72 |
| 73 | 2395·0 | 2398·3 | 2401·6 | 2404·9 | 2408·1 | 2411·4 | 2414·7 | 2418·0 | 2421·3 | 2424·5 | 73 |
| 74 | 2427·8 | 2431·1 | 2434·4 | 2437·7 | 2440·9 | 2444·2 | 2447·5 | 2450·8 | 2454·1 | 2457·3 | 74 |
| 75 | 2460·6 | 2463·9 | 2467·2 | 2470·5 | 2473·8 | 2477·0 | 2480·3 | 2483·6 | 2486·9 | 2490·2 | 75 |
| 76 | 2493·4 | 2496·7 | 2500·0 | 2503·3 | 2506·6 | 2509·8 | 2513·1 | 2516·4 | 2519·7 | 2523·0 | 76 |
| 77 | 2526·2 | 2529·5 | 2532·8 | 2536·1 | 2539·4 | 2542·7 | 2545·9 | 2549·2 | 2552·5 | 2555·8 | 77 |
| 78 | 2559·1 | 2562·3 | 2565·6 | 2568·9 | 2572·2 | 2575·5 | 2578·7 | 2582·0 | 2585·3 | 2588·6 | 78 |
| 79 | 2591·9 | 2595·1 | 2598·4 | 2601·7 | 2605·0 | 2608·3 | 2611·5 | 2614·8 | 2618·1 | 2621·4 | 79 |
| 80 | 2624·7 | 2628·0 | 2631·2 | 2634·5 | 2637·8 | 2641·1 | 2644·4 | 2647·6 | 2650·9 | 2654·2 | 80 |
| 81 | 2657·5 | 2660·8 | 2664·0 | 2667·3 | 2670·6 | 2673·9 | 2677·2 | 2680·4 | 2683·7 | 2687·0 | 81 |
| 82 | 2690·3 | 2693·6 | 2696·9 | 2700·1 | 2703·4 | 2706·7 | 2710·0 | 2713·3 | 2716·5 | 2719·8 | 82 |
| 83 | 2723·1 | 2726·4 | 2729·7 | 2732·9 | 2736·2 | 2739·5 | 2742·8 | 2746·1 | 2749·3 | 2752·6 | 83 |
| 84 | 2755·9 | 2759·2 | 2762·5 | 2765·7 | 2769·0 | 2772·3 | 2775·6 | 2778·9 | 2782·2 | 2785·4 | 84 |
| 85 | 2788·7 | 2792·0 | 2795·3 | 2798·6 | 2801·8 | 2805·1 | 2808·4 | 2811·7 | 2815·0 | 2818·2 | 85 |
| 86 | 2821·5 | 2824·8 | 2828·1 | 2831·4 | 2834·6 | 2837·9 | 2841·2 | 2844·5 | 2847·8 | 2851·0 | 86 |
| 87 | 2854·3 | 2857·6 | 2860·9 | 2864·2 | 2867·5 | 2870·7 | 2874·0 | 2877·3 | 2880·6 | 2883·9 | 87 |
| 88 | 2887·1 | 2890·4 | 2893·7 | 2897·0 | 2900·3 | 2903·5 | 2906·8 | 2910·1 | 2913·4 | 2916·7 | 88 |
| 89 | 2919·9 | 2923·2 | 2926·5 | 2929·8 | 2933·1 | 2936·4 | 2939·6 | 2942·9 | 2946·2 | 2949·5 | 89 |
| 90 | 2952·8 | 2956·0 | 2959·3 | 2962·6 | 2965·9 | 2969·2 | 2972·4 | 2975·7 | 2979·0 | 2982·3 | 90 |
| 91 | 2985·6 | 2988·8 | 2992·1 | 2995·4 | 2998·7 | 3002·0 | 3005·2 | 3008·5 | 3011·8 | 3015·1 | 91 |
| 92 | 3018·4 | 3021·7 | 3024·9 | 3028·2 | 3031·5 | 3034·8 | 3038·1 | 3041·3 | 3044·6 | 3047·9 | 92 |
| 93 | 3051·2 | 3054·5 | 3057·7 | 3061·0 | 3064·3 | 3067·6 | 3070·9 | 3074·1 | 3077·4 | 3080·7 | 93 |
| 94 | 3084·0 | 3087·3 | 3090·6 | 3093·8 | 3097·1 | 3100·4 | 3103·7 | 3107·0 | 3110·2 | 3113·5 | 94 |
| 95 | 3116·8 | 3120·1 | 3123·4 | 3126·6 | 3129·9 | 3133·2 | 3136·5 | 3139·8 | 3143·0 | 3146·3 | 95 |
| 96 | 3149·6 | 3152·9 | 3156·2 | 3159·4 | 3162·7 | 3166·0 | 3169·3 | 3172·6 | 3175·9 | 3179·1 | 96 |
| 97 | 3182·4 | 3185·7 | 3189·0 | 3192·3 | 3195·5 | 3198·8 | 3202·1 | 3205·4 | 3208·7 | 3211·9 | 97 |
| 98 | 3215·2 | 3218·5 | 3221·8 | 3225·1 | 3228·3 | 3231·6 | 3234·9 | 3238·2 | 3241·5 | 3244·8 | 98 |
| 99 | 3248·0 | 3251·3 | 3254·6 | 3257·9 | 3261·2 | 3264·4 | 3267·7 | 3271·0 | 3274·3 | 3277·6 | 99 |
| | | | | | | | | | | | 100 |

## TABLE 8. CENTIMETRES TO INCHES

1 centimetre = 0·393701 inches

|    | 0 | 1 | 2 | 3 | 4 | 5 | 6 | 7 | 8 | 9 |    |
|----|---|---|---|---|---|---|---|---|---|---|----|
| ·  | ··     | 0·394  | 0·787  | 1·181  | 1·575  | 1·969  | 2·362  | 2·756  | 3·150  | 3·543  | · |
| 1  | 3·937  | 4·331  | 4·724  | 5·118  | 5·512  | 5·906  | 6·299  | 6·693  | 7·087  | 7·480  | 1 |
| 2  | 7·874  | 8·268  | 8·661  | 9·055  | 9·449  | 9·843  | 10·236 | 10·630 | 11·024 | 11·417 | 2 |
| 3  | 11·811 | 12·205 | 12·598 | 12·992 | 13·386 | 13·780 | 14·173 | 14·567 | 14·961 | 15·354 | 3 |
| 4  | 15·748 | 16·142 | 16·535 | 16·929 | 17·323 | 17·717 | 18·110 | 18·504 | 18·898 | 19·291 | 4 |
| 5  | 19·685 | 20·079 | 20·472 | 20·866 | 21·260 | 21·654 | 22·047 | 22·441 | 22·835 | 23·228 | 5 |
| 6  | 23·622 | 24·016 | 24·409 | 24·803 | 25·197 | 25·591 | 25·984 | 26·378 | 26·772 | 27·165 | 6 |
| 7  | 27·559 | 27·953 | 28·346 | 28·740 | 29·134 | 29·528 | 29·921 | 30·315 | 30·709 | 31·102 | 7 |
| 8  | 31·496 | 31·890 | 32·283 | 32·677 | 33·071 | 33·465 | 33·858 | 34·252 | 34·646 | 35·039 | 8 |
| 9  | 35·433 | 35·827 | 36·220 | 36·614 | 37·008 | 37·402 | 37·795 | 38·189 | 38·583 | 38·976 | 9 |
| 10 | 39·370 |        |        |        |        |        |        |        |        |        | 10 |

## TABLE 9. KILOMETRES TO STATUTE MILES

1 kilometre = 0·621372 miles

|    | 0 | 1 | 2 | 3 | 4 | 5 | 6 | 7 | 8 | 9 |    |
|----|---|---|---|---|---|---|---|---|---|---|----|
| ·  | ··     | 0·621  | 1·243  | 1·864  | 2·485  | 3·107  | 3·728  | 4·350  | 4·971  | 5·592  | · |
| 1  | 6·214  | 6·835  | 7·456  | 8·078  | 8·699  | 9·321  | 9·942  | 10·563 | 11·185 | 11·806 | 1 |
| 2  | 12·427 | 13·049 | 13·670 | 14·292 | 14·913 | 15·534 | 16·156 | 16·777 | 17·398 | 18·020 | 2 |
| 3  | 18·641 | 19·263 | 19·884 | 20·505 | 21·127 | 21·748 | 22·369 | 22·991 | 23·612 | 24·234 | 3 |
| 4  | 24·855 | 25·476 | 26·098 | 26·719 | 27·340 | 27·962 | 28·583 | 29·204 | 29·826 | 30·447 | 4 |
| 5  | 31·069 | 31·690 | 32·311 | 32·933 | 33·554 | 34·175 | 34·797 | 35·418 | 36·040 | 36·661 | 5 |
| 6  | 37·282 | 37·904 | 38·525 | 39·146 | 39·768 | 40·389 | 41·011 | 41·632 | 42·253 | 42·875 | 6 |
| 7  | 43·496 | 44·117 | 44·739 | 45·360 | 45·982 | 46·603 | 47·224 | 47·846 | 48·467 | 49·088 | 7 |
| 8  | 49·710 | 50·331 | 50·952 | 51·574 | 52·195 | 52·817 | 53·438 | 54·059 | 54·681 | 55·302 | 8 |
| 9  | 55·923 | 56·545 | 57·166 | 57·788 | 58·409 | 59·030 | 59·652 | 60·273 | 60·894 | 61·516 | 9 |
| 10 | 62·137 |        |        |        |        |        |        |        |        |        | 10 |

## TABLE 10. SQUARE METRES TO SQUARE FEET

1 square metre = 10·763911 square feet

| | 0 | 1 | 2 | 3 | 4 | 5 | 6 | 7 | 8 | 9 | |
|---|---|---|---|---|---|---|---|---|---|---|---|
| ·· | ·· | 10·764 | 21·528 | 32·292 | 43·056 | 53·820 | 64·583 | 75·347 | 86·111 | 96·875 | ·· |
| 1 | 107·639 | 118·403 | 129·167 | 139·931 | 150·695 | 161·459 | 172·222 | 182·986 | 193·750 | 204·514 | 1 |
| 2 | 215·278 | 226·042 | 236·806 | 247·570 | 258·334 | 269·098 | 279·861 | 290·625 | 301·389 | 312·153 | 2 |
| 3 | 322·917 | 333·681 | 344·445 | 355·209 | 365·973 | 376·737 | 387·501 | 398·265 | 409·029 | 419·792 | 3 |
| 4 | 430·556 | 441·320 | 452·084 | 462·848 | 473·612 | 484·376 | 495·140 | 505·904 | 516·668 | 527·432 | 4 |
| 5 | 538·196 | 548·959 | 559·723 | 570·487 | 581·251 | 592·015 | 602·779 | 613·543 | 624·307 | 635·071 | 5 |
| 6 | 645·835 | 656·599 | 667·363 | 678·126 | 688·890 | 699·654 | 710·418 | 721·182 | 731·946 | 742·710 | 6 |
| 7 | 753·474 | 764·238 | 775·002 | 785·765 | 796·529 | 807·293 | 818·057 | 828·821 | 839·585 | 850·349 | 7 |
| 8 | 861·113 | 871·877 | 882·641 | 893·405 | 904·169 | 914·932 | 925·696 | 936·460 | 947·224 | 957·988 | 8 |
| 9 | 968·752 | 979·516 | 990·280 | 1001·044 | 1011·808 | 1022·572 | 1033·335 | 1044·099 | 1054·863 | 1065·627 | 9 |
| 10 | 1076·391 | | | | | | | | | | 10 |

## TABLE 11. HECTARES TO ACRES

1 hectare = 2·47106 acres

| | 0 | 1 | 2 | 3 | 4 | 5 | 6 | 7 | 8 | 9 | |
|---|---|---|---|---|---|---|---|---|---|---|---|
| ·· | ·· | 2·47 | 4·94 | 7·41 | 9·88 | 12·36 | 14·83 | 17·30 | 19·77 | 22·24 | ·· |
| 1 | 24·71 | 27·18 | 29·65 | 32·12 | 34·59 | 37·07 | 39·54 | 42·01 | 44·48 | 46·95 | 1 |
| 2 | 49·42 | 51·89 | 54·36 | 56·83 | 59·31 | 61·78 | 64·25 | 66·72 | 69·19 | 71·66 | 2 |
| 3 | 74·13 | 76·60 | 79·07 | 81·54 | 84·02 | 86·49 | 88·96 | 91·43 | 93·90 | 96·37 | 3 |
| 4 | 98·84 | 101·31 | 103·78 | 106·26 | 108·73 | 111·20 | 113·67 | 116·14 | 118·61 | 121·08 | 4 |
| 5 | 123·55 | 126·02 | 128·50 | 130·97 | 133·44 | 135·91 | 160·62 | 138·38 | 143·32 | 145·79 | 5 |
| 6 | 148·26 | 150·73 | 153·21 | 155·68 | 158·15 | 160·62 | 163·09 | 165·56 | 168·03 | 170·50 | 6 |
| 7 | 172·97 | 175·45 | 177·92 | 180·39 | 182·86 | 185·33 | 187·80 | 190·27 | 192·74 | 195·21 | 7 |
| 8 | 197·68 | 200·16 | 202·63 | 205·10 | 207·57 | 210·04 | 212·51 | 214·98 | 217·45 | 219·92 | 8 |
| 9 | 222·40 | 224·87 | 227·34 | 229·81 | 232·28 | 234·75 | 237·22 | 239·69 | 242·16 | 244·63 | 9 |
| 10 | 247·11 | | | | | | | | | | 10 |

## TABLE 12, SQUARE KILOMETRES TO SQUARE MILES

1 square kilometre = 0·386103 square miles

|   | 0 | 1 | 2 | 3 | 4 | 5 | 6 | 7 | 8 | 9 |   |
|---|---|---|---|---|---|---|---|---|---|---|---|
| · |  | 0·386 | 0·772 | 1·158 | 1·544 | 1·931 | 2·317 | 2·703 | 3·089 | 3·475 | · |
| 1 | 3·861 | 4·247 | 4·633 | 5·019 | 5·405 | 5·792 | 6·178 | 6·564 | 6·950 | 7·336 | 1 |
| 2 | 7·722 | 8·108 | 8·494 | 8·880 | 9·266 | 9·653 | 10·039 | 10·425 | 10·811 | 11·197 | 2 |
| 3 | 11·583 | 11·969 | 12·355 | 12·741 | 13·128 | 13·514 | 13·900 | 14·286 | 14·672 | 15·058 | 3 |
| 4 | 15·444 | 15·830 | 16·216 | 16·602 | 16·989 | 17·375 | 17·761 | 18·147 | 18·533 | 18·919 | 4 |
| 5 | 19·305 | 19·691 | 20·077 | 20·463 | 20·850 | 21·236 | 21·622 | 22·008 | 22·394 | 22·780 | 5 |
| 6 | 23·166 | 23·552 | 23·938 | 24·324 | 24·711 | 25·097 | 25·483 | 25·869 | 26·255 | 26·641 | 6 |
| 7 | 27·027 | 27·413 | 27·799 | 28·186 | 28·572 | 28·958 | 29·344 | 29·730 | 30·116 | 30·502 | 7 |
| 8 | 30·888 | 31·274 | 31·660 | 32·047 | 32·433 | 32·819 | 33·205 | 33·591 | 33·977 | 34·363 | 8 |
| 9 | 34·749 | 35·135 | 35·521 | 35·908 | 36·294 | 36·680 | 37·066 | 37·452 | 37·838 | 38·224 | 9 |
| 10 | 38·610 |  |  |  |  |  |  |  |  |  | 10 |

## TABLE 13, CUBIC METRES TO CUBIC FEET

1 cubic metre = 35·3148 cubic feet

|   | 0 | 1 | 2 | 3 | 4 | 5 | 6 | 7 | 8 | 9 |   |
|---|---|---|---|---|---|---|---|---|---|---|---|
| · |  | 35·315 | 70·630 | 105·944 | 141·260 | 176·574 | 211·889 | 247·204 | 282·518 | 317·833 | · |
| 1 | 353·148 | 388·463 | 423·778 | 459·092 | 494·407 | 529·722 | 565·037 | 600·352 | 635·666 | 670·981 | 1 |
| 2 | 706·296 | 741·611 | 776·926 | 812·240 | 847·555 | 882·870 | 918·185 | 953·500 | 988·814 | 1024·129 | 2 |
| 3 | 1059·444 | 1094·759 | 1130·074 | 1165·388 | 1200·703 | 1236·018 | 1271·333 | 1306·648 | 1341·962 | 1377·277 | 3 |
| 4 | 1412·592 | 1447·907 | 1483·222 | 1518·536 | 1553·851 | 1589·166 | 1624·481 | 1659·796 | 1695·110 | 1730·425 | 4 |
| 5 | 1765·740 | 1801·055 | 1836·370 | 1871·684 | 1906·999 | 1942·314 | 1977·629 | 2012·944 | 2048·258 | 2083·573 | 5 |
| 6 | 2118·888 | 2154·203 | 2189·518 | 2224·832 | 2260·147 | 2295·462 | 2330·777 | 2366·092 | 2401·406 | 2436·721 | 6 |
| 7 | 2472·036 | 2507·351 | 2542·666 | 2577·980 | 2613·295 | 2648·610 | 2683·925 | 2719·240 | 2754·554 | 2789·869 | 7 |
| 8 | 2825·184 | 2860·499 | 2895·814 | 2931·128 | 2966·443 | 3001·758 | 3037·073 | 3072·388 | 3107·702 | 3143·017 | 8 |
| 9 | 3178·332 | 3213·647 | 3248·962 | 3284·276 | 3319·591 | 3354·906 | 3390·221 | 3425·536 | 3460·850 | 3496·165 | 9 |
| 10 | 3531·480 |  |  |  |  |  |  |  |  |  | 10 |

## TABLE 14. KILOGRAMMES TO POUNDS

1 kilogramme = 2·20462 pounds

|  | 0 | 1 | 2 | 3 | 4 | 5 | 6 | 7 | 8 | 9 |  |
|---|---|---|---|---|---|---|---|---|---|---|---|
| ·· | ·· | 2·205 | 4·409 | 6·614 | 8·818 | 11·023 | 13·228 | 15·432 | 17·637 | 19·842 | ·· |
| 1 | 22·046 | 24·251 | 26·455 | 28·660 | 30·865 | 33·069 | 35·274 | 37·478 | 39·683 | 41·888 | 1 |
| 2 | 44·092 | 46·297 | 48·502 | 50·706 | 52·911 | 55·115 | 57·320 | 59·525 | 61·729 | 63·934 | 2 |
| 3 | 66·139 | 68·343 | 70·548 | 72·752 | 74·957 | 77·162 | 79·366 | 81·571 | 83·776 | 85·980 | 3 |
| 4 | 88·185 | 90·389 | 92·594 | 94·799 | 97·003 | 99·208 | 101·413 | 103·617 | 105·822 | 108·026 | 4 |
| 5 | 110·231 | 112·436 | 114·640 | 116·845 | 119·049 | 121·254 | 123·459 | 125·663 | 127·868 | 130·073 | 5 |
| 6 | 132·277 | 134·482 | 136·686 | 138·891 | 141·096 | 143·300 | 145·505 | 147·710 | 149·914 | 152·119 | 6 |
| 7 | 154·323 | 156·528 | 158·733 | 160·937 | 163·142 | 165·346 | 167·551 | 169·756 | 171·960 | 174·165 | 7 |
| 8 | 176·370 | 178·574 | 180·779 | 182·983 | 185·188 | 187·393 | 189·597 | 191·802 | 194·007 | 196·211 | 8 |
| 9 | 198·416 | 200·620 | 202·825 | 205·030 | 207·234 | 209·439 | 211·644 | 213·848 | 216·053 | 218·257 | 9 |
| 10 | 220·462 | | | | | | | | | | 10 |

## TABLE 15. LITRES TO GALLONS

1 litre = 0·219976 gallons

|  | 0 | 1 | 2 | 3 | 4 | 5 | 6 | 7 | 8 | 9 |  |
|---|---|---|---|---|---|---|---|---|---|---|---|
| ·· | ·· | 0·220 | 0·440 | 0·660 | 0·880 | 1·100 | 1·320 | 1·540 | 1·760 | 1·980 | ·· |
| 1 | 2·200 | 2·420 | 2·640 | 2·860 | 3·080 | 3·300 | 3·520 | 3·740 | 3·960 | 4·180 | 1 |
| 2 | 4·400 | 4·619 | 4·839 | 5·059 | 5·279 | 5·499 | 5·719 | 5·939 | 6·159 | 6·379 | 2 |
| 3 | 6·599 | 6·819 | 7·039 | 7·259 | 7·479 | 7·699 | 7·919 | 8·139 | 8·359 | 8·579 | 3 |
| 4 | 8·799 | 9·019 | 9·239 | 9·459 | 9·679 | 9·899 | 10·119 | 10·339 | 10·559 | 10·779 | 4 |
| 5 | 10·999 | 11·219 | 11·439 | 11·659 | 11·879 | 12·099 | 12·319 | 12·539 | 12·759 | 12·979 | 5 |
| 6 | 13·199 | 13·419 | 13·639 | 13·858 | 14·078 | 14·298 | 14·518 | 14·738 | 14·958 | 15·178 | 6 |
| 7 | 15·398 | 15·618 | 15·838 | 16·058 | 16·278 | 16·498 | 16·718 | 16·938 | 17·158 | 17·378 | 7 |
| 8 | 17·598 | 17·818 | 18·038 | 18·258 | 18·478 | 18·698 | 18·918 | 19·138 | 19·358 | 19·578 | 8 |
| 9 | 19·798 | 20·018 | 20·238 | 20·458 | 20·678 | 20·898 | 21·118 | 21·338 | 21·558 | 21·778 | 9 |
|  | | | | | | | | | | | 10 |

1 metric ton = 0·984207 ton

|     | 0 | 1 | 2 | 3 | 4 | 5 | 6 | 7 | 8 | 9 |     |
|-----|---|---|---|---|---|---|---|---|---|---|-----|
| ·   | ·· | 0·984 | 1·968 | 2·953 | 3·937 | 4·921 | 5·905 | 6·889 | 7·874 | 8·858 | · |
| 1   | 9·842 | 10·826 | 11·810 | 12·795 | 13·779 | 14·763 | 15·747 | 16·732 | 17·716 | 18·700 | 1 |
| 2   | 19·684 | 20·668 | 21·653 | 22·637 | 23·621 | 24·605 | 25·589 | 26·574 | 27·558 | 28·542 | 2 |
| 3   | 29·526 | 30·510 | 31·495 | 32·479 | 33·463 | 34·447 | 35·431 | 36·416 | 37·400 | 38·384 | 3 |
| 4   | 39·368 | 40·352 | 41·337 | 42·321 | 43·305 | 44·289 | 45·274 | 46·258 | 47·242 | 48·226 | 4 |
| 5   | 49·210 | 50·195 | 51·179 | 52·163 | 53·147 | 54·131 | 55·116 | 56·100 | 57·084 | 58·068 | 5 |
| 6   | 59·052 | 60·037 | 61·021 | 62·005 | 62·989 | 63·973 | 64·958 | 65·942 | 66·926 | 67·910 | 6 |
| 7   | 68·894 | 69·879 | 70·863 | 71·847 | 72·831 | 73·816 | 74·800 | 75·784 | 76·768 | 77·752 | 7 |
| 8   | 78·737 | 79·721 | 80·705 | 81·689 | 82·673 | 83·658 | 84·642 | 85·626 | 86·610 | 87·594 | 8 |
| 9   | 88·579 | 89·563 | 90·547 | 91·531 | 92·515 | 93·500 | 94·484 | 95·468 | 96·452 | 97·436 | 9 |
| 10  | 98·421 | | | | | | | | | | 10 |

## TABLE 17. QUINTALS PER HECTARE TO TONS PER ACRE

1 quintal per hectare = 0·0398294 ton per acre

|     | 0 | 1 | 2 | 3 | 4 | 5 | 6 | 7 | 8 | 9 |     |
|-----|---|---|---|---|---|---|---|---|---|---|-----|
| ·   | ·· | 0·03983 | 0·07966 | 0·11949 | 0·15932 | 0·19915 | 0·23898 | 0·27881 | 0·31864 | 0·35846 | · |
| 1   | 0·39829 | 0·43812 | 0·47795 | 0·51778 | 0·55761 | 0·59744 | 0·63727 | 0·67710 | 0·71693 | 0·75676 | 1 |
| 2   | 0·79659 | 0·83642 | 0·87625 | 0·91608 | 0·95591 | 0·99574 | 1·03556 | 1·07539 | 1·11522 | 1·15505 | 2 |
| 3   | 1·19488 | 1·23471 | 1·27454 | 1·31437 | 1·35420 | 1·39401 | 1·43386 | 1·47369 | 1·51352 | 1·55335 | 3 |
| 4   | 1·59318 | 1·63305 | 1·67283 | 1·71266 | 1·75249 | 1·79232 | 1·83215 | 1·87198 | 1·91181 | 1·95164 | 4 |
| 5   | 1·99147 | 2·03130 | 2·07113 | 2·11096 | 2·15079 | 2·19062 | 2·23045 | 2·27028 | 2·31011 | 2·34993 | 5 |
| 6   | 2·38976 | 2·42959 | 2·46942 | 2·50925 | 2·54908 | 2·58891 | 2·62874 | 2·66857 | 2·70840 | 2·74823 | 6 |
| 7   | 2·78806 | 2·82789 | 2·86772 | 2·90755 | 2·94738 | 2·98721 | 3·02703 | 3·06686 | 3·10669 | 3·14652 | 7 |
| 8   | 3·18635 | 3·22618 | 3·26601 | 3·30584 | 3·34567 | 3·38550 | 3·42533 | 3·46516 | 3·50499 | 3·54482 | 8 |
| 9   | 3·58465 | 3·62448 | 3·66430 | 3·70413 | 3·74396 | 3·78379 | 3·82362 | 3·86345 | 3·90328 | 3·94311 | 9 |
| 10  | 3·98294 | | | | | | | | | | 10 |

## TABLE 18. NUMBERS PER SQUARE KILOMETRE TO NUMBERS PER SQUARE MILE

### (or Square Miles to Square Kilometres)

1 square mile = 2·58998 square kilometres

| | 0 | 1 | 2 | 3 | 4 | 5 | 6 | 7 | 8 | 9 | |
|---|---|---|---|---|---|---|---|---|---|---|---|
| .. | .. | 2·59 | 5·18 | 7·77 | 10·36 | 12·95 | 15·54 | 18·13 | 20·72 | 23·31 | .. |
| 1 | 25·90 | 28·49 | 31·08 | 33·67 | 36·26 | 38·85 | 41·44 | 44·03 | 46·62 | 49·21 | 1 |
| 2 | 51·80 | 54·39 | 56·98 | 59·57 | 62·16 | 64·75 | 67·34 | 69·93 | 72·52 | 75·11 | 2 |
| 3 | 77·70 | 80·29 | 82·88 | 85·47 | 88·06 | 90·65 | 93·24 | 95·83 | 98·42 | 101·01 | 3 |
| 4 | 103·60 | 106·19 | 108·78 | 111·37 | 113·96 | 116·55 | 119·14 | 121·73 | 124·32 | 126·91 | 4 |
| 5 | 129·50 | 132·09 | 134·68 | 137·27 | 139·86 | 142·45 | 145·04 | 147·63 | 150·22 | 152·81 | 5 |
| 6 | 155·40 | 157·99 | 160·58 | 163·17 | 165·76 | 168·35 | 170·94 | 173·53 | 176·12 | 178·71 | 6 |
| 7 | 181·30 | 183·89 | 186·48 | 189·07 | 191·66 | 194·25 | 196·84 | 199·43 | 202·02 | 204·61 | 7 |
| 8 | 207·20 | 209·79 | 212·38 | 214·97 | 217·56 | 220·15 | 222·74 | 225·33 | 227·92 | 230·51 | 8 |
| 9 | 233·10 | 235·69 | 238·28 | 240·87 | 243·46 | 246·05 | 248·64 | 251·23 | 253·82 | 256·41 | 9 |
| 10 | 259·00 | | | | | | | | | | 10 |

TABLE 19. DEGREES CENTIGRADE TO DEGREES FAHRENHEIT

*Centigrade minus*

|  | −0 | −1 | −2 | −3 | −4 | −5 | −6 | −7 | −8 | −9 |  |
|---|---|---|---|---|---|---|---|---|---|---|---|
| −2 | −4·0 | −5·8 | −7·6 | −9·4 | −11·2 | −13·0 | −14·8 | −16·6 | −18·4 | −20·2 | −2 |
| −1 | 14·0 | 12·2 | 10·4 | 8·6 | 6·8 | 5·0 | 3·2 | 1·4 | −0·4 | −2·2 | −1 |
| .. | 32·0 | 30·2 | 28·4 | 26·6 | 24·8 | 23·0 | 21·2 | 19·4 | 17·6 | 15·8 | .. |
| .. | 32·0 | 33·8 | 35·6 | 37·4 | 39·2 | 41·0 | 42·8 | 44·6 | 46·4 | 48·2 | .. |
| +1 | 50·0 | 51·8 | 53·6 | 55·4 | 57·2 | 59·0 | 60·8 | 62·6 | 64·4 | 66·2 | +1 |
| +2 | 68·0 | 69·8 | 71·6 | 73·4 | 75·2 | 77·0 | 78·8 | 80·6 | 82·4 | 84·2 | +2 |
| +3 | 86·0 | 87·8 | 89·6 | 91·4 | 93·2 | 95·0 | 96·8 | 98·6 | 100·4 | 102·2 | +3 |
| +4 | 104·0 | 105·8 | 107·6 | 109·4 | 111·2 | 113·0 | 114·8 | 116·6 | 118·4 | 120·2 | +4 |
| +5 | 122·0 | 123·8 | 125·6 | 127·4 | 129·2 | 131·0 | 132·8 | 134·6 | 136·4 | 138·2 | +5 |
| +6 | 140·0 | 141·8 | 143·6 | 145·4 | 147·2 | 149·0 | 150·8 | 152·6 | 154·4 | 156·2 | +6 |
| +7 | 158·0 | 159·8 | 161·6 | 163·4 | 165·2 | 167·0 | 168·8 | 170·6 | 172·4 | 174·2 | +7 |
| +8 | 176·0 | 177·8 | 179·6 | 181·4 | 183·2 | 185·0 | 186·8 | 188·6 | 190·4 | 192·2 | +8 |
| +9 | 194·0 | 195·8 | 197·6 | 199·4 | 201·2 | 203·0 | 204·8 | 206·6 | 208·4 | 210·2 | +9 |
| +10 | 212·0 |  |  |  |  |  |  |  |  |  | +10 |
|  | 0 | 1 | 2 | 3 | 4 | 5 | 6 | 7 | 8 | 9 |  |

*Centigrade plus*

## TABLE 20. PRESSURE: EQUIVALENTS OF MILLIBARS, MILLIMETRES OF MERCURY, AND INCHES OF MERCURY AT 32°F. IN LATITUDE 45°

| Mercury in. | Milli-bars | Mercury mm. | Mercury in. | Milli-bars | Mercury mm. | Mercury in. | Milli-bars | Mercury mm. | Mercury in. | Milli-bars | Mercury mm. | Mercury in. | Milli-bars | Mercury mm. |
|---|---|---|---|---|---|---|---|---|---|---|---|---|---|---|
| 27·02 | 915 | 686·3 | 27·82 | 942 | 706·6 | 28·62 | 969 | 726·8 | 29·41 | 996 | 747·1 | 30·21 | 1,023 | 767·3 |
| 27·05 | 916 | 687·1 | 27·85 | 943 | 707·3 | 28·65 | 970 | 727·6 | 29·44 | 997 | 747·8 | 30·24 | 1,024 | 768·1 |
| 27·08 | 917 | 687·8 | 27·88 | 944 | 708·1 | 28·67 | 971 | 728·3 | 29·47 | 998 | 748·6 | 30·27 | 1,025 | 768·8 |
| 27·11 | 918 | 688·6 | 27·91 | 945 | 708·8 | 28·70 | 972 | 729·1 | 29·50 | 999 | 749·3 | 30·30 | 1,026 | 769·6 |
| 27·14 | 919 | 689·3 | 27·94 | 946 | 709·6 | 28·73 | 973 | 729·8 | 29·53 | 1,000 | 750·1 | 30·33 | 1,027 | 770·3 |
| 27·17 | 920 | 690·1 | 27·97 | 947 | 710·3 | 28·76 | 974 | 730·6 | 29·56 | 1,001 | 750·8 | 30·36 | 1,028 | 771·1 |
| 27·20 | 921 | 690·8 | 28·00 | 948 | 711·1 | 28·79 | 975 | 731·3 | 29·59 | 1,002 | 751·6 | 30·39 | 1,029 | 771·8 |
| 27·23 | 922 | 691·6 | 28·03 | 949 | 711·8 | 28·82 | 976 | 732·1 | 29·62 | 1,003 | 752·3 | 30·42 | 1,030 | 772·6 |
| 27·26 | 923 | 692·3 | 28·05 | 950 | 712·6 | 28·85 | 977 | 732·8 | 29·65 | 1,004 | 753·1 | 30·45 | 1,031 | 773·3 |
| 27·29 | 924 | 693·1 | 28·08 | 951 | 713·3 | 28·88 | 978 | 733·6 | 29·68 | 1,005 | 753·8 | 30·48 | 1,032 | 774·1 |
| 27·32 | 925 | 693·8 | 28·11 | 952 | 714·1 | 28·91 | 979 | 734·3 | 29·71 | 1,006 | 754·6 | 30·51 | 1,033 | 774·8 |
| 27·35 | 926 | 694·6 | 28·14 | 953 | 714·8 | 28·94 | 980 | 735·1 | 29·74 | 1,007 | 755·3 | 30·53 | 1,034 | 775·6 |
| 27·38 | 927 | 695·3 | 28·17 | 954 | 715·6 | 28·97 | 981 | 735·8 | 29·77 | 1,008 | 756·1 | 30·56 | 1,035 | 776·3 |
| 27·41 | 928 | 696·1 | 28·20 | 955 | 716·3 | 29·00 | 982 | 736·6 | 29·80 | 1,009 | 756·8 | 30·59 | 1,036 | 777·1 |
| 27·44 | 929 | 696·8 | 28·23 | 956 | 717·1 | 29·03 | 983 | 737·3 | 29·83 | 1,010 | 757·6 | 30·62 | 1,037 | 777·8 |
| 27·46 | 930 | 697·6 | 28·26 | 957 | 717·8 | 29·06 | 984 | 738·1 | 29·86 | 1,011 | 758·3 | 30·65 | 1,038 | 778·6 |
| 27·49 | 931 | 698·3 | 28·29 | 958 | 718·6 | 29·09 | 985 | 738·8 | 29·89 | 1,012 | 759·1 | 30·68 | 1,039 | 779·3 |
| 27·52 | 932 | 699·1 | 28·32 | 959 | 719·3 | 29·12 | 986 | 739·6 | 29·92 | 1,013 | 759·8 | 30·71 | 1,040 | 780·1 |
| 27·55 | 933 | 699·8 | 28·35 | 960 | 720·1 | 29·15 | 987 | 740·3 | 29·94 | 1,014 | 760·6 | 30·74 | 1,041 | 780·8 |
| 27·58 | 934 | 700·6 | 28·38 | 961 | 720·8 | 29·18 | 988 | 741·1 | 29·97 | 1,015 | 761·3 | 30·77 | 1,042 | 781·6 |
| 27·61 | 935 | 701·3 | 28·41 | 962 | 721·6 | 29·21 | 989 | 741·8 | 30·00 | 1,016 | 762·1 | 30·80 | 1,043 | 782·3 |
| 27·64 | 936 | 702·1 | 28·44 | 963 | 722·3 | 29·24 | 990 | 742·6 | 30·03 | 1,017 | 762·8 | 30·83 | 1,044 | 783·1 |
| 27·67 | 937 | 702·8 | 28·47 | 964 | 723·1 | 29·26 | 991 | 743·3 | 30·06 | 1,018 | 763·6 | 30·86 | 1,045 | 783·8 |
| 27·70 | 938 | 703·6 | 28·50 | 965 | 723·8 | 29·29 | 992 | 744·1 | 30·09 | 1,019 | 764·3 | 30·89 | 1,046 | 784·6 |
| 27·73 | 939 | 704·3 | 28·53 | 966 | 724·6 | 29·32 | 993 | 744·8 | 30·12 | 1,020 | 765·1 | 30·92 | 1,047 | 785·3 |
| 27·76 | 940 | 705·1 | 28·56 | 967 | 725·3 | 29·35 | 994 | 745·6 | 30·15 | 1,021 | 765·8 | 30·95 | 1,048 | 786·1 |
| 27·79 | 941 | 705·8 | 28·59 | 968 | 726·1 | 29·38 | 995 | 746·3 | 30·18 | 1,022 | 766·6 | 30·98 | 1,049 | 786·8 |

# APPENDIX I

# AUTHORSHIP, BIBLIOGRAPHY, AND MAPS

## AUTHORSHIP

The volume has been mainly written by Albert M. Hyamson (late Director of Immigration, Palestine), Lieutenant-Colonel K. Mason (Professor of Geography, University of Oxford), and Sir John L. Myres (Fellow of New College, Oxford). Contributions have been made by Professor P. A. Buxton (London School of Hygiene and Tropical Medicine), Dr. Norman White (late Indian Medical Service), Dr. J. V. Harrison (Department of Geology, University of Oxford), Mr. F. Ballard (Royal Botanic Gardens, Kew), Mrs. Grace Crowfoot, and Mrs. Margaret Kirk. Technical information and photographs have been supplied by the Admiralty, the War Office, the Colonial Office, the Meteorological Office, the Royal Geographical Society, the Palestine Exploration Fund, and others. Maps and plans have been prepared in the drawing office of the Oxford subsection under the direction of Mr. K. W. Hartland.

## SELECT LIST OF BOOKS AND MAPS

The literature of Palestine is exceptionally large. A nearly complete bibliography is P. Thomsen: *Systematische Bibliographie für Palästina-Literatur* (4 vols.: in progress 1908 *et seq.*). The following list, with very few exceptions, contains only books in English that can be easily and usefully consulted.

*The Bible* illustrates vividly the geography, and the life and customs of the beduin to-day, and is the chief source-book for the earlier history. Conversely, knowledge of the customs and life of the beduin illustrates the Bible narrative.

OFFICIAL PUBLICATIONS

His Majesty's Government has published every year an exhaustive *Report* on Palestine and Transjordan. The most recent is for the year 1939 (*Colonial, No. 166*).

For the British Administration before 1923 there are:

*An Interim Report on the Civil Administration of Palestine during the period July 1, 1920–June 30, 1921* (Cmd. 1499–1921).

*Report of the High Commissioner on the Administration of Palestine, 1920–1925* (1925).

From 1924 onwards the *Minutes of the Sessions of the Permanent Mandates Commission* report verbatim the discussions of that body on the British Government's Reports. There is much valuable material in other publications of the British Government, notably the *Reports* of successive

Commissions appointed to inquire into the disturbances, and into specific points that arose out of more general ones; in particular

> *Report on Immigration, Land Settlement, and Development*, by Sir John Hope Simpson (Cmd. 3686–1930), and several
> *Statements of Policy of the British Government.*

The annual *Blue Books* of the Government of Palestine, and the *Annual Reports* of several of the Government departments contain valuable statistics and other information. Since 1936 the Government has also published an *Annual Statistical Abstract.*

UNOFFICIAL PUBLICATIONS

The *Publications of the Jewish Agency* and its subsidiary organizations cover a wide range—political, economic, and educational. The most important are the *Memoranda* summarizing the events of the year, from the viewpoint of the Jewish Agency, which it has been accustomed to communicate to the Permanent Mandates Commission of the League of Nations.

> *Jewish Agency Reports*, issued as a rule every second year, interpret the history of the National Home during the intervening period.
> *Reports of the Executive of the Zionist Organization* to the Zionist Congress, which meets immediately before the biennial meeting of the Jewish Agency, are practically identical with the biennial reports of the Agency.
> *Report of the Joint Palestine Survey Commission* (Zionist and Non-Zionist) (London, 1928) and
> *Reports of the Experts* (New York, 1928) give much information regarding the Zionist administration.

The parallel publications on the Arab side in Palestine are on a much smaller scale.

HANDBOOKS AND GUIDES

> *Handbook of Palestine and Transjordan*, by Sir Harry Luke and E. Keith-Roach (3rd ed. 1934), is a semi-official publication, which gives much useful information.
> *Handbook of Syria, including Palestine* (1921), of the Naval Intelligence Division, deals only in part with Palestine and Transjordan. It is now necessarily out of date, but some of its material is still valuable.
> Cook, *Traveller's Handbook to Palestine, Syria, and Iraq* (6th ed. 1934), is more recent than Baedeker, *Palestine and Syria* (Leipzig, 1912).
> Fr. B. Meistermann, *Guide to the Holy Land* (1923), is written for Roman Catholics.

TRAVELS

Among many narratives of travel in Palestine and Transjordan, which often contain more than topographical description, three from the early nineteenth century are classics:

ELIOT WARBURTON. *The Crescent and the Cross* (1825: 16th ed. 1860).

A. W. KINGLAKE. *Eothen* (1844: new ed. 1921).

ROBERT CURZON. *Visits to Monasteries in the Levant* (1849: latest reprint 1916).

With these, in matter and in form, may be compared

GERTRUDE BELL. *The Desert and the Sown* (1907: 3rd ed. 1928).

## GEOLOGY AND PHYSICAL GEOGRAPHY

SIR GEORGE ADAM SMITH. *Historical Geography of the Holy Land* (25th ed. 1931).

F. M. ABEL. *Géographie de la Palestine* (Paris, 1934).

H. B. TRISTRAM. *The Land of Israel* (1865).

CARL RITTER. *Comparative Geography of Palestine* (E.T. 1866).

EDWARD ROBINSON. *Biblical Researches* (1841: 3rd ed. 1867); *Later Biblical Researches* (1856); contain pioneer work, and still have topographical value.

ELLSWORTH HUNTINGTON. *Palestine and its Transformation* (1911) deals with the controversial question of changes of climate and fertility.

G. S. BLAKE (Government geologist). *The Mineral Resources of Palestine and Transjordan* (Jerusalem, 1930).

M. G. IONIDES and G. S. BLAKE. *Report on the Water Resources of Transjordan and their Development* (1940).

Climate is discussed in W. G. Kendrew, *The Climates of the Continents* (1937); and in the *Mediterranean Pilot*, vol. v, and *Weather in the Mediterranean*, vols. i and ii.

## FLORA AND FAUNA

H. B. TRISTRAM. *Natural History of the Bible* (1867); *Fauna and Flora of Palestine* (1884): still useful.

G. E. POST. *Flora of Syria, Palestine, and Sinai* (Beirut, 2nd ed. 1932–3).

H. C. HART. *Some Account of the Fauna and Flora of Sinai, Petra, and Wady Arabah* (1891).

A. EIG. 'On the Vegetation of Palestine' (*Inst. Agric. and Nat. Hist. Tel Aviv*, Bull. No. 7: 1927); and several other papers, particularly 'On the Phytogeographical Subdivision of Palestine' (*Pal. Gov. Bot.* i. 4: 1938); 'The Vegetation of the Light Soils Belt of the Coastal Plain of Palestine' (*Pal. Gov. Bot.* i. 225: 1929).

R. F. JONES. 'Report of the Percy Sladen Expedition to Lake Huleh' (*Gov. Ecol.* xxviii. 357: 1940).

GRACE CROWFOOT and L. BALDENSPERGER. *From Cedar to Hyssop* (1932).

F. S. BODENHEIMER. *Animal Life in Palestine* (Jerusalem, 1935).

PUBLIC HEALTH

*Annual Reports of the Department of Health of the Government of Palestine*, and special reports on *Malaria in Palestine* (1918–41).

E. W. G. MASTERMAN. *Hygiene and Disease in Palestine* (1920): useful for earlier years, and includes a chapter on *Climate and Water-supply*, and an appendix on the *Water-supply of Jerusalem*.

THE PEOPLE

ERIC MILLS. *Report on the Census of Palestine of 1931* (Jerusalem, 1933): full statistics and much valuable information.

For special groups in the population, the following are useful:

D. GUREVICH. *The Jewish Population of Jerusalem* (Jerusalem, 1940) deals with a small part of a large subject.

J. A. MONTGOMERY. *The Samaritans; the earliest Jewish Sect* (Philadelphia, 1907).

P. K. HITTI. *The Origins of the Druze People and Religion* (New York, 1928).

H. C. LUKE. *Prophets, Priests, and Patriarchs* (1927): minor communities and sects.

A. GOODRICH-FREER. *Inner Jerusalem* (1904): minor sects.

ADRIAN FORTESCUE. *The Lesser Eastern Churches* (1913).

A. BERTRAM and J. W. A. YOUNG. *The Orthodox Patriarchate of Jerusalem* (1926).

HISTORY

A general sketch is in the *Encyclopaedia Britannica* (14th ed. 1926): compare the Foreign Office *Handbook on Syria and Palestine* (1920).

R. A. S. MACALISTER. *A History of Civilization in Palestine* (2nd ed. 1921): an excellent introduction to the earlier periods.

*The Cambridge Ancient History* (1923–39): details of the whole of the ancient period.

E. R. BEVAN. *Jerusalem under the High Priests* (1904).

A. H. M. JONES. *The Herods of Judaea* (1938).

C. R. CONDER. *The Latin Kingdom of Jerusalem* (1897).

GUY LE STRANGE. *Palestine under the Moslems* (1890).

W. T. MASSEY. *The Desert Campaigns* (1918); *How Jerusalem was won* (1919); *Allenby's Final Triumph* (1920).

GEORGE F. MacMUNN and CYRIL FALLS. *Military Operations: Egypt and Palestine 1914–18.* (1928–30): 2 vols. of the Official History, Egypt. Exped. Force.

A. M. HYAMSON. *The Archives of the British Consulate in Jerusalem* (1939, 1941): edited so far as they relate to Jewish contacts.

A. TOYNBEE (editor). *Survey of International Affairs* (annually): for Palestine under the Mandate; see also *Great Britain and Palestine 1915–1939* (Royal Inst. Int. Affairs: 1939).

Town Histories

C. R. Conder. *The City of Jerusalem* (1909).
W. Besant and E. H. Palmer. *Jerusalem: The City of Herod and Saladin* (4th ed. 1899).
G. A. Smith. *Jerusalem*. 2 vols. (1907–8).
C. Watson. *The Story of Jerusalem* (1912).
S. Tolkowsky. *The Gateway of Palestine* (1924): history of Jaffa.
N. Makhouly. *Guide to Acre* (Jerusalem, 1941). .

Palestine under the Mandate

P. Graves. *Palestine, the Land of Three Faiths* (1923).
W. Basil Worsfold. *Palestine of the Mandate* (1925).
F. F. Andrews. *The Holy Land under the Mandate* (New York, 1931).
N. Bentwich. *Palestine* (1934).
Paul H. L. Hanna. *British Policy in Palestine* (Washington, 1942); a well-balanced record.
J. Stoyanovsky. *The Mandate for Palestine* (1928): more technical.
M. Burstein. *Self Government of the Jews in Palestine since 1900* (Tel Aviv, 1934).
N. Bentwich (Attorney-General). *Legislation of Palestine 1918–25* (1926).
R. H. Drayton (Solicitor-General). *The Laws of Palestine* (1934).
F. M. Goadby and M. J. Dukhan. *Statement of the Law of Palestine* (Tel Aviv, 1935).
C. A. Hooper. *The Civil Law of Palestine and Transjordan* (1934).
A. Granovsky. *Land Problems in Palestine* (1926); *Land-Settlement in Palestine* (1930); *Land Policy in Palestine* (1940).
(Official.) *The Hebrew University, Jerusalem: its History and Development* (Jerusalem, 1939).
Said B. Himadeh. *Economic Organization of Palestine* (Beirut, 1938).
D. Horovitz and R. Hinden. *Economic Survey of Palestine* (Tel Aviv, 1938).
Government Departments. *Annual Reports, Annual Statistical Abstracts*, and *Blue Books*.

Few books on the political problems of Palestine are impartial. The following are useful:

Leonard Stein. *Zionism* (1932): the best general book on Zionism and its development.
George Antonius. *The Arab Awakening* (1938): an adequate presentation of the Arab case.
J. M. N. Jeffries. *Palestine; the Reality* (1939): rich in quotations from documents.
A. M. Hyamson. *Palestine, A Policy* (1942): the story of the political development of Zionism since 1917.

THE HOLY PLACES

H. T. F. DUCKWORTH. *The Church of the Holy Sepulchre* (1922).
W. HARVEY. *The Church of the Nativity at Bethlehem* (1935).
K. A. C. CRESSWELL. *The Dome of the Rock* (1924).
International Commission. *Report on the Western or Wailing Wall* (1930).

ARCHAEOLOGY

Discoveries are currently noted in the *Quarterly Statements* of the Palestine Exploration Fund.
CHARLES WATSON. *Fifty Years' Work in the Holy Land* (1915).
C. R. CONDER. *Tent Work in Palestine* (1878).
F. J. BLISS. *Development of Palestine Exploration* (1906).
PÈRE H. VINCENT. *Canaan* (1907).
P. E. F. HANDCOCK. *The Archaeology of the Holy Land* (1916).

TRANSJORDAN

For Transjordan the literature is less copious than for Palestine; but many books deal with both countries as a whole. The following, though old, are still interesting and useful:

J. L. BURCKHARDT. *Arabian Journal* (ed. Sir W. Ouseley: 1829).
E. H. PALMER. *The Desert of the Exodus* (1871). 2 vols.
H. B. TRISTRAM. *The Land of Moab* (1873).
G. SCHUMACHER. *Across the Jordan* (1885); *The Jaulan* (1888).

More recent works deal with special sites, or historical aspects.

ALEXANDER KENNEDY. *Petra, its History and Monuments* (1923).
MRS. STEUART ERSKINE. *The Vanished Cities of Arabia* (1924).
T. E. LAWRENCE. *The Seven Pillars of Wisdom* (1926); *Revolt in the Desert* (1927); political and military; compare *The Letters of T. E. Lawrence* (ed. D. Garnett, 1938): more reliable on many details than Lawrence's later books.
A. MUSIL. *The Northern Hejaz* (1926); *Arabia Deserta* (1927).
A. KAMMERER. *Pétra et la Nabatène* (Paris, 1929). 2 vols.
C. R. W. SETON. *Legislation of Transjordan, 1918–1930* (1931).
M. ROSTOVTSEFF. *Caravan Cities* (1932): good summarized accounts of Petra and Jerash included.
C. A. HOOPER. *The Civil Law of Palestine and Transjordan* (1934).
P. HITTI. *History of the Arabs* (1937).
NELSON GLUECK. *The Other Side of the Jordan* (1940): archaeological.
C. S. JARVIS. *Arab Command* (1943).

## MAPS AND CHARTS

(*a*) *Scale* 1:100,000: Survey of Palestine, published by the Department of Lands and Surveys; reprinted by the Geographical Section, General Staff, with road revision to 1939: G.S.G.S. Nos. 4078, 4079.

This is the best modern topographical map of Palestine, first published as a series of 11 maps, then 14 to cover Rafa, Beersheba, and the northern Negeb, and since revised in slightly larger sheets as a series of 12 maps. Contours are in brown at 100 metres. Topographical detail has been surveyed on the ground by plane-table and is very full, but some clarity has been lost by reproduction, water features in blue being particularly difficult to follow. The detail ends abruptly at the boundary of Palestine.

(*b*) *Scale* 1:250,000 (approx. 4 miles to an inch)

(i) Palestine in 2 sheets (North, South). Published by the Survey of Palestine in 1933; revised in 1937 (G.S.G.S. reproduction, No. 4089).

(ii) Sinai Peninsula (4 sheets); reduced from surveys between 1908 and 1914 (G.S.G.S. No. 2761). Two sheets cover parts of Palestine and Transjordan. (*a*) Sheet No. 2 (Rafah), 4th Edition, 1941; (*b*) Sheet No. 4 (Aqaba), 1941.

(*c*) *Scale* 1:500,000 (approx. 8 miles to an inch)

(i) Palestine and Transjordan. Three sheets ('Amman, Ma'an, Rutba); G.S.G.S. compilation and publication, No. 3932, dated 1933.

The Amman sheet is published in two different styles, with coloured layers, and without layers but with additional contours. The layered map is particularly clear and is the best map to show the relations between northern Palestine, northern Transjordan, and southern Syria. The unlayered map suffers from too much detail and from the closeness of the contours; many names are very difficult to read.

(ii) North Sinai (Sheet No. 3 of the Survey of Egypt 1:500,000 series, 1937); reproduction by G.S.G.S., No. 4084 (1st ed. 1941).

The sheet covers the whole of the Negeb and north-eastern Sinai as far south as Akaba, and east to longitude 37°.

(iii) Survey of Palestine Motor Map (Lands and Surveys, Palestine, 1938); G.S.G.S. No. 4046.

A very clear map of the roads and railways of Palestine in 1938, with road-plan insets of Haifa, Jerusalem, Jaffa, and Tel Aviv. Among much useful information shown are dry-weather motorable tracks, customs posts, aircraft landing-grounds, ancient and historical sites. The map should be very useful if kept up to date by new editions.

(*d*) *Scale* 1:1,000,000 (approx. 16 miles to an inch)

Palestine and Transjordan are covered by four sheets of the International 1: M series (G.S.G.S. No. 2555):

Beyrouth (Beirut): North I. 36 (3rd ed. 1943).
Esh Sham (Damascus): North I. 37 (3rd ed. 1941).
Cairo: North H. 36 (3rd ed. 1940).
El Djauf (Jauf): North H. 37 (2nd ed. 1938).

(*e*) *Scales* 1:2,000,000 *and* 1:4,000,000

Palestine and Transjordan are shown with neighbouring countries, on the Egypt sheet of the Africa 1:2,000,000 series, revised ed. 1938 (G.S.G.S. 2871); on sheet 32 (1:4,000,000), Persian Gulf, 1941 (G.S.G.S. 2957); and on a special Near and Middle East sheet on the same scale, 1941 (G.S.G.S. 4108).

(*f*) *Special Regional Maps of Transjordan*

(i) Scale 1:50,000. Air survey of the eastern approaches to the Jordan Valley; 2 sheets (North, South). G.S.G.S. No. 3939 (1933).

A clear and valuable large-scale map of the land-forms of the Ajlun highland; contours at 25-metre intervals. Names in Roman and Arabic characters. Roads and tracks are shown, but no vegetation. On the west the detail stops short at the Jordan boundary; on the north neither the Yarmuk nor the railway or Syrian boundary is shown. On the south-east Jerash and the Wadi Zerka form the limit, but the map does not include the Hejaz railway, Amman, or the road between the Allenby Bridge and Amman. An extension of this map would be invaluable.

(ii) Scale 1:50,000. Transjordan Lava Belt. G.S.G.S. 3937 (1933). A series of sheets intended to cover the region south of the Jebel Druse and compiled from air-photographs.

Only 6 sheets (Nos. 7, 9, 10, 11, 13, 14) are published. The rest appear to have been abandoned. Contours are at 10-metre intervals with 50-metre contours thickened. Tracks fit for mechanical transport, and the nature of the ground, lava, sand, mud, &c., are all clearly shown. Sheets 9, 10, 11, 14 show the country immediately east of Kasr Azrak.

(*g*) *Town Plans*

Jerusalem appears to be the only city with an up-to-date large-scale town and road plan. Those of Haifa and Jaffa–Tel Aviv have not been kept up to date with modern expansion.

(*h*) *Historical Atlas and Maps*

The *Atlas of the Historical Geography of the Holy Land* (2nd ed. 1936), a companion to Sir George Adam Smith's book, is excellent. It includes:

(i) 8 general maps of the 'Bible Lands'.

(ii) 6 general maps of Palestine (communications, geology, vegetation, &c.).

(iii) 8 maps of Palestine (4 miles to an inch).

(iv) 20 maps of Palestine at different periods of the history of Israel.

(v) 12 maps of Palestine and the Mediterranean in the Christian era.

Two special historical maps are excellent:

(i) *Roman Palestine* (scale 1 : 250,000), compiled by M. Avi-Yonah, and drawn under the direction of the Director, Department of Antiquities, 1935. Revised edition printed at the Survey Office, Jaffa, 1939. Accompanying the map is an explanatory text giving detailed authorities used in the compilation, and an index of Latin, Greek, Semitic, and modern names.

(ii) *Palestine of the Crusades* (scale 1 : 350,000), compiled, drawn, and printed under the direction of F. J. Salmon, Commissioner for Lands and Surveys, Palestine, from information supplied by the Department of Antiquities and Père Abel of the *École Biblique et Archéologique Française*. Printed at Jaffa, 1937. The text which accompanies the map gives a very good historical introduction and gazetteer.

## (*i*) Geological Maps

The best published geological maps are:

(i) *Geological Map of Palestine* (scale 1 : 250,000), by G. S. Blake, Jaffa (Survey of Palestine), 1939.

(ii) *Geological Outline Map of Transjordan* (scale 1 : 1,000,000), by G. S. Blake, forming figure 14 of *Report on the Water Resources of Transjordan and their Development, incorporating a report on geology, soils and minerals, and hydro-geological correlations*, by M. G. Ionides and G. S. Blake. London (Crown Agents for the Colonies), n.d. [1940], referred to in the bibliography of Geology (above).

## (*j*) Admiralty Charts

(i) The Mediterranean Coast of Palestine is covered by Chart No. 2634, and is described in the *Mediterranean Pilot*, vol. v.

(ii) The Gulf of Akaba appears on Chart No. 8 A. Akaba Bay is shown on the large-scale Chart 3595 (surveyed 1918: large corrections 1939). The coasts are described in the *Red Sea and Gulf of Aden Pilot*.

# INDEX

T. = Transjordan; r.s. = railway station

Aaron, tomb of, 454.
Abbasid dynasty, 102, 109.
Abbin (Ibbin), 519.
Abd el Malik, 102, 328.
Abdul Hadi, 134.
— Hamid, 137, 455, 468.
Abdulla, Emir, 403, 455, 461–4, 472.
Abila, 439.
Abraham, 321, 327, 344.
Abrek, R., 27.
Absalom, tomb of, 93.
Abu Bekr, 100, 449.
— el Azm (tomb of Samson), 317.
— Lisan, Ain, 458, 514, 518; r.s., 513.
— Nar, Wadi, 26, 382.
— Semara, Wadi, 384.
— Tayi (*see* Auda), 457.
Abyad, Ras el, railway, 361; Wadi, 24, 380.
Abyssinian Church, 148, 152; Uniates, 150–1.
acacias, 77–8, 256, 433.
Accho, Accon (Acre), 295.
*Acra* citadel, Jerusalem, 326.
Acre, 12, 33, 35, 295–300, 340; administration, 203, 206; agriculture, 245, 250–1; bay, 12, 33, 35, 111, 295, 303; climate, 47, 557 ff.; forestry, 254–5; health, 234, 237; history, 107–8, 111–14, 150, 190, 297–8; industries, 299; people, 143–4, 150–1, 186, 188, 297; plain, 12–13, 33, 68, 184, 295, 361, 367, 388; population, 189–90, 295; port, 300; prison, 207, 238, 299; railway, 300, 342, 346, 365; r.s., 362, 366, 368; roads, 300, 344–5, 378, 389; sanjak, 2; signals, 396; trade, 299–300.
Adana, air service, 393, 395.
Adassia, Bahai, 469.
addax, 79.
Aden, 145, 453.
Ader, 434.
Adloun, r.s., 363.
administration, 4, 124, 127, 130–1, 148, 158, 175, 191–219, 325, T. 402, 460, 474–81; Nabataean, 443–4; railway, 346–7.
administrative divisions, 4, 197; T. 473.
Adrianople, 109.
Advisory Councils, 191–2.
Adwan, 468.
Aelana (Akaba), 436, 438, 446, 522, 523.
*Aelia Capitolina*, 327.

afforestation, 62, 168, 216, 255–6; T. 494, 496.
Affula, history, 119; railways, 341–2, 344, 346, 348, 367, 369, 371; r.s., 368, 371; roads, 382–3, 388–9.
Afra, Seil, 417.
Afranj, Wadi, 19, 46.
African, Association, 453; — Jews, 120, 122; — Moslems, 173.
Agricultural, Bank, T. 502; — laboratories, 236, 251; — research, 250; — schools, 120, 216–19, 250; — settlements, 120–1, 124–5, 186, 211–13, 217, 239, 244, 260, 276, 334; — stations, 250, T. 494.
agriculture, 4, 12–13, 26, 56, 61–2, 81–3, 88, 144, 155, 167, 184, 186, 188, 230, 239–53, 273, T. 434, 443, 446, 482, 485, 487–95; College of, 219; Department of, 80, 195, 250–1, T. 474, 494.
agriculturists, 135–6, 247.
*Agudat Israel*, 201–2, 217.
Ahab, 18, 86, 436.
Ahad Ha'am, 159.
Ahamant, 452.
Ahaz, 86.
Ahiram, 86.
Ahmar, Wadi, 21, 417.
Ailat (Akaba), 451–2.
air, communications, 272, 307, 317, 392–5, 520–1; photographs, 399.
aircraft, 237; landing-grounds, 31, 317–18, 322–3, 395, T. 420, 521, 524; wireless stations, 396–7.
Airé, 451–2.
airfields, airports, 37, 237, 301, 303, 307, 331–2, 336, 392, 395, 397; T. 521–2.
Airways Ltd., Palestine, 393.
Ajami, 308.
Ajlun, 407–8, 452, 519, 540; council 473; court, 474; division, 473; forests, 495–6; highland, 400, 407–10, 425, 433, 513, 519; Jebel, 496; malaria, 477–8; people, 466; roads, 519–20; slag-heaps, 483; soils, 491; vegetation, 427; vineyards, 493; Wadi, 408.
Ajnadain, 450.
Akaba, 1, 21, 78, 399, 436, 463, 466, 505, 521, 522–4; epidemic post, 476; fish, 485, 523; gulf, 1–2, 10–11, 21, 33, 85, 454, 521–2; history, 119, 123, 457–8, 483, 503, 522–3; landing-ground, 521, 524; malaria, 478; roads, 344, 384–5, 514, 518, 524.

Akir, roads, 376.
Akka (Acre), 295.
Akrabbim, 21.
Aksa, Mosque El, 327–8, 536–7.
Al, El, roads, 518.
Ala Littoria, S.A., 392–3.
Albanians, 110, 136.
alcohol, 309, 485, 497.
Aleppo, 110, 114, 437, 441, 450–1, 453, 460; pine, 16, 72, 254, 256, 427, 495; railway, 343, 360, 362.
Alexander, Bishop, 153; — Jannaeus, 91, 315, 441–2; — the Great, 88, 297, 315, 437–8.
Alexandria, 95–6, 438, 453; communications, 391–3, 520.
Alexius, Emperor, 105.
Ali, 143, 455–6, 463; — el Muntar, Jebel, 45, 315–16; Wadi, 19.
Allat, 443.
Allenby, 118–19, 137, 315, 457–60; bridge, 30, 373, 386–7, 389, 513–14.
Alliance Israélite, 140, 167, 213, 217–18.
Allies, 5, 122, 124, 343, 461.
alphabet, 86.
Alpine race, 133.
Aluk forest, 496.
alum, 483.
Am Oved, 276.
Amalekites, 85.
Amarna, Tell el, 83, 297.
America, Babi converts, 144; emigration to, 175, 182–3, 187, 286, 320; Jews, 120, 122, 147, 173, 181; Moslems, 173.
American, Christians, 138, 218; Churches, 154; Colony, 155; schools, 219; tourists, 271; University of Beirut, 216, 471.
Americans, 179, 201; T. 400, 469.
Amirate of Transjordan, 399, 462, 464.
Amman, 400, 402, 409, 466, 540–1; climate, 421–3, 425, 557 ff.; council, 473; courts, 474; diseases, 477–9; factories, 484; highland, 410–11, 466; history, 91, 440, 444, 446, 450, 459–60, 462; hospitals, 476; library, 472; limestones, 484; people, 182, 469; railway, 348, 508–9; r.s., 510; roads, 340, 387, 514–15, 517–20; R.A.F., 476, 521; signals, 396; vegetation, 426–8; Wadi, 409.
Ammanitis, 410, 438.
Ammon, 85, 91, 94, 100, 410, 435–9.
Amorites, 435.
amphitheatres, T. 402.
Amra, Kasr, 430, 451.
Amsterdam, 270, 393.
Amud, Wadi, 21, 31, 383.
Anabta, r.s., 370; roads, 387.
Anatolians, 110, 133.
Anazeh, clan, 456; Jebel, 410.

Andromeda, 307.
Aneiza, Jebel, 399; Kalat, 418; r.s., 512; roads, 520.
Anglican, bishops, 115–16, 138, 153–4, 325, 329, 470; — Church, 148–9, 153–4, 470.
Anglo-French Convention, 2, 399; — declaration, 460.
Anglo-Jewish Association of London, 140, 213, 217.
Anglo-Palestine Bank, 279.
Anglo-Prussian bishopric, 153–4.
Anglo-Turkish railway syndicate, 341.
animal sacrifice, 147, 163, 201; — tax, 282.
animals, 78–80, 498; domestic, 79, 168–70, 494–5.
Anjera, 408; roads, 519.
ankylostomiasis, 232.
annuals, 64, 69, 73, 75, 78, 429.
Anopheles, 225–6, 477–8.
antelopes, 79.
anthrax, 223.
Antigonus, 91, 93; the One-eyed, 438.
Anti-Lebanon, rivers, 28.
Antioch, 152, 450; 'on the Chrysorhoas', 440, 543; 'of the Gerasenes', 440; Patriarch, 151; principality, 105–6; road, 345.
Antiochus, 119; III, 89, 440; IV Epiphanes, 89, 90, 95, 441.
Antipater, 91.
Antipatris (Ras el Ain), 27, 330.
Antiquities, Department, 195, 329, T. 472, 474; duty, 291.
anti-Zionism, 332.
Antony, 91, 443.
Apollonia (Arsur), 41.
Apollonius, 439.
Apostolic Delegate, 150.
appeal, courts of, 205, 211; T. 474–5.
apples, 242, 244, 251–2, 290, 494; Sodom, 77, 433.
apricots, 164, 243, 403, 494.
aqueducts, 36, 298–9, 378; T. 408, 443.
Ara, R., 26.
Arab, armed bands, 128, 130; College, 471; conquest, 99–100; co-operative societies, 280; cow, 168; cultivators, 244, 247, 251, 274; culture, 110, 117, 124, 156, 158, 161–2; emigration, 182, 187; Higher Committee, 127, 129; immigration, 101, 133, 187; increase, 5, 174; industries, 260–1, 263, 269, 271; labour, 274–7; Legion, 396, 400, 403, 473, 475, 524; merchants, 293; National Committees, 127; nationalism, 5, 117, 124, 332, 401–2, 455, 457, 468; nationality, 117, 134, 136, 173; outbreaks, 124–30, 341; police, 207; problem, 5–6, 130–1, 402; revolt, 119,

123, 456–7, 501, 503, 505; rule, 100–3, 448–55; schools, 142, 214, 215–16; State, 130, 402, 461, 464; terrorists, 130, 204; villages, 163–5, 220; world, 402.

—, Wadi, 407, 493, 515.

Araba, Wadi, 1, 3, 8, 10, 21, 24, 66, 77–8, 344, 385, 406, 418, 433, 449, 451, 453, 513–14, 518, 521–2.

Arabia, boundary, 399–400; communications, 340; Jews, 145; Petraea, 401, 444, 446; Roman, 444–6; trade, 291, 499; union, 402.

Arabian horse, 169; plateau, 406.

Arabic, 102, 124, 134, 136–40, 142, 145, 148–50, 154, 208, 214–15, 217, 447–8, 471–2; place-names, 6–7.

arable land, 239.

Arabs, 5–6, 133–8, 211, 220, 274, 465–8; administration, 191–3, 204; census, 173; distribution, 184, 188, 190; health, 230–2, 237; history, 99, 101, 117, 119, 123–37 passim; Jewish, 134, 136, 173; see also Moslems.

arak, 485.

Arak el Emir, 411, 541.

Aramaic, 86, 102, 134, 139, 148, 447–8.

Arar, 459.

arbitration committees, 202.

archaeology, 81, 83, 115, 159–60, 179, 200, 271, 472.

Archbishop, of Canterbury, 153–4; of Galilee, 150, 470.

architecture, 81, 93–4, 110, 157–8, 163, 218, 312; T. 443.

Ardah el Abbad forest, 496.

area, 1, 184, 239; T. 399.

Areija, R., 32.

Areopolis, 446.

Aretas, I, 441; II, 441; III, 441–2.

Arish, El, 24, 46, 110; people, 136; railway, 353; r.s., 356; road, 373–4.

aristocracy, 134.

Arjan, 408.

Arka, siege, 105.

'Armageddon', 83.

Armenia, 95, 105.

Armenian, (Gregorian) Church, 138, 148, 151–2; language, 138; library, 159; Patriarchs, 151; Protestants, 138; Uniates (Catholics), 150–1.

Armenians, 5, 133, 137–8, 173, 187, 328, 465, 469–70.

Armenoid race, 133.

Arnon, R., 85, 414–17, 435–6, 518.

Arraba, r.s., 371; roads, 382; Sahl, 17, 26, 382.

Arroub, Ain, agricultural stations, 250.

Arrub, 330; Wadi, 32.

Arsuf, 108.

Arsur, 41.

art, 81, 83, 88, 94, 157–8, 160, 443.

Artaxerxes, I, 95; II, 95; III Ochus, 88, 95.

Artemisia (wormwood), 64, 75, 256, 428, 430, 432.

artificial, teeth, 261, 270; — silk goods, 498.

artisans, 146, 155, 274.

arts, domestic, 165–7; school of, 471.

Artuf, r.s., 359.

Artus, 330.

Arus, Jebel, 15, 415.

Ascalon, 43, 45, 91, 108, 344, 374, 385.

Ascension, 329, 534.

Ashakif, Jebel, 419.

Ashari, 100.

Asher, 297.

Ashkaf, Jebel, 419.

Ashkenaz, 146.

Ashkenazim, 139–40, 144–7, 162, 201.

Asia Minor, 95, 103, 105, 107, 133, 146, 340, 437.

Asir, 463.

Asochis, plain of, 15, 25.

asphalt, 3, 347, 372.

asphaltic oil, 482.

Asphaltites (Dead Sea), 32.

ass, 79, 82, 169.

Assefat Hanivcharim, 201.

Assembly, Jewish, 201; Legislative, T. 473.

Assurbanipal, 437.

Assyrian, Catholics, 150–1; conquests, 18, 86–7, 95, 136, 147; Empire, 437.

Assyrians, 136.

Astarte, 94.

Asur, Tell, 17.

Aswit, El, 451.

Atargatis, 94.

Athens, air service, 393.

Athlit (Atlit), r.s., 354.

Atid Navigation Company, 391.

Atlit, 37; r.s., 354; roads, 345, 378; salt, 37, 256–7.

Attorney-General, 194–5.

Auda abu Tayi, 457–60, 467–8.

Augustus, 93, 96.

Auja el Hafir, El, 24; history, 117; roads, 379–80, 384.

Auja, Nahr, 13, 21, 25, 27, 41, 69, 233, 247, 309, 312, 376–7.

Auranitis, 442.

Australia, 176, 247, 392, 488.

Austria, Jews, 173–4, 179, 181.

Austria-Hungary, trade, 285.

Austrian Hospice, 259.

Austrians, 113, 298.

authorship, 581.

aviation, civil, 392–5.

Awaj, R., 515.

Awali, R., 361.

axle-loads, railway, 349–50.
Aylah (Akaba), 449, 451.
Azrak, Kasr, 399, 403, 419–20, 432, 451, 458, 520; marshes, 478; oasis, 489; salt, 484; Wadi, 411.
Azzib (Ez Zib), railway, 346, 348, 349 n., 360; r.s., 362.

Baalbek, 450, 453; Ras, 458.
Bab el Mojib, 414–15.
— el Wad, roads, 386–7.
Babi converts, 144.
Babylonia, 83, 85–7, 95, 135, 145, 340, 527.
bacteria, 252.
Baghdad, 102–3, 109, 118, 273, 389, 393, 396, 451–2, 514–15, 520.
Bagir, Jebel, 418–19.
Bagoora, horticultural station, 494.
Baha, Sir Abbas Effendi Abdul, 144, 303.
Bahais, 134, 143–4, 299, 303, 465, 469.
Baha-ullah, 144, 299.
Bahr Lut (Dead Sea), 30.
Bahsa, r.s., 365.
Baka, roads, 383.
balance of trade, 285–7, 292; T. 497.
Baldwin (King), 103, 105–6, 136, 451.
Balfour, Declaration, 122–4; forest, 383.
Balfourya, roads, 383.
ballast, railway, 349.
balsam, 23, 78, 433.
Baluah, 434.
bananas, 164, 246, 250, 253, 493.
Bandoeng, air service, 393.
banks, 276, 279–81; T. 502.
Banyas, 1, 2, 28; history, 87, 89; roads, 384.
Bar Cochba, Simon, 95–7, 338.
Barak, 17.
Barbara, roads, 374.
Barclay, Joseph, 154.
Bardaeus, Jacob, 447.
Bardawil, fishermen, 136; r.s., 356.
Barka, roads, 375.
barley, 75, 82, 243–4, 246–7, 252, 403, 479, 481, 493–4, 498.
Barsa, r.s., 365.
basalts, 15–16, 242–3, 259, 350, 372, 419, 514, 526.
basketry, 167–8, 272.
Basra, 100, 393.
Bassa, El, roads, 390.
Bat Gallim, 303.
batha, 74–5; T. 428.
bathing, 260, 303.
baths, T. 484; of Tiberias, 260, 339; Roman, 442.
Batrun, r.s., 365.
Battauf, Sahl el, 15–16, 25–6.
Battir, railway, 95, 359; r.s., 360.

Bayazid, 109.
Bayir, 420, 458–9, 520–1.
Bayit Vegan, 41.
bazaar-cities, 440–1.
Baziyeh, Ain el, 417.
Beaconsfield, Lord, 96 n.
beans, 164, 244–5; blight, 253.
bear, 79.
bed bugs, 481.
beduin, 4, 133–5, 161, 169, 171–2, 175, 200, 206–7, 225, 243, 269, 272, 401, 434, 466–8, 479–80, 485; Control Board, 473, 475; Control Law, 467; tribal law, 474–5.
beef, 168.
Beer Jacob, r.s., 355.
— Tuviya, roads, 375.
— Yakov, r.s., 355.
Beersheba, 1, 24, 318–19; climate, 48, 51–2, 59, 556 ff.; court, 206, 318; dam, 249; health, 234–5; history, 85–6, 117–19, 318, 458; population, 221, 318; railway, 342, 380; roads, 318, 340, 344–5, 379–80, 384–5; signals, 396; vegetation, 75.
— sub-district, agriculture, 239; population, 184.
bees, 433.
beetles, 79, 245, 251.
Beibars, 108, 315, 337, 452.
Beidha, Ain el, 408.
Beirut, communications, 343, 360–1, 391, 393, 395–6; cow, 168; history, 113, 117; r.s., 364; vilayet, 2.
Beisamun, Ain, roads, 390.
Beisan, 13, 319–20; agricultural stations, 250; climate, 48, 319, 559 ff.; history, 83, 87, 91, 119, 319–20, 441–2; plain, 22, 30, 63, 242–3, 249, 250; population, 221, 319; railway, 320, 341, 367; r.s., 368; roads, 320, 344–5, 389, 391.
Beit Deras, roads, 375.
— Hanun, forest, 255; roads, 374.
— Jala, population, 136, 221.
— Jemal, climate, 48, 558 ff.; school, 219.
— Jibrin, climate, 53; roads, 375, 381, 386.
— Lahiya, 45.
— Lahm (Bethlehem), 155, 320.
— Lid, roads, 373, 377, 387–8.
— Nabala, railway, 346, 351; road, 377.
— Safafa, hospital, 235.
— Vegan, 308.
— Yosef (Yusuf), r.s., 369.
bejel, 231, 480.
Belgium, 270.
Belka, division, 473; highland, 410–17, 433, 447, 451; people, 466, 468–9; sanjak, 1–2.

Belus (Naamin), R., 25, 35, 297.
Ben Hamideh forest, 496.
— Shemen, school, 218.
Benedictines, 149.
Benhadad, 437.
Beni Hasan, 468.
— Khalid, 467.
— Suheila, roads, 374.
— Sukhr, 467–8, 509.
benzine, 498.
Berenice, 438.
Berlin, Treaty of, 137, 534.
Beth Haggan (Jenin), 322.
— Horons, 19.
Beth-Pelet, history, 86.
Beth-shan, Beth Shean (Beisan), 83, 94, 319.
Bethany, theological seminary, 151.
Bethel, 85.
Bether, 95.
'Bethesda' Pool, 326.
Bethlehem, 320–1; health, 234, 236, 238; history, 108, 116, 190; Holy Places, 535; meteorological station, 48; olive-groves, 255, 320; people, 136, 149, 152, 155, 161, 182–3, 186, 320; population, 189–90, 221, 320; quarrying, 259; roads, 321, 345, 380; weaving, 167.
Bethzur, battle, 90.
Bezetha quarter, Jerusalem, 326.
Bialik, 159.
biblical times, 1, 61, 83–7, 171, 253; T. 400.
bibliography, 581–6; T. 586.
bilharziosis, 233.
Billi (tribes), 456.
Binyamina, 39, 43, 68–9; r.s., 354; roads, 377.
biological plant types, 64–5.
Bir Asluj, roads, 380.
— el Abd, r.s., 356.
— el Mishash, roads, 380.
— Taba, 1, 522.
Bira, 18; roads, 381; Wadi, 21.
birds, 79.
birth, place of, 172–3.
birth-rate, 5, 175–6, 221; T. 470.
births, registration, 175, 197, 220–1; T. 469, 470.
Birwa, roads, 389–90.
bishopric, Anglo-Prussian, 153–4.
Bishops, Anglican, 115–16, 138, 153–4, 325, 329, 470; Metropolitan, 148–9, 152; of Jerusalem, 148, 153, 325, 329; of Nazareth, 149; of Tyre, 150.
bitumen, 32, 259, 483.
bituminous limestone, 483.
Bjer, Kasr, 444.
blindness, 233–4.
Blyth, George Francis, 154.

Bnei Brak, medical services, 235–7.
Board of Higher Studies, 215.
boars, 433.
books, 581–6; T. 586.
Bosnians, 136–7, 187.
Bostra (Bosra), 436, 442, 444, 446, 449–50, 454.
botanical divisions, 65–78; T. 426–33.
boundaries, 1–2; T. 1–2, 399–401, 460.
bridges, Jordan, 373; railway, 349–50, 503; road, 372.
British, 6, 149, 154, 179, 465, 469; administration, 175, 193, 273, 328; air routes, 392–3, 395; Christians, 173–4, 218; consuls, 114–16, 197; Council, 471; Dominions, 182; electricity, 262; Government, 122–31 passim, 460–2, 472–3, 501; history, 45–6, 110–19 passim, 126, 128, 130, 298, 315, 318, 455–63 passim; imports, 289; interest, 6, 115–16; Jews, 131, 147, 173–4, 181; Ophthalmic Hospital, 234–5; Overseas Airways Corporation, 393, 395, 397; protection, 115–16, 123–4, 193; Resident, T., 472; schools, 218–19; shipping line, 391; Treasury, 281; universities, 216, 471; War Cemeteries, 158, 317, 329, 336.
broadcasting service, 160; stations, 396–7.
bromine, 256, 258–9, 272, 289–90, 292.
broncho-pneumonia, 222.
Bronze Age, 81–2; T. 434.
bubale, 79.
budgets, 193; Jewish, 201, 216; municipal, 199.
buffaloes, 168, 170.
building, 266–8, 274, 287, 291; materials, 12, 261, 290–1, 293, 347, 484.
built-on areas, 239.
Buksaseh, Seil, 414, 417.
Bulgaria, Jews, 179.
Burckhardt, J. L., 453–4.
Bureir, roads, 375.
Burg, El, 522.
burial, 201, 220.
Burka, Kasr, 419–20; Wadi, 517.
burnet, shrubby, 74–5, 428.
Buseira, 418.
bustards, 433.
But, Wadi, 414.
butter, 164, 485.
butterflies, 79.
Bweirda, Wadi, 418.
Byblos, 86.
Byzantine Empire, 97, 99, 100–1, 103, 446–8, 450.

Cabbala, 337.
Cabinet, T. 473.

Cables and Wireless Ltd., 396.
cactus, 13, 45, 63.
cadastral survey, T. 475.
Caesar, Julius, 91, 96, 443.
Caesarea (Kisarya), 12, 33, 37, 39;
 history, 93, 148, 450; people, 137;
 roads, 340, 345; vegetation, 68.
Cairo, 148, 182, 379, 393, 395–6.
calcium sulphate, 257.
Calcutta, air service, 393, 395.
calendars, 550–1.
Caligula, 96, 443.
caliphs, 100–2.
Callirrhoe, 484.
Calvary, 327.
camels, 169–70, 256, 372, 480, 485, 487,
 489, 494; food, 432, 481.
Campania, 95.
Canaan, 82, 315, 400; Jebel, 390.
Canaanites, 83, 85–6, 90, 94, 135, 297.
canals, 118; T. 492–3.
Canatha, 442.
cancer, 222.
canon law, 100, 143, 203.
Cape route to the Indies, 109, 453.
capital, 177, 195, 261–2, 273, 279, 281,
 286–7, 292–3; T. 482, 487, 501–2.
capitation tax, 448.
Captivity, 326, 332, 400.
caravan, cities, 435, 438–42; routes, 99,
 340–1, 344, 401, 415, 435–6, 439, 442,
 446, 452; trade, 99, 109, 145, 436–7,
 442, 453.
Carmel, Cape, 12, 37, 43, 300, 344–5,
 352, 378; Mount, 12–13, 16–17, 26,
 33, 35, 37, 39, 43, 60, 72, 81, 85, 111,
 119, 243, 254–5, 301, 303, 305, 340,
 344, 373, 378, 460, 539.
Carmelites, 539.
carnallite, 258.
Carnival of the Rites, 151.
Caro, Joseph, 337.
carpets, 269.
castella, T. 401–2, 444.
Castellum Peregrinorum (Atlit), 37.
castles, Crusaders', 37, 107, 452, 544.
casual labour, 186–7; T. 485.
categories of immigration, 177–8, 195–6.
cathedral, Armenian Uniate, 151; St.
 George, 154, 329; St. James, 152.
cattle, 135, 168, 170, 226, 231, 254,
 289–90, 495; -feeding cake, 264.
Caucasus, 137, 468–9.
causes of death, 222–3.
caves, 8, 12, 28, 81–2, 94, 135, 164.
cedars, 427.
cement, 257, 259, 266–8, 291, 304, 347.
censuses, 134, 141–2, 171–4, 260–1,
 292–3.
Central, Government, 191–7, T. 472–3;
 heating, 3; road (ridgeway), 345, 373,

379–84, 391; Town Planning Commission, 158, 200.
ceramics, T. 443.
cereals, 13, 20, 82, 239, 243–4, 247, 250,
 252, 254, 347, 480, 488–9, 492–3, 497.
Chabd, 421.
Chalcedon, Council of, 148.
chalcolithic frescoes, 434.
Chaldaeans, 150.
chalk, 483, 525.
challukah, 146–7.
Chalutzim, 162, 187.
Chaluzoth, 163.
chalybeate spring, 484.
Chambers of Commerce, 294.
Chancellor, Sir John, 125, 127.
charcoal burning, 63, 73, 254–5.
charitable endowments (waqf), 138, 203,
 209; organizations, 115.
charts, 589.
Chassidim, 147, 162.
Chechens, 465, 469, 478.
Chejere (Esh Shajara), r.s., 507.
Chekka (Shakkah), r.s., 365.
chemicals, 236, 261, 292, 484.
Chemin de Fer Hedjaz (Hejaz railway),
 347.
Chief, Justice, 204–5; — Rabbi, 138; —
 Secretary, 192–3, 195.
cholera, 237, 477.
Chosroes II, 99, 327, 448.
Chovevé Zion, 121.
Christian, holidays, 553; — Orders of
 Knighthood, 106, 297; — schools,
 213–15, 218–19; — sects, 148–55; —
 sites, 530–6.
Christianity, 2, 96–7, 99–100, 116, 144,
 153; T. 444, 446–8, 470.
Christians, 96–9, 101–2, 116, 134, 136–8,
 148–56, 162, 293, 320, 401, 436, 448,
 465, 470–1, 473; census, 172–4, 293;
 distribution, 188; emigration, 182–3;
 immigration, 173, 177, 187; increase,
 175–6; Maronite, 115, 150; Nestorian,
 133; wine, 264.
chronological table, 527–9.
Church Missionary Society, 470, 476.
Churches, 148–54, 470; Armenian, 138,
 151–2; Crusaders', 107, 332, 335, 531,
 538; Latin, 106, 114–16, 149–50; of
 the Holy Sepulchre, 99, 102, 327–8,
 530–5; of the Nativity, 116, 320, 535;
 Orthodox, 115–16, 148–9.
Churchill, Winston, 462.
cigarettes, 261, 265–6, 309, 485.
Cilicia, 91, 95, 105, 107, 460; Patriarch,
 151.
cinematograph, 160, 312.
Circassians, 5, 137, 143, 187, 465, 468–9,
 540, 543.
cisterns, 54, 56, 135, 225, 227, 407, 478.

citizenship, 172–4, 196, 329; T. 174;
Order in Council, 196.
Citrus Control Ordinance, 245.
citrus fruits, 13, 27, 41, 69, 80, 189,
232, 241, 243, 245–6, 249–52, 403,
494; trade, 288, 290, 292–3, 309, 343,
347.
Civil Administration, 124, 148, 158,
180, 191–2, 194, 342; aviation, 392–5;
courts, T. 474; engineering, 218; law,
100; servants, 187–8.
Claudius, 443.
Clayton, Sir Gilbert, 400.
Cleopatra, 91, 259, 323, 443.
climate, 3, 16, 47–61, 555 ff.; T. 421–5,
482, 557 ff.
climatic belts, 47; change, 61.
clinics, 231, 234–6; T. 476.
cloud, 50, 55, 423, 561; -bursts, 59.
coast, 33–46, 521–2; winds, 49–50, 521.
coastal plain, 3–4, 8, 12–13, 33–46;
diseases, 225, 232–3; history, 86–8,
118; population, 184; soils, 241–2;
vegetation, 63, 66–8, 72.
— railways, 36–7, 39, 43, 45–6, 118, 300,
306–7, 311, 317.
— roads, 36–7, 39, 41, 43, 45–6, 118,
300, 307, 311, 317, 344–5, 373–9.
coffee, 165, 293, 498.
cognac, 485.
coinage, coins, 139, 208, 281, 501–2.
College of Technology, 218.
Colonial, Audit Department, 195;
Development Fund, 502; Office, 195.
Colonization Association, Jewish, 26.
commerce, 88, 186, 284–94, 345, T.
497–9; Committee, 193.
commercial, banks, 279; — classes, 217;
— travellers, 288.
Commissions, Central Town Planning,
158, 200; financial, 149, 204; Partition and Technical, 130–1, 489;
Royal, 129–31, 292, 401, 464, 502;
Shaw, 126; Wailing Wall, 127, 537–8.
Commissioner of Migration, 196–7.
Committees, Arab, 127, 129; — for
Commerce and Industry, 193; — of
Local Communities, 201–2.
communal autonomy, 200–4.
communications, 2–3, 285, 340–98; T.
482, 503–21; coastal, 33, 36–7, 39, 41,
43–4, 46, 118, 300, 306, 311, 314, 317;
interference, 128.
conference, round-table, 131.
Confraternity of the Holy Sepulchre,
149.
conglomerates, 10, 525–6.
conjunctivitis, 233–4, 480.
conscription, 171, 175.
Consolidated Refineries Limited, 186,
270, 289.

Constantine, 97, 327, 447.
Constantinople, 103, 105, 109, 114, 117,
138, 148.
constitution, 131–2, 192, 462.
consuls, 114–16, 175, 187, 197, 218.
convalescent homes, 235, 303.
Convention, Anglo-French, 2, 399;
labour, 487.
Convents, 151–2, 264, 328, 336, 535.
conversion tables, 566–80.
co-operative, banks, 279; groups, 213,
274–5; societies, 279–80, 288, T. 502.
copper, 256, 436, 483; age, 81–2.
Coptic Church, 148, 152.
costume, 136, 160–3.
cotton, 244, 261, 269, 298; goods, 289,
293, 498.
Councils, Advisory, 191–2; Executive,
192, T. 473; General, 201–2; Holy
Places, 150; Legislative, 192, T. 462,
468; municipal, 188, 197, 199–200,
202, T. 473–4; of Chalcedon, 148;
Rabbinical, 201; Religious Community, T., 474.
courts, 139, 143, 201–6, 208, 211, 318;
T. 474–5.
Crac de Montroyal, 451; des Moabites,
452.
crafts, 81, 83, 86, 88, 165–8, 272, 471.
credit, 126, 280, 288; T. 502; banks,
279–80.
crime, 204–7.
criminal lunatic prison, 238.
Crocodile (Zerka), R., 25–6, 39, 41,
247.
crops, 60, 165, 243–7; T. 403, 493–4;
damage to, 128; diseases, 252–3, 493.
Crucifixion, 96, 326–7, 530–1.
Crusaders, 21, 136, 150–1, 297, 451–2;
castles, 37, 107, 452, 540, 544–5;
churches, 107, 332, 335, 531, 538;
crypts, 299; port, 41.
Crusades, 101, 103–8, 190, 308, 452,
483, 513, 528–9.
Culex pipiens, 481.
cultivable area, 239; T. 403, 488–9.
cultivation, 4, 18, 30, 33, 43, 46, 60,
63, 75, 183, 239 ff.; T. 402–3, 427,
487 ff.
culture, 81–2, 86, 88–9, 93, 110, 124,
133, 139–40, 145, 155–70, 181, 312,
527; T. 434, 440–1, 443–4, 472.
currency, 280–1, 502; — Board, 281,
286, 502; — notes, 208, 281, 501.
Customs Department, 195, 260; T. 474,
500; posts, T. 497.
Cyprus, 88, 108–9, 137, 151, 154, 257,
391–3, 395.
Cyrenaica, 95.
Cyrus, 87, 95.
Czechoslovakia, Jews, 173–4, 179.

Daba, Kalat ed, 414; r.s., 511; roads, 517.
Daghistani Jews, 138.
Dagon, temple of, 316.
Daher el Omar, 110, 298, 337.
Dahi, Jebel ed ('Little Hermon'), 16.
Damascus, cow, 168; Gate, 327–8; goat, 168; history, 99–103, 106, 108, 111, 114, 117, 437, 439, 441–2, 450–1, 453, 458–60; Melkite Patriarch, 150; railway, 341, 360–1, 503; roads, 340, 344; vilayet, 2.
Damianos, 148.
Damm, Kalat ed, 386.
Damour, r.s., 363; R., 361.
dams, 249; T. 443.
Damur, r.s., 363.
Dan, 1, 28, 85, 93, 384.
Dana, Jebel, 418; Seil, 418; Wadi, 483.
Danzig, Jews, 179.
Darb el Haj, 513–14, 517.
Darius, 87.
Daruzi, Ismail el, 143.
Dathin, battle of, 449.
David, 23, 82–3, 85–6, 171, 319–21, 325–6; 'City of', 326.
day, length of, 60–1.
days of rest, 552; of the week, 551.
Dbayeh, r.s., 364.
'Dead river' (Hadera, Mifjir), 26, 41.
Dead Sea, 1–2, 10, 12, 21, 23, 29, 31–2, 411, 414–15, 453; bathing, 260; climate, 48–9, 53, 557 ff.; evaporation, 31, 54–5, 77, 258; 'fruit', 77; history, 85–6, 459; roads, 385, 387, 391, 513–14, 518–19; salts, 12, 256–9, 261, 292, 484; tempests, 49; vegetation, 77.
death-rate, 175–6, 221; T. 470, 476.
deaths, causes, 222–3; registration, 197, 220; T. 469–70.
Decapolis, 91, 93, 319, 441–2.
deciduous fruits, 245, 251, 493.
decline of population, T. 402.
defence, 283; — Bonds, 284.
deficiency diseases, T. 479–80.
Deir, Wadi, 408.
— Alla, 409.
— Ballut, Wadi, 41.
— el Belah, 45; r.s., 356.
— esh Sheikh, railway, 359; r.s., 360.
— ez Zor, humidity, 423.
— Sharaf, 43; roads, 382, 387.
— Suneid, r.s., 356; roads, 374.
Delhamiya, r.s., 369.
dengue, 480.
dental clinics, 236, 276.
dentists, 235.
departments, government, 194–7; T. 474.
Deraa, history, 459–60; railway, 22, 29,

341, 346, 454, 503, 505, 508; r.s., 508–9; roads, 514, 517, 520.
desert, Area, 473; botanical region, 66, 76–8, 432–3; influence, 443–4; locust, 251; Mobile Medical Unit, 476, 479; Patrol, 475; routes, 290, 340, 389, 419, 516–17, 520.
deserts, 3–4, 8, 19–20, 23–5, 47, 135, 183–4; T. 419–21, 487, 489.
dew, 54–5, 60, 62, 564.
Development Department, T. 474, 482, 492, 502.
Dhahiriya, 380.
Dheikeh, Wadi, 415.
Dhiban, 514, 517–18.
Dhra, Seil, 417.
diamond industry, 270.
diarrhoea, 222, 224, 477.
Difleh, Nahr ed, 39.
Dilagha, Wadi, 418.
Dilb, agricultural sub-station, 251; Wadi, 19, 27.
Dionysius, 94.
Diospolis (Lydda), 331.
diphtheria, 223.
Director of Lands, T. 496.
diseases, 175, 222–34; T. 476–81; crops, 252–3, 493.
dispensaries, 235–6.
Dispersion, Jews of the, 89–90, 95–7, 123, 140, 147.
distilleries, T. 484–5.
distribution of population, 171–90; present, 183–4.
District Administration, 193; Commissioners, 197, 206; courts, 204–6; Health Offices, 220.
districts, administrative, 4, 197; T. 473.
disturbances of 1929–39, 125–30, 204, 281, 321, 341, 345, 547–9.
Dium, 441.
divisional government, T. 473.
divorce, 200.
Dleila, Wadi, 409.
doctors, 235–6.
Dodecanese, air service, 393.
dolmens, 82; T. 434.
'Dome of the Rock', 102, 327–8, 536–7.
domestic, animals, 79, 168–70, 494–5; arts, 165–7; science, 215; servants, 146, 487.
Dominicans, 149.
Dor (Tantura), 39.
Dorcas, 307.
Dothan, plain of, 17, 26.
Doughty, C. M., 454.
Dragon, St. George and, 331–2.
drainage of marshes, 13, 26, 30, 39, 63, 70–1, 168, 175, 227–8, 230, 247, 254.
drama, 157, 312.

drugs, 258, 290.
Druse, Jebel, 93, 403, 406, 419, 427, 458, 469.
Druses, 102, 115, 128, 134, 143–4, 172–3, 458, 465, 469.
dry-farming, 241; T. 488–9, 492.
Duk, Ain, 29.
*dunam*, 23 *n.*
dunes, 10, 13, 24, 26, 33, 35, 39, 41, 43, 45–6, 63–4, 68–9, 184, 225, 241, 255–6, 525.
Dung Gate, Jerusalem, 138, 327.
Dura, school, 216.
Durazzo, 105.
durra, 244, 246, 252, 493–4.
Dushara, 443–4.
Dutch air service, 392–3.
Duweihek, Seil, 417.
dyeing, 484, 498.
dyes, 258.
dysentery, 223–4, 477.

'early rains', 56.
earthquakes, 28, 32, 146, 259, 317, 332, 337, 483.
Eastern Oil Industries, 304.
Ebal, Mount, 17, 332, 382.
ecclesiastical courts, 206; law, 201.
Economic Adviser, 193, 195.
Edessa, county of, 105–6.
Edinburgh Mission Hospital, 333.
Edom, 417–18, 427, 432, 437–8.
Edomites, 135, 401, 435, 437.
education, 115, 140, 142, 156, 202, 213–19; T. 471; Committee, Jewish, 216–17; Department, 195, T. 471, 474; rate, 199, T. 474.
Egra, 442, 454.
Egypt, Church of, 152; communications, 340, 343–4, 347, 373, 379–80, 391; emigration to, 182; history, 82–90 *passim*, 95, 99–103 *passim*, 107–13 *passim*, 117–18, 434, 438, 451–2, 455; people, 137, 154, 162, 173, 176; pilgrims, 271; schools, 216; trade, 265, 285, 290–1, 499.
Egyptian, air service, 392–3, 395; Camel Corps, 403; currency, 280–1; dominion, 82; occupation, 112, 114.
Egyptians, 112, 127, 137, 173–4, 307.
Ehrer, Wadi, 506.
Ela, El, 446.
Elah, Vale of, 19–20.
Elasa, battle, 90.
elections, 201.
Electoral Law, 467.
Electric Corporation, Jerusalem, 262; Palestine, 29, 247, 262–3, 396.
electrical engineering, 218.
electricity, 261–3, 304, 309, 312.
elementary schools, 213, 217–18; T. 471.

Elijah, 301, 332, 539.
Elisha, 323.
Eloth, 436, 522–3.
Emek Hefer, 27.
— Jezreel (Vale of Jezreel), 13, 21, 85, 91, 230.
— Yaharden, r.s., 369.
— Zebulun, 303, 366.
emigration, 174–5, 182–3; T. 469.
encephalitis lethargica, 223.
Enfeh, r.s., 365.
Engeddi, 23.
engineering, 218, 273.
England, Church of, 154, *see also* Anglican Church; Crusaders, 106; trade, 288.
English, culture, 140; Jews, 120, 122; language, 139–40, 142, 208, 213, 215, 217, 219, 471; Law, 206–7; Reformed Church, 154; schools, 213, 219; travellers, 114, 271.
enteric fever, 237, 477.
enteritis, 222, 224, 477.
entertainments, 157.
entomological laboratories, 236.
Ephraim, Mount, 17.
epidemic posts, T. 476.
Eriha (Jericho), 23.
erosion, soil, 241–2, 244, 255, 487–8, 492.
Esarhaddon, 437.
Esbonitis, 410–11, 438.
Esbus, 442.
Esdraelon, plain of, 4, 8, 12–16, 26, 33, 35–6, 87, 297, 300; communications, 340, 344, 367, 371, 378, 382–3, 388–9; geology, 10; history, 83, 87, 111, 442; irrigation, 250; population, 184; soils, 242–3; vegetation, 63.
Eslamiya, Jebel (Mount Ebal), 17, 332.
Español, 140–2, 144.
estimates of population, 171–2; T. 465, 470.
Ethiopia, Jews, 146.
Ethnarchs, 90–1, 93, 96.
European, Christians, 136, 138; cows, 168; culture, 156; Jews, 121–2, 139–40, 145–6, 173, 175, 178, 180–1, 274, 285–6, 328; Moslems, 173; Powers, 114–16; tourists, 271.
Europeans, 173, 179, 188, 201, 293, 301; T. 400, 465, 469–70.
evaporation, 31, 54–5, 77, 256–8, 492, 560.
evergreen oak, 65, 72–3, 254, 428, 495.
excavation, archaeological, 81.
Excise, Department, 195, 260; duties, 257, 282, T. 500.
Executive Council, 192; T. 473.
exiles, Jewish, 87–8, 93, 95, 99, 140, 145.
expenditure, 281–3; T. 500.

experimental farm, 299.
exploration, T. 453–5; Society, 159.
export, duty, 291; merchants, 289.
exports, 245–6, 259, 264–5, 268, 270, 272, 284–6, 288, 290; T. 485, 493, 495, 497–9, 501; classes, 290, T. 498.
eye diseases, 233–4; T. 480.
Ezekiel, 87.
Ezion-Geber, 436, 438, 513, 522–3.
Ezra, 88, 93, 95.

factories, 260, 272, 299, 304, 309; T. 484–5, 487.
faculties, university, 219.
Fahma, 382.
Fajja, 377.
Fakhr ed Din, 334.
Fakhri Pasha, 456.
Fakkua, Jebel (Mount Gilboa), 13, 16–17, 389.
Falashas, 146.
Faluja, 375, 380, 385.
fanaticism, 107, 321, 332.
Far East, air service, 392.
Fara, Ain, 330; Wadi, 21.
Farah (Faria), Wadi, 17.
Fareifra, r.s., 512.
Faria, Ghor el, 22; Wadi, 17, 21–2, 30, 387.
Farivaneh, horticultural station, 250.
Farradiya, agricultural station, 250. ·
Fasayil, plain, 22.
Fashkha, Ain, 32; Ras, 31–2.
Fatimids, 102–3, 108, 143.
fauna, 78–80; T. 433.
Fawzi ed Din el Kauwakji, 128.
Feast of Tabernacles, 56, 553.
federation, Arab, 402.
fees, 199, 201, 282–3, 372.
Feinan, 418, 434, 436, 483; forest, 495.
Feisal, Emir, 119, 123, 403, 455–62, 467, 523.
Fejr, Wadi, 458.
fellahin, 4, 134–6, 157, 161, 163–5, 168–9, 187, 207, 293.
fertility, 176; of land, 126, 487.
fertilizers, 250, 258, 483.
Feshshet ed Derwish, 20.
festivals, 552–3.
figs, 13, 164, 243, 403.
Fihl (Pella), 450.
Fik, 344.
finance, 193, 281–4; T. 500–2.
Financial, Adviser, 193, 195, T. 472–3; commissions, 149, 204; Secretary, 195.
Firaun, Jeziret, 452, 521–2, 524; Khazna, 545.
firjal (syphilis), 231.
First Crusade, 103–6.
— Instance, Courts of, T. 474.

fiscal adviser, T. 472; system, Ottoman, 282, 501.
fish, 31, 79, 420, 433, 485.
Fish Gate, Jerusalem, 327.
fisheries, 270–1, 339, 485, 523.
Flavia Neapolis (Nablus), 332.
fleas, 223, 232, 481.
flies, 79, 232, 477, 481.
floods, 29, 59, 379; T. 410, 424, 491.
flora, 61 ff.; T. 425 ff.
flour, 261, 289–90, 309.
flying-boats, 392–3, 395.
fodder, 239, 244, 246, 255; see also forage crops.
fog, 54–5, 423, 561.
Folk Museum, 160.
food, 164–5, 261, 289–90, 293–4, 347, 477.
forage crops, 247, 250; see also fodder.
forestry, 253–6; T. 495–7.
forests, 70, 72, 74, 76, 239, 253–6; T. 426–31, 491, 495–7.
'former rains', 56, 59; T. 424.
fortress-city, T. 440–1.
forts, T. 435, 444.
'Forty, Tower of the', 336.
foundries, 304, 309.
Fountain Gate, Jerusalem, 327.
France, history, 111, 114–16; oil, 269; trade, 265, 285.
franchise, 199, 202.
Franciscans, 149–50, 219, 308, 334, 336.
franghi (syphilis), 231.
Franj, Ain el, 417.
Franks, 107, 334.
Frazer, 454.
Frederick, I of Germany, 107; II, 108; William IV of Prussia, 153.
French, administration, 460; culture, 140; factors, 298; hospitals, 236, 333; interest, 114–15; Jews, 120, 146, 174; language, 140, 142, 213; Mandate, 107, 461; people, 136, 149; protection, 107, 116, 123, 174; railway company, 341; schools, 159, 218–19; shipping lines, 391; Vicar, 150.
frescoes, 434, 451.
Friends' Mission Schools, American, 219.
Frontier Fence, 390.
frontier roads, 390–1.
frost, 492.
fruit flies, 79, 251.
fruit-rots, 253.
fruits, 4, 45, 70, 164, 242–3, 245–6, 250–3, 403, 480, 493–4, 498; see also citrus fruits.
fuel, 72–4, 241, 255, 343, 348, 430, 432, 483, 495.
Fuheis, 411.
Fukh-khar, Tell el, 299.

Fukra, R., 24.
fumigation, 237, 252.
fungi, 251–3.
Fureidis, El, 378.
furniture, 164, 261, 293.

Gabalitis, 418, 438.
Gabinius, 91, 319.
Gad, 400, 435.
Gadara (Umm Keis), 94, 439, 441, 520, 541, 543.
Galaaditis, 407, 438, 441.
gales, 49, 422.
Galician Jews, 161.
Galilean Jews, 136.
Galilee, 3, 8, 15–16; climate, 47, 52, 59; communications, 340, 344, 379, 390; gypsum, 257; history, 82, 91, 97, 99, 131; malaria, 228; Melkite Archbishop of, 150, 470; population, 184; quarries, 259; rivers, 25–6, 31; Sea of (Lake Tiberias), 21; soils, 243; tobacco, 246; vegetation, 72–3.
Gallipoli, 109.
Gan Yavneh, 376.
Gannim, En (Jenin), 322.
garigue, 73–5; T. 428.
Gaza, 45–6, 295, 315–17; agriculture, 250; by-pass, 374; climate, 47, 49, 54, 555 ff.; commerce, 317; court, 206; forestry, 255; Gates of, 110, 316; health, 234–5, 237; history, 82–3, 88–9, 99, 108, 110, 112, 114, 118–19, 189, 315–16, 439, 441, 458; landing-ground, 317; people, 186; population, 189–90, 221, 315; port, 317; pottery, 166; railway, 317, 342–3, 346, 348–9, 351–3; r.s., 356; roads, 317, 340, 344–5, 373–4, 380, 384; signals, 396; textiles, 269; winds, 49, 317.
gazelles, 79, 433.
Gedera, 375.
General, Council of the Jews of Palestine, 201–2, 214–17; — Federation of Jewish Labour, 213, see also Jewish Labour Federation; — Post Office, 158.
Genghiz Khan, 109.
Gennesaret, plain of, 63.
Genoese, 109, 297.
geographical divisions, 3–4.
geology, 8–12; T. 403.
George V, King, 152, 192; forest, 383.
Georgian Jews, 146, 181, 328.
Geradi, r.s., 356.
Gerasa (Jerash), 94, 99, 102, 319, 439–42, 446, 543–4.
Gerasenes, 440.
gerbils, 79.
Gerizim, Mount, 17, 147, 332, 382.

German, Colony, 155, 301, 303; — hospital, 236; interest, 115; — kultur, 140; — language, 140, 142, 213; — Lutherans, 154; — measles, 223; — schools, 213, 218–19; — Templists, 154–5, 174, 301, 328–9.
Germans, 118–19, 140, 174.
Germany, Christians, 173–4; competition, 262; Crusaders, 106; Jews, 96, 139, 146–7, 173–4, 179, 181, 261, 266, 286; trade, 288–90.
Gerrha, 438, 442.
Gethsemane, 327, 534.
Geva, agricultural station, 251.
Gevat, agricultural station, 251.
Gezer, 82, 86; Tell, 20.
Ghadir Abyad, 415; r.s., 510.
— Sultan, Wadi, 415.
Ghafar, Wadi, 407–8.
ghaffirs (watchmen), 256.
Ghar, Wadi, 23.
Gharaudel, Wadi, 418.
Ghassanids, 99, 401, 446–50.
Ghazal R., 407.
Ghazza, Wadi, 19, 24–5, 27–8, 45–6, 118, 315, 317, 374.
Ghedeir, Wadi, 409.
ghee, 495.
ghettos, 139, 145.
Ghor El, 11, 21–3, 28–9, 77–8, 410, 417–18, 423, 489, 491–3, 514, 519.
— el Faria, 22.
— es Safi, 432–3, 478, 518–19.
— Feifeh, 432.
— Seiseban, 411.
Ghuweir, Ain el, 32; plain, 31; Wadi, 418.
Ghuweiteh, Wadi, 415.
Gilbaneh, r.s., 357.
Gilboa, Mts. of, 13, 16–18, 26, 35, 389.
Gilead, 400, 403, 407, 427–8, 430; history, 91, 435–6, 438, 441; people, 466.
gilgals, 82; T. 434.
Ginoea (Jenin), 322.
gipsies, 173.
glossary, topographical, 7.
goats, 62, 72, 79, 168, 170, 254, 256, 289, 485, 489, 495; hair, 135, 166.
Gobat, Bishop, 153–4; school, 219.
Godfrey de Bouillon, 103, 105, 107, 451.
gold, 82; coin, 501.
Golden Gate, Jerusalem, 327.
Golgotha, 327.
Gomer, 146.
goods trains, 347.
Gouraud, General, 461–2.
government, 191–200, T. 461–2, 472–4; Auditor, 195; Central, 191–7, T. 472–3; clinics, 231, 234–5; departments, 194–7, T. 474; divisional, T.

473; hospitals, 235–6, 238; House, 157, 329; local, 197–200; offices, 139, 328; officials, 154, 173–4, 179, 191–2, 206, 329, 347, T. 465, 473; schools, 214–16, T. 471.
governors, T. 473.
Graeco–Roman civilization, 442–3, 446.
grain, 239, 242, 247; *see also* cereals.
grants-in-aid, 281–2, 286; T. 462, 500.
grape-fruit, 188, 242, 245.
grapes, 164, 244, 246, 252, 265, 493–4.
grape-treacle, 164.
grasses, 62–5, 68–71, 74–7, 256, 428–31.
grassland, 239.
Great Britain, emigration to, 182; trade, 288–9.
Greece, 95, 135, 137, 391.
Greek, Catholics, 470; culture, 89, 94, 440–1; islands, 109, 137; language, 94, 137, 139, 149, 446; Orthodox Church, 127, 148–9, 154; War of Independence, 112.
Greeks, 91, 136–7.
Gregorian, Calendar, 550; (Armenian) Church, 151–2.
grottoes, 8, 12.
ground-nuts, 244–5.
Guy de Lusignan, 103, 107–8, 299.
gypsum, 9–10, 12, 256–7, 483, 525.

Habbaniya, air service, 392, 395.
*Habeas Corpus*, 205.
Habimah Dramatic Company, 157.
Habis (Zerka-Main), Wadi, 414, 520.
Hadar ha-Carmel, 303.
Hadassah, hospitals, 231, 235–6; Medical Organization, 221, 236–7.
Hadera, 41, 43, 121; diseases, 230, 234; population, 221; railway, 342, 352; r.s., 354; R., 25–6, 376–7; roads, 377; vegetation, 63, 68.
Hadite, Seil, 414.
Hadrian, 97, 327, 446.
haematite, 483.
Hafireh, Jebel, 415; Wadi, 415.
Haifa, 35, 49, 186, 188–9, 237, 272, 295, 300–7, 340; administration, 199, 204; airport, 237, 301, 303, 307, 392–3, 395, 397; architecture, 157; building, 266, 303; climate, 3, 47–8, 50, 53, 55, 59, 555 ff.; commerce, 304; electricity station, 263, 304; harbour, 158, 186, 189, 283, 285, 290, 300–6, 343; health, 223–4, 228, 230–1, 234–7; history, 111, 113, 119, 190, 301; hotels, 272, 303; industries, 264, 266, 269–70, 304; olive-groves, 255; people, 141–4, 146, 150–1, 155, 188, 301; population, 184, 186–90, 221, 300; port, 305–6; railways, 306–7, 341–3, 346–52, 360, 365–7, 503; r.s., 343, 353, 362, 366,

368; roads, 307, 345, 378, 388, 514; schools, 216–19; seaplane station, 392, 395; shipping, 391; shops, 293; signals, 396–7; Technical Institute, 140, 218, 303; winds, 50, 305.
Haifa sub-district, population, 184.
hail, 60, 565.
Haj Amin el Husseini, 129, 204.
Hajaya, 467.
Hakim Bi-amrillah, 102, 143.
Halazun, R., 25.
Halhul, 18.
halophytic plants, 76–8, 243; T. 425, 431.
Hama, 437, 441, 450, 453, 460.
Hamad Ibn Jazi, 467–8.
Hamam, Jeziret el, 39; Wadi, 21, 31, 383.
Hamama, 45, 375.
Hamath, 437.
hammada, T. 426.
Hammam, Seil, Wadi, 409, 414–15.
— ez Zerka, 414, 518.
Hammeh, El, 1; railway, 346, 506; r.s., 507; springs, 259–60.
— Wadi, 408.
Hanafi Moslems, 143.
Hanakein, Wadi, 415.
Hanbali Moslems, 143.
Hanish, Wadi, 417.
Haram, El, 41.
*Haram esh Sherif*, 327–9, 536–7.
Haram at Hebron, 321, 538–9.
Harith II, El, 447.
Haritiya (Harosheth of the Gentiles), 16, 367.
Harod, Ain, r.s., 368.
*harra*, T. 426.
Harrat er Rujeila, 426, 431.
Harun, Jebel, 418, 428, 454.
— ar Rashid, 102.
harvest, 56, 135, 243, 274, 347; T. 424, 466, 485, 500.
Hasa, El, Kalat, 417, 509; r.s., 512; Wadi, 414, 417–18, 426, 483, 518, 520.
Hasb, Ain, 344, 384–5, 518–19.
Hasbani, R., 28.
Hashim, 317.
Hashimites, 401, 455, 463.
Hasmoneans, 87, 89–93, 99.
Hassadeh, r.s., 368.
Hattin, battle, 103, 107, 452; 'Horns of', 16, 379; Mount, 26.
Hauran, 115, 143–4, 400, 442, 444, 447, 458–60.
Hawarith, Wadi, 27.
Hawwatat, R., 26.
Hazor, 82.
health, 202, 220–38, T. 476–81; Department, 195, 220–1, 225–7, 233, 235–7,

294, T. 474, 476–7, 487; insurance, 278; resorts, 259–60, 337, 339.

Hebrew, 124, 139–42, 145–6, 157–60, 208, 214–15, 217; culture, 93; place-names, 6–7; schools, 141–2, 214, 216–17; Technical Institute, 218; University, 159–60, 219, 250, 325, 329.

Hebron, 4, 18, 321–2; climate, 48, 51–2, 60, 556 ff.; crafts, 166–8; forests, 254; Haram, 321, 538–9; health, 234, 236; history, 114, 126, 129, 189, 321, 451; industries, 321; people, 142, 182, 321; population, 189–90, 221, 321; roads, 322, 340, 344–5, 380, 385.

Heidan, Seil, Wadi, 414–15.

Heidar, Jebel, 15.

Heir, Tell el, r.s., 357.

Heisheh forest, 495.

Hejaz, 109, 237, 447, 455, 458, 461, 463; railway, 341, 347, 409, 414, 454, 456, 458, 478, 503 ff.

Hejira, 550.

Helena, Empress, 530.

Heliopolis, 95.

Hellenism, 89–90, 93.

hellenistic period, 438–41, 527–8, 540.

hellenization, 89, 96, 102, 401, 439–41, 443.

Helueh, r.s., 365.

Heraclius, 327, 448–9.

Hermon, 'Little', 16, 389; Mount, 2, 15, 21, 28, 85, 427.

Herod, 91–4, 259, 484, 536; Agrippa, 326; Antipas, 338, 443; Gate, 327; house of, 87, 99, 401, 442; Palace, 152, 326.

'Herodians', 93.

Herzegovina, 137.

Herzl, Theodor, 121–2.

Herzlya (Herseliya), 377.

Heshbon (Husban), 410–11, 438, 442, 518.

Hezekiah, 86, 326.

High, Commissioners, 2, 124, 128, 191–203, 206, 209, 211, 461–2, 472; — Court, 205.

Hilfsverein der Deutschen Juden, 140–1, 213.

Hindaj, Wadi, 21, 28, 384.

Hinnom, valley of, 325–6, 328.

Hippos, 441.

Hira, 100, 447, 449–50.

Hirbya, 45.

hisheh (tobacco), 493.

Histadrut Ha-Ovdim, 275–8.

historical, routes, 340–1, 344–5, 513; — sites, T. 454, 540–6.

history, 4–6, 81–132, T. 434–64; table, 527–9.

Hitler, 179, 266.

Hittites, 83, 136, 434.

Hivites, 135.

Hizb el Akha el Watani, 468.

Hoffmann, Christopher, 155.

Hogarth, D.G., 123, 456.

holidays, 208, 277, 552–3.

Holland, 270, 290.

Holofernes, 88.

Holon, 308.

Holy Cross, 99, 448, 530.

Holy Land, 1–2, 105–6, 120, 147–8, 150, 155, 178, 297–8, 530; Father Custodian, 150.

— Places, 102, 130, 132, 150, 271, 327, 530–9.

— Sepulchre, 107–8, 115; Church of the, 99, 102, 327–8, 530–5; Confraternity of the, 149; Protector of the, 107.

— War, 455.

home industries, 261, 269, 272.

Homs, 437, 441, 450, 460; railway, 360, 362.

hookworm, 232, 481.

Hope-Simpson, Sir John, 127, 261 n.

Hor, Mount, 418, 428, 454.

Horites, 135, 434.

horses, 79, 82, 101, 169–70, 341.

horticulture, 216, 250; T. 471, 494.

Hosea, 515.

hospices, 271, 308–9, 329.

Hospitallers of St. John, 106.

hospitals, 204, 235–6, 276, 328, 334, T. 476; of St. John of Jerusalem, 175, 234–5, 329.

hotels, 272.

house tax, 282, 501.

Howeish forest, 496.

Howeitat, 456–7, 459–60, 467–8, 489, 523; Ibn Jazi, 467.

Huber, Charles, 454.

Hulagu Khan, 109.

Huleh, Lake, 1, 21–2, 28, 30, 63, 71, 91, 167–8, 225, 230, 244, 247, 344, 384, 390.

Humaidha island, 521–2.

humidity, 50, 53–4, 422–3, 560.

Hummar, Ain, 428.

humus, 241–2, 254; T. 426, 489, 491.

Hungarian Jews, 179, 328.

Huni, Wadi, 483.

Hurrians, 434.

Husban, 410–11, 442, 518; Wadi, 411.

Husn, El, 407, 520; people, 466, 470; plain, 489.

Hussein ibn Ali, Sherif, 455–7, 461–3.

Husseini, 134.

hydrographic survey, T. 500, 502.

hydrophobia, 223, 234.

hydrophytes, 71; T. 425, 429, 431.

Hyksos, 82–3.

Hyrcania, 95.
Hyrcanus, 91, 93.
hyssop, 65, 164.

Ibbin (Abbin), 519.
Ibn Khaldun, 402.
— Rashid, 461–3.
— Saud, King, 128, 401, 461–3, 522.
Ibrahim, 112–13, 115, 298–9, 315, 453;
  Ain, 383; Nahr, 362; r.s., 364.
Idrisi, 463.
Idumaea, 91.
Ifdan, Wadi, 418.
igneous rocks, 526.
Ikrit, 390.
Illar, 382.
illegal immigration, 180.
*Imams* (prophets), 143–4, 174.
immigration, 5, 15, 63, 116–17, 120–1,
  124–8, 132, 145, 172–4, 176–8, 186,
  188, 195–6, 211, 237, 260–1, 266,
  269–70, 283–4, 286–7, T. 469; Arab,
  101, 133; categories, 177–8, 195–6;
  illegal, 180; incentives, 178–9; origins,
  180–1; social effects, 181–2; urban,
  184–6.
Imperial Airways, 392–3, 396–7, 520.
import duties, 257, 261–2, 266, 273, 283,
  291–2, 372, T. 497; merchants, 288.
imports, 169, 268–9, 284–5, 288–92,
  347; T. 497–9, 501.
imposts, 273.
incentives to immigration, 178–9.
income tax, 283; T. 501.
increase in population, 5, 171–2, 174–7,
  184, 285; T. 470, 488, 497.
India, 173, 176, 392.
Indians, 460.
industrialization, 5–6, 26, 125, 184, 260,
  272.
industries, 186, 260–73; T. 403, 484–7.
Industry, Committee, 193.
infant mortality, 175–6, 221–2, 236, T.
  470, 477; welfare, 236–7.
infectious diseases, 222–4, 235; T. 477.
injunction, writs of, 205.
inland towns, 318–39.
inoculation, 224, 237; T. 477.
insects, 79, 251–2.
insurance, 276–8.
interchange points, railway, 348.
interest rates, 280; T. 502.
internal trade, 292–4.
International Labour Conventions, 487.
intestinal diseases, T. 476–7.
intoxicating liquors, 261–2, 282.
investments, 261, 266, 273, 282, 286,
  293.
Irak el Menshiya, 385.
Iraq, air routes, 392–3, 520; Anglicans,
  154; boundary, 399; history, 127–8,

401–2, 462–3; Jews, 146, 181;
Mandate, 191; oil, 29, 37, 189, 269–
70, 301; people, 465, 468; Petroleum
Company, 37, 289, 366, 396–7,
475–6, 499, 516, 521; road, 189, 290,
515; trade, 290, 292, 304, 497, 499.
Irbid, 407, 466, 520; council, 473;
courts, 474; hospital, 476; malaria,
477–8; rainfall, 424; roads, 388–9,
514–16, 520; signals, 396.
Irby, 454.
Iron, Age, 82, 434, 436; — foundries,
304, 309; — goods, 498; — mines,
436; — ore, 483; — works, 299, 339.
irrigable area, 239.
irrigation, 13, 25, 27, 60, 227, 230, 239,
242–3, 247–50; T. 403, 477, 480,
491–3, 502.
Isaac, 321.
Isdud, forestry, 256; r.s., 355; roads,
344, 375.
Ishar, R., 27.
Ishkar, Wadi, 27, 41.
Iskanderuna, Nahr, 25–7, 39, 41, 43,
376–7.
Islam, 2, 100–3, 109, 143–5, 213, 444,
447–50, 457, 465, 470, 472, 528.
Ismailia, signals, 396.
Ismain, Wadi, 19.
Israel, Kingdom of, 1, 16, 18, 85–7, 147,
190, 400, 527.
Israelites, 4, 20, 83, 85, 87, 135, 147,
297, 319, 331, 401, 435–6, 513.
Issa, 467.
Issus, battle, 88.
Istanbul, 391.
Italian, air service, 392–3, 395; hospitals,
236, T. 476; school, 218; shipping
lines, 391.
Italians, 140, 149.
Italy, Christians, 173; Crusaders, 105–6;
death-rate, 176; history, 115–16;
Jews, 179; quarry-men, 259; trade,
288.
Ithriyat, Jebel, 417.
Itm, Wadi, 418, 459, 505, 513–14, 518,
522.
Ituraea, 91, 441–2.

Jaba, 166; roads, 378.
Jabal, 374.
Jabalya, 45.
Jabbok (Zerka), R., 30, 408–10.
jackals, 79, 234, 433.
Jacob, 321; — Bardaeus, 447.
Jacobite Church, 148, 150, 152, 447.
Jacob's Well, 333, 382, 387.
Jaez, Seil, 417.
Jafar, 417; Jebel, 411.
Jaffa, 12–13, 41, 45, 188–9, 237, 295,
307–11; administration, 204, 206;

building, 266; climate, 47, 49, 59, 555 ff.; commerce, 284–5, 309–10; future, 309; Gate, Jerusalem, 327–8; health, 223–4, 228, 231, 235–7; history, 85, 108, 110, 112–13, 119, 126–7, 129, 190, 307–8; industries, 309; oranges, 80, 288, 308; people, 141–2, 151–2, 155, 188, 307; population, 184, 186, 189, 190, 307; port, 310–11; railway, 43, 311, 341–2, 346–7, 348, 357; r.s., 358; roads, 43, 46, 311, 340–1, 345, 377, 386; schools, 218; shipping, 391; signals, 396; soap, 263, 309; vegetation, 62–3.

— sub-district, population, 149, 184, 221; rabies, 234.

Jafr, 420, 424, 458–9, 468, 489, 520; depression, 417–18, 420–1.

*jahel, juhal*, 144.

Jajeh, Nahr el, 362.

Jalama, 388–9.

Jalud, Nahr, 13, 21, 30, 367, 389.

Jamnia, 344.

Jannaeus, Alexander, 91, 315, 441–2.

Japan, competition, 262; trade, 290, 499.

Japanese, 201.

Japhe, Jappho (Jaffa), 307.

Jardun, Wadi, r.s., 512.

Jarmak, Jebel, 15.

Jarra, R., 27.

Jathun, Wadi, 36.

Jauf, 417 *n.*, 449, 454, 458, 463, 468.

Jauzala, Wadi, 17, 21.

Jazar, Tell, 20.

Jazi Howeitat (tribe), 456, 467–8.

Jazzar, Ahmed el, 110–11, 114, 298–9.

Jebeil, r.s., 365.

Jebusite fortress, 83, 325–6.

Jeddi, Ain, 32, 135.

Jehoshaphat, 436.

Jeida, 389.

Jemal, 455.

Jenin, 13, 17, 322; climate, 48, 555 ff.; diseases, 230, 234; forestry, 254–5; history, 322; population, 188, 322; railway, 322; r.s., 371; roads, 322, 382–3, 388; signals, 396.

Jenna, Ain, 407–8.

Jerash (Gerasa), 99, 400, 402, 407, 439–40, 446, 466, 519, 543–4; bridge, 409, 519; Circassians, 469, 543; council, 473; court, 474; diseases, 477–9; epidemic post, 476; horticultural station, 494; minerals, 483–4; roads, 519; vegetation, 427; Wadi, 409, 440.

Jeremiah, 87.

Jeria, Wadi, 411.

Jericho, 23, 322–3; agricultural stations, 250; climate, 48, 51–3, 423, 556 ff.;

history, 82–3, 119, 323, 458; hotels, 272; irrigation, 249, 323; oasis, 4, 29, 243, 323; people, 136, 323; plain, 22; population, 221, 322; roads, 323, 345, 386–7, 391; Rose of, 64.

Jerouf, r.s., 512.

Jerusalem, 18, 186, 189, 323–30; administration, 199, 203–4, 206; architecture, 157, 328–9; art, 157; Bishops of, 148, 153, 325, 329; British consul, 115; building, 266, 328; climate, 48, 51–2, 54, 59–60, 556 ff.; drainage, 330; Electric and Public Service Corporation, 262; Gates, 327–8; Girls' College, 216, 219, 471; health, 224–5, 228, 230–1, 234–6, 329; history, 82–3, 85–6, 88, 90, 94–6, 99, 102–3, 106–8, 110, 119, 126, 129, 148, 150, 189, 325, 448, 450–1, 458; Holy Places, 530–5; hotels, 272, 328–9; industries, 270, 323; kingdom of, 106–7, 315, 452; libraries, 159; medieval city, 327–8; modern city, 328–9; old city, 325–7; olive-groves, 255; Patriarchs of, 148, 150, 327, 470; people, 138, 141, 145–7, 149, 151–2, 155, 161, 188, 323, 328; population, 184, 186, 188–90, 221, 323; prison, 207; railway, 328, 341–2, 346–8, 358–9; r.s., 360; roads, 327, 340–1, 344–5, 380–1, 386; sanjak, 1–2; schools, 217–19, 328–9, 471; shops, 293; signals, 396–7; site, 325–6; town planning, 158, 328; water, 329–30.

— sub-district, population, 149, 184.

Jesse, 321.

Jesus, 94, 320, 333, 335.

Jethum, Jebel, 419.

Jewish, Agency for Palestine, 15, 124, 131, 141, 177–8, 181, 186, 192, 194–6, 211, 216–17, 250–1, 275–6, 278, 293, 325, 328–9; agriculture, 62–3, 239, 242, 244, 247, 265; Anti-Tuberculosis League, 231; Arabs, 134, 136, 173; calendar, 551; Colonization Association, 26, 214, 217; community, 200–2; co-operative societies, 280; Exploration Society, 159; Farmers' Federation, 276; festivals, 553; immigration, 5, 15, 63, 116–17, 120–1, 124–7, 132, 145, 177–82, 186, 220, 254, 260–1, 266, 284–5, 289; industries, 260–1, 264–5, 269, 271, 274; Labour Federation, 213, 216–7, 236–7, 274–7; Law, 88, 96–7, 337–8, 475; mysticism, 97, 145, 147, 337; National Fund, 211, 256; National Home, 122–4, 132, 191, 462, 472; nationality, 134, 139, 173; orphanages, 219; police, 207; problem, 5–6, 130–1, 402; quarter, Jerusalem, 328; schools, 213–18, 235;

sects, 138, 140; shops, 293; sites, 539; state, 120, 122–5, 130–1, 138; University, 219.

Jews, 5–6, 136, 138–9, 144–8, 220, 274–5, 286, 293, 312, 337, 464; administration, 191, 193, 200–2, 204; census, 171–4; costume, 161–3; culture, 122, 156–60, 181, 312; distribution, 184, 186, 188; emigration, 182–3; health, 223, 231–2, 235–7; history, 87, 89, 96–7, 101–2, 106, 116, 125–31 *passim*, 441, 448; increase, 174–6; languages, 139–42; of the Dispersion, 89–90, 95–7, 123, 140, 147; vital statistics, 176, 221.

Jezreel, history, 85, 109, 190; Vale of (Emek Jezreel), 13, 21, 85, 91, 242–3, 344, 389, 391.

Jib, El, 166.

Jibal, El, 418, 433.

Jidda, 453, 463.

Jiftlik, 387–8, 391.

*jiljiliyeh* (gilgals), 82.

Jinnis, r.s., 355.

Jisr Banat Yakub, 1, 28, 87, 111, 315, 373, 389–90.

— Damiya, 30, 373, 387.

— el Majami, 29, 367, 373, 387–9, 391, 396, 514–15; r.s., 369.

— esh Sheikh Hussein, 30, 373, 389, 516.

— Wadi Shaib, 515.

Jiya, El, r.s., 356.

Jiyashi, 419–20.

Jiyeh, r.s., 363.

*jizya*, 448.

John the Baptist, 518.

Jonah, 307.

Jonathan, 90, 319.

Joppa (Jaffa), 85, 108, 190, 307–11.

Jordan, R., 1, 21, 25, 28–30, 247; boundary, 401–2; bridges, 373.

—trench, 3, 8, 21–3; agriculture, 252; climate, 3, 47–9, 52–5, 59–60, 556 ff.; diseases, 225, 230, 232, 477–8; geology, 10–11; history, 85, 111, 114, 119; population, 225, 230, 466; railway, 367; roads, 379, 383, 386, 388, 390–1; soils, 243, 491; springs, 249, 259; swine, 79; vegetation, 64, 66, 76–7, 255, 430–3.

Josak springs, 320.

Joseph, 321.

Josephus, 23.

Joshua, 83, 85, 323.

Jounieh, r.s., 364.

Joz, Wadi, 325.

Jozeleh, Wadi, 17.

Judaea, 3, 8, 12, 15–21, 46; climate, 47, 52; communications, 19–20, 340, 345, 359, 379–80; geology, 10, 11; history,

81, 83, 88–9, 91; population, 184; rivers, 27; soils, 242; springs, 249; vegetation, 66, 72–3, 75; wilderness of, 19–20.

Judaeans, 4.

Judaeo-German (Yiddish), 139.

Judaeo-Persian, 145.

Judah, kingdom of, 1, 18, 85–7, 436.

Judaism, 2, 89, 96–7, 99–100, 125, 144, 146–7, 178, 441, 444, 447.

Judas Maccabaeus, 19, 89–90.

'Judges', 85, 307.

Judicial Adviser, T. 472–3.

*Judith, Book of*, 88.

Julian, 97; Calendar, 550.

Julis, 375.

junctions, railway, 348.

Juneh, bay, 112; r.s., 364.

Jura, El, 45–6; roads, 374, 385.

Jurf ed Derawish, r.s., 512; roads, 520.

ustice, 204–7; T. 474–5.

Justinian, 99, 321, 328, 332, 447.

Kaabna, 467.

Kabatya, 383.

Kabbara marshes, 254.

Kabr Ameir, r.s., 356.

Kabri, El, 299.

Kadas, 1, 390.

*kadi*, 203.

Kadi, Tell el, 1, 28, 53.

Kadoorie Agricultural School, 216.

Kaf, 454.

Kafarchima R., 361.

Kafkafa, 407.

Kafr Semi, r.s., 353.

— Yinis, 346, 351, r.s., 355.

Kafza, Jebel, 383.

Kaikhosru II, 105.

*Kais*, 135.

Kakun, r.s., 354.

kala-azar, 230.

Kalansawa, Wadi, 27.

Kalkilya, 377, 382; R., 27; r.s., 354.

Kallia, 260; air service, 395; roads, 387, 390–1.

Kalmoun, r.s., 365.

Kalunya, 386.

Kamun, Tell, 388.

Kana, R., 27.

Kanan, Jebel, 390.

Kantara, 342–3, 346–9, 351–3; r.s., 357, 505.

Karachi, air service, 395.

*Karaites*, 148, 328.

Karn, Wadi, 36, 362, 378.

Kasseib, Wadi, 408.

Kassir, 509, r.s., 511.

Kastal, El, 386.

Kastel, 451, 517.

Kastina, 375, 380.
Katia, 344.
Katra, 375.
Katrani, 415, 521; r.s., 512; roads, 517–20.
Kebir, Nahr el (Eleutherus R.), 438.
—, Wadi, 13, 27, 41.
Kefar Barukh, r.s., 368.
— Bilu, 375–6.
— Giladi, 384.
— Malal, 376.
— Tavor, 389.
— Yehoshua, r.s., 368.
Kefr Kenna, 74, 383.
— Lam, 39.
— Rai, 382.
— Yehoshua, r.s., 368.
— Yuba, 424.
Kefrenji, 407–8, 424; Wadi, 408, 519–20.
Kelb, Nahr el, 362.
—, Wadi, 32.
Kelt, Wadi, 20–1, 30, 323.
Kerak, 452, 466, 470, 473–4, 476, 478, 483; roads, 385, 513–14, 517–20.
—, Seil, Wadi, 414, 417, 483, 513–14, 518–19.
Kerbela, 143.
kerosene, 498.
kersenneh peas, 244, 246, 493–4.
Khabara, 483.
Khabra Abil Husein, 420.
Khalasa, El, 380.
Khaldeh, 361; r.s., 364.
Khaldi, 134.
Khaled, Wadi, 506; r.s., 507.
Khaliadiya, R., 26.
Khalid ibn Walid, 100, 449–50, 457.
khalifa, 100.
Khalil-er-Rahman, El, 321.
Khalisa, 384.
khamsin, 50.
Khan el Lubban, 381.
— Rashin, 371.
— Yunis, 46, 112, 221, 256, 330–1; r.s., 356; roads, 331, 373–4.
— Zebib, r.s., 511.
Khaneizeh, Seil, 418.
Kharasan, Wadi, 409.
Kharuf, Jebel, 24.
Khashab, R., 25.
Khatta, Wadi, 409.
Khayat beach, 378.
Khelil, Wadi, 19, 27, 380.
Khirba, El, r.s., 357.
Khirbet abu Kashta, 374.
— el Mekawar, 443.
— el Yehud, 95.
— es Sarkas, 377.
— es Suwan, 408.
— Iskander, 434.
— Meneiyeh, 436.

Khirbet Mukhayyat, 545.
— Nahas, 436.
— Naur, 411.
— Tmeiri, 430.
Khiva, 145.
Khor Mezar, 417.
Khreibeh forest, 255.
Khudaira (Hadera), R., 26.
Khurma, 463.
Kibbutz, 213.
Kidron, R., 32, 325–7, 386.
Kilwa, 434.
kindergartens, 217.
'Kings' high-road', 435.
Kinneret, 250, 389.
Kir Moab, 452, 544.
Kirjath-Arba, 321.
Kirkuk oilfields, 37.
Kiryat Amal, 389.
— Anavim, 251.
— Bialik, 366.
— el Inab, 386.
— Haim (Haiyim, Hayim), 36–7, 68, 378; r.s., 366.
— Haroshet, r.s., 368; roads, 388.
— Motzkin, r.s., 362, 366.
— Shemuel, 366, 375.
Kisarya (Caesarea), 12, 39, 340.
Kishon, Nahr, 17, 25–6, 35, 85, 91, 300, 366, 371, 378, 388; railway, 348, 360; r.s., 362, 366.
Kitchener, Lord, 455.
Kitte, 424, 519.
K. L. M. air service, 392–3.
knafe, 165.
Knights, of St. John, 106, 109, 297; of St. Lazarus, 297.
Koninklijke Lucktvaart Maatschappij (K.L.M.), 393.
Koran, 100, 144; — schools, 213.
Koreish, 99.
Kosseima, see Kuseimeh.
kouskous, 165.
Krak (Kerak), 452–3.
Krak-et-Montréal, 452.
Kub, R., 27.
Kubbet Abd es Seyyid, 417.
Kubbet es Sakhra, 327, 536.
Kubeiba, Wadi, 385.
Kubu, Wadi, 415.
Kuds, El (Jerusalem), 323.
Kufa, 100.
Kufeir, 382–3.
Kufrein, Tell, 411; Wadi, 410–11.
Kum Gharz (Khum Garz), r.s., 509.
Kuneitra, 460.
Kupat Holim Sick Fund, 236, 276.
Kurdana, Tell, 35.
Kurdistan, Jews, 181.
Kurds, 110, 137, 328.
kurkar hills, 69, 241.

Kurnub, 344–5.
Kurum, Ras el, 35, 37, 303, 305.
Kuseimeh, 24, 342, 380.
Kusheibeh, Wadi, 418.
Kuwait, 463.
Kuweira, 459.
*Kwuzah, Kwuzot*, 213.

Laban, 417; Wadi, 417.
laboratories, 234, 236–7, 251, 276, 476.
Laborde, 454.
labour, 6, 177, 186–7, 207, 213, 227–8, 273–8, T. 485–7; Department, 195, 278; exchanges, 276, 278; Immigration Schedule, 128, 177–8, 180, 186–7, 196; legislation, 277–8, T. 487.
labourers, 137.
Lachish, 83, 86, 340.
'Ladder of Tyre', 12, 33.
Ladino (Español), 140, 142, 144.
lakes, 30–2, 39.
Lakhmids, 99, 447.
land, 126–7, 132, 197; courts, 204–5, 211; -hunger, 488; -ownership, 204–5, 208–13, 255; registration, 283; Registry, 210; Settlement Court, 475; Settlement Department, 195; taxes, 282, 448, 501; tenure, 475; Transfers Regulations, 211.
Lands, Department, 195, T. 474, 502; Director, 197.
languages, 94, 109, 134, 137, 139–42, 151, 208, 218, T. 446, 471; official, 102, 124, 139, 208, 215, T. 472.
Larnaka, communications, 393, 395–6.
Latin, Church, 106, 114–16, 148–50; Convent, 333; Hospice, 308; Kingdom, 106–9, 136, 148, 315, 451–2; Patriarch, 106, 150, 327, 470.
Latrun, El, climate, 48, 52, 556 ff.; roads, 375, 382, 386–7.
'latter rains', 56, 59; T. 424.
Lausanne, Treaty of, 283, 401, 501.
lava belt, T. 399, 403, 419, 450, 514, 516.
law, 206–7; Beduin, 467, 474–5; canon, 100, 143; civil, 100; Classes, 214; Courts, 328; Electoral, 467; Jewish, 88, 96–7, 475; martial, 129; Mining, 482; Mosaic, 475; Moslem, 474–5; Organic, 462, 465, 472, 482.
Lawrence, T. E., 119, 456–60, 462, 467.
Layard, A. H., 454.
League of Nations, 6, 124, 130, 191, 193–4, 290, 400, 462, 472.
leather goods, 261.
Leban, 518.
Lebanon, 2, 15, 107, 115, 123, 143–4, 150, 191, 253, 402.
Legal Secretary, 195.
legions, 444.

legislation, 139; banking, 279; labour, 277–8, T. 487; water, T. 492, 502.
Legislative Assembly, T. 473; Council, 192, T. 462, 468.
leguminous plants, 243–4, 247, 493.
leishmaniasis, 230, 479.
Lejjun, 415, 434–4, 520.
lemons, 245.
lentils, 244, 403, 493–4.
lentisk, 65, 68, 73, 168, 427.
Leper Hospital, 235.
Lepers, Mosque of the, 332.
leprosy, 223.
Leuce Come, 439–40, 442.
Levantine population, 136–7.
*Li Vaux Moyse*, 451.
Libb, 414; roads, 518.
Libban, railway, 509; r.s., 511.
Libbeh, Wadi, 408.
Liberal Jews, 147.
libraries, 159–60, 219; T. 472.
lice, 232, 478–9.
licences, 199, 201, 282, 372; T. 500–1.
Liddan, R., 28.
lighthouses, 37, 295.
Lihyanitic kingdom, 440.
L'île de Graye (Jeziret Firaun), 452.
lime, 242, 261; burning, 63, 74, 254.
*limes* (Roman), 444.
limestones, 8–10, 225, 242–3, 249, 259, 349–50, 372, 403, 483–4, 525–6.
Linant, 454.
Lisan, El, 31; isthmus, 417; 'marl soils', 243; peninsula, 414, 513, 518–19, 521; plateau, 414.
Litani, r.s., 363; R., 2, 41, 361.
literacy, 141.
literature, 139–40, 158–9, 581.
Lithuanian Jews, 162, 174.
litigation, 202, 206.
'Little Hermon', 16, 389.
livestock, T. 485, 494–5.
*Liwas*, 473.
*Lloyd Triestino*, 391.
loams, 242, 489, 491.
loans, 279–80, 283, 287; T. 502.
locomotives, 343, 348.
locusts, 80, 251, 480–1.
Lod (Lydda), 331.
Lodz, weavers, 269.
loess, 66, 70, 242–3.
looms, 166–7.
Lorraine, Crusaders, 103.
lorries, 480.
L.O.T. air service, 392–3.
lottery-tickets, 279.
Louis VII of France, 106.
Low Countries, Crusaders, 106.
Ludd (Lydda), 331.
lunacy, 238.
Luria, Isaac, 337.

Lusan, r.s., 513.
Lussan, Jebel, 24.
Lutheran Church, 148, 154.
Lydda, 13, 19, 43, 46, 331–2; airport, 237, 331–2, 377, 392–3, 395–7, 520; history, 331–2; olive-groves, 255; people, 186, 331; population, 189–90, 331; railways, 332, 341–3, 346, 348, 350–2, 357–8; r.s., 355, 358–9; roads, 332, 344, 377.

Maan, 418, 463, 466; council, 473; court, 474; division, 473; epidemic post, 476; garrison, 475–6; highland, 417–19, 433; history, 449, 454, 459; landing-ground, 521; malaria, 478; railway, 346, 348, 350, 454, 503, 505, 508–9; r.s., 513; rainfall, 424; roads, 514, 517–18, 520; sanjak, 2; signals, 396.
Maani, Jebel, 460.
Maaruf, Jebel, 522.
Maccabaean, palaces, 326; revolt, 21, 89–90, 315, 441.
Maccabaeus, Jonathan, 297; Judas, 19, 89–90.
Macedonian colony, 439.
Machaerus, 443, 518.
machinery, imports, 289–91, 304.
Machpelah, Cave of, 321, 538.
Madeba, 544–5; council, 473; court, 474; malaria, 478; plain, 489; roads, 513–14, 517–18, 520.
Mafrak, 459; landing-ground, 521; r.s., 510; roads, 514, 516, 520.
mafruz land, 209.
Maghara, Jebel, 24.
Magharbeh, 110, 137–8.
magistrates' courts, 204–5, 211; T. 474.
magnesium, bromide, 257–8; chloride, 258–9.
mails, 392, 395, 515, 520.
Main, 414, 545.
'main rains', 56; T. 424.
maize, 244, 246–7, 252, 403.
Majali, 468.
Majdul, r.s., 355.
Majid Pasha, 468.
Majnuna, Wadi, 36.
Makaren, railway, 506; r.s., 507.
Malaka, Wadi, 19.
malaria, 26, 29–30, 224–30, 235, 477–8.
Malat, Tell el, 39.
Malih, Wadi, 17, 21–2.
Malik, R., 26.
Maliki Moslems, 143.
Malikiya, 390.
Malilheh, Wadi, 417.
malnutrition, 479–80.
Mamluks, 108–10, 112, 315, 452–3.
Mamre, oak, 253.

Manaiyoun, 467.
Manasseh, 319, 400, 435.
Manchester, emigration to, 182.
mandamus, writs of, 205.
Mandate, Palestine and Transjordan, 6, 123–32, 177, 180, 191–4, 208, 290, 292, 462, 472, 529; Syria (French), 107, 461.
manganese, 12, 483, 526.
Mangles, 454.
Mannaiyyin, 467.
Manshiya, r.s., 362.
manufactured goods, 284, 289, 291–2.
manures, 241, 244, 250.
maps, 399, 400, 587–9.
maquis, 72–3, 74–5, 254; T. 426, 428, 495.
Mar Elias, Jebel, 301, 539.
— Saba, 20.
Marcheshwan, 56.
Marissa, 94.
marketing organizations, 276, 288.
markets, 6, 245, 261, 263, 265, 269, 288, 290, 347; T. 485, 495.
marls, 8, 10, 243, 489, 491, 525.
Maronite Christians, 115, 150.
marram grass, 63, 68, 256.
Marseilles, 391.
marshes, coastal, 25–6, 35–6, 39, 63, 68–71, 168, 175, 183–4, 225, 230; Jordan trench, 21–2, 28, 30–1, 63, 77, 168, 183, 225, 230; T. 403, 419–20, 478.
martial law, 129.
Masada, 94.
Masammat, Wadi, 415.
mashaa land, 208–9; T. 475.
Mashash, Wadi, 415.
Mashhur, 468.
Masmiya el Kebira, 374–5.
masonry, 259.
massacres, 95, 106, 110–11, 456.
Massin, R., 26.
Massoudieh, see Masudiya.
Mastabeh, 409.
'mastic', 68.
Masudiya, railways, 342, 346, 348, 367, 369, 371; r.s., 370, 372; roads, 387.
Matate dramatic company, 157.
Matawila, 143.
matches, 261–2, 291, 299.
Matfana, r.s., 363.
mats, 167, 269.
Mattathias, 89–90.
Mauritius, immigrants, 180.
Mazar, railway, 353; r.s., 356.
Mazbuta waqfs, 203.
Mazhlum, 418; plain, 421.
Mazraa, 378.
measles, 223.
measures and weights, 553–4.

Mecca, 99–100, 102, 237, 327, 448–9, 451, 453, 455, 463, 503.
mechanical engineering, 218, 273.
Medaan, Wadi, 406.
Medabegh, Seil, 417.
Medayin Salih, 442, 446, 454.
Medeba (Madeba), 442, 446, 544.
Medical Officer, Senior, 197.
medical services, 195, 235–8; T. 476.
medicine, 175, 219, 290.
Medina, 99, 447–9, 454, 456, 458; railway, 341, 454, 503.
Mediterranean, botanical region, 66–74, 426–9; climate, 47–9, 55, 65; flora, 65; fruit fly, 251; race, 133; routes, 340, 343; seaboard, rivers, 25–8; steppe soil, 242.
megalithic structures, T. 434.
Megiddo, 13, 83, 86–7, 119, 340, 344, 388, 460.
Mehemet Ali, 112–14, 115, 136, 153, 453.
Meirun, 390.
Meithalun, 382.
Mejdel, 45–6; agriculture, 250, 494; people, 186, 188; population, 190, 221; rabies, 234; r.s., 355; roads, 344, 374, 383, 385; textiles, 269; weaving, 167.
Melek el Ashraf, 298.
Melkites, 150, 470.
melons, 33, 60, 164, 244, 246, 347–8, 493.
Memorial Chapel, 329.
Menahamiya, gypsum, 256.
Mendelssohn, Moses, 139.
Menshieh, 308.
mental hospitals, 236, 238.
Menzil, r.s., 512.
Merj el Ghuruk, 17.
— es Suffar, 450.
— ibn Amir (plain of Esdraelon), 35.
— Sannur, 17, 382.
Merkal, 83, 94.
Merom, Waters of (Lake Huleh), 1.
Mersa Dahab, 521.
Mersed, Ras, 31.
Merv, 103.
Mesha, 436.
Meshatta, 451, 545.
Meshek Yajur, r.s., 368.
mesophytic plants, 64.
Mesopotamia, 86, 93, 95, 99, 101, 148, 340, 437, 446, 452, 455.
Messageries Maritimes, 391.
Messianic Age, 143; Zionism, 178, 201.
metalware, 261.
meteorological stations, 47–8, T. 421; tables, 555–65.
methylated spirits, 262, 485.
Metropolitan bishops, 148–9, 152.

metrukhi land, 208–10.
Metulla, 1; roads, 345, 383–4, 391.
mevat land, 208, 210.
Mezerib, 460; r.s., 508.
Mezra, 417.
Microlithic culture, 81.
Midan, El, r.s., 356.
Middin, 417.
Middlesex Yeomanry, 460.
Midianites, 418.
midwives, 235.
Mifjir, Nahr, 25–6, 39, 41, 43, 376–7.
migration, 465; Department, 195, 207; forced, 95; seasonal, 172, 225, 466, 468–9, 478.
Mikveh Israel, 120; agricultural school, 218, 250.
Milh, Tell el, 345, 385; Wadi, 27.
Military Administration, 124, 191, 197; landing-grounds, 395.
milk, 164–5, 168–9, 479, 485.
millets, 101, 138, 200, 202.
Mills, Eric, 134, 158.
mineral springs, 259–60; T. 484.
minerals, 256–60; T. 482–4.
mines, T. 436, 482.
Minet abu Zabura, 41.
Mining Law, 482; Ordinance, 482.
ministers, T. 473.
mirage, 55; T. 423.
miri land, 208–9.
Miriam, Ain, 334, 536.
Mirza Ali Mohammad, 144.
— Yahya, 144.
Misfak, railway, 353; r.s., 356.
Mishna, 56, 338.
Mishra en Nasraniyeh, 409.
Mishrafa, 380.
Misr Airwork S.A.E., 393, 395.
mission hospitals, 333; T. 476.
missionaries, 114–16, 142, 152–3, 187, 213–14, 218, 470, 476.
mist, 54–5, 423.
Mithkal Pasha el Faiz, 468.
Mitspa, 383.
Mitwali, 143.
Mizpah, 383.
Mizra, 383.
Mizrahi, 216–17.
Moab, 400, 411, 428; history, 81, 85, 435–8.
'Moabite Stone', 436, 518.
Moabites, 91.
Moabitis, 411, 438.
Moahib, 456.
Moawiya, 102.
Mohammad, 99–100, 144, 448–9, 530; II, 109.
Mojib, Seil, Wadi, 414–17, 483, 518.
monasteries, 20, 150, 152, 321, 446, 535.
Mongols, 102, 108, 452–3.

Monophysite doctrine, 152, 447–8.
monopolies, 257, 265, 282, 289.
monotheism, 447–8.
*Montakas*, 473.
Montréal, Montroyal, Crac de, 451–2.
moon-goddess, 443.
Moors, 106.
Moriah, Mount, 326–7.
Moroccan Jews, 146; wheat, 247.
mortality, 176, 221–2, 224, 230.
Mosaic law, 475.
*mosaic* in tobacco, 253.
*Moshav Ovdim*, 211, 213.
Moslem, calendar, 550; Committee, 203; community, 202–4; festivals, 552–3; law, 474–5; rule, 450–5; sites, 536–9; Supreme Council, 203–4, 218, 236, 325, 327.
Moslems, 134, 137–8, 143–4, 154, 293, T. 465, 470–1, 474; administration, 191, 202–1; census, 171–4; costume, 161–2; culture, 156; diseases, 231–3, 235; distribution, 188; education, 213–15, 218; emigration, 182; history, 100–2, 106–7, 125–7; immigration, 177, 187; increase, 175–6; soap, 263; vital statistics, 175–6, 221–2.
mosquitoes, 26, 79, 227, 478, 481.
Moteh (Mutah), 448.
mother-craft centre, 237.
moths, 251–2.
motor, cars, 290, 341, 372, 480; mechanics, 471; transport, 273.
Mount Carmel, 12–13, 16–17, 26, 33, 35, 37, 39, 43, 60, 72, 81, 85, 111, 119, 243, 254–5, 301, 303, 305, 340, 344, 373, 378, 460, 539; Sanatorium, 231.
— Ebal, 17, 332, 382.
— Ephraim, 17.
— Gerizim, 17, 147, 332, 382.
— Hattin, 26.
— Hermon, 2, 15, 21, 28, 85.
— Hor, 418, 428, 454.
— Moriah, 326.
— of Olives, 18, 151, 325, 329, 386, 534–5.
— Ophel, 325.
— Scopus, 219, 325, 329.
— Sinai, 21.
— Tabor, 13, 16, 35, 73, 218, 344.
Mountains of Gilboa, 13, 16–18, 26, 35, 389.
Mousterian culture, 81.
Mudauwara, Kalat, 399.
Mudeiyineh, 435.
mud-flats, T. 419–20.
*mufti*, 203.
Mughar, El, 375–6; Jebel, 415.
Mukallik, Wadi, 20–1.
Mukatta, Nahr, 25, 35, 37, 367, 371, 539.

Mukaur, 518.
Mukheires, Seil, Wadi, 415, 520.
Mukhnah, Sahl, 17, 381.
*mukhtars*, 197, 220.
mulberries, 45, 164, 244.
mules, 169–70.
Mulhaqa waqfs, 203.
*mulk* land, 208–9.
municipal, councils, 188, 197, 199–200, 202, T. 473–4; courts, 205–6; Library, Tel Aviv, 159.
municipalities, 187–8, 190, 197–200.
Murad, 109; III, 523.
murine typhus, 478.
Murray, Sir Archibald, 118, 456–7.
Musa, Ain, 426; Wadi, 418, 451.
museums, 160, 299, 328–9.
Mushakka, Jebel, 35.
Musheirifa spring, 28.
Mushrifeh, El, 380.
music, 156–7.
Musil, Alois, 425, 430, 432, 454, 467.
Musrareh, R., 27.
Mutah, 99, 448–9.
Mutawwakil, 109.
Muwakkar, 451.
mysticism, 97, 145, 147.

Naamin, Nahr, 25, 35, 36, 230, 297, 366; railways, 360–1; r.s., 362, 366.
Naaneh, *see* Niana, 375.
Nabataeans, 91, 401, 437–46, 484.
Nabathu, 437–8.
Nablus, 4, 17, 332–3; administration, 203–4; agriculture, 250, 332; health, 223–4, 227, 231, 234–5; history, 85, 114, 119, 127, 189, 332; olive-groves, 255; people, 136, 147, 182, 186, 188–9, 332; population, 189–90, 221, 332; railway, 333, 342, 344, 346, 367, 369, 370; r.s., 370; roads, 333, 340–1, 344–5, 382, 387–8; signals, 396; soap, 263, 333; weaving, 167.
Nahalal, 389.
Nahalat Yehuda, 376.
Nahaliel, Wadi, 414.
Naharayim, r.s., 369.
Nahariya, 35–6; r.s., 362; roads, 378–9.
Nahr, Wadi, 387.
Najadat, 467.
Najil, Wadi, 20.
Nakb es Safi, 385.
— Shtar, 503, 508–9; r.s., 513; roads, 518.
Nakurah, 33; r.s., 363; Ras en, 1, 12, 33, 36, 345, 361, 379.
Naples, 391; (Nablus), 332.
Napoleon, 110–12, 115–16, 136, 207, 298–9, 308, 315, 336.
Nar, Wadi, 32, 53.
Nashashibi, 134.

Nasi, Don Joseph, 338.
Nasib, r.s., 510.
Nathanya, 41, 43, 121, 270, 377, 387.
National Labour Organization, 276.
National-Socialism, 179–80, 266.
nationalism, Arab, 117, 124, 332, 401–2, 455, 457, 468; Jewish, 140–1, 178, 181, 273, 275, 401.
nationality, 133–9, 172–3.
Nativity, Church of the, 116, 320, 535.
Natufian rock-drawings, T. 434.
natural increase in population, 174–7.
— sciences, 219.
naturalization, 173–4, 196.
Naucratis, 437.
Naur, Circassians, 469; roads, 518; Wadi, 411.
Nautical School, 218.
Nawibi, 521.
Nazareth, 13, 16, 333–4; Bishop, 149; climate, 48, 555 ff.; forests, 254; history, 108, 111, 119, 190, 333–4; Holy Places, 535–6; people, 150, 186, 333–4; population, 189–90, 333; rabies, 234; roads, 334, 383; signals, 396; vegetation, 72.
— sub-district, population, 184.
Nazla, 45.
'Nazzaz', 70, 241–2.
Neanderthal man, 81.
Nebajoth, 437.
Nebi Samwil, 18, 108.
Nebk, 458.
Nebuchadnezzar, 85, 87, 95, 145.
Nefud, Great, 454.
Negeb, 3–4, 8, 23–5, 183–4; climate, 47, 52, 55, 59; history, 85, 435–7; population, 184, 466; rivers, 27; roads, 379; soils, 242–3; vegetation, 66, 73, 75–6, 78.
negroid type, 136.
Neheil, Wadi, 408.
Nehemiah, 88, 93, 326, 437.
Nejd, 454, 461–2, 468, 497, 499.
Neo-Babylonians, 437.
Neolithic culture, 82.
Nero, 443.
Nes Ziona, 376.
Nesher, cement, 292, 304; railways, 344, 346, 348, 351, 360; r.s., 368; roads, 388.
Nesib el Bekri, 458.
Nessib, railway, 346–7, 349–50, 503, 508; r.s., 510.
Nestorian Christians, 133, 447–8.
Netherlands East Indies, air service, 393.
New Gate, Jerusalem, 327.
New Zionist Party, 276.
newspapers, 159, 276, 312; T. 472.
Niana, r.s., 359.

Nicaea, 105, 109.
Nicomedia, 109.
Nimr, R., 27.
Nimrin, Tell, 411, 514; Wadi, 410–11, 514.
Nisib, Nizip, 112.
nomads, 23, 134–5, 137, 172–3, 188, 243, 254; T. 401–2, 434, 465–8, 479–80, 487, 489.
non-conformists, 148.
non-Zionists, 125, 131.
Normans, 105.
Nubian sandstone, 482–4, 491, 525–6.
Nur esh Shems, railways, 344, 346, 348–9, 351, 369; r.s., 370.
Nureddin, 107.
Nuri Shaalan, 456, 458–9.
nurseries, agricultural, T. 494; day, 237; forest, 256.
nurses, 236.

oaks, 16, 65, 70, 72–4, 253–4, 427–8, 491, 495.
oases, 4, 20, 29, 77; T. 418–20, 446, 489.
oats, 244, 252, 494.
Occupied Enemy Territory Administration, 460.
ochre, 483.
octroi tax, T. 474.
Odruh, 444, 452, 459.
officials, government, 154, 173–5, 179, 191–2, 206, 329, 347; T. 465, 473.
Oghuz Turks, 103.
Ohel dramatic company, 157.
oil, 256, 263–4, 269–70, 284, 289–90, 292, 343, 348, 372, 403, 482–3, 499; Dock, 304–5; pipe-line, 29, 37, 189, 269–70, 301, 400, 419, 475, 481, 499, 514, 516; presses, 82, 263; refinery, 37, 186, 189, 301, 303; refining, 269–70; seeds, 289; storage tanks, 37, 306, 348.
Old Gate, Jerusalem, 327.
Oleander, R., 39.
Oliphant, Laurence, 121, 301.
olives, 13, 20, 28, 36, 41, 45–6, 65, 243–4, 246, 250, 254–5, 264, 403, 428; -oil, 164, 244, 263–4, 498.
Olives, Mount of, 18, 152, 325, 329, 386, 534–5.
Oman, 453.
Omar, 100, 102, 297, 327–8; ez Zahir, 298, 337.
Ommayad dynasty, 102, 143, 541.
Omri, 18, 436.
operas, 156.
Ophel, Mount, 325.
Ophir, 523.
ophthalmic disease, 233–6 329.
Or, Tel, electricity station, 263; garrison, 475.

oranges, 13, 33, 80, 164, 188, 242–3, 245, 253–4, 284, 288, 292.
orchards, 36, 45–6, 239.
orchestras, 156, 312.
Orders in Council, 192, 194, 196, 204, 206.
ordinances, labour, 277; Mining, 482; trade, 294.
Organic Law, 462, 465, 472, 482.
Orient Line, 391.
oriental, culture, 156; Jews, 136, 140, 145–6, 157, 163, 173, 188, 274; Research School, 159; 'sore', 230, 479.
orientalists, 454.
origin of immigrants, 180–1.
orphanages, 204, 218–19, 334.
Orthodox, Church, 115–16, 148–9, 154, 470; Jews, 140–1, 201, 216.
Ottoman, Bank, 484, 502; citizens, 196; codes, 206–7, 474; Debt, 282–3, 500–1; education, 213; Empire, 109–23, 134, 138, 453, 460, 469; influence, 454, 503; law, 206, 210, 247, 474, 492; Ministry of Waqf, 203; monetary system, 280; rule, 1–2, 5, 15, 110, 114, 120, 138, 171, 182, 187, 200, 282, 284, 291, 328, 341, 402, 455, 529; taxes, 282, 501; Turks, 109, 453.

palaces, 86, 93, 152, 182, 326; T. 484.
palaeolithic occupation, T. 434.
Palaestina Tertia, 318, 446.
*Palestina*, 85.
Palestine, Airways Ltd., 393; Diploma, 215; Electric Corporation, 29, 247, 262–3, 396; Jewish Exploration Society, 159; Order in Council, 192, 194, 204, 206; Potash Company, 23, 258, 289, 396, 484, 519.
Palestinian, air service, 393; shipping line, 391.
Palestinians, 5, 131, 134, 173–4, 191, 193, 196, 199–200, 207, 237, 329, 469.
Palgrave, W. G., 454.
palms, 13, 23, 35–6.
Palmyra, 446.
Paluzeh, r.s., 357.
Pan, 28.
Paneas (Banyas), 28, 89, 440.
Papacy, 106.
papyrus, 30, 71, 167.
paralysis, 481.
paratyphoid fever, 223–4, 477.
Pardes Hanna, 218, 377.
Parthia, 93–4, 99, 102, 446.
partition, 130–1, 489.
Party of National Fraternity, 468.
passenger traffic, 237, 391, 395; trains, 347.

Passover, 147, 553.
passports, 195, 197; T. 475.
pastoral industries, T. 482, 485.
pasture, 12, 239, 247, 254; T. 420, 431, 466.
patriarchal rule, T. 440, 465, 485.
Patriarchs, Armenian, 151, 327; Coptic, 152; Greek Orthodox, 148, 327, 470; Latin, 106, 150, 327, 470; of Antioch, 151; of Cilicia, 151; of Jerusalem, 148, 150, 325, 327, 470.
Patron Saint, 329, 331, 539.
peaches, 164, 251, 494.
Peake, Colonel F. G., 403.
pears, 73, 164, 242, 244, 251, 427.
peas, 65, 244, 429, 481, 493–4.
Peel Commission, 130.
Pella, 441–2, 450.
Pekiin, 136.
Pentateuch, 147.
Peoples' Crusade, 103.
Peraea, 91, 401, 442.
Perdiccas, 439.
periodicals, 159, 312.
Permanent Committee on Geographical Names, 6.
Permanent Court of International Justice, 194.
persecutions, 96, 116, 147.
Persia, 87–8, 95, 101, 110, 290, 304, 393, 395, 448, 451.
Persian Empire, 437, 527; Gulf, 48, 392, 421, 438, 442; Jews, 95, 146, 174, 328.
Persians, 99, 109, 136, 143, 297.
pests, 79–80, 251–3; T. 480–1.
Petah Tikva, 120–1, 188, 334; administration, 199, 202, 206; population, 189–90, 202, 221, 334; rabies, 234; railway, 342, 346, 351; road, 334.
Peter the Hermit, 103.
petitions, 205.
Petra, 545–6; history, 91, 99, 145, 402, 437–9, 441–3, 446, 454, 459; vegetation, 428, 430.
*Petra Deserti* (Kerak), 452.
*Petra Incisa* (Atlit), 37.
petrol, 258, 291, 372.
petroleum, 12, 482.
Pharaoh's island (Jeziret Firaun), 522.
Pharisees, 93–4.
Phasael, 91, 93.
Philadelphia (Amman), 91, 319, 439, 440–2, 444, 446, 540–1.
Philip Augustus of France, 107–8.
Philistia, plain of, 13, 27, 33, 43, 45–6, 86, 340.
Philistines, 19–20, 83, 85, 119, 135, 307, 319, 331.
Philo of Alexandria, 96.
*Phlebotomus* (sandfly), 230, 479–80.
Phoenicia, 39, 86, 88, 437.

Phoenicians, 436.
phosphates, 12, 242, 483, 491, 525.
Pietists, 147.
pilgrim road, 513–14, 517.
pilgrims, 102–3, 114–15, 144, 150, 152, 237, 271, 309, 320, 327, 451, 453–5, 503, 523, 530.
pine, Aleppo, 16, 72, 254, 256, 427, 495.
Piraeus, 391.
Pisans, 297.
*pistacia*, 429–30, 495.
place of birth, 172–3.
place-names, 6–7, 107.
plant, diseases, 252–3, 493; Protection Service, 251–3; types, 64–5.
plantations, 27, 70, 243–4, 250, 256, 491; damage to, 128.
plough, 63, 82.
ploughing, 56, 242; T. 424, 485.
Plumer, Viscount, 125–6.
plums, 242–3, 251–2, 494.
police, 126, 173–4, 179, 187, 207, 396, T. 475, 500; Department, 195, 207, 372.
Policy, Statement of, 131–2.
Polish, air service (Polskie Linje Lotnieze, L.O.T.), 392–3; Jews, 146–7, 162, 173–4; weavers, 269.
polytheism, 448.
Pompey, 91, 95, 319, 441–3.
pools, 54, 135, 225–6; T. 403, 478, 489; of Siloam, 325–6; of Solomon, 320, 330, 380–1.
'poor tax', 448.
popular culture, 160.
population, 4–5, 46, 61, 132, 190, 221, 225, 230, 293, T. 402, 465, 482; decline, T. 402; distribution, 171–90; estimates, 171–2, T. 465, 470; increase, 5, 171–2, 174–7, 184, 285, T. 470, 488, 497.
Port Said, air service, 393, 395.
ports, 33, 35, 37, 41, 49, 189, 236–7, 295–317; T. 436, 522–4.
Portugal, 106, 144.
Portuguese sea-power, 109, 453.
Post Office, 208; Savings Bank, 280.
postage stamps, 139, 208.
Postmaster General, 397.
Posts, Department, 195, 396–7; T. 474.
potash, 12, 242, 256–9, 272, 289–90, 292, 491; Company, 23, 258, 289, 396, 484, 519.
potassium chloride, 257–8.
pottery, 165–6; early, 82–3, 86, 90, 435.
*Praetorium*, Jerusalem, 326.
precipitation, 562–3.
Presbyterian Church, 148.
Press Bureau, 193.
pressure, atmospheric, 48; T. 421.
priesthoods, 88–9, 93–4; T. 440.

Prime Minister, T. 473–4.
Prince Line, 391.
Princes, Crusade of the, 103.
printing, 159, 337.
prisons, 207, 238, 299, T. 475; Department, 195, 372.
production costs, 257–8, 261.
professions, 146, 186, 275, 282.
property rate, 199.
Proselytes of the Gate, 96.
Protector of the Holy Sepulchre, 107.
Protestant Churches, 148.
Protestants, Armenian, 138.
Ptolemais (Acre), 295, 297, 319, 340, 438, 442.
Ptolemies, 89, 95, 297, 315, 438–9.
Ptolemy, II, 439; Philadelphus, 439.
public, health, 220–38; vehicles, 372; Works Department, 195, 330, 372, T. 474, 503, 515.
publishing, 159.
puisne judges, 204.
*Pulisata* (Palestine), 83.
Pumping stations (oil pipe-line), 515, 517.
Punon (Feinan), 418.
Puteoli, 95.

Qalqilia (Kalkilya), r.s., 354.
Qaqun (Kakun), r.s., 354.
quarantine, 236–7.
quarries, 259, 349; T. 484.
quarrying, 207, 259, 261.

Raanana, 377.
Rabaa, r.s., 357.
Rababi, Wadi, 325.
Rabba (Areopolis), 446.
Rabbath Ammon, 91, 438–9, 540.
Rabbi, Chief, 138.
Rabbinical Council, 201; Courts, 201.
rabies, 169, 234, 236.
Rachel, Tomb of, 539.
radio-communication, 521.
Rafa, 1, 33, 43, 45, 48; forestry, 256; history, 89, 118, 256; railway, 342, 346, 348, 352; r.s., 356; roads, 373–4, 384.
rails, 349–50.
railways, 256, 345–72, T. 346, 349, 454–5, 503–13; history, 341–4, 503–5; workshops, 36–7, 303, 348, 366.
rainfall, 3, 8, 12, 16, 18, 19, 24, 27, 56–61, 75–6, 225, 241, 243–4, 249, 253, 255; T. 421, 424, 487–9, 493.
*Rais al Ulema*, 203.
Rajel, Wadi, 420.
Rajib, 407–8; Wadi, 408.
Rakkat (Tiberias), 338.
Ram, Jebel, 418–19.

Rama, 389–90.
Ramallah, 4, 18, 335; broadcasting station, 396–7; crafts, 166–7; history, 335; olive-groves, 255; people, 182–3, 335; population, 221, 335; rabies, 234; roads, 381–2; schools, 219, 335; teachers' training centre, 216.
Ramat Gan, 264.
Ramin, 387.
Ramleh, 13, 46, 335–6; history, 190, 336; people, 152, 186, 336; population, 189–90, 335; rabies, 234; railway, 336, 342; r.s., 359; roads, 336, 340, 344, 373, 375–6, 386, 387; signals, 396; soap, 263.
— sub-district, 184.
'ramp valley' theory, 11.
Raphia (Rafa), 89.
Ras el Ain, 27, 330; railway, 342, 346, 351; r.s., 354; road, 344; Wadi, 409.
Rashayideh beduin, 135.
Rasheida, 467.
Rashida, r.s., 356.
Rashidiya, 417, 467.
rates, 199–201; T. 474.
Ratiya plain, 421.
raw materials, imports, 289, 291.
Rayak, 360.
Raymund of Toulouse, 105.
Reading power-station, 309, 312.
rebellions, Arab, 127–9.
reclamation, 30, 184, 227, 247.
Red Sea trade, 438, 442, 453.
re-exports, 497, 499.
reformatories, 207.
Reformed Churches, 154.
refugees, 171, 175, 178–9, 187, 266.
Régie (monopoly), 265.
Rehavia quarter, Jerusalem, 328–9.
Rehovot, 46, 121; administration, 206; agricultural research, 219, 250–3; diseases, 224, 234; population, 221; r.s., 355; roads, 376.
Reimon, 519.
Reina, 334, 383.
relapsing fever, 223, 479.
religions, 81, 88, 97, 143–55, 172–3, 178, 208; T. 435, 443–4, 448, 470.
Religious Communities Ordinance, 200, 202; Community Councils, T. 474; courts, 203, 206, T. 474; festivals, 208, 233, 552–3; freedom, 208.
Remtha, 489, 520.
Renaud de Châtillon, 452, 544.
Reparatrices, Convent of the, 151.
research, 218–19, 236, 250–1.
reservoirs, 226, 249, 326, 330.
respiratory diseases, 222.
retail shops, 293–4.
Reuben, 400, 435.
revenues, 281–3, T. 500; municipal,

199, T. 474; roads, 372; university, 219; Waqf, 203.
Revisionist Party, 276.
Rhodes, 94, 109, 393.
rice, 165, 293, 498.
Richard Cœur de Lion, 19, 107–8, 297, 299, 308, 336.
— of Cornwall, 108.
ridgeway, 340, 344–5, see also central road.
'rift valley' theory, 11.
Riga, Jebel, 418.
Rishi, Jebel, 518.
Rishon le Zion, 121, 221, 234, 264; roads, 374, 376.
Riyashi, Wadi, 409.
Rmeileh, r.s., 363.
road, accidents, 372; -making, 207, 503; material, 12, 372; tax, 501; Transport Ordinance, 372.
roads, 344–5, 372–91; T. 385, 389, 400, 419, 513–20.
Robert, of Flanders, Count, 105; of Normandy, 105.
rock-drawings, T. 434.
rock salt, 31, 256–7.
Rockefeller jr., John D., 160, 329; Museum, 160, 163.
rocky soil steppe, 429–31.
Rogel, Ain, 325–6.
rolling-stock, 343.
Roman, Arabia, 444–6; Catholic Church, 128, 148–50; Curia, 150; Palestine, 90–4; period, 90–9, 402, 528, 540; roads, 341, 344–5, 444, 513, 518; rule, 441–3; Wadi, 25.
Romaneh, r.s., 357.
Romania, church, 148; death-rate, 176; Jews, 116, 120, 174, 179; ships, 391; trade, 289–90, 499.
Romans, 97, 135–6.
Rome, air service, 393; revolt against, 94–5.
Rosh Pinna, 121; garrison, 475; roads, 384, 390; tobacco, 246.
rotation of crops, 244, 250; T. 493.
Rothschild, Baron Edmond de, 121, 217, 264; Evelina de, School, 217; Hadassah Hospital, 235.
Roumi, 148.
round-table conference, 131.
routes, historical, 340–1, 344–5.
Roy, El, r.s., 368.
Royal, Air Force, 119, 126, 336, 400, 421, 476, 521; Commission, 129, 130–1, 292, 401, 464, 502; Flying Corps, 523; Geographical Society, 453; Navy, 129, 547–9.
Rubadiya, Wadi, 21, 31, 383.
Rubin, Wadi, 25, 27, 45–6, 69, 233, 375.
Rufeifan Pasha, 468.

rugs, 269, 485.
Rumeideh, 321.
Rumeileh, r.s., 363.
Rumeimin, Wadi, 409.
Rumman, 469; Wadi, 409.
Rummana, R., 26.
Rural Property tax, 246.
Rusaifa, 469, 478, 483, 494; r.s., 510.
Russia, Christians, 148, 173; history, 115–16, 137; Jews, 120–1, 146–7, 162, 173–4, 334; pilgrims, 271; trade, 265, 285.
Russian, drama, 157; monastery, 321; Orthodox Church, 115–16, 148; ships, 391; Turkestan, 145.
Russo-Turkish war, 468–9.
Rutba, 514, 520.
Ruwalla tribe, 420, 456, 458–9, 463, 468.

Sab, Wadi, 385.
Saba, Wadi Bir es, 19, 27, 318.
— Biar, 450, 458.
sabbaths, 552.
sabkha, 77, 431.
Sabkhet el Bardawil, 136, 353.
— Ghudian, 418.
Sacred Shrines, guardian, 149.
sacred trees, 72.
sacrifice, animal, 147, 163.
Sadducees, 93.
Safad, 4, 336–8, 539; earthquakes, 146, 337; forestry, 254–5; health, 234–5, 337; history, 111, 126, 190, 337; people, 142, 145, 150, 153, 182, 186, 336; population, 189–90, 221, 336; roads, 338, 341, 344, 378, 390; school, 217; signals, 396; weaving, 167.
Safi, Tell es, 375.
Safiriya, Es, r.s., 357–8.
Saida (Sidon), r.s., 363.
Saideh, Seil, 415.
Saif ed Din, 452.
St. Andrew's Church, 154, 329.
St. Bernard, 106.
St. George, 331–2, 539; Cathedral, 154, 329; monastery, 20; School, 219, 329, 471.
St. Gregory the Illuminator, 151.
St. James, 148, 152; Cathedral, 152.
St. Jean d'Acre, 295, 297.
St. John, Church, 316; Hospitals, 175, 234–5, 329; Knights of, 106, 109, 297.
St. Lazarus, Knights of, 297.
St. Paul, 96, 297, 443.
St. Peter, 96, 307.
St. Stephen's Gate, Jerusalem, 327–8.
Saitanik, R., 361.
Sakib, 519.
sakye layer, 241.
Saladin, 106–8, 150, 297, 331, 336, 338, 452.

Salameh, Wadi, 255.
Salesians, 149, 219, 334.
Salihiya, Es, 28.
Salman, Wadi, 19.
Salmanah, r.s., 356.
Salt, Es, 424, 461, 466, 470, 473–4, 476–8, 484, 493, 515.
salt, deposits, 484; -lake, 136; -marsh, 31, 425; monopoly, 257, 262, 282; -pans, 37, 256–7; -quarrying, 261; river, 26, 41; -steppe, 431.
salts, 12, 29, 242–3, 249–50, 257–8, 261, 489.
saluki, 169.
Samakh, 22, 119; railways, 341, 344, 346–50, 367, 503, 505–6; r.s., 369, 506; roads, 383, 391; signals, 396.
Samaria, 3, 8, 15–18; climate, 16, 52; history, 81, 86, 91, 93, 95, 111, 147, 190, 460; malaria, 228; population, 184; rivers, 27; roads, 340, 379, 382, 388; soils, 242; springs, 249; Woman of, 333; vegetation, 16, 66, 72, 75.
Samaritans, 87, 97, 136, 147–8, 332–3.
Samarkand, 145.
Samaweh, Jebel, 24.
Samma, Wadi, 407–8, 515.
samne, 485, 495, 498.
Samra, r.s., 510.
Samson, 20, 110, 316–17.
Samt, Wadi, 19–20.
Samuel, 108, 335; Sir Herbert, 124–5, 191, 462.
sanatoria, 231, 329.
sanctuary-city, T. 440–1.
sand-flies, 79, 230, 479–80.
sand-fly fever, 480.
sandstones, 10, 12, 403, 484, 525–6.
sand-storms, 51.
sanitation, 163, 175, 232, 253.
Saracens, 21, 94, 99, 107, 297, 337, 452.
Sarafand, 39, 250; Cantonment railway, 346, 357.
Sarar, Wadi, 19, 27, 46; railway, 342, 359; r.s., 359.
Sargon, of Assyria, 85; II, 437.
Sarida, R., 27, 41.
Sarona, 47, 155, 560–1, 565.
Sasa, 390.
Sassanids, 446.
Saudi Arabia, 399–400, 402–3, 497, 499.
Saul, 18, 85, 319.
Savings Bank, 280; certificates, 284.
Sawafir el Gharbiya, 375.
— esh Sharkiya, 375.
Sbeirri, Wadi, 408.
scale insects, 79–80, 252.
schistosomiasis, 223, 233.
school, gardens, 471, 494; medical services, 235.

schools, 140–2, 152, 154, 156, 159, 167, 204, 213–19, 276, 328, 334; T. 471.
sciences, 218–19, 236.
scirocco winds, 50–2, 54–5; T. 422–3.
Scopus, Mount, 219, 325, 329.
Scorpion cliffs, 21.
scorpions, 481.
Scotland, Church of, 148, 154, 329.
Scots College, 219.
Scythians, 319.
Scythopolis (Beisan), 91, 319, 441–2.
sea-fish, 270–1.
seaplane stations, 237, 307, 392, 395, 522.
seasonal migration, 172, 225, 466, 468–9, 478; tracks, 372.
Sebastiya, r.s., 370.
Sebustya (Samaria), 43, 190; r.s., 370; roads, 340, 382.
secondary schools, 213, 216–19; T. 471.
Secretary, Chief, 192–3, 195; Financial, 195; Legal, 195; of State for the Colonies, 191–2, 194.
security, 281, 283, 345; T. 474–6.
Sefei, Wadi, 414–15.
Seir, mountains of, 417–19.
Sejera, 74.
Sela, Selem (Petra), 438, 451.
Seleucids, 89, 315, 438–40.
Seleucus Philopator, 89.
self-sufficiency, 273.
Selileh, Wadi, 409.
Selim I, 109–10, 453.
Seljuk Turks, 103, 105, 107, 109.
Semak, R., 31; Tell es, 37.
seminaries, theological, 150–1.
Semites, 134.
Semmu, 407; Wadi, 408.
Senik, r.s., 363; R., 361.
Senineh, Wadi, 417.
Sennacherib, 437.
Sepharad, 144.
Sephardim, 95–6, 140, 144–5, 163, 201.
Sergius, 449.
Servizi Marittimi, 391.
sesame, 244, 246, 264.
settlement, agricultural, 120–1, 124–5, 186, 211, 213, 217, 239, 244, 260, 276, 334; peace, 460–4.
'Seven Sisters' hill, 386.
sex ratio, 221.
Shaalan dynasty, 463.
Shababik, R., 28.
Shabah, Tell, 419.
Shafi Moslems, 143.
Shaftesbury, Earl of, 116.
Shahabi, Jebel, 522.
Shahyan, R., 28.
Shaib, Wadi, 410, 514–15.
Shajara, Esh, r.s., 507.
Shakkah, r.s., 365; Ras esh, 362.

Shallala, Wadi, 522.
Shammar, Jebel, 454, 461–3.
Sharia courts, 202–3; T. 474.
Sharia, Wadi, 27, 384.
Sharon, plain of, 12, 26, 33, 37, 39, 41, 43, 47, 62, 63, 70, 74, 184, 241, 352, 387, 460.
Shatta, r.s., 368.
Shaw, Sir Walter, 126.
Sheba, Queen of, 145–6, 436.
Shechem (Nablus), 17, 85, 189, 332–3, 340.
sheep, 79, 168, 170, 254, 289, 485, 489, 495, 498.
Sheep Gate, Jerusalem, 327.
Shefa, Jebel, 414.
Shefa Amr, 221, 378.
Shehab, 458, 460.
Sheikh Zowaid, r.s., 356.
Shell Company, 270.
Shellal, Nahr, 406.
Shellala (Ghazza), R., 27.
Shems, Ain, 83.
Shephelah, 12, 20–1, 27, 46–7, 53.
Shera, Esh, 418, 433, 489, 491.
Sherm Dhaba, 521.
— Mujawan, 521.
Shermeh, Wadi, 415.
Sherrar, Wadi, 21.
Shia Moslems, 105, 109, 143.
Shimron, 383, 389.
shipping, 272, 295, 391.
ship-repair depot, 306.
Shita, Wadi, 411.
Shittim, valley of, 411.
Shobek, 418, 451, 459; roads, 514, 517–18, 520.
shopkeepers, 155, 182, 274–5, 292; T. 469.
shore, vegetation, 67–8.
Shubaicha, plain, 420.
Shubash, R., 21.
Shulchan Aruch, 337.
Shunet Nimrin, 514.
Shuni, Esh, 407, 515, 518.
Shukeifat, Seil, 415.
Siagha, Ras, 545.
sick funds, 236–7, 277.
Sideir, Wadi, 415.
Sidon, 113, 340, 344, 438; railway, 361; r.s., 363.
signal communications, 395–7.
Sihon, 435.
Sik gorge, 454, 545.
Sikh, Jebel es, 16.
Sileh, 371; r.s., 372.
silk, 244, 261, 269.
Siloam, Pools of, 325–6; tunnel, 86, 326.
Simeon, 85, 332.
Simon, 90; the Tanner, 307.
simoom, 50.

*sim-sim*, 403.
Sinai, 1–2, 78, 80, 82, 110, 117, 135–6, 243, 439, 442, 466, 522; Mount, 21; railway, 349, 353.
Singapore, air service, 392.
Sir, Ain es, 411; Wadi, 411, 469.
Sirhan, tribe, 467; Wadi, 400, 403, 418–20, 426, 432, 446, 449, 454, 458, 463, 468, 489.
Sitmar, 391.
Sitt, R., 26.
Siyona (Nes Ziona), 376.
sleepers, 349–50.
Sleikhat, Wadi, 408.
Sleit, 467.
small-pox, 223, 237, 480.
Smith, Sir Sidney, 111, 299.
snakes, 79.
snow, 3, 60, 425, 564.
soap, 260–1, 263–4, 284, 299, 309, 333, 498.
Socialist-Zionists, 217.
Socony Vacuum Company, 270.
sodium chloride, 250, 257–9.
Sofara, Wadi, 408.
soil, erosion, 241–2, 244–5, 487–8, 492; temperatures, 62.
soils, 3–4, 16, 22, 29, 66, 68–70, 74–5, 239–43, 250, 254; T. 426, 487, 489–91.
*Solel Boneh*, 276.
Solomon, 82, 85–6, 145, 147, 319, 326, 330, 436, 483, 522; Pools, 320, 330, 380–1; Song of, 330.
Sor, Jebel, 418.
Sorek, vale of, 27.
South Africa, air service, 392.
Southampton, communications, 391–3.
sowing, 56; T. 424.
Spain, Sephardim, 95–6, 139, 144–5, 337.
Spanish Procurator, 150.
spelling of place-names, 6–7.
spinning, 166–7.
spirits, 485, 500.
spleen-rates, 228; T. 477–8.
springs, 8, 12, 16, 26–9, 56, 135, 225, 249, 320, 323, 325–6, 330, 332, 337, T. 407, 410–11, 414, 417, 443, 492; hot, 31–2, 257, 259, T. 408, 414, 483–4; mineral, 259–60, 339, T. 484.
Stafford, Sir Robert, 113.
stamp-duty, T. 501.
standard of living, 171, 207, 222, 274; T. 488.
State Forests, 255; T. 496–7.
Statement of Policy, 131–2.
Statistics, Office of, 197; vital, 220–2; T. 476.
Stephen of Blois, 105.
steppes, 66, 70, 75–6, 242; T. 426, 429–31, 487, 489.

*stipa* steppe, 76, 428.
storax, 72–4, 254, 428.
storms, 59; T. 424.
stratigraphical table, 525–6.
Straus Health Centres, 236.
strikes, 127, 276–7, 310, 547–8.
stud farm, 299.
students, 177, 179, 214, 219; T. 472.
Subhiyeh, Seil, 415.
submarine cable, 396.
Sudan, 154, 182, 195.
Suez, 505; Canal, 46, 117–18, 342, 454, 522–3.
Suf, 407, 409; Wadi, 440, 519.
sugar, 165, 291, 498.
Sukhneh, 469.
Sukreir, r.s., 355; Wadi, 27, 45–6, 233, 375.
Suleiman, 114, 299, 327, 336, 453.
sulphur, 256–7, 482; Quarries Limited, 396.
sulphurous springs, 484.
Sultan, Ain es, 323; Birket es, 326; Tell es, 323.
Sumeil, Wadi, 408.
sun-god, 443.
Sunin, Jebel, 82.
Sunni Moslems, 105, 109, 143; T. 465, 470.
sunshine, 562.
Supreme, Court, 204–5; Moslem *Sharia* Council, 203–4, 218, 236, 325, 327.
Sur (Tyre), r.s., 363; Wadi, 20.
Suraa, Wadi, 249.
Surveys Department, 195; T. 502.
Suwa, 450.
Suwaga, r.s., 511.
Suweileh, 410, 469; roads, 515, 518–19.
swamps, 29–31, 71, 184, 225–7, 230.
Swedish Reformed Church, 154.
'Sword of Allah', 449.
Sycaminon (Haifa), 301.
synagogues, 89, 94, 96, 102.
*synedria, synodoi*, 91.
syphilis, 231–2, 480.
Syria, air service, 392–3; boundary, 1, 399, 401, 406; camels, 169; history, 86, 89–91, 93, 99, 101, 103, 105–6, 109–15, 120, 123–4, 128, 437, 452–3, 455, 460–1; Mandate, 107, 191; people, 5, 135, 151, 154, 162, 182, 465–6, 468; railways, 343, 346–8, 360, 503, 506; roads, 373, 379; shipping, 391; trade, 269, 289–91, 497–9; union with, 124, 401–2.
Syriac, 102, 150, 152.
Syrian, Catholics, 150–1; Jacobite Church, 447; Orphanage, 219; Orthodox Church, 152.
Syrians, 19, 21, 127, 136, 174, 469.

Taamireh, 135.
Taanach, 83.
Taba, Jebel, 418.
Tabarja, r.s., 364.
Tabernacles, Feast of, 56, 553.
Tabgha, 48, 383, 561, 565.
Tabor, Mount, 13, 16, 35, 73, 218, 344.
Tabriz, 144.
Tafileh, 417–18, 452, 459–60, 473–4, 476, 478; roads, 513–14, 517–18, 520.
Taif, 463.
Talaat Pasha, 455.
Talal, 459.
Talbieh quarter, Jerusalem, 328.
*Talmud*, 97, 146, 338; Jews, 147; *Torahs*, 217.
tamarisks, 63, 65, 71, 76–8, 254, 256, 429, 431.
*tamattu* tax, 282, 501.
Tamerlane, 109, 453.
Tancred, 105.
tanning, 260, 321; T. 430.
Tantura, 37, 39, 43, 352, 378; r.s., 354.
Tarbikha, 390.
tarbush, 161, 163.
Tarfawiyat, Wadi, 415.
tariffs, 193, 261, 273, 290–2; T. 497.
Tarkumiya, 386.
Tarshiha, 36.
Tarshish, ships of, 436.
Tatars, 452–3.
Taurus Mts., 450–1.
Tawahin, Wadi, 409, 519.
Tawahiya, 468.
taxation, 171, 199, 201, 217, 273, 282–3, 288; T. 448, 454, 474, 500–2.
Tayibeh, 408, 424; Wadi, 407–8.
tea, 165, 291, 498.
Teachers' Training Colleges, 216.
Tebuk, 449.
Technical, Commission, 130; Institute, 140, 218, 303; schools, 216, 218.
Teheran, air service, 393, 395.
Teim, Wadi et, 28.
Teis, Wadi Ain et, 408.
Tekoa, wilderness of, 20.
Tel Aviv, 12, 25, 37, 41, 43, 186, 188–90, 237, 266, 295, 311–14; administration, 199, 202, 204, 206, 314; agriculture, 251; air service, 393; architecture, 157, 312; art, 157, 160, 312; building, 266, 312, 347; climate, 3, 47, 558, 560, 564; electricity station, 263, 312; health, 223–4, 230, 234–7; hotels, 272, 311; industries, 270, 312; Jewish demonstrations, 127; labour exchange, 278; library, 159, 312; people, 141–2, 146, 188, 312; population, 184, 186–90, 221, 311; port, 314; r.s., 358; road, 342; schools, 216–17; shipping, 391; shops, 293, 312;

signals, 396; trade, 309–10, 312–14; vegetation, 62, 64; water-supply, 247, 312; winds, 314.
telegrams, 139, 208, 395.
telegraphs, 195, 395–7; T. 474.
telephones, 395–7.
temperature, 50–3, 422, 557–9.
Templars, 106, 297, 332, 335, 337.
Temple, 86–7, 89, 93, 97, 147, 326–8, 536.
temples, 94–5, 442, 444, 536.
Templists, German, 154–5, 174, 301, 328–9.
tents, 135.
terebinth, 16, 65, 72–4, 428.
*terra rossa*, 242–3; T. 426, 489, 491.
terrace cultivation, 82, 241–2, 244; T. 434–5, 487.
terrorists, 130, 204, 548.
Teutonic Knights, 106, 297.
textiles, 261, 269, 312.
Thamudaeans, 446.
theatres, 276; Roman, 442.
Theodorus, 441–2, 449–50.
Thomma, Jebel, 411.
Thothmes III, 83, 190, 297, 434.
thunder, 56, 60, 425, 565.
Tiberias, 15, 16, 22, 31, 260, 338–9, 539; climate, 48–9, 52, 55, 337, 556 ff.; earthquake, 146; electricity station, 263; forestry, 255; history, 107, 190, 338; Lake (Sea of Galilee) 1, 15, 21–2, 28, 30–1, 49, 55, 75, 119, 237, 247, 257, 259, 344, 383, 389; people, 142–3, 186, 338; plain, 31; population, 189–90, 338; rabies, 234; roads, 379, 383, 390–1; seaplane station, 237, 392, 395, 397; signals, 396; springs, 257, 259–60, 339.
Tiberius, 96, 338.
Tiglath-Pileser IV, 437–8.
Tileh, Seil, 418.
Tilul, El, r.s., 356.
timber, 62, 254–5, 290, 349–50, 432, 495, 498.
time, 550.
Tin, R., 26.
Tina, 342.
Tinf, Jebel, 399.
Tira, 377; r.s., 353.
Tiran island, 521.
Tireh, r.s., 353.
tithe, 204, 282–3, 501.
Titus, 94, 327.
tobacco, 244, 246, 253, 261–2, 265–6, 282, 289–90, 299, 484–5, 493, 497, 500.
Tobiads, 437.
Tobias, 439, 541.
Toghra, r.s., 510.
Togrul Beg, 103.
tomatoes, 60, 164, 244–6, 253.

*tombac* (tobacco), 493.
tourists, 155, 271–2, 286, 320; T. 472.
town planning, 158, 200, 328.
towns, 187–90, 318–39.
*Tozereth Haaretz*, 273.
trachoma, 233, 235.
tracks, ancient, 341, 344; seasonal, 372.
trade, 273, 284–95, 497–9; balance, 285–7, 292, T. 497; Department, 195, 260; -routes, 99, 437–9, 443–4, 447, *see also* caravan routes; schools, 216, 218–19; unions, 275.
trading organizations, 276.
traffic, offices, 372; railway, 347–8.
training colleges, 216–17, 471.
Trajan, 444.
transit trade, 290, 304; T. 499.
Transjordan Frontier Force, 230, 281–2, 396, 475–6, 500.
transport, 273, 372, T. 475, 483, 485, 498; costs, 257–8, 372.
travellers, 114, 271; T. 400, 425, 454.
Treasury, 195, 281.
Treaty, of Berlin, 137, 534; of Lausanne, 283, 401, 501.
trends of industry, 272–3.
tribal courts, 206, 318; T. 475.
Tribunal, Special, 205.
Tripoli, county of, 105–6; history, 113–14; railway, 343, 346–7, 349, 360, 362; r.s., 365.
trunk, air routes, 392–3, 395; telephones, 395–6.
Tubas, 383.
Tubeik, Jebel, 420.
tuberculosis, 222–3, 230–1, 235, 481.
Tuffa, R., 21, 31.
Tuleilat Ghassul, 434.
Tulkarm, 17, 43, 216, 234, 254–5, 339; railways, 339, 342, 344, 346, 348, 351, 367, 369; r.s., 354, 370; roads, 339, 344, 387–8; signals, 396.
— sub-district, population, 184.
Tulul ed Dahab, 409.
Tulunids, 102.
tunnels, 349–50.
Tur, Et, 386.
Tur, Jebel et (Mount Gerizim), 17, 332; (Mount of Olives), 18; (Mount Tabor), 13, 16.
Turan, Jebel, 16, 255.
Turban, Jebel, 418.
Turkey, 137; communications, 343, 391, 393, 395; trade, 269, 291.
Turkish, currency, 280; language, 137–8, 213; rule, 448–55; Tobacco Monopoly, 265.
Turkomans, 137, 465, 469.
Turks, 102, 103, 105, 109, 111–13, 116–19, 137, 173, 298, 318, 453, 455–60, 503, 522.

Twelfth Imam, 143–4.
typhoid fever, 223–4, 477.
typhus, 223, 478–9.
Tyre, 88, 108, 340, 344, 361, 436, 438; 'Ladder of', 12, 33; Maronite Bishop of, 150; r.s., 363.
Tyropoeon valley, 325–7.

Ujal, Tell (Gaza), 19, 45, 317.
*ulema*, 161.
Umm Awiya, Jebel, 410.
— Beghak, Wadi, 20.
— ed Daraj, 407–9, 519.
— el Amad, 463.
— el Kharruba, Ras, 22.
— es Semmak, 410–11.
— Gadid, Jebel, 418.
— Keis, 520, 541.
— Kuseir, 520.
Umma, Ain, 482.
Umrkaa, 419.
underground water, 4, 8, 12, 28, 247.
unemployment, 275, 278.
Uniate Churches, 148, 150–1.
Union of Soviet Republics, Jews, 174.
Unitarianism, 147.
United Kingdom, 174, 176; trade, 285, 289–90, 499.
— States of America, 115, 155, 173–4, 181, 219, 221, 265, 488; trade, 289–90, 292, 499.
University, Hebrew, 158–60, 219, 250, 325, 329.
urban development, T. 446, 472; immigration, 184–6, 220; malaria, 224–5, 228, 478; property tax, 199.
Urfa, 146.
Urtas, 155.
Usdum, Jebel, 31, 257, 385.
Uweinid, Jebel, 420.

*Vaad, ha-Hinnukh*, 214; — *ha-Kehillah*, 201; — *Leumi*, 201, 214, 216–18.
vaccination, 223, 237; T. 480.
Valley, of Death, 119; of Fire, 53.
vassals, 443, 447, 457.
vegetable oils, 263–4.
vegetables, 33, 164, 244–6, 250, 252, 480, 491, 493–4.
vegetation, 16, 29, 61–78, 239; T. 425–33, 487.
vehicles, 372.
veiling, 162.
venereal diseases, 231–2, 235; T. 480.
Venetians, 109, 297.
Via Dolorosa, 328, 534.
Vicar, French, 150.
Victoria, Queen, 153.
village schools, T. 471.
villages, Arab, 163–5, 220.

vines, 13, 23, 241–3, 250, 252, 403, 493–4.
Virgin's Fountain (spring), 325–6, 334, 535; House, 334, 535; Tomb, 534.
visas, 195, 197.
visibility, 54–5; T. 423.
vital statistics, 220–2; T. 476.
vitamin deficiency, T. 479–80.
volcanic activity, 10–11, 15; rocks, 8, 419, 431.

wages, 261, 274, 277–8.
Waheida, Ain, r.s., 513.
Wahhabis, 462–3, 467–8.
Wailing Wall, 125–7, 138, 326, 537–8.
Waira, 451.
Wakkas, R., 28.
Wala, Wadi, 414–15, 520.
Walid, I, 451; II, 451, 545.
Wallin, G. A., 454.
*waqf*, 138, 203–4, 208–9, 474.
War, Cemeteries, 158, 317, 329, 336; Crimean —, 116; — of Independence, Greek, 112; — of 1914–1918, 5, 45–6, 62, 72, 117–20, 137, 224, 254–5, 315, 318–19, 342, 345, 395, 455–60, 503, 523; — of 1939, 127, 129, 245, 343, 345, 347–8, 350, 402, 505, 523.
Warsaw, air service, 393.
Wasit, 521.
water, area, 1, 184, 239; conservation, 443, 487; legislation, 492, 502; -mills, 411; -points, 489; purity, 330; -softening plant, 353; -supply, 4, 8, 12, 28, 54, 61, 118, 135, 225–7, 247–50, 256, 349, 407, 410, 481, 492, 503; -table, 487; -trains, 353.
Watut el Khatalin, 410.
Wauchope, Gen. Sir A., 127.
'Way of the Sea', 28, 315, 340, 343–4, 435, 441, 451.
*wazir*, 100.
wearing apparel, 261, 289.
weaving, 166–7.
weeds, 63, 77, 244, 427, 431.
weights and measures, 553–4.
Wejh, 456–8.
wells, 13, 28, 41, 46, 56, 225–7, 249–50, 466, 471, 492–3.
Wends, 106.
*werko*, 282.
wheat, 22, 82, 244, 246–7, 252, 289, 403, 479, 493–4, 498.
wildernesses, 19–20, 29.
Wilhelma, 155, 377.
willows, 71, 76, 429, 431.
winds, 47, 49–51, 305, 314, 317, 421–2, 521, 555–7.
wine, 244, 260, 264–5, 282, 284, 293, 320, 484–5, 500; presses, 82.
wireless stations, 396–7, 524.

Women's International Zionist Organization, 218, 237.
woodland, 253–4, 256.
wool, 166, 169, 261, 269, 485, 495.
woollen goods, 498.
workmen's compensation, 277.
workshops, 260–1, 269, 272; railway, 36–7, 303, 348, 366.
wormwood (*Artemisia*), 64, 75, 428, 430–2.
writs, 205.
Württemberg, Templists in, 154–5.

xerophthalmia, 479–80.
xerophytic plants, 64–6, 75–8; T. 428–9.
X-ray, 236, 476.

Yabis, Wadi, 408, 520.
Yaguz, 409.
Yaman (tribe), 135.
Yarkon (Auja), R., 25, 27.
Yarmuk, R., 1, 29, 101, 247, 403, 406–7, 492, 506.
Yemen, 99, 145–6, 447.
Yemenite Jews, 138, 142, 145–6, 156, 161, 163, 174.
Yesna, Wadi, 408.
Yezid, 449, 451.
Yibna, 46, 344, 352, 376; r.s., 355.
Yiddish, 139–42, 217.
Yosef (Yusuf) Tel, r.s., 368.
Young, Arabs, 117; Men's Christian Association, 329; Turks, 117, 455.
Yusha, Jebel, 409–10, 515.
Yusur, 344.
Yutm (Itm) Nijad, Wadi, 418–19.

Zahar, Wadi, 407, 494.
Zahrani, R., 361.
Zaid ibn Harithah, 449.
*zakah*, 448.
Zarnuka, 376.
Zebrika, r.s., 356.
Zeid, 455.
Zeimar, Wadi, 17, 26, 43, 339, 370–1, 387.
Zeiyad, Wadi, 408.
Zeizun, r.s., 508.
Zeklab, Wadi, 408, 493, 520.
Zeno Cotylas, 441.
Zenon, 439.
Zephathah, valley of, 19.
Zerka, Ain ez, 414; garrison, 475; iron ores, 483; Kalat, 409, 521; Nahr, 25–6, 30, 39, 41, 247, 376–7; malaria, 477–8; people, 469, 478; railway, 509; r.s., 510; signals, 396; Wadi, 406–10, 483–4, 515, 519.
Zerka-Main, Wadi, 257, 414, 483–4, 518, 520.
Zerubbabel, 88.

Zib, Ez, 35–6; railway, 343, 346–9, 360; r.s., 362; roads, 378, 390.
Zichron Jacob, 26, 39, 69, 121; r.s., 354; roads, 377–8.
Zikhron Yakov, r.s., 354.
Zion, 83, 326.
Zionism, 116, 121–3, 140, 272, 401.
Zionist, Education Council, 214; headquarters, 329.

Zionists, 125, 126–7, 130–1, 162, 178, 180, 183, 187, 196, 217, 276, 286.
Zirin, 190.
Ziza, depression, 414; landing-ground, 521; r.s., 511; R., 509; roads, 517, 520.
Zohar, 97.
Zumeili, Wadi, 384.
Zuweira, Ras ez, 385.